FROM SCHMELT CAMP to
"LITTLE AUSCHWITZ"

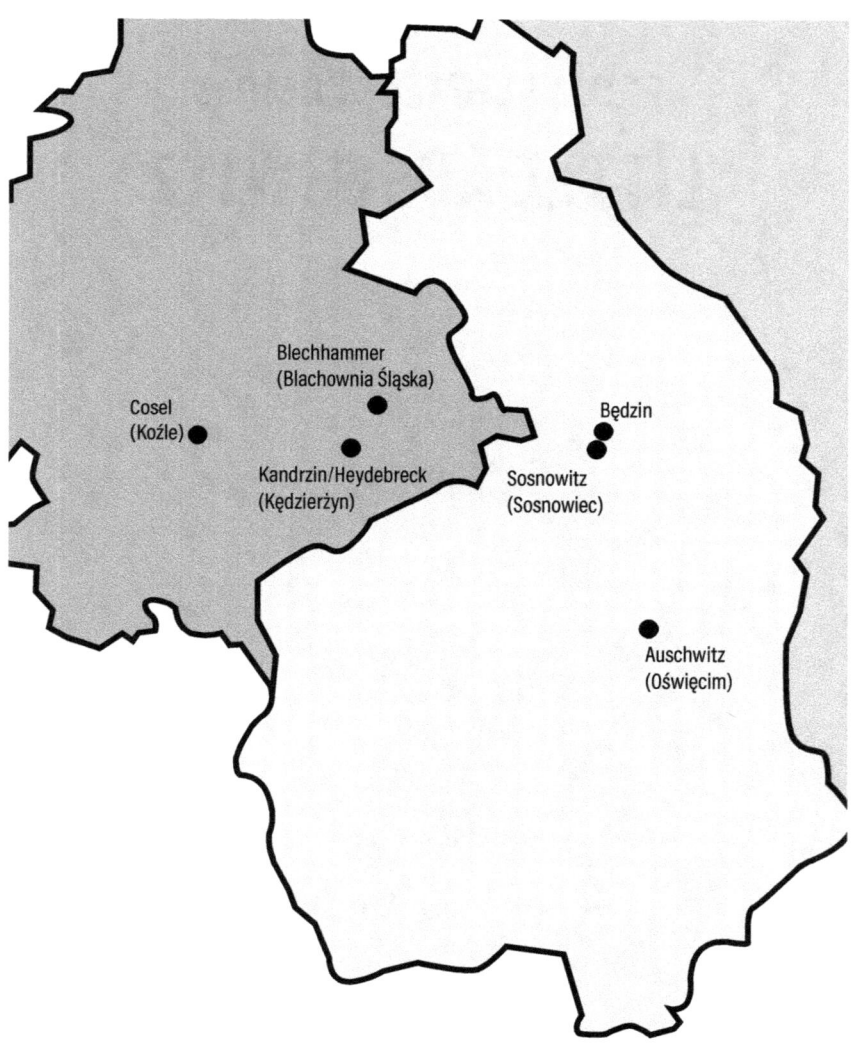

Area map, October 1939.

FROM SCHMELT CAMP to
"LITTLE AUSCHWITZ"

Blechhammer's Role in the Holocaust

Susanne Barth

Purdue University Press • West Lafayette, Indiana

Copyright 2025 by Purdue University. All rights reserved.
Printed in the United States of America.

Cataloging-in-Publication Data is available from the Library of Congress.
978-1-61249-955-0 (hardback)
978-1-61249-954-3 (paperback)
978-1-61249-956-7 (epub)
978-1-61249-957-4 (epdf)

This volume is an abridged version of the thesis "The Oberschlesische Hydrierwerke and the Auschwitz Subcamp Blechhammer, 1939–1945" (Oldenburg University, 2020).

Cover: *One big oak tree without leaves*; Halyna Lakatosh/iStock via Getty Images Plus

NE PAS VOIR
On ne doit pas voir.
On doit pas savoir.
On ne doit pas comprendre.
On ne doit pas entendre…
Le silence.
Le terrible silence
de l'indifférence
de l'homme
pour l'homme.

NOT TO SEE
You don't need to see.
You don't need to know.
You don't need to understand.
You don't need to listen to…
The silence.
The terrible silence
of man's indifference
towards man.

JACQUES ROZENBERG (1922–99),
ARTIST AND AUSCHWITZ SURVIVOR

Poem taken from the book *Hommage Jacques Rozenberg. Sa pensée, sa peinture*, edited by Andrée Caillet-Rozenberg, Gant 2005, with friendly permission of Andrée Caillet-Rozenberg.

CONTENTS

Preface ix

Introduction 1

1. Building the "Tower of Babel": The Oberschlesische Hydrierwerke as a Beneficiary of Jewish Forced Labor 20
2. Establishing a Reign of Terror: The First Schmelt Camp in Blechhammer, March–September 1942 34
3. A New Camp, New Prisoners, New Dimensions of Brutality 47
4. "Rationalization" or Annihilation? The Camp at the Intersection of Two Conflicting Policies in 1943 65
5. Blechhammer's New Role in the Holocaust in Eastern Upper Silesia 85
6. Becoming "Little Auschwitz": The Takeover of Blechhammer in April 1944 98
7. Life Under the SS 116
8. Exposure to Allied Bombings and the Exacerbation of Violence in Summer 1944 136
9. Hangings Without a Witness? On the Vicissitudes of Relating Traumatic Memories 144
10. "A Cynical Joke": Enforced Theatrical and Musical Performances 173
11. The Massacres of January 1945 181
12. The Death March 194
    Epilogue: Surviving Blechhammer—A Look at Collective and Individual Strategies 207
    Conclusion 244

Abbreviations	*249*
Notes	*251*
Unpublished Sources	*313*
Bibliography	*319*
Index	*341*
About the Author	*349*

PREFACE

THIS BOOK ATTEMPTS TO REFRAME THE HISTORY OF THE CAMP FOR JEWS AT Blechhammer (today Blachownia Śląska), one of many "forgotten" camps on the Holocaust's deplorable map.

In sharp contrast to its "mother camp" Auschwitz-Birkenau, the site of the former Blechhammer satellite is now largely overgrown by forest and is probably visited more often by herds of wild deer than by tourists. Those familiar with the camp are typically locals or the next of kin of victims and survivors. Accordingly, it was the story of my great-grandfather that inspired me to write a doctoral thesis on Blechhammer. He was arrested by the Gestapo in June 1941 for having publicly criticized Nazi Germany's attack on the Soviet Union. He was shipped from southern Germany to Auschwitz, where he was detained until August 1941. Then he was conscripted to highway construction works "on probation." From spring 1942, he was assigned to building the industrial complexes in Heydebreck (Kędzierzyn-Koźle) and Blechhammer. He managed to escape in January 1945 with British prisoners of war he had befriended. After the war, he wrote a manuscript on the horrors he witnessed and experienced but unfortunately found no publisher. Over the years the manuscript was lost, he passed away, and his story only lived on through what my grandmother told us.

I'm indebted to many individuals and institutions who made this research project possible.

First, I would like to extend my heartfelt thanks to all those whose family members were interned in Blechhammer and who shared these life stories with me. I'm especially grateful to the late Charles Hayward, a former British prisoner of war at Blechhammer, and his son Tony, for granting me an interview in 2010, and to Simone Millard Spira.

Edward Haduch of the Blechhammer-1944 Association (Stowarzyszenie Blechhammer-1944), a local initiative in Kędzierzyn-Koźle to commemorate the victims of the Blechhammer camps, is a fount of knowledge on the region's difficult history. He and a group of fellow volunteers tirelessly excavate and preserve objects, gather archival sources, and reach out to survivors and their families for information, to maintain a museum. He started to exchange information with me from an early stage in my research, and I cannot thank him enough for his wonderful support.

A European Union Holocaust Research Infrastructure (EHRI) Fellowship at the Netherlands' Institute for War, Holocaust and Genocide Studies (NIOD) in Amsterdam in June 2012 enabled me to see some of the oldest and highly crucial testimony on Blechhammer by Dutch Jewish survivors. Thanks to Karel Berkhoff and other researchers and staff at the NIOD, my stay was extremely fruitful.

I'm immensely grateful for having been awarded a Claims Conference Saul Kagan Fellowship in Advanced Shoah Studies in 2012–2013. The feedback I received from the incredibly knowledgeable and helpful members of the academic board, like Steven T. Katz, Dalia Ofer, David Silberklang, and Jolanta Ambrosewicz-Jacobs, and also from the other fellows, gave important new impetus to my project.

I equally wish to thank the University of Oldenburg's history department for providing me with a position based on a stand-alone project grant by the German Research Association (DFG) from 2013 to 2015 and from 2016 to 2017.

Many thanks to Yad Vashem for a two-week research fellowship for PhD candidates at the International Institute for Holocaust Research in June 2014. All the staff, and especially Eliot Nidam, did their utmost to help me access a wide array of sources. I'm particularly grateful for the unique opportunity to discuss my project with Yehuda Bauer during my stay in Jerusalem.

A junior fellowship at the Vienna Wiesenthal Institute for Holocaust Studies (VWI) in 2015–2016 provided much needed long-term access to specialist libraries and the USC Shoah Visual History Archive. My special thanks to the University of Vienna's library staff. The amazing work of the VWI's directors, Éva Kovać and Béla Raśky, filled my eight months' tenure with vibrant, highly interesting events, ranging from group discussions and public presentations commented on by accomplished scholars to talks by international Holocaust researchers. I particularly wish to thank Sybille Steinbacher for the invitation to present my project in one of her higher seminars at the University of Vienna and for her competent feedback. Fruitful exchange was equally provided by the other fellows, and I especially benefited from thoughtful advice by Rory Yeomans, Volha Bartash, and Paul Weindling.

I likewise extend my gratitude to the Fondation pour la Mémoire de la Shoah for granting me a doctoral fellowship in 2017–2018, and to Dominique Trimbur for organizing a very stimulating workshop in Paris.

I wish to thank Wendy Lower, Waitman Wade Beorn, and Steven Tyas for inviting me to a workshop on complicity and collaboration at the United States Holocaust Memorial Museum in summer 2014. The two weeks in Washington, D.C., were very productive, also due to the great support of the archive and library staff, and especially Elizabeth Anthony, who facilitated access to the International Tracing Service (ITS) database. I'm also indebted to the Claims Conference for enabling my participation in a workshop for British and Israeli PhD students at the Wiener Library in London in June 2015. Many thanks to the insightful commentators, among others Dan Michman, Christopher Dillon, and Mary Fulbrook, and to Christine Schmidt, who introduced the participants to the ITS.

This project drew on a wide variety of sources in many archives and libraries in Europe, Israel, and the United States. I thank all staff members for their assistance. I'm particularly grateful to the head of the Archive of the State Museum Auschwitz-Birkenau in Oświęcim Wojciech Płosa for his expert advice and generous provision of materials.

Furthermore, special thanks to Linda Margittai and Ari Joskowicz for translating Hungarian and Hebrew sources, and to Uwe Höpken of the "euthanasia" Memorial (Gedenkstätte Alte Pathologie) in Wehnen for helping with the first preparations for this project (and for brewing Frisian tea on rainy days). I likewise thank my family for their continuing support.

I feel very honored that my dissertation was awarded the Prix Fondation Auschwitz–Jacques Rozenberg, 2021–2022. I extend my deepest gratitude to the members of the Fondation Auschwitz and the Fondation Jacques Rozenberg, and especially to Baudouin Ferrant and Andrée Caillet-Rozenberg.

Finally, I wish to thank Andrea Gapsch, the director Justin Race, the editorial board, and the whole team of Purdue University Press for their fantastic assistance in turning my dissertation into a book.

INTRODUCTION

LEO B. WAS BORN INTO A JEWISH ORTHODOX FAMILY IN SOSNOWIEC IN 1918. When Nazi Germany invaded Poland in fall 1939, he was conscripted for forced labor duties. He witnessed how the Germans publicly humiliated his father by shaving off his beard. Leo continued to live in the ghetto established in Sosnowiec with his family, until the first deportation waves to Auschwitz began. He and his family were among the twenty-two thousand Jews from Sosnowiec, Będzin, and Dąbrowa who were rounded up in sports fields on August 12, 1942, for selections. Leo's mother was shot immediately, while his father and his siblings were either murdered in Auschwitz or transferred to labor camps. Leo was the only family member allowed to remain in the ghetto, as he worked for the German Army. In March 1943 he, too, was sent to labor camps. After only three months in camp Gräditz (Grodziszcze), Leo became unfit to work due to a leg injury. Despite being granted a short period to recover in a so-called camp for convalescents at Brande (Prądy), Leo's name was swiftly put on a list for Auschwitz. His life was saved by the intervention of a Jewish overseer, who secretly added him to a transport to Blechhammer (Blachownia Śląska). The hard labor exacerbated the problems with his leg, which had not fully healed. However, Leo managed to continue working with the help of a female inmate, who passed on food to him. The takeover of the Blechhammer forced labor camp by Auschwitz in April 1944 turned him into a concentration camp prisoner. When the Blechhammer prisoners were evacuated to Buchenwald in January 1945, Leo was unable to go on the march. He was liberated in the camp's infirmary by the Red Army on January 28, 1945, and was eventually reunited with his surviving brother and sisters.[1]

Leo B.'s story is unique, yet representative of the fate of tens of thousands of Jewish women and men who had been ghettoized in the region the Germans referred to as "Eastern Upper Silesia."

Up to 120,000 Jewish residents of formerly Polish parts of Silesia, the Cieszyn area, and northern parts of Lesser Poland, which had been annexed by Nazi Germany in October 1939, were concentrated in a small strip of land deemed inappropriate for German settlement. While the non-Jewish parts of the ethnically diverse population of Silesia were screened for their suitability to become "Germans," the Nazis intended to remove all Jews from the outset.[2] When initial plans to deport the Jews to the Polish-Soviet borderlands had to be abandoned due to logistical impediments, it was decided to temporarily exploit their labor in ghetto workshops and camps. Growing numbers of young people were arrested in the ghettos to be detained in a secluded system of forced labor camps set up all over Silesia and Sudeten by Himmler's Special Commissioner Schutzstaffel (SS) Brigadeführer Albrecht Schmelt from fall 1940. The so-called Schmelt camps operated outside the concentration camp system but were closely connected to Auschwitz. Next to providing the German war industry with cheap labor, they were integral to the anti-Jewish policy. The internment in Schmelt camps permitted Nazi authorities to control healthy, young ghettos inhabitants they considered likely to put up resistance.[3] By the end of 1942 more than 50,500 people, almost half of the region's Jewish population, had been arrested and transferred to camps under this policy. Most importantly, the conditions in Schmelt camps effected soaring mortality rates of up to 95 percent, which decimated young, able-bodied women and men even before the onset of the large deportation waves from the ghettos to Auschwitz in 1942 and 1943.[4]

Immediately after the invasion of Poland, the Reich Security Main Office (Reichssicherheitshauptamt, RSHA) under Reinhard Heydrich ordered the establishment of Jewish councils, a relic of the Middle Ages, with the sole purpose of carrying out German orders. In Sosnowiec, an umbrella organization known as the Central Office of the Jewish Councils of Eastern Upper Silesia (Zentrale der jüdischen Ältestenräte in Ostoberschlesien) was formed to supervise all Silesian Jewish councils. The Central Office was headed by Moshe Moniek Merin (1906–1943), a commercial broker with a polarizing personality. Like Chaim Rumkowski in the Łódź ghetto, Merin pursued the strategy of "salvation through labor." Both were convinced that a thriving ghetto economy, coupled with the provision of laborers to German businesses, would save parts of the Jewish communities, at the cost of sacrificing those who were unable to work. However, as Dan Michman has pointed out, the Jewish councils were not self-governing bodies, as they had virtually no leeway for action. Merin was held personally responsible for the proper implementation of German directives he received from Hans Dreier, who represented the Gestapo Kattowitz (Katowice) in the Sosnowiec ghetto.[5]

From October 1940 at least one male member of a Jewish family was obligated to work in a camp. This order coincided with the delegation of Jewish labor affairs from employment agencies to the Office of the Special Commissioner for the Deployment of Foreign Labor, Albrecht Schmelt. The so-called Schmelt Office was a major driving force behind the expansion of forced labor camps and ghetto workshops. The profits were seized by the German state, and Schmelt also embezzled considerable amounts of money. A central transit camp in the Sosnowiec ghetto served as a collection point for those conscripted for labor duties in camps. The Germans requested ever greater contingents of workers from the Jewish councils. Moreover, Schmelt's deputy, SS Obersturmbannführer Heinrich Lindner, together with the Gestapo and German police units, frequently raided the ghettos to have people arrested for labor camps.[6]

The Schmelt Office closely collaborated with Fritz Todt's Reich Highway Company (Reichsautobahngesellschaft, RAB). Sybille Steinbacher and Wolf Gruner even posit that the Schmelt Office came into existence as a result of Himmler's order of September 12, 1940, to supply the RAB with Eastern Upper Silesian Jews. Todt's enterprise was in charge of constructing "thoroughfare IV," a fast-track route to the Ukraine built in preparation for the attack on the Soviet Union. As this road was considered crucial to the planned Operation Barbarossa, and the RAB suffered from labor shortages, the RAB was allocated thousands of Jewish workers by Schmelt to complete the segments running through Silesia.[7] The RAB and the Schmelt Office indeed became tightly knit together in several respects. An employee of the RAB's building supervisory board at Breslau (Wrocław) named Haunschild became Lindner's right-hand man in regard to selecting Jewish workers or killing those on the spot they deemed unfit during their visits to camps. The RAB administered the camps it set up along thoroughfare IV themselves. Its civilian camp leaders, who could be notoriously cruel, were partnered with order police guards provided by the Schmelt Office.[8] In late 1941 the construction of industrial sites was prioritized over the completion of the highways, and the RAB was delegated the building supervision of arms production facilities. The company allocated its Jewish inmates to these projects. Hitler's "architect" Albert Speer, who inherited most positions held by Todt after his death in February 1942, intensified the exploitation of Jewish labor by playing out his simultaneous functions as minister of arms and ammunition and head of the RAB. Having urged Himmler to permit the Schmelt Office to extract Jewish men from western deportation trains before they reached Auschwitz in fall 1942, he offered the Highway Company's camps as transit centers. Haunschild was a key figure in selecting the deportees, many of whom subsequently augmented the RAB's own workforce.[9] By the end of 1942 the RAB was utilizing about five thousand Jewish inmates, 10 percent of all able-bodied Jews held in Schmelt camps at the time.[10]

In January 1942 a protocol of the Wannsee Conference stipulated that Jews involved in important war work were to be temporarily exempted from the Final Solution. In Eastern Upper Silesia, the first deportations of those unfit for work, or unemployed, to Auschwitz began. In parallel with the onset of mass murder, Schmelt further expanded his camp system. The selections in the ghettos, which were made by Dreier and Schmelt Office staff, equally forced more and more able-bodied women and men into labor camps.[11] The number of Schmelt camps almost tripled during what Bella Gutterman called the "fall peak" of 1942.[12] Altogether, there were up to 160 Schmelt camps in Silesia and 19 in Sudeten.[13] These seemingly contradictory developments were in fact part and parcel of the same murderous plannings. The paramount role of the Highway Company in the policy of "annihilation through labor" was implied by a paragraph in the protocol of the Wannsee Conference stating that the able-bodied Jews were to be taken eastward while constructing roads. It was assumed that the overwhelming majority would perish in the process.[14] Although the road-building work was gradually stopped in Silesia (but continued in the Ukraine, where a camp system similar to Schmelt's evolved),[15] the conditions in the newly established industrial Schmelt camps were no less lethal.

The Schmelt camp set up in Blechhammer in spring 1942 adjacent to one of the Third Reich's most important synthetic fuel facilities, the Oberschlesische Hydrierwerke (Upper Silesian Hydrogenation Works, OHW), was emblematic of the last phase of Schmelt's system. At a crucial turning point in the anti-Jewish policy, the camp was at the intersection of the full implementation of the Final Solution and the industrialists' requests for more laborers. Consequently, it began to serve a dual purpose. First, it supplied workers to a plant, which produced fuel for the German Navy and the Luftwaffe. Second, Blechhammer took over important functions connected to the mass murder of the Eastern Upper Silesian ghetto population and Schmelt camp inmates.

The pivotal role played by camps like Blechhammer in the Shoah remains largely unexplored by scholarship in the field.[16] The almost complete absence of studies on individual Schmelt camps left many central aspects of the Holocaust in Eastern Upper Silesia in obscurity.[17] As a result, a narrative developed that (mis-) construes the Schmelt Office's actions as lifesaving to Jews. At the core of what Yehuda Bauer referred to as an "extreme functionalist" argument lies the contention that Schmelt's economic interests had slowed down or even averted the genocide.[18] Andrea Rudorff thus identifies the Schmelt camps as "unintentional safe havens" (*nicht intendierte Überlebensorte*), where the Jewish inmates purportedly survived, while their next of kin were deported to Auschwitz.[19] Stephan Lehnstaedt even posits that Schmelt had been opposed to the Final Solution, and that the mass deportations had only commenced after his dismissal in 1944.[20] By contrast, Steinbacher points out that Jewish labor deployments and mass murder were intrinsically linked to one another. However, her groundbreaking work on Schmelt's system did not delve deeper into the actual conditions prevailing inside these camps, and neither did it arrive at approximate death tolls to support her argument.[21] Moreover, the identities of both the perpetrators and the victims remain diffuse in most studies on the subject.

The relevance of microhistories is underlined here. They add precision and clarity and help to discern between singular phenomena and standard practices. Schmelt's parallel system, its relation to the Auschwitz concentration camp, the internal organization of these camps, their changing functions, the different perpetrator groups, and their interactions can only be fully comprehended by examining individual camps. Microhistories also permit a victim-centered perspective and the reframing of the prisoners' responses to the atrocities they were confronted with.

Considering the abundance of sources, it is surprising that camps like Blechhammer are still categorized as "forgotten camps." Sadly, the lack of camp studies equally led to the omission of the victims of the Schmelt camps from public commemoration.

Following Saul Friedlander's concept of an integrated history, this microhistory on Blechhammer combines contemporaneous documents and judicial interviews with survivor testimony to achieve a more balanced view.[22] Next to fact-centered accounts that Lawrence Langer termed "common memory," witness testimonies enhance our understanding of the inflicted trauma with their inherent layers of "deep memory."[23]

A previously untapped document collection on the OHW in the German Federal Archives Berlin-Lichterfelde sheds new light on the plant's ruthless exploitation of Jewish and other unfree labor. The original OHW company files were taken over from the former German Democratic Republic's Dornburg archive in 1993 but only became accessible to the public in 2008.[24] Most documents pertaining to the activities of the Schmelt Office have been destroyed. To a certain extent, the modalities of the Jewish work deployment can be derived from files from the OHW, the RAB, the Council of Jewish elders of Dąbrowa, regional administrations, and the police president of Sosnowiec.[25] Despite attempts by the SS to burn most compromising evidence, a small fraction of Auschwitz prisoner records has nonetheless been preserved.[26] A wealth of witness accounts and life writing collected by archives beginning in 1945 was evaluated.[27] The introduction of video testimonies in the 1980s opened a fresh perspective on the Shoah by facilitating a more differentiated view of the human suffering inflicted by the experience. Survivors who had repressed their memories for decades began to tell their stories for the first time. The Fortunoff Video Archive at Yale University in 1982 spearheaded this new trend and led to the creation of similar databases. With an estimated eight hundred relevant video testimonies, these archives provide the largest corpus of source material on the Blechhammer camp.[28] The increased public interest in the Holocaust resulted in a surge in autobiographies by survivors, some of whom were former Blechhammer prisoners.[29] Several trials and pretrial investigations in Poland and Germany regarding members of the Schmelt Office, camp leaders, and SS men produced judicial interviews by Jewish survivors, as well as perpetrators.[30]

The Blechhammer camp is ideally suited as a case study to examine the multifaceted roles played by Schmelt camps in the Shoah. Its later transformation into an Auschwitz subcamp allows a comparative view of the differences and similarities between the concentration camp and Schmelt's seemingly autonomous system. As an industrial camp,

Blechhammer likewise illustrates the far-reaching connivance and complicity of senior executives, factory guards, and civilian foremen in the Holocaust.

When the Highway Company was delegated the building supervision of the OHW in early 1942, it relocated up to fourteen hundred Jewish prisoners to set up the new Schmelt camp at Blechhammer. Originally the plant had been built in Silesia for the ideological purpose of "Germanizing" the area through industrialization. However, conscriptions to the front disrupted the regime's plans for increasing the number of Germans in the borderland region, and the OHW had to draw on foreign and unfree labor instead. Next to workers from Axis states or Nazi-occupied countries, the OHW received British, French, and Soviet prisoners of war, as well as Polish and Jewish penitentiary prisoners. Contrary to the other categories of laborers, the allocation of the Jewish Schmelt camp inmates was a direct result of the Highway Company's building supervision. Around the same time, Albert Speer became the director of the Highway Company after Todt's sudden death in an explosion. Speer was a frequent visitor at the OHW and facilitated the transfer of more and more Jewish inmates.[31] He equally initiated the stopping of western deportation convoys en route to Auschwitz to extract additional Jewish men for Schmelt camps in fall 1942.[32]

Founded in summer 1939 pursuant to the Nazi regime's autarky program, the OHW plant was fully privatized in 1942. The main investors were Preussag, Reichswerke-Hermann-Göring, and the Upper Silesian Hard Coal Syndicate.[33] The managing director, Max Josenhans (Wildbad, Württemberg, 1893–St. Petersburg, Florida, 1966), had previously been a chief engineer at IG Farben's Leuna plant. Based on his recommendations, IG Farben chose Auschwitz-Monowitz as the site of its synthetic rubber factory in 1941. The OHW's plans for a second hydrogenation works on the same site did not materialize; however, it closely cooperated with IG Monowitz.[34]

The Nazi Party tightly scrutinized all enterprises with the help of senior members of the management, who guaranteed a high level of compliance among the workforces. At the OHW, a key figure in this respect was the corporate lawyer and deputy director Dr. Heinrich Schlick. He officially represented the Nazi Party and its branch organizations and acted as counterintelligence officer. He reported any nonconformist behavior to the Gestapo and was authorized to interrogate foreign and unfree laborers suspected of alleged sabotage, or espionage. Schlick simultaneously commanded the works police (*Werkschutz*), comprising 150 men.[35] Originally intended to protect factories against theft, these private guards were transformed into auxiliary policemen reporting to Himmler's security police (*Sicherheitspolizei*, Sipo) after the outbreak of war. They closely monitored the growing numbers of non-German laborers on industrial sites and were permitted to kill alleged saboteurs on the spot from summer 1944. Jewish inmates were among their main victims.[36] The dangerous alliance between industrialists and the works police effectively turned senior executives into accomplices in the regime's genocidal policies.[37] Despite their undeniable collaboration in atrocities, the factory guards are rarely the foci of newer historiographies. Consequently, the scholarship on this perpetrator category is still shaped by the East German anti-capitalist rhetoric of the Cold War era.[38] However, it is important to keep in mind that both overlooked groups significantly impacted the survival chances of Jewish inmates, and that their influence remained a constant in industrial camps under Schmelt and Auschwitz alike.

In marked contrast to the concentration camps, Schmelt camps were guarded by the order police (*Ordnungspolizei*, Orpo). Some 233 police officers and 169 police veterans of the Sosnowiec police administration that Himmler had created in 1940 to control the Jewish ghettos were put at Schmelt's disposal. The policemen were reinforced by ethnic German auxiliaries. The guards were under the command of Higher SS and Police Leader (HSSPF) of Silesia, Heinrich Schmauser.[39] While the order police's collaboration in *Einsatzgruppen* (Sicherheitsdienst [SD] killing squads) shootings, ghetto liquidations, and deportations has been widely researched, their tenures in labor camps for Jews remain a considerable lacuna.[40] During their deployment in Schmelt's system, they established a new dimension of violence. The police murdered countless inmates by way of the so-called death bath procedure (*Totbadeverfahren*). The victims were exposed to cold water until heart failure set in, they drowned, or they died of hypothermia. This despicable killing method presumably originated in the Mauthausen subcamp Gusen in fall 1941.[41] There is contention among historians over whether these water-induced murders were directly connected to Himmler's 14f13 directive of May 1941 to have unfit concentration camp prisoners killed, and the subsequent experiments with gassings in Auschwitz.[42] Contrary to Auschwitz, where this method was not commonly applied, water-induced murders had become the terrifying hallmark of the Schmelt camps by spring 1942 at the latest. The superior of the police guards at Blechhammer, guard duty officer (*Wachhabender*) Walter Rettinghausen, made such excessive use of the death bath procedure that the prisoners, in a cynical allusion to the Jewish ritual bath *mikvah*, called him *Mikvenik*.[43]

It is unclear when selections of unfit prisoners for Auschwitz were introduced into Schmelt's system. Gruner and Steinbacher assume that sick inmates had been systematically killed beginning in November 1941, analogous to the order by HSSPF Katzmann to murder the unfit in Eastern Galician labor camps along thoroughfare IV. Rudorff recently rebutted this contention due to a lack of evidence.[44]

Survivor testimonies corroborate that frequent selections were already taking place when the Blechhammer camp was set up in March 1942.[45] The selections were made by police guard duty officer Rettinghausen. Schmelt's deputy Lindner likewise listed inmates for Auschwitz during his weekly inspections. Both the members of the Schmelt Office and the order police guards had received preliminary training to this effect. Schmelt and most of his staff were police officers and had become members of the SD by joining the SS. In addition to frequent ideological training, they had participated in racial screenings and in the expulsion of Jews and Poles during previous engagements in "settlement centers" established by the SS Race and Settlement Main Office (Rasse- und Siedlungshauptamt) in late 1939.[46] The order police units stationed in the annexed territories were systematically prepared for carrying out mass killings by SS "experts" starting in 1940.[47]

The order police's deployment in Schmelt camps was not an interruption, but rather a seamless continuation of their collaboration in the Holocaust. Before they were pulled out of the camps in February 1943 to be allocated to more pressing tasks, such as ghetto liquidations and guarding deportation convoys, they trained the civilian Schmelt camp leaders in making selections and carrying out water-induced murders. Schmelt Office staff and members of the order police instructed the civilians in a special SD school set up in Blechhammer for this purpose. It is unknown how many schools of this kind existed in Silesia, as this phenomenon remains a blatant research gap.[48]

The police guards were replaced by Wehrmacht convalescents and veterans. To ensure the continued exploitation of Jewish unfree labor, Speer had urged Himmler to permit the use of soldiers in Schmelt camps. The concept of Wehrmacht guards spearheaded by the Schmelt camps was introduced in the concentration camp system from December 1943.[49] Although not explicitly ordered to carry out mass killings of civilians, the Wehrmacht had become entangled in the Holocaust at an early stage of the war. The level of its complicity depended on the attitudes of lower echelon leaders and individual decisions.[50] In Blechhammer the soldiers were delegated supporting roles, like escorting and supervising prisoners during work. They received no preliminary ideological training, and they were too diverse to generalize on their attitudes toward Jews. Their behavioral spectrum thus ranged from hostility to indifference to support. Individual soldiers assaulted inmates on their own initiative. However, contrary to the police guards' systematic violence, such attacks were rare.[51]

The dual function of camps like Blechhammer is exemplified here once more: they provided the war economy with a constant influx of workers while inexorably decimating the Jewish inmates by selections for Auschwitz or camp killings. The perpetrators in charge of these duties were interchangeable.

The civilian camp leader of Blechhammer was Dr. Erich Hoffmann, a lawyer and agricultural engineer born in Breslau in 1897. Hoffmann had been sentenced to two years in prison for criticizing the Nazi Party in 1936 and was banned from party membership and the Wehrmacht henceforth. Upon his release in 1938, he was placed at the Highway Company as a clerk and worked his way up to camp leader. His designated tasks included the procurement of food and the coordination of the prisoners' work deployment. However, the utilization of Jewish unfree labor fundamentally changed the position of RAB camp leaders from administrators to powerful arbiters over life and death. Despite his apparent adverse attitude to the Nazi Party, Hoffmann was infamous for his vicious attacks against the Jewish prisoners. From early 1943 he carried out water-induced killings, and he assisted police guard duty officer Mareck, who had remained in Blechhammer as the last police representative, in making selections. Hoffmann was executed by Poland in 1948 for the crimes he had committed in Blechhammer.[52] Male and female civilian camp leaders were characteristic of the Schmelt camps. Both the practice of water-induced killings and the utilization of civilians were immediately abolished with the Auschwitz takeover.

Similar to concentration camps, Schmelt camps equally had a so-called self-administration of the prisoners (*Häftlingsselbstverwaltung*). It was a crucial tool in the hands of the German camp leadership to split up solidarity among the inmates by giving privileges to a small fraction of them. On top of the hierarchy were the Jewish elders, who like the Jewish councils in the ghettos often faced ethical dilemmas. They were unable to truly represent their comrades' interests, as the Germans forced them to carry out orders directed against the prisoners.[53] Throughout the camp's existence, the position of Jewish elder was held by Karl Demerer. Born in Vienna in 1901, the merchant had relocated to Katowice in Poland in 1928. While visiting his mother-in-law in Sosnowiec in 1940, he was arrested in the streets, and thereafter passed through several Schmelt camps. Demerer had a rare talent for creating a sense of community among the inmates and was renowned for his "diplomatic" way of dealing with the camp leadership.[54]

The overall living conditions in Schmelt camp Blechhammer were worse than in concentration camps. Blechhammer used standard RAB barracks fitted with two-tiered bunk beds. By order of the Highway Company, camps for Jews had to be run three times above capacity. Consequently, three prisoners had to share a bed. The inmates only received two hundred grams of bread and some soup, nearly half of the rations handed out in Auschwitz. They wore civilian clothes with a sewn-on blue and white Star of David. The daily wear and tear, coupled with a lack of opportunities to wash, turned them into filthy rags, and the prisoners became infested with body lice. They were assigned to menial labor on the OHW construction site for up to twelve hours a day. German and ethnic German civilian overseers often maltreated or even killed prisoners without being reprimanded.[55] While it is commonly assumed that only a small fraction of them classified as fervent Nazis, the regime had nonetheless succeeded in instilling the idea of Jews as universal enemies in the population. Especially the ethnic Germans were under a certain pressure to prove that they were "good Germans," which sometimes culminated in an exaggerated demonstration of being "good Nazis."[56]

Notwithstanding the OHW's relentless demands for more Jewish workers, the company did nothing to prevent their gratuitous deaths on the construction site. A major cause of lethal accidents was the policy of "warlike building." Introduced by the Reich

Office for Economic Development in July 1941, it stipulated that buildings should be constructed by using a minimum amount of material and manpower. By order of the Highway Company's building supervisory board at Breslau, the OHW further radicalized this policy by opting out of standard safety precautions, such as using scaffolds or handrails. The predominant victims were Jewish prisoners who, unlike other categories of foreign and unfree workers, were not permitted to reject hazardous work.[57]

Jewish prisoner physicians tended to their sick comrades in a camp infirmary. As Schmelt only tolerated a sick rate of 2 percent, a small fraction of the estimated 30 percent of the inmates in need of treatment were actually admitted. Others avoided the infirmary, as the patients were at high risk of being selected for Auschwitz transports by the police or camp leader Hoffmann.[58] The doctors' capacity to provide genuine aid was limited by the camps' intrinsically annihilatory nature, and there was hardly any leeway to protect the patients from selections or other forms of murder. Those refusing to carry out killing orders put their own lives in the balance. When faced with the dilemma of adhering to the Hippocratic oath or being compliant to save their lives, the physicians made different decisions.[59] As Primo Levi pointed out, inmates whose positions placed them in a "gray zone" between the perpetrators and the victims should not be judged for their involvement in events beyond their control.[60] In areas where there was less external pressure, individual behaviors may nonetheless be evaluated.[61] The work of the Jewish medical staff was regularly checked by an SS physician from Auschwitz.[62] Interestingly, the SS never interfered with the selections in the infirmary. As of spring 1943, SS physicians from Auschwitz visited Schmelt camps at three-month intervals to select working prisoners.[63] This development coincided with the SS Economic Administration Main Office's (WVHA) order to delegate selections at the ramp, and in work details at Auschwitz from SS block leaders to physicians to increase the number of prisoners that could be made available to the war economy.[64]

During a dysentery outbreak in summer 1942, an SS physician narrowly averted the shooting of all Blechhammer inmates ordered by the Schmelt Office to contain the spread of the disease. Nazi ideology construed Jews and others labeled "racially inferior" as "endemic carriers" of contagious diseases and postulated their annihilation. This notwithstanding, wiping out entire prisoner populations was not regarded as an appropriate measure even by SS standards. Following the SS doctor's moderating intervention, the infected Blechhammer inmates were isolated. Many nonetheless died, and those who still tested positive after a few weeks were gassed in Auschwitz.[65] The Schmelt Office likewise pursued more radical policies than the Auschwitz administration in medical issues regarding female inmates.

From April 1942, about one hundred Jewish women worked in Blechhammer's kitchen and laundry. They were detained in a secluded barrack to prevent contacts with the male prisoners. Unlike the men, the women spent a comparatively short time in Blechhammer, as they were sent to production sites specifically created or modified for female inmates.⁶⁶ Especially the younger women were exposed to sexual violence by German camp personnel. A Czech German chef, who supervised the female inmates in the kitchen, and camp leader Hoffmann frequently raped women. In contrast to the rape of male prisoners, the assaults not only humiliated the victims, but they also entailed the risk of unwanted offspring. The women's reproductive capability was regarded as a threat to the purity of the "Aryan race." The perpetrators could easily conceal the official crime of "race defilement" by the process of genocide. As Himmler's directive of 1941 to murder pregnant Jewish women was equally implemented in Schmelt camps, Hoffmann sent several female inmates to Auschwitz who were expecting his children.⁶⁷ In spring 1943 the WVHA issued the order to kill the babies but leave the mothers alive.⁶⁸ Schmelt nonetheless continued to have pregnant women murdered either directly in the camps or by sending them to Auschwitz. No intervention by the SS physicians from Auschwitz seems to have occurred in these gender-specific cases.⁶⁹

On May 21, 1943, Himmler ordered the deportation of all Jews in Reich Germany and the Protectorate of Bohemia and Moravia to "the east," regardless of their employment status.⁷⁰ However, Speer's demands that the number of concentration camp prisoners should be raised in support of the war effort resulted in a special arrangement for the inmates of Schmelt camps. Himmler ordered the closure of Schmelt's ghetto workshops and bringing the most important of his labor camps under the administration of either Auschwitz or Gross-Rosen. Camps not vital to the war effort were to be disbanded, and the prisoners should be killed in Auschwitz.⁷¹ The mass deportations from the ghettos commenced in June 1943 but were temporarily brought to a halt by Zionist resistance groups. They held the Sosnowiec ghetto against the Germans until mid-August 1943, when it was finally liquidated.⁷²

During the uprising in the Sosnowiec ghetto, Blechhammer began to play a crucial role in the deportation of the Eastern Upper Silesian Jews to Auschwitz. It took over the function of the central transit camp of Sosnowiec, which had become unavailable. Whole families from smaller ghettos were subsequently sent to Blechhammer, where Heinrich Lindner and Haunschild selected them for either death in Auschwitz or work in Schmelt camps. Babies born in the transit camp were instantly killed. Similarly, pregnant women from Sosnowiec were presumably drowned in a washroom barrack.⁷³ The inmates of several disbanded Schmelt camps simultaneously passed through Blechhammer. On average, no more than one-third of the prisoners were picked for work, irrespective of their physical state. The overwhelming majority were killed in Auschwitz, as Himmler had commanded.⁷⁴ From August 2, 1943, a permanent new transit camp was established in camp Annaberg (Góra Świętej Anny), the place the Schmelt Office had been relocated to from Sosnowiec. It operated until the end of March 1944, when the Schmelt camp system had largely been dismantled.⁷⁵ The use of Blechhammer and

Annaberg, which were both administrated by the Highway Company, exemplifies the intense collaboration of Speer's private enterprise in the Holocaust. In these camps, perpetrators not directly linked to Auschwitz made selections and destined the greater part of those passing through them for death in the gas chambers. Blechhammer evidently also served as an entity where newborn babies and individual groups of women were instantly murdered.

The Jewish elder Karl Demerer succeeded in rescuing about thirty boys, who were between eleven and fifteen years old, from the transit camp by bribing Hoffmann. His thirteen-year-old daughter Halina and twelve-year-old son Heinrich had been brought to Blechhammer at the start of the liquidation of the Sosnowiec ghetto together with his wife. The Schmelt Office had granted him this privilege in return for his service as a Jewish elder. In the following months, more juveniles arrived in Blechhammer who had erroneously been selected for labor camps by Schmelt representatives. The children first served as calfactors and later formed a work detail of their own.[76] They were frequently molested by Hoffmann's deputy Pfeiffer, who lured them into his apartment by inviting them for free meals. The abuse of children was ubiquitous in concentration camps, and the Schmelt camps evidently were no exception.[77]

From late 1942, so-called camps for the sick and convalescent (*Kranken- und Erholungslager*) were set up in Schmelt camps like Annaberg and Brande. They initially were meant to comply with Speer's call for preserving the prisoners' capability to work to boost the war economy. Emaciated inmates were temporarily given more food, and some of them returned to labor camps. Those not regaining their ability to work within a given period were sent to Auschwitz. The sick camps were nonetheless gradually transformed into killing facilities and mere collecting points for Auschwitz transports. Blechhammer functioned as one of the last sick camps in the period September 1943 to March 1944.[78] Unfit prisoners from other camps were locked into a former washroom barrack without any medical attention, until sufficient numbers had been gathered for a transport. Blechhammer equally began to operate a punishment camp. The prisoners sent there for alleged transgressions were simply added to the sick to be killed in Auschwitz.[79] Similar to the transit camp, the modified variant of a sick camp established in Blechhammer was intrinsically linked to the implementation of the Final Solution in Eastern Upper Silesia. Instead of providing medical care to sick and unfit prisoners, its only purpose was to have them killed in the gas chambers in great numbers. The sick camp was simultaneously used for sending up to two-thirds of the inmate population of disbanded Schmelt camps to Auschwitz, regardless of their physical state.[80] Along the same lines, prisoners sentenced to punishment camps were now simply murdered.[81] Blechhammer was placed at the end of a continuum moving from genuine aid to the sick to their large-scale, unspecific murder. The sick camp equally turned Blechhammer into a major cog in the wheel of the genocidal machinery of death at Auschwitz, annihilating not merely the ghetto population but increasingly also the inmates of labor camps.

Owing to the OHW's significance in the war economy, Blechhammer was among the forty-three Schmelt camps about to be incorporated into the satellite systems of Auschwitz and Gross-Rosen. On the eve of the Auschwitz takeover in spring 1944, thirty-two hundred out of the twenty-five thousand Schmelt prisoners who were still alive then were detained in Blechhammer. Despite the apparent increase in the camp's inmate population, it becomes strikingly obvious that the overall number of Schmelt camp prisoners had decreased by 50 percent compared to the previous year. The percentage of prisoners who perished between January 1943 and April 1944 must have been even greater, if one considers that the last able-bodied men and women from the liquidated ghettos were forced into these labor camps on top of the existing inmate population. Figures suggest that together with the roughly nine thousand western deportees imported into Schmelt's system in fall 1942, there could have been up to seventy-five thousand prisoners in these camps between 1940 and 1944. A mere twenty-five thousand thereof were subsequently transferred to the concentration camp system. Consequently, the overall deaths incurred by the Schmelt camps must have come close to fifty thousand. An estimated fifty-five thousand people were deported to Auschwitz from the Eastern Upper Silesian ghettos, and most of them were immediately killed in the gas chambers. Evidently, almost equal numbers were murdered in Auschwitz and perished in camps.[82] Therefore, the Schmelt camps were not a ticket to life, as some historians suggest,[83] but they played a fundamental role in the Shoah. The inmates not only succumbed to emaciation and sickness but were systematically decimated by way of the water-induced murders, maltreatment, and selections for Auschwitz. Despite the soaring mortality in the camps, the Schmelt Office still managed to satisfy the industrialists by providing fresh contingents of Jewish workers. At the OHW, Jewish inmates represented the largest group among the approximately ten thousand foreign and unfree laborers in 1943.[84]

Schmelt's system was dismantled in spring 1944. Known as "Little Auschwitz" among the SS, Blechhammer was transformed into a subcamp on April 1, 1944, and developed into the second largest satellite, with a prisoner population of four to six thousand.[85] Auschwitz has become a universal symbol of unspeakable crimes against humanity. The fact that the Auschwitz takeover was regarded as a considerable improvement by many Blechhammer prisoners makes the horrors of the Schmelt camp phase palpable. The inmates appreciated the initially higher food allocations and better hygiene.[86] However, the implementation of a full administrative apparatus rapidly institutionalized the concentration camp's modus operandi, resulting not only in a drastic increase in staff and departments, but also in a stricter drill and new forms of punishment.

All Auschwitz subcamps reported to the commandant of Monowitz, Heinrich Schwarz. Blechhammer's first camp leader was SS Hauptsturmführer Otto Brossmann

(Brawin, 1889–Lohr/Main, 1957), a schoolteacher from Sudeten with previous service times in Auschwitz and the Jaworzno subcamp. The inmates considered him a "sadist" who viciously maltreated them. (His death sentence by Poland was converted into a prison sentence in 1950.)[87] In November 1944 Brossmann was replaced by Untersturmführer Kurt Klipp (Cologne, 1907), a merchant and Army officer who joined the SS in 1936. Following deployments in Flossenbürg, Lublin, and Auschwitz, he remained in Blechhammer until the evacuation. From February until April 1945, Klipp was a camp leader in Bergen-Belsen, where he died of typhus.[88] The camp was guarded by the Seventh SS Death's Head Battalion, commanded by the camp leader of Blechhammer. Due to personnel shortages, many of the Wehrmacht guards stationed in the camp in 1943 were incorporated into the SS guard battalion.[89] Comradeship evenings were meant to create a sense of unity among the "genuine" SS and the Wehrmacht guards. In industrial subcamps, they evidently served to foster the mutual relations with the entrepreneurs as well. Thus, OHW deputy director Heinrich Schlick was a frequent visitor to such evenings in the Blechhammer camp.[90]

The camp came under the full control of the SS Economic Administration Main Office (Wirtschafts–Verwaltungshauptamt, WVHA) under Oswald Pohl. Since late 1943, Pohl had issued several decrees in response to Albert Speer's calls for increasing the work productivity of concentration camp prisoners to boost the German war effort. His directives to camp commandants stipulating that the living conditions of the prisoners should be ameliorated nevertheless remained on paper.[91] The effects of Speer's "rationalization" efforts on the concentration camps have been controversially discussed by historians. Donald Bloxham and Ulrich Herbert contend that from 1944 pragmatism had overruled ideology, and the mortality of Jewish inmates in industrial subcamps had not differed significantly from that of other foreign workers.[92] Christian Gerlach erroneously assumes that there had been no selections for the gas chambers in subcamps and therefore, they had been the "best option" for Jews during the Holocaust. He equally claims that the policy of "annihilation through labor" had not applied to Jewish prisoners.[93] In marked contrast, both Christian Wagner and Stefan Hördler find that inmate mortality rose from early 1944 due to the increased workload and unchanged adverse living conditions, as well as systematic murders. Wagner regards the SS Economic Administration Main Office as symbolic of the fusing of genocide and labor.[94] Yehuda Bauer and Steven T. Katz question the very notion of "economic rationalization" regarding Jewish labor, as great numbers of skilled workers were murdered on the spot, and those detained in labor camps quickly lost their ability to work due to emaciation. They view Jewish work deployments as purely annihilatory in nature.[95] Contrary to the idea of punitive labor in the early concentration camps, Wolfgang Sofsky attributes some economic purpose to the work in industrial subcamps but equally stresses its potentially lethal character.[96]

At Blechhammer the death tolls remained extremely high, at an estimated 87 percent, despite the slight improvements effected by the Auschwitz takeover.[97] Jewish prisoners were three hundred times more likely to die than Germans, ethnic Germans, and foreign laborers with a similar status at the OHW.[98] Two groups of Jews, whose identities were not disclosed, and who were neither visibly marked nor affected by the anti-Jewish legislation, were held in Blechhammer camps between 1941 and 1944: Jewish "Palestinian" prisoners of war (POWs) serving in the British Army and penitentiary prisoners. A comparison of their fatalities showed that the work coupled with malnourishment alone was not a decisive factor. All three had to cope with a similar type and amount of work, and the penitentiary prisoners received the same food allocations as the Jewish concentration camp prisoners. Surprisingly, their mortality did not exceed 14 to 20 percent, until their transfer to Auschwitz under the Ministry of Justice's "annihilation through labor" act in summer 1944.[99] The POWs, who could top up their German rations with Red Cross parcel food, had a death rate of 2 to 3 percent.[100]

The disproportionately high mortality of Jewish prisoners in subcamps like Blechhammer can only be explained by the repercussions of the Final Solution. The systematic murders of sick and emaciated inmates in the camp or in Auschwitz, coupled with assaults by guards and civilians, were the main causes of death. The two "invisible" groups of Jews were affected by neither the Nazis' annihilatory policies nor the excessive violence exerted against visibly marked Jewish prisoners on the OHW construction site.

Malnourishment, combined with insufficient clothing and poor hygiene, continued to cause physical deterioration and diseases. However, the permanent supervision by an SS medical orderly (*Sanitäts-Dienstgrad*, SDG), who reported to the chief physician of Auschwitz III, Horst Fischer, and the area chief physician (*Standortarzt*) of Auschwitz, Eduard Wirths, added a further ramification to the already difficult work of the Jewish doctors of Blechhammer.[101] As was standard practice in Auschwitz since winter 1941, the SDG regularly murdered severely ill or injured prisoners using phenol or cyanide injections.[102] Up to three times a month, he listed prisoners not expected to recover within a couple of days for Auschwitz transports. The working prisoners were selected in three-month intervals during roll calls.[103]

Notwithstanding the high death tolls, Jews represented one-third of the total OHW workforce in 1944 and continued to be the largest group among the unfree laborers. At the time, Jews were the only category of workers that could be replaced immediately by drawing on the enormous reservoir of people who were deported to Auschwitz from across Europe.[104] Diametrically opposed to the paramount importance of Jewish laborers in Silesia and Speer's alleged economic "rationalization" efforts stood the OHW management's connivance and active collaboration in their atrocious treatment. Under the leadership of deputy director Dr. Heinrich Schlick, the works police relentlessly reported Jewish inmates to the SS under trumped-up charges. A leading role in this was played by Blechhammer's Political Department, which was superintended by Monowitz and headed by SS Unterscharführer Otto Ewald Albin Schmidt (Großberndten, 1906). Schmidt was responsible for filing penal reports to the RSHA in Berlin, via the Political Department at Monowitz, to request permissions for floggings, or executions. He was infamous for pressing the inmates into making false "confessions," and some died under his torture.[105] The first hanging of a Blechhammer prisoner took place in September 1944. It was staged as an "exemplary" punishment by the SS, and the surviving witnesses of this execution were so deeply traumatized that they remained unable to render a precise account of the event and of the other hangings that followed.[106] Therefore, it was impossible to construct a historical narrative on this crucial phase in Blechhammer. Instead, the memory fragments have been used to circumscribe the executions, as Saul Friedlander has suggested.[107]

Lower echelon SS men frequently murdered prisoners on the construction site and instigated more violence toward Jewish inmates among the civilian workers. Moreover, newly enacted decrees on plundering permitted civilian foremen and the OHW works police to lynch Jewish inmates on the spot.[108] The temporary work deployment of Ukrainian auxiliary policemen at the OHW plant, who had participated in mass shootings of Jews in Kharkiv, led to further brutal killings.[109] The prohibition against using shelters cost the lives of hundreds of Jewish prisoners when the fuel facility began to be targeted by strategic Allied air raids beginning in summer 1944. Bombing victims received no medical treatment but were gassed in Auschwitz.[110] By order of Hitler, Jewish prisoners were forced to clear delay-action bombs and combat dangerous fires. Such "suicidal" work details invariably suffered heavy losses.[111]

Scholarship on the industrialists' motives for exploiting Jewish labor mostly assumes that companies expected to save wage costs, but low productivity coupled with additional financial obligations toward guards had made them unprofitable.[112] Two years into employing Jewish laborers, the OHW nonetheless explicitly stated that they were utilized to have a wide profit margin, and because they could not leave their place of work at will. A crucial aspect, which has been overlooked by most scholarly works on the subject, is that wages were substantially lowered by reduced output factors (*Minderleistungsfaktoren*). They offered a legal loophole for entrepreneurs to circumvent the Labor Front's stipulation that standard wages had to be paid to foreign and unfree laborers to prevent them from becoming more attractive than German workers. Reduced output factors are common practice in the construction sector to compensate delays caused by unforeseeable adverse events. In Nazi Germany, the industrialists set fixed reduced output factors that always applied to specific groups, often even before the start of their work deployments. The factors corresponded to their status in the Nazi racial hierarchy. The companies thus paid 60 percent of the standard wages for British POWs and 40 percent for Jewish prisoners. Silesian entrepreneurs adopted the reduced output factors set by the Reich Highway Company, whose dominant role in shaping the conditions of Jewish labor is stressed here once more.[113] The utilization of Jewish workers was indubitably initiated by the Nazi regime, but it would not have been realized without the industrialists' consent. Although the contracts with the SS euphemistically stated that unfit prisoners would be sent back to Auschwitz, it was an open secret at the OHW that they were killed.[114] Richard Overy fittingly described this as an "unavoidable complicity" in the Nazi regime's crimes from which both sides drew their benefits.[115]

The deadliest cooperation between the OHW factory guards and the SS occurred during the evacuation of Blechhammer on January 21, 1945. Under the command of OHW deputy director Schlick, the works policemen shot ninety Jewish prisoners who refused to go on the march. Most of them were prisoners from the Jaworzno and Gleiwitz subcamps who had been rerouted to the camp. In the following days further massacres by the SS and retreating Wehrmacht soldiers ensued.[116] These events illustrate the close intertwining of the industrialists with the Nazi regime's genocidal policies, especially during the final phase of the war.[117] Notwithstanding the atrocities committed in Blechhammer, camp leader Klipp decided to disobey superior orders by HSSPF Schmauser to murder the three hundred infirmary patients, and they were eventually liberated by the Red Army on January 28, 1945.[118] The rapid Soviet advance likewise prevented the murder of the sick in other subcamps like Monowitz.[119] However, Klipp's motives for sparing the infirmary remain obscure. The Blechhammer case nonetheless shows the leeway for action available to SS leaders during the chaotic evacuation phase, and it refutes Blatman's concept of "local liquidation units" purportedly sent into the deserted camp to carry out Schmauser's order belatedly.[120]

Some historians posit that the paramount goal of the death marches had been to secure workers for the armaments industry.[121] Others, like Yehuda Bauer, classify the death marches as a continuation of the genocide by other means after the gassings had ceased.[122] Both contentions hold true for the Blechhammer death march, albeit from a gendered perspective. Although one-quarter of the male prisoners died on the two-week march to Gross-Rosen and Buchenwald, they were still regarded as a labor force that could be allocated anew to war work in the west.[123] All of the approximately seventy female inmates of the march reached Buchenwald alive but were no longer deemed necessary as workers. Their subsequent transfer to Bergen-Belsen fully subjected them to an extremely agonizing form of mass murder by neglect, starvation, or typhus.[124]

The prisoners of Blechhammer responded in complex ways to the unprecedented circumstances of their internment. During both the Schmelt camp and the Auschwitz phases, almost identical survival strategies were applied. The most central, and the most contentious, collective strategy was the bribing of the German camp leadership and guards by the Jewish elder Demerer. At times he succeeded in saving the lives of individual prisoners, but he could not avert the Nazis' genocidal plans, nor the omnipresent camp brutality. Bribery was ubiquitous in camps and ghettos alike and defined the relations between the representatives of Jewish communities, or Jewish camp elders, and the Germans. Bribery was always Janus-faced, as the camp leadership also coerced the Jewish elder to pay bribes under threats of committing further atrocities. Corruption was thus used as another form of spoliation by the Germans. Both the Schmelt camp leader and the SS demanded a fixed monthly "salary" from the prisoners, in addition to extra benefits, such as alcohol, cigars, and even a car.[125] About 5 percent of the prisoners were able to procure lifesaving extra food, clothes, or medicines through barter with other workers at the plant. Some construed their bartering as a form of resistance, as securing their physical survival defied the annihilatory policy of the Nazis.[126] Bribery and bartering were invariably intertwined, as the required sums of money and luxury items had to be acquired through large-scale trafficking operations under the aegis of the Jewish elder.[127] Another important lifeline was contacts with foreign and unfree laborers ready to share food or pass on letters and parcels from family members at home.[128] A small fraction of the inmates managed to escape or survived in other Blechhammer camps under an assumed identity.[129]

Mental strategies, also known as "spiritual resistance," also played a role in coping with the camp conditions. The term refers to attempts to counterbalance dehumanization and degradation in Nazi camps and ghettos through religious, nonreligious, cultural, or educational activities.[130] However, its generalized assumption of inmate solidarity does not sufficiently reflect the sharp dividing lines within the highly stratified camp population, as these practices were not always available to a broad mass of prisoners. Moreover, drawing on inner resources to survive was a very personal affair, which took on different shapes in different individuals and depended on their previous life experience.[131] Political activists, like the members of a small communist cell in Blechhammer, found it easier to integrate their suffering into a broader narrative of the collective struggle against Nazism. They taught juvenile inmates to increase their survival chances by showing solidarity.[132] The firm belief in a speedy Allied victory likewise offered a form of escapism from the grim realities of the camp and helped many to keep up their morale.[133] The Germans prohibited any form of religious practice and deliberately staged executions and collective punishments on Jewish high holidays. Observant Jews, who were a minority among the inmates of Blechhammer, still found ways of keeping their prayer routines, often with the assistance of nonpracticing functionary prisoners. By keeping track of holidays, they restored a sense of time in the other prisoners.[134] It is often assumed that religious Jews coped better with the atrocities they experienced, as they accepted them as a "divine punishment."[135] However, the Nazis' annihilatory ideology did not discern between practicing and secular Jews, and some lost their faith while witnessing the horrors of the camps. Others returned to religion to find consolation or to reconnect to their former lives.[136] The manyfold facets of religious practice indubitably played a crucial role in the struggle for survival of individuals and groups.[137]

Blechhammer was one of the most important camps in Schmelt's system at a time when the Final Solution began to be fully implemented in Eastern Upper Silesia. It is a shocking example of how a private enterprise put its infrastructure and personnel at the disposal of Nazi authorities to facilitate mass murder. This book seeks to illuminate the central role played by so-called forgotten camps outside of the concentration camp system in the Shoah. Just as for the Schmelt camps, the diverse perpetrators involved in the genocide are all too often overlooked. The book endeavors to further the general understanding of the scope of their crimes, the new killing methods they introduced and proliferated, and their remarkably smooth interchangeability. Moreover, it urgently calls for the integration of these perpetrators into Holocaust scholarship. Blechhammer exemplifies how the exploitation of Jewish workers under Schmelt and Auschwitz alike was invariably intertwined with the policy of "annihilation through labor." The exorbitant mortality of the Blechhammer prisoners defied alleged "rationalization" efforts and was rooted in the regime's unchanged genocidal plans against the Jews.

Himmler infamously prided himself on the fact that the Nazis' obliterated crimes would forever remain an "unwritten page of glory" in German history. Writing the truly inglorious history of Blechhammer hopefully will contribute to plucking the Schmelt camps from scholarly oblivion and to including their victims in Holocaust remembrance.

I

BUILDING THE "TOWER OF BABEL"

The Oberschlesische Hydrierwerke as a Beneficiary of Jewish Forced Labor

Kandrzin (today Kędzierżyn-Koźle) was a sleepy little town situated between Breslau (Wrocław) and Gleiwitz (Gliwice). Most of its seven thousand inhabitants were railroaders. The region had seen a quick succession of Polish, Bohemian, Austrian, and German rule since the foundation of a royal seat in the neighboring village Slaventzitz (Sławięcice) by the Piast duke Wladisław in 1245. The Prussian princes of Hohenlohe-Öhringen, distant relatives of the British queen Victoria, rose to power in the mid-eighteenth century. They intensified the local production of sheet metal, iron, and tin. Blechhammer (Blachownia Śląska), a village south of Kandrzin, was the site of a sheet metal works.

After the First World War and the ensuing downfall of the tsarist Russian Empire and imperial Germany, the Silesian borderlands were claimed by the reemerging Polish state and the newly established Weimar Republic alike. Both used a local ethnic group with a mixed Polish German background as a lever. They either saw themselves purely as Upper Silesians (Pojęcie Górnoślązak) or identified themselves with Poles or Germans. They spoke an ethnolect of Polish with borrowings from Czech and German that was never standardized in written form. Also known as "Water Poles" (Wasserpolen) because they lived by the River Oder, their allegiance often fluctuated between Poland and Germany, depending on which side was more influential at a given time. Between 1919 and 1921 the political struggle between Germany and Poland led to three uprisings on Silesian territory. In March 1921 a plebiscite was finally held, in which a narrow majority of 59 percent of Upper Silesians voted to belong to Germany. The Polish nationalist camp questioned this result and started a military campaign to gain Silesian territory under the leadership of Wojciech Korfanty. In November 1921 the League of Nations decided to divide Silesia into a German part and a Polish part. Poland received

29 percent of the area, containing 46 percent of the population and 75 percent of the coal mines. The eastern parts of Silesia with the addition of Silesian parts of Ciezyn thus formed the autonomous voivodship Silesia. The western areas formed the German province Upper Silesia, with Oppeln as an administrative center. Kandrzin and Blechhammer therefore remained under German rule.[1]

The Weimar Republic required the princes of Hohenlohe to have their property administered by a trust. Between 1932 and 1942 the trustee sold one-fifth of their vast woodland territory to private owners and the state.[2] Twelve hundred hectares of this land were acquired by the regional administrator (*Landrat*) of Cosel in summer 1939, who offered it to the OHW, a synthetic fuel plant being planned.[3] It was projected to increase the population of Kandrzin, which the Nazis had renamed Heydebreck, to eighty thousand by way of industrialization.[4]

These steps pertained to the Nazi regime's Germanization program in Upper Silesia, which fused economic incentives with ideologically loaded population policies. Infrastructural developments, such as the construction of the Oder-Danube canal, were coupled with the concept of increasing Upper Silesians' birthrates and attracting German workers to the region to form a "stronghold" against Poland. The strategy was equally intended to gain more control over roughly half a million Upper Silesians, whose fluid national identity (*schwebendes Volkstum*) was viewed with suspicion.[5]

The production of synthetic fuel was a cornerstone of the Third Reich's striving for autarky from imported goods, such as crude oil. Representatives of the IG Farben concern had sponsored Hitler's 1933 election campaign in return for a ten-year price guarantee for the synthetic fuel produced in its Leuna plant. They also convinced the dictator that economic autarky was crucial to the preparation of war. Carl Krauch, one of IG Farben's chief chemists, was installed as the general plenipotentiary for special questions of chemical production at the Reich Office for Economic Development. He played a leading role in the drafting of the Second Four-Year Plan of 1936 and its amended six-year version of 1937. The plans called for an increase in the production of goods relevant to the war effort, most importantly fuels, artificial rubber (*Buna*), aluminum, and explosives. Consequently, new hydrogenation plants were built; among them was Blechhammer.[6]

In March 1939 the Nazi regime conceptualized the OHW (initially also known as Schlesien-Benzin) as Germany's largest hydrogenation plant with an expected annual output of over one million tons of fuel. The goal was to fully privatize the concern; however, the Office for Economic Development's search for investors was complicated by the requirement to pay a high stock capital, as well as the plant's borderland location. The Upper Silesian Hard Coal Syndicate (Oberschlesisches Steinkohlesyndikat) thus blatantly refused to become a shareholder until Polish coal mines had been conquered. Its spokesperson, Dr. Alfred Pott, who represented the Upper Silesian Miners' Association, had already indicated in March that the borderlines would be drawn anew soon.⁷ When the invasion of Poland granted access to these resources six months later, the syndicate played a decisive role in their exploitation and the transfer of coal from the annexed Polish parts of Silesia to western Germany.⁸ The syndicate held 30 percent of the OHW shares, and Pott chaired the company's supervisory board. The syndicate's initial reluctance had prompted Hermann Göring to threaten that his enterprise would completely take over the OHW. Reichswerke Hermann-Göring eventually only acquired 30 percent of the shares; and another 15 percent were held by Preussische Bergwerks- und Hütten AG (Preussag).⁹ IG Farben was only a minor investor, but the OHW used its patent hydrogenation techniques and drew on the experience of some of its leading scientists, who became OHW employees. IG Farben simultaneously set up a chemical plant in Heydebreck for refining the by-products of the OHW facility's coal to fuel hydrogenation, like phenols.¹⁰ The construction of the OHW began in June 1939 under the building supervision of Mineralöl-Bau, an IG Farben associate specializing in the design and engineering of fuel plants, which also functioned as a holding corporation until full privatization was achieved.¹¹ Contracts between the OHW, the German Navy, and the Luftwaffe foresaw the annual production of up to two hundred thousand tons of fuel oil and kerosine.¹² Although the planned output was never fully reached, the plant's decisive role in the German war effort is underlined here.

The OHW's managing director was Max Josenhans (Wildbad, Germany, 1893–St. Petersburg, Florida, 1966), who had been a chief engineer at IG Farben's Leuna hydrogenation plant. Josenhans was known for giving public speeches in praise of Hitler to his employees, but he avoided to join the Nazi party proper through his membership in affiliated organizations, such as the German Labor Front (Deutsche Arbeitsfront, DAF).¹³ The Nazi regime did not make it a requirement that senior executives be party members until 1942. Josenhans is a good example of the smooth integration of industrial elites into the Nazis' command economy, whose hierarchy and abolition of trade unions gave them almost unlimited control over their workforce.¹⁴ He was not immediately in charge of the work deployment of foreign and unfree labor. Therefore, his name did not appear on relevant documents, which made it fairly easy for him to claim after the war that he had resisted discriminatory treatment of them due to an adverse attitude to Nazism.¹⁵ The following facts rebut this self-exculpatory contention.

Josenhans spearheaded the industrialization of the territory around the newly built Auschwitz concentration camp. Following a field trip to the area in fall 1940, he chose Auschwitz as an "ideal" location for an additional OHW synthetic fuel facility specifically because of the nearby camp complex. His account indicates that the industrialists not only knew of the planned eviction of the local Jewish and Polish population and their transfer to camps but welcomed the opportunity to seize their property. Josenhans also alluded to the medieval "eastern colonization" (*Ostkolonisation*) by Germans that the Nazis used as a pretext for claiming Polish territory. This notion is further underlined by his derogatory description of the Polish parts of Silesia and their inhabitants:

The inhabitants of Auschwitz, especially the children, make a very miserable impression. Apart from the large marketplace, the town itself makes a very wretched impression.... The Jews and Poles, if industry is established here, will be turned out, so that the town will then be available for the staff of the factory. For this reason, it will not, at least at first, be necessary to build many dwellings, because an adaption of the existing houses, at least to a certain extent, will probably be possible. A concentration camp will be built in the immediate neighborhood of Auschwitz for the Jews and Poles.... While the territory around Auschwitz cannot, from a scenery point of view, be described as bad, it is of course from a cultural and civilizational point of view entirely unopened. Every German who goes there is, therefore, a colonist.[16]

The Reich Office for Economic Development had required IG Farben to build a synthetic rubber (*Buna*) plant in Silesia in return for permitting it to construct another facility in western Germany. IG Farben at first considered a site near Breslau and then presented a plan to Carl Krauch in July 1940 to install two *Buna* plants in Upper Silesia, one adjacent to the OHW in Blechhammer, the other next to its own chemical plant in Heydebreck. Combining the two facilities was deemed efficient and cost-effective, as the *Buna* production relied on certain by-products of coal hydrogenation, such as hydrogen. Krauch, who curiously doubted that Silesia would remain under German control in the long term, postponed the undertaking.[17] Meanwhile, both IG Farben and the OHW contemplated an expansion to Auschwitz independently of one another. In January 1941 a conference was held in Ludwigshafen to negotiate their possible collaboration. IG Farben's Dr. Ambros, who knew the area only from studying maps, had Josenhans outline the results of his exploratory tour. IG Farben eventually opted for the Auschwitz site and proposed financial participation in the OHW's Blechhammer and future Auschwitz plants of 30 percent.[18] Krauch supported these plans; however, the Ministry of Economic Development prioritized the production of *Buna* and postponed the construction of a second OHW hydrogenation works in Auschwitz-Monowitz due to labor shortages.[19] The extra facility envisaged by the OHW did not materialize in the end. Archival sources nevertheless corroborate the close cooperation between the two concerns and clearly refute Bernd Wagner's contention that IG Farben had attempted to eliminate a competitor by expanding to Monowitz.[20] Historians hold conflicting views on whether IG Farben specifically chose Auschwitz as a production site to utilize concentration camp prisoners or for logistical purposes.[21] Prison labor was not crucial to Josenhans in 1940–1941 at any rate, but he certainly was a driving force behind IG Farben's decision to move to Monowitz, the future site of Auschwitz's largest subcamp.

The OHW maintained close relations with IG Farben's Monowitz plant, which was admired as an ideal by the management. When Dr. Dürrfeld of IG Farben Monowitz reported power shortages in September 1943, Josenhans offered at once to supply the plant with electricity from Blechhammer's own power station.²² Indirectly, the OHW thus also supported the Germanized town of Auschwitz itself, which relied on the electricity and water provided by IG Farben.²³

By recommendation of Carl Krauch, Josenhans was awarded the war service medal, first class with swords (*Kriegsverdienstkreuz*), for his contribution to the war effort in July 1942.²⁴ Josenhans's opportunistic conformity with Nazi ideology is likewise illustrated by the fact that he regularly made use of a Jewish prisoner from the Blechhammer camp to have a shave and a haircut.²⁵ His loyalty to the Nazi regime ended abruptly when the Red Army approached Blechhammer in January 1945. Feigning illness, he made for the west with a company car, while the rest of the OHW management had been ordered to defend the factory. A former employee saw him cross the River Neisse (Nysa): "The vehicle was stacked with alcohol, tobacco, butter, a large wireless etc. Dr. Beyer and I checked the vehicle, we were threatened with revolvers by the personal employees of the director, they were intoxicated."²⁶

Josenhans headed back to his old workplace at Leuna in Saxony, where he was earmarked as an expert for the construction of demo oil plants by the American scientist Dr. L. L. Hurst in spring 1945. To avoid capture by the Soviets, he moved to Ulm in the American sector and filed for denazification. The court ruling declared him a follower of the Nazi regime, and he was fined US$400. In August 1947 Josenhans, together with the chemists Otto Ambros and Walter Dürrfeld from IG Farben Monowitz, was brought to the United States under the Joint Intelligence Objectives Agency's Paperclip program, which permitted one thousand German scientists enter the country under temporary military custody in return for lending their support in the "arms race" with the Soviet Union.²⁷ Josenhans denied his membership in Nazi Party organizations and claimed that he had always held democracy in high esteem.²⁸ After working for fuel plants in Louisiana and Pittsburgh, his military custody ended, and Josenhans was screened by the Federal Bureau of Investigation for his suitability as a Komitet Gosudarstvennoi Bezopasnosti (KGB) double agent in October 1951.²⁹ He retired in 1958 and resettled to Florida with his second wife. They both died in 1966.³⁰

Dr. Heinrich Karl Schlick (Karlsruhe, 1905–Mannheim, 1977) was a corporate lawyer who joined the OHW in 1941 as a proxy and head of the personnel office and became deputy director in August 1944.³¹ He was at the top of a perfidious surveillance network set up by the Nazi regime to suppress resistance and to ensure compliance at the workplace. Contrary to Josenhans, Schlick showed an early commitment to the Nazi Party, which he joined in 1938. Ironically, it was his over-eagerness to please Nazi leaders that brought him to Silesia against his will. Shortly after starting a job at the IG Farben affiliate Hoechst AG in Frankfurt in fall 1940, Schlick denounced a colleague and confidant of the district leader of Hesse, Jakob Sprenger, for procuring goods on the black market, allegedly to protect the Nazi Party's reputation. His intrigue backfired and led to his dismissal in January 1941. Moreover, Sprenger was so infuriated that he banned Schlick from the district of Hesse.[32] Schlick consented to relocating to Upper Silesia to work at IG Farben's Heydebreck plant in February 1941 but was seemingly placed at the OHW straight away. IG Farben still paid him until April 1942; however, his salary in Silesia was significantly lower. Schlick played up this incident after the war to portray himself as a "victim" of Nazi persecution and claimed that he had been constantly scrutinized by Nazi authorities. In his denazification trial, the mayor of Ludwigshafen even stated that Schlick had put up "active resistance against the Hitler dictatorship."[33]

The OHW files prove otherwise: Schlick hardly acted like an intimidated victim of political persecution but in fact was directly in control of the oppressive apparatus installed by the Gestapo and the Nazi Party in enterprises, and he maintained excellent relations with higher echelon functionaries and SS men. As the Nazi Party's official representative at the plant, he organized ideological schoolings; distributed the viciously anti-Semitic pamphlet *Parole der Woche* (Slogan of the week), issued by Goebbel's Ministry of Propaganda; and coordinated the activities of all party members in the workforce.[34] He closely cooperated with the propaganda office of the Upper Silesian district leader in Ratibor, whose newsletter he passed on to the management. Toward the end of the war, the office also broadcast radio propaganda to lull the OHW workforce into a false sense of security.[35]

Schlick administered all camps housing foreign and unfree laborers. He was frequently invited to SS comradeship evenings in the Auschwitz subcamp at Blechhammer from 1944. Apparently the SS leadership was eager to foster their relations with the industrialists they supplied with unfree labor. On such evenings, they were entertained by the Jewish camp orchestra.[36] Schlick received a special invitation to a New Year's Eve party from camp leader Klipp. The card cynically read: "Do you have the intention to spend the last hours of the year laughing? Would you like to welcome the New Year with a smile? Then you shall be our guests on our comradeship evening on New Year's Eve."[37]

Despite his close connection to the Blechhammer subcamp, Schlick conspicuously avoided visiting Auschwitz. He declined several offers by IG Farben executives to accompany them to Monowitz, such as the one from Dr. Bertrams of IG Leuna who, in June 1944, planned to make a stopover in Blechhammer before proceeding to Auschwitz. On his return, Dr. Bertrams strongly advised Schlick to see the barrack camps at Monowitz and use them as an inspiration for Blechhammer.[38]

As a "politically reliable" senior executive, Schlick was appointed as counter-intelligence officer. These officers served as Gestapo auxiliaries from 1939 to avert alleged sabotage, espionage, and revolts. They illustrate the intensified collaboration between industrialists and the Nazi regime during the war.[39] A former OHW employee related that Schlick had constantly monitored the staff's conduct for ideological conformity and had thus been known as "the greatest Nazi intriguer" at the plant.[40] His primary victims were nonetheless foreign and unfree laborers, and especially the Jews. Under Schlick's command, the OHW works police (*Werkschutz*) reported countless non-German workers to the Gestapo or the RSHA in Berlin for punishment. By initiative of IG Farben, factory guards were equipped with machine guns by the Wehrmacht to combat espionage and sabotage from 1937 and were eventually subordinated to Himmler's Sipo in 1943.[41] The OHW works police comprised 150 men under the leadership of Kurt Karl Schumann, a baker born in Lauchstadt (Merseburg) in 1903 and a member of the Nazi Party and the SS. They were authorized to interrogate suspects before handing them over to a branch of Gestapo Oppeln in Heydebreck for reprimanding.[42] A decree issued in summer 1944 permitting the factory guards to lynch alleged looters on the spot led to numerous killings out of hand.[43] The works policemen's collaboration in atrocities climaxed during the evacuation of the OHW. Under the command of Schlick and Schumann, they assisted SS units in shooting at least ninety Jewish prisoners in the Blechhammer subcamp, who refused to go on a death march on January 21, 1945. On January 23, they liquidated twenty-five Polish penitentiary prisoners who had dodged a forced march to the Gross-Rosen concentration camp. Both Schlick and Schumann were held in British remand custody in 1947, but a trial did not take place, as key witnesses residing in the Soviet sector could not be heard.[44] These incidents exemplify the fusing of senior executives and auxiliaries with the Nazis' genocidal policies: a lethal relationship that became more and more pronounced toward the end of the war.[45]

Notwithstanding his record, Schlick managed to be denazified in 1948, but he remained unemployed until 1951. He coerced IG Farben into allotting him a generous pension and compensation for his enforced relocation to Blechhammer by threatening to disclose compromising information about the concern's complicity in the Nazi regime's crimes. Despite his Nazi past, Schlick was appointed as a judge in postwar West Germany.[46]

THE DEPLOYMENT OF FOREIGN AND UNFREE LABOR AT THE OHW

From the outset, the construction of the OHW plant required more manpower than was realistically available at the time. Labor shortages had ailed the German economy well before the outbreak of war. It is estimated that by 1939 the economy was short over one million workers. The Nazi regime opted to import foreign labor into Germany to replace men conscripted to the front rather than calling up German women for work, as had been done in the First World War. By 1945 approximately 9.5 million foreign and unfree workers had been deployed in Germany.⁴⁷ Only a small minority of these laborers voluntarily rendered their services to Nazi Germany. The level of coercion and their overall treatment varied fundamentally depending on their country or region of origin and the latter's current diplomatic relations with Nazi Germany, the course of the war, and their status as defined by Nazi racial policies.

Non-Germans eventually constituted 60 percent of the OHW's workforce. The multitude of foreigners speaking many languages, coupled with the high chimneys, evoked allusions to the biblical Tower of Babel not only among the Jewish prisoners.⁴⁸ A POW from New Zealand also drew parallels to the bondage of the Jews in Egypt: "This is how Pharaoh built his ruddy pyramids. There's all sorts—British, German Army prisoners, French Army P.O.W.s, French civilians, Dutch, Russians, Jews, Poles, Italians, Palestinians—a pukka Tower of Babel it is!"⁴⁹

Next to foreign workers from Axis states and Nazi-occupied territories, the OHW utilized unfree laborers. The term "unfree labor" generally characterizes different types of involuntary work carried out under the threat of punishment. This includes indentured labor imposed by states, such as prison labor or work deployments of prisoners of war.⁵⁰ The groups that the OHW referred to as "guarded work details" (*überwachte Arbeitskolonnen*) belonged to this category in Blechhammer: British (including Jews from Palestine), French, and Soviet prisoners of war, penitentiary prisoners (among them Polish Jews), "night and fog" prisoners from western Europe, German Wehrmacht prisoners, and Jewish inmates.⁵¹ Their mortality rates were ten to three hundred times higher than those of Germans and ethnic Germans, and groups of foreign workers with a similar status. British and French POWs had the lowest death toll with 3 percent, followed by penitentiary prisoners at 14 to 20 percent. Soviet POWs had an estimated mortality of 60 percent. The Jewish inmates' death rate was disproportionately high, at 87 to 95 percent.⁵² The major underlying causes were malnourishment, overcrowding coupled with a lack of sanitary facilities, maltreatment, outbreaks of infectious diseases, bombings, and hazardous work. Selections for Auschwitz and camp killings invariably intertwined the industrial work deployment of Jews with the Final Solution.

The OHW management did not name reasons for employing Jews. However, company files corroborate that they explicitly used unfree laborers, as they were cheap and unable to leave their workplace at will. OHW executives argued that these benefits outweighed the stricter regulations on their upkeep and guarding.⁵³ Contracting companies, whose own staff was usually restricted to a handful of experts, were obliged to accept the foreign and unfree workers provided by the plant.⁵⁴

The wage costs were significantly lowered by reduced output factors (*Minderleistungsfaktoren*). Normally these are applied in the construction sector to avoid paying overtime for work delayed by unforeseeable events. Nazi-era entrepreneurs used them as a legal loophole to circumvent the Labor Front's stipulation to pay standard wages to non-Germans to prevent foreign and unfree workers from becoming more attractive than Germans. Each year the industrialists set fixed reduced output factors for different categories of laborers, which always applied and were determined by Nazi racial ideology, not the actual work performance. The reduced output factor indicated the percentage of the wages still payable by companies. British POWs had the highest factor among the unfree laborers at 60 percent. Within the three years of their deployment, the reduced output factors for Jewish inmates steadily declined, from 60 percent in 1942 to 40 percent in 1944. Jewish labor was thus assigned the lowest economical value, analogous to Jews' status in Nazi ideology. The Silesian entrepreneurs usually adopted the factors set by the Reich Highway Company, which played a dominant role in the utilization of unfree labor.[55]

The OHW's own German and ethnic German workforce never exceeded twenty-five hundred. Contractors added another ten thousand workers. The influx of foreign and unfree labor into Blechhammer started in 1940 and peaked at twelve thousand in late 1943. Their number remained constant throughout 1944, while more and more Germans were drafted to the front. Consequently, the total workforce dropped from 24,000 to 20,790, turning non-Germans into a majority with almost 60 percent.[56] Jewish prisoners represented the largest group among all foreign and unfree workers, with nearly six thousand in 1944. In parallel to the large-scale mass murder at Auschwitz, Jews were the only type of laborers still allocated to the OHW at the time. The growing importance of Jewish unfree labor is exemplified here.[57]

THE HIGHWAY COMPANY AS A CATALYST FOR THE OHW'S UTILIZATION OF JEWISH PRISONERS

The OHW's comparatively late use of Jewish unfree labor was indelibly linked to the transfer of the building supervision from Mineralöl-Bau to the RAB in spring 1942. The RAB had drawn on Eastern Upper Silesian Jews from mid-1940 to complete segments of thoroughfare IV (*Durchgangsstrasse* IV), a fast-track road to the Ukraine built in preparation for the planned attack on the Soviet Union.[58] The nature of the RAB's exploitation of Jewish workers was shaped by swift policy swings in the region.

In the wake of the invasion of Poland in September 1939, Germanization plans for the annexed Silesian territories foresaw the expulsion of the approximately 120,000 Jewish inhabitants to the Polish-Soviet borderlands in the General Government, as was done with Austrian and German Jews. Objections by General Governor Hans Frank, coupled with logistical impediments, led to a change of course in February 1940. The Jews were forced to relocate to the so-called eastern strip, a stretch of land formed by the western parts of Lesser Poland that had been annexed to the Kattowitz (Katowice) district, and the southwestern part of the Kielce administrative district. The area was considered unsuitable for German settlement, as it was mostly inhabited by Poles. Large parts of the Jewish population were concentrated in the three cities Sosnowiec, Będzin, and Dąbrowa.[59]

The "Aryanization" of Jewish property and unemployment caused pauperization, even more so as the Jewish communities had to shoulder the costs of health-care facilities and social services alone. Unlike in ghettos like Warsaw and Łódź, the Germans did not pursue a starvation policy in Eastern Upper Silesia, in order to maintain a certain work productivity. Hunger was nonetheless commonly experienced.[60] By order of the leader of the RSHA, Reinhard Heydrich, Jewish councils (*Judenräte*) had to be established in every community from September 1939. The term *Judenrat* derived from the heads of Jewish religious communities (*kehillot*) in the Middle Ages. Dan Michman argues that the Nazis deliberately revived this expression to allude to the diminished status of Jews before the emancipation. The councils were mere puppet institutions pressured to execute Gestapo orders under the threat of death.[61] Criminal inspector SS Hauptsturmführer Hans Dreier, who led the Gestapo Kattowitz's department of Jewish affairs,[62] oversaw the Jewish councils. In January 1940 an umbrella organization, the Central Office of the Jewish Councils in Eastern Upper Silesia, was formed. It was headed by Moshe (Moniek) Merin (1906–43).[63] The commercial broker and representative of the Revisionist Party in his hometown, Sosnowiec, was a controversial person and reputedly a highly indebted gambler.[64] Most former communal representatives refused to work with the Germans, and those who did were typically perceived as "traitors" and "collaborators" by their contemporaries. It should, however, be acknowledged that their leeway for action was minuscule.[65]

Labor deployments were central to both the Germans' anti-Jewish policy and the Jewish councils' survival strategy. Gestapo and police forces frequently rounded up ghetto inhabitants following the introduction of general labor conscription in October 1939. Regional employment agencies began to establish special Jewish labor divisions. The Jewish councils were obligated to provide specific contingents of laborers on demand and were punished if the respective quotas were not met. Initially, it was possible to buy oneself out of labor conscriptions. Consequently, it was the less resourceful parts of the ghetto population that were predominantly affected by forced labor duties. The workers received 35 percent of their earnings; the rest was intended to finance the work of the Jewish councils. However, as the money was transferred to a fund administered by German authorities, the councils only received negligible sums.[66]

Merin maintained close contacts to the Jewish elder of the Łódź ghetto, Chaim Rumkowski. They both embraced the (illusionary) strategy of saving parts of the Jewish population through labor deployments at the cost of sacrificing the "unproductive."

This contentious preemptive cooperation with the Nazis was supported by most Eastern Upper Silesian rabbis but provoked the vehement resistance of Zionist youth organizations.[67] Merin initiated the establishment of ghetto workshops manufacturing goods vital to the German war effort. As the main beneficiaries of its output, the Germans were usually interested in a thriving ghetto economy. Merin, like Rumkowski, hoped to defer mass deportations in this way.[68] On September 12, 1940, Himmler nonetheless ordered the concentration of the able-bodied Eastern Upper Silesian Jews in labor camps to make them work in quarries and build roads. This order pertained to the construction of thoroughfare IV and presumably resulted in the formation of a special SS agency that was delegated the management of all future Jewish work assignments in the area: the Office of the Special Commissioner for the Deployment of Foreign Labor in Eastern Upper Silesia (Dienststelle des Sonderbeauftragten des Reichsführers-SS für den fremdvölkischen Arbeitseinsatz in Ostoberschlesien).[69] The Office's staff mainly comprised former police officers, who had become members of the SD by joining the SS. The conspicuous fact that most of them had previous service times in "settlement centers" of the SS Race and Settlement Main Office (Rasse- und Siedlungshauptamt) indicates that they were concerned not primarily with labor affairs, but with the removal of the local Jewish population, euphemistically referred to as "desettlement" (*Aussiedlung*) by the Nazis.[70] On October 15, 1940, Himmler appointed SS Brigadeführer Albrecht Schmelt as head of the Office, which was henceforth informally called Schmelt Office.[71] Born in Breslau in 1899, the radio operator of the merchant Navy joined the Nazi Party in 1930 and jump-started his career after Hitler's rise to power. He became the police president of Breslau in 1934 and, having entered the SS in June 1939, worked for an ethnic German resettlement office (*Einwandererzentralstelle*) in Cracow from October 1939. Two of his coworkers in Cracow, chief inspector Hentschel of the police administration and the order policeman Lieutenant Baesler, later also joined the Schmelt Office. From July 1942, Schmelt was simultaneously installed as chief administrator (*Regierungspräsident*) of Oppeln.[72] His visits to the Office, located in a private house in Sosnowiec already occupied by the Gestapo, were rare. The most prominent member of the Office was Schmelt's deputy SS Obersturmbannführer Heinrich Lindner. Born in Breslau in 1893, he was the superior of the police guards and responsible for the training of the civilian camp leaders. Lindner was infamous for his fervent anti-Semitism and cruel treatment of Jews. When speaking to Jews, he either turned his back to them or covered his mouth.[73] Helen Israel, one of two Jewish secretaries employed by the Schmelt Office to translate the letters of Polish laborers for censorship, described him as "a pit bull, a man-eater."[74] His pre–Schmelt Office activities are largely unknown; however, two Jewish survivors stated that he had commanded SS units that shot five hundred Jewish POWs from the Soviet-occupied parts of Poland in Biała Podlaska near Lublin in February 1940.[75] He was mainly in charge of providing the industrialists with Jewish workers and played a paramount role in selections in camps and during ghetto liquidations.[76] The work deployment of female prisoners was managed by SS Hauptsturmführer Alfred Ludwig, who was transferred to the Schmelt Office from a resettlement commission for ethnic Germans in Sosnowiec in June 1941. Born in Kreuzburg (Kluczbork), Upper Silesia, in 1902, the criminal police officer joined the Nazi Party in 1921, the *Sturmabteilung* (storm troopers; SA) in 1928, and the SS in 1931.[77] Furthermore, an ethnic German schoolteacher from Romania, Friedrich Karl Kuczinsky, headed the Office's division of Jewish affairs.[78]

After a brief period of collaboration with a regional employment agency, the headquarters of the RAB's building supervisory board at Breslau (Oberste Bauleitung Reichsautobahnen, OBR) immediately connected with the newly founded Schmelt Office in fall 1940. Dr. Werner Schulz, who had been entrusted with managing the RAB's Jewish work deployment, frequently met with Lindner and Hentschel. In October 1941, Schulz was replaced by Walter Tschechne, a senior civil servant formerly employed by the Breslau Rail directorate.[79] Gruner's and Steinbacher's assumption that the Schmelt Office was created to serve the RAB's interests is confirmed by the fact that employees of the Highway Company assisted Schmelt's staff in crucial tasks. The OBR Breslau's social ombudsman Albert Hitschler selected Jewish women for the Highway Company together with Alfred Ludwig.[80] An elderly RAB employee with a limp named Haunschild oversaw the recruitment of male Jewish workers. His identity could never be verified, but as he constantly combed camps for laborers with Heinrich Lindner, he was widely known by the inmates, who referred to him as "the slave trader" or "the horse dealer."[81]

Hitschler's postwar claims that Jewish workers had been treated like Germans in RAB camps until Schmelt took over were false.[82] Albert Youra, who had been conscripted to build up the RAB camp Auenrode (Osiek Grodkowski) in October 1940, reported hard physical labor, scanty food rations, and a lack of sanitary facilities. The only noticeable difference after the transfer of authority from employment agencies to the Schmelt Office was that the camp was fenced in, and the sign reading "RAB camp" was changed to "forced labor camp for Jews."[83] The Jewish laborers were then urged to send letters home pretending that everything was "fine."[84] The RAB's building supervisory board at Breslau continued to administer their camps for Jews with its own staff. The civilian camp leaders simultaneously rendered their services to Broemel & Sohn, a grocery wholesaler.[85] Wilfried Broemel, born in 1901, became a wealthy man when he expanded his father's shop in Breslau in 1940 and began to specialize in supplying Nazi Party institutions and labor camps with food. Twenty RAB-run camps, among them Blechhammer, as well as IG Farben in Auschwitz-Monowitz, were clients of his. The company thrived thanks to generous loans from the petrochemical industry, including from Mineralöl-Bau and Benzol-Vereinigung des Ostens (Eastern Benzole

Association). In 1943 Broemel's profits amounted to 1.5 million RM. His success was not even hampered by a temporary arrest for poisoning customers with rotten spinach.[86]

Coinciding with the Schmelt Office's foundation, at least one able-bodied member of a Jewish family had to work in a camp. As word of the horrific conditions in these camps had spread in the ghettos and people were reluctant to sign up for such deployments, this order was soon followed by enforced mass conscriptions. All Jewish men of Chrzanów aged between eighteen and fifty years, for instance, had to register for labor camps in November 1940. By the end of the year, approximately twenty-eight hundred people were being held in Schmelt camps.[87] In February 1941, Schmelt ordered the Central Office of Jewish Councils to muster all men between eighteen and fifty-five for their ability to work and to create a card index with their personal details. Employment in one of the ghetto workshops Schmelt set up in parallel to the camps only temporarily exempted young people from camp internments.[88] The pressure on Moshe Merin grew as Schmelt urged him to withdraw food stamps from the next of kin of those evading labor conscriptions, while the ghetto population branded him a "traitor" for luring people into camps. Majer Brzeski, who ran the Central Office's labor division, publicly resigned in protest against Merin in spring 1941.[89] The Nuremberg Laws were implemented in the annexed territories in June 1941, and from September, the Eastern Upper Silesian Jews were required to wear the yellow Star instead of the white armband with the blue Star of David. The Gestapo used any violations of the new laws as a pretext for sending ghetto inhabitants to Schmelt camps.[90]

A former Jewish secondary school in Sosnowiec served as a central transit camp (*Durchgangslager*), from where able-bodied women and men were distributed among Schmelt camps after a medical examination by members of the Sosnowiec SD. Judging peoples' age only by their looks, they often picked under sixteen-year-olds. The Germans held the families of those evading labor conscriptions in an in-between camp (*Zwischenlager*) next to the transit camp and transferred them to Schmelt camps if their relatives failed to show up.[91]

In January 1942 the infamous Wannsee Conference marked the formal beginning of the Final Solution. The protocol stated that Jews doing important war work were to be exempted until they could be replaced by Soviet POWs. However, the assumption that the majority of these workers would die while "building roads" unmistakably underlined the lethal character of Jewish labor assignments and the collaboration of the Highway Company that was in charge of road construction.[92] As a result, the Schmelt Office announced that people employed in ghetto workshops were no longer freed from conscription to labor camps and that the workshops would soon be closed.[93] On February 15, 1942, Jews from Bytom were among the first victims of the gas chambers of Auschwitz.[94] In April the Schmelt representatives Lindner and Kuczinsky demanded a list of ten thousand "unproductive" ghetto inhabitants from Merin for the first wave of deportations to Auschwitz in May. Merin was made to believe that this measure would save the working Jewish population.[95] Inadvertently, the Central Office of Jewish Councils thus contributed to the Nazis' preliminary goal of liquidating the unfit while concentrating the young and the able-bodied in Schmelt camps. This ensured that resistance was contained and eased the planned mass deportations.[96] By August 1942 about thirty-five thousand Eastern Upper Silesian Jews had been murdered in Auschwitz.[97] Hans Dreier, Heinrich Lindner, and Friedrich Kuczinsky were predominantly responsible for the selections. They frequently maltreated or killed especially the smaller children in the process. They were also present during a mass roundup of twenty-two thousand Jews in sports fields in Sosnowiec, Będzin, and Dąbrowa on August 12, 1942, during which numerous people died of exhaustion or mistreatment.[98]

The disbanding of workshops and selections forced more and more able-bodied ghetto inhabitants into Schmelt camps. The Highway Company benefited from this drastic development, as it could draw on a growing reservoir of Jewish laborers at a time when it increasingly turned to the supervision of crucial armaments projects under construction, such as the OHW at Blechhammer. Notwithstanding its growing demand for Jewish workers, the RAB only considered them as temporary replacements for the Soviet laborers that they expected to keep more permanently. In the second half of 1941, Eastern Upper Silesian Jews were thus required to set up transit camps for Soviet POWs that were managed by the RAB.[99] The Highway Company nonetheless received a reimbursement of 800,000 RM from Schmelt for the training and upkeep of Jewish construction workers in a camp in Klettendorf (Klecina) in winter 1941–1942. It also augmented its Jewish workforce to approximately 5,128, indicating an increase of 1,205 by late 1942.[100] As one of the Schmelt Office's most important clients, the Highway Company exploited roughly 10 percent of the Jewish women and men interned in these camps then.[101] However, it is important to remember its role in decimating the able-bodied Jewish population through labor implied by the protocol of the Wannsee Conference.

2

ESTABLISHING A REIGN OF TERROR

The First Schmelt Camp in Blechhammer,
March–September 1942

IN NOVEMBER 1941 THE OHW ANNOUNCED THE EXPECTED ARRIVAL OF FIF-
teen hundred Jewish builders provided by the Breslau section of Organisation Todt,
a multinational pioneer organization founded by Fritz Todt in 1938 and merged
with the Highway Company in spring 1942.[1] However, it was not until March 10, 1942,
that the first group of about seventy Jewish boys and men was transferred to Blechhammer from the RAB-run camp Gogolin. The first camp for Jews initially consisted
of three barracks in the proximity of a provisional settlement area for the plant's foreign workforce, called a *Dorflager* (village camp). One barrack accommodated the German camp personnel; the other two were gradually filled with the newly arriving Jewish
prisoners, whose number soon reached about 200.[2] By July 1942, the prisoner population had increased to 1,410.[3]

The camp had a dual leadership. It was administered by a civilian RAB camp leader
and guarded by members of the German order police. The policemen were under the
command of a guard duty officer (*Wachhabender*), who reported to Schmelt's deputy,
Heinrich Lindner. Both authorities closely collaborated, thereby blurring the boundaries of individual culpability.

The order police (*Ordnungspolizei*) were founded in 1936 by the newly appointed
chief of the German Police, Heinrich Himmler. Owing to the color of their uniforms,
they were also known as the "green police" (Grüne Polizei). Their commandant, Kurt
Daluege, was committed to achieving Himmler's goal to merge the police with the SS.
The order policemen received intensive ideological indoctrination to this effect. Another important role in this respect was played by the HSSPFs, who were installed in
every German district from September 15, 1938, to coordinate joint operations of the
SS and the police. By 1941, 65 percent of all order police officers had joined the Nazi

Party, and 30 percent had become members of the SD by entering the SS. From September 1939, the order police participated in the racial war against Jews and Slavs. They reinforced SD killing squads (*Einsatzgruppen*); were involved in mass shootings, executions, and "resettlements"; and guarded deportation trains, camps, and ghettos.[4]

The order police units deployed in the annexed Polish territories had systematically been prepared for carrying out mass killings by SS "experts" from 1940.[5] Those assigned to guard duties in Schmelt camps underwent further training in SD schools, whose head instructor was Heinrich Lindner.[6] The police guards of Blechhammer belonged to a unit of the police administration of Sosnowiec created by Himmler in November 1940 to control Jewish communities in the "eastern strip." They were under the command of Heinrich Schmauser, the HSSPF of Silesia. In April 1942, 169 police veterans and 233 active police officers were at his disposal for guard duties in Silesian forced labor camps. Their immediate superiors were Schmelt's deputy Heinrich Lindner and a high-ranking member of the order police in Sosnowiec named Raszewski.[7] The Blechhammer guards comprised eight police officers. They were reinforced by ethnic Germans from Bessarabia, who spoke Yiddish with the inmates and broken German among each other.[8] To mitigate their escalating personnel shortages, the chief of the order police, Daluege, had been permitted to recruit six thousand ethnic German auxiliaries into their ranks in 1940.[9] Several hundred of them were allocated to the police chief of Sosnowiec to guard ghettos and Schmelt camps.[10] They predominantly stemmed from Bessarabia and Bukovina and had been imported into the annexed territories during the so-called Buchenland-Aktion of fall 1940. Only a small fraction of the 250,000 ethnic Germans from these areas was sent to Upper Silesia under the regime's Germanization program. This was partly due to Silesian district leader Josef Wagner's opposition but was equally linked to the region's high level of industrialization, disqualifying it for agrarian resettlement projects.[11] Extended stays in transit camps for ethnic Germans left many disillusioned. The men were either conscripted into the Wehrmacht or signed up for the Waffen-SS, the SS, or the order police.[12] They served as guards in concentration camps and supported local police units in rounding up and killing Jews. Although the exact numbers of ethnic German collaborators in Nazi crimes cannot be arrived at, historians assume that the Holocaust could not have happened without their assistance.[13]

The commanding guard duty officer (*Wachhabender*) of Blechhammer was Walter Rettinghausen (also Rettinghaus), a police officer and member of the SD Sosnowiec, whose identity could not be verified. He supervised the police guards and was authorized to punish the prisoners.[14] Alluding to the Jewish ritual bath *mikvah*, the inmates cynically nicknamed the man in his mid-thirties Mikvenik, due to his key function in murdering prisoners by way of the so-called death bath procedure (*Totbadeverfahren*). He also used the washroom for brutal beatings that most of his victims did not survive.[15] Moreover, Rettinghausen terrorized the prisoners at nights by forcing them to stand outside in the cold for hours.[16]

"A BEAST IN HUMAN SHAPE": CAMP LEADER ERICH HOFFMANN

Dr. Erich Walter Fritz Hoffmann, a lawyer and agricultural engineer, born in Breslau on June 24, 1897, and executed by Poland in 1948, served as camp leader of Blechhammer for almost two years, until the Auschwitz takeover ended his reign of terror. It was not only due to his comparatively long and continuous tenure that his name was etched into the memories of Blechhammer survivors. Described as a "beast in human shape," Hoffmann was notorious for his vicious temper and sadistic acts of cruelty.[17] The prisoners gave him the Yiddish nickname *Moishe Huhn* (Moishe the chicken), as his antics and high-pitched voice reminded some of a mentally disturbed boy in their village who believed he was a rooster. Hoffmann knew of his nickname and set his dog on the inmates whenever he overheard it.[18]

Interestingly, Hoffmann was neither a fervent Nazi nor a member of the SA or the SS. On the contrary, he had been banned from membership in the Nazi Party and its branch organizations, in addition to being declared unworthy of serving in the armed forces (*wehrunwürdig*).

Hoffmann started his career by joining a voluntary Catholic labor service (Freiwilliger Katholischer Arbeitsdienst) in 1932, but he automatically became part of the National Socialist Reich Labor Service (RAD), which took over the church's institution in 1933–34. He joined the National Socialist Party (NSDAP) in April 1936. Three months later, Hoffmann's alleged "Catholic attitude" prompted him to make derogatory remarks about the RAD and the party. He was dismissed and sentenced to two years in prison. His cousin later claimed that the Hoffmann family had had "a strong dislike" of the Nazi Party.

Hoffmann served his full prison term in Breslau-Kletschkau and was released in 1938. He remained excluded from party organizations and the Wehrmacht henceforth. Being considered persona non grata by the NSDAP nevertheless posed no significant obstacle for recruitment

Camp leader Dr. Erich Hoffmann, Munich, 1946.
(*Source:* StA M SpkA K 739)

into Fritz Todt's ambitious highway project.[19] Thus, Hoffmann was placed at the RAB by his local employment agency in summer 1938. By 1941 he had worked his way up from simple office clerk to camp leader, apparently without encountering any faith- or ideology-related conflicts. He had already gained some experience as an RAB camp leader when he was assigned the administration of the camp for Jews at Blechhammer in July 1942. He remained an employee of the RAB throughout his tenure, while rendering his services to the family-run grocery wholesaler Broemel & Sohn, which supplied the camp with food. Hoffmann's immediate superior was the RAB's Walter Tschechne.[20]

The use of Jewish unfree labor fundamentally changed the position of RAB camp leaders from plain administrators to powerful arbiters over life and death. Their surprisingly swift transformation into accessories to genocide and murderers in their own right was carried out by members of the SD branch of Sosnowiec. In SD schools, like the one established in Blechhammer in fall 1942, male and female camp leaders attended preparatory courses.[21] Although camp leaders and guard duty officers were equals in hierarchical terms, the influence of the police on the behavioral patterns of the RAB administrators should not be underestimated. As Himmler's "police-soldiers," who had been drilled to wage a merciless war against "inferior" peoples, they fostered the indoctrinating work of the SD training and, above all, introduced office clerks like Erich Hoffmann to maltreatment, torture, and manslaughter.[22] In his Munich trial in 1947, Hoffmann obviously lied when he claimed his designated job had merely been to manage the distribution of food to the inmates and to coordinate their work deployment at the OHW.[23] In addition to his participation in and initiation of killings, he was involved in selecting inmates for Auschwitz.[24]

Hoffmann's deputy, Wilhelm Pfeiffer (born in 1911), was chiefly responsible for food allocations.[25] In stark contrast to Hoffmann, Pfeiffer was described as a good-natured and generous person, who often handed out extra food portions to weak prisoners. The fact that he did not participate in camp atrocities or selections indicates that there was no pressure on the civilian camp personnel in this respect. However, Pfeiffer reportedly played on his status to molest young, male inmates.[26]

THE FIRST CAMP AT DORFLAGER

Inmates assigned to building up Schmelt camps from scratch generally had to endure very harsh conditions.[27] The prisoners setting up the future camp for Jews at Blechhammer were driven to clear trees and erect barracks at a rapid pace, while being constantly beaten by the police guards. In the first weeks, they had to sleep outdoors on plain wooden boards, and there was no running water, sanitary facilities, or electricity.

Still lacking a camp kitchen, they only sporadically received a bowl of unwashed spinach. Later the daily rations amounted to about two hundred grams of bread, some ersatz coffee, and soup.[28] The food was of poor quality, and the allocations were almost half of those handed out to concentration camp prisoners. Hoffmann was infamous for selling off the better part of the prisoners' food rations, leaving merely the unpalatable portions for their consumption, such as rotten vegetables and horse meat.[29]

Efforts by Jewish "Palestinian" prisoners of war held near Ehrenforst to aid the starving inmates were radically stopped by guard duty officer Rettinghausen. The POWs used to throw food to the inmates when they were driven past the camp on a truck. One day Rettinghausen shot at the soldiers and apparently forced the truck driver to take a different route henceforth.[30]

When the camp had been set up, there were two types of wooden barracks, identical to the ones used by the Highway Company for its German workers. The smaller barracks had six chambers and the larger ones twelve. Each chamber was five meters long and four meters wide and equipped with two-tier bunk beds and lockers. Owing to Todt's order to operate camps for Jews at three times above capacity, up to thirty prisoners slept in one chamber, and three men had to share a bed.[31]

The inmates wore civilian clothes and were initially permitted a limited number of spare shirts and underwear, as well as some toiletries. Higher quality garments and most of their other possessions were confiscated by the camp leader and guards upon arrival. German camp personnel reportedly pocketed valuables and clothes from the inmates' luggage.[32] A white Star of David was sewn on their jackets and trouser legs. Schmelt camps had their own system of prisoner numbers, consisting of a letter and a number. The numbers were not tattooed, but merely attached to the prisoners' clothes. It is unclear whether the inmates received a new number in each camp or retained a specific number throughout their imprisonment. The letter might have corresponded to the first letter of the camp's name. Only two Blechhammer survivors stated their Schmelt camp number in testimonies. The initial letter was a "B" as in Blechhammer, but it could also have referred to the first letter of their surnames.[33] Eastern Upper Silesian Jews were allegedly marked by the letter "O" for *Ostjude*.[34]

Until fall 1942, Jewish prisoners were still allowed to write and receive letters and parcels. The mail was censored, and valuables were mostly seized by the Germans. Inmates who had been sent money therefore tried to sew it into their clothes before the guards could confiscate it, and they destroyed the relevant letters immediately. The exchange of letters and postcards nevertheless provided an opportunity to keep in touch with family members in the ghettos and other Schmelt camps for a certain time.[35] Gruner's contention that the Schmelt Office had prohibited the reception of mail from spring 1942 is refuted by a report by the Sosnowiec police department of May 1942. The report states that Schmelt representative, Alfred Ludwig, instructed the police to prevent the relatives of inmates from handing over parcels themselves. He did not object to the delivery of mail as such, but excoriated the unrest stirred up by such visits.³⁶

The so-called self-administration of the prisoners (*Häftlingsselbstverwaltung*) implemented in the Schmelt camp system was analogous to that in concentration camps. It was a crucial tool in the hands of the German camp leadership to split up the solidarity among the inmates by giving privileges to a small fraction of them. On top of the hierarchy were the Jewish elders, who like the Jewish councils in the ghettos often faced ethical dilemmas. They were unable to truly represent their comrades' interests, as the Germans forced them to carry out orders directed against the prisoners.³⁷ Throughout the camp's existence, the position of Jewish elder was held by Karl Demerer. Born in Vienna in 1901, the merchant relocated to Katowice in Poland in 1928. While visiting his mother-in-law in Sosnowiec in 1940, he was arrested in the street. His wife and two children remained in Sosnowiec. Having passed through several Schmelt camps, he joined a transport of 350 men from camp Ottmuth (Otmęt) that was assembled to build up Blechhammer. Guard duty officer Rettinghausen appointed him as Jewish elder due to his good command of German. Demerer was very popular among fellow inmates and was renowned for his "diplomatic" way of dealing with the camp leadership. Bribery was his favored strategy for mitigating the guards' violence and saving the lives of individual prisoners.³⁸

While most regular inmates struggled for sheer physical survival, the functionary prisoners were granted access to music and entertainment. As in the concentration camps, this privilege symbolized their higher status and reflected the extreme hierarchy deliberately created by the Nazis to split up the inmate solidarity in camps.³⁹ On Friday and Saturday nights, Demerer organized so-called soirées in the office block (*Schreibstube*) featuring recitations, arias performed by an opera singer from Warsaw, and Yiddish theater plays. On Sunday afternoons, an impromptu show was put on by some of the inmates who were able to play an instrument, sing, or dance. The artists also performed in the barracks of the regular inmates afterward. Unlike the SS, neither camp leader

Jewish elder Karl Demerer. (*Source:* YVA photo archive 3883_3505.jpg)

Hoffmann nor the police guards let themselves be entertained by prisoners. Hoffmann thus permitted the soirées and impromptu shows but never attended them himself.[40] They were not used for singing or composing revolutionary songs. Unlike Brande and Seibersdorf (Zebrzydowice), Blechhammer had no camp song.[41]

Camp leader Hoffmann oversaw the prisoners' work deployment. At the OHW plant, the building supervisory board of Breslau, represented by the building technical department (BTA) on site, and OHW deputy director Dr. Heinrich Schlick coordinated their allocation to contractors. Each detail had a head of column (*Kolonnenführer*), the equivalent to an Oberkapo in the Schmelt camp system.[42] A typical day in summer started at 3:00 a.m., and a roll call was held half an hour later. At 4:00 a.m. the police guards marched the details to the factory, where they were assigned to literally backbreaking jobs, such as carrying cement sacks. A survivor recalled: "We simultaneously carried one sack on our backs, and another under our arms. It required superhuman strength. We poured the cement into buckets, while balancing on narrow, shaky scaffolds, or moving along steep riverbanks, sometimes we fell into the water."[43]

Consequently, a juvenile prisoner suffered from hernia. The prisoners received no protective clothing, such as gloves, when having to unload bricks, whose sharp edges cut their hands. The weight of iron poles they had to transport on their bare shoulders caused bleeding wounds.[44] While the order policemen guarding the prisoners were quite restrained on the OHW site, German, and particularly ethnic German, overseers frequently maltreated or even killed them. Ethnic Germans, who represented 17 percent of the total OHW workforce,[45] reputedly exerted more brutality against Jews than German foremen. The survivor Israel Rosengarten assumed that they had been driven by an inferiority complex, a constant urge to prove they were equal in value to the Germans.[46] One of the Water Polish masters was nicknamed *lopotka*, Polish for "shovel," as this was his preferred object to maltreat prisoners with. Another one was known as "the Murderer" among the inmates.[47]

Medical treatment was very limited. Prior to the ghetto liquidations, the few Jewish physicians permanently allocated to Schmelt camps often commuted between several camps to tend to inmates. Although Schmelt's system operated outside the concentration camp system, an SS area chief doctor (*Stabsarzt*) from Auschwitz regularly supervised the Jewish physicians. Until fall 1942, severely ill patients could be referred to the Jewish hospital in the Sosnowiec ghetto depending on the Schmelt Office's consent. Camps without a Jewish physician appointed so-called paramedics. In Blechhammer, this position was held by the dentist Simon Wallner from Wadowice.[48] Standard drugs had to be ordered from the Schmelt Office, which usually delivered only a small fraction of the required medicines. Surgical instruments were likewise rare. An estimated 30 percent of the prisoners were temporarily or permanently unfit to work. However, as Schmelt only tolerated a sick rate of 2 percent, most of them received no treatment. This rate also could be lowered at the camp leaders' discretion; in Blechhammer, it was not to exceed 1 percent, and there even was a "zero-sick-policy" in camp Seibersdorf. Admittance was restricted to those unable to stand or having a temperature above 39°C. The others were urged to continue to work and often died on the construction site as a result. The infirmary's reputation as an "antechamber to Auschwitz" also deterred many from seeking medical aid.[49]

The initial practice of permitting emaciated or ill Schmelt camp inmates a short period of recovery back in the ghettos was abandoned at the turn of the year 1941–42.[50] Evidently this option was no longer available to the prisoners of Blechhammer, to whom selections for the gas chambers of Auschwitz had already become a terrifying routine in spring 1942.[51]

Himmler's directive of April 1941 to murder sick and unfit concentration camp prisoners, code-named 14f13, reverberated throughout Schmelt's system. Schmelt camps were never visited by the physicians involved in the program to "euthanize" disabled and mentally ill patients in German health-care facilities known as Aktion T4, who began to select unfit prisoners in the concentration camps and subsequently gassed them in the same "sanatoriums" at Sonnenstein, Hartheim, and Bernburg that were used for the T4 murders. From December 1941, nonmedical camp personnel were authorized to make selections in support of the premeditated deployment of T4 physicians in the death camps of Aktion Reinhardt, Sobibór, Bełżec, and Treblinka.[52] Despite the apparent similarities, the tendency to draw a line of continuity between T4, 14f13, and the Holocaust is increasingly put into question.[53] Recent studies point to the prevalence of economic aspects in Aktion T4 murders, as opposed to the ideologically motivated killings of 14f13 and the Holocaust.[54]

Auschwitz started to create independent structures for murdering sick prisoners from August 1941. A single transport of 575 mainly non-Jewish Polish prisoners left the camp for Sonnenstein (Saxony) on July 28, 1941. Following first experiments with lethal injections and gassings with cyanide pellets, a sick transport to Sonnenstein was retained in Auschwitz to be gassed along with six hundred Soviet POWs on September 3, 1941.[55] The September gassings marked the beginning of frequent selections in the Auschwitz camp infirmary.[56] In spring 1942 the SS Economic Administration Main Office (WVHA) ordered the extension of selections to working prisoners and the killing of those who were emaciated and weak. In Auschwitz the first selection of this kind was made on May 4, 1942. Prisoners in the subcamps were regularly selected by SS personnel from the main camp.[57]

Historians assume that Schmelt camp inmates were among the earliest victims of gassings in Auschwitz.[58] However, the precise start of selections in Schmelt's system has never been verified.[59] The police guard duty officers were authorized to select prisoners for Auschwitz transports, and they increasingly drew on the civilian camp leaders' assistance. Schmelt's deputy, Heinrich Lindner, and Haunschild equally scrutinized the prisoners during their weekly visits: "Those looking lackluster, and who were unable to stand upright, or look straight into the 'slave trader's' eyes, disappeared as 'Muselmen' and were never seen again."[60]

Lindner, who rated illness as "sabotage," often shot sick or weak prisoners on the spot on these occasions.[61] The Schmelt Office's staff had long been familiarized with selection processes due to their involvement in "racial" screenings and the expulsion of Jews and Poles while working for SS "settlement centers." As members of the SS and the SD, they underwent regular ideological training.[62] Following their deployment in the annexed territories, the order police units had been prepared for carrying out mass killings by SS "experts" from 1940.[63] Together with the civilian camp leaders, the police guards were further instructed in special SD schools.[64]

In parallel to the gassings, unfit Schmelt camp inmates were murdered by way of the death bath procedure. They were exposed to cold water until heart failure set in, were drowned, or died of hypothermia. In Blechhammer, guard duty officer Rettinghausen mainly carried out these despicable killings. He also targeted inmates he intended to punish.[65] This killing method most likely originated from the Mauthausen subcamp Gusen, where unfit inmates were disposed of in this way between September 1941 and January 1942 due to the temporary suspension of transports to the T4 gassing facility in Hartheim.[66] Unlike in Gusen, water-induced murders remained a constant in Schmelt's system and were further intensified in 1943. To keep the sick list numbers low, inmates were also strangled or battered to death.[67]

The camp killings produced large numbers of bodies. Unlike concentration camps, the Schmelt Office did not use crematoria but instead buried the deceased in communal cemeteries or in designated places in the vicinity of camps. In the first half of 1942, dead Blechhammer inmates were interred in a Polish cemetery adjacent to an OHW camp for foreign laborers in a forest (*Waldlager*) that also included a communal grave for seven Soviets.[68]

THE FEMALE PRISONERS

Unlike in Auschwitz, where females represented only one-third of all registered prisoners and were not assigned to work deployments until 1942, Schmelt had Jewish women from the Eastern Upper Silesian ghettos conscripted for forced labor from late 1940 and established special camps for them.[69] Some were held in camps for men, like Blechhammer, to do household chores.[70] On April 9, 1942, the first one hundred Jewish women were transferred to Blechhammer from the RAB-run camp Klettendorf (Klecina), where they had been sewing uniforms for the Wehrmacht. They were housed in a single barrack in a fenced-off area of the camp adjacent to the Jewish elder's office.

Because there were so few of them, they could sleep in a bed of their own and were even forbidden to share a bed. During the winter this apparent privilege proved disadvantageous, as it was harder to stay warm at night. The women's daily routine started with the cleaning of the barracks in the mornings, before they split into groups to work in the scullery and the laundry or to sweep the streets. The women in the laundry washed the male prisoners' clothes, which they handed in once a week. Another barrack was set apart for sewing and mending. The kitchen staff had to prepare cabbage for the lunch of camp functionaries not going out to work. In the evening they got the men's hot meals ready.[71] The women spent comparatively short times in Blechhammer before being relocated to production sites specifically created or modified for women, while new arrivals took their place in the kitchen and the laundry. Haunschild also sent women to Blechhammer who had become too weak to work in factories.[72]

Gender is increasingly perceived as a decisive factor in determining the treatment and survival chances of male and female Holocaust victims.[73] Women in Schmelt camps appeared to have been at higher risk of being selected for Auschwitz transports, even if they were able to work. Several survivors related that "excess" women in transit camps had been sent to Auschwitz, and there were gender-specific selections in the camps targeting fit women.[74] Another factor was rape by German camp personnel. Sexual violence against women, men, and children was ubiquitous in Nazi camps.[75] However, unlike male victims of sexual assaults, Jewish women were typically killed to prevent "racially undesirable" offspring endangering the "purity of the Aryan race."[76] As the official crime of raping those considered "racially inferior" could be concealed by the ongoing genocide that legitimized the murder of these women, Steven T. Katz posits that the Nazis' annihilatory policy was a catalyst for assaults against female prisoners.[77] The subject of rape is often excluded from narratives on the Holocaust, based on the erroneous assumption that Nazi laws on "race defilement" (*Rassenschande*) prevented Germans from sexually assaulting Jewish women.[78] Numerous survivor testimonies and judicial interviews corroborate the abuse and ensuing murder of female inmates of Blechhammer who had become pregnant. Himmler's 14f13 directive of 1941 stipulating that pregnant concentration camp prisoners should die was likewise implemented in Schmelt camps and sealed the victims' fate.[79]

As access to the women's secluded quarters was restricted to a small fraction of the male personnel, they were the key perpetrators. One of them was the Czech German chef A. Alois, an employee of the Highway Company who supervised the women in the kitchen. He habitually coerced younger female prisoners into having a relationship with him. If the respective woman did not obey, he punished the others, such as by forcing them to stand outside in the snow.[80] At times the victims were ostracized by their female comrades, who misconstrued the abuse for a genuine affair. When Alois once overheard a woman scolding one of his victims for her "relationship," he almost beat her to death. A tall, sturdy man in his early twenties, Alois also mistreated male inmates. When he dished out the evening soup to the starving men and they pushed forward too much, he occasionally emptied out the soup bowls into their faces or hit them with a frying pan.[81] His behavior toward men nevertheless had a different quality, and he tended to reconcile with his male victims by giving them some extra food or cigarettes.[82] According to a postwar statement by Erich Hoffmann, he had saved Alois from being arrested by the police several times, but he did not mention for which allegations.[83]

The teenage girls formed a group distinct from the female prisoners in their twenties and thirties, who were mostly married with children.[84] Erich Hoffmann, whose wife and sons lived in Breslau, preyed on these inexperienced young women, especially if they were pretty and spoke German. He frequently came into the scullery asking for "very proper" girls to tidy up his apartment. When Hoffmann picked seventeen-year-old Rosa Schwarzberg and her friend Sala Fischel one day, Rosa fainted, terrified of what awaited her. Rosa fled from his apartment when her friend had suddenly disappeared, but she was dragged back inside by a furious Hoffmann. He wiped off the dust from a table and angrily smeared it onto her face. In the following weeks, Rosa was forced to clean for Hoffmann, assisted by Sala's sister, as Sala refused to carry on the work. Rosa was so desperate that she volunteered for another camp but had to return to Blechhammer a year later. Hoffmann immediately recognized her and threatened that she would stay for good this time. She then learned that Hoffmann had raped Sala Fischel and had ordered her sent to Auschwitz, as she became pregnant with his child. The Jewish elder Demerer facilitated Rosa's permanent transfer to a camp in Schatzlar the next day.[85] More "cleaning girls" shared Sala Fischel's fate after a few weeks in Hoffmann's service. Officially, they were selected for being "sick," but it was an open secret that they had become pregnant from rape. One way to avoid being targeted by Hoffmann was lacking knowledge of German. The Polish-speaking inmate Gucia Ferst thus refused to learn German, even if this put her at risk of being punished for not following orders promptly because she did not understand them.[86]

"SENT OFF TO AN UNKNOWN DESTINATION": THE MASS KILLINGS OF DYSENTERY PATIENTS

Shortly after the start of Hoffmann's tenure in July 1942, dysentery broke out in the Jewish camp and in a neighboring camp for Soviet POWs. During his Munich trial in 1947, Hoffmann blamed his alleged predecessor, whose identity remains unclear, for the outbreak. He also claimed that the disease had been caused by a lack of hygiene on the OHW construction site, not by the adverse sanitary conditions in the camp. OHW files nevertheless corroborate that the dysentery had spread from the two camps in question.[87] Public health authorities quarantined the inmates of both camps from mid-August.[88] On the day the quarantine was put into effect, the Jewish work details had already set out for the construction site. Around noon they were abruptly marched back to the camp, following orders by the Schmelt Office to liquidate them. The guards first made the prisoners exercise in the washroom barrack before ordering them to dig graves. They were narrowly saved by the intervention of the SS medical officer from Auschwitz, who routinely supervised the Jewish prisoner physicians' work. He demanded that Dr. Ritter, a Jewish head surgeon interned in camp Königshütte (Chrzanów), be transferred to Blechhammer immediately. Dr. Ritter apparently managed to convince the Germans that the dysentery had spread from the Soviet POW camp, not the Jewish camp, and that it would suffice to isolate those carrying the disease. The sick were held in a fenced-in compound, and the forest surrounding the camp was disinfected with lime.[89]

The events in Blechhammer seem to correspond with the likewise averted plans for shooting Jewish Schmelt prisoners, who had contracted typhus during their deployment with Organisation Todt in Russia in 1941.[90] Schmelt's radical killing policy was doubtless in line with the Nazi concept of annihilating those considered "racially inferior" and "endemic carriers" of contagious diseases.[91] However, even by SS standards it was considered inappropriate to wipe out the entire prisoner population of a camp. In both cases, Schmelt was thus urged to adopt a more selective method practiced in Auschwitz during outbreaks, which primarily targeted those among the infected who did not recover within a given time.[92]

Nevertheless, the prospects of Blechhammer inmates who had contracted dysentery were bleak, as they received no proper medical treatment. Among the few survivors was sixteen-year-old Sol W. He related how the Jewish prisoner physicians had to improvise to compensate for the lack of medicines, like dispensing charred bread to their patients as a remedy.[93] When the quarantine had been lifted, a list of the names of all remaining dysentery patients was drawn up, and they were successively removed from the camp. The inmates were made to believe that they would be taken to the Jewish hospital at Sosnowiec. Healthy inmates hoping to escape from Blechhammer in this way even bribed camp orderlies to get their names on the list. A survivor later disclosed the true fate of the prisoners on these transports: "Two cars with fifty to sixty people (among them one woman, Dr. Trammer's wife) drove off. Two hours later, the cars returned with all their belongings, their boots, and coats. As it turned out, all these people had been taken to the nearby town of Cosel, the central point for the segregation of transports of western Jews. I later met Dr. Trammer's wife, who was on that transport, in another camp. She told me that she had been the only one to get out alive, as she was an office worker. The others had been sent off to an unknown destination."[94]

This "unknown destination" was Auschwitz. The source indicates that the dysentery victims were added to deportation convoys from western Europe, which were frequently stopped in Cosel at the time to extract able-bodied men for Schmelt camps. The unfit prisoners were then sent on to Auschwitz with the elderly, the women, and the children on board to be killed.⁹⁵ At least another 120 prisoners were sent to their deaths in this way. Moreover, Erich Hoffmann tricked thirty emaciated inmates into volunteering for transports by claiming that they would go to a "convalescent camp."⁹⁶ Rosa Schwarzberg, one of Hoffmann's unfortunate "cleaning girls" desperate to leave the camp, followed the Jewish paramedic's advice to join a transport purportedly heading to Sosnowiec. Rosa was confined in an isolation barrack for one week, until enough dysentery patients had been gathered for a transport. Before the transport went off, the barrack was inspected by Hoffmann. On seeing Rosa, he went pale and exclaimed in surprise, "You, too?" but did not keep her back. In her video testimony, Rosa Schwarzberg did not go into further detail about what happened to that particular transport. As she eventually went to camp Eichthal (Dąbrówka Górna), there must have been another selection for fit prisoners.⁹⁷

By September 1, 1942, 409 prisoners out of the 1,410 still accounted for in July had died.⁹⁸ When the quarantine was lifted six weeks after the outbreak, another 700 inmates were relocated to Schmelt camps in Sudeten. Approximately 300 prisoners remained in Blechhammer to build up a new camp.⁹⁹

3

A NEW CAMP, NEW PRISONERS, NEW DIMENSIONS OF BRUTALITY

IN SEPTEMBER 1942 THE FIRST JEWISH CAMP AT *DORFLAGER* WAS DISBANDED, and a new one was set up on the grounds of the so-called *Bahnhoflager* ("railroad camp"), situated a few hundred meters from the Ehrenforst train station. The decision to relocate the camp was not, however, related to the dysentery outbreak, but had been contemplated from the outset. Postwar, self-exculpatory claims by camp leader Erich Hoffmann that he had initiated the inmates' transfer to a "better" camp were false.[1] Negotiations on the lease of land for new barrack camps between OHW director Riedmüller, Dr. Urbanek of the OHW social department, and Dr. Carstaedt, who acted on behalf of the Hohenlohe Trust, had already taken place in February 1942. Having long run out of building space on the territory previously acquired from Prince Hohenlohe, the OHW now found itself under increasing pressure to comply with General Plenipotentiary Krauch's directive to construct barracks for another eight thousand people by the middle of the year. The allocation of laborers was tied to the provision of adequate housing facilities, and an increase in the workforce was deemed necessary to meet Göring's recent demands for an increase in the production of synthetic fuel. Therefore the relocation of the new, enlarged Jewish camp was not just a logistical requirement, but was regarded as an important contribution to the Third Reich's large-scale war effort.[2]

It was soon agreed to use a stretch of 4.2 square kilometers of forested land situated east of the road leading from the Ehrenforst railroad station to Ehrenforst village. Yet only the southern part of what was to become the *Bahnhoflager*, comprising approximately one-third of the total camp area, was designated as a camp for Jews (*Judenlager*). Prince Hohenlohe's concerns about prisoners trespassing on his hunting grounds were only short-lived, as head engineer Otto Stoltzenburg, who represented the Highway Company's building supervisory board at the OHW, was quick to assure him that the camp for Jews would be surrounded by a 2.5-meter-high barbed wire fence.[3]

The ranks of the severely decimated Blechhammer inmates were augmented by approximately six hundred Jewish men from the Netherlands, Belgium, and France, who began to arrive in the camp between October and December 1942, after the quarantine had been lifted. Owing to a request for ten thousand additional Jewish laborers for industrial sites in Silesia by the Ministry of Armaments and War Production under Albert Speer, Himmler authorized Schmelt to extract men from western deportation convoys en route to Auschwitz.[4] Following the launch of mass deportations of Dutch, Belgian, and French Jews, Speer apparently sought new ways of supplying the war economy with skilled workers from western Europe. His intention to replace the Polish Jews with deportees from western Europe possibly led to the transfer of seven hundred Eastern Upper Silesian Blechhammer prisoners to Sudeten when the first camp was disbanded.[5] During the so-called Cosel period,[6] deportation trains were stopped by Schmelt representatives in the freight depot of Cosel (Koźle), a town situated about forty miles northwest of Auschwitz, to take off able-bodied men aged between about sixteen and fifty-five.[7] Those over fifty were taken off when there were few younger men and sent back to the train when there were plenty. As a rule, Schmelt representatives only judged the men's age by their looks, so that younger and older persons were taken, or those younger looking were not.[8] An estimated 9,015 western deportees were thus selected by Schmelt Office staff between August 28 and December 10, 1942. A mere 700 of these men survived. There were no female survivors, even though a small number of the women were selected for work when the trains had terminated in Auschwitz.[9] As Schmelt camps operated independently from Auschwitz and its subcamps, the men were selected in Cosel, not on the ramp of Birkenau. The Cosel stops thus facilitated the unprecedented import of western deportees into a secluded camp system designated for Eastern Upper Silesian Jews.

The Cosel period was divided into three phases. The first involved Himmler's official permission and ended on October 7, 1942. The second phase was illicitly carried out by Schmelt representatives on their own initiative between October 18 and December 10, 1942. A third phase ensued in fall 1943.[10]

Between August 28 and November 9, 1942, seventeen transports from France were stopped in Cosel, and approximately thirty-five hundred men were made to get off.[11] Jewish emigrants from Austria and Germany, who had fled to southern France, represented a majority in the eight convoys departing from Drancy between August 31 and September 16, 1942. They had fallen victim to a raid on foreign Jews carried out in the unoccupied part of France between August 26 and 28 with the Vichy regime's approval.[12] Among them were numerous artists or members of political resistance movements. They had often endured imprisonment in the early Nazi concentration camps and had fled to the South of France after the invasion to avoid capture by the Germans, and in the hope of reaching a safe destination from Marseille. Some rendered their services to the American Emergency Rescue Committee, initiated by German writer Thomas Mann in 1940 to enable those on the Gestapo blacklist to immigrate to the United States. Owing to their artistic talents and previous camp experience, they typically played leading roles in the prisoner administration or camp theaters and orchestras in Schmelt camps.[13] On the last French train stopped in Cosel on November 9, 1942, were mainly Jews holding citizenships previously excluded from deportations. This predominantly affected 609 Romanian Jews, who had been arrested in a major raid on September 24, 1942, and Greek Jews rounded up on November 5, 1942. On April 1, 1944, 1.6 percent of Blechhammer inmates held Romanian citizenship and presumably stemmed from these final roundups in France.[14]

Between August 31 and October 12, 1942, six Belgian convoys from Mechelen/Malines had a stop in Cosel, and an estimated 1,975 men were seized by the Schmelt Office. Most of the people on board had been arrested between July and September 1942 as a result of major roundups in Antwerp and Brussels. The deportations were temporarily suspended in October 1942, as the Belgian police ceased to collaborate in any further arrests.[15]

An estimated 3,540 male deportees from the Netherlands were taken off in Cosel between August 28 and December 10, 1942. They represented the largest group among the "Cosel men."[16] The August and early September transports had a halt in Liegnitz (Legnica), where the deportees were tricked into writing postcards to their relatives. The messages were intended to keep up the myth of Jews being "resettled" to the east and to prevent resistance to the deportations. This perfidious method was widely practiced by the Nazis. The order police guards escorting the trains collected the mail and posted it on their return to the Netherlands from Auschwitz. Most of the senders had already been murdered in the gas chambers by then.[17]

The Dutch and Belgian deportees were still boarded on passenger trains. They usually arrived in the early mornings and were torn from their sleep by Schmelt's staff, who entered the compartments demanding that all younger men should step out. They removed those who did not obey at once from the trains by force. They were assisted by SS men and order police guards escorting the trains. Up to three hundred men, one-third of an average convoy, were extracted in Cosel. Schmelt's deputy Heinrich Lindner made a first selection on the station's platform. Then the men had to squat on their luggage with raised arms, until trucks took them to transit camps.[18] The separation of families caused turmoil and was occasionally met with resistance. On the Westerbork transport of August 31–September 2, a woman approached an SS man and demanded her husband back. The SS guard began to whip her without responding to her request, and she dared to slap him in the face. Stunned by her unexpected reaction, the SS man permitted her husband to return to the train.[19] Schmelt camp leaders evidently attended the selections when they required workers, and they supervised the male deportees on the platform. Erich Hoffmann was thus seen in Cosel on October 5, 1942, when the first Westerbork deportees destined for Blechhammer arrived.[20] French convoys consisted of cattle cars, and deaths or suicides commonly occurred on these transports. In Cosel, the younger male deportees were rounded up in a field next to the freight station. The SS and Schmelt representatives encircled them with utmost brutality, ordering them to lie flat on their faces.[21] The survivor Jules Fainzang later described the ensuing selection process, which reminded him of depictions of a slave market: "Three German officers thus approached us, headed by a civilian with a limp, carrying a notebook in one hand and a little cane in the other: '*Mund aufmachen*', 'open your mouth', the civilian told one of our comrades, and he inspected his teeth using his cane to hold his mouth open. A scene from a movie I had watched in Anvers before the war came to my mind, *Capitaine Blood* with Errol Flynn. On a slave market a slave trader made the same gesture. However, here, unlike in the film, it was not done to see if the slave was in good health, but only to check if he had gold teeth!"[22]

The "official" phase of the Cosel period ended on October 7, 1942, when Auschwitz commandant Hoess cabled to Eichmann that deportation trains from Westerbork were to be routed straight to Auschwitz henceforth to prevent Schmelt from meddling in the transports.[23] However, the Schmelt Office did not comply with Hoess's demands and continued to extract male deportees. Both the Dutch convoy of October 5–7 and the one of October 16–18 carried a record number of men in the appropriate age group. An estimated 1,120 men were taken off these two transports alone.[24] The October peak pertained to the concerted disbanding of all fifty Jewish labor camps on Dutch soil on October 2 and 3, 1942. The camp inmates and their next of kin were transferred to Westerbork to be deported. An additional five thousand Jews arrested in a large-scale raid in Amsterdam constituted a major "reserve" for deportations in the following weeks.[25] In his postwar trial, Hoess stated that he had objected to the Cosel stops, as they delayed the trains and allegedly enabled escapes.[26] Given the growing pressure on concentration camps to put ever larger numbers of prisoners at the disposal of the war industry, he presumably also began to perceive Schmelt as a rival skimming off potentially fit men.[27] Along the same lines, the Schmelt Office was compelled to find ways of circumventing these restrictions to satisfy the demands of industrialists, whose production sites operated outside of the concentration camp system. One of the most influential clients in this respect was the Reich Highway Company.

Apart from two transports from Malines and Drancy, the illicit Cosel stops carried out between October 18 and December 10, 1942, mainly targeted Westerbork deportees. As Lindner could no longer draw on the large-scale support of SS and police units, he picked fewer men in the desired age group. His staff applied various strategies to prevent any unrest during the separation of families. The selected men were now assured that they would be reunited with the women and children later. Young men were tricked into leaving the trains under the false pretense that everyone would receive refreshments, and they were served first. Immediately after they got off, the trains departed.[28] Unlike before, Schmelt's staff politely asked for volunteers for labor camps instead of removing the men by force. Those who declined the offer were permitted to stay on the trains.[29] The most crucial—and disturbing—new development was the exchange of healthy men for sick, emaciated, and even dying Schmelt camp inmates.[30] The camp leaders now simply transported their unfit prisoners to Cosel on trucks and added them to the trains. The victims of the dysentery outbreak in Blechhammer were among the first to be affected by this practice.[31] Westerbork deportees were shocked to see prisoners being loaded onto the train they had just been taken off on October 18, 1942, the start of the unauthorized stops. Among them were Dutch inmates who, like themselves, had been made to step out in Cosel only weeks before and were now about to be murdered in Auschwitz. They gave them the last advice to eat up all the food provisions they still had before the guards in the transit camps could take them away. Two weeks later a Dutch survivor witnessed how twenty "ghastly looking" Jews were put on the train.[32] The Schmelt camp inmates added to the trains presumably warned the other deportees what awaited them in Auschwitz. Three young women who had been on the first Westerbork transport with an unauthorized Cosel stop on October 16–18, 1942, thus refused to enter the gas chamber, and pleaded for their lives. They were shot on the spot by SS men.[33] A British POW and medical officer placed on a deportation convoy in Cosel to return to the Blechhammer POW camp gave a disturbing account of the despair of the women, children, and elderly people on board, who had suddenly realized that they would be killed.[34]

The Schmelt Office's efforts to obfuscate the ongoing Cosel selections by replacing the missing men with equal numbers of unfit prisoners were nonetheless futile, as the illicit extraction of deportees was noticed in Auschwitz. Hoess's complaints to Eichmann eventually prompted HSSPF of Silesia Schmauser to act against Schmelt's staff.[35] Survivors of the last stop of December 10, 1942, testified that a large part of the able-bodied men already selected for Schmelt camps had been ordered to return to the train and travel on to Auschwitz. This was likely the result of Schmauser's intervention.[36]

Evidently the unauthorized Cosel stops were resumed in the late summer and fall of 1943.[37] From March to July 1943, convoys from Westerbork rode to Sobibór. Between August 24, 1943, and November 16, 1943, seven trains were rerouted to Auschwitz.[38] Numerous interrogation reports by former policemen guarding these transports in 1943 corroborate selections by SS men in Cosel, who exchanged fit men for sick and emaciated prisoners.[39] Camp leader Erich Hoffmann seized on the renewed Cosel stops for sending sick Blechhammer inmates to Auschwitz. He added 350 prisoners to a Westerbork convoy on September 1 and an unknown number of typhus convalescents on September 16, 1943.[40] The modus operandi established during the Cosel selections apparently served as a model for similar stops in stations near larger camps situated along the major deportation routes toward Auschwitz in late 1943. Again, Westerbork convoys were primarily targeted. A Czech SS unit thus pulled out fit men from a train stopped in Königshütte. The same was done in Sosnowiec, and sick inmates were added to replace the missing men. During a stop near Kattowitz, younger women were selected with the men.[41] It is unclear whether the Schmelt Office carried out the unauthorized stops of 1942 and 1943 entirely on its own, as Hoess had claimed. The office must have been informed of the incoming deportation trains beforehand by either the Gestapo or HSSPF Schmauser. Possibly Schmelt was notified of the transports as part of his function as chief administrator of Oppeln. It is also unknown who instructed the Oppeln Rail Directorate to bring trains to an unscheduled halt in Cosel. The numbers of fit men extracted during the stops of 1943 are impossible to arrive at. There were either no survivors or none who gave testimony.

The unauthorized phases of the Cosel stops reflect the crude reality of the policy of "annihilation through labor," as Schmelt representatives disposed of sick and emaciated inmates while simultaneously drawing on a reservoir of fresh workers. Except for a small fraction, most of these men succumbed to the murderous conditions in Schmelt camps. Many of the unfit prisoners taking their place on the trains had been made to step out of such convoys only weeks before, when they were in good physical shape. The Cosel men, and particularly the Dutch deportees among them, had staggering death tolls of up to 95 percent and often did not even make it through their first winter in Silesia. Survivors linked this extreme mortality to the traumatic, sudden separation from their families in Cosel, which profoundly impacted their will to persevere.[42] The Cosel selections were the first face-to-face encounter with the Germans. The brutality exerted by Schmelt representatives while forcing men off the trains not only was humiliating, but suddenly made the deportees grasp the disturbing realities of the Final Solution. Dutch Jews typically had no previous knowledge of the death camps or did not believe in their existence.[43] The Westerbork deportee Gabriel Zvi Lifschitz had even employed a former Buchenwald inmate in his household before the occupation of the Netherlands. This encounter had prompted him to read books about German concentration camps. He nonetheless felt that nothing could have prepared them for the ordeal of the labor camps that was to follow.[44] During the unauthorized Cosel stops, a young man deported from Westerbork thus unsuspectingly decided to stay on the train. It was only at the ramp of Birkenau that he suddenly realized that most of his fellow deportees were about to be gassed. Panic stricken, he nevertheless found a way of hiding in the camp and smuggled himself onto a transport to Buchenwald three days later.⁴⁵ Similarly, French deportees often opted to ignore reports about Nazi concentration camps and mass killings spread by Communist underground papers such as *Unzer Wort* and *J'accuse*.⁴⁶

Some survivors remained unable to integrate the Cosel selections into their memories for the rest of their lives. The Viennese cartoonist Bil Spira, whose Drancy convoy was stopped in Cosel on September 6, 1942, completely omitted the selection in his autobiography penned over fifty years later. He merely described his arrival in the Sakrau (Zakrzów) transit camp. Ernest Koenig, who also was on this transport, wrote his memoirs around the same time. Contrary to Spira, he gave a detailed account of the SS men's crude acts of violence, which culminated in the murder of a little girl who had accidentally gotten off the train during the selection process. Spira, like many others, seems to have suppressed his traumatic memories.⁴⁷

The testimony of Léon Zyguel is an even more tragic example. The then teenage boy was pulled out of a Drancy convoy with his brother and father. Decades later, he went into schools to tell his story. He related the unscheduled stop, but then immediately jumped to the tattooing of his number in Auschwitz or one of its subcamps. He apparently fused the memory of the Cosel selection with that of his registration as an Auschwitz prisoner, which must have taken place two years later. He seemingly had no active recall of details of the Cosel stop and the internment in Schmelt camps that followed, but nevertheless stressed that this had been a turning point in his life:

> When we arrived in Poland, the doors were thrown open. To my fifteen-year-old mind, my life had been turned upside down. I didn't know where I was. The interpreters arrived and told us: "All men aged between sixteen and fifty get off the train." My father and my brother got off. I got off with them, and the train continued, carrying off the elderly and the children, the women too. My sister, who had been arrested with us, was on that train that left for Auschwitz. We never saw her again. Like I was told, I went into the hut where the prisoner was, who was going to tattoo my number. I stepped up to him to tell him that I was Zyguel. I laid my arm down on the table, like this, as he was looking at his lists and numbers. He told me "From now on, you'll be 179084."⁴⁸

The missing memories in both Bil Spira's life writing and Léon Zyguel's oral history report illustrate the destructive force of the Shoah and make the ongoing struggles of survivorship palpable. They were the result of a coping mechanism found in many Holocaust survivors, who repressed their traumatic memories for the sake of rebuilding their lives.⁴⁹

Various camps administrated by the Reich Highway Company served as collection points for those selected in Cosel. The men traveled up to fifty miles on open trucks driven by Dutchmen who had volunteered to work in Germany. The most frequently used transit camps were Sakrau (Zakrzów), Annaberg (Góra Świętej Anny), Johannsdorf (Jaśkowice), and Ottmuth (Otmęt).[50] The western deportees were conspicuously kept off the usual transit points for Eastern Upper Silesian Jews in the ghettos of Sosnowiec and Będzin. The crucial role of the RAB as a key facilitator of the exploitation of Jewish forced labor is underscored here once more. The Highway Company's representative, Haunschild, visited transit camps on the same day, or the day after, transports had passed through Cosel, to register the men according to their professions. He had all the men lined up in front of him and made them walk. When asking for their professions, Haunschild ridiculed those with "typically Jewish" occupations, prompting some to state that they were farmers. Most of the deportees were distributed among Schmelt camps within the next few days or weeks.[51]

The first group of Cosel men in Blechhammer stemmed from the transport that had left Westerbork on October 3 and was stopped in Cosel on October 5, 1942. Two hundred men had been split between the Annaberg and Sakrau transit camps. The Sakrau group was transferred to Blechhammer on October 11, followed by the one from Annaberg on October 15. The first French deportees arrived in the beginning of the month via Ottmuth. Haunschild allocated 25 out of the 175 men extracted from the thirty-eighth convoy that had left Drancy on September 25, 1942, to Blechhammer. Haunschild together with Erich Hoffmann selected 150 carpenters in Niederkirch (Dolna) on October 14 and an extra 350 men from Johannsdorf on October 19. With the arrival of further Dutch Jews from Eichthal (Dąbrówka Górna) and Klein-Mangersdorf (Magnuszowice) on December 4 and 5, the number of prisoners reached 900 in late 1942.[52] Only a few barracks had been erected when the first groups arrived, and some of them were still inhabited by non-Jewish Polish and French laborers, who were gradually moved to *Dorflager*. One of the Jewish inmates' first tasks was to fence in the new camp with barbed wire fetched from the deserted old camp for Jews. Under constant beatings by the guards, they built additional barracks and beds and made footpaths in the camp.[53]

Especially the Dutch Jews had staggering death tolls in the first winter, not only due to the hard labor, but also because they could not adjust to the camp conditions mentally. A decisive factor was their lack of Polish language skills, which inhibited their integration into social networks the Polish Jews had established, for example to acquire and share extra food. The Dutch often felt discriminated against by Polish Jewish functionaries and by the ethnic German overseers on the construction site, who tended to give out instructions in Polish. Unlike Polish Jews, who were still allowed to receive parcels from their relatives, the western Jews were barred from this lifeline.[54] Blechhammer was no exception in this respect. The Degussa plant at Gleiwitz, which had set up a Schmelt camp in spring 1942, canceled its plans for replacing Eastern Upper Silesian Jews with western Jews, as most of the "Cosel men" were rated as unfit for work by March 1943. They were removed from the camp and presumably murdered in Auschwitz. Jews from the Sosnowiec ghetto replaced them.[55]

POLICE GUARD VIOLENCE AND ITS PROLIFERATION THROUGH THE SD SCHOOL BLECHHAMMER

Guard duty officer Walter Rettinghausen was assigned a deputy, whose identity remains unclear. He was a tall, gaunt man with bowlegs and a blunt face with a moustache, who came to Blechhammer from camp Ottmuth (Otmęt). The inmates called him "The Blue Angel," as his face had become bluish from alcohol abuse, and "to be blue" in German also means "to be drunk." When he was intoxicated, he ferociously maltreated the inmates.[56] He often flogged prisoners to death. One of his victims was a former medical student from The Hague, whom he killed in this way because his body was covered in lice. When the prisoners returned from work, he stood at the camp gate dealing out blows "like a clockwork." At night he chased them out of their barracks to check on the "cleanliness" of the beds. He had a peculiar habit of lowering his voice, rather than screaming, when addressing prisoners.[57]

In late 1942, a so-called SD school (*SD-Schule*) was set up in Blechhammer. It served as a training center for order police guards and future male and female civilian camp leaders. The theoretical instructions were given in a barrack near the Jewish campkitchen. The training, which lasted up to six weeks, also included "field lessons" in the camp. The main instructors were Schmelt's deputy, Heinrich Lindner, and a police officer named Knauer.[58] Knauer's identity could never be verified, but he was closely connected to Lindner, with whom he regularly inspected camps. In early 1943 Knauer was replaced by SS Sturmbannführer Knoll, a member of the SD and the Schmelt Office.[59]

The survivor Salomon Lierens related his encounter with a class of policemen who were led around Blechhammer: "There was a special barrack, the *Lehrschulbaracke*, where the gentlemen were instructed how to get the highest productivity out of us on the smallest food rations. They made excursions around the camp with twenty to thirty men of the *Grüne Polizei*. People were dying like rats, but they had enough human material to replace them immediately."[60]

The expansion of the Nazi apparatus of oppression, coupled with men being drafted to the front, increasingly caused the regime to draw on women, especially after the collapse of the eastern front in 1942–43.[61] The Schmelt Office thus began to install female camp leaders in camps for women. One of them was Margarethe Neugebauer. Born in Breslau in 1906, she had been conscripted to Luftwaffenbaupark Ost by an employment agency in June 1943 and accepted the offer to become the camp leader of Klettendorf. Prior to her appointment, she attended a three-day course in Blechhammer's

SD school. In a court hearing in 1962, Neugebauer stated that Knoll had advised his students to treat the inmates with absolute ruthlessness, irrespective of their physical state. Camp leaders were to list inmates for Auschwitz transports if they were ill, were unfit for work, or had transgressed rules. Neugebauer professed ignorance of the fate of the female prisoners she had selected for Auschwitz. It can nonetheless be gleaned from her statements that female camp leaders were equally familiar with the practice of water-induced murders. Although it was hardly the place for a budding romance, she started an affair with Heinrich Lindner during the training in Blechhammer, and they eventually got married. Her career went smoothly, and she soon took over camp Güntherbrücke (Swojczyce).[62]

The SD schools are an entirely unexplored field. Therefore, it is unknown how many schools existed, when they were introduced, and whether they were restricted to Schmelt's system. In addition to fostering the police guards' collaborative functioning in the Holocaust, the training of civilians in selections and murders seems to have been a preparatory step in the planned withdrawal of the order police from the Schmelt camps to make them available for newly formed rapid response units.[63] By training civilian camp leaders, the school propagated the police guards' violence. Blechhammer's role in the recruitment of civilians for tasks directly connected to the Final Solution is exemplified here.

The establishment of the SD school also exacerbated the guards' brutality, who had license to punish or kill prisoners without permission from a superior authority. The school's instructor, Knauer, was placed in Blechhammer permanently. He mistreated the prisoners during work and encouraged Hoffmann to attain high productivity by laying into work details.[64] The prisoners were often beaten for petty infractions, such as not having shined their shoes or wearing filthy clothes, even though it was well known to the guards that they had neither shoe polish nor soap. One inmate was flogged simply because he had forgotten to put on his cap when queuing for the evening soup.[65] An average forty prisoners had to report to the police guards each night for alleged transgressions during work. They were dealt up to one hundred whip lashes. By contrast, typical floggings under the Auschwitz administration did not exceed twenty-five lashes.[66] Work details were also collectively punished, for example if individual prisoners had been caught smoking at work.[67] In October 1942 newly arrived inmates were ordered to empty a latrine with buckets. One of the inmates slipped while holding a full bucket in his hands, and a supervising police guard was soiled. Infuriated, the guard tossed the inmate into the open trench of the latrine, from which he was unable to extricate himself. Rescue attempts by a fellow prisoner were stopped by the guard, and the inmate slowly drowned in the excrement.[68]

After schooling in violence in Blechhammer, a police guard named Pietsch was appointed guard duty officer of a new Schmelt camp in Seibersdorf by Lindner in fall 1942.

The grocer from Neisse (Nysa) was a member of the Sipo and an officer of the reserve army. The inmates described him as a "fanatic anti-Semite" and nicknamed him "The One with the Whip," as he incessantly made use of his riding whip. In Seibersdorf, he was infamous for ill-treating the sick.[69] The police veterans tended to be more lenient. The inmates even had a laugh with a sixty-three-year-old police guard with a hunchback, who shouldered an old-fashioned rifle that appeared bigger than himself. To tease him, the inmates marched along very fast, as the old man could hardly keep up.[70]

Rettinghausen prepared Hoffmann for the time after the police's departure by letting him assist in the water-induced murders committed in the washroom barrack each night.[71] The camp leader was nonetheless susceptible to bribery. The Jewish elder thus managed to save five prisoners Hoffmann intended to murder for having written letters about the conditions in the camp.[72]

THE EXPANSION OF THE CAMP'S INFRASTRUCTURE DURING THE "FALL PEAK"

In preparation for the camp's projected enlargement it was staffed up, and the infrastructure was adjusted accordingly. The Cosel stops and the start of deportations in the ghettos led to a massive influx of new prisoners into Schmelt's system, which Gutterman referred to as the "fall peak." Blechhammer's inmate population doubled, from nine hundred in December 1942 to about two thousand in spring 1943.[73]

The Jewish elder was given a deputy named Ems. The German Jewish veteran of the First World War had fled to the Netherlands after the Nazi rise to power. He was pulled out of a Westerbork convoy in Cosel and came to Blechhammer via Annaberg on October 16, 1942. The Schmelt Office staff appointed him because they liked his military, Prussian-style attire. Ems reputedly was a well-mannered intellectual who despised bribery, which is why he did not hold his post for long. He was made the superior of all heads of columns instead and tirelessly drilled the prisoners like soldiers. This earned him the nickname Yeke Potz, "German fool" in Yiddish.[74] In December 1942, a Dutch Jew with Polish roots called Jozef Niewes (also Piet Nieuwes) became the new deputy. Niewes, born in Slachzince in 1894, had emigrated to the Netherlands and became a renowned manufacturer of hats in Amsterdam. When the Germans invaded the country in 1940, his factory was expropriated, and he fled to southern France. Niewes was deported from Drancy to Auschwitz in August 1942. When the train was stopped in Cosel, Heinrich Lindner first appointed him as Jewish elder of camp Annaberg, then sent him to Blechhammer. He was put in charge of all camp personnel and the kitchen, while Demerer oversaw the prisoners' work deployment.[75] Niewes was a polarizing figure described by a survivor as "a combination of a merchant and a thief."[76]

Niewes replaced the previous Jewish cook, who was blamed for reselling camp provisions to local farmers, with two new ones, Grynzeiger and Szmulek Band from Oświęcim. Especially Band was infamous for his short temper and authoritarian leadership style toward the female kitchen staff.[77] Both cooks infuriated fellow inmates, who called them "murderers," as they sold the margarine intended to be used in the soup to certain prisoners for money.[78] A new camp kitchen comprising three barracks was ready in October 1942. It could only be accessed via a neighboring camp for female Soviet workers. Until it had been completed, the prisoners, much to Hoffmann's dislike, enjoyed a short period of high-quality meals allocated by a German staff canteen. Later their diet consisted of unpeeled potatoes in a soup made of spinach and pearl barley.[79] The bread rations were raised from two hundred to three hundred grams, served with a topping of margarine or molasses. Apart from a fortnightly distribution of milk, no dairy products were handed out, even though butter and soft cheese were made in the camp. In fall, pumpkins, white cabbage, and beetroots supplemented their diet. On special occasions, like Hitler's birthday, the soup contained pieces of meat.[80] As in most camps, the bread rations for the following day were handed out with the evening soup. As only few had enough self-discipline to retain some of that bread for the next day, most inmates were marched to work on an empty stomach and devoured the lunchtime soup the OHW had introduced in July 1942 to boost work performance. Made of rotten vegetables, the OHW's "bunker soup" notoriously caused digestive problems and edema. Instead of increasing the prisoners' productivity, the extra meal thus merely exacerbated their physical state. This notwithstanding, the OHW charged contracting firms, who were obligated to supply their Jewish workers with the broth, 0.10 RM per portion.[81]

Hoffmann aggravated the food situation by mismanagement and embezzlement. He often procured large quantities of perishable goods, which soon began to decay, and not only resold food but misappropriated ration stamps the OHW issued to the prisoners.[82] Low wages and poor accommodation made the Highway Company an unattractive employer; thus those who signed up as camp leaders often had previous convictions or were alcoholics. The RAB was forced to dismiss a camp leader for embezzlement or permanent intoxication practically every month. Their dishonesty further diminished the survival chances of the prisoners, who depended on the rations. Most companies nevertheless refrained from reporting them to the police to avoid public scandal.[83] In one exceptional case, the Gestapo arrested the camp leader of Sackenhoym for distilling alcohol from the prisoners' sugar allocations.[84] Under the Auschwitz administration, the Blechhammer inmates not only received higher standard rations on paper, but they were also more likely to find them in their bowls.[85]

Mimicking the Jewish ghetto militia, the Schmelt Office used Jewish policemen (*Lagerpolizisten*) to supervise the prisoners. Blechhammer's two Jewish policemen,

Dennenbaum and Rauch, wore caps with a white band and were armed with whips. In the "gray zone" between the German camp leadership and the prisoners, they each chose a different path.[86] Jumbo Dennenbaum was one of the few Jewish survivors of the railroad construction works in Russia organized by Organisation Todt in winter 1941–42.[87] After his recovery, he was sent to Blechhammer in fall 1942 to serve as a shoemaker and camp policeman. Jumbo was popular, as he used his controversial position to help other inmates. When he was ordered to flog a prisoner in the washroom barrack, he only pretended to hit him. By whipping the sink, Jumbo created a typical noise for the German police guard, who usually waited outside. He told his victims to scream as loudly as possible and to hold their backs as if they were in great pain afterward.[88] Rauch, by contrast, dealt out real blows and was considered a "sadist" by fellow inmates.[89] In the evenings he punished those he caught queuing for a second helping of soup.[90] The teenage inmate Wolf W., who served as Rauch's calfactor, reported that he had mistreated him.[91] Rauch also assisted the police guards and Hoffmann in water-induced murders and was ordered to strangle a female inmate.[92] He was installed as a head of a column in camp Landeshut (Kamienna Góra) in spring 1944. After the war, Rauch was allegedly put on trial, and he was executed in Paris.[93]

Toward the end of 1942 the construction of the OHW plant had progressed, and more and more contracting companies were demanding to be allocated Jewish workers. A new detail was formed in response to each of these requests. The work details, comprising about fifty men, were supervised by Jewish heads of columns (*Kolonnenvorstände*), equivalent to head Kapos in the concentration camp system. They were assisted by foremen (*Schieber*) and were installed or dismissed by the Jewish elder and the camp leader. A certain percentage of the prisoners were offered this position due to their formerly privileged social status. All heads of columns donned riding breeches and boots and carried a whip. Demerer tried to keep beatings to a minimum and occasionally took away their whips. Nevertheless, the pressure to maintain a high pace at work under the scrutiny of German overseers left most heads of columns no other choice than to maltreat their comrades. Their dilemma was an intrinsic part of the Nazis' strategy to break up solidarity among the prisoners. Therefore, some declined such positions.[94] On Sundays, the heads assembled for a special roll call parade in particularly elegant clothing. To the ordinary inmates, whose civilian clothes had been reduced to filthy rags, this demonstration exemplified the vast social divide within the camp population.[95]

However, individual heads of columns, like Joseph ("Jopie") Braasem, gained the sympathy of their comrades. Born in Amsterdam in 1919, he had been deported from Westerbork on September 7, 1942. He came to Blechhammer in October 1942 from Ottmuth and was soon appointed as the head of a column. Braasem had been a boxer and was a real muscleman, whose strength even impressed the Germans. He succeeded in making them believe that he was very tough on fellow inmates when, in fact, he only pretended to hit them. Like Jumbo the policeman, Braasem told his victims to scream, while hardly touching them.[96] His way of tricking the Germans inspired others and, contrary to the intended dehumanizing effect of the floggings, this particular "whipper" renewed their moral strength: "He managed to satisfy the sadistic Nazi supervisors with a deceptive display of flogging which did not harm the victim badly. He always managed to build up a sweat and pretended to breathe heavily during the whipping acts to deceive the Nazi supervisors that he applied the full force of the whip."[97] Only a few of the punishing functionary prisoners could act as convincingly as Braasem. This often resulted in collective punishment by Hoffmann or Knauer.[98]

The sanitary facilities remained primitive, with only three washroom barracks fitted with basins, and no showers. At least three hundred men were forced to share a washroom, and it was of little use that two medical orderlies were ordered to check on the prisoners' personal hygiene in the mornings, since the men could barely clean their upper bodies. As the growing number of inmates overburdened the laundry, their clothes were only irregularly washed and propelled the spread of body lice and fleas. Despite frequent disinfection, the latrines remained a source of infectious diseases.[99] Every Sunday the prisoners, usually those considered "intellectuals," had to empty them using buckets.[100]

Following the dysentery outbreak, Dr. Ritter was permanently installed as camp physician. His predecessor, the dentist and "paramedic" Wallner, was transferred to Brande (Prądy). Wallner was deported to Auschwitz when the Jewish hospital in Sosnowiec, where he had been a patient, was liquidated in summer 1943.[101] Blechhammer's small dental practice was taken over by Maurice Perlman, a Romanian Jew from Paris, who was among the first French "Cosel men" imported into the camp in early October 1942.[102] Dr. Ritter was loathed for making use of the riding whip handed out to all Jewish physicians by the police guard duty officers to force inmates in need of treatment out of the infirmary.[103] The physicians were under no obligation to comply with Schmelt's instructions to hit their patients. In Brande, for instance, the Jewish doctors only used their whips for beating dust out of jackets.[104]

The infirmary continued to suffer from a chronic lack of medicines and equipment. Camp leader Hoffmann deemed the bandaging of injured prisoners a "waste of material," as they were about to "go to the ovens" anyway. A newly arrived Westerbork deportee thus offered 300 RM to Demerer so he could clandestinely procure dressing material.[105] Similarly, when three female prisoners asked for painkillers in the infirmary, Hoffmann and guard duty officer Rettinghausen used this as a pretext for flogging the women and the medical staff. Surgical instruments were extremely rare in Schmelt camps and were not even provided in urgent cases. In Blechhammer, a prisoner's crushed leg had to be amputated with an ordinary saw and an axe; the patient died a few days later.[106] In camp Markstädt (Laskowice), a kitchen knife was used for surgery.[107]

With the launch of mass deportations from the Eastern Upper Silesian ghettos in 1942, the referral of Schmelt prisoners to the Jewish hospital of Sosnowiec was no longer permitted.[108] In late October 1942, the Schmelt Office purported that admittance to the hospital was impossible due to "overcrowding."[109] Around the same time, Haunschild instructed prisoner physicians in Brande that treatment in the Jewish hospital was now out of the question. This order meant certain death for critical patients, who were simply taken to Auschwitz henceforth: "Anyone who does not get back to their feet here, must die. If anybody needs surgery you cannot perform in the camp, discard of them, we have got plenty of that stuff!"[110]

In October and November 1942, so-called camps for the sick and convalescent (*Kranken- und Erholungslager*) were established in some Schmelt camps like Ottmuth and Annaberg, which were meant to partly take over the Jewish hospital's functions. Admittance was restricted to sick or injured prisoners expected to regain their full ability to work within a short span of time. As those not recuperating fast enough were killed in Auschwitz, only a small fraction survived these facilities.[111]

The prisoners who died in Blechhammer, mostly as a result of camp killings by Rettinghausen and Hoffmann, were now buried in a spot in the forest about 500 meters from the new camp. The owner of the land, Prince Hohenlohe, permitted the establishment of a designated Jewish cemetery that was marked by a sign with the Star of David. Next to Abram Blachinskzi, a camp shoemaker commonly known as *der shister*, three "Cosel men" from the Netherlands volunteered for the burial detail: Arthur Salomons, Salomon Lierens, and Hartog Ereira. The detail was free to perform burial rites and was not supervised at the graveyard. The men wrapped the bodies in a blanket

Jewish "graveyard" in the forest near Blechhammer after the war.
(*Source:* "The Jewish Graveyard," APMO)

before lowering them into a 1.8-meter-deep excavation with a foundation of sand and pine branches. They also placed pine branches on the faces of the deceased and then covered them with earth. Finally, the grave was marked by a wooden board with the person's name, date of birth, and date of death.¹¹² When a Polish War Crimes Commission inspected the graveyard after the war, many name plates were still legible and facilitated the identification of the victims.¹¹³

"NO SPORT FOR THE MALNOURISHED": LABORING ON THE OHW SITE

Construction at the OHW synthetic fuel plant was 30 percent complete in late 1942. Jewish prisoners predominantly cleared forests for new buildings, paved roads, and constructed fuel tanks and railroad lines. Due to personnel shortages, the OHW required them to work on two Sundays a month. They typically had to unload building material then.¹¹⁴ While working winter hours, they rose at 4:00 a.m. and were allocated to details during the roll call one hour later. Many weakened prisoners seized this opportunity to slip into a different detail assigned to lighter work.¹¹⁵ Details performing piecework especially had high death tolls, as the unloading of cement sacks and other heavy material was strictly supervised by the police guards and foremen, who demanded a fast pace. There were no breaks until the task had been finished, which caused many inmates to collapse. Teenagers in particular were at high risk of dying of exhaustion.¹¹⁶

Skilled workers were in great demand. The Highway Company's representative, Haunschild, and camp leader Hoffmann frequently combed other Schmelt camps for such experts, who were promised cigarettes and better clothes. The latter consisted of old Czech military uniforms, worn by members of Organisation Todt since the outbreak of war. Later they were clad in black uniforms with a sewn-on white Star of David.¹¹⁷ Regular prisoners often pretended to be skilled laborers, as the latter had more favorable working conditions and received larger food rations. Contractors like AEG therefore tested the inmates' work before accepting them. A Jewish crane operator even oversaw one hundred British POWs and Wehrmacht prisoners, until a works policeman complained to the OHW about the inappropriateness of a Jew commanding non-Jews. The prisoner was sent to a penal commando unit as a result.¹¹⁸

Altogether, the treatment and workload of skilled and unskilled Jewish laborers did not differ significantly. As the French Jewish survivor Etienne Rosenfeld pointed out, even skilled work was "no sport for the malnourished." Rosenfeld fought a fruitless battle with his German overseer to treat him more respectfully. He ignored the master's orders when he addressed him as a "bloody Jew," only to be viciously maltreated each time. His courage notwithstanding, he had soon earned himself the dubious reputation of being "the most beaten man" in the camp.[119]

German engineers were entitled to have Jewish calfactors for stocking stoves and cleaning their offices. Regular German workers also required them to heat up their lunch and do their dishes in return for food leftovers. This practice exemplifies the low status of Jewish prisoners, who were considered "servants" or even "slaves" by the German workforce.[120] Calfactor jobs were occasionally offered as a "reward" to prisoners, as they involved only light work. The Dutch "Cosel man" Jonas Pampel, who was acclaimed for his enormous physical strength, was one of them. With unease he noted that "while I sat there, I saw the others perishing, and I only had to stock the stove and heat up the soup."[121]

"GET RID OF THIS TRASH!": THE INTENSIFICATION OF AUSCHWITZ TRANSPORTS

In late 1942 Rettinghausen and Hoffmann sent an average of two hundred prisoners to Auschwitz each month. They added fit prisoners to the sick for alleged "transgressions." When a transport left Blechhammer, Rettinghausen once drily remarked: "Get rid of this trash!"[122]

When Schmelt's deputy Lindner was in the camp, he also listed female prisoners he deemed unfit, or "bad" workers for Auschwitz. Ida Frydman, who worked in the kitchen, narrowly escaped this fate. Like many other women, she suffered from edema in her legs, as they had to stand all day. Barely able to walk, she had remained in her barrack one day, when Linder suddenly inspected the camp. She was saved by fellow inmates, who immediately carried her into the kitchen and concealed her swollen legs with a potato sack.[123] On another occasion, Lindner supervised a roll call in the women's camp and made every tenth female prisoner step forward. The women were sent to Auschwitz despite being fit for work. These murders must be classified as gender-specific, as there were no selections of this kind in the men's camp.[124]

In stark contrast to Auschwitz subcamps, a private driving company called Hancke was hired to take the selected prisoners to Auschwitz. The drivers received a list with the names of the prisoners they should hand over to the Auschwitz administration. In winter, many emaciated inmates froze to death during the ride on open trucks, as their shoes and clothes had been taken away.[125] The drivers thus invariably became accessories to their murder. This practice underscores two characteristics of the Schmelt camp system: first, the large-scale involvement of civilians in the genocide, and second, a rather careless, overt demonstration of the ongoing mass murder of the Jews.

A novel development was the addition of unfit prisoners to western deportation convoys during the illicit Cosel stops between October and December 1942. Blechhammer seized this opportunity to transport infirmary patients to Auschwitz on December 5, 1942.[126] They were exchanged for male deportees on a Westerbork convoy reaching Auschwitz in the early hours of December 6. Danuta Czech stated that out of the 811 listed passengers on the train, 795 were instantly murdered in the gas chambers.[127] However, it is important to keep in mind that during this particular time, Schmelt inmates died in Auschwitz alongside or instead of those named on the deportation lists.

4

"RATIONALIZATION" OR ANNIHILATION?

The Camp at the Intersection of Two Conflicting Policies in 1943

I N 1943 THE SCHMELT CAMPS WERE AT THE INTERSECTION OF SPEER'S "RATIOnalization" efforts to gain more Jewish workers for the war economy and the full-scale implementation of the Final Solution in Eastern Upper Silesia. These seemingly conflicting policies, on the one hand, led to a concentration of Schmelt prisoners in Blechhammer, while most other camps were disbanded. On the other hand, Blechhammer began to play a decisive role in the organized mass murder of the Jewish ghetto population and the killing of sick and unfit Schmelt camp inmates. The exchange of the police guards for Wehrmacht soldiers applied to both developments. The policemen were needed to carry out ghetto liquidations and deportations, whereas the soldiers facilitated the continuing exploitation of Jewish labor.

THE WITHDRAWAL OF THE ORDER POLICE GUARDS

In February 1943 Wehrmacht soldiers replaced the police guards of Blechhammer to make them available for new tasks. Their guard duty in Schmelt camps had only been an episode in the police forces' long-standing collaboration in the Holocaust.

Special police battalions were formed in Poland in September 1939, comprising active and veteran order police officers. They carried out mass shootings and executions alongside the SD killing squads (*Einsatzgruppen*), escorted deportation convoys, and guarded camps and ghettos.[1] In an effort to augment their ranks, Hitler decreed the establishment of police training battalions. As policemen were not conscripted to the front, there were many volunteers. An astonishing twenty-six thousand men joined the training battalion set up in Silesia in October 1939 alone. After one year of military drill and ideological schooling, outstanding marksmen among them were drafted into the police battalions. Starting in September 1941, Himmler replaced SS police divisions supporting Waffen-SS units with police battalions. In the annexed territories, auxiliary police forces were included in this policy. In addition to front service, the police battalions were once more involved in mass killings of civilians.[2]

Preserved fragments of correspondence between HSSPF Schmauser and Himmler in April 1942 corroborate that they had plans for assigning the 233 policemen, and 169 veterans currently on guard duty in Schmelt camps to these battalions. Schmauser went to great lengths to withhold his police guards, arguing that their authoritarian leadership style could not be exuded by civilians in a comparable manner and that their withdrawal would not merely sabotage German war production in general but Minister Speer's "giant" new project at Blechhammer in particular.[3] Schmauser eventually succeeded in retaining the police guards for almost another year.

The chief of the order police, Daluege, called for the transformation of police battalions into rapid response units, so-called police guard battalions (*Polizei-Wachbataillone*). They should facilitate more flexible deployments in areas considered vital to the war effort, such as combating sabotage and espionage and hunting down escaped POWs. At the same time, normal policing was to be reduced to a minimum. Daluege ordered every inspector of the order police to set up at least one guard battalion in his district by drawing on all available police officers, the students of police academies, and Eastern European auxiliaries. On September 29, 1942, Schmauser reported to Schmelt the formation of guard battalion number I of Silesia, commanded by Major Zauner of Kattowitz. Its four divisions were recruited from staff of the police administrations of Sosnowiec, Gleiwitz, Oppeln, Troppau, and Breslau, as well as the police veterans' academy of Bunzlau. Altogether, there were 109 men equipped with eighty-five rifles, six submachine and machine guns, and twelve bicycles. They had already been sent to Lemberg (Lvov) and Tarnopol to carry out raids and suppress "revolts" in POW camps.[4]

In a meeting between Schmauser and Schmelt on November 28, 1942, Schmelt insisted on deploying one section of the Oppeln division of the guard battalion in the annexed regions Warthenau, Loben, and Blachstädt from December, to reinforce local police combating partisans.[5] The training of new recruits had been adapted to the altered requirements. Curricula now included the subject of "evacuations," a euphemism for deportations of the Jewish population.[6] In February 1943 the Silesian guard battalion was transferred to Warsaw and Marseille, the first of several deployments outside Silesia.[7] It was then that Schmauser's policemen were finally pulled out of Blechhammer to serve in the guard battalion. In October 1943 they were sent to the former Warthenau (Zawiercie) ghetto, which had been liquidated on August 20, 1943, to protect confiscated Jewish property against "looting partisans."[8] Fighting alleged "partisans" was usually a pretext for mass killings of civilians. In total, at least 130 police and police guard battalions are known to have existed during the Second World War, and it is estimated that they participated in the murder of up to half a million people.⁹

To Speer's Ministry of Armaments and War Production, finding replacements for the police guards became a top priority. The Schmelt Office promptly required new personnel, not only to ensure the continued work deployment of Jews in the already existing industrial camps, but also to realize Speer's plans for intensifying the exploitation of Jewish labor even further. Speer's idea to use convalescents and veterans of the Wehrmacht did not resonate well with Himmler. He nevertheless received Himmler's permission to try out the new scheme in Schmelt camps, as they operated outside of the concentration camp system. The Schmelt camps thus spearheaded the use of soldiers as guards. By December 1943 Speer had convinced Himmler to deploy soldiers in concentration camps to mitigate the increasing lack of SS personnel in the rapidly expanding subcamp systems.¹⁰

Contrary to the policemen, the Wehrmacht guards were not to interfere with the internal affairs of the Schmelt camp administrations. In Blechhammer they were not permitted to enter the camp compound, but merely oversaw the territory from watchtowers to prevent escapes. Direct contacts with the prisoners only occurred when the soldiers escorted them to the factory and supervised work details. They were not authorized to reprimand the inmates.¹¹ A single police representative nonetheless remained in the camp. Seemingly the concept of a dual camp leadership split between a police guard duty officer (*Wachhabender*) and a civilian administrator was not affected by the police's general withdrawal. This presumably pertained to the police's monopoly on all Jewish affairs. Similarly, the presence of a Gestapo officer was obligatory in concentration camps.¹²

Blechhammer's previous guard duty officer, Rettinghausen, was promoted to inspector-general of the Schmelt camps in Silesia. Unlike Rettinghausen, who had been infamous for torturing prisoners to death, his successor, Hauptwachtmeister Mareck, was very restrained. Therefore most Blechhammer inmates perceived the exchange of the order police as a considerable improvement. Aside from camp leader Erich Hoffmann's outbursts of violence, life in Blechhammer became notably quieter and more predictable.¹³

The Wehrmacht guards were either aged veterans or convalescents, who went back to the front as soon as they had recovered. Owing to their relatively short tenure in the camp, the names of individual guards were rarely corroborated by survivor testimonies. The soldiers' attitudes toward the prisoners varied markedly, ranging from indifference to supportiveness to hostility. Some reportedly mistreated prisoners during work. However, in contrast to the policemen's overt brutality, assaults by soldiers were not the rule.¹⁴ The elderly, physically impaired veterans tended to be more passive, except for an eighty-year-old who, despite having difficulties walking, dealt out blows incessantly.¹⁵ The guards' swift relocation to the front usually prevented them from reporting prisoners for infractions. Notwithstanding the prohibition against maltreating prisoners, some soldiers reprimanded transgressions on the spot by forcing the Jewish heads of column to mete out the punishment.[16] The soldiers also found themselves under considerable pressure to maintain a high level of productivity in their details. If they appeared too lax, German foremen could report them.[17]

A certain proportion of the guards openly demonstrated their opposition to the Nazi regime. When soldiers escorting prisoners to work overheard them saying that the acronym for Oberschlesische Hydrierwerke, OHW, stood for *Ohne Hoffnung weiter* (continue without hope), they comforted the prisoners by changing it to *Ohne Hitler weiter* (continue without Hitler).[18] Two survivors independently confirmed that a commanding Wehrmacht officer intervened in the collective flogging of Jewish camp physicians ordered by Hoffmann in summer 1943. He instructed the camp leader that the Wehrmacht would not tolerate the ill-treatment of prisoners. Two days later he was removed from his post.[19] It is hard to generalize about the knowledge soldiers deployed in Schmelt camps had of the Holocaust. Contrary to the SS and police forces, Wehrmacht soldiers received no ideological training. Therefore, this category of guards demonstrated a wide behavioral spectrum.[20] Dr. Wollenberg, a German Jewish physician and veteran of the First World War who served as a "paramedic" on the construction site, dared to discuss the Final Solution with a group of soldiers. During work breaks, they sat together in a hut Wollenberg was supposed to heat. One day the guards spoke of their apprehension about returning to the front and remarked to Wollenberg how lucky he was to lead a "carefree life" in the camp. When he told them about the selections for Auschwitz, the soldiers became quiet.[21]

"THE MAIN THING IS TO KEEP THE CHIMNEYS SMOKING": ENFORCING A HIGHER PRODUCTIVITY

From 1942 Speer endeavored to boost the war production by reorganizing resources and manpower.[22] His "rationalization efforts" palpably reverberated throughout the OHW's work routines.

As of spring 1943, the engineer Otto Stoltzenburg managed the deployment of foreign and unfree labor at the OHW on behalf of the Highway Company's building supervisory board in Breslau. He acted as an intermediary between camp leader Hoffmann and the OHW personnel office headed by Dr. Schlick. The group leader of the Nazi Party, who followed the credo that the most important thing was "to keep the chimneys smoking," was infamous for his cruel treatment of foreign and unfree workers.[23] Moreover, the sweeping order to draft all German masters and foremen into the voluntary works police increased the pressure on these laborers, whose work performance and overall conduct were constantly monitored.[24] In April 1943 Stoltzenburg informed the OHW that it would be allocated five hundred Jewish electricians and electrician helpers, who were deemed crucial to the progress of construction works, from the General Government. As the Jewish electricians had to be detained separately from the "western" Jews, the OHW negotiated with Prince Hohenlohe the lease of an extra 6.2 hectares of woodland adjacent to the present camp. He agreed but prohibited complete deforestation.[25] The prisoners therefore called this camp section "Abessynia," as it was so densely forested. It comprised barracks twenty-six to thirty-two.[26] There were now about twenty-five hundred prisoners in the *Bahnhoflager* compound for Jews. The rest of the area was inhabited by Polish and Italian workers.[27] Blechhammer held approximately 5 percent of the 50,570 Jewish prisoners in Schmelt camps accounted for in early 1943.[28] In the course of the year, the influx of further inmates from disbanded Schmelt camps increased Blechhammer's Jewish prisoner population to about thirty-two hundred, making them the largest group of foreign and unfree laborers, representing 16 percent of the total OHW workforce. These figures stress the growing importance of Jewish labor in the Silesian war economy.[29]

The daily workload of all laborers increased significantly. In late 1943 Dr. Urbanek of the OHW social department noted that the forty-eight-hour week had largely been replaced by a sixty-hour week, plus overtime. He added that entrepreneurs in Auschwitz had introduced the sixty-hour week from the start.[30] The Jewish inmates worked up to twelve hours daily. They were granted a twenty-minute lunch break, providing there was no urgent work to be done. Visits to the latrines required the permission of the Wehrmacht guards, who checked how long the prisoners were absent and sometimes refused to let them go at all. Occasionally heavy rainfalls provided a welcome interruption of the work. When the rain set in while they were at the plant, the inmates were allowed to shelter in buildings under construction. If bad weather conditions prevented the details from leaving the camp, they were assigned to alleged "maintenance work," while Hoffmann lived out his sadistic urges, such as by forcing them to crawl in the mud.[31] A newly introduced roster required the Jewish prisoners, inmates of the work education camp (AEL), and French POWs to alternately work on one Sunday every three weeks.[32] However, instead of granting the prisoners some urgently needed rest on those Sundays off work, they were given chores around the camp. In June 1942 the SS WVHA decreed that concentration camp prisoners should work part-time on Sundays. If companies ran no regular Sunday shifts, they were to do maintenance work in the camp. Schmelt camps seem to have complied with this stipulation. In addition to giving them the extra work, Hoffmann seized every opportunity to maltreat them. On one Sunday the intoxicated camp leader was exasperated to see a group of inmates sunbathing in front of their barrack. He started to chase them with a club, yelling, "So, you bloody gits think I will let you become fat from being idle!" Whoever could not run away fast enough was severely beaten, and numerous emaciated inmates died of exhaustion in the process.[33]

The amount of work inexorably consumed the strength of the malnourished prisoners. Many developed hunger edemas, which made every step painful and put them at great risk of being sent to Auschwitz. During the morning roll call, the heads of columns encouraged weakened inmates to leave their detail, not out of sympathy, but rather to rid themselves of the burden of driving them on all day and attracting the guards' attention.[34] The Jewish elder Demerer at times placed convalescents in columns with a lighter workload. He thus saved the life of a prisoner suffering from pneumonia who had been urged to leave the infirmary after only two days due to an impending selection.[35] Prospects were bleak for inmates in a state of physical and mental deterioration who were unable to leave a heavy workers' column, especially if they had a ruthless German overseer. They simply collapsed from exhaustion. The survivor Leo Weiniger delineated how he saw his comrades being worked to death while struggling for his own life: "With a clear mind and a bleeding heart, I registered this indescribable misery and suffering. But I was helpless myself, and too weak to lift my feet, shuffling along, bent with back pain. My age was estimated at forty years, and I was twenty-four years old. But I was not ready to die like a dog, and without a grave, not before I had witnessed the defeat of the monsters who, slowly but surely, let us perish."[36]

During an annual meeting of Silesian industrialists in November 1943, the output factor for Jewish labor was lowered to 50 percent, 10 percent less than in the previous year.[37] Around the same time, Oswald Pohl of the WVHA instructed the commandants of concentration camps to support the war effort by increasing the food rations and ameliorating the overall conditions for the prisoners. He nevertheless made it clear that this was not done on humanitarian grounds, but simply to exploit their bodies more effectively: "We need to be concerned about the prisoners' well-being, not out of false mawkishness, but because we require them with their arms and legs, because they must contribute to enabling the German people to win a great victory."[38]

It is obvious that Pohl merely paid lip service to Speer in this matter. Moreover, as commandants could reshape or ignore superior orders at their discretion, these improvements largely remained on paper.[39] In the Schmelt camps, the food allocations stayed below the standard rations of concentration camp prisoners.[40] In Blechhammer, mismanagement led to a temporary abundance of food in spring 1943. Having cut down the potato allocations in the year before at the expense of the prisoners' lives, Hoffmann suddenly had great contingents left when new potatoes were delivered. For two weeks he granted unlimited access to the potato cellar. Tragically, many prisoners died as a result of hyperphagia during this time.[41] Toward the end of the year the nutritional value of the already thin Blechhammer soup further decreased. It was made of unpeeled beetroots, and even the starving prisoners could hardly eat it.[42] The malnourishment caused a pronounced obsession with food. If a prisoner happened to find solid particles in his soup, he showed them to the others, and they were counted and closely examined. The most talked about subject was nevertheless bread, as in most camps.[43]

The winter of 1942–43 was particularly severe, and the death tolls soared due to a chronic shortage of clothes and shoes. The prisoners' worn-out civilian clothes hardly offered any protection against the biting cold, and they were issued no gloves. Moreover, most of them were short of one piece of clothing or another.[44] The only source of fresh clothes was Auschwitz, whose administration put the belongings of murdered Eastern Upper Silesian Jews at the Schmelt Office's disposal. The Highway Company encouraged its camp leaders to make use of these goods.[45] Leo Weiniger recounted the agony of being exposed to extreme weather conditions, which caused many of his comrades to die:

> I had underpants, a vest, no socks, shoes with broken soles; I stood in the snow like that all day with my bare feet. To go along with this, I had a torn pair of trousers one could see my knees shining through, and a ripped shirt with missing sleeves. This is how I spent an entire Upper Silesian winter. All winter, day after day, we stood outdoors in the snow and ice-cold wind, nearly frozen; the sensation of the soaking wet rags went through marrow and bone. Hundreds more stood there like me, but few are still alive to tell their story.[46]

The gradual process of freezing to death typically started with a numbness in the extremities, and the victims ultimately collapsed. Their fate was sealed by the Wehrmacht guards who, under constant beatings, forced them up and made them work until they died.[47]

The camp hierarchy imposed by the Germans was designed to divide the prisoners by giving functionaries certain privileges.[48] A widely visible, distinctive feature of functionary prisoners was their proper appearance. The two Jewish elders Demerer and Niewes wore tailor-made riding costumes and high-quality fabrics. In view of the life-threatening wintry conditions, these inequalities did not resonate well with the regular inmates.[49] Warm indoor workplaces were sought after and easier to find outside the OHW plant. In January 1943, for instance, Blechhammer prisoners helped to set up the brothel (*Bordell-Baracke*) the OHW had been required to establish for Polish laborers.[50] Until the Auschwitz takeover in April 1944, Blechhammer prisoners were equally assigned to housing projects for IG Farben and OHW employees in Heydebreck. IG Farben's close cooperation with the Auschwitz administration regarding the allocation of prisoners for the Monowitz and Fürstengrube subcamps notwithstanding, its chemical plant at Heydebreck never made use of Jewish labor. Consequently, the Blechhammer inmates did not work on IG Farben's construction site itself. A former IG Farben executive's statement on the purported rotation of Auschwitz prisoners between the sites at Heydebreck and Monowitz was erroneous.[51] A detail of fifty Blechhammer inmates worked for the Polish contractor Tills & Blume in Heydebreck. As the site was too remote from the camp to march, they commuted by truck. Alongside Polish and Italian laborers, they had to unload bricks and sacks of cement.[52] While decorating houses in Heydebreck, some of the prisoners encountered the spouses of OHW and IG Farben staff, who often secretly passed on food to them. When their guard had become ill and they were left almost unsupervised, an engineer's wife extended her help to Dutch Jewish inmates. She asked her neighbors for spare food to make them lunch and chatted for hours about her hometown, Hamburg. When one of the prisoners learned that her former home there had been bombed, he wrote a Dutch saying on a tile in her house that moved the woman to tears: "Even when there's storm and rain outside now, one day the sun will be shining again."[53]

Additional rationalization measures at the OHW, like the policy of "warlike building" (*kriegsmäßiges Bauen*), posed a lethal threat especially to the Jewish inmates. Introduced by the Reich Office for Economic Development in July 1941, this policy stipulated that the amount of material and manpower used for constructing buildings should be reduced to a minimum. By order of the head of the RAB building supervisory board of Breslau, Müller, the OHW further radicalized this instruction by opting out of standard safety precautions, such as using scaffolds and installing handrails.[54] Even if this practice seemed to affect all workers, it was predominantly Jewish prisoners who fell victim to foreseeable accidents of this kind. Unlike other workers, they could not refuse such "suicidal" jobs. The survivor Hessel Goldberg gave a harrowing account of the deadly conditions they had to work in: "The four of us were painting a roof in building 56. The British, French, and Italians had all refused to do the job, as the Germans did not want to set up a scaffold, because they needed everything done in a hurry.... The work was life-threatening, and Reuter [one of the four inmates] fell off, and was killed immediately."[55]

Missing handrails caused several casualties among the prisoners. When two prisoners had to carry a beam up an unsecured staircase, one of them slipped and fell three floors to his death.[56] Similarly, a young inmate was killed by a fall from the fifth floor of the OHW power station while carrying a steel girder up a narrow staircase. Salomon Staszewski, the column's Jewish head, had tried in vain to dissuade the German master from letting the prisoners work in these conditions. Staszewski was removed from his post by the Jewish elder, but the German personnel on the construction site were not made accountable for the boy's death. Demerer seems to have projected the blame onto the functionary prisoner, as he had no control over the German overseers. This certainly contributed to the postwar phenomenon of incriminating functionary prisoners for injustices ultimately committed by Germans.[57] Prisoners working at great heights, such as welders, often sustained fractures by falling off scaffolds. They were rarely given the time to heal but were murdered in Auschwitz. Thus, even if they survived the accident, their injuries equaled a death sentence.[58]

Accidents at work became rampant, due to the increased pace demanded by the Germans. Consequently, injured, dying, or dead inmates had to be taken back to the camp on a wheelbarrow each day.[59] A similar development was noticeable on several construction sites of Mineralöl-Bau, an affiliation of IG Farben in charge of supervising the OHW site until 1942. When confronted with the soaring number of prisoners who had died in work accidents due to a lack of safety precautions, one of the company's engineers bluntly remarked that considering the many soldiers killed at the front, "victims of work" (*Arbeitsopfer*) behind the lines did not count.[60] In October 1943 a particularly terrible accident cost the life of a juvenile inmate from Rotterdam, who was burned over three-quarters of his body after falling into a condenser. The infirmary staff could do nothing to alleviate his agony.[61] Having to work without protective gear, like gloves, invariably led to injuries. During the winter months the inmates carried metal poles with their bare hands in temperatures below the freezing point, and pieces of skin stuck to the metal. Unloading bricks in a human chain without gloves also caused severe cuts and wounds. The prisoners of work detail number fourteen (Isolierbetrieb Fuchs) were predominantly occupied with insulating tubes with glass wool. As they had not been provided with protective clothing, they all suffered from skin irritations, and some became unfit for work because of abscesses.[62]

Maltreatment at work was another underlying cause of prisoners becoming unfit or dying. The Wehrmacht guards were supposed to protect the prisoners against "illicit" assaults by German civilians. However, they mostly turned a blind eye to the German overseers' ubiquitous brutality or even instigated violence themselves.[63] An eighteen-year-old Wehrmacht soldier thus cold-bloodedly worked two Jewish inmates to death. He and an Upper Silesian foreman forced them to shoulder a four-meter steel girder around a building, until they both collapsed dead. The killings seemed to have been carried out as a kind of sadistic pastime, as one of the perpetrators checked his watch and coolly remarked to the other that the whole procedure had only taken twenty-five minutes.[64]

In the prisoners' perception, the Germans tended to divert their aggression against the Jews if things did not work according to plan.[65] Next to ill-treating the inmates, German masters and foremen evidently committed murders on their own initiative. In the winter of 1943 a Jewish prisoner assigned to the OHW contractor Kies AG was thrown into a river and pushed underneath its frozen surface until he drowned. The victim, an antiquarian from Amsterdam, was killed for dropping two of the four rocks he was carrying.[66]

The Upper Silesian overseers at the plant exhibited a broad behavioral spectrum toward Jewish prisoners. Owing to their "fluid" national identity, they often fluctuated

Depiction of a notorious Upper Silesian overseer by Bil Spira. (*Source:* IWM ART 17123)

between assaulting prisoners and offering their support. Many reportedly shared food with Jewish inmates, facilitated escapes, or smuggled letters—especially if prisoners spoke Polish or originated from the same area as themselves.[67] Their efforts to appear "German" were perceived as comical by the inmates. One foreman was even portrayed in a cartoon by the Austrian Jewish artist Bil Spira.[68] His name was unknown to the inmates, but he was easily identified by the word he used the most: *pierunje*, Polish for "damn." This man, a member of the Highway Company, was intoxicated most of the time and kicked the inmates with his boots.[69] Despite having been classified as "Germans," the position of Upper Silesians remained vulnerable, allowing some Jewish inmates to fend off their vicious attacks. The Jewish head of column Joseph Braasem, for instance, dared to stop an Upper Silesian from beating a juvenile prisoner in his detail with an iron bar without incurring punishment himself.[70]

The harsh treatment of the Jews at the plant was a well-known fact even to the family members of employees. The wife of an OHW engineer once complained to Otto Stoltzenburg about the maltreatment of Jewish inmates, and his only reply was that they had to be treated this way, as they were Jews.[71] The Highway Company's social ombudsman in Breslau Hitschler was aware of the frequent assaults on Jewish prisoners by German guards and foremen on virtually all construction sites under the company's supervision. Hitschler nevertheless claimed that he had been unable to restrain the ubiquitous violence.[72] Curiously, camp leader Erich Hoffmann, who was notorious for his cruelty himself, once made a stand against a certain German master who incessantly mistreated prisoners. As the master had ignored his numerous warnings, Hoffmann withdrew all Jewish work details from the construction site and retained them in the camp for several days, until the man had been rebuked. This was the only known protest by camp personnel against assaults on Blechhammer inmates. Yet Hoffmann's paradoxical reaction was unlikely to have been based on sympathy with the Jews.[73] Physical violence remained integral to the work deployment of Jews in industrial camps and was often the cause of their deaths.[74]

THE REINFORCEMENT OF JEWISH MEDICAL PERSONNEL AND THE FIRST TYPHUS OUTBREAK

The influx of inmates from liquidated Schmelt camps into Blechhammer steadily increased the number of Jewish physicians, who came along with them, to twelve. Their capacity to provide genuine aid was limited by the camps' intrinsically annihilatory nature, and there was hardly any leeway to protect the patients from selections or other forms of murder. Those refusing to carry out killing orders put their own lives in the balance. When faced with the dilemma of adhering to the Hippocratic Oath or being compliant to save their own lives, different physicians made different decisions.[75] As Primo Levi pointed out, those inmates whose positions put them into a "gray zone" between the perpetrators and the victims should not be judged for their involvement in events beyond their control.[76] In areas where there was less external pressure, individual behaviors may nonetheless be evaluated.[77] The increase in physicians in Blechhammer in 1943 made the prisoner patients much more aware of the marked differences in the treatment they received, and they often excoriated the medical personnel for their alleged or actual shortcomings. The most common accusations against the doctors were centered around the issues of gratuitous violence, embezzlement, and corruption—all of which were generated by the inherent logic of the Nazi camp system.

On January 26, 1943, the inmates of a disbanded camp at Seibersdorf (Zebrzydowice) arrived in Blechhammer, together with their camp physician, Dr. Isaac Cohensius from the Netherlands. Cohensius was about to graduate from medical school when his wife was called up for deportation in mid-August 1942. He followed her to camp Westerbork and received special permission to take his final exams in return for joining one of the first deportation convoys to the east. He was one of thirteen Jewish physicians deported in 1942 who were denied the right to stay in Westerbork granted to most senior medics. He passed the exams and swore the Hippocratic Oath on August 28, 1942. On the evening of their wedding on August 31, he and his wife were deported. It was the second Dutch convoy stopped in Cosel. He was pulled out of the train and separated from his wife, who died in Auschwitz. Cohensius served as a camp physician in the Niederkirch transit camp until October 1942, when he was sent to a newly formed camp in Seibersdorf, along with two hundred fellow Westerbork deportees.[78]

The Blechhammer inmates disliked Cohensius, as he, like Dr. Ritter, whipped patients.[79] In his postwar memoirs, Cohensius related the inner conflicts plaguing him as an inexperienced doctor who tried to fulfill his medical obligation to care for his patients while being coerced to comply with Seibersdorf's "zero-sick-policy." To him, the camp infirmaries were nothing but a "show" the Germans put on for the Red Cross, and the Jewish physicians had no choice but to cooperate in the mass murder of their comrades.[80]

Shortly after Cohensius arrived, Dr. Moses Auerhahn was sent to Blechhammer. He became head surgeon and treated female inmates. In stark contrast to Ritter, he had a kind personality, showed compassion for his patients, and tried to admit as many of them to the infirmary as possible. Despite the limited means available, survivors stated that Auerhahn was eager to provide the best care that he could.[81]

In April Dr. Jerzy Iwanter arrived with inmates from Laurahütte (Siemianowice Śląskie). Having converted to Catholicism, the general practitioner from Warsaw had reputedly avoided contacts with Jews before his internment in Nazi camps. As in Laurahütte, he was very hard on the sick in Blechhammer. Some inmates described him as a "terrible man" and even as a "beast." Iwanter exploited the system of corruption prevailing in the camps for his own benefit and only admitted patients for treatment in return for several pounds of butter and other delicacies. In marked contrast to his emaciated comrades, Iwanter had a corpulent figure, and he was nicknamed "the elephant." His progressive obesity even prevented him from using a stethoscope properly. For every extra week a patient stayed in the infirmary, he demanded more goods, such as butter, cigarettes, apples, or tomatoes. Those lacking the means to procure these coveted items from "second economy" markets were denied medical treatment, even if they were gravely ill. These inequalities further deepened the divide between the inmates. Less resourceful prisoners felt that while the needy "died like rats," those who paid the most were helped first. On the other hand, there were extraordinary acts of solidarity among some of the prisoners, who collectively gathered the sums to cover a comrade's treatment.[82]

Ironically, some functionary prisoners were permitted to use the infirmary as a "hotel" when they wanted a break from work. Thus, for the price of one diamond a head of column was allowed to take a fourteen-day "vacation" in the infirmary, as he disliked the rainy weather outside.[83] Just like the kitchen staff, the medical personnel frequently embezzled the patients' food, which consisted of one liter of mashed potatoes or semolina. The regular inmates were outraged about doctors taking advantage of the most vulnerable among them: "They stole food from people unable to eat bread anymore, and who depended on this tiny liter of food. Are these thieves not murderers acting on bad intentions? Who should we have complained to? To the guard shouldering his rifle, the posts with machine guns or to the commandant who always had his whip ready? To the functionaries who always wished these things did not happen? . . . Our hatred of the functionaries within our own enclosures was greater than of those planning our annihilation from outside."[84]

Despite the growing number of camp physicians, the medical supplies remained wholly insufficient. As one doctor put it, the only "medicine" available to them was to encourage their patients to go on living.[85] Treatment in the strict sense of the word was only possible by procuring the required medications from "second economy" vendors on the construction site. Again, this option was primarily available to more resourceful prisoners, as illustrated by the following example. A French Jewish inmate in a mixed marriage still maintained contacts with his wife in France with the help of French Service Travail Obligatoire (STO)workers. This connection proved lifesaving when he suffered a total physical breakdown in June 1943. The camp doctors advised him to take insulin and offered to acquire the respective doses for 400 RM from a clandestine source. His wife promptly forwarded the money to pay for the injections, and he made a full recovery.[86]

With the reinforcement of the infirmary staff, medical orderlies began to be recruited as well. These were usually prisoners with no prior medical training. Helping in the infirmary was a way of receiving long-term treatment without payment. Sixteen-year-old Kurt Klappholz was on the brink of suffering a breakdown due to the heavy work on the OHW site. As a last resort, he asked for admission into the infirmary to recover for a few days. Dr. Iwanter at first rejected him and warned him of an impending selection. Even though he grasped the true implications of the selections for the first time, Klappholz insisted on being taken in for treatment. Iwanter offered to make him an orderly to protect him from being selected but demanded sexual favors in return. From then on, Klappholz was frequently abused by Iwanter. Incredibly, he still decided to keep his "superb job," as it provided him with extra food, and he did not have to set out to the construction site anymore. His daily chores included waking the sick and distributing bread and water. He also had some messenger duties, and while handing out sick lists to the barrack elders, he often managed to steal some of their food to keep alive.[87] It was usually younger men and boys who were forced into sexual relationships with functionary prisoners. The case of Kurt Klappholz is a good example of how more "privileged" inmates took advantage of the juvenile prisoners in their desperate struggle for survival and exposed them to various forms of sexual violence.[88]

Twenty-year-old Jules Fainzang from Belgium had already been Iwanter's orderly in Laurahütte, and he continued to assist him after their transfer to Blechhammer. He nonetheless opted to work on the construction site during the day and only helped out during the nightly admission. In return, Fainzang received some extra food and the privilege of a "room" of his own: a tiny, windowless cubicle in the infirmary used as a storage closet for bandaging material. Unlike Klappholz, he did not report any sexual assaults by Iwanter in his autobiography.[89]

Three female auxiliary nurses worked in the women's ward in return for a double soup ration. Hoffmann, who seldom interfered with the male infirmary staff, was a regular visitor to the women's ward. One of the nurses, Fanny Pillersdorf from Będzin, had dyed her hair blonde before being arrested, and Hoffmann was friendly to her when he patrolled the infirmary. However, as soon as the dye began to grow out, his behavior changed completely. He frequently screamed at her for alleged shortcomings and once even had her flogged for not having made the beds neatly enough.[90]

In May 1943 two inmates contracted typhus. They were kept isolated until the Schmelt Office ordered camp policeman Rauch and a paramedic to strangle them, as there was no time to take them to Auschwitz.[91] The Schmelt Office often used such blatantly violent methods to conceal outbreaks of infectious diseases in order to prevent quarantines and subsequent loss of income. Haunschild thus shot ten prisoners, eight of whom had typhus, while recruiting workers in camp Gräditz (Grodziszcze).[92] By August, Blechhammer nonetheless was in the grip of a full-fledged typhus outbreak, and a quarantine became inevitable. The inmates were disinfected in a barrack normally used for delousing blankets, and those who had contracted the disease were isolated in a fenced-off part of the infirmary.[93]

In the middle of the outbreak, another crisis concerning Dr. Ritter emerged, which ultimately led to his murder in Auschwitz. Survivor testimonies rendered two different versions of what happened. In the first version, mainly corroborated by Dutch Jewish witnesses in the early postwar years, Dr. Ritter purportedly had a fight with Demerer and attempted to have him killed by swapping his blood sample with that of a typhus patient, so he could become Jewish elder himself. The sample tested positive in the laboratory, but Demerer could prove that Ritter had manipulated the samples with the help of an SS medical officer who was called into the camp. Ritter and his wife were then deported to Auschwitz, along with the physician Dr. Simons and several paramedics.[94] The second version originated from the Munich trial of Erich Hoffmann in 1946, in which Karl Demerer appeared as a key witness for the prosecution. He and the other witnesses unanimously blamed Hoffmann for Ritter's assumed death. They stated that Ritter's wife had rejected sexual advances by Hoffmann, and both had been deported. The witnesses named Dr. Ritter's refusal to carry out Hoffmann's orders to kill patients as an additional reason. Before sending him on a transport to Auschwitz with Dr. Simons, two paramedics, and several blind prisoners, Hoffmann allegedly searched his quarters for valuables.[95] Ritter's brother-in-law Ezriel Rabinowitsch also testified in the Munich trial. He learned of Ritter's presumed death from relatives transferred to the camp after his disappearance but made no statement about the circumstances leading to his murder.[96] In video testimony, he later accused Demerer of having sent the Ritters to their deaths because Demerer's alleged mistresses were jealous of Mrs. Ritter's good looks. As Rabinowitsch was not present at the camp himself, this scenario does not seem very credible.[97]

It is difficult to judge the veracity of the other two conflicting narratives. The first version construed Ritter's death as the result of a power struggle between functionary prisoners. Ritter's penalty for challenging the Jewish elder was self-inflicted, while Demerer was portrayed as the victim. However, the fact that he turned to an SS physician to intervene for him and to reprimand Ritter and his spouse in this drastic way also made Demerer partly responsible for their murder. Lethal conflicts of this kind were a ubiquitous phenomenon in Schmelt camps and concentration camps alike. They were fueled by the unfair hierarchy imposed on the inmates by the German camp leadership.[98] In Brande, a Jewish camp physician tried to get rid of an unwanted colleague by adding him to a list for Auschwitz. This was averted by the camp leadership, and the physician was brutally killed in the end.[99] The second version, told by Demerer himself, completely omitted him from the course of events. Hoffmann was accused of molesting Ritter's wife, issuing killing orders for sick prisoners, and stealing his property. The camp leader had undoubtedly committed numerous crimes of this kind. Nevertheless, the witnesses possibly intended to emphasize his "base motives," which were a prerequisite for indicting Nazi perpetrators with murder in western German courts.[100] Moreover, Hoffmann tried to call Demerer as a witness for the defense and invited him to his apartment several times before the start of the trial. He could have played on Demerer's inadvertent entanglement in the developments leading to Ritter's murder to blackmail him.[101] In the immediate postwar era, there was a tendency to incriminate Jewish functionaries for their alleged collaboration in the Holocaust, which might have led Demerer to fear for his life. The alternative narrative of Hoffmann's trial fully vindicated Demerer and permitted him to make a damning statement, which ultimately brought the former camp leader to the gallows.[102]

However, the shadows of the past did not disappear with Hoffmann's death. Two decades later the fate of the second physician deported with Dr. Ritter was the focus of criminal investigators. Dr. Simons, a veteran of the First World War, had been a camp doctor in Gleiwitz (Gliwice). He was sent to Auschwitz via Blechhammer for the attempt to save a female inmate by concealing her pregnancy.[103] In November 1963 a relative of Dr. Simons charged Karl Demerer with the murder of Dr. Ritter and Dr. Simons. In March 1963 Demerer had abruptly left his place of residence in Germany. The German attorney general found out that he was living in Israel on a tourist visa. The Israeli police department offered to press charges against him, but no legal steps ensued, as the claimant was deceased. A year later, Demerer gave testimony on his time in Blechhammer to the Israeli police. The Ritter affair was not addressed.[104] The repercussions of Ritter's murder reverberated throughout most of Demerer's life after the camps, irrespective of the actual or assumed degree of his involvement. Despite his unquestionable popularity among Blechhammer prisoners, Demerer experienced the common dilemma of functionary prisoners, on whom some survivors took their revenge for crimes committed by German perpetrators, who in turn attempted to project the blame on the functionaries.[105]

During the epidemic, three more camp physicians arrived. The first was Dr. Bernhard Littwack from a Schmelt camp near Katowice, who started out as a paramedic before taking over Ritter's position as chief physician.[106] In August he was joined by Dr. Wolf Lajtner, a survivor of the railway construction works carried out by Jewish inmates for Organisation Todt (OT) in Russia in the winter of 1941–42, and Dr. Wollenberg from Berlin.[107] Dr. Lajtner had asked to be transferred to Blechhammer from Parschnitz, a camp for women, to meet his parents there. Police guards escorted him and four girls from Parschnitz on the train journey. He then learned that the female prisoners were about to be murdered, as they had contracted tuberculosis, and two suffered from a mental disorder. Screaming incessantly, the mentally ill girls were locked into a washroom barrack, and Hoffmann finally ordered Lajtner to kill them by noon. As he refused to do this, they were strangled by a Jewish camp functionary. For having disobeyed his orders, Hoffmann added Lajtner and his wife Erna Ellert, who had followed him to Blechhammer as a nurse, to a sick transport to Auschwitz on September 1, 1943.[108]

It was the first of four transports taking the victims of the typhus outbreak to Auschwitz.[109] Altogether, Hoffmann selected 350 prisoners, among them typhus patients as well as elderly people, children, and pregnant women from the transit camp operated by Blechhammer at the time. Trucks took them to a railroad station to be added to a deportation train. As the date of the transport corresponds with the third phase of the Cosel stops, it may be assumed that the sick were taken to the freight depot of Cosel to wait for a Westerbork convoy carrying 1,004 deportees. When the train arrived, Lajtner and his wife carefully laid those unable to walk in the cattle cars. Hoffmann, who had personally accompanied the trucks in his own car, was infuriated by their tender treatment of the prisoners. In a fit of rage, he got on one of the trucks, threw some of the sick on the ground, and brutally trampled them to death. The convoy reached Auschwitz-Birkenau at midnight.[110] It is unclear how many fit men had been taken off in Cosel in exchange for the 350 Blechhammer inmates. Some 502 people of this transport were selected for work in Auschwitz; the others, including 160 children, were immediately killed in the gas chambers.[111] Some of the women deported from Blechhammer were among the 247 females selected for work in Auschwitz. They were brought into the bunker of the main camp and were led into Block 10 in the afternoon, where their hair was cut. Afterward they received prisoner uniforms and tattoos. The women then learned that they were in a block for medical experiments.[112] The SS physicians Carl Clauberg, Horst Schumann, and Eduard Wirths experimented with different forms of sterilization in Block 10, exposing the women to high doses of X-rays, injections in the fallopian tubes, or ovariectomies. Many of their victims died in extreme pain or suffered from health problems for the rest of their lives.[113]

Erna Ellert and her husband were among those shuttled toward the killing facilities, and she later gave a harrowing account of what she experienced there: "We were immediately led into the gas chambers after having been forced to get undressed. We owe our lives to the lucky coincidence that I managed to convince Hauptsturmführer Wirt [Wirths] that my husband and I were not sick but had accompanied the transport as nurses. I had hardly put my clothes back on when I heard the no longer human wailing of the approximately 350 suffocating inmates from Blechhammer."[114]

Having narrowly avoided the same fate as Dr. Ritter and Dr. Simons before him, Dr. Lajtner was first allocated to an execution commando unit in Auschwitz as a physician and was later transferred to Monowitz.[115]

The last transport with typhus patients left in mid-September. The victims were locked in the isolation ward the night before. A young convalescent desperate to save his life made an escape attempt early in the morning. Hoffmann collectively blamed the camp physicians for his disappearance and had all medical personnel flogged. He then threatened that five doctors would be sent to Auschwitz if the missing boy could not be retrieved by 11:00 a.m., the trucks' scheduled time of departure. The boy was finally found in a barrack. He was beaten and forced to climb onto one of the waiting trucks. The transport was probably added to a Westerbork convoy of 1,005 people on September 15, 1943.[116]

On September 16, 1943, Dr. Gossner of the Public Health Board instructed the OHW to have all workers, including Jews, inoculated against typhus. The OHW contractors nevertheless considered it a gratuitous waste of their time and money to have foreign laborers vaccinated during work. Their demands to deduct the missing hours from the laborers' payrolls were rejected by the OHW, which reiterated that precautionary measures of the Health Board were beyond its control and also affected the German workforce.[117] The vaccine probably derived from one of the plants maintained by the Wehrmacht in Cracow and Lemberg (L'viv). The Polish biologist Rudolf Weigl had developed a typhus vaccine during the First World War and was forced to render his services to the Nazis after the invasion of Poland. He used his position at the Behring-Institute in Lemberg to save Jewish scientists from deportation by offering them employment and to smuggle doses of typhus vaccine into the Warsaw ghetto. The so-called Weigl vaccine nevertheless only provided partial immunity to the disease, causing milder and less fatal attacks. Some of the jabs destined for the SS and the Wehrmacht were manipulated, offering no protection at all.[118] The Jewish prisoners of Blechhammer were inoculated by their camp physicians. As some of them contracted typhus afterward, a survivor suspected that the Germans had meddled with the vaccines in order to kill them. Despite prisoner experiments with typhus in Auschwitz and Buchenwald, it seems nonetheless unlikely that the inmates of Blechhammer were deliberately infected. Apparently these cases occurred due to "vaccine failure" or to "breakthrough disease" caused by a wild type of virus despite an inoculation. The outbreak was contained in the fall.[119]

Despite the reinforcements, only four doctors were allowed to work in the infirmary along with the head physician Dr. Littwack. The others were forced to set out to the construction site as paramedics.[120] When typhus erupted in camp Gräditz in mid-February 1944, Dr. Littwack, Dr. Rosenthal, Dr. Jakubowitsch, Dr. Cohensius, and Dr. Wollenberg were sent there to help. In postwar testimony, Dr. Littwack alleged that the Schmelt Office had transferred the Jewish physicians to this camp with the intention of killing them by way of a typhus infection. All Blechhammer physicians sent to Gräditz did indeed contract typhus, and Dr. Rosenthal died of it. The vaccination of September 1943 had obviously failed, or the OHW had received the doses manipulated by Weigl.[121]

THE DELEGATION OF WATER-INDUCED MURDERS AND THE INTERVENTION OF AUSCHWITZ IN THE SELECTIONS

The new guard duty officer, Mareck, oversaw the selections in the infirmary together with Erich Hoffmann. Their primary victims were patients unfit for work for more than four to six weeks. This policy also targeted inmates who had had several shorter stays in the infirmary and went back to work in between. They could be put on a transport list even though they were working full-time again. The infirmary was often emptied of all patients, unless the camp physicians managed to warn individual prisoners or discharged them in time before a selection.[122] Inmates saved by untimely discharge often reproached the medical staff for the abrupt termination of their treatment, until they realized that it had been done for their own good. A prisoner electrician with a severe leg injury incurred by a fall from a scaffold, for instance, was sent back to work after seven days in the infirmary, despite requiring the assistance of comrades to walk. His initial anger with the camp physicians turned into gratefulness the following day, when he found the infirmary almost empty.[123]

Mareck delegated the water-induced murders his predecessor Rettinghausen had carried out excessively to Erich Hoffmann. The camp leader had been familiarized with this cruel killing method by the SD and had gained more practical experience by assisting Rettinghausen in 1942. Now that the police guards were no longer available, Hoffmann increasingly drew on the enforced collaboration of Jewish functionary prisoners. The Jewish elder Demerer was thus required to attend up to fifty murders of this kind.[124] The survivor Aron Schlos witnessed numerous murders in the washroom barrack through the window of his room and had to remove the bodies the next morning.

He stated that Hoffmann had randomly chosen three to five prisoners each day. During the postwar trial of Hoffmann, Schlos described the killing procedure in painful detail: "The respective prisoners had to get fully undressed, and were then hosed with cold water, until they were dead. The torment of taking them from life to death usually lasted for two hours. The hose was inserted into the mouth of those who had survived this procedure, until the water pressure caused their organs to rupture, or their head was held into a water-filled barrel, until they had drowned."[125]

At the end of 1943, Hoffmann had two inmates from a newly arrived transport from Königshütte (Chorzów) killed in this manner for an escape attempt. He purportedly offered one hundred cigarettes to any prisoner ready to assist him.[126] Using prisoners as their own comrades' henchmen was part of a perfidious strategy commonly pursued in Nazi concentration camps, which aimed to drive a wedge between the inmates.[127] As there were no public executions in Schmelt camps, the intended effect was somewhat diminished. However, most of the prisoners were pressed into cooperating and had to continue with their gruesome tasks even if they were relocated to different camps. A former camp policeman of Brande (Prądy), Icek Rosenzweig, was appointed head of column when he came to Blechhammer in late 1943. Just like the camp leader of Brande, Hoffmann coerced him into drowning or strangling inmates under threat of sending him to Auschwitz.[128] He was feared by the other prisoners, who reproached him for his role as an alleged accessory. His status as a half-Jewish German further contributed to the negative image of him. The child survivor Leo B. recounted how Rosenzweig nearly killed him in a fit of rage by hitting his fist against his heart, while the two Jewish elders stood by helplessly.[129]

Coinciding with the WVHA's order to delegate selections at the ramp and in work details at Auschwitz from SS block leaders to physicians to increase the number of prisoners that could be made available to the war economy, SS doctors from Auschwitz began to intervene in the selection process in Schmelt camps.[130] As of spring 1943, they visited Blechhammer in three-month intervals to select working prisoners and encouraged Mareck and Hoffmann to participate.[131] All work details had to run in front of the SS physicians, who checked the blood circulation of those unable to keep up by piercing their legs with pencils. Some among the selected were sent to a convalescent camp and returned to Blechhammer alive. However, most of them were murdered in Auschwitz.[132] The Wehrmacht guards were required to list prisoners they found to be unfit or working slowly. Survivors reported that they were reluctant to earmark prisoners and preferred to swap weak inmates between details to conceal their lower productivity for a while. The pressure to maintain a high pace at work nonetheless cost the last reserves of emaciated prisoners, and they were prone to fall victim to one of the next selections.[133] In winter 1943 female inmates in their forties and fifties had to step forward during a roll call. They were collectively added to a sick transport to Auschwitz despite being fit to work.¹³⁴ Gender-specific decimations of healthy women were common in Schmelt's system. The order to murder the middle-aged women appears to have been part of the preparations for the Auschwitz takeover, analogous to the transfer of one hundred younger female prisoners to Peterswaldau, a future Gross-Rosen subcamp, in January 1944.¹³⁵

Occasionally women were taken to Schmelt camps to work despite being pregnant. Others became pregnant while in the camps, due to either rape or consensual relationships. The Schmelt Office complied with the WVHA directive to murder pregnant women that had been introduced in the concentration camps in spring 1941. In a revised version issued in mid-1943, the WVHA demanded the babies be killed but the mothers be kept alive.¹³⁶ Schmelt nonetheless continued to have pregnant women murdered either directly in the camps or by sending them to the gas chambers. No intervention by Auschwitz physicians ensued.¹³⁷ Schmelt's unrestrained killing policy resulted in a particularly tragic incident in Blechhammer. In early 1944, a pregnant woman and her husband, who had been hiding in the liquidated ghetto of Sosnowiec, were arrested and transferred to Blechhammer. The woman worked in the kitchen at first but was added to a sick transport to Auschwitz as soon as her pregnancy was noticed. When the transport had left, her husband immediately hanged himself.¹³⁸

Parallel to the growing number of prisoners and victims, the already existing burial detail was staffed up. In January 1943 Jonas Pampel and Levie Barmhartigkeid from the Netherlands were transferred to Blechhammer from Seibersdorf, where they had also acted as gravediggers. The two friends worked on the construction site during the day and helped to bury the dead in the evening. They usually performed a ritual washing of the bodies and said *Kaddish*, the traditional prayer for the dead.¹³⁹ The deputy Jewish elder Niewes, who also carried out Jewish burial rites, temporarily had the same function.¹⁴⁰ Even though every other form of religious practice was strictly prohibited, the German camp personnel did not interfere with the burials. The dead of the Schmelt camps therefore could still be laid to rest with a certain dignity compared to camps like Auschwitz. Curiously, the members of the burial detail were rarely observant Jews themselves. However, practicing the rites for the dead obviously drew a line of continuity to religious traditions the Nazis aimed to eradicate along with the Jewish people and represented a particular form of spirituality that could still be upheld in the camps.¹⁴¹

5

BLECHHAMMER'S NEW ROLE IN THE HOLOCAUST IN EASTERN UPPER SILESIA

On May 21, 1943, Himmler decreed that by June 30, 1943, all Jews still living in the German Reich and in the Protectorate of Bohemia and Moravia had to be taken to "the east," or to Terezín. This new policy also targeted Jews working in crucial sectors of the war economy, who had previously been exempted from deportations. However, special arrangements were to be made for the inmates of Schmelt camps. According to the former Auschwitz commandant Rudolf Hoess, Himmler ordered Schmelt's ghetto workshops closed down and brought the most important of his labor camps under the administration of either Auschwitz or Gross-Rosen. Camps not vital to the war effort were to be liquidated, and the prisoners should be killed in Auschwitz.[1] Approximately one-fifth of the Schmelt camps were thus preserved. Contrary to Hoess's claims, a small fraction of the inmates of the disbanded camps was distributed among the remaining Schmelt camps. Schmelt's deputy Heinrich Lindner and RAB representative Haunschild selected an average 20 to 30 percent of the prisoners for work. The others were sent to their deaths, irrespective of their physical state. Lindner and Haunschild still made them believe that they would be transferred to a "sanatorium" in camp Annaberg.[2]

By contrast, networks of labor camps in East Galicia and the Warthegau similar to those set up by Schmelt in Silesia were all liquidated by fall 1943, and almost none of the inmates were left alive.[3] This deviating strategy reflected Upper Silesia's paramount importance in arms production and Speer's call for an increase in the economic output and the rationalization of manpower and resources. Speer demanded that Himmler should raise the number of inmates in concentration camps and put them at the disposal of the war industry to an even greater extent than before. Consequently, Schmelt camps not involved in vital war work were disbanded, and a certain percentage of the inmates were relocated to industrial sites considered crucial to the war effort. Between September 1943 and July 1944, forty-three Schmelt camps were taken over by Auschwitz and Gross-Rosen. Both significantly expanded their subcamp system in the process of complying with the war economy's apparent need for workers. However, Himmler failed to reach his envisaged target of having an extra two hundred thousand prisoners transferred to concentration camps.[4]

Adolf Eichmann was delegated to schedule the deportations of the Jews of Eastern Upper Silesia with Gestapo Kattowitz, headed by Rudolf Mildner at the time.[5] Documents on the respective agreements between Eichmann and Mildner have not been preserved, but Blechhammer obviously began to play a crucial role in the Holocaust in Eastern Upper Silesia. As one of the remaining camps, Blechhammer was not only enlarged, but it simultaneously facilitated the selections and subsequent murder of parts of the ghetto population, as well as the transfer of sick and unfit inmates from disbanded Schmelt camps to Auschwitz.

THE TRANSIT CAMP (DULAG)

Following Himmler's May order, the ghettos were liquidated, and a new wave of transports to Auschwitz set in. But not all of them went straight to the death camp. Next to able-bodied young women and men, whole families were sent to Blechhammer. During the uprising in the Sosnowiec ghetto, Schmelt's central transit camp (*Durchgangslager*, Dulag) became unavailable for selections. Therefore, Blechhammer temporarily took over its functions between June and August 1943. A fenced-off section with two barracks was used to segregate those still deemed fit for work from their children, younger siblings, or elderly relatives. The able-bodied were distributed among Schmelt camps, whereas the others were murdered in Auschwitz after a few days or even hours in Blechhammer. Simultaneously, weakened inmates of the camp were added to the Auschwitz convoys.[6]

The first transport of this kind originated from the ghetto of Strzemieszyce. The Germans had ghettoized the local Jewish inhabitants, who mostly worked in nearby camps, in 1940. In June 1942, four hundred people were deported to Auschwitz. The head of the Central Office of the Jewish elders in Sosnowiec Moshe Merin conducted a census among the remaining population and issued new working papers to approximately one thousand people. One year later, on June 15, 1943, all ghetto residents were deported to Auschwitz, except for some able-bodied young men, who were sent to Blechhammer by passenger trains. On arrival, they had to hand in their valuables, take a shower, and exchange their clothes for worn-out rags. The Highway Company's representative,

Haunschild, came the next morning to take down their names and professions. Those who remained in Blechhammer were very supportive of one another and continued to form a group of their own.[7]

The town Kłobucko in the district of Kielce had a Jewish population of about sixteen hundred in prewar times. After the German occupation, it was first part of the General Government but then incorporated into Eastern Upper Silesia in November 1939. Many Jews from bordering communities fled the General Government to seek refuge in the town, as the conditions there seemed more tolerable. By March 1940, Kłobucko's Jewish population had reached over two thousand. In October 1941 a ghetto was established, and the inhabitants were required to work in camps the Germans set up in the vicinity. One of these camps, located in the village Zagórze, was regarded as a "safe haven." It attracted volunteers not only from Kłobucko but also from nearby towns like Zabrze. Between June 21 and 22, 1942, the ghetto of Kłobucko was liquidated, and all but seven skilled workers and their families were marched to Krzepice to be selected and deported to Auschwitz. As a great number of people had gone into hiding before the liquidation, the Germans set up tailor's and shoemaker's workshops in the former ghetto and its surroundings to lure those in hideouts back into closed settlements. For want of alternative options, they returned to the workshop camps. The Zagórze camp soon numbered five hundred workers. It was disbanded in July 1943, along with the rest of the workshops and camps in and around Kłobucko. All remaining Jewish inhabitants, including children and the elderly, were taken to Blechhammer by train.[8]

The families spent the night together in barracks, which were so crowded that some had to sleep outside. When Blechhammer prisoners came to the fence of the transit camp to beg for bread, they got a first impression of what awaited them. A survivor recalled that there was a cynical poster reading *"Arbeit macht das Leben süß"* ("work makes life sweet"). The next day Haunschild arrived for the selections. He was accompanied by "a very choleric *Obersturmbannführer*," possibly Heinrich Lindner. The selection process was extremely stressful, as it took place in the summer heat and the deportees had no access to water. The men were separated from the women, and pregnant women, those over forty years old, and little girls were pulled out. In the end, six hundred men from Kłobucko were selected for work, twenty-six of whom stayed in Blechhammer. When they learned that the unfit women and children would be sent to Auschwitz, the situation escalated. Crying and screaming for each other, families desperately tried to stay together, while the Germans set their dogs on them.[9] Smaller children were taken away from their mothers so the women could be sent to work camps. Wailing for their mothers, the children were retained in Blechhammer for up to a week, until the next trucks left for Auschwitz. Not only the women were confronted with the "choiceless choice" of either dying with their children or leaving them to their fate alone.[10] A father from Kłobucko was likewise forced to hand his little son over to an elderly woman he knew from his hometown in order to survive. Both the little boy and the woman perished in Auschwitz. Some of the pregnant women gave birth in the transit camp. Their babies were drowned immediately.[11]

In this desolate situation, people offered jewelry to the Jewish elder Karl Demerer and his deputy Jozef Niewes, imploring them to save their children or other relatives. By bribing camp leader Hoffmann, Demerer succeeded in rescuing about thirty boys below the age of sixteen out of a total of two hundred children who passed through the transit camp. The Jewish functionary prisoners of Blechhammer knew all too well where the transports were going, as Demerer had been to Auschwitz two or three times with Hoffmann, and they did their best to save as many as possible. With Hoffmann's permission, the children were hidden until the transports had left. They later served as calfactors in the camp, where they stoked stoves, made coffee, or ran errands.[12] Those lacking the means to pay bribes occasionally made daring attempts to protect their next of kin. Thus, a woman from the Zagórze work camp approached a Schmelt representative directly after her former Jewish elder had declared that he could do nothing for her twelve-year-old nephew. She gave the boy shoes with high heels, so he appeared taller, and showed his hands to the German official, arguing that he could work. Thanks to his aunt's intervention, the boy was indeed allowed to remain in Blechhammer, as a cleaner.[13]

At times older siblings succeeded in saving their younger brothers or sisters. Two adult sisters from Kłobucko smuggled their eleven-year-old sister through the selection by having her wear boots with high heels and a long skirt, so she looked older. All three were sent to a Schmelt camp together. However, their thirteen-year-old brother Art was not selected for work. When he realized that he was about to be separated from his sisters, he threw himself on the ground and pleaded with Demerer to be given a job. The Jewish elder took pity on him, remarking that someone with so much courage and will to live deserved to be saved. Together with four other rescued boys, Art was hidden in a washroom barrack until the transport had gone. Demerer persuaded Hoffmann to make the boy a messenger between his and the camp leader's office, and he survived.[14]

The Jewish population of Sosnowiec was among the last to be ghettoized, on March 15, 1943. The Germans' plans to fully liquidate the ghetto by June 23–24, 1943, were hampered by an uprising of Zionist resistance fighters under the leadership of Vebek Śmetana. Twelve thousand people, including Moshe Merin and his assistant, had been taken to Auschwitz in a first wave before the deportations were brought to a halt. The ghetto was held against the Germans until the beginning of August, when SS and police units were reinforced. The crushing of the revolt resulted in the deportation of another thirty thousand residents of Sosnowiec and its twin city Będzin to Auschwitz.[15] Some of the younger ghetto inhabitants were shipped to Blechhammer in cattle cars to be selected for Schmelt camps. There were also children and pregnant women among the able-bodied. On arrival, they had to take a shower and exchange their own clothes for used ones. The pregnant women were led into a separate washroom barrack. A survivor reported that she had heard their screams and suspected that they had been mistreated. Possibly they were even murdered, like a group of unfit women who passed through Blechhammer in winter 1943. The ensuing selection was carried out by two men. One of them must have been Lindner, assisted by someone with a missing eye, who meted out blows to those not standing up straight. The men and women considered fit for work spent between one day and several weeks in Blechhammer before being transferred to various Schmelt camps. The others were sent to Auschwitz.[16]

The inmates of at least seven to eight disbanded work camps passed through the transit camp in parallel to the ghetto inhabitants. A transport of about one thousand women from Bautrupp Saybusch arrived in Blechhammer, but only two hundred of them were selected for a camp in Neusalz (Nowa Sól).[17] The proportion of inmates from liquidated camps rated as "fit" was typically very low, implying that the majority were murdered in Auschwitz irrespective of their physical ability to work.[18]

Fifteen-year-old Sara Chrapot was transferred to Blechhammer from a dissolved camp in Ziechenicze with her brother and sister. Recalling what a cousin had told her about Treblinka, she expected to be gassed on arrival. When they all had to line up in rows of five to be selected, Sara hid in the back. She and her sister were held in one of the transit barracks, together with elderly people from the ghettos. In her postwar testimony, she mentioned that one of the men in the barrack had offered her bread in return for sexual favors, to which she agreed. Consensual sexual barter was a common phenomenon in ghettos. However, the practice was discontinued in the Schmelt camps, as men and women were strictly kept apart. Sara was sent on to Neusalz after a few days, while her sister managed to escape from the transit camp. Her brother, who had been taken to a different barrack, was presumably murdered in Auschwitz.[19] Altogether, approximately six hundred women considered fit for work passed through the transit camp, but only a small fraction stayed in Blechhammer.[20]

From August 2, 1943, a permanent new transit camp was established in camp Annaberg (Góra Świętej Anny), the place the Schmelt Office had been relocated to from Sosnowiec. It operated until the end of March 1944, when the Schmelt camp system was largely dismantled.[21] The use of Blechhammer and Annaberg, which were both administered by the Highway Company, exemplifies the intense collaboration of Speer's private enterprise in the Holocaust. In these camps, perpetrators not directly linked to Auschwitz made selections and condemned the greater part of those passing through them to death in the gas chambers. Blechhammer evidently also served as an entity where newborn babies and individual groups of women were immediately murdered.

THE UNPLANNED FORMATION OF A CHILDREN'S DETAIL IN THE AFTERMATH OF THE GHETTO LIQUIDATIONS

Resulting from Blechhammer's temporary role as a transit camp, a small group of under-sixteen-year-olds were held in the camp who had either erroneously been selected by Schmelt representatives, because they looked older than they were, or had been smuggled in through bribery. The total number of children in Schmelt camps is unknown.

By contrast, hundreds of thousands of children and teenagers were deported to concentration camps. However, the majority were almost immediately murdered, like the first Jewish children arriving in Auschwitz in early 1942 from Eastern Upper Silesia. As the demand for more laborers grew, deportees on certain transports from Slovakia and France, including children, were registered as workers without prior selections. Their survival chances were nevertheless minuscule. With the introduction of regular selections at the ramp in summer 1943, children were gassed upon arrival. An unknown number of unregistered teenagers had nevertheless been smuggled into work details of adult prisoners. In 1944 children were temporarily held in the transit camp of Birkenau with their parents to await their deaths. Occasionally another selection was made, and a few older children were assigned to work details or were sent on to other camps. Some of the children were abused for medical experiments. Out of an estimated 6,700 Jewish children registered in Auschwitz, a mere 451 survived.[22]

The first children in Blechhammer were the Jewish elder's son and daughter, Heinrich and Halina Demerer. They lived in the Sosnowiec ghetto with their mother until the liquidation commenced in May 1943. Karl Demerer had pleaded with the Schmelt Office for a long time to be granted permission to take his family to Blechhammer. The Schmelt representative, SS Obersturmführer Alfred Ludwig, eventually offered to save his wife and children from being deported as a "reward" for his service as Jewish elder. Amid the ongoing mass deportations to Auschwitz, the Demerers were escorted to the Schmelt Office's headquarters in Sosnowiec to have lunch with Ludwig. Later, an SS guard boarded a passenger train to Ehrenforst (Sławięcice) with them, from where they were driven to Blechhammer by car.[23] The Demerers were nevertheless not allowed to live together as a family. Thirteen-year-old Halina and her mother had to move to the women's camp section, and twelve-year-old Heinrich was accommodated in a barrack with functionary prisoners, the cook, the hairdresser, and a shoemaker. During the day he assisted the shoemaker in his workshop. In a postwar memoir, he delineated how a profound sadness had overcome him when he learned that his former friends from Sosnowiec had all perished in Auschwitz. Curiously, he never mentioned the arrival of dozens of other children from the ghettos in Blechhammer.[24]

The thirty boys rescued from the transit camp by the Jewish elder in summer 1943 were between eleven and fifteen years old. The children had calfactor jobs in the camp and later also worked on the OHW construction site. When the inmates of camp Reigersfeld (Birawa) were transferred to Blechhammer in 1943, the number of children rose to fifty.[25] Teenagers deported from Drancy and selected for work by Haunschild during the "Cosel period" in 1942 were also taken to Blechhammer in the course of 1943. In August 1943 a group of twenty-two boys aged between eleven and seventeen from the Będzin ghetto had been selected to work in Karwin, a Schmelt camp in a part of Moravia incorporated into Upper Silesia. When it had become clear after a few days that they could not cope with the heavy labor, they were sent to Blechhammer as well.[26] The boys formed a detail of their own and lived together in a room of a barrack. The child survivor Gunter Faerber, who was in the group from Karwin, recalled that they were so exhausted from the work that they did not even start fights among each other. They usually communicated in Yiddish, as other languages, such as German or Polish, were considered undesirable. Those unable to speak Yiddish thus quickly had to learn it.[27]

The growing pressure on concentration camps to support the war effort resulted in an order by Himmler that all juvenile prisoners should learn a trade. In 1942 a school for masonry was established in Auschwitz-Birkenau to train Jewish and non-Jewish boys.[28] Similarly, a small fraction of teenagers from Blechhammer were sent to a trade school to attend five-week programs. However, the children put at the disposal of contracting companies at the OHW free of charge as alleged "apprentices" were mostly allocated to menial jobs, such as unloading cement sacks, instead of being trained.[29] About twenty of the boys aged eleven to fourteen were deployed in a work detail of their own to fetch firewood from the forest surrounding the camp. They also had to clean tree roots of soil after a tractor had pulled them out.[30] They were supervised by a Wehrmacht guard who, according to Jewish camp physician Wollenberg, was "a well-meaning and good-hearted person," who cared for the boys "like a father." As soon as the detail had reached the forest, he would make a little shelter for the children and let them sleep in it while he collected the firewood himself. Later the children were distributed among adult work details as calfactors. Wollenberg felt they were being "spoiled" by everyone, and especially by the British POWs, who showered them with chocolates and sandwiches. He apparently underrated the paramount importance of the extra food to the children's survival. Above all, Wollenberg excoriated their lack of education and manners and the fact that none of the adult prisoners ever reprimanded them for their "inappropriate" behavior. To survive, many of the children had started to pilfer, and they bartered on the construction site, just like the adults.[31] More than anyone else, the children seemed to reflect the effects of the enforced change of paradigms in the Nazi camps, where moral values had become corrupted and previous notions of good and evil had been reversed. At second glance, Wollenberg's criticism was not so much directed against the children as against the adult prisoners, whose struggle to stay alive had compelled them to adapt to the new, gruesome realities. The adults were too preoccupied with the heavy work and their own existential crises to organize clandestine teaching for the young inmates, as was done in ghettos like Terezín and the "family camp" at Birkenau.[32]

Even worse, the adult prisoners were unable to protect the children from molestation by the German camp personnel. The sexual abuse of children in concentration camps was commonplace, and evidently the Schmelt camps were no exception.[33] Hoffmann's deputy Wilhelm Pfeiffer often handed out extra food rations to the boys. However, Pfeiffer's generosity was not based on altruism, but merely a trick to lure the young prisoners into his apartment so he could abuse them. His "appetite for boys" was well known among the adult inmates. He had a habit of going into barracks in the evenings to distribute biscuits and prunes among the children, and he invited some of them to his place in the old camp kitchen for free meals and "some fun." One of them was Art G., then fourteen years old, who had accepted Pfeiffer's invitations several times, along with his friends. It was only after a while that he realized that some of his friends were being molested on these occasions, and he stopped going there. The fifteen-year-old messenger Kurt Moses was frequently abused by Pfeiffer. One time a fellow inmate on night guard duty found his bed empty and had the camp searched for young Kurt. At 2.30 a.m. he was finally seen coming out of Pfeiffer's quarters. He pleaded that he not be punished for his absence, asserting that he was "a powerless slave." The juvenile prisoners avoided speaking about the abuse among each other.[34] Wilhelm Pfeiffer appeared as a witness in the postwar trial of Erich Hoffmann in Munich but was never charged himself.[35]

THE TRANSFER OF FEMALE PRISONERS TO FUTURE GROSS-ROSEN SUBCAMPS

In preparation for the beginning of the dissolution of Schmelt's system, large numbers of female Blechhammer prisoners were relocated to camps for women, which were gradually taken over by the Gross-Rosen concentration camp. As of spring 1943, female Blechhammer inmates were transferred to Schatzlar (Žacléř) in Sudeten to work in a spinning mill. In the summer others were sent to a newly opened camp for women in Langenbielau (Bielawa), comprising a spinning mill and an ammunition factory. The latter claimed very high death tolls due to exposure to toxic explosives. Some of the women passing through the Blechhammer transit camp in the late summer were also transferred to a spinning mill in Neusalz (Nowa Sól) in Lower Silesia. By the end of the year, fifty-five hundred female inmates of former Schmelt camps had been incorporated into the Gross-Rosen satellite system. They represented about two-thirds of Gross-Rosen's total female prisoner population.[36]

Shortly before the takeover of Blechhammer in January 1944, the Auschwitz administration demanded that 100 of the camp's 160 female prisoners leave. As the destination was unspecified, none of the women volunteered. The Jewish elder thus took the painful decision to put the names of his own wife and daughter on top of the transport list to gain the other women's trust. There was a strict selection for young women with good eyesight and apt hands, as they were supposed to regulate timers for bombs. The camp they were taken to was Peterswaldau (Pieszyce), an ammunition factory with a newly established camp for women, which was about to become a subcamp of Gross-Rosen. The takeover was finalized in April 1944. One of the women from Blechhammer was appointed Jewish elder in Peterswaldau. However, Karl Demerer only learned that his wife and daughter were still alive and where they had been taken when Schmelt representative Alfred Ludwig came by for an inspection several weeks later.[37] On the very morning of the women's departure, one hundred young females from Będzin replaced them.[38] They were transferred to Blechhammer from a camp set up after the liquidation of the ghetto of Będzin in August 1943, which had just been disbanded.[39]

THE CAMP FOR THE SICK AND CONVALESCENT (*KRANKEN- UND ERHOLUNGSLAGER*) AND THE PUNISHMENT CAMP (*STRAFLAGER*)

Following the launch of ghetto liquidations in the summer of 1942, the Schmelt Office no longer permitted the referral of critically ill prisoners to the Jewish hospital of Sosnowiec. Alternatively, special units for the sick and convalescent were set up in several Schmelt camps from late 1942. Their function was highly ambivalent. At first they undoubtedly reflected the WVHA's short-lived attempts to comply with Speer's demand to support the war economy by boosting the prisoners' output. However, within several months they were transformed from care units providing limited medical aid into mere collection points for Auschwitz transports and additional killing facilities.[40]

The first sick camps were established at Ottmuth (Otmęt), Annaberg (Góra Świętej Anny), and Sakrau (Zakrzów). Initially there was a triage of the patients into convalescents and emaciated prisoners likely to regain their full ability to work after some "feeding up," those expected to recuperate within a given period of time, and gravely ill or injured inmates. The latter were invariably murdered in Auschwitz, while the other two groups stood a certain chance of returning to labor camps alive. Especially Annaberg, which served as a sick camp from November 27, 1942, until June 1943, still had a fairly good reputation among the inmates.[41] In Parschnitz (Poříčí, Sudeten), a sick camp began to be built on the grounds of the Alois Haase factory in 1943. It was only completed on February 4, 1944, one month before the takeover by Gross-Rosen.[42]

Brande (Prądy) exemplifies the gradual transformation of a sick camp into a killing center. With the cessation of highway construction, the former RAB camp was turned into a camp for the sick in December 1942. Guard duty officer Kurt Bruno Pompe, together with a civilian camp leader named Thien, selected prisoners who had not recovered after six weeks for transports to Auschwitz. The victims were isolated days before a transport without receiving any medical care. Pompe and Thien frequently exposed them to very cold water, which caused fatalities. The practice of water-induced murders was intensified from April 1943, when Schmelt's deputy Heinrich Lindner was deployed in Brande. Almost every night, unfit prisoners whose beds had been marked with a red cross were drowned in the washroom by Pompe or died of hypothermia. Under threats of sending them to Auschwitz, he coerced two Jewish functionaries, the camp policeman Icek Rosenzweig, and a head of column to collaborate. When Brande was dissolved at the end of August 1943, Pompe, Rosenzweig, and the Jewish medical staff were relocated to Blechhammer.[43] From then on Rosenzweig, a half-Jewish German, was forced to commit murders for Hoffmann. Thus, he and the camp policeman Rauch once had to strangle a young female prisoner. After the war, Rosenzweig was charged with murder before a Jewish Honor Court in a displaced persons' camp.[44] These courts primarily had a cathartic function to alleviate the moral dilemma facing Jewish communities by having to integrate former functionary prisoners, who were perceived as "collaborators." Rosenzweig's case is a drastic example of the German perpetrators' attempts to incriminate their victims, whose leeway for action was minuscule.[45] Forcing prisoners to assist in the murder of their comrades was also part of a perfidious strategy in Nazi camps to break up their solidarity.[46]

Blechhammer operated a sick camp from September 1, 1943, until the Auschwitz takeover in April 1944. In stark contrast to its predecessors, Blechhammer was merely used as a collection point for transports to Auschwitz. The incoming prisoners were no longer segregated by triage and received no medical attention.[47] This signaled the end of the Schmelt Office's feeble concessions to Speer's call for higher work productivity.[48] The camp infirmary compound was extended to barracks thirteen and fourteen. The adjacent washroom barrack was stripped of all sanitary facilities and transformed into a gruesome isolation cell for prisoners from Blechhammer and other Schmelt camps who had been selected for Auschwitz.[49] Tragically, some prisoners "volunteered" for the sick camp, as they had lost their will to live entirely. The sick were kept naked on straw bedding in despicably unhygienic conditions. Once a day, half a food ration was thrown in through a window. Their ordeal often lasted for weeks, until sufficient numbers had been gathered for a transport. An average of four hundred prisoners were sent to Auschwitz on each of these occasions.[50] Nobody was permitted to enter the barrack.

Individual prisoners nonetheless tried to catch a glimpse of their friends or relatives through the window and were horrified by what they saw: "Locked up like wild animals, they did not wash, defecated in the room, and touched the smaller part of our rations. On visiting them, I had the impression of being in a zoo. Their facial expressions were really savage and made them look even worse."[51]

Reprehensibly, the inmates were still made to believe that they would be transferred to the Jewish hospital of Sosnowiec and could go home later, even though the hospital had already been liquidated in June 1943. Blechhammer survivor Gucia Ferst, who worked in the kitchen, became a firsthand witness to several incidents in the sick camp. She related how, one day, a group of girls arrived in that camp section who were overjoyed, thinking they would return to their homes. They were all murdered in Auschwitz a few hours later. Camp leader Erich Hoffmann committed a series of atrocities in the sick camp. One of the victims was a prisoner selected for Auschwitz who managed to hide under a barrack roof until the transport had left without him. Hoffmann started a feverish search, and when he finally found the man, he killed him in an utterly brutal fashion. Ferst could see from the kitchen window how the prisoner's skull split open under Hoffmann's boots, and his brain was splattered over the ground.[52] Hoffmann also ordered Pompe to strangle two pregnant women immediately after his arrival from Brande. During his brief tenure in Blechhammer, Pompe supervised the female inmates.[53]

Unlike in Brande, mass killings of the unfit in the camp itself were an exception. One such case occurred in winter 1943, when a transport of sick female prisoners arrived. Sensing what was in store for them, the women started to panic. The camp personnel apparently decided to murder them on the spot by using the death bath procedure. Gucia Ferst saw how the female prisoners were led into a washroom barrack, where they were sprinkled with cold water. For some time she heard their screams, then the women became quiet. Later some of the prisoner physicians were called to confirm their deaths.[54] Similar ad hoc killings are known to have taken place in Auschwitz, whenever individual deportees tried to warn others about entering the gas chambers.[55]

The events in the sick camp made the reality of the Shoah palpable to the other prisoners: "We could not believe what happened in Auschwitz in the beginning, then we saw transports with naked people from other camps going through Blechhammer, they had no dignity left. . . . Those transports made their mark, we finally realized this was no joke."[56]

The sick camp began to be used for sending up to two-thirds of the prisoners of disbanded Schmelt camps passing through Blechhammer to Auschwitz. They were killed without necessarily being unfit for work.[57] Their large-scale murder complied with Himmler's May order to liquidate the majority of the Schmelt camps, and Blechhammer facilitated these final steps in the annihilation of the Eastern Upper Silesian Jewry.[58]

The sick camp had an added function as a punishment camp (*Straflager*). This was a new development in the Schmelt camp system. The prisoners usually were sent to punishment camps for a limited time to be reprimanded for various offenses by way of hard labor, and they subsequently returned to their regular workplaces. However, the punishment section at Blechhammer only served to detain inmates supposed to be sent to Auschwitz for transgressions, such as escape attempts. On average, up to one hundred prisoners were held in the camp for this purpose. Hence, two formerly separate entities in Schmelt's system, camps for the sick and punishment camps, were fused into a single facility with the sole purpose of murdering the respective inmates.[59] In rare cases, another selection for the fit was made in the sick camp, when there was an urgent need for laborers. A Schmelt representative with a limp, probably Haunschild, once pulled out a considerable number of prisoners from the roughly four hundred men about to be sent to Auschwitz. This saved the life of a healthy prisoner from camp Sackenhoym, who was supposed to go to Auschwitz for punishment.[60]

Similar to the transit camp, the modified variant of a sick camp set up in Blechhammer was intrinsically linked to the implementation of the Final Solution in Eastern Upper Silesia. Instead of providing medical care to sick and unfit prisoners, its only purpose was to have them killed in the gas chambers in great numbers. The sick camp was simultaneously used for sending up to two-thirds of the inmate population of disbanded Schmelt camps to Auschwitz, regardless of their condition.[61] Along the same lines, prisoners sentenced to punishment camps were now simply added to the sick to be gassed in Auschwitz.[62] Blechhammer was placed at the end of a continuum moving from genuine aid to the sick to their large-scale, unspecific murder. The sick camp turned Blechhammer into a major cog in the wheel of the genocidal machinery of death at Auschwitz, annihilating not merely the ghetto population, but increasingly also the inmates of labor camps.

CONCLUSION: THE CLOSING CHAPTER — BLECHHAMMER DURING THE FINAL PHASE OF THE SCHMELT CAMP SYSTEM

Owing to the OHW's significance in the war economy, Blechhammer was among the forty-three Schmelt camps about to be incorporated into the satellite systems of Auschwitz and Gross-Rosen. On the eve of the Auschwitz takeover in spring 1944, 13 percent of the twenty-five thousand Schmelt prisoners who were still alive were detained in Blechhammer. Despite the apparent increase in the camp's inmate population, it is strikingly obvious that the overall number of Schmelt camp prisoners had decreased by 50 percent compared to the previous year.[63] The percentage of prisoners who perished between January 1943 and April 1944 must have been even larger than suggested by the aforementioned figures, if one takes into account that the last able-bodied men and women from the liquidated ghettos were forced into these labor camps on top of the existing inmate population. Altogether, the number of Schmelt prisoners could have reached seventy-five thousand (including nine thousand "Cosel men" imported from western Europe), implying a total death toll of fifty thousand. Considering that an estimated fifty-five thousand people were deported from the Eastern Upper Silesian ghettos, it must be concluded that camps like Blechhammer were responsible for the murder of nearly half the Jewish population in the area.[64]

Speer's pressure to enforce higher productivity contributed to an increase in the mortality of the Jewish prisoners, whose general living conditions deteriorated, and who were subjected to violent assaults as well as a hazardous work environment. The intensification of the murders of sick and unfit inmates was facilitated by the perpetrators' interchangeability. The delegation of killings and selections from authorities such as the SS or the Gestapo to civilian auxiliaries was a typical development linked to the intensifying lack of personnel toward the end of the war.[65] Interestingly, the Schmelt Office did not draw on the Wehrmacht guards to commit these atrocities.

Following Himmler's decision to liquidate the ghettos, Blechhammer's transit camp became a key point for segregating the Jewish population. Utilizing the infrastructure of a privatized industrial concern, members of the Schmelt Office and the Reich Highway Company, who were not directly connected to the Auschwitz concentration camp, selected children, pregnant women, and the elderly for death in the gas chambers. The camp for the sick and convalescent, with its added function as a punishment camp, merely served as a collection point for Auschwitz. Both the transit camp and the sick camp were used to send most inmates of disbanded Schmelt camps to their deaths. Evidently, Blechhammer was integral to the implementation of the Shoah in Eastern Upper Silesia in 1943. The purportedly "economically" motivated exemption of a small fraction of Schmelt camp inmates from the deportations to Auschwitz in summer 1943 was by no means lifesaving. With mortality rates of up to 95 percent, camps like Blechhammer were not "sanctuaries" but part and parcel of the annihilatory policy relentlessly pursued against the Jews.[66] Countless young, able-bodied men and women had perished in these camps long before the onset of mass deportations decimated the ghetto inhabitants. Their exorbitant death tolls were just not in line with the German economy's alleged need for Jewish workers. Rather than supporting the war effort in a meaningful way, the Schmelt camps served to concentrate, weaken, and eliminate those among the Jewish population who were the most likely to put up resistance.[67] The active role played by Schmelt's staff in selections and murders in camps and ghettos in 1942 and 1943 clearly refutes the common narrative that the Schmelt Office had slowed down or even resisted the Nazis' genocidal plans in the region to extract more profits from Jewish labor.[68] In summary, Jewish work deployment in Schmelt camps and the Holocaust were not conflicting policies, but closely correlated with one another.[69]

6

BECOMING "LITTLE AUSCHWITZ"

The Takeover of Blechhammer in April 1944

THE AUSCHWITZ ADMINISTRATION STARTED NEGOTIATIONS REGARDING the takeover of Blechhammer on December 15, 1943, during an official visit by Heinrich Schwarz, the commandant of Auschwitz III.[1] Over the following months Schwarz, the Gross-Rosen commandant Hassebroek, and HSSPF Schmauser prepared for the incorporation of up to twenty-five thousand Schmelt inmates into their subcamp systems. In the end, Auschwitz gained fifteen new satellites and Gross-Rosen twenty-eight.[2] On March 12, 1944, Gerhard Maurer, the head of the WVHA's work deployment department, came to Blechhammer to discuss the future use of prison labor with the industrialists.[3] At the end of March the first inmates from disbanded Schmelt camps arrived in Blechhammer, among them Borsigwerke, Malapane, Peiskretscham (Pyskowice), and Bobrek.[4] On Saturday, April 1, 1944, Blechhammer was transformed into an Auschwitz satellite. Heinrich Schwarz personally attended the first roll call, remarking to the prisoners that he had never seen so much misery and dirt. Interestingly, Schmelt's deputy, Heinrich Lindner, was present during the takeover.[5] The Schmelt Office's headquarters had been relocated to Annaberg after the liquidation of the Sosnowiec ghetto in 1943. With the final dismantling of its camp system, the Schmelt Office turned to the management of Polish labor until January 1945. Annaberg was still used for sorting and mending the shoes of murdered Eastern Upper Silesian Jews. Schmelt was forced to retire in 1944 under allegations of embezzlement. He committed suicide in 1945. Lindner was arrested after the war and killed himself before his impending extradition to Poland in 1949. Some of their coworkers were tried in 1967 but received no prison terms.[6]

The Highway Company's administration of the camp was also terminated in April 1944. Both camp leaders left Blechhammer within the first month of the takeover. Erich

Hoffmann allegedly had ten trucks filled with food supplies removed from the camp before the SS arrived. He returned to his hometown, Breslau, until January 10, 1945, when he fled to southern Germany with his family. He then worked as a truck driver for the police in Pasing near Munich. Hoffmann filed for denazification before a Munich court in April 1946, but moved to Nordhorn, Lower Saxony, a few months later, hoping to be denazified quicker in the British sector. His second denazification in Northern Germany went smoothly, yet the Munich court, which was still probing his case, issued an arrest warrant in November 1946. Hoffmann was tried in absentia on July 23, 1947. Karl Demerer and other former Blechhammer prisoners were called as witnesses, and Hoffmann was sentenced to ten years in a penitentiary. Meanwhile, Hoffmann was arrested in the British sector and was extradited to Polish authorities on October 14, 1947. On May 25, 1948, the Polish District Court of Gliwice sentenced him to death. Hoffmann was hanged in Gliwice on November 13, 1948.[7]

The organizational structure of Blechhammer was adapted to that of the Auschwitz concentration camp, resulting in the implementation of an almost identical administrative apparatus and a massive increase in camp personnel. Among the SS, Blechhammer soon became known as Little Auschwitz (*Klein-Auschwitz*).[8] Altogether, six departments were established.

The first one was the Commandant's Office (Kommandantur), represented by the camp leader, SS Hauptsturmführer Otto Brossmann. The schoolteacher from Sudeten (born in Brawin in 1889) joined the Nazi Party and the SS in November 1938. Until the start of his tenure in Blechhammer on April 1, 1944, he had served in Auschwitz and the Jaworzno subcamp.[9] Survivors described Brossmann as a "sadist," who frequently mistreated the prisoners and carried out floggings himself.[10] He was arrested by Poland in December 1948. A death sentence by the district court of Cracow was converted into a prison term, leading to his acquittal on January 4, 1950. He died in Lohr/Main in 1957.[11]

Brossmann was replaced by Untersturmführer Kurt Klipp on November 9, 1944. The merchant (born in Cologne in 1907) and cavalry and infantry sergeant of the reserve entered the SS in October 1936 and joined the Nazi Party a year later. He had a successful career, with deploy-

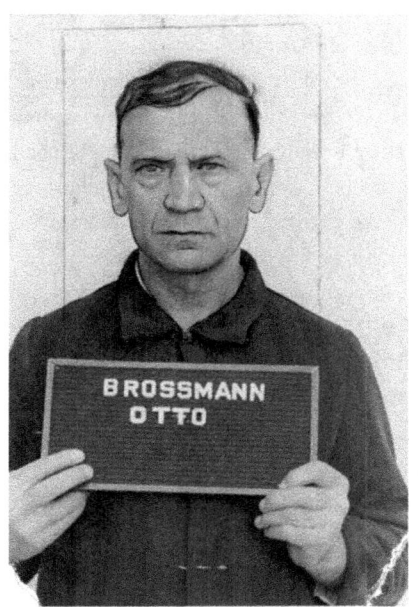

SS camp leader Otto Brossmann.
(*Source:* IPN Kr-11-1-261-1-1)

ments in the Dachau and Flossenbürg concentration camps. In June 1942 he was appointed camp leader of an SS POW camp in Lublin and later held the same position in the SS labor camp Truppenübungsplatz Heidelager in Dębica. Oswald Pohl of the WVHA paid out a 500 RM bonus to Klipp in December 1943 for "loyal services," and he received a "Yule candelabra" from Himmler. He was also awarded the war service cross (*Kriegsverdienstkreuz*) with swords. The thumb and index finger of his left hand were missing. Klipp, who was married and had a daughter, was a member of the SS Lebensborn. From August 1944, he spent a brief period in Auschwitz, before coming to Blechhammer. After the evacuation, he served as a camp leader in Bergen-Belsen. Klipp was arrested by the British in April 1945 but died of typhus in the Oerbke internment camp before being put on trial.[12]

All camp leaders of Auschwitz satellites reported to the commandant of Monowitz (Auschwitz III) Heinrich Schwarz, whose superior was SS Gruppenführer Richard Glücks of the WVHA in Berlin.[13]

The camp leader commanded the seventh SS Death's Head Battalion (Totenkopf-Bataillon) of Blechhammer, one of seven battalions formed in May 1944 by Schwarz to serve in larger Auschwitz subcamps. The Blechhammer guards were overseen by SS Oberscharführer Klingberg, a sixty-year-old from Breslau.[14] Conscriptions of SS men to the front, coupled with rising prisoner numbers, led to the utilization of foreign collaborators and Wehrmacht soldiers in concentration camps. Following the successful deployment of soldiers in Schmelt camps, Speer convinced Hitler to make ten thousand convalescents and over-forty-year-olds from an Army unit retreating from the Crimea available for guard duties in spring 1944. The influx of soldiers increased when Himmler gained control over the reserve army in October 1944. The soldiers were only incorporated into the SS in September 1944 and eventually represented more than half of all camp guards.[15] The Wehrmacht guards already stationed in Blechhammer since early 1943 were taken over by the SS and reinforced with newly assigned soldiers, who had undergone a few days' training in Auschwitz.[16]

The camp leader had a deputy, the second-in-command or *Rapportführer*, whose superior was Obersturmführer Vinzenz Schöttl, the leader of the protective custody camp department (*Schutzhaftlager*) of Auschwitz III. The department managed the prisoners' work deployment, prepared daily strength reports, and was authorized to carry out punishments.[17]

The first second-in-command of Blechhammer was Unterscharführer Hans Stefan Olejak, born in Kunzendorf, Upper Silesia, in 1918. His career in the SS was the result of an early commitment to ethnic German political organizations. He joined the ethnic German party Deutsche Partei at age seventeen and volunteered for a paramilitary unit, the Volksdeutscher Selbstschutz,[18] which the Germans established on Polish soil when war broke out. The unit assisted the SS and SD in raids and executions before

R. u. S.-Fragebogen

(von Frauen sinngemäß auszufüllen)

Name und Vorname des SS-Angehörigen, der für sich oder seine Braut oder Ehefrau den Fragebogen einreicht:

Dienstgrad: *W.-Scharführer* SS-Nr. _____

D. B. Nr. _____

Name (leserlich schreiben) *Kurt Klipp*
in SS seit *19. Oktober 1936* Dienstgrad: *W.-Scharführer* SS-Einheit: *Stab. K.L. Dachau*
in SA von _____ bis _____, in HJ von _____ bis _____
Mitgliedsnummer in Partei: _____ in SS: _____
geb. am *19. September 1908* zu *Köln a/Rhein* Kreis: _____
Land: _____ jetzt Alter: *29 Jahre* Glaubensbek.: *gottgläubig*
Jetziger Wohnsitz: *Dachau* Wohnung: *Augsburgerstr. 57 I*
Beruf und Berufsstellung: *W.-Scharführer*
Wird öffentliche Unterstützung in Anspruch genommen? _____
Liegt Berufswechsel vor? _____
Außerberufliche Fertigkeiten und Berechtigungsscheine (z. B. Führerschein, Sportabzeichen, Sportauszeichnungen):
Führerschein 3, Reichssportabzeichen.

Ehrenamtl. Tätigkeit: _____
Dienst im alten Heer: Truppe _____ von _____ bis _____
    Freikorps . . . . _____ von _____ bis _____
    Reichswehr . . . _____ von *1.10.1929* bis *22.2.1935*
    Schutzpolizei . . . _____ von _____ bis _____
    Neue Wehrmacht _____ von *23.2.1935* bis *30.9.1936*
Letzter Dienstgrad: *Unteroffizier*
Frontkämpfer: _____ bis _____ verwundet _____
Orden und Ehrenabzeichen einschl. Rettungsmedaille: *Dienstauszeichnung 4 u. 12 jähr. Dienstzeit*
Personenstand (ledig, verwitwet, geschieden – seit wann): *verheiratet seit 24. März 1934*
Welcher Konfession ist der Antragsteller? *gottgläubig* die zukünftige Braut (Ehefrau)? *evang.*
(Als Konfession wird auch außer dem herkömmlichen jedes andere gottgläubige Bekenntnis angesehen.)
Ist neben der standesamtlichen Trauung eine kirchliche Trauung vorgesehen? Ja – nein.
Hat neben der standesamtlichen Trauung eine kirchliche Trauung stattgefunden? Ja – nein.
Gegebenenfalls nach welcher konfessionellen Form? *evangelisch*
Ist Ehestandsdarlehen beantragt worden? Ja – nein. _____
Bei welcher Behörde (genaue Anschrift)? _____

Wann wurde der Antrag gestellt? _____
Wurde das Ehestandsdarlehen bewilligt? Ja – nein.
Soll das Ehestandsdarlehen beantragt werden? Ja – nein.
Bei welcher Behörde (genaue Anschrift)? _____

SSV R 1 SS-Vordruckverlag W. F. Mayr, Miesbach

Curriculum vitae of SS camp leader Kurt Klipp (p. 1). (*Source:* BArch R 9361/III-98175)

Curriculum vitae of SS camp leader Kurt Klipp (p. 2). (*Source:* BArch R 9361/III-98175)

Raum zum Aufkleben der Lichtbilder.

Curriculum vitae of SS camp leader Kurt Klipp (p. 3). (*Source:* BArch R 9361/III-98175)

Nr. 2 Name des leibl. Vaters: Klipp   Vorname: Konrad
Beruf: Obergerichtsvollzieher i.R.   Jetz. Alter: 85 Jahre   Sterbealter: —
Todesursache: —
Überstandene Krankheiten: —

Nr. 3 Geburtsname der Mutter: Liermann   Vorname: Mathilde
Jetz. Alter: 70 Jahre   Sterbealter: —
Todesursache: —
Überstandene Krankheiten: —

Nr. 4 Großvater väterl. Name: Klipp   Vorname: Cloos, Heinrich
Beruf: Gendarmerie-Wachtmeister   Jetz. Alter: 182 Jahre   Sterbealter: 85 Jahre
Todesursache: Lungenentzündung
Überstandene Krankheiten:

Nr. 5 Großmutter väterl. Name: Theys   Vorname: Elisabeth
Jetz. Alter: 182 Jahre   Sterbealter: 88 Jahre
Todesursache: Altersschwäche
Überstandene Krankheiten:

Nr. 6 Großvater mütterl. Name: Liermann   Vorname: Adam
Beruf: Förster, Rentner   Jetz. Alter: 114 Jahre   Sterbealter: 67 Jahre
Todesursache: Gasschlag
Überstandene Krankheiten:

Nr. 7 Großmutter mütterl. Name: Liermann   Vorname: Katharina
Jetz. Alter: 110 Jahre   Sterbealter: 67 Jahre
Todesursache: Unterleibskrebserkrankt
Überstandene Krankheiten:

a) Ich versichere hiermit, daß ich vorstehende Angaben nach bestem Wissen und Gewissen gemacht habe.
b) Ich bin mir bewußt, daß wissentlich falsche Angaben den Ausschluß aus der SS nach sich ziehen.

Dachau (Ort), den 23. Februar 1937 (Datum)

Kurt Klipp.
(Unterschrift)

Die Unterschrift der zukünftigen Ehefrau bezieht sich nur auf Punkt a

Curriculum vitae of SS camp leader Kurt Klipp (p. 4). (*Source:* BArch R 9361/III-98175)

Himmler had its members recruited into SS and party organizations in November 1939. Olejak, then an unskilled worker without employment, thus joined the Waffen-SS in December 1939. Due to cardiac insufficiency, he was transferred to the SS and served as a block leader in the men's quarantine camp in Auschwitz-Birkenau from May 1940. In January 1942, Olejak was decorated with the war service cross, second class with swords and got promoted to *Unterscharführer* eight months later. He was appointed second-in-command of the Jaworzno subcamp in June 1943, until his transfer to Blechhammer in April 1944. He left Blechhammer together with Otto Brossmann to become the camp leader of the Tschechowitz subcamp in November 1944. In May 1945 he was captured by British troops while serving in an SS tank artillery battalion; he was released in June 1948. In July 1976 he was put on trial for crimes committed on the Jaworzno death march but was acquitted by a West German court due to lack of evidence. He had mood swings spiraling into "ravaging fury" at times.[19] He could be very hard on the prisoners but also had a lenient side.[20] A Jewish survivor, who had worked in a spinning mill with Olejak before the war, rated his behavior as "correct" but intimidating.[21]

Olejak was replaced by Oberscharführer Karl Czapla, who arrived in mid-October 1944 from Auschwitz-Birkenau, where he had held the position of second-in-command of the men's quarantine camp BIIa. Czapla, an unskilled laborer born in Bismarckhütte, Upper Silesia, in 1911, had worked in the subscription office of a local newspaper, the *Oberschlesischer Kurier*, before joining the SS in April 1940. After only two months, kidney disease terminated his deployment in the SS Death's Head Regiment Ostmark in Prague, and he took up guard duties in concentration camps in Ebelsberg, Oranienburg, Hinzert, and Fallersleben. In August 1942 he was appointed second-in-command of the Dębica labor camp and came to Birkenau in April 1944. Czapla spent three years in Allied custody after being captured in June 1945. He was tried before a French Military Court in Rastatt for crimes committed in Blechhammer and Birkenau but was acquitted in May 1948. He also walked out of the Frankfurt Auschwitz Trials as a free man and died during another trial in 1976.[22] Czapla is a good example of the rapidly advancing careers of ethnic Germans in the SS during the war years.[23] He was not associated with atrocities in the camp itself but reportedly shot prisoners during the evacuation in 1945.[24]

The second-in-command was assisted by several block leaders. Block leaders, usually with the rank of *Unterscharführer*, were located at the bottom of the SS hierarchy. They had the most direct contacts with the prisoners, as they counted them during roll calls, dealt out punishments, and oversaw the blocks. One of them, SS Rottenführer Karl Masseli, managed the prisoners' work deployment and acted as the main intermediary between the camp leadership and the OHW plant. He reported to the independent subdepartment IIIa for work deployment at Auschwitz.[25] Born in Stephanshain/Gross-Strehlitz (Strzelce Opolskie), Upper Silesia, in 1907, the blacksmith joined the

R. u. S.-Fragebogen
(Von Frauen sinngemäß auszufüllen!)

Name und Vorname des SS-Angehörigen, der für sich oder seine Braut oder Ehefrau den Fragebogen einreicht:

Hans Olejak

Dienstgrad: SS Uscha. SS-Nr.:

Sip.-Nr.:

Name (leserlich schreiben): Hans Olejak   353853

in SS seit: 16.12.1939   Dienstgrad: SS Unterscharführer   SS-Einheit: Kdtr.Au.III

in SA von _____ bis _____, in HJ von _____ bis _____

Mitglieds-Nr. in Partei: _____   SS-Nr.: _____

geboren am: 9.8.1918   zu Kunzendorf   Kreis: Bielitz

Land: Ober-Schlesien   jetzt Alter: 26 Jahre   Glaubensbekenntnis: ggl.

Jetziger Wohnsitz: Blechhammer   Wohnung: Arbeitslager/Bahnhoflager

Beruf und Berufsstellung: Textilweber

Wird öffentliche Unterstützung in Anspruch genommen? nein

Liegt Berufswechsel vor? nein

Außerberufliche Fertigkeiten und Berechtigungsscheine (z. B. Führerschein, Sportabzeichen, Sportauszeichnung):
Führerschein Kl.2

Staatsangehörigkeit: Deutsch   Volkszugehörigkeit: Deutsch

Ehrenamtliche Tätigkeit:

Dienst im alten Heer: Truppe _____ von _____ bis _____
Freikorps . . . . _____ von _____ bis _____
Reichswehr . . . . . . _____ von _____ bis _____
Schutzpolizei . . . . . _____ von _____ bis _____
Neue Wehrmacht . . . _____ von _____ bis _____
Waffen-SS . . . . . . _____ von 16.12.1939 bis _____

Letzter Dienstgrad: SS Unterscharführer

Frontkämpfer: _____ bis _____; verwundet: _____

Orden und Ehrenzeichen einschl. Rettungsmedaille:
Kriegsverdienstkreuz Kl.2 mit Schwerter

Personenstand (ledig, verwitwet, geschieden — seit wann): ledig

Welcher Konfession ist der Antragsteller? ggl.   die zukünftige Braut (Ehefrau)? r.k.
(Als Konfession wird auch außer dem herkömmlichen jedes andere gottgläubige Bekenntnis angesehen.)

Ist neben der standesamtlichen Trauung eine kirchliche Trauung vorgesehen? ja — nein.
Hat neben der standesamtlichen Trauung eine kirchliche Trauung stattgefunden? ja — nein.
Gegebenenfalls nach welcher konfessionellen Form? _____

Ist Ehestandsdarlehen beantragt worden? ja — nein.
Bei welcher Behörde (genaue Anschrift)? _____

Wann wurde der Antrag gestellt? _____
Wurde das Ehestandsdarlehen bewilligt? Ja — nein.
Soll das Ehestandsdarlehen beantragt werden? ja — nein.
Bei welcher Behörde (genaue Anschrift)? _____

Curriculum vitae of deputy camp leader Hans Stefan Olejak (p. 1). (*Source:* BArch R 9361/III-144120)

Lebenslauf:
(Ausführlich und eigenhändig mit Tinte geschrieben.)

Ich Hans Olejak bin am 9. August 1918 in Kunzendorf b/ Bielitz als Sohn des Fabriksmeisters Johann und dessen Ehefrau Rosa geborene Tomik geboren. Vom 6. bis 14. Lebensjahr besuchte ich die Volksschule und mit sehr gut bestanden. Mit 16 Jahre ging ich in die Lehre und erlernte das Textilhandwerk. 3 Jahre war ich bei einer Firma, aber weil ich ein Deutscher war so bin ich erwerbslos geworden bis zum Polenfeldzug. Nach dem Polenfeldzug bin ich freiwillig zum Selbstschutz gegangen und von dort wurde ich am 16. Dezember 1939 zur Waffen SS eingezogen. Am 1. September 1942 wurde ich zum SS-Unterscharführer befördert und am 30. Januar wurde mir das Kriegsverdienstkreuz 2. Klasse mit Schwertern verliehen. Jetzt bin ich Kommandantur Angehöriger vom K.L. Auschwitz III. und versehe meinen Dienst im Arbeitslager Blechhammer.

Olejak
SS-Uscha.

Curriculum vitae of deputy camp leader Hans Stefan Olejak (p. 2). (*Source:* BArch R 9361/III-144120)

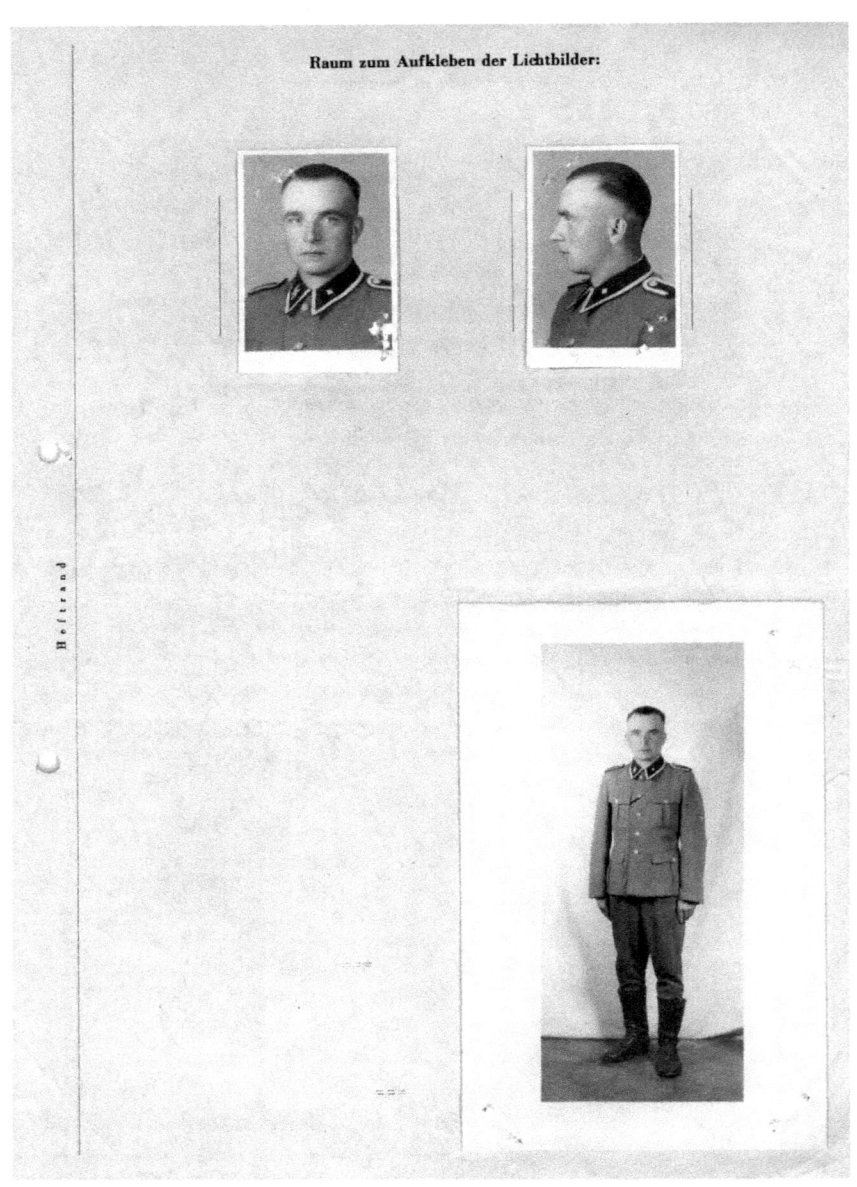

Curriculum vitae of deputy camp leader Hans Stefan Olejak (p. 3). (*Source:* BArch R 9361/III-144120)

Waffen-SS in 1940 but then served as a concentration camp guard in Sachsenhausen and Auschwitz. From early 1942, Masseli was responsible for work deployments in Jawischowitz and later Lagischa. He claimed he had been transferred to Blechhammer due to a dispute with the cook, which had also earned him three days of detention in Auschwitz. He admitted to having smacked prisoners in the face. Masseli was captured by the Soviets, extradited to Poland, and sentenced to five years in prison for having been a member of the SS and an Auschwitz guard. In 1958 he and his family moved to West Germany. He appeared in two trials about Blechhammer, in 1973 and 1977.[26]

Blechhammer had one of five detachments of the Political Department (Politische Abteilung) of Auschwitz. It was headed by SS Unterscharführer Otto Ewald Albin Schmidt, born in Großberndten in 1906, whose superior was Johann Taute of the detachment in Monowitz. Political departments represented the police in concentration camps and were subordinated to the Gestapo and the Reich Security Main Office (RSHA). They kept prisoner records, led interrogations, filed penal reports to Berlin, and oversaw executions.[27] Schmidt was infamous for torturing prisoners until they signed alleged "confessions" or died from his abuse.[28] He was involved in the shooting of stragglers on the death march of January 1945. After the war, the butcher from Goslar was recognized by a Blechhammer survivor who lived in the same town. The witness stated that Schmidt had avoided capture by pretending to be a regular soldier.[29] However, as Schmidt had officially been reported as missing and was eventually declared dead, investigations regarding his case were soon closed.[30]

Auschwitz and its satellites were supplied with food by the wholesaler Deutsche Lebensmittelwerke, which replaced Blechhammer's previous supplier, Broemel & Sohn. The camp kitchen was overseen by an SS man of small stature, nicknamed "Napoleon" or "Bonaparte." His real name could have been SS Sturmmann Johann Repczuk, a former guard who joined the Auschwitz administration in December 1942.[31]

The clothes depot of Blechhammer was headed by Adolf Schindler, born in Einsiedel, Sudeten, in 1921. Due to a head injury he incurred while serving in the Waffen-SS in Russia in 1942, he was allocated to managing clothes and furniture in Oranienburg, Dachau, and Auschwitz. From spring 1944, Schindler was housing manager (*Unterkunftsverwalter*) in Blechhammer and supervised the shoemaker's, carpenter's, and tailor's workshops as well as the clothes and furniture supplies. He was infamous for letting prisoners freeze to death.[32] He was captured by US troops in Austria but released from custody three and a half months later.[33]

Apart from Monowitz, there were no SS physicians in the subcamps. Their tasks were partially taken over by SS medical orderlies or Sanitäts-Dienstgrade (SDG), who, except for a short introductory course at the SS Sanitätsschule in Oranienburg, received no medical training. They supervised the prisoner physicians and admission into the infirmary, made selections, and administered lethal injections. The SDG reported to the chief physician of Monowitz, whose superiors were the area chief physician (Standortarzt) of Auschwitz, Eduard Wirths, and Enno Lolling of the WVHA's Office for Sanitation and Camp Hygiene in Berlin.[34] Four SDGs were installed in Blechhammer in quick succession. The first was Oberscharführer Herbert Scherpe (1907, Gleiwitz) who only stayed for one month. The butcher, who had been an SDG in Auschwitz, purported that he had asked to be transferred to the subcamps after experiencing a "moral dilemma" while carrying out an order to murder children with phenol injections. He was sentenced to four and a half years in prison by a Frankfurt court as an accessory to murder in at least seven hundred cases.[35] His successor until September 1944 was Sturmmann Peter Quirin (1902, Fischbach), a miner and early member of the Nazi Party, who enlisted in the SS in 1937 and in the Waffen-SS in 1942. He started to train as an SDG in Oranienburg in March 1943 and spent a short time in Auschwitz. Quirin later claimed he had tended to SS guards in Heydebreck between November 1943 and November 1944. He denied not only his deployment in Blechhammer but also his ensuing transfer to Jawischowitz. Blechhammer inmates described him as particularly cruel. He was captured after the war and held in custody until February 1948.[36] It seems that Quirin changed places with the acting SDG of Jawischowitz, the Bavarian Sturmführer Kaufmann, who filled the gap until the arrival of Hauptscharführer H. Müller in November 1944.[37]

The utilization of non-Jewish criminal Kapos, so-called Berufsverbrecher (BVer), was novel. Marked with green triangles, they had volunteered to serve in the Sachsenhausen concentration camp in return for an early release from prison. From May 1940, they were also placed in Auschwitz.[38] One of the Kapos, Walter Redock (Liegnitz/Leszno, 1906–Osterode, 1973), who assisted Schindler in the clothes depot and the crematorium, had been imprisoned in Darmstadt for murder since October 1939.[39] He showed excessively violent behavior toward the Jewish inmates. Another murderer, the Polish Kapo Felix, supervised the SS kitchen. There was a single Roma among them, whose name was Manni or Mouni. Sentenced to twenty-five years in prison for forgery, he was a gifted musician, a talent he had in common with the other two Kapos, who all performed in the Jewish camp orchestra from fall 1944.[40]

"AUSCHWITZ CAME TO US": THE IMPLEMENTATION OF AUSCHWITZ RULE IN BLECHHAMMER

The announcement of the impending Auschwitz takeover stirred up fears in the prisoners that they would all be murdered. The then teenage inmate Israel Rosengarten was relieved to learn that they would not be taken to Auschwitz, "but Auschwitz came to us."⁴¹ Others viewed the change in leadership with indifference: "Both pursued the same goal: our disappearance. It did not make a difference to me whether their uniforms were yellow or green."⁴²

On April 8, 1944, the Saturday before Easter, a van with thirty prisoners, who were experts in tattooing and normally worked in the reception office (*Aufnahmebüro*) of the Political Department of Auschwitz, came to Blechhammer. The order that all prisoners were to take a shower caused a panic, as rumors had spread of the gas chambers in Auschwitz being camouflaged as showers. The prisoners calmed down when the first cohorts returned from the washroom barracks alive. Later, they were clad in blue-and-white striped uniforms that had been sent over from Auschwitz. The new uniforms also came with a fresh set of underpants, a shirt, and a piece of cloth instead of socks. The barracks were thoroughly cleaned, and the old straw mattresses were burned to get rid of the lice. The regular inmates noted with satisfaction that the Jewish elder and prisoner functionaries were now required to wear the same uniform as themselves and had their heads shaved.⁴³ The female inmates received blue-and-white striped dresses and headscarves but retained their hair.⁴⁴

The prisoners were then called up in alphabetical order to be tattooed. Blechhammer inmates were issued general Auschwitz numbers and numbers of the A-series. From preserved Auschwitz documents, 3,970 numbers of male prisoners could be retrieved: 3,946 of the general series between 10435 and 201142, and 24 of the A-series between A-35 and A-17530. On the day of the actual takeover, 3,056 male and 200 female prisoners were in Blechhammer. The tattoos not only had a psychological impact by making the inmates feel branded like cattle, but also diminished their chances of escaping and caused skin inflammations.⁴⁵

The tattoos almost proved fatal to the female prisoners, who had erroneously been given numbers already held by prisoners in another subcamp. The new camp leader's radical plans to liquidate them all in Auschwitz to set the records straight could narrowly be averted by the Jewish elder. Brossmann eventually accepted Demerer's bribes and had the women's old numbers crossed out and replaced with fresh ones.⁴⁶ The initial numbers of 132 female prisoners tattooed in April 1944, ranging from 76330 to 76462, have been retrieved. Danuta Czech assumed that not all of the two hundred women registered at the takeover received numbers, as they had been murdered in Auschwitz for being "unfit for work." On May 1, the second set of numbers of the lower 79000 series was tattooed. As was common in Auschwitz, the numbers of deceased prisoners were reused. Some of the Auschwitz prisoners previously registered under the numbers later given to the female inmates had been murdered by phenol injections between October 1941 and August 1943.⁴⁷

Contrary to the Schmelt Office's overt demonstration of violence, the SS took precautions to shield the inmates from public view. The work details were no longer permitted to march along a main road to the OHW factory but had to use a newly paved footpath through the forest.⁴⁸

Moreover, fifty-four prisoners of the mason's detail were ordered to build a four-meter-high concrete wall around the camp. The wall consisted of slabs the prisoners fabricated by filling concrete into special forms. Some inmates decided to seize this opportunity for a lifesaving act of sabotage. They manipulated the concrete so it would not harden properly and made "emergency exits" in strategic spots of the wall, which could easily be broken up in case of a mass evasion. The soft spots in the wall allowed prisoners to escape into the forest when returning SS units set the camp on fire during the evacuation of January 1945. Finally, electric wire was fixed on top of the concrete wall, and a searchlight was installed above the entrance gate by the Dutch Jewish camp electrician, Maurits Bremer.⁴⁹

Rachel Brukner Frydrych with her husband, Arie Frydrych, showing the two numbers tattooed on her arm. (*Source:* YVA photo archive 3883_3617.jpg)

Camp gate and wall. (*Source:* APMO 10764.jpg)

As the Auschwitz administration prohibited interments, a mobile crematorium with a capacity of three to five bodies was set up in early summer. Between the takeover and the crematorium's delivery, the bodies were taken to Auschwitz.[50] The crematorium at Blechhammer was meant to relieve the crematoria of Auschwitz.[51] It was operated by a professional burner formerly employed by a Jewish cemetery in Vienna and his assistant. Schindler and Kapo Walter Redock oversaw their work.[52] It is unclear why Schindler, who represented the Administration Department, was delegated this function and not the Political Department, as was the rule in Auschwitz.[53] The ashes were first buried near the camp and then sold to local farmers as fertilizer.[54] The former burial detail and the orderlies of the infirmary were required to carry the dead to the crematorium.[55] Witnessing the burning process was extremely disturbing to the then sixteen-year-old orderly Kurt Klappholz, but he later stated that the dead were still treated with dignity.[56] In July 1944, young Kurt and his comrade Jules Fainzang were given the gruesome task of cleaning out the oven, as the accumulated human ashes extinguished the flames. Fainzang recalled the harrowing procedure: "The conversation was held as if it had been about the oven of a bakery. . . . In the end, my throat was filled with the ashes of our comrades. By the time of the evening roll call, the oven was burning again. Life and death continued in the rhythm of the camp."[57]

The crematorium's nauseating smell and widely visible flames made the passing of fellow prisoners more palpable than before.[58] The Jewish elder's teenage son Heinrich even related that he and other inmates had been unable to eat when the oven was burning.[59]

The mobile crematorium. (*Source:* APMO 4355.jpg)

THE ARRIVAL OF AUSCHWITZ PRISONERS

Following the liquidation of the Eastern Upper Silesian ghettos, Blechhammer drew on Auschwitz prisoners. In March 1944 a group of Jewish men from Greece arrived.[60] They had been deported to Auschwitz from Salonika and other German- and Bulgarian-controlled areas in Thrace and eastern Macedonia between March and August 1943. As the SS had projected that it would gain 10,000 Greek Jews as laborers, 8,025 men and 4,732 women out of the 46,061 deportees were left alive. By 1944 their number had shrunk to 2,469; 517 of them were men detained in subcamps. Out of the approximately 18 percent selected for work, 3 percent survived the Holocaust.[61] The exact number of Greek Jews in Blechhammer is unknown. Records show that in January 1945, two Greek survivors were liberated in Blechhammer, and the Auschwitz personnel file of one Greek Blechhammer prisoner could be retrieved.[62] As the anti-Jewish legislation in western Greece had only been implemented one month ahead of the first deportations of March 1943, most people on the transports remained unsuspicious about their imminent murder. The surviving Greek Jews took longer to adjust to the realities of the concentration camps, and suicide rates were high. They also experienced communication problems, as most only spoke modern Greek and medieval Spanish. However, many had studied French in Alliance Schools.[63] During the first evening roll call in Blechhammer, no one could make out where the newcomers were from, until a prisoner inquired whether anyone spoke French. An elderly Greek gentleman stepped forward, and they had a conversation. He still harbored the belief that he would see his wife and children again if he worked well, and the Blechhammer prisoner did not have the heart to tell him the truth.[64]

On July 9 or 10, 1944, 528 men from the so-called family camp (*Familienlager*) BIIb at Auschwitz-Birkenau were sent to Blechhammer. They stemmed from two transports of Jews from Terezín (Theresienstadt), in December 1943 and May 1944. The family camp was the result of a propaganda campaign intended to keep the myth alive that Jews were put to work and not killed. The SS guaranteed these deportees from the Czech Protectorate, Germany, Austria, and the Netherlands that they would not be selected and did not have to work for six months. They nonetheless faced terrible conditions in Birkenau, with scanty food rations, a lack of drinking water, and poor hygiene. Five thousand Jews from an earlier transport in September 1943 were gassed in March 1944 following the false announcement that they would be taken to a labor camp in Heydebreck. The members of the December transport witnessed their murder and expected to be killed as well when Mengele made selections for alleged work deployments in early July 1944. Altogether, thirty-five hundred men and ninety boys aged fourteen to sixteen were selected for subcamps like Fürstengrube and Blechhammer. The others were murdered on July 11–12, 1944, and the camp was liquidated.[65] Otto Deutsch was among those destined for Blechhammer. He related how they were driven past their camp in Birkenau and still could not believe that they had survived: "To the present day, it has never been explained to me why we (the December transport of 1943) were so lucky to have escaped alive from Auschwitz-Birkenau."[66]

Despite higher food allocations and slightly improved conditions, the new arrivals soon felt their physical strength dwindling and were wary of the risks posed by the frequent selections.[67] The survivor Oto Hostovsky described their ensuing misery in Blechhammer: "For here, the hunger is even worse than in Auschwitz, because we did not work so hard there. But here, we get up early, work very hard during the day and go to bed very late. Thus, we lose more and more weight each day."[68]

Two-thirds of those sent to labor camps from BIIb in July 1944 perished. Out of the family camp's total population of 17,517, merely 6 percent survived.[69]

In November 1944 the first and only non-Jewish prisoners arrived from Auschwitz. Up to eighty French resistance fighters arrested near Vosges for partisan activities in so-called Maquisards groups had been deported to Auschwitz via the Dachau concentration camp between October 25 and November 24, 1944.[70] Their commander, Henri Dolmaire, was taken to a POW camp for officers in Munster (Oflag VI).[71] The order to shoot all Maquisards upon capture issued by the German Army High Command in summer 1944 was not immediately carried out by all Wehrmacht and SS units. Therefore, some were still handed over to concentration camps.[72] In Blechhammer, the French, who were in a poor physical condition, were housed in a separate barrack. French-speaking Jewish inmates contacted them during roll calls to offer their support.[73] One of the Maquisards reported that a Jewish prisoner had regularly passed on food and cigarettes to him, which he received from French POWs on the construction site. One day, however, the prisoner was caught and sent to a penal work detail.[74] When the Maquisards contracted typhus, the conductor of the Jewish camp orchestra, Czaczkes, helped some of them to recover by accepting them into the ensemble, where they ate better.[75] Owing to the Maquisards' presence, Blechhammer presumably was the only Auschwitz subcamp ever inspected by the Red Cross. To prevent contacts between the inspector and the Jewish inmates, the SS sent everyone out to the OHW site. The soup was made thicker to evoke the impression that the inmates were "well-fed." Immediately after the inspection, a Jewish prisoner was hanged. One witness stated that the victim had attempted to speak to the inspector; another related that a prisoner who normally worked in the camp had pilfered wire on the construction site.[76] According to a report by an inspector of the International Red Cross, Dr. Landolt, who visited the camp in January 1945, fifty Maquisards were still alive. Contrary to postwar claims by the International Red Cross that they had been unaware of the ongoing genocide at Auschwitz, Dr. Landolt's report corroborates his knowledge of the atrocious treatment of the Jewish inmates of Blechhammer and the mass killings of those unfit for work.[77] The Maquisards were separated from the Jewish prisoners when the evacuation trek reached the Gross-Rosen concentration camp in February 1945. Some of them hid in the camp and were liberated by the Red Army.[78]

7

LIFE UNDER THE SS

"FROM HELL TO HEAVEN"? ALLEGED AND ACTUAL IMPROVEMENTS TO THE LIVING CONDITIONS

Increased food rations and more hygiene after the Auschwitz takeover deceived many inmates, including the Jewish elder Demerer, into believing that life in Blechhammer would improve.[1] One survivor even thought that they had come "from hell to heaven."[2] However, these changes were only short-lived, and the stricter Auschwitz drill posed additional dangers.[3] The food allocations were initially raised to four hundred grams of bread and one and a half liters of soup a day but were soon reduced to pre-Auschwitz standards of three hundred grams of bread and one liter of watery soup accompanied by three boiled potatoes, or three-quarters of a liter of thick soup. The prisoners also received small quantities of either molasses, margarine, or sausage, and some milk once every two weeks. In the mornings a half-liter of unsweetened ersatz coffee was distributed. Sugar was usually put into the soup or disappeared entirely.[4] The WVHA's instructions of fall 1943 to issue "nutritious dishes," not soups, remained on paper.[5] Moreover, the soup was now prepared with a dry mix of kohlrabi peels and nettles that came in bags labeled "For Jews and Russians Only." Given the mixture's poor quality, the prisoners joked that the SS should have written "For Pigs Only" on the packages.[6] As the average daily rations did not exceed fourteen hundred calories, those unable to procure additional food quickly declined and developed hunger edema.[7] Sofsky places the root of the SS's failure to genuinely improve the prisoners' living conditions in concerns that they would put up resistance if they regained their physical strength.[8] The takeover only made a difference to skilled laborers, who became eligible for heavy workers' rations amounting to 600 grams of bread on workdays, and 400 grams on weekends, plus weekly allocations of 250 grams of margarine, 100 grams of butter, and 300 grams of canned meat.[9]

The barracks were now called blocks, and each had a Jewish block elder who reported to an SS block leader. The block elders distributed all meals in the barracks, so that the prisoners no longer had to queue and endure the kitchen staff's chicanery. The mental effects of starvation nonetheless still made some believe that they were receiving less food than the others, and they projected the blame onto the block elders, who allegedly skimmed off the margarine and fished out the potatoes while fetching the soup barrels from the kitchen.[10] Admittedly, block elders, as in most camps, withheld food in order to hand out second helpings to individual prisoners who bribed them or did them favors.[11] In Blechhammer, the Jewish elder was even forced to intervene when some block elders procured ladles holding less than the prescribed liter and pretended they were handing out full rations. Some prisoners were so infuriated that they started fights with their block elders. Consequently, Demerer installed a head block elder to ensure even soup distributions.[12] A bakery in Heydebreck that delivered the inmates' bread also embezzled loaves. When an SS man discovered that each batch of one hundred loaves was short one, he required them to add half a loaf extra for every prisoner at Christmas.[13]

The fact that not all prisoners possessed bowls and spoons further complicated the food distribution. Having to eat their soup out of washbasins with four to six others, these unfortunate prisoners viciously struggled for their proper share.[14] Scales were built to cut the bread loaves into six even pieces. The procedure was watched intently by all inhabitants of a barrack, who often fought over morsels of bread.[15] The starvation prompted some to eat garbage. A prisoner once even caught an SS man's cat and devoured it after steaming the animal in one of the plant's hot tubes.[16] In August 1944 the OHW constructed a new potato cellar and a luxurious stable for pigs, chicken, and rabbits for the SS. The work was done by twelve Soviet POWs, who for several weeks slept in the cellar's foundation. Jewish inmates later tended to the animals and often seized the opportunity to have some of their food, which was significantly better than the prisoners'.[17]

In summer 1944 the Blechhammer prisoners were subjected to a food experiment with artificial sausages that were to be tested before being offered to the German population. The Auschwitz administration's central laboratory at Rajsko took samples from those who developed adverse intestinal reactions.[18] Since 1939, the BioSyn Society had striven to fabricate a protein-rich meat replacement from yeast grown on sulfite wastewater, a by-product of the viscose rayon industry. The project had been closely linked to the SS from the outset, and Himmler had the first sausages tried out on concentration camp prisoners in Mauthausen, Dachau, Buchenwald, and Sachsenhausen

Map of the Blechhammer subcamp in 1944. (Author's adaptation of a hand-drawn map found in StA Wü 2012-009.)

between summer 1943 and 1944. The tests were halted due to severe gastroenteric infections caused by mycotoxins. The Blechhammer prisoners probably received the sausages that came from a rayon-producing plant in Hirschberg, Upper Silesia, operated by Phrix works of Wittenberge.[19] It is unclear why they were the only Auschwitz prisoners to be included in this experiment. As Wirths, the area chief doctor of Auschwitz, only tried out baker's yeast on malnourished prisoners, a connection to the artificial sausage experiments seems unlikely.[20]

The newly established clothes depot under the SS man Schindler and Kapo Walter Redock distributed prisoner uniforms and shoes that were fetched from Auschwitz by truck. Schindler also allocated furniture procured by the OHW plant. About twelve prisoners worked in the camp's tailor's, shoemaker's, and carpenter's workshops. They led a comparatively privileged life, living in two-bedroom quarters with mattresses and receiving better food.[21] Schindler notoriously acted out his sadistic urges by sprinkling prisoners with cold water and letting them freeze to death outside. In December 1944 he forced a whole block to spend the night kneeling naked in the snow to reprimand them for "untidiness." At least twenty inmates died as a result.[22] Swinging from one extreme to another, he once gave a new prisoner a job in the shoemaker's workshop simply because he had the same surname as him.[23]

Parts of the prisoners' new uniforms were soon lost, either because they bartered them for food or they disappeared in the camp laundry.[24] Pneumonia became rampant in the winter, when the inmates had to endure endless roll call parades in their thin and often wet clothes.[25] The WVHA half-heartedly recommended precautions against the cold, like keeping roll calls as short as possible, not shaving the prisoners' hair, and allowing them to insulate their coats and caps with newspapers, but these were not implemented.[26] The prisoners of Blechhammer were even punished for using empty cement sacks from the construction site as insulation underneath their coats and in their shoes. The SS, who considered this practice "sabotage," hit them with bamboo sticks to detect the rustling of cement sacks and flogged those who wore them. Most prisoners were nevertheless ready to take this risk to have some lifesaving protection against the cold. Another negative side effect of the sacks was that they aggravated the symptoms of scurvy, a skin condition caused by malnutrition.[27] As no gloves were issued, the prisoners tried to warm their hands in their pockets, until the SS ordered that they be stitched up in winter 1944.[28] The survivor Philip Venetianer was severely maltreated by Kapo Walter for fabricating a pair of gloves and a headband from the seam of his blanket.[29]

The wooden soles of the textile shoes issued to the inmates tended to split, causing painful sores and edema that could lead to septicemia.[30] The use of pieces of cloth instead of socks, known as "Russian socks," as Soviet POWs were required to wear them, further exacerbated the problem. As the prisoners had to hand in their shoes to the block elders at night, the "socks" frequently disappeared. Auschwitz only replaced broken shoes when they were sent in, not missing ones.[31] Marching and working in bad, or even without, shoes put the inmates at great risk of being selected for Auschwitz due to limping and injuries. The child survivor Arno Lustiger lost his father, a very tall man, only because there were no shoes in his size in Blechhammer's depot, and he was sent to the construction site barefooted. He was admitted into the infirmary due to sore feet and fell victim to a selection.[32] Only skilled or functionary prisoners were entitled to wear shoes with a leather sole, like the carpenters who worked at great heights. They were not just safer, but permitted a normal gait, whereas the prisoners wearing wooden shoes shuffled along painfully.[33]

The same standard RAB barracks continued to be used, but the bunk beds received a third tier. All prisoners of a work detail were housed in the same barrack, whose chambers had to be cleaned by two inmates, the so-called *Stubendienst*, each morning. As the SS provided no brooms, the prisoners fabricated some out of birch twigs.[34] Blechhammer had central heating powered by the OHW plant since late 1943. The radiators were briefly put on in the mornings and in the evenings. Some prisoners therefore turned them back on for more warmth. When the OHW power station was destroyed by bombs in fall 1944, the barracks remained unheated, at the cost of prisoners' lives.[35] The SS ordered that all barracks be painted to combat lice but left it to the inmates to clandestinely procure the paint from the OHW construction site. The block elders promised extra food to those who brought them paint. As a result, the barracks were decorated in many different colors, and the beds were even adorned with images, like fruit or swans. By order of the SS, the name and number of each prisoner had to be written on the respective bed to make it easier to punish those hiding forbidden items in their straw mattresses.[36]

The overall hygiene was improved considerably by the presence of more washroom barracks and the construction of a bathhouse with showers. During the summer, makeshift outdoor showers were also used. Supervised by a functionary prisoner, all work details were to wash themselves once a fortnight. However, as there were only fourteen shower heads for details of an average thirty prisoners, they barely got wet. After the shower, they were treated with a disinfectant ointment and a barber shaved off their body hair. As their clothes were laundered on shower days, the prisoners had to spend the night in their shirts and underwear. Although the laundry had been enlarged and staffed up to twenty-five female prisoners, the clothes were seldom returned clean. The OHW were required to build a disinfecting chamber to eliminate body lice from the prisoner uniforms and blankets with cyanide gas. Nevertheless, the prisoners were covered in lice and typically spent the evenings removing them from the seams of their clothes.[37] Most inmates nonetheless welcomed the improved hygiene. Being able to wash more often was perceived as a return to civilization and a factor contributing to their survival.[38] Others found the confrontation with their emaciated bodies unbearable. Two brothers thus avoided looking at each other while they were naked under the shower.[39]

Several barbers were appointed to shave their comrades and were given extra bread. As they continued to work on the construction site, some offered their services to British POWs and German civilian laborers for additional food.[40] One of the barbers, Simon Blein from the Netherlands, even gained such a good reputation among German workers that OHW director Max Josenhans called him into his office, requesting a shave and a haircut in return for cigarettes.[41]

The quest for more cleanliness was foreseeably misused by the SS. Each night an SS block leader patroled the barracks to find prisoners with unwashed feet. Most fell into this category due to broken shoes, and they were severely punished, such as by having to stand outside all night.[42]

WORK ROUTINES

On April 20, 1944, the new camp leader, Brossmann, instructed the OHW employees and contractors about changes regarding the work deployment of Jews. He and OHW deputy director Dr. Schlick reiterated that the Jewish details were no longer to be supervised by guards to facilitate their more flexible use and to increase their productivity.[43] However, it would be misleading to believe that the SS left the prisoners alone during work. Next to the chain of guards surrounding the OHW factory, several SS patrols on bicycles were on the lookout for prisoners transgressing the rules or not seeming to work fast enough. Calling them the "Flying Brigade," the inmates used the code word "six" to warn each other of their presence.[44]

One of the SS block leaders specifically screened the construction site for bartering prisoners. Unterscharführer Paul Veittes (Neuss, 1903), who had been transferred to Blechhammer from the Monowitz subcamp, was infamous for his excessively cruel punishment of those he caught trading goods.[45] If he found on prisoners bread other than the type distributed in the camp, he dried it and then knocked out their teeth with it.[46] He caused the inmate Sam Weinstock to lose his hearing simply because he had been given a bread roll by his foreman.[47] He regularly invited himself to drinks with Jewish functionary prisoners and confided to them that he had been a convict: "He was the worst of them all.... He told us that he had been in jail for one and a half years in normal times. He came at eight p.m. and left at four a.m. With watery eyes and a foamy mouth, he would sit there and tell us of all his crimes. We fell asleep, but it did not bother him."[48]

The prisoners of Monowitz gave him the nickname "The Lion of Buna" due to his flaming red hair and predator-like behavior, and that name spread to Blechhammer.[49]

Prisoners working in a shop at Blechhammer in 1944.
(*Source:* YVA photo archive 44BO9.jpg.)

Veittes apparently knew of his nickname and even had a picture taken of himself posing with the head of a stuffed lion. According to some functionary prisoners, his premature return to Monowitz in spring 1944 resulted from Jewish elder Demerer offering Brossmann a considerable sum of money to have him removed. Paul Veittes was executed by Poland on November 14, 1949.[50]

Veittes's replacement, nicknamed "Tom Mix" by the inmates because he reminded them of a cowboy, was no less cruel than his predecessor. He was a hollow-faced, tall, and slender man in his thirties with bowed legs, who always carried a pistol on each hip and a riding whip. Obsessed with firearms, he loved to let his pistol spin around his finger. While patrolling the construction site, he sneaked up behind prisoners with his whip. Many died from his vicious beatings. When he spotted a prisoner not standing up straight and aligned at roll call, he simply shot him.[51] Tom Mix was infamous for his overly meticulous searches for contraband goods and even made work details stand naked in public: "On the construction site, one had the impression of being in a western movie. While working quietly among the others, suddenly an SS man would appear and command us to raise our arms and stand with our backs to each other, then he searched us. We often had to get completely undressed, irrespective of the male and female civilians passing by the road. 'Tom Mix' enjoyed this the most. Woe to the prisoner he found money on, or anything else."⁵²

These scenes were also registered by British POWs, who were appalled by the SS man's behavior.⁵³ Tom Mix was never officially identified. As he had a good command of Dutch, he might have originated from a western German borderland region.⁵⁴ The survivor Heinz Joseph stated that his Kapo knew the SS man from the Rhineland, where he had been in the stock-trading business in his civilian life.⁵⁵ Some Blechhammer survivors as well as the SS man Masseli suggested his name had been Hermann Leinkenjost.⁵⁶ The *Unterscharführer* was born in Langendreer (Bochum) in 1903 and was killed by a bullet through the head in Schmiedefeld near Breslau on April 19, 1945. Masseli considered Leinkenjost a fervent anti-Semite and a "very bad character" on the verge of insanity. Before his transfer to a unit defending Breslau, Leinkenjost indicated that he preferred suicide over being taken prisoner and thus always carried two hand grenades.⁵⁷ It is unclear whether Blechhammer's Tom Mix was identical with an SS man with the same nickname who participated in the second experimental gassing of unfit inmates and Soviet prisoners in Auschwitz in September 1941.⁵⁸

Another block leader in addition to Masseli, Veittes, and Tom Mix was an ethnic German from Romania.⁵⁹ In marked contrast to his SS comrades, he encouraged the prisoners when they marched out of the gate by shouting in Yiddish "*es geit tsu nile*," indicating that the war would soon come to an end.⁶⁰ The leader of block eight was fifty-year-old Oberscharführer Rieger, who the prisoners called "Grandpa." He was also known as *Bettenbau*, for he checked whether the beds were made according to rule. An SS man nicknamed "The Boxer" almost knocked out a prisoner's teeth with a knuckleduster when he found a scrap of newspaper on him that he had used as a handkerchief.⁶¹ Further names of block leaders corroborated by testimonies were Neumann, Kesler, and Emil Taubert.⁶²

Due to their marked heterogeneity, it is difficult to generalize about the collaboration of the Wehrmacht soldiers, who largely made up the camp guards and surrounded the OHW territory during work. Unlike the order police or SS men, the soldiers were not systematically indoctrinated with Nazi ideology, and many would not have been eligible to enter the SS by previous standards. Nonetheless, while serving in the Wehrmacht they had been familiarized with the Judeo-Bolshevism narrative, and parts of the Army evidently participated in the Holocaust.⁶³ Several studies show that the number of shooting incidents involving soldiers in concentration camps commonly did not exceed that of the SS, who had become a minority.⁶⁴ The only reported shooting in Blechhammer was carried out by SS Unterscharführer Johann Trunz, who killed two prisoners during an escape attempt on June 1, 1944.⁶⁵ The prisoners perceived the convalescent or veteran soldiers as less dangerous than the SS: "They were a far cry from the Auschwitz SS thugs—they were decrepit, elderly soldiers shambling under the weight of their basic rifles, clearly unfit to serve the Fatherland in active service at the front in any of the many theatres of war."[66]

A few soldiers tried to help by handing out food to the prisoners or starting a friendly conversation.[67] One such man was Heinrich Schäfer (Wartenberg, Sudeten, 1891), who had been drafted into a *Landesschützen* battalion in May 1944 and was incorporated into the SS only one month later. After one day in Auschwitz, Schäfer was deployed in Blechhammer and remained there until the evacuation. A Blechhammer survivor testified that his wife had been half-Jewish, and he had been very sympathetic. Nevertheless, Schäfer evidently participated in the shooting of prisoners after his transfer to Dautmergen, a satellite camp of Natzweiler, in February 1945.[68] Two Blechhammer survivors recounted that they had visited a guard named Hermann Täuser from Rheinbach after the war out of gratitude for his support. He reportedly had warned the prisoners of the SS he was about to join against his will.[69]

To thwart such undesirable relations, the SS rotated the soldiers continuously.[70] Most Blechhammer guards were thus exchanged monthly.[71] More importantly, experienced SS men were to set a practical example of brutality. SS Oberscharführer Claessen, presumably a police officer from Hamburg, was sent to Blechhammer from Auschwitz to drill the guards accordingly. They later stated that he had been utterly cruel and sadistic and had frequently rifle-butted the inmates. A similar role was played by SS Sturmmann Heinrich Tille (Schossendorf, Bohemia, 1893), who came to Blechhammer in June 1944.[72] One of the guards regularly had his dog attack prisoners. When the person was lying on the ground, he would act out his sadistic urges, such as by showing the prisoner bread he was not allowed to have.[73]

Jewish Kapos were urged to drive their comrades at a great pace during work and faced severe punishment if their details were "unproductive." A Kapo was thus kicked between the legs by a German master simply because he had allowed his detail a short rest. Many weakened prisoners collapsed, dead, as a result of the constant overworking.[74] As under Schmelt, Ems oversaw all Kapos. A non-Jewish criminal named Bick was one of three head Kapos.[75]

Skilled workers were in huge demand, and their slightly better living conditions prompted some prisoners to pass themselves off as professionals despite the risk of punishment.[76] Strength reports to Auschwitz suggest a sudden increase in skilled laborers at the OHW from 150 to 300 in early December 1944.[77] One of their privileges was permission to wear company overalls. After the takeover, the SS insisted that Jewish skilled laborers had to be clearly distinguishable from the civilian workers to prevent escapes. As a result, they were clad in Italian military uniforms, so-called Badoglio dresses, that had been left behind after the Italian surrender.[78] Contracting companies tended to treat prisoners with coveted qualifications more respectfully and were interested in keeping them. The Dutch Jewish survivor Louis Waterman was a sought-after expert in the construction of pipelines. The Pollems company went to great lengths to win him back when he and five other skilled prisoners were retained in the camp as a punishment for having worked unsupervised in a place beyond the chain of SS guards. Pollems managed to be allocated an SS guard just for the six experts, so they could continue working for the company. Considering the SS personnel shortage at the time, this was a remarkable achievement.[79] By contrast, IG Farben's chemical plant at Heydebreck discontinued the use of Jewish Blechhammer prisoners for constructing a housing estate. In a postwar statement, IG Farben claimed it had been unable to comply with Auschwitz's requirement to erect a four-meter-high fence around its industrial site due to a lack of barbed wire.[80]

The significant impact of companies on the conditions of Jewish work deployment is exemplified by the case of the Czech contractor Smely from Prague. In spring 1944 the company began to construct three firehouses for the OHW and was assigned the newly formed Jewish work detail number thirty-eight. The Czechs collectively sabotaged the building project in resistance against the Nazi regime and thereby transformed the Jewish prisoners' work from deadly peril into lifesaving bliss. Having erected a few brick walls to shield them from view, the Czechs mainly bartered goods that were rationed in Silesia but still available in the Protectorate. They invited the Jewish prisoners to free meals and played cards with them. They only had to pretend that they were working when German overseers came along. The Czech Jewish survivor Ernest Koenig assisted a mason in the peculiar task of building a brick wall and deconstructing it at the same time to prolong the construction period of the houses. To Koenig, the Czechs' sabotage was reminiscent of the legendary tales of the soldier Schwejk. To the prisoners' regret, their detail was assigned to a different contractor building air-raid shelters in June 1944. The months with Smely had provided them with fresh reserves of strength to endure the renewed hardships to come.[81]

The takeover made Blechhammer prisoners eligible for productivity bonuses (*Prämienscheine*), which the WVHA had introduced in May 1943 pertaining to Speer's calls to boost the war economy. Entrepreneurs were expected to acquire bonuses worth up to 10 RM from Auschwitz to reward prisoners who demonstrated above average productivity and took no sick leaves.[82] The prisoners perceived the bonuses as cynical, as the goods they were able to purchase with them were of little use: "We got mustard, for example, and you had to imagine the piece of meat to go along with it; then also shampoo for washing our hair, probably to annoy us, as our heads were as bald as a snooker ball. Rarely, it was Russian tobacco or cigarettes."[83]

During a meeting of Silesian entrepreneurs using Auschwitz prisoners and the inspectorate of the military district VIII B in Kattowitz on December 11, 1944, the industrialists eventually demanded that the bonuses be abolished. Their radical idea to split the prisoners into three categories according to their productivity and reward those in the first two groups with more food, which would be deducted from the third group, with the lowest output, was rejected, as even by SS standards the allocations to the last group would have been insufficient. Auschwitz nevertheless tolerated the companies' lowering the reduced output factors for concentration camp inmates from 50 to 40 percent. At a time when prisoners reported that they had been pushed to their absolute physical limits, the entrepreneurs were obviously intent on further reducing wage costs. In the case of the OHW, another underlying reason was bankruptcy. The plant had already stopped paying out wages to regular German employees in November 1944 but seemingly still made its payments to Auschwitz. During the same meeting, the industrialists terminated the piecework system for concentration camp prisoners.[84] They normally worked on a time-rate but were occasionally assigned to piecework when unloading goods. However, unlike POWs, Jewish inmates were not permitted to return to their camp when a specific task had been completed. The highly paced work also led to increased mortality, as emaciated prisoners used up their last physical reserves.[85] German overseers were often behind such cases of overworking. Notwithstanding the Jewish inmates' obvious malnourishment, they expected them to show the same productivity as British POWs, who almost exclusively had performed piecework since 1943 and were eager to leave the factory early. A German master thus promised the Kapo of a Jewish detail that his men would be allowed to rest if they finished a job as swiftly as the British. However, when the exhausted inmates lay down as agreed, a German engineer alerted a guard, who beat them for being "lazy." Even worse, the master insisted on a higher work pace the next day, arguing that the piecework experiment had shown that the prisoners were capable of higher productivity.[86]

Despite soaring mortality rates, Jewish prisoners made up one-third of the total OHW workforce of approximately fifteen thousand and had become the largest group among the unfree laborers by late 1944.[87]

NEW FORMS OF PUNISHMENT

Unlike Schmelt, Auschwitz required the WVHA's formal authorization of all punishments. Penal reports sent to Berlin via the Political Departments of Blechhammer and Monowitz had an average turnaround of four weeks. The Auschwitz commandant Rudolf Hoess named the following standard forms of punishments: floggings, detention, collective punishments, transfer to a penal commando unit, and executions. Floggings normally took place in the blocks and typically did not exceed twenty-five lashes. They were thus significantly more lenient than under Schmelt.[88] The practice of prisoners being appointed to flog their comrades continued under Auschwitz. The names of the Dutch Jewish prisoners Joseph Braasem and Maurits Broeks frequently appeared in penal reports in this context. Braasem was known for only pretending to hit and remained very popular among fellow prisoners, whereas Broeks did not refer to his controversial task in his postwar testimony.[89]

Blechhammer had a detention cell, and prisoners were similarly transferred to Auschwitz's infamous Block 11. Contrary to Hoess's claim that detentions did not exceed forty-five days, the Blechhammer prisoner Szaja Finkelstein was sentenced to five months of detention in Auschwitz for smoking near petrol tanks. His fate remains unclear.[90] Collective punishments affected either work details or blocks and took on different forms. The inhabitants of a block once had to hit each other for emptying the latrine bucket during the night, for example.[91] Work details were often subjected to penal exercising coupled with constant beatings and long nocturnal roll calls for bartering or alleged low productivity. Escapes were punished by penal exercising and the withholding of the evening soup for the whole camp.[92] Penal work details (*Strafkommandos*) were first introduced in Auschwitz in 1940 and generally equaled a death sentence. The respective inmates had to perform hard labor on the run under the strict supervision of extremely vicious guards and Kapos.[93] In Blechhammer, the SS predominantly made penal commandos toil in the factory's smoldering section (*Schwelerei*), where brown coal was refined to tar and middle oil. At a depth of 150 meters, the inmates had to unload coal without any protection against the dust. Most died of respiratory diseases in a matter of weeks.[94] The child survivor Israel Rosengarten, whose life was saved because a Jewish Kapo helped him to change into another detail, related his ordeal in this commando unit: "The *Meister* there were extremely cruel and, deep down under the earth, far away from the others, yelling frantically, they stood next to us like devils. We were beaten all day long."[95]

A special penal camp (*Straflager*) was operated by an Auschwitz subcamp established at Bismarckhütte (Chrzanów) in September 1944. An unknown number of Blechhammer prisoners accused of pilfering or eating food reserved for Germans were taken to this camp on November 8, 1944, along with 120 men from other Auschwitz subcamps. The penal camp's approximately 200 prisoners did construction work, while the guards set their dogs on anyone not moving fast enough. The penal prisoners were transferred to Monowitz before the evacuation of Bismarckhütte on January 18, 1945, and some were liberated by the Red Army.[96] Eliazer Content, who was caught stealing a V-belt he intended to exchange for food, recounted how Blechhammer's Political Department under Schmidt pressed him into "confessing" a more serious infraction that brought him to the penal camp: "He asked what I wanted to do with that belt, and I answered, 'Swap it, because I was hungry.' Then Schmidt said: 'You were going to sell it to the Poles for cigarettes, of course!' A Jewish boy, who worked in his office as a typist, told me to just say 'yes.' I did not trust him, said 'no' and was beaten until I finally said 'yes.' A few weeks later, I was sent on *Straftransport* to Bismarckhütte."[97]

In addition to the "official" forms of punishment authorized by the WVHA, spontaneous violence against the prisoners was commonplace.[98] In an especially brutal public demonstration, several prisoners who had attempted to escape were forced to lie flat on their stomachs with bound hands. Water bowls were placed in front of their heads, and they slowly drowned in them.[99] During the winter, many prisoners died of hypothermia or pneumonia when the SS made them stand naked outside their barracks.[100]

THE INFIRMARY

The infirmary was now under the control of an SS medical orderly (*Sanitätsdienstgrad*, SDG) who constantly monitored the admittance of patients and the Jewish physicians' work. The SDGs were primarily concerned with what Hoess referred to as "nonmedical activities," namely selecting unfit prisoners and murdering sick prisoners with phenol or cyanide injections.[101]

A new Jewish chief doctor was appointed. Dr. Alfred Hyrsz, formerly the chief physician of a hospital in Prague, had been incarcerated in Dachau and Auschwitz for being a Communist. His extremely emaciated body shocked the other physicians, but Hyrsz predicted that they would soon look the same.[102] Shortly afterward, Abram Szeftel arrived with two hundred prisoners from the disbanded Schmelt camp Markstädt. He had worked in the Jewish hospital in the Sosnowiec ghetto until it was liquidated on June 24, 1943. Having tried in vain to hide his ten-year-old son in the hospital, Szeftel was arrested, and the boy perished. He first served as a paramedic, before being put in charge of the female prisoners' ward. Dr. Iwanter remained chief physician of the interior medical section, and Dr. Auerhahn continued as head surgeon. Altogether, fifteen prisoner physicians tended to almost four thousand inmates. However, only seven of them were permitted to work in the infirmary, while the rest had to go out to the construction site as paramedics.[103] All of the infirmary staff nevertheless had access to higher quality food prepared by their own cook, and Dr. Hyrsz was even served breakfast in bed by the orderlies.[104]

The orderlies Kurt Klappholz and Jules Fainzang were reinforced by two comrades. Maurice Moshe Szmidt, who had been transferred to Blechhammer from Borsigwerke in March 1944, contracted scabies and was admitted into the isolation ward. As he required long-term treatment, he was offered a job in the infirmary to prevent him from being sent to Auschwitz. He thus scrubbed the floors, emptied latrine buckets, bathed patients, and distributed bread and water. He also took the bread rations of severely ill prisoners into his safe keeping, until they had regained their appetite. If they died, he was entitled to their ration. In addition, he got an extra half liter of soup.[105] The second was Efraim Roseboom, a Dutch Jew, who had become so weakened that he tried to avoid work on the construction site by pretending to faint during the march-off. After seven months, he decided to help in the infirmary instead.[106] Iwanter took on the juvenile prisoner Kurt Baum as his clerk, who later considered him a "war criminal" for denying treatment to patients who were unable to bribe him.[107]

From July 1944, Jindřich Flusser, a medical student from Prague who had been among the five hundred prisoners sent to Blechhammer from the liquidated "family camp" at Auschwitz-Birkenau, served as Dr. Iwanter's assistant. Initially selected for the gas chambers by Mengele due to emaciation, Flusser's determination to live prompted him to smuggle himself into a group of prisoners bound for Blechhammer. Shortly before the transfer he contracted dysentery, and he was immediately admitted into the infirmary upon arrival. He made a quick recovery, and Iwanter offered him a post. Flusser assumed that Dr. Iwanter, who was on bad terms with his colleagues, had chosen a student like him because he did not perceive him as a competitor. Although Flusser had not completed medical school, the Blechhammer patients greatly benefited from his participation in research on the effects of malnutrition undertaken by a group of Jewish scientists in Terezín. He discovered that a vitamin B deficiency caused swollen salivary glands, a phenomenon he later called "Terezín symptom." He also diagnosed so-called Bitot's spots, lesions on the conjunctiva in the shape of a triangle caused by a lack of vitamin A, in many Blechhammer prisoners. His efforts to aid the prisoners soon clashed with Dr. Iwanter's harsh methods, who claimed that dysentery resulted from "overeating" and prescribed his patients a strict fast. Their food rations were eaten by Iwanter who, weighing 240 pounds, became "pink as a fattening pig." During his internment in Terezín, Flusser had studied the use of sulfonamides in the treatment of dysentery. He turned to Kurt Bachmann, a prisoner in the clerk's office (*Schreibstube*) who had contacts with communist foreign workers at the OHW plant, to procure the medicine. There were only enough doses to treat three patients daily, and Flusser decided to administer it to young prisoners in the early stages of the disease, whom he expected to have the highest survival chances. Eventually all patients benefited from the sulfonamide treatment of the few. In return for curing the non-Jewish criminal Kapo of the neighboring SS kitchen, Felix, of dysentery, Flusser was permitted to "steal" vegetables from the SS compound during the daily lunchtime nap of Felix's guard. Flusser took advantage of each of Dr. Iwanter's absences from the infirmary to distribute cabbage and carrots to dysentery patients, and the vitamins helped many to recover. Flusser was henceforth called "Dr. Zelinka," derived from the Czech word for "vegetables."[108]

The dentist Dr. Perlman was assisted by a colleague from Berlin named Starepolski. The order issued by Auschwitz to extract the gold teeth of diseased prisoners increased their workload. The SDG passed the teeth on to a dental laboratory in Auschwitz, where the gold was melted before being deposited in the German National Bank (Reichsbank) by the WVHA.¹⁰⁹

The SDG further complicated the already difficult work of the prisoner physicians. Each morning when he entered the infirmary, the physicians had to stand to attention. On his first day in the infirmary, Dr. Szeftel was unaware of this rule and continued to tend to a prisoner patient when SDG Quirin appeared. Quirin hit Szeftel hard in the face, muttering that now he knew how to behave.¹¹⁰ Chief doctor Hyrsz did his best to appease the SDGs, who frequently assaulted patients, by treating them to a special breakfast goulash that was prepared by the young orderly Kurt Klappholz according to a recipe of his mother's.¹¹¹

The physicians only received medical supplies if they bribed the SDGs with cigarettes originally destined for the sick prisoners.¹¹² The medical services nonetheless slightly improved under the SS.¹¹³ With the onset of Allied bombings in July 1944, the infirmary was enlarged by another barrack, and a makeshift operating theater was installed. According to instructions from Dr. Hyrsz, camp electrician Maurits Bremer and a fellow inmate built an operating table out of an old car. The vehicle was procured by the SS man Schindler, who in return demanded that furniture be made for him out of its remnants. The two prisoners were given sick leave to construct the table and were rewarded with a two-week "vacation" in the infirmary on double food rations. The grim realities of the camp soon caught up with them when an impending selection, during which all patients were taken to Auschwitz, abruptly ended their stay after ten days.¹¹⁴

The SDG made selections in the infirmary up to three times a month. The night before, he collected the patients' medical records. The next morning, trucks arrived from Auschwitz, SS men blocked the infirmary's entrance, and all patients still able to stand were lined up naked in front of their beds. The SDG inquired about their profession and when they expected to start working again. He retained the records of those who were sent to Auschwitz, usually prisoners requiring more than a few days' treatment or with serious medical conditions.¹¹⁵ Efraim Roseboom, who later became an orderly in the infirmary, saved his life during a selection by claiming to be a mechanic, a job in great demand, and by reassuring the SDG that he could return to work the next day. Roseboom and a boy with a fractured leg were the only survivors of the thirty-two patients then in the infirmary.¹¹⁶

The physicians knew how the gassings were carried out from Jewish elder Karl Demerer, who attended every selection and who had received details on the mass murder from the SS camp leader.¹¹⁷ The Jewish doctors' leeway in this respect was extremely limited. However, individual prisoners could occasionally be saved from the gas chambers by discharging them in time. Perniciously, such rescue attempts were often connected to bribery.¹¹⁸ By contrast, Dr. Szeftel risked his life to prevent the admission of a friend into the infirmary before an impending selection under the very nose of the SDG.¹¹⁹

The SDG inspected working prisoners every two to three months during roll calls. Making them stand with bare upper bodies, he took down the numbers of those who looked emaciated.[120] Every roll call nevertheless posed the risk of being earmarked for Auschwitz: "During the roll call, the keen eye of the *Sturmbannführer* searched for those who appeared to be the weakest. Almost all of us were weak and undernourished. The feeblest usually stood in the back rows. Some were so weakened that they had to be supported by the prisoners standing next to them or behind them in order not to collapse. If one was found to be too weak, he was listed for an Auschwitz transport. On Sundays, selections were even stricter."[121]

Therefore, the prisoners who had been transferred from Auschwitz warned the others about the gassings and advised them to always present themselves as "strong" and "healthy."[122] The machinery of death at Auschwitz ceased to operate in late November 1944, resulting in the termination of selections in Blechhammer.[123]

In parallel to the Auschwitz transports, the SDG murdered smaller numbers of sick prisoners with lethal injections. In July 1944 SDG Quirin, assisted by Dr. Iwanter, killed twelve male patients who were over fifty years old.[124] Another victim was a juvenile prisoner with a complicated leg fracture. He knew he was going to be murdered and said Kaddish for himself in front of the other inmates.[125] The killings intensified during a typhus outbreak in October 1944. As soon as the first cases had been confirmed by the SS laboratory in Rajsko, SDG Müller and Dr. Iwanter administered deadly injections to twenty infected inmates. During a staff meeting, Dr. Hyrsz reproached Dr. Iwanter for collaborating in the killings and warned him that he would be held accountable for his deeds one day.[126]

Contrary to the Schmelt camp phase, when the refusal to carry out killing orders had put the Jewish physicians' own lives at stake, the administration of lethal injections was voluntary under Auschwitz. Dr. Iwanter's motives for lending his assistance to the SDG remain unclear. A possible underlying reason could have been his early conversion to Catholicism and denial of his Jewish origins.[127] As he was under no coercion, his actions should be placed outside of Primo Levi's "gray zone."[128] The case of Aron Kremer, a journalist from Paris, who worked in the infirmary because he had done some medical studies, exemplifies the latitude for action available to Jewish medical staff in this issue. When the SDG asked him one day to give lethal injections to bedridden patients, Kremer simply refused.[129]

The murder of typhus patients did not prevent the spread of the disease. The SS turned to even more drastic measures by ordering the camp policeman, Rauch, to burn infected prisoners even if they were still breathing.[130] Following one of the last selections in November 1944, all but a few remaining typhus patients were taken to Auschwitz.[131] The young prisoner Wolf W. narrowly avoided being added to the transport after having spent eleven days in the typhus isolation ward by repeatedly telling the SS that he was fit for work, until they let him go.¹³² Similarly, Hermann Siegfried was discharged before a selection and survived a day at work with the help of a sympathetic German foreman. After his return to the infirmary, he fully recovered.¹³³

In a spectacular case in July 1944, SDG Quirin strangled a Jewish girl named Hirschberg from Będzin. She was the only survivor of a brutal raid by the German police on her family's hideout in a barn. The police took the profoundly traumatized girl to Blechhammer during a roll call. Before she was locked into the washroom barrack, she called out to the SS that they were all murderers. Dr. Auerhahn spent the afternoon with her and listened to her story—then Quirin murdered her.¹³⁴

The female prisoners were treated in a separate ward by Dr. Szeftel. The SS strictly prohibited other men from entering, and deputy camp leader Olejak once even attacked Szeftel when he left the ward after his shift. When Szeftel explained himself in Polish, Olejak, who belonged to a mixed Polish German minority, had a violent fit that was seemingly rooted in his conflicting "fluid" national identities: "I replied in Polish for, as a Silesian, he spoke this language. In an outburst of anger, he threw himself upon me, but luckily, he restrained himself and merely uttered a curse and called me names. The SS man Olejak had the worst reputation in the camp."¹³⁵

The Auschwitz takeover led to the introduction of Himmler's modified directive to no longer kill pregnant prisoners but only their babies, which had not been implemented under Schmelt.¹³⁶ The SS instructed the Jewish doctors to terminate pregnancies whenever possible. They thus induced premature labor in one less advanced pregnancy, and the child was born dead. Another woman gave birth to a healthy baby but was forced to suffocate it in order not to be sent to Auschwitz.¹³⁷

THE FEMALE PRISONERS

The women sent to Peterswaldau in January 1944 were gradually replaced with female prisoners arriving along with the men from disbanded Schmelt camps. Their block elder, Witka, mistreated them so ferociously that Demerer had her replaced by the Czech Jewish inmate Irma. Within the women's segregated compound were their key workplaces, the kitchen, the scullery, and the tailor's shop. Supervised by male criminal Kapos, the women worked for up to twelve hours daily. They were awakened for roll calls at 4:00 a.m., which, despite their small number, could last for up to three hours. Some female prisoners had to clean the SS quarters or did the gardening work for SS officers and also tended to their rabbits and poultry. The prisoners in the laundry were given clothes from the SS households to wash on Sundays.¹³⁸ The kitchen staff was overseen by the Jewish cook Band, who persistently ignored Dr. Auerhahn's instructions to let the women sit down during work to prevent swollen legs. Many developed health problems, as they had to stand all day.¹³⁹

At lunchtime, the female inmates received half a liter of soup, and in the evenings, half a liter of ersatz coffee and a piece of bread with some margarine, marmalade, or sausage. Those working in the kitchen often pilfered extra food, which they smuggled through the fence to help male prisoners.[140] A detail of eight women was assigned to fetch bread from a local bakery three times a week. While loading the loaves on a truck, they could secretly eat some of the bread, and they passed on their regular rations to fellow inmates.[141] There were no floggings or executions of female prisoners, perhaps because this would have required Himmler's permission.[142] Nevertheless, the women were frequently maltreated, had their food rations taken away, were left standing in the cold, or were sent to Auschwitz as a punishment. Prior to going to their deaths, their heads were shaven.[143]

The female prisoners continued to be exposed to various forms of sexual violence. Under Auschwitz rule, the perpetrators were non-Jewish criminal Kapos and the SS. Kapo Walter Redock, a convicted murderer, supervised the women in the clothes depot and the tailor's shop. He assaulted female prisoners while they cleaned his room and had them punished if they were not compliant. He thus reported Rozka Kam to the SS for a trumped-up infraction after she had rejected his advances. She was told that she would be sent to Auschwitz and was forced to stand at the camp gate for a whole day. In the end, the transport left without her, but she had no explanation for her rescue.[144]

Kapo Walter often harassed and beat the women when they were taking a shower and forced a female office worker to have an affair with him. Another cleaning girl, Sali Montag, stated that Redock deliberately left money and chocolate lying around in hopes of catching her stealing. He once accused her of having taken a perfume flask, although it was still in its place. One day the SS man Schindler sent her to pick berries in the forest. As her legs were too swollen to walk in clogs, she asked him for proper shoes. Schindler only gave her the shoes after beating her, and Kapo Redock severely mistreated her again the next day. As a result, she recurrently suffered from severe headaches and developed a facial paralysis. Unbeknownst to her, the long-term physical impairment inflicted by Walter had sealed her fate. When she sought help in the infirmary, the prisoner physicians told her that they were no longer permitted to treat her, as she had already been put on a list for Auschwitz. The evacuation of the camp narrowly saved her life, but she never recovered from the paralysis.[145]

The SS men regularly forced the women to stand naked on roll call parade while making sexually offensive remarks about their looks. When the summer uniforms were distributed in early 1944, the female prisoners had to pick them up naked in front of the SS.[146] The head of the Political Department, Otto Schmidt, reportedly punished a girl renowned for her beauty in the washroom barrack by stripping her naked and beating her. Her injuries were so severe that she was added to an Auschwitz transport four weeks later.[147] Some female inmates consented to trade sexual favors for food with SS guards. They were not only ostracized by the other women but were at risk of being sent to Auschwitz for their illicit contacts. These seemingly "consensual" relationships must clearly be characterized as a particular form of sexual violence.[148]

THE FORMATION OF A CHILDREN'S WORK DETAIL

The takeover augmented the number of children in the camp. Twenty boys under age sixteen were transferred from Auschwitz in spring, where they had merely spent two months. In July 1944, more boys from the liquidated family camp at Birkenau followed.[149] Rumors that all children of Blechhammer would be gassed prompted the Jewish elder, whose teenage son also lived in the camp, to suggest the formation of a children's work detail to the SS. The detail thus set out to the construction site with armed SS guards and three adult prisoners as Kapos. The adults were a certain Klapisch from Paris, a pianist from Warsaw named Borenstein, and the student Ernest Koenig.[150] The children's detail regularly caused an outcry among the foreign and unfree workers: "Even in the realm of slaves we lived in, nobody had seen anything like it before. The columns of English and French prisoners of war we encountered on the way called out to the SS 'shame' and 'boches'. All foreign laborers who saw us booed and cursed the SS. Even the German workers unambiguously demonstrated their contempt for what they saw."[151]

The hard labor on the OHW construction site caused many young prisoners to die of exhaustion. The Jewish elder's son Heinrich and his friends had to leave the work detail after two days, as the fast four-mile march to the factory had already been too demanding.[152] Others were not that lucky. Only three of the twenty boys from Auschwitz survived the first four months in Blechhammer. One of them was Ludwig Hamburger. In a harrowing account given during a postwar interview, he delineated how a friend died while working next to him. The boy complained about a bad headache, then became disoriented and collapsed. Hamburger pulled him to the roadside but was stopped by an SS man, who ordered him to just let the boy lie, adding that he would soon share the dead boy's fate. Hamburger found it very disturbing to see the collapsed children being discarded "like sacks." He related that many teenagers had been suicidal and that, unsure whether they would meet again, he had said goodbye to a friend each day. Next to being overworked, the children were also maltreated by SS guards. Hamburger was once stopped by an SS man who, asking what was three times seven, played a perfidious game with him. When he gave the correct answer, "21," the SS man dealt out that number of blows to him for no apparent reason.[153]

The young prisoners tried to alleviate their despair with happy childhood memories and stories about perseverance that they had once read in books.[154] These reveries apparently played an important role in their struggle for survival.[155]

Ernest Koenig, one of the adult prisoners who accompanied the detail, gave a rather euphemistic account of the children's work deployment. In an autobiography penned fifty-six years later, he claimed that the children had only performed light work, on a voluntary basis. He recounted how a five-year-old boy of his detail allegedly started to play with an SS guard, who carved boats and planes out of wood for him.[156] However, neither this incident nor the presence of such young children in the detail were corroborated by other testimonies.[157]

During the summer, ten of the eleven- to fourteen-year-olds were temporarily sent into the forest to gather branches and tree rods.[158] The children's detail was finally disbanded after twenty-nine of the fifty youths had been killed in an air raid in September 1944. The surviving boys were distributed among adult columns. The adult prisoners were aware of children working alongside them, but only a few still had the stamina to spare them the hardest labor.[159] The Blechhammer survivor and cartoonist Bil Spira was deeply moved by the working children, whom he documented in several drawings that he passed on to a British POW in 1944.[160]

In late 1944 the SS planned to send the remaining boys to Auschwitz. The Jewish elder and his son Heinrich gave conflicting testimonies on how these plans were averted. In Karl Demerer's version, the children had been rescued by a member of the Highway Company's building supervisory board at Breslau, the engineer Hans Mertens. Demerer persuaded him to make the SS believe that the boys were urgently needed on the construction site, and they were given little jobs.[161] Surprisingly, Mertens never confirmed the story, which could have eased his denazification.[162]

Heinrich Demerer related that his father had arranged for the children to take over the chores of the block elders by arguing that the adult prisoners could thus support the German war effort in their full strength.[163] This version was supported by the testimony of another child survivor, Art G., who stated that following a period of hard labor on the OHW site, they only worked in the camp from fall 1944.[164]

8

EXPOSURE TO ALLIED BOMBINGS AND THE EXACERBATION OF VIOLENCE IN SUMMER 1944

IN MAY 1944 THE ALLIES LAUNCHED A CAMPAIGN TO DESTROY GERMAN OIL facilities to diminish the German armed forces' fighting power. The OHW was targeted by strategic aerial bombings operated by the 15th wing of the US Army Air Force from July 1944.[1] The construction of air-raid shelters only began in June 1944. The OHW's belated reaction to the imminent threat of air attacks put it under considerable pressure, and the Jewish inmates assigned to this task experienced "catastrophic" conditions characterized by overworking and physical assaults. During this time more prisoners fell victim to selections or committed suicide than before.[2] The Blechhammer prisoners were reinforced by a Jewish masons' detail from Birkenau that was meant to fortify the plant's petrol tanks.[3]

Jews, like the other non-German laborers, were barred from air-raid shelters. The OHW issued directives on scattering during daytime alerts in July 1944, stating that the Jewish prisoners were to seek cover in cellars, in buildings under construction, under bridges, or in the open.[4] The company prohibited the entire workforce to seek shelter before the second air-raid signal had sounded.[5] However, the Jewish prisoners were always the last group allowed to leave their workplace, which rarely gave them enough time to reach cover before the bombings started.[6] Full of contempt for this German policy, a British prisoner of war noted in his diary: "A shame the Jews have to stay and work during a raid."[7] British POWs, who had secret radios, occasionally warned the Jewish prisoners of impending air raids. However, the information, often passed on in rudimentary German in the style "Today—boom, boom!," was of little value given the limited protection available to both groups.[8]

Jewish prisoners trying to enter bomb shelters were forcefully driven out by the Germans. It seemed cruel to the Jewish prisoners that there were even shelters for tools at the OHW, while they were denied access to the buildings they helped to construct.[9] During one of the first raids, on August 7, several Jewish prisoners were beaten out of a shelter reserved for the staff of the Highway Company. Minutes later a direct hit killed the seventy people inside. The prisoners construed this incident as a "divine punishment."[10]

At first the SS locked Jewish details into an unroofed, concrete enclosure. They saw the airplanes circling above them while their guards withdrew into shelters.[11] Some Jewish prisoners joined foreign workers taking cover inside the huge OHW chimneys that were in the center of the bombers' target area.[12] Others crept into boats and pipes, fled into deserted houses, or used one-man shelters by the roadside. The most dangerous place was outside. One prisoner lying flat in a field was almost buried by the sandy ground thrown up by the impacts. Others were killed by shrapnel or the air pressure of detonating bombs.[13] Later, when most German workers left the OHW site during the raids, the SS permitted the Jewish inmates to use the empty bomb shelters and the lower floors of the plant's power station.[14] The artist Bil Spira delineated the horror of enduring an air attack in an unfinished shelter without doors: "We were about one hundred men, tightly packed together. Suddenly, an immense air pressure pushed us so hard against the walls that we could not breathe. For half a minute, I stared into wide opened eyes and reddening faces, and I thought I would suffocate. Then the pressure was released, but this experience left a deep impact. On the same evening, I managed to depict the scene on a large piece of packing paper. I saw it before me as if the horror and fear of death had etched it into my senses like a photograph."[15]

While the bombings renewed the prisoners' hopes of a speedy liberation, they also posed a deadly risk. The deaths of comrades inadvertently caused by the Allied air strikes were perceived as particularly tragic but nevertheless unavoidable.[16] The bombings claimed about 180 Jewish casualties.[17]

The initial attacks of July 3, 7, and 9, 1944, merely targeted a railroad line. The first heavy raid came on August 7, when thirty B-24s and B-17s bombed the plant's southern part, killing at least fifty-four Jewish prisoners. Among them were twenty-nine boys of the children's detail, who were buried underneath a collapsed roof.[18] On August 11 the strikes were aimed at underground fuel tanks. Tragically, Jewish work details sheltered in the empty tanks, deeming them safe due to their air-tight doors. Twenty-four prisoners died when one of the tanks received a direct hit.[19] Another one hundred prisoners lost their lives during an attack on August 27. The main victims were the prisoners of the smoldering detail, who worked six floors underneath the OHW power station. All of them were killed when the power station was destroyed.[20] Others perished under the bombs, unable to find a place to take shelter in time. The survivor Oto Hostovsky recalled this tragic day:

> We are the last ones at work and watch everybody around us running and seeking cover. We go to "our" shelter nearby—"ours" because we have been working on it for almost two months. In the view of the Nazis already inside the shelter, this does not qualify us for entering it. They immediately chase us out with clubs and wooden boards. Swiftly, we run into the forest, barefooted as the wooden shoes are a hindrance. From afar, we hear the planes' engines. We have not reached our destination yet, and the planes are already above us. Bombs are being dropped. One of them explodes fifteen meters away from me. The air pressure knocks me to the ground, I get buried underneath soil and clay. I gather all my remaining strength to dig myself out as quickly as possible and run to the nearby forest shelter. I hardly make it inside when a firework starts over Blechhammer. After two hours, it is all over.... On the way back to our place of work, we find our dead comrades. They faced the raid outside, and the air pressure caused by the bombs exploding near them has ruptured their intestines. They are mutilated beyond recognition—we can only identify them by their sewed-on numbers.[21]

Two more major raids, on September 13 and December 18, were followed by ten lighter ones, in October and December.[22] While the non-Jewish workers hurt by bombs were tended to in local hospitals, the Jewish victims only received treatment in the camp infirmary or were taken to Auschwitz if they had severe injuries.[23] German paramedics denied them medical aid and even mistreated them: "During a raid, bombs fell on an unfinished building we sheltered in. Everybody jumped out of a window, and I was hit in the neck by a large brick and lost consciousness. Bleeding and twisted, I remained lying on the ground. A short time later, German paramedics arrived, asking what was wrong with me. When they realized I was Jewish, they started to hit me in the face and left me behind on the ground, due to my 'treacherous' blood."[24]

German orders that all missing prisoners had to be accounted for after bombings often kept the details at the factory until late at night. The dead were taken away on handcarts, covered with cement sacks.[25] Some were never retrieved, or only weeks later. As a result the OHW grounds were strewn with decaying bodies. Once a Jewish prisoner found a piece of striped cloth and could make out the silhouette of a body in a field, already swarming with insects. He then helped to unearth the unfortunate comrade's remains.[26] British POWs, who were blamed for the air raids by the Germans, had to look for Jewish inmates who had perished. This experience left a mark. One of the POWs, George Didcock, wrote in his diary after finding a Jewish prisoner's body: "I've got a bad, cold, miserable feeling."[27] The Jewish medical orderlies were even forced to search the debris for arms or pieces of skin on which the tattooed numbers could still be discerned.[28]

However, not all missing prisoners were dead. Some escaped during the air raids, when the prisoners were left unguarded. In late August the OHW reported several escapes by Jewish prisoners facilitated by the carelessness of its German workforce, who left their civilian clothes and company ID cards in open lockers.[29]

The Jewish prisoners had to carry out additional bombing-related tasks, most of which were highly dangerous. A small Jewish detail overseen by a Roma criminal Kapo assisted in the preparation of a smoke screen in a special laboratory. They worked together with Wehrmacht convalescents, who regularly passed on bread to them and whose German foreman was rather sympathetic.[30]

In summer 1944 Blechhammer set up a Jewish fire brigade to combat fires at the plant caused by bombings. Similar fire brigades were established in Auschwitz, Sachsenhausen, and Buchenwald from 1941.[31] Following several weeks of training, the Blechhammer brigade was permanently on call in a hut on the construction site. The first time the alarm was sounded after a heavy air raid, they decided to stay in their hut in an act of passive resistance, until a German sergeant threatened to have them shot for sabotage.[32] The prisoners were often sent into hazards nobody else dared to tackle. For instance, the directors of the OHW contractor AEG once demanded that the Jewish firefighters extinguish the flames in one of their buildings, where oxygen bottles were stored that already had begun to explode.[33] Similarly, an intoxicated SS man ordered the brigade to dismantle a wooden scaffolding around the burning power station after a direct hit on August 7.[34]

The Jewish bomb-clearing detail experienced exorbitant death tolls. Following a decree by Hitler of October 1940 that Jewish prisoners should clear delay-action bombs, such details were established in Auschwitz and other concentration camps.[35] In Blechhammer, a bomb-clearing detail existed from July 3, 1944. Perniciously, the SS asked for "volunteers," who mostly signed up for this task because they were promised double food rations.[36] Others felt they had nothing left to lose, like a boy sentenced to death for pilfering, whose last wish it was to have more bread. However, the extra rations were seldom handed out. Six Jewish prisoners were normally allocated to a German expert to dig out the bombs, remove the detonators, throw them into a ditch, and destroy them in a controlled explosion. The Germans merely supervised this process from a safe distance. At least half of the detail's sixty prisoners were killed by exploding bombs.[37] Jonas Pampel was the only survivor of a group of six prisoners digging out a bomb in December 1944. His life was saved because he went to the latrine shortly before the bomb detonated. Initially, he and his friend Levie Barmhartigkeid had found it amusing to scare their SS guards by handling the bombs in a rather reckless fashion. Following the death of his five comrades, Pampel asked to leave the detail, but he was forced to continue.³⁸ Other prisoners, who were only temporarily assigned to the detail, were lucky to get out alive.³⁹ The Blechhammer detail also had to remove bombs on neighboring industrial sites at Reigersfeld (Birawa) and IG Farben Heydebreck.⁴⁰

At the start of the air raids, it became apparent that the OHW plant's three chimneys were not fully covered by the smoke screen. Therefore, the SS asked for Jewish volunteers to shorten the chimneys by thirty meters, in return for three bonus vouchers a day.⁴¹ The work, beginning on August 3, 1944, was closely monitored by British POWs, who were concerned about the Jewish inmates' safety and even moved to tears by their plight.⁴² All the Jewish volunteers survived the dangerous task, but they never received the bonus vouchers. Moreover, their demonstration of outstanding courage prompted the SS to allocate them to the bomb-clearing detail.⁴³

On a different note, Blechhammer's Political Department was responsible for the ill-treatment and attempted lynching of two American pilots, who were captured after bailing out of their plane when it was shot down on August 22, 1944. Their lives were spared by a member of the Luftwaffe, who apparently objected to Hitler's order of June 1944 to kill Allied pilots who were shot down on the spot.⁴⁴

THE EXACERBATION OF VIOLENCE IN SUMMER 1944

The bulk of survivor testimonies corroborates a surge in violence against Jewish inmates after the Auschwitz takeover. An SS directive prohibiting the punishment of prisoners in public, and their maltreatment, led the SS men patrolling the construction site to conceal their clubs in briefcases, so they could unobtrusively carry out floggings in a special hut.⁴⁵ Nevertheless, brutal killings and assaults frequently took place in full view of the other workers. Prisoners were murdered when others in their detail escaped or for working too slowly, for instance.⁴⁶ The SS block leaders also took down the prisoner numbers of those reported by German foremen for infractions such as talking to civilians. They were punished upon their return to the camp and often died of their injuries. In one case, six inmates were nearly whipped to death for not saluting the Wehrmacht guard of French prisoners of war.⁴⁷ Regarding these direct punishments, German masters' reports were forwarded to the Political Department of Auschwitz and the WVHA in Berlin. The over one hundred preserved penal reports concerning Blechhammer give evidence of the ideologically loaded complaints accusing Jewish prisoners of being "obstinate and lazy" or "arrogant and provocative."⁴⁸

From late 1943 the work deployment of sixty Ukrainian auxiliary policemen, who had participated in mass shootings of Jews in Kharkiv between 1941 and 1943, led to further brutalization. Many of these men had belonged to the right-wing Ukrainian People's Militia (OUN) supporting Stepan Bandera.⁴⁹ When the three thousand auxiliary policemen of Kharkiv were temporarily released from service, they volunteered for employment in the German war industry. New laws were enacted that exempted such "politically reliable" Soviet workers from the discriminatory *Ostarbeiter* decrees.[50] Several assaults on Jewish prisoners at the OHW correlate with the auxiliary policemen's presence in Blechhammer. In early 1944 a Ukrainian killed a Jewish prisoner with an iron bar to extract his gold teeth. Shortly after this incident, two Ukrainians threw a Jewish inmate off a scaffold for the same reason. All three were hanged in Blechhammer's work education camp (AEL). The punishment was related to the theft of gold teeth, not to the murder of Jewish inmates.[51] Similarly, a Ukrainian welder working at great heights persistently nudged his young Jewish assistant Kurt Baum trying to make him fall off.[52] In fall 1944 the Ukrainian auxiliaries were once again drafted into German police units in Silesia.[53]

After the onset of Allied air strikes in summer 1944, strict decrees on "plundering" and "sabotage" were implemented that gave license to lynching and shooting out of hand.[54] In addition to the SS, the OHW works police and German civilian workers played a key role in these killings. The child survivor Ludwig Hamburger recalled the dangerously tense atmosphere at the OHW: "The foremen and supervisors were all murderers. They were the scum of Germany. They beat us at work ... for everything, for the least. They said we were saboteurs. And many of my friends, many of our comrades have lost their lives. If they lost a screw, if they dropped something ... it was too heavy for them, it was called sabotage and they were murdered."[55]

On October 27, 1944, a detail comprising one hundred prisoners was machine-gunned by the SS for sabotaging the war effort by working "slow." Eddie Willner was the only survivor, as he sought cover and was pulled into a nearby hut by a Jewish paramedic, who tended to his head injury.[56] Furthermore, an SS guard and a German foreman took the lives of two juvenile inmates, who had pilfered a piece of wire, in a particularly despicable fashion. Rating the minor theft as "sabotage," they ordered the boys to sit in a huge cement mixer and killed them by switching it on.[57] On another occasion, six hundred Jewish electricians were slightly reluctant to start their Sunday shift, and their German foreman instantly reported them to the SS for alleged "sabotage" and even "insurgency." They were punished with hour-long penal exercises and floggings, causing many weakened inmates to die.[58]

The works police, headed by OHW deputy director Dr. Heinrich Schlick, constantly scrutinized the non-German workforce on the construction site. They did not hesitate to murder Jewish inmates on the spot based on trumped-up accusations under the new decrees. Nathan Prochownik was nearly shot for alleged "espionage" simply because he was waiting for a German worker outside his hut to exchange food with him. Prochownik's life was saved through the intervention of his German foreman, who pretended to beat him hard. Meanwhile, the works policeman reported him to the Political

Department for begging bread from German girls and "race defilement." Despite being tortured by Political Officer Schmidt, Prochownik vehemently denied the accusations, and the works police's fabricated story was dropped.[59] Similarly, Ernest Koenig narrowly escaped a public lynching after the works police and SS guards caught him transporting tin plates for German workers, unaware that the workers had stolen them. Preparations were made to hang him on the construction site. The ad hoc execution was stopped by concerns that the German workers would later also be charged for theft.[60]

Plenipotentiary for the Work Deployment of Foreign Labor Fritz Sauckel decreed that extra shifts should be run to compensate work interruptions during air raids. However, as security concerns precluded late shifts, the SS still required the OHW to extend the full hourly payments for the Jewish prisoners. The OHW, in turn, instructed German foremen to extract more productivity from the prisoners at a greater pace. Consequently, cases of overworking became rampant.[61] An ethnic German master forced a prisoner detail to unload a truck containing twenty tons of rocks in three hours under threat of being accused of sabotage. Three inmates died while trying to accomplish this impossible task.[62] A foreman from Sudeten intended to work two teenage prisoners to death. The two usually shouldered heavy pipes, with a Soviet POW holding up the middle. One day the foreman ordered the Soviet prisoner to let the boys carry a pipe alone, and they almost collapsed. A German overseer, who knew them, came to their rescue and placed them in another detail.[63]

Most Germans working at the OHW knew that unfit Jewish prisoners were gassed in Auschwitz.[64] Despicably, some intentionally harmed prisoners so they would fall victim to a selection.[65] One of these prisoners was Lion Gosler, whose German foreman caused him a septic wound by deliberately dropping a rock on his foot. A Jewish physician luckily managed to warn him of an impending Auschwitz transport during his treatment in the infirmary.[66]

Moreover, the German overseers urged the Jewish Kapos to constantly hit their comrades, while simultaneously beating and kicking the prisoners themselves.[67] The inmates' deteriorating physical state triggered more violence. Leo Weiniger delineated the vicious attacks on those suffering from edema caused by malnutrition: "The pain was unbearable, especially the water in the legs, and in the swollen faces no human traits were recognizable anymore. The *Meister* made nasty remarks about these unfortunate men, who were in a physical and mental shock. They did not have the strength to stand upright, let alone to work."[68]

Between late May and September 1944 the British POW George Didcock recorded in his diary several assaults by German civilians on Jewish prisoners: "One of the Jews beaten up and nearly killed this morning.... Saw a German knocking a Jew terribly today."[69] Karl Masseli, the SS man managing the prisoners' work deployment, admitted their frequent ill-treatment by German overseers. His claims that some overseers had been rebuked by the camp leader were nevertheless not corroborated by survivor testimony.[70] Auschwitz commandant Rudolf Hoess attributed the widespread brutality on industrial construction sites to the war-related decrease in skilled German workers and company directors losing control over their employees.[71] However, it is important to remember that it was senior executives like Dr. Schlick—who were at the top of a surveillance apparatus planted in all concerns by the Nazi regime and who commanded auxiliary forces, such as the works police—who cooperated in the maltreatment, lynching, and mass killing of Jewish prisoners.

Richard Overy sees the Allied air raids and the ensuing deterioration of the overall living standards as being at the root of the growing German aggression against Jews and other foreign laborers in 1944.[72] In addition to the aforementioned factors, the escalation of violence in Blechhammer in summer 1944 was notably fueled by the new decrees on looting and sabotage. These enactments provided a legal framework for manslaughter that evidently encouraged "ordinary" Germans to commit atrocities against other human beings, who had been labeled as "inferior."

9

HANGINGS WITHOUT A WITNESS?

On the Vicissitudes of Relating Traumatic Memories

P‍UBLIC EXECUTIONS BY HANGING WERE FIRST INTRODUCED UNDER THE Auschwitz administration. Unlike the over one hundred penal reports on minor infractions, no evidence of even a single death sentence has been preserved. Due to the complete lack of official documentation resulting from the destruction of incriminating evidence by the SS in early 1945, the only available sources for reconstructing the executions in Blechhammer are survivor testimonies and judicial interviews of perpetrators. In addition, a British POW's war diary corroborates some dates of hangings.

While largely providing consistent facts on most other aspects of the camp's history, the bulk of witness accounts conspicuously produced extremely conflicting information on the executions. The sudden distortion of testimony regarding the hanging incidents points to a massive trauma inflicted on the survivors, who were forced to witness these atrocities. Trauma interferes with memory and often leads to the creation of "split-off" fragments that cannot be integrated into one's life story. Another typical reaction is to suppress such unwanted, painful memories. However, the longer these memories remain repressed, the more distorted they will become. As the Holocaust survivor and psychiatrist Dori Laub has pointed out, the Shoah was "an event without a witness." Many former inmates failed to become witnesses to their own story because they remained incapable of embedding their traumatic experiences in their biographies. Moreover, the system of Nazi camps created a dehumanizing frame of reference, which contributed to the process of derealization and depersonalization.[1]

The repression of memories or disjointed and ruptured recollections reflect the "ineffable" experience of the Holocaust. These testimonies preclude the usual gathering of facts to create a coherent historical narrative. Instead, they convey the loss and destruction effectuated by the Shoah. By following the accounts as they become tainted or cease to provide information at all, layers of what Lawrence Langer termed "deep memory" emerge that enhance our understanding of the immense and unprecedented breakage of a frame and the survivors' desperate struggle to communicate the "incommunicable."[2]

When facing extreme emasculation, a group may start to recall as fact what they wished had happened. Such collective "myths" were prevalent in the testimonies of former Blechhammer prisoners. Holocaust memories also form part of a collective memory, and "myths" evidently played an important role as unifying symbols. Identifying these symbols thus tells us more about a specific group than about the event itself.[3] Survivors with repressed memories were particularly susceptible to integrating such legendary complexes, deriving from the "conformist group memory" of their comrades, into their own stories. The group memory had attained greater credibility than their individual recollections, leading some to replace their, perhaps more accurate, recall of details with that of a particular group.[4]

Most testimonies corroborate a basic storyline, such as recounting in many variations the execution of a young man who was hanged twice because the rope had broken, and the hanging of two prisoners whose Kapo was also hanged for having defended them. There were presumably more hangings, but the information was very incongruent. The precise number of executions, the dates, and the victims' identities are impossible to arrive at.

The tainted memories of the Blechhammer hangings show that the Holocaust will never be fully explicable, and we can only attempt to circumscribe the void by analyzing the trauma fragments from a multitude of angles. Distorted memories may bring to the fore what invariably will remain "indeterminate, elusive, and opaque." They force us to accept the limits of the historical representation of the Holocaust, and that there will never be a "complete" narrative with a "redemptive closure."[5] This apparent lacuna nonetheless symbolizes the most central, intrinsic element of the Shoah: the destruction.[6]

The SS carefully planned and staged each of the hangings, and all staff members supposedly were present at or actively participated in the executions. Of the few SS men of Blechhammer ever interrogated in courts, none gave identical information on the number of hanged prisoners and the circumstances of their deaths. Primo Levi felt that the need to repress the memories of atrocities united the perpetrators and the victims in a "paradoxical analogy." Contrary to their victims, the perpetrators intended to suppress feelings of guilt. The widespread use of euphemisms created to cover up their crimes also helped to relieve the SS men's consciences, along with the consumption of alcohol during and immediately after killing operations.[7] In a state of intoxication, humans generally show impaired perceptual judgment, awareness, memory, and decision-making, and the amount of information they are able to recall is reduced.[8] Drinking following acts of violence equally fostered camaraderie and cemented the alleged "righteousness" of their collective moral transgressions.[9] Jewish prisoner artists were forced to stage theatrical performances on the very evening of executions in Blechhammer.[10] To the SS men, these events offered another opportunity for distraction and maintaining a self-image of being "cultured" and "civilized."[11]

The veridical memories still retained by the perpetrators were often manipulated by deliberate fabrications they told either to be acquitted or to blend into the postwar society more easily. They typically applied a twofold strategy of feigning complete or selective amnesia and disclaiming personal responsibility for their actions by pleading that they were obeying superior orders. In the beginning, the falsifying of accounts was still done consciously, but the more often lies were told, the more the boundaries between truth and fiction became blurred.[12] Feigning amnesia and fabricating lies may both affect the veridical memory. The unreported true information is likely to be repressed and replaced with the manipulated information over time. To create a false memory, the veridical memory is nevertheless needed to recall the correct information before altering it.[13] For reasons diametrically opposed to those of their victims, the SS men therefore equally failed to become witnesses of their own crimes.[14]

Otto Brossmann and his deputy Hans Stefan Olejak were responsible for the first hangings in September and October 1944. Neither was interrogated about the executions. The second camp leader, Kurt Klipp, died before he could be tried.[15] Klipp's deputy Karl Czapla appeared in the Frankfurt Auschwitz Trials in 1960. He disclaimed all responsibility by claiming that staff from the Auschwitz main camp had carried out the hangings. The presence of external personnel was not corroborated by any other sources and appears to be a fabrication:

> I witnessed two executions by hanging in Blechhammer. Two prisoners, who had made an escape attempt before my time and had been sent to the Political Department of Auschwitz, returned in the beginning of December accompanied by three SS men from Auschwitz, and they were hanged in the presence of all inmates. The verdict was read out before the execution by an *Oberscharführer*, whose name I have never known, as he belonged to the Political Department of Auschwitz. The gallows had been especially set up for these two prisoners. This was the only execution I witnessed during my whole time in Auschwitz.[16]

Sixteen years later, Czapla was questioned again. By then most details of the executions had sunk into genuine or feigned oblivion in his mind. It is noteworthy that he carefully avoided even mentioning the word "Auschwitz." Rather than incriminating anonymous others, he changed his strategy and portrayed himself as an innocent bystander. In his statements, he generally tried to create the impression that he had been a friend and benefactor of the prisoners, and he obviously succeeded in convincing the judges. He was acquitted twice and, had he not died, would probably also have walked away from his third trial as a free man. "I cannot remember precisely these days who read out the verdict and who carried out the execution. I only know that the whole camp was assembled during the execution. I was present, too, but had nothing to do with the execution."[17]

The former SS block leader Karl Masseli admitted that there had been one hanging, connected to the smuggling of explosives. He did not mention the breaking of the rope and used the strategy of selective amnesia regarding any other hangings: "A prisoner was hanged, as he had brought gunpowder into the camp. I have no remembrance of any other executions."[18]

The guard Heinrich Schäfer had been in Polish custody immediately after the war but was never questioned about executions. In 1964 the Jewish Blechhammer survivor Erwin Lagus contacted Simon Wiesenthal, the famous Nazi hunter, urging him to start investigations into crimes committed in the camp. As Lagus had had friendly relations with Schäfer in Blechhammer, he wanted him to appear as a witness. Schäfer sent him a letter stating that he did not remember much about the camp and was unable to provide the names of SS men or details of executions. Taking the role of a mere bystander, Schäfer briefly recounted the hanging with the snapped rope: "I only witnessed a single execution as a guard, but the rope broke and [he] was hanged once more."[19]

The former SS man Adolf Schindler went into complete denial when he was confronted with a Jewish witness's accusation that he had supervised the second hanging. He not only claimed that there had never been any executions but also tried to pretend that the crematorium, where the bodies of the hanged were usually burned under his auspices, did not exist.[20]

All other perpetrators conspicuously stressed that they had participated in a *single* hanging only, when they must have been involved in many more. This understatement was undoubtedly intended to downplay their culpability. The phenomenon seems to correlate with the overstating of numbers apparent in some survivor testimonies. To Dori Laub, the latter symbolized the "unimaginable breakage of a frame" experienced in the camps.[21] It is also known that the memory for traumatic events may amplify over time due to flashbacks.[22] Contrary to the victims, the perpetrators, in their quest for vindication, obviously produced a reverse effect by reducing their memories.

The perpetrators represented a "memory community" characterized by feigned (and partly genuine) amnesia, lies, and denial antithetical to that of the survivors. The nature of the trials, especially in Western Germany, permitted them to evade personal responsibility and contributed to their exculpation from state-sponsored mass murder.[23] The almost total absence of truthful confessions on their part left the survivors as the only witnesses, whose statements were often put into question by the culprits' persistent and widely accepted denials. The trauma inflicted by the perpetrators complicated the act of witnessing for the victims or even made it impossible.

George Didcock, a British POW assigned to a Blechhammer working party in fall 1943, kept a diary throughout his Italian and German captivity. From April 1944, he made regular diary entries about the treatment of Jewish prisoners he encountered on the OHW construction site. He noted the hangings of five prisoners on four occasions between September and December 1944. It was not unusual that British POWs gathered information on what would later be called the Holocaust, but none of the other POWs in Blechhammer mentioned any hangings in interviews or autobiographies.[24] It was impossible for any bystander to watch the executions with their own eyes, as the camp for Jews was surrounded by a massive concrete wall and was situated several miles from the British POW camps. However, many British POWs had clandestine contacts with Jewish inmates for bartering or simply offering their assistance. Didcock never disclosed who told him about the hangings, possibly to protect his contact person and himself in case his diary should fall into the hands of the Germans. What renders this diary so valuable is that in contrast to all other available sources, it is a contemporaneous document. Whoever gave Didcock the information, it was still "raw." He thus came closest to being what Dori Laub referred to as an "outsider-witness," somebody detached enough to remain unaffected by trauma.[25] He did not provide ample details, but the dates are more likely to be accurate, as British POWs had access to calendars. The diary corroborates the hanging of one prisoner for the possession of explosives on Yom Kippur, September 27, 1944, during which the rope snapped. Interestingly, the entries do not confirm the hanging of three other prisoners at the same time:

> September 28, 1944: A Jew was hung last night, a detonator was found on him, the rope broke with his weight, so he had to wait while they found another, all the camp had to watch it.
> October 15, 1944: Two of the Jews were hanged last night for pinching.
> October 26, 1944: Another Jew hung last night.
> December 3, 1944: Jew hanged last night for pinching rubber.[26]

The historian Russell Wallis construes Didcock's diary entries on atrocities against Jews as symptomatic of a particular "chatter culture" among British POWs, who had allegedly become increasingly desensitized to the ubiquitous acts of cruelty committed by the Germans. He suggests that there had been no direct contacts between Didcock and Jewish inmates. Didcock's diary nonetheless clearly corroborates "second economy" barter, which presumably involved Jewish prisoners. As his writing was the only archival source by British POWs documenting the hangings, this information was unlikely to have been based on rumors spread in POW camps.[27]

"AN EXEMPLARY PUNISHMENT": THE TRAUMA OF THE FIRST HANGING

The first public execution of a prisoner in Blechhammer was deviously conceived of by the SS as an "exemplary punishment" for alleged insurrection. However, many prisoners felt that the SS had merely sought a scapegoat following the onset of Allied air raids.[28] What made this first execution so disturbing to watch was that the rope broke as soon as the young prisoner had been hanged. He was forced to climb up on a chair placed on a table, the noose was put around his neck, and the chair was kicked off, whereupon he abruptly fell to the ground. This traumatizing incident, corroborated by most of the testimonies, was certainly no coincidence, but part of a cynical strategy applied by the SS to cause a maximum shock effect on the prisoners and the condemned person. A perfidious ingredient of the whole scenario was the sudden hope that the victim would be spared, as the execution had failed. Nearly all witnesses were convinced that this was stipulated by an international law or an old tradition. Jewish elder Demerer recalled how he had approached the camp leader to ask him to pardon the man. Numerous survivors confirmed his appeal for mercy. Two witnesses erroneously stated that Demerer had been a lawyer (he was a merchant), thus indirectly underscoring the rightfulness of his cause.[29] Others claimed that the victim had asked to be pardoned himself.[30]

Curiously, such a law never existed. There is nonetheless a widespread ancient belief that an innocent person sentenced to death might be saved by divine intervention preventing the execution. Despite some documented cases in Britain and the United States of condemned persons having been pardoned after multiple failed attempts to execute them, the principle of "double jeopardy" has at no time applied to death sentences.[31] Nonetheless, the SS cruelly played on the prevailing assumption that the victim would be pardoned to torment the prisoners. According to several survivors, the camp leader sneered at Demerer and replied that international law did not apply to Jews.[32] Although there was no legal framework for pardoning the prisoner, the camp leader obviously intended to demonstrate to the inmates that they had been deprived of all human rights.

Similar "failed" executions were staged in other Nazi camps, such as Pustków. In this camp, an escapee was hanged on a hook, which immediately broke off the wall. The assembled inmates also expected the condemned to be pardoned, but the hook was fastened once more, and he was hanged a second time.[33] These events underline the changed function of executions in concentration camps. Rather than deterring prospective perpetrators from committing crimes, they primarily served as a means of total degradation.[34]

The "failed" execution in Blechhammer plunged the prisoners from feelings of horror into tentative optimism and then, ultimately, humiliation and emasculation. An additional trauma was caused by having to witness the hanging for a second time. The extraordinarily traumatizing hanging likely contributed to the distortion of the survivors' memories and also impacted their recall of the following executions. Some prisoners decided to avoid watching the other hangings altogether.

Several survivors stated that the victim of the first execution was Jacob Fresco, a young man from the Netherlands they had known well.[35] According to information from the Dutch Red Cross and the Jewish Council gathered after the war by the Netherlands' Institute for War Documentation (RIOD), Jacob Fresco was born in The Hague in February 1922. He married Carolina de Wind on August 25, 1942. She was deported from Westerbork on August 28, 1942, and was murdered upon arrival in Auschwitz on August 31, 1942. The RIOD considered it an established fact that Jacob Fresco was hanged for sabotage on the eve of Yom Kippur 1944.[36] However, there were also witnesses who stated that the hanged man had been the chemistry student Rudolph Raphaelson, a German emigrant to the Netherlands who had volunteered for the bomb-clearing detail in Blechhammer. His identity was not verified by institutions after the war.[37] These witnesses equally claimed to have known the victim well or even to have been friends with him. The survivor Jules Fainzang described the shocking moment when he realized that the condemned was somebody he believed to be an old acquaintance of his: "I was trembling when I recognized Rafaelson, Ringel's friend; the three of us had formed an inseparable trio in Laurahütte two years earlier. An SS officer read out the verdict. I do not recall having understood anything of it. I had to pull myself together in order not to faint at the sight of brave Rafaelson behind the dangling noose, a table in front of him."[38]

The victim's identity will remain elusive. To the survivors, a name nevertheless became crucial when telling their story. As Henry Greenspan has pointed out, names are an indispensable tool to render a terrifying crime tellable to others by transforming it into a human "tragedy" they can relate to. By restoring a victim's identity, the individual is thus not only saved from oblivion but also stands out from the anonymity of mass atrocity. Seeing a friend die instead of a stranger implied closer emotional ties and evoked compassion equivalent to the shock the survivor experienced during the hanging. Being able to provide the victim's proper name and his alleged traits of character likewise increased the credibility of one's story—to oneself and to others. However, it is important to remember that the communicable parts of the "tragedy" only represent a fragment of what the witness experienced and that a sole, seemingly identifiable, victim may symbolize the suffering of many others who remain nameless.[39] Along these lines, several witnesses gave additional information about the victim's personality. His youth and innocence were particularly emphasized. Most stated that he had been about twenty years old.[40] He was further described as tall, well-built, and brave, with a "childlike face." His unusual calmness and docility at the gallows, where he stood "like a lamb," prompted some to suspect that the SS had administered a drug to him before the execution.[41] A survivor, who thought the victim had been Raphaelson, recalled how that person had once shared a piece of bread with him.[42] A gesture like this constituted a supreme act of altruism in the universe of the concentration camps.

The memory for traumatic events may also amplify over time as a result of flashbacks or reexperiencing. These memories are nevertheless prone to distortion, especially when the information is focused on perceptual details, such as colors or sounds.[43] A good example of this is the statement given by the survivor Abram Stone in a pretrial investigation thirty years after the event. A part of his recollections of the hanging was a vivid mental picture in which the victim wore bright red socks at the gallows.[44] Under the Auschwitz administration all prisoners had to use a piece of cloth instead of socks. And even if the victim had clandestinely acquired such socks, the SS would have confiscated them upon his arrest. Similarly, two other survivors recalled that the Jewish camp orchestra had played during executions. One of them mentioned that it had played the popular tune "Lilli Marleen."[45] Although the abuse of prisoner orchestras for such purposes was ubiquitous in many concentration camps, none of the other witnesses corroborated the playing of music during hangings in Blechhammer. These survivors might have erroneously fused their memories of the hangings with those of the ensuing theatrical performances. Memory failure is often based on schematic processing. Schemes are organized knowledge structures based on individual sets of beliefs, values, and expectations that the brain utilizes to interpret what we perceive. Due to the constructive rather than reconstructive nature of perception and comprehension, we add components to or alter what we perceive to render it more understandable.[46]

Most testimonies corroborate that the condemned was caught with an explosive substance he had picked up from the construction site. This was independently confirmed by the diary of the British POW Didcock and the judicial interview of the SS man Karl Masseli.[47] However, the prisoners did not believe the SS's story of a bombing plot. Instead, they described the victim as a person with a naïve curiosity about unusual objects, who probably did not even realize that he was carrying hazardous material.[48] The head of Blechhammer's Political Department, Schmidt, forced the prisoner under torture to sign a "confession" that he had intended to blow up the camp.[49] The testimonies were unclear about the length of the victim's detention before Berlin confirmed the death sentence.[50] As the prisoners had typically lost their sense of time in the camps, they found it hard to keep track of specific dates.[51] The formal turnaround for reports sent from Blechhammer to Auschwitz and the WVHA in Berlin was usually four weeks. A time frame of one month seems realistic, due to the likely connection between two major air raids on August 22 and 27 and the hanging.[52] On the day of the execution, the prisoners were confronted with a gallows on their return from work. Some recalled that the SS had led the condemned onto the assembly court when they had all lined up for the roll call. Others were convinced that he had stood in a row next to them and had been forced to step forward.[53] As the latter version would imply that the prisoner still went out to work, it was probably erroneous. The memory of the unsuspecting victim being taken straight from their midst could have been evoked by the unexpectedness of the event. The notion of the seemingly random calling of his number further enhanced the feeling of total subjugation to an arbitrary power. This sentiment is exemplified by the following excerpt from video testimony by the survivor Ernest Koenig, who could only render a generalized account of the hangings: "Hanging was particularly impressive, and it was intended to be so because it was always a big show. All the camp had to assemble and had to look at the persons. Very often, they did not know until their number was called up that they are going to be hanged, so it was very fear-inspiring, and the SS made a big show of it."[54]

Except for the SS block leader nicknamed Tom Mix, individual perpetrators participating in the execution were rarely identified. Tom Mix reportedly kicked off the chair the victim stood on and attached a new rope after the first hanging had "failed."[55] Higher echelon SS personnel were only sporadically incriminated.[56] When asked for the names of SS men involved in the executions during a pretrial investigation in 1976, a witness pointed out that the prisoners had been too exhausted to focus on the perpetrators: "One should not forget that these executions took place when we returned from the construction site, we were hungry and deadly tired. After having stood on roll call parade for over an hour, it is possible that one did not pay attention to the faces of SS men."[57]

Another possible explanation could be the effect known as "memory narrowing." Witnesses to traumatic events tend to exhibit improved recall for central details, in this case the condemned prisoner at the gallows, and worse recall for peripheral ones.[58] The assumption that SS men were seldom perceived as individual actors is affirmed by the statement of a survivor who argued that the SS had committed crimes collectively and it was hard to single out those more guilty than the others. "'Tom Mix' was usually present at executions, along with other SS men. The gentlemen had the executions carried out by prisoners. I cannot give you the name of an SS man I saw during executions. You must look at it this way that the SS had a collective guilt of these crimes."[59]

Several survivors explicitly named two Jewish Kapos who supposedly participated in the execution. Enforced collaboration in the killing of fellow prisoners was part of a commonly applied Nazi strategy intended to divide the inmates and turn functionary prisoners into accessories to their crimes.[60] In one version corroborated by two testimonies, the victim's block elder, a certain Schwarzbaum, put the noose around the boy's neck the first time. He allegedly refused to hang him a second time, and thus Tom Mix took over.[61] In a second version, the Kapo in question was a Dutch prisoner named Jacques Presser. He hanged the boy both times but was said to have asked the camp leader to pardon the victim when the rope had broken.[62] Survivors judged such functionary prisoners differently. Some reproached them for having volunteered to participate in the hanging process; others saw them as the victims of the SS perpetrators, who were ultimately responsible for these atrocities.[63]

Trauma and humiliation were felt for different aspects of the first execution. The snapping of the rope was a shock to most witnesses.[64] The camp leader's subsequent refusal to pardon the victim caused great moral anguish and a feeling of dehumanization and emasculation, a state of mind in Holocaust survivors that Langer called the "diminished self."[65] Jacques Grinband recalled: "We were there, . . . without a voice, with an empty stomach after a laborious day, incapable of saying a word. We pondered what we were in their eyes. No, not human beings, . . . I demand one minute of shame for humanity."[66]

The time between the first and the second hanging, while the victim was forced to wait for the new rope, was experienced as the most devastating. The victim was often portrayed rather idealistically as a hero, who went to his death with great calmness and bravery. This was doubtless intended to honor the condemned, who had suffered such utter humiliation at the hands of the SS, but it also made it easier for the survivors to keep their emotional distance. Individual testimonies nevertheless corroborate a more realistic, albeit disturbing perspective. Ernest Nives delineated the agony of having to watch the panic-stricken man die: "I saw gallows for the first time, we were surrounded by machine guns, they made a show for us. . . . We were agitated, numb, saw the terror in Raphaelson's eyes, we did not know what to do. . . . You were helpless having to watch how your own friend is being killed because a guy behind you is pointing a machine gun at you."[67]

Estimates of the approximate time span between the first and the second hanging varied significantly, depending on the emotional strain inflicted by the situation. While to some the second hanging came in swift succession to the first, others stated that up to thirty minutes had elapsed: "The rope broke and the poor boy had to stand at the gallows and wait for half an hour until a stronger rope had been fetched. This was the most terrible thing I have ever experienced. He looked at us helplessly, and we could hardly bear the sight of him, as we were left standing helplessly around him. The situation was so unbearable to us that any minute during this waiting in silence, I feared to lose my nerve."[68]

Only one survivor rendered a harrowing account of the actual dying process: "Our unfortunate comrade clings to his life, he makes a few kicks into the air, then it is over.

He moves no more. It is horrible to watch: his violet face, his rolled back eyes, his tongue hanging from the opened mouth."[69]

The trauma of the hanging also caused psychosomatic symptoms. One witness stated that he had been unable to eat for several days afterward.[70] Heinrich Demerer, the Jewish elder's teenage son, fainted during the execution.[71] The survivor Bil Spira recalled that he and many other prisoners had wept.[72]

Surprisingly, two witnesses immediately realized that the breaking of the rope was a fraud. Their narratives were thus much more distanced and downplayed the shock effect. The first account, written shortly after the liberation in 1945, emphasized the prisoners' wish for revenge:

> It was the first time I witnessed a hanging; I had often seen people being beaten to death, but this was something new.... I thought the rope did not look very strong and, as it turned out, it was not. He listened to the verdict quietly, then he was hanged, but not for long, the rope snapped. This had, of course, been a nasty trick by the SS.... It took at least twenty minutes until the new rope had been fetched. The young man must have departed from this world with awful thoughts.... We had to watch the last twitches of the guy and cadaver-to-be. He deeply impressed most of us, however hardened we had become by then. It was quiet in the rooms, and our thoughts went out to this young man with the childlike face, who had died so bravely and without uttering a sound. In many faces one could make out the wish for revenge.[73]

In the second account, an excerpt from an autobiography published in 2013, the breaking of the rope was construed as a form of resistance against the SS of the Jewish functionary prisoners involved in the hanging. The attempt to rescue the victim was sabotaged by the Nazis' violation of "international law": "Evidently, the helpers must have tampered with the rope, on the assumption that no man can be hanged twice. They should have known that the Nazis would not recognize any such law."[74]

In contrast to this, a survivor who had mentally blocked out the executions but could not avoid registering the dead bodies the SS left hanging for at least another day kept suffering from recurring nightmares in his later life and showed signs of "survivor's guilt": "They left the bodies hanging there for days to teach us a lesson. A horrific sight that still haunts me. I have nightmares about them staring at me, asking, 'Why did you make it? Why did I end this way?'"[75]

Feelings of guilt and self-recrimination may indicate a failed attempt to recount traumatic memories. Through a narrative of guilt, survivors typically tend to make an incommunicable incident more "retellable" to others, as this is a feeling non-Holocaust victims can relate to.[76]

Several testimonies contained phrases characteristic of the normative urge to tell an "upbeat" story found in postwar settings of the United States and other Western countries. These survivors complied with their audiences' expectation that they would transform their traumatic past into a positive message for the future. At the same time, it was considered undesirable to show any hostility toward former perpetrators or to be unforgiving of their crimes.[77] As a result, we often find statements loaded with genuine contempt and anger, yet adorned with a more appeasing vocabulary, which in its violent clash with the rest of the sentence seems like an oxymoron. Survivors equally came under pressure to adapt their life stories to a mythology of martyrdom and heroism based on the notion postulated by Emanuel Ringelblum that moral integrity had prevailed in the nihilistic universe of the camps. Moreover, they were portrayed as messengers from a "different world" that eludes our comprehension.[78] The testimony of Felix G., recorded by the Fortunoff Video Archive, illustrates his inner struggle to cope with the traumatic experiences and their psychological repercussions, the disdain for the Nazi atrocities that caused them, and the urge to satisfy external expectations to formulate a heroic, positive narrative: "I pitied the SS for their stupidity, for doing incomprehensible things. Hanging was a recreation to them, revolting. It was a world of folly and absurdity. I was a witness to this different universe. The Germans had taken everything except our inner liberty of judgement. I never cried in camps. I am no longer capable of shedding tears because of the camps!"[79]

Similarly, having delineated his total impotence in the face of the renewed hanging of the first victim, the survivor Ernest Nives stressed how, contrary to the Nazis, the prisoners had succeeded in retaining their humanity: "But we still did not crack, the essential victory over the SS was being civilized, unlike the Germans."[80]

THE FORMATION OF A LEGENDARY COMPLEX: A HEROIC SPEECH AT THE GALLOWS

In response to the humiliation and dehumanization effected by the first execution, certain survivors subliminally started to construct a legendary complex which to them became an alternative reality they firmly believed in. Other former prisoners, typically those with repressed memories, began to embed the legend into their own narratives. In extreme situations, in which humans feel overpowered, impotent, and exposed to a merciless, hostile, and unpredictable outside world, a group may construct a mental counterbalance by recounting as a true event what they *hoped* would have happened, but that never actually did happen.[81] For the Blechhammer inmates, this event possibly was a speech by the victim(s), relaying various messages in different languages. Some were patriotic and even anti-German, others encouraging or very personal. As the speeches were related in so many variants and attributed to several prisoners, some or all might have been fictional. In the following, an attempt is made to show the broad spectrum of memories and possible ways of interpreting them without questioning the truth they doubtless held for the survivors.

The overwhelming majority of the speech's patriotic versions referred to the Netherlands, and most contained anti-German elements as well. The survivors who integrated them into their testimonies were all Dutch Jews. The speech was delivered either before the first hanging attempt or when the broken rope was replaced. Two testimonies given during a pretrial investigation in 1976, in which the German prosecution specifically asked for information about Tom Mix, recounted a direct verbal and physical confrontation of the victim with this person. The following dialogues may therefore be the result of the effect known as "witness contamination," the motivational distortion of memories intended to support other witnesses or investigators, or of false memories produced by leading questions.[82] "The boy cried, 'Cheer up, boys, long live the Queen!' As I said before, 'Tom Mix' had a good command of Dutch, and I had the impression that he understood the boy's words. 'Tom Mix' leaped towards the gallows, and I saw how he knocked over the chair; in the same instance the rope snapped."[83]

"After the first hanging, he called out, 'Dutch comrades, have a safe trip back home!', then 'Tom Mix' said, 'Shut up, bloody git!' He and the prisoners kicked off the chair and he suffocated."[84]

A third testimony, given between 1945 and 1947, posited a more daring conversation between the victim and the camp leader. Interestingly, the incident of the broken rope was omitted: "Before the hanging he said, 'Boys, I hope you have a safe trip back to Holland!' 'Shut up,' the *Obersturmführer* cried. He answered, 'Die!', having nothing to fear anymore."[85]

An exceptional Zionist variant of the speech was rendered in the video testimony of a former Polish Jewish prisoner who had emigrated to the United States: "They was hanging a guy and he fell down two or three times, he fell down, the rope slipped off or whatever, but they still hanged him. I'll never forget the words what he said, '*Kinderlakh* (kids), I'm just going *haym* (home), we should have a *Yiddishe medine* (a Jewish State).'"[86]

The way he mixed Yiddish words with English may be regarded as typical of the postwar "multi-glossic" and no longer multilingual usage of the Yiddish language. A shift to Yiddish in testimony indicates that the survivor intended to emphasize the symbolic value of the language rather than convey any relevant information. Sometimes Yiddish is deliberately used to commemorate those native speakers who perished or to enact one's Jewishness.[87] Switching to other languages during an interview also implies that the survivor is literally going back to another time of his life in the past.[88]

Two purely anti-German speeches were attributed to the victims of later hangings by former Polish and Belgian Jewish inmates. The first was allegedly delivered by a Polish Jewish prisoner named Katz: "He behaved heroically, as he called out loud and in German while standing by the gallows, 'Comrades, look at me, I am dying here as an innocent, but the Germans have lost the war and will soon be brought to the gallows themselves.'"[89]

The second speech given by one of the victims during the "hanging of three" also included an obligation to commemorate and to testify, rendering the prisoners' death more meaningful: "One said, 'Brothers, bear witness and speak the truth. Hitler and the German nation will be damned forever. I love you, brothers!'"[90]

All these speeches may be subsumed as "heroic memories," diametrically opposed to what Langer defined as "unheroic memories." The survivors who implanted this legendary complex into their life stories mentally converted humiliation into courage and impotence into triumph. A peculiar addition was the patriotic element predominantly found in the testimonies of Dutch Jews who had resettled in the Netherlands after the war. Apparently they felt a need to affirm their allegiance to their country of origin and the royal family, while at the same time underlining that they had not been mere victims, but part of a joint resistance effort against the German oppressors. Along the same lines, the anti-German speeches seemed to express the hope of retaliation against the Nazis and that the hanging of their fellow comrade would be avenged by the Allies. Patriotism was completely absent from Polish Jewish testimonies, which is probably why they fell back on anti-Nazi or Zionist speeches.

Testimony rendering nonpatriotic speeches either contained a universally encouraging phrase, in part identical with the those found in the patriotic accounts, or they assured the prisoners that the war would soon end. In the first category, the sentence "Have a safe trip back home" was used the most frequently, along with "Cheer up."[91] Both of these rather trivial lines may not seem very appropriate as someone's last words before an execution; however, the survivors imbued them with a special meaning: "Before the second hanging the boy cried, 'Have a safe trip back home, comrades!' He will never return home himself—the tightening of the noose mutes his last words... words that will remain a constant memory and reminder of the unknown comrade to all of us who survived."[92]

The victim, whose life was about to be taken, thus appeared to convey a twofold message. First, he reassured his fellow prisoners that they would eventually survive the concentration camps and return to their old lives. This kind of wishful thinking was likely connected to the secret hopes and daydreams of many a prisoner, despite the unbearably cruel reality surrounding them.[93] Second, and most important for postwar memories, his words either seemed to reinforce the "guilt" of having survived or served to relieve survivors of that very guilt. The latter effect is illustrated by the following testimony from a Dutch survivor, who stressed that the victim had wished them well for their future in liberty without any reproach or envy: "Before he died, Rafaels gave a speech, despite having been ordered to stay silent. He wished us a speedy liberation and a happy reunion with our families."[94]

A highly unusual version of the speech that did not fit into the context of the others was rendered in Ernest Koenig's autobiography. The victim's last words allegedly were, "Say hello to my mother!"[95] As the author had almost become the victim of a lynching himself, he might have put the words into the condemned prisoner's mouth that had been on his own mind then.

To others, the victim's speech struck a different chord, namely that of the imminent ending of the war and liberation. The following variant was attributed to one of the three prisoners hanged at the same time. It becomes obvious how the message conveying hope of liberation is given more credibility in the form of the speech. "The victim cried out, 'The war will soon be over!' We believed him."[96]

In an additional paragraph following his description of the first hanging, the survivor John Steiner aggregated a plethora of possible versions in a seemingly inexorable succession of executions of victims, who all gave heroic, heartening speeches: "Almost every Sunday, these cruel and unskilled hangings took place.... The condemned comrades died heroically, without complaining or whining (in contrast to some of the major war criminals hanged in Nuremberg). Before being hanged, some of the comrades shouted encouragement to us: 'Persevere, it will not last forever... be courageous... keep your heads up, don't despair... don't forget us.' These young men died as true heroes."[97]

Despite formulating a detailed narrative of the first execution, Steiner was clearly still incapable of integrating the emerging fragments of his traumatic memories. Overwhelmed by the returning "split-off" memories, it appeared to him that there had been an interminable routine of "failed" hangings.[98] The flow of disjointed trauma fragments was stopped short by the imperative to tell a "positive" story. His obscured recall of numerous, faceless victims dying in agony was thus transformed into an account of "heroes," whose bravery at the gallows elevated them above the "whining" Nazi perpetrators.

Juxtaposed with the legendary complex of "heroic memories," there remained an almost equal number of recollections reflecting "unheroic" hanging scenarios.[99] The victim was described as intimidated, scared, and helpless.[100] Some survivors recalled that instead of giving a daring speech, he had "begged for mercy."[101] Others emphasized that he had been very quiet, possibly even sedated, and had died "without uttering a sound."[102] Survivors reporting such bleak variants of the execution seem to have coped better with the traumatic experience. They felt no need to construct an "uplifting" story but were able to integrate the shocking event into their narratives. There is an obvious link between the trauma of the "failed" hanging and the belief in a heroic speech. Therefore, neither of the two survivors aware of the "trick" used that element of the speech in their accounts.[103]

THE IMPORTANCE OF YOM KIPPUR

The highest Jewish holiday, Yom Kippur, the Day of Atonement, was certainly not chosen at random by the SS for staging the first and most traumatic hanging. Although only a few prisoners were observant Jews, most of their nonpracticing comrades were aware of the holiday and its meaning.[104] On this day, when according to Scripture the sins of the repentant are forgiven and it is decided whether they will be "written into the Book of Life" or not (Leviticus 16:30), the execution scenario resembled a symbolic act of "divine judgment." Survivors often underscored the victim's innocence by comparing him to a child and by pointing out that he had been a good person, who was "as docile as a lamb." When the rope broke, there was a sudden chance that his life would be preserved. By not granting him any mercy, the SS literally put themselves in the place of the biblical God: a God who failed to intervene. Therefore, the hanging led some of the religious prisoners to doubt the divine existence: "When we returned from the roll call, I passed by a barrack in front of which a heated debate went on. They were religious Jews who had spent the day fasting as good as they could, for it was Yom Kippur, the Day of Atonement. The Nazis had deliberately chosen this day for the execution. The people were crying: 'Where is God? Where is God? How can he allow this to happen? Is there a God? If he lets this happen, is it a proof of his weakness, or of his indifference, or of his non-existence?'"[105]

The survivor Dr. Alfred Meier wrote a poem about the first execution in which Yom Kippur was the central thread. He elaborated on the existential questions arising from the Day of Atonement in a concentration camp setting, when none of the prisoners could be sure to survive the next day or even the next hour, and they reflected on the obscure fate of their next of kin. In this pensive mood, the sight of the gallows by itself already tore apart their "heart and mind" with pain. The execution violently disrupted their inner, spiritual dialogue. The author also emphasized the innocence of the victim, whose only "crime" had been his Jewishness, and whose suffering was representative of that of all other prisoners. Although the breaking of the rope was omitted, he also included a nonpatriotic variant of the speech that was fused with the religious component of the prayer for the dead:

> "*Kommt Kameraden gut nach Haus*" ("*Comrades, have a save trip back home*")
> *Das Schma Jisroel alsdann;* (*followed by the Sh'ma Yisrael;*)

Kein Laut der Klage, dann ist's aus. (No sound of woe, then it is over.)
O, dass ein Gott dies ansehen kann. (Oh, that a God can watch this.)

Instead of recounting a legal dispute between the prisoners and the camp leader, Meier had the biblical God abstain from saving the victim on the Day of Judgment. The poem seems to reflect the characteristics of Langer's "diminished self" in the aggravated state of theological, not merely psychological, crisis:[106]

Nur langsam dann der Platz sich leert, (The yard empties only slowly,)
Das Herz ist krank von Leid, (The heart is sick with pain,)
Was dieser Tag an Weh beschert, (How much woe this day held for us,)
Gerichtstag war, Jom Kippur heut. (It was Judgement Day, Yom Kippur today.)[107]

Aside from a handful of functionary prisoners who worked in the camp office (and clandestine "chroniclers of the Holocaust"), most inmates had no access to calendars and were consequently left with "no sense of time." The prohibition against reading and writing also disrupted the traditional practice of literate societies of marking days and keeping a register of events. Religious Jews nevertheless managed to keep track of the holidays. Apart from the spiritual connotation, high holidays such as Yom Kippur thus served as a point of reference also to nonobservant Jewish prisoners when it came to dating important events in the camp. When asked for the date of the second execution, many survivors counted onward from the last fixed date they knew, Yom Kippur. Occasionally they placed both executions on this day. Sometimes other holidays were mentioned instead, such as Rosh Hashanah or even Christmas.[108] During the temporary, enforced "illiteracy" of the Holocaust, Jewish inmates fell back on a different form of mnemonic techniques typically found in cultural settings that bar access to writing, in which religious holidays or natural cycles are used to define times and events.[109]

THE HANGING OF THREE PRISONERS

Most testimonies on the presumed second public execution corroborated a similar course of events. Two prisoners picked up a piece of wire on the construction site after an air raid, intending to use it as a shoelace, a belt, or a handle for their food bowls. They were caught, and an SS man forwarded a report to Berlin. When their Kapo tried to defend them, he was accused of being an accessory to sabotage. All three were taken to Auschwitz and returned one or two weeks later to be hanged in Blechhammer. None of the survivors gave a specific date for the executions. Some were convinced they had been carried out on Yom Kippur; according to others it had been on a Saturday in

October or November.¹¹⁰ The British POW George Didcock noted in his diary that two prisoners were hanged on October 14, 1944. This was presumably the date of the second execution.¹¹¹

As during the first hanging, the SS perpetrators were seldom identified, as the prisoners focused on the condemned. One survivor stated that the execution had been supervised by the leader of the Political Department, Schmidt. Another thought it had been Adolf Schindler, the head of the crematorium.¹¹² The first camp leader, Otto Brossmann, reportedly oversaw the hangings, indicating that they took place before the change of leadership in early November.¹¹³

The child survivor Kalman Landau (Niwka, Upper Silesia, 1928) was the only one to visually reframe the hanging, in a drawing made in a children's home in Switzerland in summer 1945. His still very childlike artistic style clashes violently with the motif of the execution scene. He depicted second-in-command Olejak reading out the verdict in the foreground. Landau rendered a minute description of the peculiar type of gallows used in Blechhammer. It was a makeshift construction made out of two concrete pillars like the ones used in the camp wall and a steel rail. Only one other survivor recalled this important detail.¹¹⁴ The three condemned prisoners stood on chairs placed

Kalman Landau's depiction of the hanging of three prisoners in Blechhammer in 1944. (*Source*: AfZ, ETH Zurich, Kalman Landau, *3 Heftlinge ferurteilt zum Galgen*, drawing, 1945, S Biographien und Sachthemen/78)

on tables. The hanging scene nevertheless stays in the background, and only one of the prisoners, possibly the Kapo, has distinct features. The other two victims are hardly distinguishable.[115]

The rest of the testimonies also remained vague about the other two victims' identities. The alleged nationalities attributed to them ranged from Dutch, Belgian, or Polish, to Turkish. Among the corroborated names were Izak Cohen, Napkowski, and Tuchschneider or Tuchenschneider from Będzin.[116] Most survivors were nevertheless certain that the Kapo executed with them had been a French Jewish lawyer from Paris named Roger Ochshorn, Oxhoorn, Oxon, or Ochs, and many provided details on his personality and appearance, describing him as a "charming guy" and a "noble person."[117] In stark contrast to the relative anonymity of the two other victims, the Kapo was portrayed as a sort of a superstar: "Ochsen, a friend of mine, he was French and a real enigma. Tall, blond, handsome, he could have been an actor, but he was a lawyer."[118] Unlike the functionary prisoners who volunteered as helpers during the executions, the French Kapo was associated with virtues such as solidarity and courage. Once again, the survivors utilized alleged names, personality traits, and episodes from that person's life to make the "tragedy" more tellable.[119]

Unlike for the first hanging, most prisoners seemed to have been aware of the impending executions and the transfer of the three men to Auschwitz for interrogation. When the gallows were set up, they were mentally prepared to face a "new nightmare," as the survivor Nathan Prochownik put it. The hangings were carried out in an unspectacular fashion, and there were few detailed descriptions. In both video testimony and his autobiography, Prochownik emphasized the rational calmness of the Kapo at the gallows, as opposed to the two other, allegedly Sephardic, prisoners, who turned to prayer in "apathy": "One month later, three gallows were erected. I stood in the front and saw all details of this new nightmare. All three climbed on the table, without any resistance or cry, the two others seemed apathic, Oxon was very calm and controlled. When the guards put the noose on his neck, he demanded that they place it under the Adam's apple and not above it, and they obeyed. This time no broken ropes. The bodies were left hanging for several days, they took on a violet color."[120] "The two Sephardic Jews had no idea what was going on, they were reciting the Sh'mah."[121]

After the war, a surviving father and his sons related the Kapo's story to the French Féderation des Internés, Resistants et Deportés in Paris. This was the beginning of a veritable personality cult. His presumed Auschwitz prisoner number was reconstructed by fellow survivors tattooed at the same time he was and engraved on memorabilia, such as medals and emblems designed by a certain Dr. Uzan. They were worn by a group of Blechhammer survivors to commemorate the Kapo and his sacrifice, his attempt to save two others. Later, members of this group tried to verify the alleged prisoner number, 178284, only to find out that it had belonged to a different person. The Kapo's name showed up in neither deportation lists nor any other documents.[122]

The group then refashioned him into a universal symbol of all the nameless victims who perished in the Holocaust. This process was reminiscent of the military tradition of erecting memorials to the Unknown Soldier: "He remains a mystery, what a great symbol of the phantoms we have become, of all the anonymous numbers who died with dignity and courage."[123]

The personality cult around the Kapo ultimately spread beyond the circle of Blechhammer survivors. Julian Hirshfeld, who had no connection to the camp, received a button cover with the Kapo's presumed prisoner number in a displaced persons' camp in Paris. He later stated that it had been made in honor of a certain Charles Oschkor, who had given his life to save two comrades.[124] Until the 1970s, a "heroic" narrative was the hallmark of the way the war was commemorated in France, and Jews were not perceived as victims unless they had been involved in resistance activities. Jewish Holocaust survivors therefore adapted their remembrances to this paradigm.[125]

The Kapo's special commemoration as a unifying symbol notwithstanding, it is unclear whether the legendary "hanging of three" really took place in this way, or whether it was the result of a collective mythmaking process.[126] The war diary of the British POW Didcock, who noted down the execution on the day after it was carried out, conspicuously restricts the hangings to two prisoners at the same time.[127] As the two other victims could barely be described by the majority of survivors, it might be possible that there was only one prisoner at the gallows, and the Kapo was then hanged along with him.

POSSIBLE ADDITIONAL HANGINGS

The testimonies corroborating further executions were extremely conflicting and provided scanty details. Often the information was restricted to estimates of the number of possible hangings. These ranged from three to fifty.[128] In the most extreme version, fourteen prisoners were allegedly hanged in one night during a penal roll call as retribution for the murder of a German general.[129] The stating of much higher numbers than seem plausible is a phenomenon often found in survivor testimonies. To Dori Laub, this symbolizes the massive impact an event had on the witnesses. Beyond factual accuracy, such apparent memory failures most disturbingly convey to us the shattering effects of exposure to acts of extreme violence.[130]

A third execution of one or more prisoners for an escape attempt was corroborated by four survivor testimonies and a judicial interview by the second-in-command, Karl Czapla. Henri Kichka, who had only mentioned the hanging of three prisoners in his video testimony in 1994, delineated two more executions in an autobiography penned twenty years later. Next to the hanging with the snapped rope, he described how an escapee who was caught was made to stand on the assembly court with a card around his neck reading, "I am back again." Before being hanged, he had to crawl on all fours, crying "I am back again," until he fainted.¹³¹

The child survivor Walter Spitzer recalled that three prisoners were hanged for an escape attempt. One of them died very slowly, as his neck did not break, and he strangled in a seemingly endless agony.¹³² A prisoner's suffering due to slipped gallows was confirmed by other testimony.¹³³ A third witness stated that two prisoners had been hanged for the escape of three others on a truck. The executions took place during a penal roll call that lasted for two days.¹³⁴ Another survivor's testimony confirmed the hanging of one escapee without providing any further information, and Czapla's interview supported the hanging of two for the same reason.¹³⁵

Six testimonies described the hanging of a single prisoner for pilfering. This incident could be identical to the fourth execution of December 2, 1944, noted by British POW Didcock in his diary.¹³⁶ Four witnesses unanimously stated that the victim had been a certain Srulek Katz from Katowice. He was accused of sabotage for having picked up a piece of wire he used as a shoelace.¹³⁷ According to one of the testimonies, the victim allegedly gave a daring, anti-German speech by the gallows.¹³⁸ Heinrich Demerer confirmed the hanging of a Polish Jew for pilfering wire in his postwar autobiography. He remembered that the SS had whipped prisoners who tried to turn their faces away shortly before the execution.¹³⁹ A sixth testimony by Kurt Klappholz corroborated the hanging of a prisoner for pilfering wire to make a handle for his bowl. Klappholz particularly stressed the fact that the victim had been a Bulgarian deported from France and had been the first Sephardic Jew in the camp, who, unable to speak the common vernacular Yiddish, could not make himself understood.¹⁴⁰

In his autobiography, Maurice Obréjan listed two more hangings that were not confirmed by anyone else. He might have confused these incidents with executions in other camps. Both victims were allegedly punished for complaining about the conditions in the camp. The first one stepped forward during a Red Cross inspection, and the second wrote a letter to the Hungarian ambassador.¹⁴¹ Only one other testimony corroborated the hanging of a prisoner for pilfering wire immediately after a Red Cross inspection, which could have been scheduled on December 2, 1944, the date of the presumed fourth execution.¹⁴²

REPRESSED MEMORIES VERSUS THE OBLIGATION TO BEAR WITNESS

Often the brain's first reaction to traumatic events is to erect a barrier against the overwhelming information, rendering our psychological abilities ineffective. Trauma predominantly interferes with the process of forming a conscious, verbal narrative of an experience, thus preventing survivors from becoming "witnesses to their own story."

Traumatic episodes are prone to become disconnected from memory by defense mechanisms such as amnesia, denial, splitting, derealization, and depersonalization. The knowledge of the trauma nevertheless lingers on in the subconscious, but it is usually fragmented and difficult to retrieve coherently. Unwanted memories may also be actively inhibited. The longer traumatic memories in a repressed state remain untold, the more distorted they will become.[143]

At a certain time in their lives, Blechhammer survivors with repressed memories of the hangings felt compelled to testify about their experiences in the camp, either because they appeared as witnesses at a trial or were responding to the effects of unsettling sociopolitical developments, such as the rise of Holocaust deniers. They were faced with a twofold dilemma. First, the memories they had blocked from their consciousness tended to surface in the form of isolated fragments or split-offs that were difficult to integrate into a comprehensive narrative. Second, they had to come to terms with the traumatizing effects of confronting the "demons of the past."

During the demanding process of retrieving traumatic memories for the sake of bearing witness, survivors were susceptible to incorporating information provided by other former prisoners into their narratives or to replacing their fragmentary memories with those of others. While it is normal that memories be continually revised, those with vague or missing recollections will compensate for their deficits with "conformist group memory." Fellow survivors were regarded as a highly credible source, and adopting their memories, including the legendary complexes involved, rendered their own accounts more "acceptable."[144] Implanting the memories of others might also have been a compromise between being able to tell a conformist narrative to an audience and not having to confront the trauma. These survivors did not fully "own" their stories, and they only partly abandoned the realm of silence of many decades that had become "a fated exile, a home, a destination, and a binding oath."[145]

Testimonies of this kind rarely delineate the hangings concisely, but instead focus on situations and routines not directly linked to them, thereby circumventing the traumatizing memories as such.

The popular actor and Blechhammer survivor Robert Clary only began to speak about his experiences in 1980, with the intention of countering Holocaust denial and neo-Nazism, and he joined the Holocaust Education Program of the Wiesenthal Center. When he gave video testimony to the Shoah Visual History Archive in 1994, he had told his story to schoolchildren numerous times before. He elaborated more on the second hanging, recounting how two prisoners pilfered wire and were executed with their "Belgian" Kapo. However, he did not focus on the "heroic" Kapo but on the SS man Tom Mix, whom he blamed for maltreating and killing the condemned prisoners. While the hangings remained peripheral to his account, the general personality, habits, and crimes of this particular SS man gained in importance. Clary seems to have had poor recall of the first hanging and chiefly reiterated that it had been preceded by a two-hour-long speech, and that the body had been left hanging all night. He mentioned numerous other hangings without describing them. Traumatic memories abruptly started to interfere with the "conformist" storyline as Clary recounted how he had to watch the bodies of the hanged while on night guard duty: "Suddenly, there were corpses, I don't want to see that, I'm frightened, Mama!"[146]

In his autobiography, published seven years later, Clary added more details to the first hanging but still omitted central features, such as the breaking of the rope, Yom Kippur, and the speech. He nevertheless addressed the traumatic impact of this hanging: "I stared with horror as the man's hands and feet were bound. He was lifted onto a stool and the noose was put around his neck. The stool was kicked out from under him. A faint moan came from his throat the moment before his neck snapped.... That was the first time I saw it happen, and the shock was unbearable. I couldn't sleep that night, and for days afterwards my mind kept replaying the horror of the hanging."[147]

Tom Mix continued to be at the center of his description of the second hanging. The number of hanged prisoners was increased to four. He added some character traits about the Kapo but was still unable to render his name and did not portray him as a "hero": "Tom Mix ranted at us that these four dirty Jews had better be a lesson to all of us not to steal German property, or we would wind up like them on the scaffold. Standing there, we endured his abuse for two hours and then saw the stools being kicked out from under the feet of the men. That particular Kapo, unlike Goldberg, was loved by everyone. It broke our hearts to see this gentle man hanged."[148]

A similar example of implanted memories is Stanley B.'s version of the first hanging. He likewise gave few details on the hanging itself and did not include the speech. He mentioned that he had no personal recollections of the executions and that he had used a friend's memories instead. Trauma fragments nonetheless penetrated the narrative, when Stanley indicated that he had seen the rope breaking *three* times: "The picture of this hanging, his falling down three times, is still on my mind, a horrible experience."[149]

A phenomenon often found in late testimonies and predominantly affecting survivors with repressed memories is that the (tainted) features of several different executions were mingled into a single event. Memory fragments of their own coalesced with "group memories," relating the gist of the hangings disjointed from the normal succession of events. Such a chronological compression of incidents usually indicates that a collective process of mythmaking is at work. The two "legendary" victims, the Dutch boy and the Kapo, became unifying symbols of all other hanged prisoners.[150]

Kurt Baum had repressed his memories of the camps for over forty years in order to be able to start a new life. Then, aware of "forces trying to rewrite history," he felt compelled to speak about his experiences. In his first video testimony of 1988, he suddenly brought up the topic of the hangings himself but was still incapable of rendering a precise account. He linked the hangings to the selections for Auschwitz held during roll calls, stressing that the victims had been executed for being unfit for work.

INTERVIEWER: "How long did you stay in Blechhammer?"
KURT BAUM: Yes, I can recall specifically, and I want to mention a couple more things about the camps. Roll calls were an additional torture after ten hours of work. Frequently after a roll call, a few numbers were read, and we had executions right on the roll call. And we were supposed to watch while some poor comrade was executed by hanging for something that he supposedly did . . . like he refused to obey orders. Usually, he refused to obey orders because he collapsed, he couldn't work anymore. And so, he was reported, and a few days later his number came back from HQ, execute him to state an example.[151]

Nine years later, he had incorporated a combined version of the hanging of three prisoners and the breaking of the rope in his narrative, while still referring to inmates dying of exhaustion. Most of the "conformist group memory" was derived from the first hanging in ample detail, yet without the heroic speech. He embedded the implanted memories into two camp routines, the march back from work and the distribution of the evening soup:

> When you came back from work to assembly square, sometimes people did not make it back from work, and I saw a few executions and, somewhere, we had a surprise, and there was one gallows, two gallows, three gallows standing there, right in the center of the assembly square. And the camp commander would read some numbers, and then he would . . . a prisoner would come to the center, and then he would read some trumped up, ridiculous charges about sabotage or whatever it may be, and then the prisoner would be executed by hanging. . . . One day, a hanging took place of three people, and the prisoner stood on the stool, the stool was kicked away, and the rope broke. And in the Middle Ages, this was considered a God's judgement, you know, the man wasn't meant to go, he's going free, but not in Blechhammer. The SS commander got very mad and sent another guard to the kitchen, and he took about five minutes, the guy came back with a rope about that thick, and the man was executed a second time. This time the rope did not break, and we had to march by him, and then we had our soup distribution and our bread distribution.[152]

In his autobiography published in 2004, the artist Walter Spitzer compressed the key elements of the first and second hanging even more. He made the French Kapo plead for the life of the Dutch boy to prevent him from being hanged anew. At the end of the account, Spitzer pointed out that he had not been able to eat or sleep after witnessing the hangings, and that he had tried to block images of the executions from his mind with the help of recollections from his childhood, to "chase away from my spirit at any cost what I had seen a few hours earlier." Most aspects of the two "conformist" legendary complexes were represented:

A young Dutchman climbed on the chair. In a firm voice he wished us "good luck" and a safe trip back home in German. The noose was put on his neck, the chair was kicked away and, oh wonder, the rope broke. The Dutchman fell violently on the ground, his hands tied behind his back. The SS started all over again. The rope broke a second time. In this moment, a prisoner named Oxhoorn stepped forward: "I'm a barrister from Paris. An international law stipulates that a broken rope means the convict must be pardoned." The SS ridiculed him, told him to come, then attached the noose around his neck, and both were hanged. I was petrified, my throat was tight, I was on the brink of fainting, horrified to see someone executed I knew personally—I made his portrait he had sent to his wife in France.[153]

THE REFUSAL TO BECOME A WITNESS

a. Not Witnessing as an Act of Self-Preservation

Several inmates deliberately decided that they did not want to become witnesses to the atrocities committed in the camp. During their internment, they developed various strategies to avoid monitoring disturbing scenes. Active nonwitnessing partly spared them the process of repressing painful memories afterward, but it certainly did not completely exclude them from it. Such prisoners were aware that there had been one or more hangings, but they were unable or unwilling to recall the events. Instead, they gave evasive explanations for their alleged absence: "There were two hangings, I forgot about the details, perhaps more. I could skip such things quite often as I had to arrange the deputy Jewish elder's stamp collection."[154]

"I heard there were other executions [in addition to the first one], as I was sometimes called out to the factory out of hours, I might not have been in the camp on such occasions."[155]

Others, like Ben Fainer, had blocked out violent scenes from their minds a long time before the start of public executions. Fainer stated that he had initially done this in order not to rob the victims of their dignity and added that, in retrospect, he realized he had also tried to preserve his own humanity. In the next sentence, he was nevertheless confronted with the emergence of his numbed "impromtu [sic] self" of the camp.[156] Having grown more and more indifferent to the suffering of others, he had ultimately stopped turning away from cruelties, as this would only have "wasted energy." In search of an explanation for his lack of compassion, he concluded that "maybe your heart has to harden in order to survive." Fainer gave no description of the hangings but repeatedly stressed how the images of the dead bodies still haunted him, provoking feelings of guilt for having survived. In the end, his decision to ignore the executions did not spare him from suffering mental trauma.[157] Similarly, Raphael Montezinos, who had consciously witnessed the first hanging and could provide details of it in his testimony, decided to look away during the following execution. In his memory, the incident he had avoided witnessing was transformed into something even more terrible. In the end, he was convinced that seven prisoners had been hanged at the same time on Yom Kippur.[158]

The child survivor Felix Weinberg likewise applied a mental technique to keep away disturbing memories, but the unexpected snapping of the rope during the first execution suddenly caught his attention. Almost seventy years later, he wrote about the execution in a seemingly very detached, emotionally uninvolved way. However, the fact that he was convinced that the rope had snapped twice, and that the prisoner was hanged three times, reflects the deep traumatic impact the event had on him: "I tried my usual device again of blanking my mind—looking without seeing or registering—but was disturbed by a gasp from the assembled crowd when the rope snapped, and the man fell on the stage. Incredibly, the entire action was replayed for a second time, with the same result.... On the third attempt, with a new rope, the poor man died at last."[159]

Siegfried Parsser unsuccessfully tried to avoid watching the hangings by standing in the back row. The SS pulled him out and dragged him to the front, forcing him to witness the execution with open eyes and a smiling face. As a result of this traumatic and humiliating experience, he remained incapable of giving an account of the execution in later life.[160]

b. Not Witnessing Out of Resistance

A fundamentally different reason prisoners refused to witness the executions was to protest against the SS and to show their solidarity with the victims. The outstanding incident described in the following provides the most congruent testimonies but seems to never have been integrated into the collective group memory. Therefore, only a minority of survivors referred to it, mainly those who were active participants in the protest, and a few who misunderstood, and consequently misremembered, what had happened. It must have been during the final preparations for the second hanging that a group of prisoners, among them Czech survivors of the liquidated Auschwitz family camp, made a brave stand against the SS. When the verdict was read out, they left the assembly court to openly protest against the execution, thereby provoking reprisals by the SS.[161] A survivor recalled: "As a sign of protest, we tried to leave the courtyard, but then the guards started shooting in the air."[162]

Some managed to return to their barracks, while others in the crowd tried to move away from the gallows, causing turmoil among the assembled men. The SS guards began to shoot into the barracks to drive the prisoners out by force. A witness stated that one prisoner had been shot in this way. Others claimed the SS had not aimed at them and nobody had been hurt.[163]

It is astonishing that this truly courageous act of resistance was misinterpreted for cowardice by individual prisoners, who thought the others had "stolen themselves away," as they could not bear to witness the execution. Memories of the ensuing shootings became fused with those of the execution the inmates were forced to watch immediately afterward. Thus, a survivor testified that the prisoners taken out of the barracks had been beaten by the SS and at least one of them had been hanged as well.[164] According to two testimonies, the SS fired shots at the bodies of the hanged.[165] Others reduced the shootings to disciplinary measures intended to keep the prisoners standing on parade.[166] In the memory of one prisoner, the SS started to shoot after the rope had broken during the first execution. In his opinion, this was done to prevent an uprising, but the prisoners all remained quiet.[167]

The unrest among the prisoners caused by the protesting group trying to push away from the main body and the SS guards' fierce reaction to it were misconstrued as mass hysteria and were even perceived as a threat to their lives by some inmates, who obviously did not comprehend the general context of the scene. They were led to believe the SS would murder all inmates.[168] One of these witnesses, Ernest Koenig, had narrowly escaped from a lynching by the works police and the SS only weeks before the execution. The fear of death experienced then must have overwhelmed him at the sight of the gallows. In a general remark on hangings, he stressed that the worst moments were the minutes before a person was put to death who would have had a rich and fulfilling life still ahead of him. In his mind, the purpose of public executions was the constant renewal of terror in the prisoners.[169] "It seemed as if the gallows had only been set up to distract our attention and they wanted to shoot us, as the machine guns on top of the watchtowers were turned in semicircles. Somewhere in the background, one group pushed against another, who pushed back in return. The sound of the trampling feet caused by their motion grew louder, giving those who stood in the front and at the sides the impression that one group was being hurt. But the panic that had broken out, ebbed down."[170]

Perhaps owing to the fact that this genuinely heroic act was only fully understood by the minority of prisoners involved in it, it was either misrepresented or missing in most testimonies. Thus, instead of drawing on this event, most survivors preferred to incorporate a different story of heroism and resistance, ultimately formed into a collective legendary complex, into their own memories.

THE FEMALE PRISONERS

Detained in a secluded camp section, the women of Blechhammer had only clandestine contacts with their male relatives, spouses, or friends through the wire. Only male functionary prisoners working in the camp and office staff regularly met with the female inmates. The women themselves were not subjected to public punishments but were forced to watch those of the men from their enclosed compound. Most female survivors claimed that the SS had ordered them to watch the executions from their camp. However, testimonies rarely went into details on individual hangings, but rather emphasized the repeated occurrence of executions. To a female survivor it even seemed that there had been a hanging "every day."[171] The women appeared uninformed about the precise circumstances of the executions. The majority were unable to state under which allegations the prisoners had been hanged. Contrary to the men, they frequently stressed that the Germans had hanged someone "to have fun."[172]

Only two of the women rendered accounts from which basic elements of the executions described by male survivors were identifiable. In her video testimony, Esther Drexler indicated her disinclination to witness the public punishments of the men. She then related an unusual encounter with an SS man before the first hanging without going into more detail about the actual event: "I don't know how they knew it's Yom Kippur, I don't know. And once a German came into the hut, the house, to the room where I was sleeping, and he said, 'I know the day today, it's Yom Kippur, but one will go, [points her finger upwards] they will hang somebody.'"[173]

The second testimony, by Helen Pinczewski, was equally restricted to information regarding the context of the hanging of one prisoner, possibly that of Katz, but omitted the execution as such. Following a general description of the men's proneness to sores caused by missing shoelaces on their clogs, the account stated that a prisoner was executed for using a piece of wire as a shoelace, and the female inmates had to watch.[174]

The women's assumed ignorance might have been partly due to their remoteness from the men's camp and the resulting restricted flow of information, but it also became strikingly apparent that they tended to avoid witnessing the executions. This process was assisted by the spatial distance of the gallows from the female prisoners' barracks. It also seems unlikely that the women were subjected to the same scrutiny as the men. During the hangings, the SS men must have gathered in front of the gallows rather than supervised the female inmates, and they probably did not risk punishment for not watching. One female survivor apparently had repressed all memories of the executions and claimed that the women had not been allowed to leave their barracks during such times.[175] Another woman stressed that she had been afraid of the hangings, and that she had first been confronted with the sight of dead bodies after the evacuation in Bergen-Belsen.[176]

To some, the suffering of the male prisoners, who were often their next of kin, generally weighed heavier than their own, and the "moral injustice" of having to witness such atrocities filled them with bitterness.[177] The understating of female suffering and the women's refusal to witness the hangings illustrate the adjustment of testimony to social expectations of "appropriate" gender behavior. Rendering a concise account of the atrocities seemingly did not fit into the typical roles attributed to women at the time, which were largely centered around the ideals of "mothers" and "caregivers."[178]

It is noteworthy that the female survivors obviously remained excluded from the legendary complexes reproduced in the testimonies of most men. And they made no effort to complete their missing or repressed memories with episodes derived from the pool of collective group memories created, shared, and dominated by the male survivors. The only exception is the testimony of Rachel Brukner Frydrych, whose husband was a former prisoner in Blechhammer as well. Her account of the executions resembles those of the male survivors and features the two "signature" hangings of the Dutchman, whose rope snapped, and the two prisoners and their Kapo. The fact that she quoted dialogue between the Jewish elder Demerer and the SS camp leader at the gallows, which she could not possibly have heard from the women's enclosure herself, further hardens the assumption that her testimony was largely based on the memories of her husband.[179]

10

"A CYNICAL JOKE"

Enforced Theatrical and Musical Performances

THE CAMP THEATER

Shortly after the start of his tenure in November 1944, the new camp leader Kurt Klipp ordered the establishment of a camp theater.[1] Enforced theatrical performances were commonplace in concentration camps. They were meant to convey a false sense of "normality" to the outside world and were also intended to lower the risk of insurgencies by offering some light relief to the prisoners.[2] Following the replacement of SS guards with Wehrmacht soldiers and ethnic German auxiliaries toward the end of the war, entertainment grew in importance to create comradeship.[3] When public theaters were closed in fall 1944, the SS increasingly relied on camp performances.[4]

Klipp's deputy Karl Czapla, who portrayed himself as a great connoisseur of the arts, directed the theater. He even made the prisoners believe that he had been an art critic for a local Silesian newspaper, when in fact he had merely managed the subscriptions.[5] His overeagerness to enact his alleged cultural "superiority" was typical of many SS men.[6]

The prisoners had ambivalent feelings about the theater. To the child survivor Israel Rosengarten, the staging of performances for people who were on the brink of death was nothing but humiliating:

> Overall, this cabaret was an unspeakably misplaced, outrageous, terribly cynical joke, of course. We were forced to participate in order to feel good, to have a little, miserable party.... No one in the camp objected to humor in general; each opportunity for making fun of somebody was welcomed.... However, many attending

the cabaret were in a worse shape than myself. They were mortally ill and could not stand straight, were shaky and about to die.... We had all lost our families. We had no future; we had no lives. We were disillusioned by this moment signaling the last phase of our destruction.[7]

The performances invariably formed part of the SS men's "perverse logic" to maintain a self-image of being "cultured" and "civilized" while simultaneously committing atrocities.[8] This notion was underscored by the requirement to stage plays on nights following an execution. The presence of cheerful SS men, who were enjoying themselves after a hanging, was unbearable for the Jewish prisoners: "In this model camp, model feasts of murder were held, interrupted by music and theatre performances.... The first row was reserved for the *Hauptsturmbannführer* and his staff who had found it worthwhile to spend the evening among their archenemies."[9]

They could not help but identify the theater shows with the acts of violence that preceded them: "It was extraordinarily ironic for Nazi officers to enjoy the performances of the Jewish artists they intended to destroy.... The SS ensured we did not forget that we were in a Nazi concentration camp by staging much less amusing performances, usually on Sunday afternoons, which we all had to attend. Performances of flogging punishments and horror shows of executions by hanging were carried out."[10]

The psychiatrist and Holocaust survivor Viktor Frankl felt that art had been "grotesque" against the backdrop of the camps, while stressing the importance of humor in the prisoners' struggle for self-preservation.[11] Along these lines, the prisoner artists themselves were committed to helping their comrades forget their misery for awhile. They were nevertheless aware that they were part of an SS strategy to make the perpetrators appear more "humane," and that many prisoners were too exhausted to even attend the performances.[12]

The theater was set up in a barrack adjacent to the female inmates' compound. The camp electrician, Maurits Bremer, installed above the stage a searchlight of the same type that was used on the camp wall.[13] Klipp ordered the prisoners to pilfer the rest of the equipment from the OHW. They therefore smuggled out paint and bales of blackout cloth to fabricate costumes and a curtain.[14] The necessary curtain rail was stolen from the factory by concealing it in the middle of a detail of one hundred marching prisoners.[15] As in most camps, the prisoner artists were housed together in one barrack and were given leave from their work to rehearse. They also received more food.[16] They also benefited from the "entrance fee" of one cigarette per visitor. Performances were given on Saturday and Sunday nights to an audience of six to eight hundred people. A new program was put on every three or four weeks.[17] The SS men were always placed on the right side of the auditorium, and behind them sat the female inmates. The Jewish elder and the male inmates were kept on the left. Even during the performances, the prisoners were beaten by block elders attempting to restore "order." The theater therefore offered neither an opportunity to meet female prisoners, as Demerer claimed in postwar testimony, nor a respite from the camp's ubiquitous violence.[18]

The permanent cast consisted of twenty-five prisoners. The artistic director was Hartog Soep, also known as Harry Pos, who performed as an actor, singer, and dancer. Born in Amsterdam in 1916, he had been taken off a Westerbork convoy on October 16, 1942. Following internments in the Schmelt camps Sakrau and Bobrek, he came to Blechhammer on March 28, 1944. He survived several death marches to Gross-Rosen, Buchenwald, and Bissingen, until he finally managed to escape. After the war, he emigrated to New York.[19] Fellow actor Robert Clary described Harry Pos in the following way: "He was only five feet tall, even shorter than I, and he had the biggest nose I had ever seen. He would have been ugly were it not for his marvelous soft brown eyes. Out of this tiny man came a strong and beautifully trained voice. Harry, I soon learned, was the star of the camp and was admired by everybody."[20]

Klaus Wolfsohn, a clerk in the Political Department, was the technical director. The scenery was made by accomplished artists. David Brainin (Kharkiv, 1905) had studied art and choreography in Paris and became a dancer in a Russian troupe. From 1931, he specialized in stage design. Brainin was taken to Drancy in June 1942 and deported shortly thereafter.[21] His wife perished in Auschwitz. The young prisoner Walter Spitzer was overjoyed to assist Brainin in painting the scenery for a play titled *Under the Bridges of Paris*. Spitzer not only received an extra piece of bread in return but was grateful to learn from one of the "big and famous" from Paris.[22] Brainin's fate after the evacuation of January 1945 remains unclear.

Wilhelm "Bil" Spira (Vienna, 1913–Puteaux, Paris, 1999) had made his debut as a stage designer in the anti-fascist ABC (short for Alsergrund Brettl City) Cabaret troupe in Vienna. Spira joined the cast in 1935 with his friend, the well-known author Jura Soyfer,[23] whom he had met while working as a cartoonist for the newspapers *Arbeiter-Zeitung* and *Wiener Tag*. Ahead of the ABC's last performance before Austria's incorporation into the German Reich in March 1938, Spira managed to write "Hitler can kiss our ..." on the scenery, but he had to remove the phrase, as director Hans Margulies feared reprisals by the regime. In Blechhammer, Spira had the courage to allude to the decline of the Nazi regime under the very noses of the SS. While making gesture drawings (of a series of poses), he let the sun rise out of a sinister sky above the barbed wire fence on the last sheet of paper. This time it was Jewish elder Demerer who became nervous, but Spira's only reply was, "If the SS doesn't mind, why should you?"[24]

Among the lead actors was Peter Sturm (Josef Michel Dischel, Vienna, 1909), who simultaneously functioned as the artists' block elder. He also participated in the ABC Cabaret between 1936 and 1938, when he was taken to Dachau and Buchenwald for being a Communist. He illegally immigrated to France after his release in 1939 and was deported from Drancy in summer 1942. The death march brought him back to Buchenwald, where he supported the Communist underground organization in taking over the camp in April 1945. He cofounded a Communist theater in Vienna after the war and moved to East Berlin in 1956. Sturm became a cast member of the German Theatre (Deutsches Theater) under the direction of the Buchenwald survivor Wolfgang Langhoff. He appeared in more than fifty cinema and television productions, among them the adaptation of Bruno Apitz's novel *Nackt unter Wölfen* (Naked among wolves), based on the true story of a child secretly kept alive by Buchenwald inmates. In 1961 Peter Sturm was awarded the Art Prize of the German Democratic Republic. He died in East Berlin in 1984.[25] His exceptional acting talent and fairness as a block elder earned him great respect in Blechhammer. Bil Spira praised his enormous versatility as an actor, a quality that also helped him to survive the reality of camps.[26] To Robert Clary, the time he spent rehearsing with Sturm seemed like "paradise in hell."[27]

Robert Clary (Robert Max Widerman, Paris, 1926) was the youngest of fourteen children. His Jewish orthodox parents had moved to Paris from Poland in 1921. From an early age he performed as a singer and tap dancer. He was pulled out of a Drancy convoy in September 1942 and assigned to the Schmelt camp Ottmuth. His parents and most of his siblings were murdered. Clary was transferred to Blechhammer in April 1944. Following his liberation in Buchenwald in April 1945, he pursued a singing career in France but then discovered his talent for acting during a tour in the United States. He starred in numerous movie and television productions as well as theatrical plays. Robert Clary is probably best known for his role as French POW Lebeau in the popular television series *Hogan's Heroes* (1965–1971). In Ottmuth, his singing performances had already earned him extra food, and the camp cook, who had taken a liking to him, inadvertently gave him the nickname "Didi," meaning to say *dis donc* ("hey you") in French. Before the camp theater was set up in Blechhammer, Clary entertained functionary prisoners. Later, Clary usually played the female parts because of his small stature. Wearing a straw wig and a skirt, he liked to perform Marlene Dietrich songs as well as traditional Yiddish pieces. He also danced with David Brainin.[28] The two had developed a special "Apache" dance for the play *Under the Bridges of Paris,* alluding to the gangsters of the Paris underworld.[29]

Hartog Salomon Ereira from Amsterdam was famous for his remarkable voice. He performed for British POWs during work and for functionary prisoners at the Jewish elder's soirées before joining the theater cast.[30]

The first theater play was presented like a television show. A replica of a TV, a box with an eye and an ear, was part of the scenery. Then there was a special Christmas show written by Harry Pos and Klaus Wolfsohn, titled *A Prisoner's Dream*. It started with an inmate (Harry Pos) falling asleep on the building site and dreaming of a trip around the world, to the tune *Ein Lied geht um die Welt*.[31] In his dreams he traveled to Amsterdam, where a clog dance was performed amid a field of tulips, then he moved on to

London, where he was greeted by stiff Englishmen. In Paris he walked over Montmartre, and he eventually saw Robert Clary and David Brainin waltzing through Vienna. Finally, the prisoner was woken up by a Kapo and resumed his work. The show was such a success it was performed more than ten times, until the day before the camp was evacuated.[32] During one of the shows the lyrics of a song alluding to the Russian proverb that a broom can shoot like a rifle if it is God's will caused great confusion among the SS. Camp leader Klipp remarked to Demerer: "It was a very nice show, but is it really possible that a broom can shoot if it is God's will? Isn't that complete nonsense?"[33]

In a 1976 interrogation report, Czapla claimed he had given a daring speech to the Jewish inmates after one of the theater performances, encouraging them to persevere, as liberation was close at hand. This incident had evidently contributed to his acquittal by a French military tribunal at Rastatt in 1948.[34] Several survivors indeed confirmed that a member of the SS had addressed them in a way that could be understood as criticism of the Nazi regime.[35] Robert Clary associated Czapla's speech with a general improvement in the camp conditions and the decision to have a theater:

> Upon his arrival, [he] made a speech telling us not to despair, not to give up hope, that we were human beings, and one of these days we would be free. We couldn't believe our ears. We had heard a German officer saying things nobody in his position would dare to say without being shot instantly for treason. It was a remarkable, brave thing for him to do, and we never understood how he got away with it. Life in camp changed somewhat. Tom Mix no longer woke us up at some godforsaken hour to exercise. And the new lieutenant decided that we should have a theatre.[36]

Others, like Leo Weiniger, were clear about the unchanged brutality, despite attempts by individual SS men to appear in a more favorable light: "After the show, which had really been a great artistic achievement, a noncommissioned officer of the SS gave a speech. He said he admired the brilliant performances the inmates had been able to present. That did not keep him from hanging three prisoners the next day."[37]

THE CAMP ORCHESTRA

Music, as an "existential human need," played a crucial role in camp life. Its function was even more ambivalent than that of the camp theater. A softly played tune or a song could have a powerful effect, as memories of a former, better life were instantly brought to mind and feelings of solidarity and emotional warmth were created. In stark contrast, the SS men abused music to humiliate their victims. Prisoner musicians invariably became entangled in this abuse and were consequently attributed an ambivalent role as well.[38] Camp orchestras (*Lagerkapellen*) were integral to concentration and death camps. In Auschwitz, music was deliberately played during the selections of new arrivals to convey a false sense of normality.[39] The orchestra of Blechhammer was established simultaneously with the theater at the start of Klipp's tenure in November 1944.[40] Blechhammer was one of five Auschwitz subcamps with an orchestra, next to Monowitz, Fürstengrube, Gleiwitz I, and Golleschau.[41] The orchestra was supervised by deputy camp leader Karl Czapla, who in a postwar trial prided himself on having founded it on his own initiative to offer "joy and entertainment" to the prisoners. He only spoke of Sunday concerts, conspicuously refraining from naming the orchestra's more sinister functions.[42] Perniciously, prisoner ensembles in Nazi concentration camps were equipped with instruments originating from the depots of goods confiscated from those who had been murdered or incarcerated. Occasionally the SS allowed ordering instruments and notes from music stores, but had the prisoners pay for them.[43]

Klipp appointed Georges Czaczkes (also known as Johnny Georgeslo, Gelati, Moldova, 1914) as the conductor when he learned that he was a renowned violinist. The child prodigy had been sent to Vienna for lessons with the violinist Robert Pollak, and he gave his first concert at seven years of age. Czaczkes went on to study music in Vienna and became a professional musician and composer. Following the annexation of Austria, Czaczkes fled to Paris in 1939; he was deported from Drancy in 1942. He came to Blechhammer via Laurahütte. Czaczkes played for the French radio symphony orchestra in Paris after the war. As his Stradivarius had been confiscated upon his arrival in the Annaberg transit camp with the blunt remark "You won't need a violin to die," he received a new instrument from Blechhammer's depot of looted goods. Contrary to the actors, the musicians still had to work, but they were given time off for rehearsals and were assigned to lighter tasks. Czaczkes was granted small privileges, like a room of his own in the orchestra's barrack and higher quality food. When he contracted anthrax, the SS even called a German doctor into the camp.[44]

Unlike most other camp orchestras, Blechhammer had a mixed ensemble. One of the female members was the violinist Polly Reinveld, who performed in Brussels after the war.[45] Some of the other musicians whose names can be reconstructed were the Viennese Weiss (violin), the Dutchman Frankenhuis (trumpet), the Simons brothers from Brussels, J. de Hond, and multitalented Harry Pos. They were joined by the three criminal Kapos Walter, Manni, and Felix. The convicted murderers Felix and Walter were excellent guitarists, and especially Walter Redock impressed with his blues. Manni was a Romani, who had been sentenced to twenty-five years in prison for forgery. His repertoire encompassed gypsy airs and Yiddish songs, and he played the balalaika.[46] The orchestra became a lifeline for six of the French Resistance fighters who were detained in Blechhammer from fall 1944. Following a typhus outbreak, most of the Frenchmen were in a deplorable condition. The camp orchestra thus offered them a chance to recuperate on higher food rations. Czaczkes even kept a Frenchman in the ensemble who had only pretended to be a musician. He henceforth held a violin in his hands without playing during performances, until an SS man noticed the trick. Czaczkes nevertheless was able to persuade the SS man that he was indispensable for copying notes.[47]

It was the orchestra's daily obligation to play when the prisoners passed the camp gate in the morning and evening.[48] Under the merciless scrutiny of the camp leader and his deputy, swift marching music was meant not only to speed up the prisoners' steps but also to expose those who were too weak to keep up. Holocaust survivors often drew parallels between the industrial process of mass murder and the emaciated inmates' forced movements to mechanical marching tunes.[49] It was enough to have pulled off one's cap too slowly to be maltreated by the SS at the gate.[50] Many emaciated prisoners had to mobilize their last bit of strength to avoid such attacks and then fell out when they were out of view. Most work details thus swiftly disintegrated once they had left the camp.[51] The survivor Oto Hostovsky delineated how the music at the gate formed part of a tormenting daily ritual that could potentially end the inmates' lives: "Each morning when the block elder chases us out in the frost, when we have nowhere to hide anymore, when we stand at roll call for over one hour, back-to-back, until the SS man on duty makes us go off to the factory in rows of five to the tune of the parading march, ... death is handing out its visiting cards to us."[52]

These humiliating encounters at the gate were the most frequent contacts between regular prisoners and the orchestra, and the forcefully played music inflicted suffering on both sides. However, unlike in the women's camp in Birkenau, the inmates of Blechhammer showed no open hostility toward the musicians.[53] Feelings of guilt were commonly experienced by surviving prisoner musicians. Possibly this was the reason Czaczkes denied in his postwar interview that the orchestra had ever played at the gate.[54]

The music was not randomly picked. The marches were intended to assert German dominance over the prisoners and to create a certain military order. In Blechhammer the Prussian grenadiers' march *Fridericus Rex* was usually played. Based on Carl Loewe's 1837 musical version of a ballad by Willibald Alexis (1798–1871) dedicated to the Prussian king Frederick II, Ferdinand Radeck composed this march in 1860. Nazi propaganda portrayed the historical figure of King Frederick II as an exemplary, strong military leader, culminating in the picture *The Great King*, directed by Veit Harlan (*Jud Süß*).[55] The orchestra even had to play when the prisoners were driven on the death march in January 1945. The only difference was that the musicians carried their food canisters, and they played in a more subdued and somber manner. Their instruments were taken along on sleighs pulled by prisoners.[56]

It is unclear whether Blechhammer's ensemble had to perform during executions, as was the case in numerous concentration camps.[57] There were only two testimonies stating that the orchestra had played the popular wartime song *Lili Marleen* after a hanging.[58] As none of the other survivors confirmed this, it seems more likely that the two witnesses had inadvertently fused their traumatic memories of the execution with the theater shows given immediately afterward, during which the musicians also had to play. By staging such shows after executions, the SS perverted music into an instrument of degradation and robbed it entirely of its positive qualities. A former Blechhammer prisoner recalled: "Later that evening [after the hanging], we had to listen to a concert, and while Harry Pos was singing, one could see the dead bodies dangling outside."[59]

As in Auschwitz, the camp orchestra had to entertain the SS on comradeship evenings (*Kameradschaftsabende*), which were regularly held in a festival hall. As Jews were banned from the SS quarters, Czapla concealed the musicians' identities by dressing them in grey civilian suits and white shirts and covered their shaved heads with caps. Occasionally there were joint performances of SS men and Jewish prisoners.[60] A frequent visitor was the OHW deputy director Schlick, who seemingly was invited by the SS to foster their mutual relations.[61] There were no private performances for individual SS men like the ones requested by Mengele in Auschwitz.[62]

As in the preceding years, Demerer continued to organize soirées for functionary prisoners to provide them with some cultured entertainment. Such evenings also inspired political and philosophical disputes.[63] Next to classical music, Yiddish songs were an important part of the soirées.[64] Contrary to the classical pieces, they formed a bridge between the intellectual and nonintellectual functionaries. Yet these musical performances remained the prerogative of a few that underscored their higher status in the camp strata.[65] Kapos Walter, Felix, and Manni performed during the functionaries' social gatherings. The medical orderly Jules Fainzang related how he had been deeply touched by Manni's interpretation of a German children's song about a boy's dream of owning a horse: "A magic sound filled this sinister room like rays of sunlight. A spell-binding tenor voice sang in German: 'Mamatchki, schenk mir ein Pferdchen / Ein Pferdchen wäre mein Paradies.' ... These words made tears run down my face. How were the Germans capable of exterminating hundreds of thousands of Jewish children, if they cared so much for their own children? Was it possible that the German language, that seemed so cruel when flung at us day in day out, possessed other tonalities, too?"[66]

The regular prisoners rarely enjoyed the positive aspects of music unless they sang songs among themselves. Several prisoners from the Netherlands thus made up a love song dedicated to the female inmates of Blechhammer, who risked their lives to pass on food to the men. The lyrics, revolving largely around bread, were sung to the popular tune of "I Can't Give You Anything but Love, Baby."[67] In late 1944 the Jewish prisoners were involuntarily exposed to musical propaganda primarily intended to raise the crumbling morale of German workers. By order of the SS propaganda office of Ratibor, Dr. Schlick continuously played them records with operettas and light popular tunes.[68] Listening to this music evoked painful memories among the inmates of happier days in their former lives, of their "paradise lost."[69]

11

THE MASSACRES OF JANUARY 1945

H IMMLER BEGAN TO TAKE PRECAUTIONARY MEASURES FOR SECURING the concentration camps in June 1944 by issuing a directive that allowed the HSSPFs to seize control from the SS commandants in the event of an insurgency or evacuation. Camp leaders received evacuation guidelines from the district leader of Silesia, Fritz Bracht, on December 21, 1944. Nevertheless, the vast majority of the Auschwitz prisoners were not removed from the area for almost another month, in line with the Ministry of Armaments and Ammunitions's order to keep production facilities running for as long as possible.¹ The launch of the Soviet offensive on January 12, 1945, swiftly cut off most of Bracht's intended marching routes. Moreover, Himmler's failure to issue sweeping orders to evacuate the camps prevented a concerted retreat. Oswald Pohl of the WVHA eventually instructed the HSSPF of Silesia, Heinrich Schmauser, to start the evacuation process of Auschwitz and its satellites.² On January 19, 1945, Schmauser commanded that all sick prisoners be liquidated.³

Blechhammer was the last Auschwitz subcamp to be evacuated.⁴ The roaring of the Russian artillery had been audible for several days when rumors about the evacuation of Gleiwitz spread, and the Blechhammer prisoners expected their camp to be next. Notwithstanding the undeniable signs of the impending German retreat, the camp leadership tried to convey a sense of continuity. In a speech to the prisoners on Saturday, January 20, second-in-command Czapla claimed that the camp would not be evacuated. A theater performance staged to distract the inmates was promptly interrupted by a Soviet air raid. On the same evening, camp leader Klipp assured the Jewish elders that they would stay in Blechhammer but announced only two hours later that the camp would be evacuated as soon as groups marching out of Gleiwitz on January 18 had arrived. Three blocks in the Abessynia section were cleared to enable the approximately twenty-three hundred inmates from Gleiwitz I, III, and IV to get some soup and sleep after a strenuous three-day march without any food.⁵ A smaller group of these prisoners was driven to Blechhammer on trucks. Curiously, the SS required them to conceal themselves with blankets during the ride.[6] Early the next morning, another two to three thousand inmates evacuated from Jaworzno/Neu Dachs on January 17 followed. All these treks had been rerouted to Blechhammer due to combat activity.[7]

The SS had already murdered large numbers of inmates on each of these treks. SS Unterscharführer Hans Stefan Olejak had been the second-in-command of Jaworzno from June 1943 until April 1944, when he started his tenure in Blechhammer. He claimed he had been appointed camp leader of the Tschechowitz subcamp in November 1944. Survivors of Jaworzno nonetheless stated that he had returned to their camp and had shot twenty prisoners en route to Blechhammer. However, his renewed presence in Blechhammer was not corroborated by former prisoners.[8]

On the morning of Sunday, January 21, preparations for the march began.[9] The SS intended to take the inmates from Gleiwitz, Jaworzno, and Blechhammer to the Gross-Rosen concentration camp in separate treks and then ship them to Buchenwald by train from there. The infirmary patients and the female inmates were permitted to stay behind.[10] These plans were disrupted by the spontaneous decision of thousands of prisoners to fight for their lives by awaiting the Red Army in the camp. This rebuts the common assumption that only the sick had remained.[11] It is estimated that in addition to the fifty-nine thousand Auschwitz prisoners who were driven on death marches, nine thousand stayed behind.[12] The experience of those who remained has never been the focus of scholarly works, and there is not even a proper designation for the unprecedented and dangerously unpredictable power vacuum the prisoners struggled to survive in. The arrival of the prisoners from Gleiwitz and Jaworzno was a major catalyst for the escalation of violence that ensued. The Germans' violent attempts to crush the Blechhammer "revolt" resulted in several massacres, which are delineated in the following sections, along with the prisoners' responses to these assaults.

MURDERS BY THE CAMP SS AND FACTORY GUARDS ON JANUARY 21, 1945

When the Gleiwitz prisoners were woken at 6:30 a.m. for the morning roll call, they were informed that their group would be the first to leave, at 9:00 a.m.[13] After several sleepless nights in the cold, their limbs had painfully stiffened up during the short rest in bunk beds. Knowing they would not be able to endure another leg of the march, hundreds remained in their bunks.[14] Only about seven hundred Gleiwitz prisoners attended the roll call. Due to the pandemonium caused by the new arrivals and the SS men's haste to move westward, overall discipline had become unprecedentedly lax. More Gleiwitz prisoners thus seized the opportunity to go into hiding. Numerous

Blechhammer prisoners were prompted to follow their example after hearing their harrowing accounts of mass shootings en route. The arrival of trucks loaded with the bodies of those killed on the way to Blechhammer shockingly confirmed these reports.[15] The SS subsequently departed with no more than one-third of the original Gleiwitz trekkers and made no effort to retrieve the missing men.[16]

Unlike those involved in the Gleiwitz treks, the Jaworzno prisoners had not received anything to eat upon arrival in Blechhammer. Knowing that the prisoners had been going without any provisions for days, the SS promised them food on the condition that they line up for the march.[17] Under the impression of the horrors of the past days and the heavy losses they had suffered, the Jaworzno prisoners were desperate to dodge another march at any cost.[18] They had witnessed how the SS had brutally killed fellow prisoners trying to hide in the mines of Jaworzno with grenades. A survivor recalled that the SS had "bribed" the rest of the inmates with bread and salami to prevent any resistance. He assumed that they were using the same strategy now to "trick" them into another death march.[19] Therefore, many opted to retreat into hideouts, such as the barrack roofs, instead of queuing for food.[20]

Forced to change their plans due to the Jaworzno inmates' noncompliance, the SS prepared the Blechhammer trekking group for marching off first. When the Blechhammer prisoners were allocated their provisions for along the way, some of the starved Jaworzno inmates started to pilfer bread loaves and raided the food depots.[21] Klipp commanded his deputy Czapla and another five SS guards to open fire on the prisoners. In a postwar trial, Czapla claimed that they had merely shot in the air, and that he had personally tended to a prisoner who had "accidentally" received a bullet in his leg.[22] His story was an obvious fabrication, as a survivor witnessed how he shot a prisoner at close range.[23] An SS man placed in front of the shoe depot fired at any prisoner near him.[24] They were supported by the non-Jewish criminal Kapos, who had been armed with rifles and clad in SS uniforms to escort the march.[25]

The newcomers' "revolt" evoked fear of reprisals in the Blechhammer prisoners; however, it also emasculated the SS and encouraged many to stay behind and hide.[26] There was no organized resistance to the evacuation as in Buchenwald, as Blechhammer lacked an active underground movement.[27] Therefore, most fit inmates and functionary prisoners left the camp, expecting the others to be killed.[28]

The approximately 130 to 150 female prisoners were in a similar dilemma when the SS advised them to stay in the camp if they did not feel capable of making a highly paced march. Suspecting that all remaining women would be murdered, only thirty of them dared to accept this offer.[29] Tragically, most of the women who went on the march later perished in the infamous "reception camp" of Bergen-Belsen.[30] Their barrack was nonetheless seen as a sanctuary by a group of male prisoners, who hid there in the hope of avoiding the march.[31]

A diverse group of Jewish inmates aged between seventeen and fifty-one eventually stayed behind.[32] Some of the fifty Maquisards still accounted for in January 1945 remained in the camp, but their fate is unclear.[33]

When the Blechhammer group finally departed at noon, all "hell broke loose," as a survivor put it.[34] Crazed with hunger, more and more Jaworzno prisoners gathered to force their way into the bread storeroom. They devoured their first food in days, despite SS guards starting to machine-gun them from the watchtowers.[35] Around 3:00 p.m., those prisoners from Jaworzno that the SS had been able to assemble by force were marched out of Blechhammer, while the looting continued.[36]

Unprecedented in the camp's history, the retreating SS delegated the plant's works police under the command of OHW deputy director Schlick authority over the remaining prisoners. The SS instructed the works police's leader Kurt Karl Schumann to crush the "rebellion." He had up to 150 armed men at his disposal and could also draw on a unit of eighty SS men in charge of securing the OHW plant, who were commanded by SS Hauptscharführer Bruno Palla. Schumann, and SS Obersturmbannführer R. Kügler, the head of the SS propaganda office in Ratibor, supervised the renewed shootings in the camp.[37] At least ninety prisoners were shot on this day.[38] A postwar interrogation report by a British War Crimes Group clearly corroborates that Schlick knew of the massacre and presumably gave the respective shooting orders. On January 23, 1945, Schlick was involved in the liquidation of Polish penitentiary prisoners that German authorities had been unable to transfer to Gross-Rosen in time.[39] These incidents exemplify the fusing of the industrialists and factory guards with the regime's annihilatory policies. Especially in the last phase of the war, lower echelon auxiliaries, such as the works police, as well as civilians were delegated tasks previously executed by the SS or the Gestapo.[40] Both Schumann and Schlick were released in 1947 after a few months in British remand custody. Their case was closed, as key witnesses residing in the Soviet sector could not be interrogated.[41]

The looting prisoners showed signs of what Langer called "impromptu self," a self-preserving survival mode that temporarily eclipses one's moral values.[42] Many survivors, like Hans Rehfisch, not only struggled to come to terms with the atrocities they witnessed but also found it difficult to relate to their actions later in life: "We must have tread over dead people, it was horrible. I suppose we were crazy."[43]

THE INFIRMARY PATIENTS' EXCEPTIONAL PROTECTION

Approximately three hundred sick prisoners were left behind in the camp infirmary. Three of the Jewish prisoner physicians of Blechhammer, Dr. Pollak, Dr. Flescher, and Dr. Szeftel, stayed with them.[44] During the interim, they were the last representatives of the SS-imposed "self-administration" of the prisoners.⁴⁵ Although the infirmary was the only place still regulated by certain rules, the physicians did not interfere with the fit prisoners' affairs.

Before the evacuation, the SS ordered that all patients still able to walk were to assemble in front of the infirmary. Having heard rumors of the liquidation of sick inmates by the new arrivals from Gleiwitz and Jaworzno, the Blechhammer prisoners feared that they would meet a similar fate. To their surprise, the SS merely checked whether the inmates were genuinely unfit to march and sent them back to their beds.⁴⁶ Camp leader Klipp reportedly issued a written note to the infirmary staff confirming that the sick prisoners were not to be harmed by anyone.⁴⁷ His motives for not carrying out Schmauser's directive to murder the sick, issued two days earlier, remains obscure. Evidently the treatment of unfit prisoners varied from camp to camp. The rapid Soviet advance thus prevented a full-scale massacre of the sick in the Auschwitz main camp and in Birkenau. The infirmary of Monowitz was not touched at all. In an act of preemptive obedience, the SS shot unfit inmates in Gleiwitz I on January 18, 1945, and burned the infirmary patients of Gleiwitz IV alive.⁴⁸

Unlike camp commandants, subcamp leaders were not authorized to revise or ignore superior orders from Berlin. Contrary to Wachsmann's theory of "autonomous" subcamp leaders, there is no evidence that directives from the commandant of Monowitz, Heinrich Schwarz, who superintended all Auschwitz satellites, were not implemented by Blechhammer in normal times.⁴⁹ Klipp's written note indicates that he had received Schmauser's order but decided not to execute it. Possibly he intended to speed up the evacuation, or his own disability (his left hand had been maimed in combat) may have made him reluctant to massacre the infirmary patients.⁵⁰ His noncompliance was likely triggered by the temporary power vacuum created by the unorganized retreat.⁵¹ Nevertheless, Klipp obeyed the sweeping order to shoot "recalcitrant" hiding prisoners and subsequently delegated this task to the factory guards and the Wehrmacht. The brutal murders of those in hiding were probably rooted in widespread fears of prisoners leaving the camps to take revenge on the German population.⁵² Klipp also had all prisoners murdered who became unfit en route to Gross-Rosen.⁵³

The infirmary patients' reactions to the impending evacuation differed considerably. Some forced themselves to march, others deliberately stayed behind, and some were mentally or physically incapable of making decisions at all. Most were invariably aware of the intrinsic logic of the Nazi camps that anyone unfit for work was condemned to death. Therefore, it was expected that prisoners unable to march would be killed. As a survivor put it, the "fear of death" led many fellow patients to leave the infirmary despite their poor state of health: "All fit prisoners go on this transport—they are joined by the ones from the infirmary who are still able to limp along a little. No one would give a penny for the lives of the rest of the sick who stay behind. The fear of their probable deaths helps many comrades to get back on their feet.... Yes, to live on, these living corpses go on the march."[54]

Tragically, the sick prisoners who had joined the trek hoping to stay alive were systematically murdered en route. On as many as ten occasions, SS guards took these inmates to remote places, such as rubbish dumps or cemeteries, and shot them.[55] Those among the gravely ill who were still sufficiently conscious were painfully aware that they might be killed. However, their physical state precluded any other options apart from staying in the HKB. Typical diseases were pneumonia or gangrene.[56] Others, like Oto Hostovsky, were extremely emaciated and began to turn into "Muselmen." Hostovsky was one of the few survivors of the liquidated family camp BIIb in Auschwitz-Birkenau and was transferred to Blechhammer in July 1944. He had spent over a month in the infirmary due to exhaustion and malnourishment when the camp was evacuated. In postwar testimony, Hostovsky indicated that the other prisoners had not chosen between life and death but merely between a fast and a slow death.[57]

By contrast, some lightly injured or convalescing prisoners reckoned their survival chances would be higher if they stayed in the infirmary, as did a number of healthy inmates hiding among them.[58] Similarly, a medical orderly was prompted to remain in the infirmary after helping to unload a truck bearing the bodies of Gleiwitz prisoners shot en route.[59] When the Blechhammer group left, the gate of the fence surrounding the infirmary was locked and was guarded by a prisoner. The guard nonetheless let twelve of his comrades enter in return for tending to the sick.[60] As the SS did not check the so-called *Schonungsblock*, the section where terminally ill prisoners were left unattended in despicably unhygienic conditions, some inmates used it as a hideout.[61]

The infirmary was not affected by the massacre outside. When the last SS men had left with parts of the Jaworzno group, Dr. Flescher seized the opportunity to come to the aid of the shooting victims. The medical staff also registered the tattooed numbers of those killed in the massacre to secure the evidence of the atrocities committed in the camp.[62] As the SS had turned off the electricity and water, the orderlies melted snow to prepare soup and potatoes for the sick.[63]

THE RETURN OF THE CAMP SS AND THE MASSACRE OF JANUARY 22

After a night in nearby Heydebreck (Kędzierzyn-Koźle), the Blechhammer trekking group was ordered to head back toward Blechhammer, only to be rerouted to Gross-Rosen again within a few miles of the camp on January 22. Klipp had Czapla assemble a patrol to investigate whether the Russians already held the camp.[64] Seven male and female prisoners, two of the criminal Kapos, and eleven SS men set out by truck. Shortly after their departure, the group was marched back to the camp.[65]

The patrol's initial preparations for a return soon coalesced with hasty efforts to destroy compromising evidence and culminated in a large-scale massacre of prisoners hiding in the camp.[66] First the seven prisoners belonging to the patrol had to tidy up the SS quarters. A short while later it became clear that the camp would be left for good, and they were ordered to load documents on handcarts. The SS forced eighteen prisoners they had caught hiding in the camp to pull the carts. When an SS man remarked that fifteen men were sufficient, the surplus three were simply shot. Meanwhile, a member of the SS formerly in charge of the food allocations nicknamed "Napoleon" searched the camp kitchens and killed several hiding prisoners.[67]

Around 3:00 p.m., the SS set their quarters and the Political Department on fire. They threw hand grenades into some of the prisoners' barracks from the watchtowers and shot at anyone escaping the flames. The Blechhammer guards' superior, SS Oberscharführer Claessen, had belonged to the group's rearguard platoon (*Nachkommando*), but then followed the patrol back to the camp.[68] Infamous for his cruelty, he even bayoneted those who were shot to make sure they were dead. Four prisoners lying among the dead were still alive and jumped up when he approached them. Claessen then shot them in front of the camp wall.[69] SS Rottenführer Karl Masseli also participated in the massacre.[70]

Kapo Walter made all women vacate their barrack to hunt down male prisoners in hiding.[71] But not all of them had left when the SS set fire to the building. Several women were shot as they ran out to seek cover in the nearby potato cellar. Among the shooters was the SS man overseeing the clothes depot, Adolf Schindler.[72] Great numbers of hiding prisoners sheltered in the potato cellar during the massacre. Others broke through the four-meter-high camp wall and escaped into the forest.[73] Their lives were saved by the weak spots in the concrete that the mason's detail had deliberately inserted during the wall's construction in April 1944.[74] A small group of inmates used a wardrobe to reach an unmanned watchtower and fled into the woods. The SS pursued them with dogs, and some were shot. The rest of the group managed to hide in a deserted house until the arrival of the Red Army.[75] Interestingly, German OHW workers seem to have been present during the massacre. A female prisoner and her two daughters were thus warned to leave the camp immediately by a German laborer and fled into the forest. Polish workers they encountered on the main road offered to harbor them in their camp.[76] When the SS finally left, they put a lock on the camp gate.[77] Up to 108 prisoners fell victim to the massacre of January 22, 1945.[78]

THE MEDICAL STAFF'S EFFORTS TO SAVE THE SHOOTING VICTIMS, JANUARY 22–23

Thanks to heavy snowfall and a change in the wind direction, the surviving inmates soon managed to extinguish the fires. Thus, only the SS quarters and individual barracks near the watchtowers were destroyed completely.[79] The prisoners began to search for injured comrades trapped underneath the ruins of collapsed barracks. The camp was strewn with the bodies of the shot.[80] A part of the infirmary had been hit by a hand grenade, but no one was hurt, and the barrack remained intact. The renewed shootings nonetheless led to a sharp increase in the number of dead and injured prisoners hiding outside. Two prisoner physicians from Gleiwitz volunteered for the infirmary. However, the medical staff's capacity to provide genuine aid was extremely limited, as the SS had confiscated their surgical instruments and supplies. In aid of comrades who were bleeding to death, some prisoners even cut up their own shirts and trousers.

The next day, January 23, four of the orderlies were sent to the now deserted campsites of British and French POWs a few miles' away to search for dressing material. This undertaking was quite risky, as the Germans were still patrolling the roads. It was hoped that doctors' coats with a sewn-on red cross would offer them at least some protection. It did not take long until two of the orderlies were stopped by elderly members of the home guard (*Volkssturm*), who were suspicious of the striped uniforms underneath their coats. One of the prisoners managed to scare the home guards away by making them believe that their SS guards had just fled from the approaching Russians. When the two reached the British POW camp, they were almost shot by works policemen involved in a massacre of Polish convicts in hiding.[81] Eventually, French POWs offered some of their medical supplies to the HKB. Many of the wounded and the sick nevertheless died, and the piles of unburied corpses grew.[82] When a prisoner detail ordered to collect those shot en route returned with the bodies of another two hundred Blechhammer inmates, a mass grave was excavated. The pit was left open to preserve the evidence for the Soviets.[83]

WEHRMACHT KILLINGS: JANUARY 24–25, 1945

From Wednesday, January 24, Blechhammer was temporarily in the crossfire of the Soviet artillery and the Wehrmacht, and grenades exploded in the camp.[84] An air raid claimed the lives of several prisoners, whose barracks had received direct hits.[85] During the night of January 24–25, two vehicles carrying Wehrmacht soldiers arrived.[86] They may have belonged to a unit of soldiers on leave to work in the armaments industry (*Wehrmachtsurlauber*) that had been reactivated on January 23, 1945, to reinforce the local home guard. They were joined by an anti-aircraft battalion stationed in Blechhammer since summer 1944.[87] Purportedly there were also collaborating Georgians among the soldiers.[88] They killed about fifty prisoners hiding in the potato cellar.[89] The soldiers took up to 150 inmates out of the camp for an unclear purpose, only to shoot them in the end. Some survivors related that they had intended to use them as a "protective shield" or to build a bridge. Their bodies were found in the nearby forest later.[90]

Between 780 and 1,000 prisoners, predominantly those from Jaworzno and Gleiwitz, were marched to a school building before being added to a trek to Gross-Rosen.[91]

During the roundup, a group of Jaworzno prisoners escaped through the hole in the camp wall. They were eventually arrested by the police and sent to Gross-Rosen. Unlike most other groups, they were not transferred to Buchenwald but to Leitmeritz, a subcamp of Flossenbürg.[92]

In the middle of the massacre three prisoners, who had barricaded themselves in a former workshop, narrowly escaped death when they mistook the Germans for Soviet soldiers and erroneously gave themselves away:

> We fell silent. Steps drew close, but they were the steps of a single soldier. We heard the screams of fear and shooting from more distant barracks. A new manhunt had begun. The soldier outside hammered against our barrack door, yelling that we should come out. We remained silent but picked up massive lumps of iron from the floor of the room that appeared to have been used as a workshop. We silently agreed to kill the soldier if he came in. As the barrack stood isolated from the others, the soldier was unsure what to do, and he must have sensed that we would attack him, if he tried to catch us. Cursing, he left, and did not ask his comrades for assistance, as we had feared.[93]

THE INFIRMARY'S CONTINUED PROTECTION DURING THE WEHRMACHT ONSLAUGHT

Firing shots into the infirmary barrack's ceiling, the soldiers demanded that all patients assemble outside within two minutes. In postwar testimony, Dr. Szeftel stated that he had succeeded in persuading the soldiers that he was not permitted to move the patients, and they had left.[94] In a different variation of this story, Dr. Pollak allegedly saved the inmates by claiming that they all had typhus.[95] Whichever version is accurate, the infirmary patients were left unscathed in the end. Only a few patients registered the soldiers' presence, as most of them were too numb to respond to their demands.[96]

Daniel Blatman's contention that on January 26 a "second wave" of unknown members of the SS or the Wehrmacht shot most of the sick prisoners and burned them in a ditch was not corroborated by any testimony. Evidently there were numerous survivors from the infirmary. The details of the killings he ascribes to Blechhammer seem more or less consistent with Danuta Czech's account of the massacre of unfit inmates in Tschechowitz-Vacuum on January 21, 1945.[97] The fact that the soldiers did not even enter the infirmary refutes Blatman's theory of "local liquidation units" specifically delegated to carry out Schmauser's order to murder the sick in Blechhammer.[98] It seems more plausible that they intended to check the infirmary for hiding, fit prisoners. Notwithstanding the atrocities undoubtedly committed by the soldiers in the camp, their paramount task appears to have been to transfer the hundreds of hiding prisoners from Gleiwitz, and Jaworzno to Gross-Rosen. They largely followed the orders issued by camp leader Klipp on January 21: to march off the fit prisoners, if necessary by force, while sparing the sick and the women. On January 24, Klipp's group reached Ziegenhals (Głuchołazy), a town situated forty miles from Blechhammer.[99] As Klipp had a mobile wireless radio with an average range of one hundred miles, the Wehrmacht may have received his instructions beforehand.

Although not explicitly commanded to carry out mass killings of civilians, the Wehrmacht had become entangled in the Holocaust at an early stage of the war. Its level of complicity depended on the attitudes of lower echelon leaders and individual decisions. The Blechhammer case underlines the continuum of perpetration, which moved from supporting roles, like rounding up prisoners, to active initiatives to kill.[100] This scenario likewise exemplifies the apparent leeway available to Klipp during the evacuation, whose decision to safeguard the sick was not overruled by the HSSPF's superior order. Consequently, other SS camp leaders must have had the same latitude for action and could equally have protected their most vulnerable prisoners from such gratuitous acts of brutality.[101]

The Wehrmacht units left the camp gate open when they departed. The prisoners' first attempts to leave the camp on their own were nonetheless thwarted by the unsafe situation outside and the presence of German patrols. Despite the possibility of another return of the SS, the camp paradoxically seemed to offer more protection at this point. A group of inmates who had fled into the forest during the massacre therefore quickly returned after stumbling over the victims of the Wehrmacht shootings.[102]

SURVIVAL IN NO-MAN'S LAND AND (SELF-) LIBERATION: JANUARY 26–28, 1945

The Germans' ultimate withdrawal from Blechhammer signaled the end of the camp's existence. Now that liberation seemed more feasible than ever, the prisoners found themselves at the intersection of falling into "anarchy" and regaining control over their lives after years of extreme oppression. During this watershed, no one took the place of the former Jewish elder Demerer, who had been renowned for his just leadership style. As all functionaries had gone on the march, the SS-imposed "prisoner self-administration" no longer regulated the distribution of essential goods, like food and fuel. As Primo Levi, who remained behind in the infirmary of Monowitz, put it, "the rhythm of the great machine of the lager" had been extinguished with the departure of the SS.[103] When the camp's internal and external boundaries became more permeable, the enforced prisoner community gradually disintegrated. The presence of the newly arrived inmates sped up this process.

Following the disappearance of their greatest enemies, the SS, some prisoners ironically began to perceive fellow comrades as a threat instead. The sudden access to large quantities of long-missed goods led certain inmates to commit excesses. They slaughtered the pigs formerly kept by the SS, and fights erupted when one group found sugar in a depot. Amid the dead, they prepared meals on the embers of burned barracks. Countless prisoners literally ate themselves to death in this "paradise in hell," as the survivor Vilem Hostovsky called it.[104] After a period of extreme starvation, hyperphagia was a typical reaction. The increased energy level also caused aggressive behavior and mood swings. Those still in control of themselves watched their comrades in disbelief, while concerns about their own safety grew.[105] The survivor Ernest Koenig delineated the almost surrealistic scenes in the camp: "They were emaciated, fantastically dressed, and driven by an animal craving for food. They sat in front of the fires, cooked, and stirred their soups, and ate [...]. Most were unable to digest the food and vomited. [...] I saw twice how prisoners pulled scorched corpses into the fire to use them as fuel."[106]

Contrary to the infirmary patients, the fit prisoners rarely reflected on the process of feeling "human" again before or during the liberation. Their disdain for those in an alleged "anarchic" state nevertheless betrays a change in their self-perception. These prisoners typically explained their survival by their having "kept their wits."[107]

The medical personnel made no effort to guard the food depots against looters either, but merely secured enough supplies for their patients.[108] The five remaining prisoner physicians and their orderlies were overburdened with the growing numbers of the wounded, so that the approximately three hundred infirmary patients received very little attention. Food was not distributed regularly, and the patients were desperate for water. The barrack floors were soiled, and the dead were not even removed from the beds. Like Primo Levi in Monowitz, those among the sick still able to get up began to care for the others. They crawled outside to fetch snow for their thirsty comrades. Those in better shape left the camp during the day to look for food. The furniture and wooden boards of empty barracks were burned to heat the infirmary and to boil potatoes. The food and warmth, coupled with the apparent withdrawal of the Germans, filled the inmates with new hope of survival. Eating and chatting late into the night, they started to make plans for the future again.[109] Meanwhile, others passed away almost unnoticed. Oto Hostovsky recalled the final days in the infirmary amid the dying: "I crawl off my bunk, trying not to touch the dead hand stretched out widely from the bed below. Then I try to close the dead eyes, but they refuse, maybe they would like to see the newly won freedom. They are yellow, anxiously and expectingly gazing into the air."[110]

The vast numbers of decomposing bodies became a grave concern. In line with (ultra-) orthodox interpretations of the Holocaust at the time, a rabbi among the prisoners construed their protracted suffering as a "divine punishment" for not abiding by the religious law to bury the dead. He convinced two inmates to remove the body of a man who had been lying in front of their barrack door for days. When they lifted him up, they noticed that he was still alive. Incredibly, the prisoners managed to nurse him back to health.[111] Such individual efforts notwithstanding, the unburied corpses caused numerous inmates to leave. The desire to escape the "chaotic" and "unbearable" situation in the camp was the decisive impetus for actively seeking to liberate themselves days before the "official" liberation.[112]

The dissolution of the camp's repressive framework permitted more personal agency, resulting in the formation of smaller groups pursuing individual goals. Some autonomously terminated their prisoner status by leaving the camp permanently and changing into civilian clothes. About forty prisoners thus roamed the forest, occasionally asking German civilians for food. One day an elderly German offered to take them into his house but then denounced them to the police. Luckily their civilian clothes helped them to pass themselves off as foreign laborers, and they were released. The group was found by Soviet soldiers while hiding in a deserted German workers' camp.[113] Others ventured into the area around the camp in search of the Russians to speed up the liberation. On Friday, January 26, prisoners encountered the first Soviet soldiers in a nearby village. Enthusiastically, they brought Russian cigarettes and a Soviet cap back into the camp to prove to fellow inmates that liberation was near at hand.[114]

When a Soviet patrol finally reached the camp on Sunday, January 28, 1945, some survivors experienced this liberation as an "anticlimax": "They probably did not realize themselves that they were part of 'a historic moment,' that they were about to liberate a camp. Moreover, this camp indubitably was just one in a whole series of camps they had seen."[115] Another reason for feeling "disappointed" at the liberation was the fact that the war had not ended yet, and the survivors could only be repatriated months later.[116]

Unlike Auschwitz, Blechhammer was not used for filming propagandistic liberation scenes, which rarely reflected the survivors' genuine experience.[117] The generous help extended to them by the Soviets was nonetheless greatly appreciated, despite some communication problems. As there were Jews among the soldiers, they spoke Yiddish with the prisoners, but not all of them were familiar with this language.[118]

The sick prisoners still dreaded the possible return of the SS, despite the soldiers' assurances that they were safe now.[119] To Oto Hostovsky, the day of their liberation was like a "rebirth" that restored their status as human beings, who were once more entitled to all the things that make life worth living: "eating, sleeping, dreaming, going wherever, and whenever you please."[120]

Having lived in a world without mercy, the prisoners were grateful for the tender care they received from Soviet nurses and doctors. They were showered with chocolates and cigarettes and were provided with nourishing meals three times a day. The sick were immediately relocated to the better-equipped SS infirmary adjacent to the camp and then transferred to the Soviet military hospital of Częstochowa two weeks later.[121] Another eighty-two prisoners died within the first days after the liberation, of disease or as a result of the injuries inflicted by the SS, the works police, and the Wehrmacht. They were buried in the camp's mass grave.[122] In mid-February 1945, the survivors were taken to a central collecting point in Gleiwitz, and they were repatriated in the summer.[123] The joy of liberation was tainted by the inescapable truth that most of their family members had perished. The survivor Mendel Meyer only began to grasp that he was all alone now when he returned to his former home in the Netherlands: "In the evening, there happened to be a car heading towards Hoogeveen giving me a lift back home. Then came the greatest disappointment when there was no one left anymore."[124]

Approximately five hundred prisoners perished during the interim, about 25 percent of those in hiding. Roughly the same percentage of inmates was killed on the march from Blechhammer to Gross-Rosen.[125] Thus the decision to remain behind did not substantially increase the prisoners' immediate survival chances. Their earlier liberation from the Nazi camp system was unquestionably a crucial advantage. The lives of the infirmary patients, who appear to have been the least likely to survive, were seemingly spared by the order of an individual camp leader—who nevertheless did not hesitate to have all unfit prisoners murdered en route.

12

THE DEATH MARCH

Blechhammer was the last Auschwitz subcamp to be evacuated, on January 21, 1945. Comprising approximately four thousand prisoners, it also was the largest group moving westward along the border with Sudeten.[1] Bracht granted the Auschwitz columns special priority, as they were perceived as a security threat. To ensure a swift passage, they were allowed to use major roads. Civilian groups were to yield to the prisoners and maintain a ten-mile distance to avoid direct encounters. The SS guards were to obliterate evidence of the crimes committed by the so-called shooting service, the men designated to kill stragglers.[2]

Before leaving Blechhammer, the inmates received two loaves of bread, some margarine, and ersatz honey. Most wrapped themselves in their two blankets to ward off the biting frost. Some also insulated their thin prisoner uniforms with empty cement sacks. The soles of their wooden shoes were soon covered in ice, and the frozen canvas lining caused frostbite. Those who had been able to grab leather shoes during the raid on the clothes depot had thus significantly increased their survival chances.[3] Around noon the line of trekkers, measuring several miles in length, was assembled on the main road. As they marched off, Demerer encouraged the prisoners by calling out to them that they were "going home," now that the German retreat had begun. The fact that the SS already wore civilian clothes underneath their coats gave even more credibility to his words.[4] The French Maquisards went along to Gross-Rosen, but only a small fraction survived the evacuation.[5] Prior to marching off, the SS announced that they would shoot anyone who fell out.[6] It is still a matter of debate whether the killing of stragglers was based on superior orders or local initiatives. A preserved document from the commandant of Stutthoff corroborates that there was an order to kill escapees and prisoners who refused to march.[7] The fact that similar shooting orders were given out before the evacuation of penitentiaries and POW camps points to higher echelon decision-makers.[8]

Sixteen SS men formed the so-called rear guard platoon (*Nachkommando*) that followed the tail of the line to shoot stragglers. Among them was Oberscharführer Claessen, the superior of Blechhammer's guard battalion, who reputedly killed numerous prisoners.[9] The bodies were removed by a "clean-up detail" (*Aufräumkommando*), comprising four prisoners, who left Blechhammer one day after the evacuation. They had to haul the first shooting victims back to the camp on carts. The remaining prisoners later buried them in a mass grave.[10]

The Blechhammer camp personnel had been reinforced with SS men from Gleiwitz and Jaworzno, so that about one hundred guards supervised the trek. They were joined by members of the home guard at a later stage of the march.[11] Survivors stated that the former Wehrmacht guards, who had only been recruited into the SS in summer 1944, were quite restrained. One guard even announced that he would not use his rifle.[12] The key shooters were predominantly found in the ranks of the "genuine" SS, who patrolled the columns on motorbikes. The head of the Political Department, Schmidt, and Tom Mix were often named in this context. They were assisted by the armed criminal Kapos. In particular, Walter Redock and a Kapo named Heinrich Krudwig, who allegedly "wore the swastika with pride," participated in killings.[13]

The group was headed by a horse-drawn cart carrying Karl Czapla, who had injured his foot on the first marching day, as well as some luggage. Bracht had permitted the procurement of such vehicles for the SS men's belongings. Ironically, the Jewish prisoners had had to pay for the horse and cart they were not allowed to ride on themselves. Czapla also bought a handcart to transport the orchestra's instruments. It was pulled by prisoners in the rear of the group, who received some food in return. Occasionally inmates unable to walk could rest on it.[14] On the way to Heydebreck, where they spent the first night in a deserted Italian workers' camp, passing British and French POWs reassured the prisoners that they would soon be liberated by the approaching Red Army. This prompted many to devour their food rations at once, unaware that they would only get scanty provisions en route. Only the functionary prisoners had access to hot drinks and frugal meals. In Heydebreck, the prisoners learned of the Soviet conquest of nearby Oppeln (Opole) from a foreign laborer, and they enthusiastically chanted the Buchenwald anthem.[15]

THE TREK'S SEPARATION, JANUARY 22–30, 1945

On January 22, the camp leader was ordered to march the prisoners back to Blechhammer. A short distance from the camp, a renewed Soviet advance forced the group back in the direction of Gross-Rosen. Having lost a whole day through making this detour, Klipp attempted to cross the River Oder via a bridge one mile from Reigersfeld

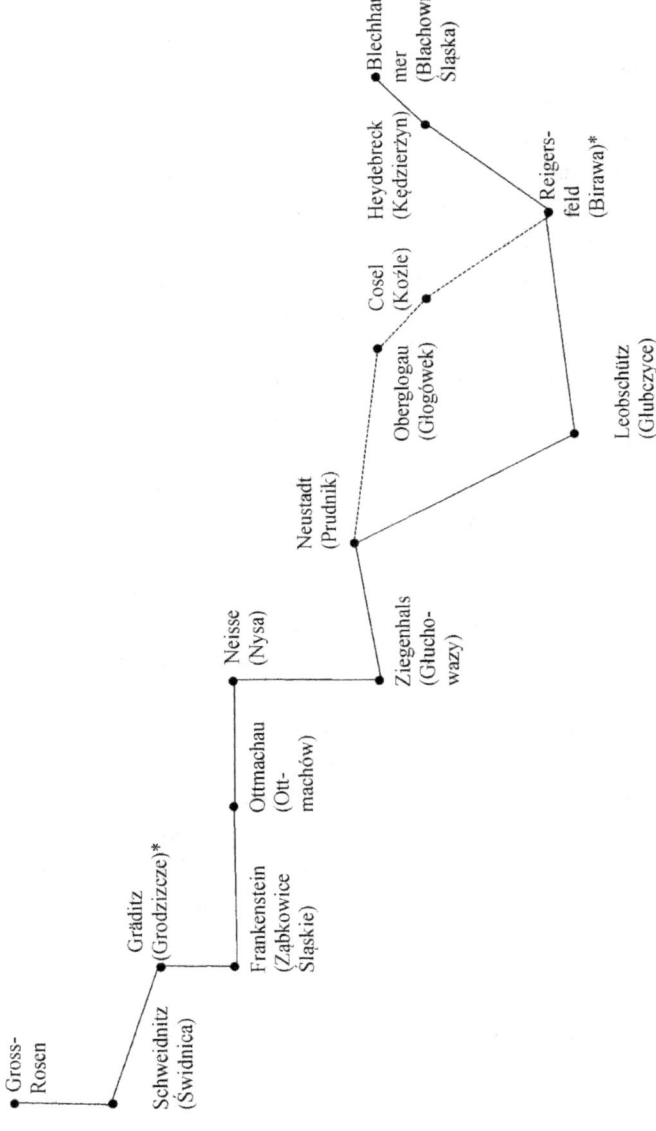

Route of the Blechhammer death march, January 21–February 2, 1945.

(Birawa). It was past midnight, and the home guard had already wired the bridge for demolition. They only waited until about thirty-six hundred prisoners had crossed the bridge before triggering the explosion. Therefore, around four hundred prisoners in the rear were cut off from the main body and were taken on a different route in the following days. The main body marched on to Leobschütz (Głubczyce), where they slept in an empty restaurant.[16]

Twelve SS guards led the split-off group, including forty female prisoners, north toward Cosel. After they spent a night in a barn, a farmer prepared boiled potatoes for them. On January 23 they crossed the Oder near Cosel and marched westward to a sugar factory in Hotzenplotz, Oberglogau (Głogówek). The prisoners enjoyed the warmth given off by the machines and ate the sugar residue left in the cauldrons. They stayed there for another day, while some of the SS men set out to find the main body. In the evening, they received one hundred grams of bread and some soup.[17]

Meanwhile, the main body had advanced over twenty-five miles, from Leobschütz (Głubczyce) to Neustadt (Prudnik) on January 23, and from Neustadt to Ziegenhals (Głuchołazy) on January 24. Contrary to the smaller group, they were driven on at a high pace, and the occasional distribution of potatoes was so uneven that many remained without food. Consequently, they used up their entire bread provisions. Only those volunteering to pull the handcart and sleighs were issued a half liter of soup. The lack of access to drinking water forced them to eat snow. A prisoner desperate to quench his thirst by drinking from a well was even rifle-butted by an SS man.[18] Marching in temperatures below −30°C without hot meals and liquids, combined with eating snow, caused hypothermia. Peripheral body parts were affected by severe frostbite and often became necrotic, as the prisoners had no gloves, and their canvas shoes literally froze to their feet. Frostbite was often the reason prisoners were shot en route. Only a few were still disciplined enough to ration their bread and knew remedies against the cold, such as rubbing themselves with snow.[19]

The split-off group reached Neustadt on January 24. They spent the night in an Auschwitz subcamp for Jewish women, who had been evacuated on January 19.[20] From January 25, they followed the same route as the main body, which was still about ten miles ahead of them.[21] To them, the march resembled a "funeral" from then on, as they were confronted with dead or dying members of the main trekking group on the roads. A prisoner shot in the head by Schmidt remained alive and conscious. The small group found him sitting in a ditch with a heavily bleeding head injury and had to watch while he was shot dead by another SS man.[22] With the Russian gunfire becoming more distant, the prisoners' hope of a swift liberation dwindled, as did their will to continue the horrendous march west. Some had given themselves up from the start and ate all their provisions to indulge in a long-missed feeling of saturation, before letting themselves fall on the road to be shot.[23] A group of teenage inmates kept each other going by sharing pleasant childhood memories and reveries of a return to their previous, happy lives.[24] Others found the strength to go on in defiance. Leo Weiniger related his constant inner struggle to endure the strain of marching: "It was so tempting to just let oneself fall in the snow. But I wanted to live now that I had come this far. I knew what happened to those falling out, and that many let themselves fall only to end this inhumane suffering."[25]

Prisoners trying to help others who could not keep up were forced to surrender them to the SS shooters. Rafael Lewin supported a friend suffering from frostbitten toes and fell back with him to the tail of the group, where they were targeted by the rearguard platoon. One of the SS men pursued them until the friend collapsed, then shot him. The SS man also aimed his rifle at Lewin, who narrowly saved himself by slipping into another prisoner column.[26]

Wehrmacht convoys frequently sped by, driving prisoners off the road, who often sustained fractures or sank into muddy ditches as a result. If they could not get back on their feet immediately, they were shot by SS guards. The Viennese cartoonist Bil Spira fainted after colliding with a military truck and would have been shot without the assistance of his friend, the actor Peter Sturm. Sturm laid him on a sleigh with baggage that he was pulling with several others, until Spira had regained his senses. Throughout the march, Sturm had been using the sleigh to secretly permit injured comrades to take a short rest. Luckily Spira got away with a sprained ankle, and Sturm advised him to conceal his limping by leaning on the sleigh.[27]

On January 26 the small group reached Neisse (Nysa). The following day a heavy snowstorm forced them to leave the road to Ottmachau, and the SS became so disoriented that they decided to march the prisoners back to Neisse.[28] Numerous prisoners perished in the masses of fresh snow, as they were unable to get back on their feet again. Maurice Moshe Szmidt recalled how the group passed them by, helpless and numb: "I still hear the screams of those falling into the deep snow, crying for help. As if we had been driven by the devil, no one turned around who heard these screams that were carried away by the wind."[29] The exhausted prisoners were given a rest on January 28, and local residents distributed some soup and potatoes. But the distance to the main body had increased even more.[30]

The conditions in the large group rapidly deteriorated, as the SS ceased to hand out provisions. They also prohibited the starved prisoners from eating the food offered by Polish and German civilians en route. During a stop in Mittwaldau, Czapla shot at prisoners who were fighting for potatoes, killing three of them. Another prisoner was shot for running back to a Pole distributing potatoes. The SS likewise forbade German villagers to give bread and milk to the inmates, claiming that they were "English spies."[31] Crazed with hunger, one prisoner even dashed into a bakery and grabbed several loaves of bread. Similarly, a group of prisoners tore a shopping bag from the hands of an elderly woman and devoured the contents in a hurry.³² During the nights in barns, they ate grain and horse feed or secretly milked cows. The young artist Walter Spitzer was once caught breaking into a cowshed. He offered to make a portrait of the farmer in return for letting him go, but the man preferred to have his best horse portrayed instead. Satisfied with the painting, the farmer gave Spitzer some soup and bread. Others dared to knock on doors and ask for food and water, and most of the farmers responded in a kind and helpful way.³³

THE TREK'S REUNION

On January 30 those in the large trekking group were given their first day of rest, to wait for the split-off group. They were reunited in a village between Frankenstein and Gräditz. During the rest, a farmer's wife caught a prisoner stealing a handkerchief from her washing line. She denounced him to the SS, and he was shot. The body was taken to the town hall, where there already was a cart loaded with prisoners killed en route.³⁴ The small group was appalled by the deteriorating state of their comrades in the main group, whose diet had largely consisted of snow. The overall conditions were exacerbated by the now larger group. Karl Masseli, the SS man in charge of organizing quarters and food, often made decisions with fatal consequences for the prisoners. He usually rode ahead on a bicycle to find a place for the night.³⁵ On the joint group's first night together near Gräditz, Masseli distributed several groups among different barns. One group of one thousand prisoners was forced into a barn that could only hold two hundred people. The SS simply shot some of the prisoners who did not fit into the building and left the remainder outside in the frost. Many either died due to overcrowding or froze to death outside. Those who survived the night in front of the barn suffered from severe frostbite and often lost several toes. The next morning, the SS ordered the prisoners to pile up the bodies of those shot the other night and add them to the ones who had died inside the barn. Dying inmates were placed on top of the pile and shot by the SS.³⁶

Casualties through overcrowding frequently occurred, when too many prisoners were forced into small barns. An average of sixty prisoners were trampled to death or slowly suffocated each night. Instead of offering some rest, the nights were thus almost unbearable. The survivor Leo Weiniger remembered during one such night that it was his birthday. When he mentioned this to a comrade lying next to him, the man told Weiniger a story as a gift: "That was the most beautiful birthday present of my life. This man was in the same physical and moral state as myself, and I don't know how he found the strength to bring up something as wonderful as this. The storyline, his way of recounting it to me, were extraordinary, almost sanctified. Everything became blurred, I forgot about my pain and the hunger, there was only this voice telling me everything so that I could picture it. In the end, I cried, something the SS had been unable to achieve with their blows."³⁷

The following morning, he found that the storyteller had passed away.

MASSACRES OF UNFIT PRISONERS

Prisoners unable to walk began to be systematically massacred from January 23, when the main group had reached Neustadt (Prudnik). According to a Polish witness, who had been forced to dig graves, the SS shot them in a field close to the village Niemysłowice and buried them in Łąką (Gräflich-Wiese). The bodies of thirty-four men, who could be identified as Blechhammer inmates by the numbers on their uniforms, were exhumed by a Polish War Crimes Commission in spring 1946. The remains of another twenty-eight Blechhammer prisoners were found in the Jewish cemetery of Prudnik. In most cases, the postmortems revealed shots in the neck.³⁸ In Mittwaldau, unfit prisoners were taken to a rubbish dump on a cart and shot there. On another occasion, the SS asked local farmers to bring weak inmates into a forest on sleighs, so they could kill them with hand grenades.³⁹

Around January 31, somewhere between Gräditz and Schweignitz, the SS offered prisoners finding it difficult to walk a ride to Gross-Rosen on horse-drawn carts. Up to forty prisoners were on the carts when they suddenly left the main road.⁴⁰ Abraham Schaufeld, who suffered from a painful cut in his foot, was among them. At dusk the carts stopped at a cemetery, and the SS told them to descend and get undressed. Grasping what awaited them, some of the inmates started to cry. Schaufeld quickwittedly took cover behind a tombstone, while the others were shot. Bereft of his shoes, he made his way barefooted to a nearby farm and hid in a haystack. Around midnight the farmer discovered him and handed him over to the local police station. The police took him to the barn where his group had stayed overnight, and he continued the march the next day.⁴¹ Hartog Tertaas also survived this massacre, with a shot in the stomach, and returned to the trek.⁴²

ARRIVAL IN GROSS-ROSEN AND BUCHENWALD, FEBRUARY 2–7, 1945

It was on February 2 around midnight that the Blechhammer group reached Gross-Rosen. In a postwar statement, the Jewish elder Karl Demerer related that when they approached the concentration camp, Klipp offered him one of his pistols so he could escape with his son. Demerer declined out of solidarity with his fellow prisoners but never found a satisfactory explanation for Klipp's unusual offer.⁴³

From mid-January, Gross-Rosen had been transformed into a crucial transit and rerouting camp for tens of thousands of prisoners evacuated from Auschwitz and its satellites. The new camp annex for Auschwitz evacuees, Erweiterungslager Auschwitz, comprised ten still unfinished barracks in a muddy field that could not realistically accommodate the masses of incoming prisoners. Extreme overcrowding, irregular food distributions, a lack of sanitary facilities, and endless roll calls made Gross-Rosen seem like a hell to the new arrivals.[44]

On entering the blacked-out camp, the Blechhammer trekkers were greeted by the surreal scene of barefooted musicians playing Strauss while standing ankle-deep in the mud. Criminal Kapos from Gross-Rosen then viciously beat them into the barracks, which had been stripped of the usual bunk beds to hold more people. There was still barely enough room to stand. One of the Kapos caused a mass panic among a group of prisoners jammed into a barrack when he hit them with a shovel. Pushing toward the back of the barrack, they eventually broke through the wall. Laughing, the Kapo threw their bread rations into the barrack and disappeared, leaving many prisoners without any food. The next morning the prisoners were assembled for a roll call in a muddy court that lasted eighteen hours. They were constantly maltreated by a Kapo and SS men, who killed several prisoners, until bread and soup were distributed. Some inmates were so desperate, they electrocuted themselves on the wire. The sick and the dying were simply cast underneath the barracks, where water accumulated and they drowned.[45] Admittance into the camp infirmary of Gross-Rosen was no longer granted, as it had reached the limits of its capacity with over three thousand inmate patients. The Auschwitz annex lacked the urgently required facilities to treat sick prisoners.[46]

During a roll call, Karl Demerer noted that eight hundred prisoners had perished on the march from Blechhammer to Gross-Rosen. A member of the SS rearguard platoon stated that there had been one thousand casualties. Another four hundred prisoners lost their lives during the five days in Gross-Rosen.[47] The bodies of the Blechhammer prisoners shot on the last leg of the march were later brought to the camp's crematorium.[48]

On February 7, the prisoners were taken to Buchenwald in open cattle cars. Apart from a single bread allocation when they boarded the train, they received no food during the four-day journey. The train reached Weimar during an air raid and was bombed. The prisoners took cover underneath the train or in a nearby field, and some managed to escape. The journey and the bombings caused another two hundred deaths. Following a foot march to Buchenwald, the prisoners were disinfected, shaved, and issued new uniforms. As there were not enough uniforms left, some had to spend several days wrapped only in a blanket while waiting for their old clothes to be cleaned. Buchenwald was overburdened by the masses of evacuated incoming prisoners. The few barracks of the so-called Little Camp (Kleines Lager) were operated at five times above their capacity, leading to deaths by suffocation. The prisoners also slept in washroom barracks and makeshift tents. The scanty food allocations often did not get through.

Some Blechhammer survivors reported that during their eight-day stay, they had lived on two servings of cold soup. The extreme conditions caused up to eighty deaths per day. Sick prisoners began to be murdered by lethal injections on a large scale.[49]

The majority of the former Blechhammer prisoners were swiftly transferred to various subcamps of Buchenwald, Dachau, or Flossenbürg, and they often had to endure another death march, until they were liberated in spring 1945.[50] By order of Himmler, all remaining Jewish inmates of Buchenwald were evacuated to Terezín in April 1945. He later dismissed his plans to use them as hostages, and they were liberated by the Red Army. Only the Communist Jewish prisoners of Blechhammer managed to stay in Buchenwald, as they joined the camp underground movement's insurgency leading to (self-) liberation. Among them were Peter Sturm, who had previously been interned in the camp in 1938, and Kurt Bachmann.[51]

THE FEMALE PRISONERS

Over one hundred female inmates marched off from Blechhammer with the men on January 21. Dressed in male prisoner uniforms, they mingled with the men despite attempts by the SS to keep them in a separate column in the front.[52] At night the women shared the quarters of functionary prisoners or the SS, and they thus had access to regular meals. Occasionally they were locked into sheds, and they seized the opportunity to drink warm milk from cows. Male friends or relatives often tried to support women struggling to keep up. The mother of a female prisoner was nevertheless shot on the first day of the march.[53] Precise numbers are not available, but a survivor estimated that almost all female prisoners had reached Gross-Rosen alive.[54] There, they were taken to overcrowded barracks with other female prisoners. The women fought for bread and only received some soup on the third day in the camp. Contrary to the men, none of the female inmates reported any violent assaults or hour-long roll calls.[55]

From Gross-Rosen, the women were shipped to Buchenwald on February 7, together with the men. After a brief stay, they were transferred to Bergen-Belsen, a so-called reception camp (*Aufnahmelager*) predominantly for female prisoners. From March 1944, Bergen-Belsen had mainly served as a collection point for unfit prisoners, who were left to die or were killed by lethal injections. By early 1945 it had become a camp for the dying (*Sterbelager*), where the prisoners awaited a slow and agonizing death from almost total neglect. Twenty-five thousand women evacuated from Auschwitz and its subcamps arrived in the camp between December 1944 and March 1945. The former commandant of Auschwitz-Birkenau, Josef Kramer, was installed in Bergen-Belsen. He further reduced the women's food allocations. Starvation and typhus caused staggering mortality rates, with eighteen thousand deaths in March alone. A few days before the camp was handed over to British troops on April 15, 1945, the food allocations stopped entirely, and the women were left without drinking water, as the SS refused to fix a water pump after it was damaged by bombs.[56]

Upon arrival in Bergen-Belsen, the female prisoners from Blechhammer were whipped, and they had to spend the first day in an open field in the snow. There was only a bucketful of rainwater to quench their thirst after the four-day train journey. In the evening, they were issued civilian clothes. The barracks were so full that some women slept outdoors. Apart from morning roll calls, they were left to themselves. Being unable to wash, the prisoners were infested with body lice. Soon many of them had contracted typhus and died of it without receiving any medical attention. The women were often so emaciated and weakened by starvation and illness that they were no longer able to stand or walk but could only crawl. Ida Russ, who had come from Blechhammer with her mother and sister, said that their suffering had been so immense that they had only prayed for death. They all had typhus but lived to be liberated by the British. However, Ida's mother passed away after eating canned meat, and her sister died shortly afterward. Ida Russ was later sent to a sanatorium in Sweden, where she learned that her father and brother were still alive.[57]

Precise death tolls are impossible to arrive at. A female survivor stated that most women evacuated from Blechhammer perished in Bergen-Belsen.[58] By transferring these fit women to Bergen-Belsen, the SS invariably destined them for death, as they were no longer required as a workforce. Following the cessation of mass killings by poison gas, in camps like Belsen the survivors of the death marches were murdered by extreme neglect.[59]

FLIGHTS EN ROUTE

Historians disagree about whether there was a sweeping order to kill prisoners for escape attempts on the march, as stipulated by the directive found in Stutthoff.[60] Prisoners in the Blechhammer trekking group were evidently not punished for trying to escape, either because there was no superior order to do so or because the camp leader did not execute it en route. Escaping was never easier than during the march, as the prisoners were often unguarded, and the SS had stopped counting them. However, in the wintry conditions escapees depended heavily on the support of the local population, whose reactions were difficult to predict.[61] Although denunciations were common, "manhunts" for escaped prisoners, which occurred in parts of western Germany, were not corroborated.[62]

Escapes were often related to extreme exhaustion. For these prisoners, the risk of falling out and being shot during the march seemed greater than escaping. The teenage prisoner Felix G. thus spontaneously jumped into a ditch because he felt too weak to carry on. A German boy following the group as a "spectator" denounced him to the SS. He was rifle-butted back to the column, resulting in a partial loss of hearing.[63] Others hid in the haystacks of the barns they had spent the night in. The SS were well aware of this and searched the hay with their bayonets or hayforks each morning. Sometimes they fired off shots. The farmers were usually present, and most gave away hiding inmates. The screams of those stabbed or hit by a bullet could still be heard by the assembled prisoners outside.[64] Policemen or the home guard checked the barns once more after the group's departure; however, if they discovered escapees, they simply made them return to the march.[65]

Those who remained undetected could rarely avoid encounters with the farmers. Three prisoners were even invited for dinner into a farmer's house after he had found them in his barn. Unfortunately, the prisoners were noticed by a Wehrmacht soldier asking for food at the farm, who then added them to a group from Monowitz.[66] Marcus Samuel Frank was handed over to the local mayor immediately after being caught on a farm. The mayor initially intended to portray himself as the prisoner's "rescuer" to the advancing Soviet troops but then decided to send him to a prison in Breslau. Frank fled, hid once again in a haystack, but was discovered after one week because he was so weak that he fell off a ladder in the barn. He was arrested and interned in a Gestapo prison in Neisse. A few weeks later, he was taken to the Mauthausen and Dachau concentration camps. Frank escaped from another death march in spring 1945 and was finally liberated by US troops near Innsbruck in Austria.[67] Heyman Joseph Leefsma took the desperate decision to hide his father in a barn in the straw, as he had become too weak to walk without help, and Leefsma feared that the SS would shoot him. The surviving son never learned what his father's fate was.[68]

The evacuation permitted some prisoners to finally put their escape plans into practice. A group of twenty teenagers had been organizing their flight from Blechhammer from late 1944. They stole civilian clothes from the tailor's workshop but postponed the escape, as members of the group became sick. Some of these prisoners were among the split-off group that spent the night of January 23–24, 1945, in a sugar factory in Oberglogau. Two of them hid in an empty vat, put on their civilian clothes, and made it to the Russian front.[69] Similarly, Sam Silberberg managed to slip into a column of French POWs who passed by the Blechhammer group on January 26, because he had continuously worn parts of a uniform given to him by a French POW at the OHW factory. Their highly paced march nevertheless made him pass out. His outfit was so convincing that retreating units of the Ukrainian Vlasov Army, who found him unconscious, carried him to a French field kitchen, where he received the first hot meal in days. Silberberg then went to Neisse to be reunited with his mother, who was hiding in a monastery. His father, who continued the march alone, did not survive.[70]

The unplanned escape of Henry S. exemplifies the importance of civilians as flight facilitators and rescuers. Henry had lost two toes to frostbite after two or three days of marching, and his foot began to turn septic. The SS ordered a guard to take him into a forest and shoot him. The two started a conversation on the way, and when the guard learned that Henry was only eighteen, he did not have the heart to kill him. He fired a shot in the air, shook Henry's hand, and wished him good luck. Henry asked for help at a farm and was indeed taken in by a family, who hid him in their barn. For their own safety, they burned his prisoner uniform and clad the boy in a German military uniform, insisting he should pass himself off as an ethnic German. A few days later, Henry's deteriorating health forced them to take him to a hospital. Nuns nursing the patients helped him to conceal his tattooed prisoner number with a bandage. Shortly after the patients' evacuation to southern Germany, Henry recovered and volunteered in the hospital. Still pretending to be an ethnic German, he found himself in a dilemma when he was assigned to distribute food to a group of concentration camp prisoners in March 1945. He was terrified that there might be people among them who would recognize him. Henry only dared to reveal he was Jewish well after the arrival of American troops in April 1945.[71]

THE EVACUATION OF BLECHHAMMER IN CONTEXT

Blechhammer's evacuation was characterized by extremes, ranging from massacres to the rescue of the infirmary patients. These events raise many questions, some of which will never be fully answered. In the havoc of the German retreat, camp leader Klipp evidently seized on the temporary power vacuum to carry out or ignore superior orders at his own discretion.[72] His written order to leave the infirmary patients alive contradicted HSSPF Schmauser's killing directive. Nevertheless, even the Wehrmacht soldiers and other auxiliaries followed Klipp's instructions after his departure. Klipp's latitude for action and far-reaching control seemingly rebut Blatman's concept of a second wave of "local liquidation units" wielding "limitless power." Presumably due to a source error, Blatman uses the example of atrocities allegedly committed in Blechhammer's infirmary to support his argument.[73] Klipp's order to shoot prisoners who refused to go on the march shows similarities to the preserved Stutthoff directive. It was the basis for the recurrent mass shootings of prisoners by SS men, the works police, and soldiers in the evacuated camp, and it instigated further acts of brutality.

In marked contrast to his efforts to safeguard the infirmary patients, Klipp had all unfit prisoners on the trek ruthlessly killed. Similar to the shooting of stragglers, it is unclear whether these murders were in response to superior orders or were randomly carried out by individual guards.[74] The fact that such atrocities were committed on virtually all evacuation treks of concentration camps and the shooting orders were corroborated by the guards of penitentiary subcamps and prisoner of war camps harden the assumption that higher authorities were behind them.[75]

The deaths of prisoners caused by a lack of food and water, overcrowding, and hypothermia probably occurred outside of the framework of written orders.[76] The relatively bearable conditions in Blechhammer's small split-off group seem to indicate that these mortalities increased with the number of prisoners on a trek and were connected to the poor organizational skills of the responsible SS guards.

The purpose of the death marches has generated controversy. Strzelecki posits that the paramount goal of the SS was to relocate Jewish laborers to the west in support of the war industry.[77] Scholars such as Yehuda Bauer and Eduard Kolb consider the death marches and reception camps a continuation of the genocide by other means when the gas chambers had ceased to operate.[78] From a gendered perspective, both contentions are confirmed by the Blechhammer death march. Although one-quarter of the male prisoners was killed en route to Buchenwald, most survivors were almost immediately allocated to work in industrial subcamps. By contrast, almost all female prisoners survived the march, but their transfer to Bergen-Belsen equaled a death verdict. The women were thus fully subjected to the alternative forms of mass murder described by Bauer and Kolb, whereas the male prisoners were kept alive as a labor force.

EPILOGUE

SURVIVING BLECHHAMMER

A Look at Collective and Individual Strategies

BOTH THE SCHMELT CAMPS AND THE CONCENTRATION CAMPS WERE CHARacterized by total arbitrariness, excessive violence, and the policy of annihilation. Coupled with malnourishment and privation, they often resulted in apathy and defeatism. The dehumanizing frame of reference contributed to a disintegration of the prisoners' personalities and affected their decision-making capabilities. Mental and physical survival thus strongly depended on finding ways of keeping one's body and spirit intact.[1]

The Blechhammer prisoners used a wide variety of collective and individual strategies to improve their survival chances. These encompassed overarching structures under the auspices of the Jewish elders, predominantly bribery and large-scale bartering, also with the SS. Trading, pilfering, and trafficking were crucial to individual inmates as well. Many prisoners established close contacts with other groups of foreign and unfree laborers, who would give them food or pass on clandestine letters to their families. A small fraction of prisoners managed to escape or hide in other camps.

Mental strategies, also known as "spiritual resistance," also played a role in coping with the camp conditions. The term refers to attempts to counterbalance dehumanization and degradation in Nazi camps and ghettos through religious, nonreligious, cultural, or educational activities.[2] However, its generalized assumption of inmate solidarity does not sufficiently reflect the sharp dividing lines within the highly stratified camp population, as these practices were not always available to a broad mass of prisoners. Moreover, drawing on inner resources to survive was a very personal affair, which took different shapes in individuals and depended on their previous life experience.[3] These strategies included political resistance, religious practice, and the spreading of "good news" about the course of the war. The production of clandestine artworks was a mixture of both strategies, and it equally served as a means of preserving evidence of the events in the camp for posterity.

"A PACT WITH THE DEVIL": DEMERER'S SYSTEM OF BRIBERY

In postwar testimony, Jewish elder Karl Demerer often prided himself on having saved vast numbers of inmates from certain death and on having improved the conditions in the camp by way of bribery. Numerous survivors confirmed that his preferred strategy had been to bribe the camp leader and other German functionaries with money and expensive gifts. Corruption was a typical phenomenon found in concentration camps and was equally commonplace in ghettos. It thus became a decisive factor in the relations between prisoners and German camp personnel. Bribery nonetheless could not alter the total arbitrariness prevailing in a camp system designed to subjugate and eventually murder the inmates. In a state of emasculation, the Jewish elder attempted to regain a certain level of control over lower echelon German functionaries and might have succeeded in rescuing individuals at times.[4]

However, it was an illusion to believe that the Nazis' genocidal policies could be altered in this way. Just like the heads of Jewish councils in the ghettos, Demerer must have been fully aware of the fact that sooner or later all prisoners would be sent to their deaths. His apparent talent for what survivors referred to as "diplomacy" notwithstanding, Demerer was required to pay a high price for winning small victories. In postwar accounts of former Jewish functionaries, the impact of bribery was often greatly exaggerated, to the point that the real hierarchy of the camp was turned upside down. Along with bartering, bribes were regarded as the most crucial factors of survival, and they were inextricably linked to one another. In the memory of survivors, these two strategies combined allegedly allowed the Jewish elder to gain sufficient control of German camp officials to avert maltreatment, punishments, and even executions. Relating "heroic" stories of daring and provocative behavior, such survivors conveyed the image of an almost invincible Jewish elder capable of saving prisoners at will.

Nonetheless, bribery was always Janus-faced, as the Germans coerced the Jewish elder to pay bribes. Corruption was thus used as another form of robbing the inmates of their last possessions, and it enabled the Germans to enrich themselves.[5] It is not surprising then that Schmelt camp leaders were equally as susceptible to bribes as the SS, and the change of leadership following the Auschwitz takeover made no difference in this respect. A survivor pointed out: "We were not dealing with honest people, who would have been impressed by heroes, but with profiteers trying to avoid being sent to the front."[6]

Under the threat that prisoners would be murdered or sent to Auschwitz, Demerer had to pay the first camp leader, Erich Hoffmann, a monthly "salary" of 500 RM and supply him with cognac and cigarettes.[7] The inmates even bought him a car to appease his violent temper.[8] The deputy Jewish elder, Jozef Niewes, described his daily "obligation" to procure alcohol for Hoffmann: "Each day he had long forgotten what he had been given the day before. If we did not bribe him, once again dozens of people would be killed. I gave him plenty to drink, and once he was intoxicated, I could get out the ones destined for the gas chambers. That was a nerve-wrecking task."[9]

After the Auschwitz takeover, the prisoners continued to give a fixed monthly sum to the new SS camp leader, Otto Brossmann, whose regular income averaged 285 RM a month. Brossmann demanded additional pricey gifts, like a fur coat for his mistress. The second-in-command and the head of the Political Department also received monthly payments of around 400 RM. Similarly, the criminal Kapo Walter Redock pressed the Jewish inmates into procuring alcohol or chocolate for him.[10] Occasionally the camp leaders gave the Jewish elder an ultimatum for paying large amounts of money: "One day, we received an order to collect 2,000 RM. They knew precisely we had money, and it had to be extended within so and so many days. If the money was not delivered, the whole camp would be punished within three days. Of course, the 2,000 RM were handed over, plus several liters of Jenever."[11]

Under Schmelt, the police guards often killed newly arrived prisoners so they could pocket their valuables. They also came into the barracks at night to take away the wedding rings they were still allowed to wear. One guard infamously cut off the fingers of those unable to remove their rings fast enough.[12] The SS men also enriched themselves with the prisoners' property. The survivor Maurits Broeks once watched an SS guard hide two bags containing three thousand diamonds underneath the roof of a barrack.[13] Corruption was so widespread that the German camp personnel felt entitled to have the prisoners pay for gifts to their own families. In 1943 police guard duty officer Mareck thus expected Demerer to collect 1 RM from every inmate to pay for his daughter's wedding.[14] Shortly before Christmas 1944, the SS camp leader Kurt Klipp announced that he would punish the whole camp unless the prisoners provided him with alcohol for the holidays. Demerer nevertheless tried in vain to procure the alcohol from the OHW's "second economy" vendors. All prisoners were urged to find an alternative source. Eventually a teenage prisoner persuaded an ethnic German worker to sacrifice his personal reserve of three bottles, and Klipp was satisfied.[15]

As Demerer was under constant pressure to collect the necessary bribes, a general fund was maintained to facilitate prompt responses to the camp leadership's recurring threats. Demerer thus regularly confiscated money from inmates gathering for gambling nights, and he pleaded with newly arrived prisoners to donate their valuables.[16] Bartering nonetheless constituted the main source of money and goods. Bribery and clandestine barter were interdependent in complex ways. Prisoners involved in bartering were expected to contribute to the bribing fund, while the clandestine exchange of goods was made safer by bribing German guards, who let the respective work details pass unchecked. Those who were caught could often avert the filing of a penal report by offering their contraband goods to guards. The German camp personnel were typically eager to acquire luxury items they no longer had any access to in "first economy" markets due to war-related rationing, such as English cigarettes, chocolates, and perfumed soap, which the Jewish inmates obtained from British POWs.[17] According to Jan T. Gross, the shortage of goods in combination with the discriminated against group of the Jews offering such desirable items as bribes, formed a crucial basis for corruption.[18]

In summer 1944 the Jewish work detail assigned to the Czech building company Smely, a commercial hub of Blechhammer's "second economy," was thrice threatened with being deported to Auschwitz. Suspecting that these prisoners possessed plenty of food that had been rationed in Silesia, the camp leader required Demerer to pay a ransom of US $5,000 so they could stay in Blechhammer.[19]

The system of bribery promoted corruption in the camp itself, particularly in the infirmary. Certain prisoner physicians only treated patients in return for bribes and warned them of impending selections for Auschwitz. Drawing a line of continuity back to the ghettos, the poorer people, who were among the first to be sent to labor camps, were also more likely to fall victim to diseases and selections as prisoners. The corruption in the camp therefore exacerbated the cleavage between "privileged" inmates with access to valuables and desirable goods and those without the means to pay for medical aid.[20]

It is difficult to judge the veracity of the overall effectiveness of the Jewish elders' bribery. Demerer's contention that his bribes had turned Blechhammer into a "sanatorium" certainly does not reflect the crude reality of the camp. Demerer and other Jewish functionary prisoners frequently stressed that bribes had enabled them to carry out floggings themselves. The punishing inmates had merely pretended to hit their victims while leaving them unscathed. However, the delegation of corporal punishment to prisoners was ubiquitous in Nazi camps and therefore not related to corruption. Next to survivor testimonies stating that guards had often been bribed with cigarettes so they would leave the room where floggings were carried out and leave the victims to be spared the rest of the punishment, there were also accounts of severe or fatal beatings. It was equally common that the guards or the camp leader took over if the floggings were being carried out too leniently.[21] Altogether, bribery at best restrained some guards' brutality for a while, but it rarely had the capability to prevent murders, executions, and Auschwitz transports on a larger scale.[22]

In some cases, Demerer did indeed save individual prisoners, such as the teenage boys from the Eastern Upper Silesian ghettos passing through Blechhammer in summer

1943 who later formed the children's detail.[23] He also averted the SS leadership's plans to kill the female inmates, as they had been tattooed with the wrong numbers in April 1944. In postwar testimony, Demerer delineated the delicate process of testing the new camp leader, Brossmann, for his susceptibility to bribes after the prisoners had collected jewelry and gold worth US $5,000:

> I started to talk to him, and he suddenly asked, "Now, tell me Demerer, if I wasn't camp commandant and you weren't Jewish elder, who do you think would win the war?" I said, "Us, of course." Then he looked at me and asked, "Who do you mean by 'us'?" "Us Germans, *Herr Kommandant*." He pulled out his cigarette box, I remember it as if it were yesterday, and offered me a cigarette, lighted it for me and I smoked with him. I returned to the subject of the women: "*Herr Kommandant*, I need to ask you for a huge favor, please help me." He said, "What do you want?" ... "Leave the women in the camp. I found something I have to hand in to you anyway. It was hidden in the clothes depot (I could not tell him that I had collected the money and gold from the people, after all), among the old clothes taken away from people when they were given prisoners' clothes I found a parcel with gold, and jewels, and dollars, I don't even know how much it is, I didn't count. It's of no use to me, so you should take it, *Herr Kommandant*, maybe you need it, and perhaps you can do something for the women." He looked at me in a strange way and said, "Where is the parcel?" I led him to the depot and gave him the parcel. He took it, opened it, had a good look at it all, put it in his pocket and said, "Does anyone else know about it?," and I said, "No, *Herr Kommandant*, not a soul knows, just me." "And you will keep quiet?" "I'll keep quiet, *Herr Kommandant*, I give you my word as a former Austrian officer." Then he said, "The women will stay."[24]

Demerer purportedly succeeded in saving another ten inmates from being sent to Auschwitz and prevented the executions of eight prisoners.[25] He seemingly also had the extremely violent SS block leader Paul Veittes transferred to another camp.[26] The survivor Joseph Braasem related that he had made use of Demerer's bribing fund to withhold a sick transport to Auschwitz in 1944 to save his nephew, who was among the selected patients. This incident was not corroborated by any other testimonies.[27]

In late 1944, Jewish functionary prisoners intensified their relations with lower echelon SS men. On the initiative of the Jewish Kapo Max Goldfaden, the SS men were invited to gambling nights in the prisoners' barracks. Among them was the infamously brutal Tom Mix, who was bribed in an unobtrusive way by the Kapos to appease him. Pretending to borrow gambling money from him, they paid him back with an added pack of cigarettes. The prisoners usually let the SS men win the card games and gave them plenty of drinks, hoping to get small favors from them. They were also treated to exclusive goods obtained through bartering, like English cigarettes, meat, and sausages.[28] To regular inmates, these evenings seemed like "insanity at its peak": "The bloodthirsty hangmen who terrorized us by day and night and might send us to the gas chambers tomorrow, were sitting there with us to play a game and have a chat, as if they were our best friends."[29]

As Gross has pointed out, bribery establishes a social bond. In a pernicious way, this was also true for the grotesque and uneven relationship formed between Jewish functionary prisoners and German camp personnel. The repercussions of corruption reached beyond liberation. In fall 1946 Demerer and the former cook Samuel Band were invited to Erich Hoffmann's Munich apartment several times, purportedly to drink beer and smoke cigarettes together. Hoffmann apparently intended to urge the former Jewish elder to vindicate him in his pending denazification trial and also named him as a witness when he was charged with the murder of Blechhammer inmates in November 1946. Demerer ultimately became a witness for the prosecution and made it clear to the judge that his meetings with Hoffmann had not been of a "friendly" nature, as the former camp leader had claimed. It is unclear how intense these postwar interactions between Demerer and Hoffmann were. A possible link might have been Hoffmann's deputy, Pfeiffer, who, like Demerer, lived in Bayreuth in the immediate aftermath of the war. The ties formed through bribery in the camp obviously prompted Hoffmann to demand such favors from former prisoners. Once again, corruption was coupled with blackmail. Hoffmann presumably threatened to incriminate Demerer in Dr. Ritter's murder in 1943 if he did not comply. Demerer maneuvered himself out of this dilemma by calling on the support of other Blechhammer survivors, who testified on his behalf.[30]

HELP FROM CIVILIAN AND UNFREE WORKERS

Clandestine donations of food and clothes from civilian and unfree laborers constituted a crucial lifeline for the Jewish prisoners. Next to the material aspect, these gestures of solidarity boosted their morale. Many established regular contacts or even friendships with those willing to provide aid. Nevertheless, only a small fraction of about 5 percent of the Jewish work details offered an opportunity for such contacts. The prisoners thus strove to be placed in these details and often shared the food with fellow inmates unable to meet other laborers themselves.[31]

As of summer 1940, Blechhammer had three working parties of British and Dominion POWs from Stalag Lamsdorf.[32] Numerous survivor testimonies corroborate that they readily passed on food, items from Red Cross packages, and clothes to Jewish prisoners.[33] As they also helped Soviet POWs and Soviet civilian workers (*Ostarbeiter*), their key motivation seems to have been to mitigate the palpable suffering of those attributed a low status in the Nazi racial hierarchy. Former British POWs often described the misery of these groups, and especially of the Jews, in postwar accounts or life-writing. Explanations for extending their help were not normally given.[34]

The image of British POWs as selfless and heroic rescuers of Jewish inmates, conveyed among others by John Castle's 1954 autobiography about his time at Monowitz, *The Password Is Courage*, has recently been brought into question. The British historian Russell Wallis argues that the POWs primarily donated their German rations to Jewish prisoners because they disliked this food and lived on what they received in Red Cross parcels instead.[35] The POWs unquestionably preferred the food in the parcels over the unpalatable German meals; however, Red Cross parcels were only distributed on a regular basis and in sufficient quantities from early 1943 and were the only source of nutrition after the stop of German allocations in late 1944. Moreover, inspectors of the International Red Cross found that most British POWs in German captivity were underweight, and the prisoners frequently stated that they felt hungry.[36] This was the case even though they often gave to prisoners "luxury" items from their Red Cross parcels, like chocolates, cigarettes, and perfumed English soap, that they could have used to barter for extra food for themselves. These facts clearly point to a considerable degree of altruism in the British POWs' aid-giving.

In his study on the Monowitz subcamp, Joseph R. White construed British aid as a form of protest against the Nazis' policy of dehumanization and the violation of human rights epitomized by the atrocious treatment of the Jews.[37] The Jewish prisoners commonly perceived the British POWs as extremely privileged, but they, too, interpreted their generosity as acts of solidarity.[38]

Seeing the British as representatives of the western Allied forces, the Jewish prisoners occasionally even turned to them for help against German assaults. The survivor Rachel Brukner Frydych significantly overestimated the British POWs' influence on the Germans by ascribing the departure of Blechhammer's first camp leader Erich Hoffmann to their intervention after the female prisoners had informed them of a collective flogging in their camp. Hoffmann evidently had to leave his post as a result of the Auschwitz takeover in 1944.[39] However, the British POWs did openly demonstrate their contempt for the Jewish child labor practiced at the OHW. Apart from protesting loudly, all they could do was to shower the children with chocolates and sandwiches.[40] The inextricable link between the material assistance British POWs provided to Jews and their overt rejection of Nazi ideology is underscored here. These incidents apparently refute Wallis's contention that British aid-giving to Jews had not been fused with political protest, as was the case in their support of Soviet POWs.[41]

British aid was of particular importance to Jewish prisoners from the Netherlands. Unlike the Polish Jews, they could not draw on the support of civilian Polish workers, as they did not speak their language. Most nevertheless had a good command of English, and some built long-term relations and even friendships with the British. Hessel Goldberg from Amsterdam, for instance, befriended a POW named Tommy, and they became so close that Goldberg felt he had cared for him "like a father."[42]

A special role was played by Jewish prisoners of war from Mandate Palestine, who had been captured in Greece or North Africa while volunteering to serve in the British Army. They formed separate working parties, but the British government made sure that they were treated in line with the Geneva Conventions.[43] Blechhammer had a "Palestinian" detail from December 1941, whose camp was situated in Ehrenforst, near the later Schmelt camp. The POWs immediately connected with the Jewish inmates after their arrival in spring 1942. They passed on war news to them in Yiddish and Hebrew and supplied them with food.[44] These encounters were highly emotional for the Jewish inmates: "One day in 1942, on the way to *Dorflager*, we saw a group of Jewish POWs wearing British uniforms. While passing us by, they told us they were Jews from Palestine. In our misery, we could not imagine that there were indeed Jews left who did not share our plight. It was very moving and a moment of great joy."[45]

The POWs usually showered the Jewish inmates with bread and cigarettes during work.[46] Their attempts to throw food to the inmates when they were driven past their camp on trucks each morning were brutally thwarted by police guard duty officer Rettinghausen. He fired several shots at the trucks one day and forced the drivers to take a different route thereafter. This was the only reported case of POWs being reprimanded for helping Jewish prisoners in Blechhammer.[47]

The dangers involved in accepting food from POWs were invariably greater for the Jewish inmates. However, most of them felt that obtaining extra food outweighed the possible risk of being flogged, the usual punishment for such clandestine contacts.[48] The British POWs were presumably aware of the negative repercussions their help could bring to Jewish prisoners. Wallis's allegation that certain British POWs had only given food to Jewish inmates with the intention to inflict punishment or even death on them as a pernicious variant of anti-Semitism needs to be taken with a grain of salt.[49] His argument reduces the Jewish inmates to passive recipients of British aid and does not acknowledge their autonomous decision-making capabilities, which might have been infringed by starvation at times but still remained intact.[50] And after all, the "Palestinian" POWs, who were unlikely to have been motivated by a hatred of Jews or indifference to their plight, never refrained from helping the inmates due to concerns about their safety.

The psychological merits were presumably greater than the material benefits. R. Stoppelman stressed in postwar testimony that the food obtained from British POWs had not only sustained his brother and himself but encouraged him to persevere. In postwar testimony, he expressed his gratitude to a POW whose identity was unknown to him: "An English prisoner of war gave me plenty of food. I took half of it back to the camp for my brother, who did the same for me. That was the advantage of working in different details, one time he had something, and another time I did. This was a decisive factor in keeping up our spirits. Many thanks to this Englishman and the English! I will never forget this!"[51]

Admittedly, not all encounters between Jewish inmates and British POWs were positive. A small fraction of Jewish survivors explicitly reproached the British for having denied them their support. However, even this apparent criticism simply reveals once more the central importance of British aid in the perception of Jewish prisoners and the sometimes exaggerated "moral" expectations projected onto the POWs.[52] Those relating negative experiences with POWs typically had no command of English at the time and might not only have been less successful in asking the British for food but were prone to misunderstand their answers. The French-speaking Jewish prisoner Nathan Prochownik was thus convinced that British POWs had called him names, while admitting that he had had no knowledge of English then.[53] In a rare case, a British POW who had lost his family in an air raid started to attack Jewish prisoners.[54] Although a narrative developed in wartime Britain that fused ancient anti-Jewish stereotypes with Jews as "war mongers," leading some parts of the population to link the persecution of European Jewry to economic motives, the POWs at no time supported the Nazi regime's genocidal policy. Therefore, this POW's behavior was possibly linked to post-traumatic stress rather than anti-Jewish sentiments.[55]

Overall, former Jewish prisoners predominantly portrayed British POWs in a positive light, and many ascribed their physical and mental survival to their aid-giving. It is impossible to judge the veracity of these contentions; however, they seem to form part of a myth offering an explanation to the survivors themselves for having stayed alive while others perished.[56]

Blechhammer maintained a penal commando unit of French prisoners of war from summer 1943, most of whom were punished for escape attempts. They experienced harsher living conditions than regular western Allied POWs but were still entitled to Red Cross parcels.[57] Although they stayed no more than two months in the commando unit, some befriended Jewish inmates. French language skills naturally eased these encounters.[58] Jules Fainzang, a Polish Jew raised in Belgium, received a can of sardines on the first day he worked alongside a French POW, and the two became close friends.[59] The Belgian Jewish prisoner Leo Weiniger felt that the French penal POWs were more sympathetic than the British, as they had to endure hardships themselves. He appreciated their gestures of solidarity when they saluted Jewish details on the march to work.[60]

Despite struggling for survival in the most adverse conditions themselves, the Soviet POWs held in Blechhammer since September 1941 reportedly shared food with Jewish inmates.[61] The Jewish prisoners, in turn, also risked their lives to aid the Soviets.

Aron Goldfinger once gave a piece of bread to a Soviet POW who was so starved that he had begun to eat grass. Goldfinger was caught by an SS man, who threatened to send him to Auschwitz. His German overseer managed to talk the SS man out of making a report, but he still knocked out Goldfinger's teeth with his rifle butt.[62]

Foreign laborers of various nationalities conscripted for work at the OHW also aided Jewish prisoners. Their help was predominantly extended to prisoners originating from the same countries or able to speak their language. Many French STO (Service de Travail Obligatoire) workers thus supported French Jews.[63] A Jewish inmate regularly received bread from Polish workers he still knew from his hometown, Dzialozun.[64] Similarly, some Dutch laborers were ready to exchange money Dutch Jews had smuggled into the camp into Reichsmark to enable them to barter food.[65] Workers of the Czech building company Smely, which had been a safe haven for Jewish prisoners during the construction of firehouses in summer 1944, continued to provide the Czech Jewish prisoner Ernest Koenig with bread, even after his detail had been deployed elsewhere. Koenig managed to unobtrusively pick up the extra food each day by pretending that he had to transport a log to the Czechs that he carried on his shoulders. In retrospect, he considered the additional piece of bread a key factor of his survival.[66] In early 1942 a foreman from Luxemburg eased the plight of twenty Jewish prisoners in his detail in a similar way by supplying them with leftovers from the German kitchens at the plant every day. The food simultaneously improved the survival chances of other inmates, as the members of this detail shared their regular German food allocations with them.[67] A Jewish detail assigned to maintenance work in a foreign laborers' camp at the *Dorflager* in 1943 was also secretly given food passed through windows or hidden in garbage bins.[68]

Thousands of German civilian workers were confronted with the suffering of Jewish prisoners every day. Possible motives for offering help could be a general dislike of the Nazi regime or political resistance against it. German Communist workers' material aid to Jewish inmates, for instance, was fused with political debate.[69] Others carefully eschewed discussing their political views, but they still conveyed their contempt for the Nazis by giving food to Jewish inmates or allowing them to sleep during work.[70] An adverse attitude to the regime, however, did not always imply unwavering support of Jews. Despite alleging that he was an "anti-Nazi," and that his cousin was imprisoned in a concentration camp, a master persistently threatened to have a Jewish inmate in his detail hanged for "sabotage." He only refrained from reporting the prisoner because he was the only one who could understand his speech, which was impaired by damaged vocal cords.[71] An ethnic German worker who handed out bread to Jewish inmates out of compassion for their misery nevertheless made it clear that he considered the Jews "parasites" that should be removed from society.[72]

Giving leftovers to individual Jewish prisoners was not necessarily politically motivated. To the survivor Simon Grinband, receiving spare food from Germans, "like a beast is given a handful of hay," symbolized his dehumanized status.[73] Along these lines, a group of Wehrmacht convalescents left their bread and soup rations to a Jewish prisoner they worked with, simply because the food was not to their taste. Unlike their master, who comforted the Jewish prisoner by telling him that the war would soon be over, the convalescents avoided personal contacts.[74] Another typical example of this attitude is that of a seventy-year-old Upper Silesian foreman, who left the crusts of his sandwich to the only German-speaking Jewish inmate in his detail, as he found them too hard to chew.[75] Often physically impaired or elderly German overseers rewarded prisoners with food for assisting them. A German invalid master used a Jewish prisoner as his personal assistant and gave him bread in return, while openly demonstrating his anti-Semitic sentiments by saying that the Jews were "terrible," but the inmate in question was an exception.[76]

Others had become disillusioned with the Nazi regime and started to help Jewish prisoners as a form of "revenge" for the loss of family members or their health. The German master of a detail of electricians, supposedly a member of the Nazi Party, clandestinely supplied the Jewish inmates under his supervision with food and clean clothes after his wife, his two sons, and his mother had perished in an air raid. When one of the inmates was wounded in a bombing, he arranged medical help for him from British POWs.[77] Similarly, an elderly master "retaliated" against the regime for his having sustained a jaw injury and losing two sons at the eastern front, by treating the inmates in a humane way. The master always demanded twice the number of prisoners he would have required for unloading bricks, so they could work in two shifts. While one group was working, the other was allowed to rest and received food from him.[78]

With the Red Army advancing westward, the Jewish inmates noticed that higher echelon German employees tried to appear more "friendly." To their astonishment, a group of inmates ordered to fix broken windows in an office of the OHW administration after an air raid were offered sandwiches and apples. However, the prisoners were apprehensive about touching the food, as they expected to be accused of theft afterward. Eventually some office workers handed the food to them directly, while pretending to be shouting at them. They seemingly did this to be protected against denunciation from colleagues.[79] German help occasionally entailed punishment for the Jewish prisoners. A civilian worker passed on two kilograms of bread to a Jewish inmate so he could distribute it among the children in his detail. The inmate was caught, a penal report to Auschwitz was made, and he was flogged.[80]

In summary, German help was interwoven with a complex network of compliance and collaboration with the regime and rarely the result of genuine resistance to it. As

Doris Bergen has pointed out, the dividing line between "rescuers" and "perpetrators" was often blurred, and the one did not necessarily contradict the other.[81]

CLANDESTINE LETTERS AND PARCELS

Jewish inmates from Eastern Upper Silesia were permitted to receive letters and parcels from their families in the ghettos until the end of 1942. Following protests by the next of kin of prisoners who had learned of the abhorrent conditions they had to endure, the Jewish Councils regularly sent parcels with food and clothes to Schmelt camps as well.[82] By contrast, Jews from western Europe arriving in Blechhammer from October 1942 were prohibited from corresponding with the outside world. The lack of extra provisions resulting thereof increased their risk of starvation or of contracting diseases like pneumonia.[83] Most of the men pulled out of deportation trains in Cosel were aware that their next of kin were not alive anymore. However, some still had family members in western Europe living in mixed marriages or in hiding, as well as non-Jewish friends whom they tried to contact. As the official way of communicating by mail was barred, the Jewish inmates approached civilian workers from their home countries, asking them to smuggle out letters in return for money or goods. Whenever a civilian worker was due to go on a holiday back home, the exchange could be arranged. A local farmer even turned his house into a clandestine "post office" through which all correspondence passed. The civilian couriers facilitated the influx of news from the outside world. Apart from asking for material support, it was of great importance to the inmates to learn about the fate of their family and friends at home, while sparing them details of their lives in the camp. It was nevertheless only a minority of prisoners who regularly sent and received mail.[84]

Occasionally, German civilian workers offered to mail letters abroad from Upper Silesia using their own addresses.[85] The Jewish prisoner Maurits Stodel used several Dutch couriers between December 1943 and June 1944 to contact his non-Jewish sister-in-law Mina in Amsterdam. He wrote letters on empty cement sacks that he then passed on to Dutch workers going on holidays. As Stodel did not have the means to pay the couriers in advance, his sister-in-law was obligated to remunerate them, usually in the form of shaving blades and soap. Stodel managed to be sent parcels with food and warm clothes by Mina on a weekly basis. In a postwar interview, he was moved to tears when delineating the couriers' efforts to establish this lifeline for him. He also acknowledged the considerable risk his sister-in-law and his brother, a member of the Dutch underground movement, had been willing to take and stressed that the food parcels had not only helped to secure his physical survival, but had also strengthened his will to endure the hardships of the camp.[86]

Some Jewish prisoners, like Felix G., found an opportunity for writing letters but had no surviving relatives or friends. Help could nevertheless come from unexpected sources. As Felix's family had been deported with him from Belgium, he could think of no one else to write to than a former math teacher from Brussels he had admired during his school years, when a Belgian worker offered to smuggle out a letter prior to going on his holidays. Two weeks later, Felix was overjoyed to receive a parcel with chocolates, cookies, cigarettes, and canned meat from the teacher.[87]

Clandestine letters were often the last signs of life their next of kin got from prisoners, as illustrated by the case of Maurice (Moritz) Young. The Young family had Czech roots and had settled in Vienna but had to leave the country following Austria's annexation by Nazi Germany in March 1938. Maurice emigrated to Paris and the rest of the family to the United Kingdom. Maurice was deported to Auschwitz and eventually transferred to Blechhammer, where he met the British POW J. A. Fox. Fox consented to pass on a message to Maurice's relatives in Britain with the help of his sister at home. His sister was indeed able to contact Maurice's family and sent a reply to her brother, who had been transferred to another camp in the meantime. Fox returned to Britain after the war, whereas Maurice's fate remains unknown. Desperate to learn more about his whereabouts, the Young family wrote to Fox directly and on May 23, 1945, received the following letter from him:

> I saw Maurice with a party digging air-raid shelters. We started a conversation when Maurice asked if I knew Sheffield. You must understand that it was a Jewish lager, so he was not allowed to write to anyone, that is why I had to be careful how I wrote, or else it would not have gone through. I was moved to another lager after fourteen days, and I made enquiries about some Jews he worked with after receiving my sister's letter. As my sister told you, we were forced to march. I'm afraid that a lot of the Jews weren't strong enough to do it, but I cannot tell you what happened to them. The camp Maurice was in was the Jewish lager Blechhammer O.S. The camp was deserted on January 29, I last saw him in May 1944.[88]

Although Maurice was never found by his family and presumably perished in the Shoah, his example illustrates how couriers, like J. A. Fox, facilitated the spreading of information from inside the Nazi camps to the outside world and enabled Jewish prisoners to circumvent the ban on communicating with friends and relatives.

Some couriers took advantage of the prisoners' precarious status and pocketed the money or valuables handed over by relatives, while making the intended recipients believe that they had not received anything.[89] The Dutch Jewish prisoner Samuel Abrams was even told by a worker from the Netherlands whom he had paid for delivering a letter to his mother, who lived in a mixed marriage, that she had been deported. As his mother was his only remaining family member, Abrams was devastated. When he returned home after the war, he learned that his mother had lived in her house all the time, and the driver had never gone to see her.[90] A French STO likewise embezzled parcels passed on to him by the wife of a Jewish inmate living in France. He even wrote false letters to her in the inmate's name to receive more goods and money. The STO only aroused the woman's suspicion when he asked her for cigarettes, unaware that her husband was a nonsmoker.[91]

Even if the couriers worked according to plan, the risk of being caught by German guards remained. The prisoner Paul Weil, for example, was reported to Auschwitz when a French civilian laborer picked up a letter for him.[92] Another prisoner was purportedly hanged for having written to the Hungarian ambassador to complain about the conditions in the camp.[93]

ESCAPES

Under Schmelt and Auschwitz alike, prisoners were killed for escape attempts. The only difference was that during the Schmelt camp phase, the respective offenders were murdered on the spot, whereas the SS men were required to obtain formal permission for an execution from Berlin. Collective punishments were common in both systems. Sources corroborate three unsuccessful flight attempts in 1943, all resulting in the prisoners' deaths.

A young inmate hid inside the camp to escape at a later point in time. While the Wehrmacht guards were searching for him, all male prisoners were flogged. When the hiding prisoner had been found a few hours later, the prisoners were ordered to assemble once more to watch as camp leader Hoffmann set his dog on him in a deadly attack.[94] A particularly tragic escape attempt was made by a juvenile convalescing from typhus on September 13, 1943, who fled from the camp infirmary the night before he was supposed to be sent to the gas chambers of Auschwitz. Hoffmann had all Jewish physicians and medical orderlies flogged and threatened to send five of them to Auschwitz if the boy was not retrieved in time for the transport. The unfortunate prisoner was found a short while later. Before being forced to climb onto the truck to Auschwitz, he was severely mistreated.[95] In late 1943 two prisoners trying to escape when their transport from Königshütte (Chrzanów) arrived at Blechhammer were caught, and Hoffmann had them killed using the infamous death bath procedure.[96]

At least eleven escape attempts could be established for the Auschwitz subcamp phase, seven of which apparently succeeded. Considering the much stricter precautions taken by the SS against escapes, these numbers are astonishing. The tattooed numbers and shaved heads thwarted flights, and only few prisoners still dared to put their escape plans into action. Moreover, most inmates were no longer in a physical or mental state to cope with a flight situation. Successful escapes strongly depended on the assistance of civilians, with whom prior arrangements had to be made.[97]

Shortly after the takeover of April 1944, a French Jewish prisoner fled from his work detail. The new SS administration evidently intended to set a deterrent example to the other prisoners by making them stand at the factory gates for hours while guards searched the territory with dogs. Rumors spread among the intimidated prisoners that they would be severely punished, perhaps even sent to the gas chambers. When the escapee had not been found before dusk, the details had to return to the camp. Instead of being allocated their soup rations, the prisoners were collectively punished with a roll call lasting all night. Around midnight, the first inmates collapsed from exhaustion. Hungry and cold, they were marched straight off to work the next morning. On their return in the evening, they received some soup but were immediately taken back to work again, after almost thirty hours without sleep. The escaped prisoner was presumably never found.[98] In September 1944 Samuel Montag escaped from the factory using to a premeditated plan he had worked out with the Polish civilian laborer Jerzy Grzybowski from his hometown, Będzin. Grzybowski knew Montag's family, who lived in Będzin under an assumed identity, and regularly passed on bread from them. He was ready to facilitate Montag's escape, so he could hide with his relatives. Montag seized one of the frequent air raids to run into a nearby forest and change into the civilian clothes deposited there by Grzybowski. After nightfall, Grzybowski led him to the hideout, where Montag remained until the end of the war. Grzybowski was declared a Righteous Among the Nations by Yad Vashem in June 1989.[99] Similarly, a prisoner from Olkusz escaped with the help of his foreman, with whom he had established friendly relations. Despite being interrogated and beaten by the SS, the members of his work detail did not betray his whereabouts.[100]

The risk of being caught was high, and those acting as flight facilitators were not always trustworthy. A Czech foreman who promised civilian clothes to a prisoner intending to flee eventually denounced him. He and a fellow prisoner who were supposed to deliver the clothes to him were detained by the SS and told that they would be hanged. It was only thanks to the Jewish elder's bribing fund that the SS refrained from reporting the incident to Auschwitz, and the two were released.[101] Chil Feder's painstakingly planned escape was canceled when the SS found 500 RM and a forged photo ID card with his name on it with his comrade Josef Lajtner, who had procured the money and false papers from a German civilian in exchange for fifteen diamonds. It is unclear whether the German reported the two prisoners to the SS, but he took advantage of the situation by embezzling two-thirds of the money he had received for the diamonds.[102]

During air raids, the German workforce often left their belongings behind unguarded. Some prisoners seized these opportunities to escape with the help of stolen

ID cards and clothes, without the risk of involving a third party.[103] The workers' carelessness was lifesaving to a prisoner from Wadowice, whose foreman had reported him to Auschwitz after an argument. Fearing that he would be sentenced to death, the prisoner did not return to the camp but spontaneously grabbed civilian clothes and took off from the factory. The other prisoners had to stand on the assembly court until the SS announced hours later that the escapee had been found. To his great surprise, a survivor learned years later that the escape had succeeded, when he met the former prisoner in Poland after the war.[104]

In late 1944 three inmates escaped on a truck, and the whole camp was punished with a roll call lasting two days. Two of them were caught and hanged in December 1944.[105] On another occasion, the SS tormented a recaptured escapee by placing a card around his neck reading "I am back again" and making him call out this phrase while crawling over the assembly court on all fours.[106]

One day before the evacuation, on January 20, 1945, there was a last, evidently successful, flight from the camp during a Soviet air raid.[107]

HIDING AMONG POLISH LABORERS: THE SANDBERGS

An unusual story of survival is that of the Jewish couple Jenny and Abe Sandberg, who smuggled themselves into a Polish workers' camp in Blechhammer. Using forged papers, they had fled from the Częstochowa ghetto prior to its liquidation in 1942. Pretending to be non-Jewish Poles, they applied to the local employment agency for work and were sent to Blechhammer. Unlike the other Poles, the Jewish couple could not rely on food parcels from relatives at home, and they had to live on the scanty amount of money and ration stamps they received for their work. An ethnic German's remark that Jenny had "Jewish looks" aroused the others' suspicions, and she was ostracized. As no one wanted to work with her anymore, she volunteered for cleaning chores and teamed up with another "outcast," a woman with a limp. The ethnic German continued to harass the couple and eventually denounced them to the Gestapo. The Sandbergs assumed that he had done this to appear more "German." Fortunately they managed to convince the Gestapo officer interrogating them that they were Poles. The Polish workers became more friendly after this and shared some of their food with them. One day a non-Jewish friend of her family recognized Jenny. A Communist friend of her husband immediately intervened, threatening to kill the man if he did not keep quiet. Jenny was pregnant and would have been killed if her Jewish identity had been disclosed. She eventually gave birth to a healthy daughter in a hospital in May 1943. The German midwife was not sympathetic; however, Jenny was comforted by a nun, who suggested she name the baby Maria. The child was taken care of in a nursery for foreign laborers' babies, so Jenny could resume her cleaning duties. The baby was treated comparatively well, and Jenny was permitted to visit her after work. Like the other Polish laborers, the Sandbergs were not evacuated from the OHW in January 1945 but awaited the arrival of the Red Army.[108]

THE EXCHANGE OF "GOOD NEWS"

In a report to the Gestapo in February 1943, the OHW's counterintelligence officer, Dr. Heinrich Schlick, rated the British POWs as the group constituting the greatest security threat to the works. In line with Nazi ideology, Schlick blamed the Jews for inciting acts of "sabotage" among the British by spreading war news: "Due to their intelligence and close contacts to other foreigners, something that cannot be avoided on a giant construction site, they [the Jews] pose a considerable risk in terms of counterintelligence. Therefore, we are presently contemplating to have them exchanged, especially when taking into consideration . . . that their work productivity is so low."[109]

In reality, the exchange of news was a reciprocal affair. British POWs frequently relayed the latest BBC news they had received with their secret wireless radios to Jewish inmates, who in turn passed on what they had heard from foreign or German laborers.[110] These multifaceted contacts allowed the Jewish prisoners to keep updated on crucial turning points of the war, like the Italian surrender, the D-Day landings, the assassination attempt on Hitler, and the Soviet advance.[111] Reports indicating German defeat and a timely liberation strongly fostered the prisoners' will to survive.[112] Their enthusiasm was nevertheless tainted by the uncertainty of whether they would live to see the end of the war.[113]

When French POWs broke the news of the Allied landing of June 1944 to a group of French-speaking Jewish inmates, they joined in their euphoria. The Jewish survivor Jules Fainzang recalled how the German guards temporarily lost control following a POW's exclamation that Paris had been liberated: "They were all dancing on the tables, and I cried with joy. . . . Although the situation got worse for us, the advance of the Red Army and the Allies strengthened our courage."[114]

In addition to speaking or listening to other laborers, the Jewish prisoners gathered information from German newspapers that they secretly peeked into during work breaks or fished out of garbage bins. They often fought over newspapers that had been smuggled into the camp.[115] In a rare case, a Jewish prisoner risked his life when he acquired a radio from a French STO to listen to the BBC.[116] In the barracks, heated debates ensued about the correct interpretation of German military reports.[117] Veterans of the First World War among the prisoners were even attacked for doubting the overly positive prognoses of younger comrades: "If someone gave a non-optimistic prognosis, he would not be talked to anymore, for optimism was crucial to our morale."[118] The firm belief in exaggerated "good news" about the alleged end of the war was a form of escapism characteristic of the Nazi camps. As the prisoners could not hope to be released one day, they had no future to look forward to and consequently were prone to apathy and losing their sense of time. Liberation narratives motivated many to persevere.[119]

Under the SS, the barracks were regularly searched for newspapers. A prisoner was severely maltreated simply for having used a piece of a paper as a handkerchief.[120] In August 1944 Dr. Schlick, together with Blechhammer's Political Department, attempted to charge the Jewish Kapo Max Voss with sabotaging the war effort. Voss had relayed news from foreign stations passed on to him by the Wehrmacht soldier Ernst Meyer to fellow prisoners and POWs. In their report to Auschwitz, the OHW deputy director and the head of the Political Department claimed that Voss had undermined the POWs' work morale and strengthened their "spirit of resistance." Max Voss was sentenced to twenty-five lashes as a result. The soldier was interrogated by Dr. Schlick but apparently not reprimanded.[121] The OHW management and Nazi authorities were aware of German workers asking Jewish prisoners for war news, as they did not trust the official radio broadcasts or newspapers anymore. In January 1945, Dr. Schlick even suggested to the propaganda officer SS Obersturmbannführer Kügler publishing at least *some* real facts, deeming this measure less harmful than not reacting to the news spread by foreign laborers and prisoners.[122] Jewish prisoners nevertheless were cautious in their conversations with Germans and tried not to confront them with too many unpleasant developments.[123] Nonetheless, the survivor Louis Waterman dared to tell his German overseer that Germany was facing defeat: "'We can't lose with Hitler and Göring,' the Meister said. I answered that they were only two men, and he laughed. In the evening, he returned with a letter saying his house had been bombed. He admitted that I might have been right."[124]

Especially toward the end of the war, some German OHW workers openly demonstrated their support of the Allied advance. A German overseer thus informed a Jewish prisoner in his detail of the D-Day landing and reassured him that he would soon be able to go home.[125]

SPIRITUALITY

Contrary to other unfree laborers, concentration camp prisoners and the inmates of Schmelt camps were forbidden to hold religious services, to gather for prayers, and any other form of practicing their religious beliefs. Religious artifacts brought into camps by the inmates were confiscated and destroyed. Moreover, the Nazis frequently used Jewish holidays to stage executions or collective punishments, and observant Jews were prevented from fasting on Yom Kippur under allegations of "sabotaging" the German war effort. The coalescence of "racial" anti-Semitism with anti-Judaist violence explicitly directed against religious symbols, including the desecration and burning of synagogues, epitomizes the massive impact of thousands of years of metaphysical relations between Jews and non-Jews. The Nazis' "racial" anti-Semitism was inextricably linked to the religiously motivated Christian anti-Semitism of the past and adopted its demonizing images of Jews.[126] In Blechhammer, a minority of observant Jews were juxtaposed with a majority of inmates who, whether or not they had been raised in a Jewish religious home, were not practicing their religion or remained indifferent. Some lost their faith while witnessing barbaric acts of cruelty committed by the Germans in ghettos and camps; others turned to religion to find consolation. Religious life was possibly more widespread in camps than is revealed by testimonies and took on multifaceted forms. Reducing religiousness to acts of "spiritual resistance" and martyrdom elides the central importance of religious practice in a narrative of individual survival.[127]

Religious gatherings had to be held in secrecy. During the Schmelt camp phase, camp leader Hoffmann frequently had religious artifacts, such as phylacteries (*tefilin*), confiscated and buried on the camp's rubbish dump. However, the religious prisoners stoically dug them out and reused them.[128] One of the camp policemen and head of the burial detail, known as the *shister*, regularly invited rabbis and other observant inmates to his room, where he clandestinely kept *tefilin* and a prayer shawl (*tallith*). Curiously, the *shister* was not religious himself, yet he took the risk of facilitating prayer services. To the religious prisoners the opportunity for prayers offered a chance for retaining their self-respect in a dehumanizing environment.[129] On Friday nights, Shabbat services were held in numerous barracks. The prisoners set a watch to warn them of patrolling guards. The Jewish elder's son, Heinrich Demerer, related that he had been invited to join the Shabbat prayers of French Jewish inmates when he happened to pass by their barracks. Hesitant at first, as he did not know any French prayers, he stayed with them the whole evening and pledged to return the following week. However, not all observant prisoners tolerated the presence of nonreligious comrades during their prayer times.[130]

The female prisoner Gucia Ferst retained her usual prayer routine in the mornings and in the evenings, believing that God would help her to survive. Her unbroken faith inspired other women, who gathered around her to reconnect to traditional forms of spirituality they had known from home, to what they referred to as *yiddishkayt*. On Fridays they got together in their barracks, exchanging memories of the way the Shabbat had been celebrated in their families. Keeping track of upcoming holidays also helped prisoners maintain a certain sense of time.[131]

On Yom Kippur, many of the religious prisoners tried to keep the traditional fast, and they sold their bread rations to fellow inmates for cigarettes. The Jewish elder had food rations distributed early on such occasions to enable the observant to eat before the beginning of the fast. However, aware of the high holidays, the German guards attempted to prevent them from fasting. On Yom Kippur 1943, police guard duty officer Mareck personally checked that everyone finished their rations and punished those who disobeyed by withholding their food stamps. In 1944 the SS administration chose the Day of Atonement for a particularly traumatizing hanging. After the execution, those refusing to collect their food rations were viciously maltreated by the guards.[132]

As the representatives of an anti-religious ideology, the SS frequently humiliated observant Jews by questioning the existence of a deity.[133] When a new transport of Polish Jews, many of whom were religious, arrived in Blechhammer, the SS confiscated their prayer books and artifacts, piled them up, and set them on fire. Some tried to rescue pages of Scripture from the flames, while others exclaimed in despair that there was no God if he allowed this to happen. Eventually a Blechhammer prisoner who had witnessed the scene convinced them that the SS merely intended to rob them of their dignity and that their faith did not depend on the possession of religious artifacts.[134]

Christmas was one of the rare occasions on which the prisoners received meat. It was typically pork and therefore was rejected by some religious prisoners. Others deemed it acceptable to eat nonkosher food in order to survive.[135] While nonobservant prisoners often reproached the religious ones for gratuitously risking their lives by attempting to adhere to a kosher diet, this proved advantageous at times. When the SS distributed artificial sausages to test them on the prisoners, the religious inmates abstained from eating them, and thus they were not affected by the severe digestive problems that soon afflicted the other prisoners.[136]

It has been suggested that observant prisoners found it easier to cope with the everyday atrocities experienced in camps, as they were able to integrate these events into a long-standing history of suffering of the Jewish people and perhaps even accepted them as a form of divine punishment. This included the notion of sacrificing one's life to sanctify the name of God, known as *Kiddush ha-Shem*.[137] However, *Kiddush ha-Shem*, a form of martyrdom in response to forced conversion in the Middle Ages, intrinsically differed from the situation of Jews under the Nazis. As Steven T. Katz has pointed out, the Nazi genocidal policy precluded "a separation of the Jew from Judaism," denying conversion as an option to save one's life. Nazi racial laws aiming to eradicate the Jewish people, not merely Jewish religious and cultural life, did not discern between practicing and secular Jews, and both were murdered indiscriminately.[138]

In (ultra-) orthodox thinking, the reality of the Holocaust was shaped by the metahistorical reality of Scripture. The Nazis were considered the evil tools in God's hands to punish the nonobservant Jews. Some believed that their plight could only be ended by repentance (*teshuvah*).[139] Numerous Blechhammer inmates with a religious upbringing were confronted with severe theological crises or a complete loss of faith while in the camp. Sam Silberberg, then a teenager, began to reject his ultraorthodox father's interpretation of the Holocaust as part of a divine plan, and he found the idea of the Germans claiming the same God as the Jews unbearable: "I could not make use of the notion of one God at a time when the Wehrmacht... had the inscription on their belt buckle '*Gott mit uns*.'" During the death march, his father's spirituality nevertheless constituted a source of hope, until he decided not to flee with his son, as the two of them had planned to do a long time before the march. Feeling obligated to commemorate the anniversary of a relative's death according to religious laws, the father continued the march alone, while Sam Silberberg escaped. When he learned that his father had perished, he blamed his piety for his death.[140]

Even to religious prisoners, the brutality of the camps was hard to reconcile with their beliefs.[141] In the aftermath of the hanging on Yom Kippur in 1944, for instance, a dispute arose among a group of orthodox Jews on whether God could exist if he allowed such acts of cruelty to happen.[142] While some of the pious prisoners were bereft of their faith, individual nonreligious inmates returned to their spiritual roots to feel closer to family members they assumed were dead. Reciting Yiddish prayers from their childhood was a way of commemorating their next of kin, and it gave them some comfort. The survivor Nathan Prochownik compared his prayers to "bottled messages cast into the ocean," hoping these would somehow reach his family, if he entered into a dialogue with the God, who had allowed them to be murdered but spared his own life:

> At night in the block, I was overwhelmed by a sinister sense of foreboding that my parents and siblings were dead. I felt an immense loneliness that would remain with me forever. I pondered whether there was a Supreme Being.... One evening I felt the desire to pray in Yiddish and to use the colloquial words I had heard from my mother, when she expressed her joy or anger, and also when she had implored the Lord. Perhaps I would be reunited with her and the rest of the family through the agency of this being above us that was so hard to perceive?[143]

Faced with death, even nonreligious prisoners commonly fell back on some form of ritual practice. A member of the bomb-clearing detail, for instance, recalled that he had always "trusted in God" while handling delay-action bombs.[144] Moreover, certain events related to the violent deaths of Nazis were construed as manifestations of "divine judgment" by the broad mass of the nonobservant camp inmates. One such occasion was a direct hit on a shelter reserved for German staff during an air raid, killing everyone inside. Only minutes before the bomb fell, a group of Jewish prisoners had been chased out of that shelter. An inmate who witnessed the scene remarked to his friend, "'You know, I'm gonna start believing in God again. A hundred times we escaped death, but this was direct intervention.'"[145] Another time, members of the Hitler Youth were driven past a detail of Jewish prisoners, and they started to chant Nazi slogans. One of the boys jumped off the truck before it had come to a halt and was fatally hit by the vehicle. Many prisoners perceived this as a divine punishment.[146]

Jules Fainzang, who was not observant himself but had received religious tuition in a *cheder* as a child, was eager to share his knowledge of the Bible with others lacking this education. Among his "students" was the prisoner physician Dr. Iwanter, who had converted to Catholicism early in life. Fainzang's biblical stories served a similar purpose as the recounting of novels or movies he was familiar with—namely, to ease the strenuous foot march between the camp and the factory by distracting himself and fellow inmates. He also alluded to biblical figures in difficult situations, a phenomenon commonly found among religious inmates. For example, while the prisoners were toiled up a steep hill, he narrated the story of Moses and the exodus from Egypt.[147]

POLITICAL RESISTANCE: COMMUNISTS

Blechhammer had a small yet influential group of up to four active Communists. They never managed to rally other prisoners behind their cause, mainly because most of their comrades were too exhausted to engage in political ideas, let alone resistance activities.[148] However, they tried to improve the conditions in the camp by countering the Nazis' strategy to split up the prisoners' solidarity. Two prominent members of this group were Kurt Bachmann and Peter Sturm.

Bachmann (Düren, 1909–Cologne, 1998) worked in the Jewish elder's office, the *Schreibstube*.[149] He also volunteered to become a medical orderly in the camp infirmary.[150] During a dysentery outbreak, Bachmann clandestinely procured sulfonamides for the patients.[151] He had joined the Communist Party of Germany (KPD) in 1932 and participated in an underground resistance movement until he fled to France with his wife, Alice, in 1938. After the German invasion of 1940, Bachmann restored his contacts with the Communist underground but was arrested and deported with his wife from Drancy in 1942. Alice was murdered in Auschwitz, while Kurt Bachmann was pulled out in Cosel and went through numerous Schmelt camps before coming to Blechhammer. Following his liberation in Buchenwald, he returned to Germany and cofounded the Association of the Persecuted by the Nazi Regime (Vereinigung der Verfolgten des Naziregimes). He also was part of the KPD leadership until the party was banned in 1950. Bachmann then became a journalist and worked as a political correspondent for the weekly paper *Die tat*. Almost two decades later, in 1968, he was one of the founding members of the German Communist Party (DKP), which he chaired until his death.[152]

The Viennese actor Peter Sturm (Vienna, 1909–East Berlin, 1984) had been a member of the Communist Party of Austria. Following his arrest in May 1938, he had been interned in Dachau and Buchenwald for one year. He fled to France and was deported from Drancy in summer 1942. His contacts with the camp's Communist underground organization permitted him to remain in Buchenwald following the evacuation of Blechhammer, and he helped to overthrow the SS in April 1945. He voluntarily settled in East Berlin after the war.[153] Sturm utilized his long-standing camp experience to teach a group of fourteen teenage prisoners how to improve their survival chances. Setting a personal example, he emphasized the importance of personal hygiene and discipline. They also learned to protect one another against assaults by the SS and the risk of selections by sharing food with those whose rations had been withheld due to sickness, and by supporting weak comrades during the march to the OHW. Kurt Baum was one of these teenagers, and he related that many of them attributed their survival to Peter Sturm, who had given them a feeling of belonging and of not living in "a jungle."[154] When Sturm was offered the controversial position of block elder in late 1944, he reluctantly accepted after Kurt Bachmann convinced him that the opportunity to help others outweighed the risk of being drawn into the Nazis' perfidious system of inequality and corruption. As a block elder, Sturm was soon renowned for his justice, and he managed to have the teenage inmates be assigned to lighter work.[155] For example, he distributed food leftovers according to an alphabetical list, so that all prisoners received their share. Peter Sturm is said to have saved more than one life and was an inspiration to many: "In this world of violence, contempt and injustice he was the only one who respected the principles of human rights. In his barrack, humanity, equality, and fraternity prevailed."[156]

During the death march, Sturm kept himself going in spite of the adverse conditions by comparing his struggle to survive with the combat of the Soviet soldiers. Drawing a line of continuity from the death march back to his decision to fight Austro-Fascism and Nazism in the prewar years, he was able to integrate his suffering into the joint Communist effort to create "a better world."[157]

Non-Communist Jewish prisoners were reportedly helped by German Communist OHW workers, who supplied them with food, medicine, and money.[158] Under the Nazis, the KPD had split up into small, underground cells, whose members no longer engaged in open resistance but turned to individual demonstrations of nonconformist behavior.[159] Some deliberately sought contacts with foreign laborers at the workplace.[160] These relations could have negative repercussions for the Jewish prisoners, as illustrated by the case of Josef Wolmark. He was reported to Blechhammer's Political Department in October 1944 for accepting a German foreman's offer to exchange money and valuables for bread and cigarettes. The German, allegedly a Communist, was arrested by the Gestapo, and Wolmark had to sign a trumped-up confession stating that he had indirectly supported the Communist organization. He was sentenced to twenty-five whip lashes by Berlin.[161]

The Jewish Communists in Blechhammer apparently did not join forces with non-Jewish communist workers. Attempts by British intelligence to use foreign laborers as "Trojan horses," who would form a bridge with German Socialists and Communists and create upheaval among the workforce, evidently failed, as the level of resistance among German workers was generally very low.[162]

"ALMOST NO ONE DIED OF HUNGER"? CONFRONTING THE MYTH OF BLECHHAMMER'S "SECOND ECONOMY"

"Our good Jews had money, gold and jewels and could procure anything they wanted, anything they wished for, on the construction site—butter, coffee, milk, eggs, sugar, sardines, sausages, everything. Many had money and shared with one another, thus Blechhammer really was not a hunger camp. Almost no one died of hunger."[163] This statement made by Jewish elder Karl Demerer in 1973 is the centerpiece of a myth whose key message is that thanks to the black market, very few inmates had died of starvation. Curiously, in a judicial interview held nine years earlier, Demerer had stated that there had hardly been any deaths in the camp but explained this by the fact that emaciated and unfit prisoners had regularly been taken to Auschwitz to be killed.[164] The narrative that death by starvation had been rare was predominantly supported by former functionary prisoners.[165] Their contention that up to 75 percent of the prisoners had been able to barter for extra food is rebutted by the testimonies of regular inmates, reducing this number to a mere 5 percent.[166] Only a few possessed the means and stamina to engage in such deals, and these prisoners were aware of their special status: "We, the privileged ones, a very small minority, managed to make contacts with civilians of all nationalities who worked there."[167] Feelings of guilt likely prompted former functionaries to fabricate a self-exculpatory narrative of a camp where everyone allegedly had enough to eat. These stories might equally have been rooted in fears of being put on trial or being ostracized by fellow survivors.[168]

Regardless of the exact numbers of those involved, the act of bartering undoubtedly played a key role in the memory of survivors. They often described in minute detail how they earned their first money or food and managed to establish clandestine contacts with other workers. Bartering raised their self-esteem, as it enabled them to regain some control over their lives. Access to more and higher quality food increased their survival chances; at the same time, it defied the Nazis' policy of annihilating the Jews. These prisoners thus created another myth, centered on their inner strength, cunning, and enterprise as the sources of their survival.[169]

In wartime Germany, trading or offering services outside of formal sectors had become an essential part of everyday life. The rationing of goods along with the devaluation of money fostered the so-called second economy. This affected not only the German civilian population but also large parts of the foreign and unfree workforce.[170] The term "black market" is commonly found in testimony, but it seems inappropriate in this context due to its association with illegal or criminal activities. During the war, operators of the second economy supplied goods and services of an absolutely legal nature that were no longer available in "first economy" venues.[171]

Despite the risk of punishment, Jewish prisoners soon became integral to Blechhammer's second economy. Although their precarious status prevented them from acting on equal terms with civilian workers, they carved out a niche for themselves as interlocutors due to their foreign-language skills. Only a few work details offered a chance for establishing such contacts with other laborers without being scrutinized too closely by German guards. To some prisoners, favorable settings for safe barter outweighed harsh working conditions, and they volunteered for seemingly unattractive commando units.[172] Most deals required starting capital, usually in the form of valuables prisoners had smuggled into the camp, like their wedding rings or cash money.[173] Less resourceful prisoners had to make a much greater sacrifice: their own food rations. One of these was sixteen-year-old Israel Rosengarten. For eight consecutive days, he sold his entire bread allocation to fellow inmates. With the 6 RM he earned in this way, he bought a higher-quality bread loaf from foreign laborers and resold it for 8 RM in the camp. He kept up the same system for several months, until he had saved enough money to buy three or four loaves of bread. Following this life-threatening period of almost total deprivation, he could finally purchase bread for himself. The additional food meant a lot more to him than just filling his empty stomach: "Gaining food all by myself was a symbol of my resistance and it strengthened my ability to survive.... The feeling of triumph was magical. I had outwitted the monsters who wanted to kill us."[174] Another prisoner pursuing the same strategy was caught by the SS when he sold his sausage ration to a fellow inmate for 3 RM in order to procure some bread from a foreign worker.[175] Others took over cleaning chores in the barracks and resold the extra food they received.[176] Some prisoners sold their clothes, cigarette allocations, bonus vouchers, or pilfered tools.[177]

A main target group for bartering were the British and French POWs. As they mainly had to live on dried or canned food from Red Cross parcels, they craved fresh fruits, vegetables, bread, and eggs. When their German rations ceased in late 1944, the British increasingly depended on bartering to sustain themselves.[178] Fresh products were offered by Czech and Polish laborers, who in turn were interested in obtaining Red Cross package items such as chocolates, cigarettes, and soap. In order to exchange their goods, both groups used multilingual Jewish inmates as intermediaries. Hoping to acquire essential food, as well as medicine, shoes, and clothes, the deprived Jewish prisoners built up an impressive network of civilians to help them procure almost anything the British wished for. The Jewish inmate Nathan Prochownik even managed to persuade German workers to buy powder for preparing a blancmange, when a

British POW had told him of his craving for the dessert. The Germans received a share of the prunes Prochownik was offered by the POW. The transaction was repeated several times, until Prochownik had earned enough prunes to barter an extra bread ration. Prochownik nevertheless found it hard to relate to the superficial concerns of the POW, considering the murderous realities in the camp for Jews: "It was a tough blow for him not to have a blancmange, while in a few meters' distance we were dying like flies, lacking everything."[179]

The British were also very keen on onions. As the author of a food column in the Lamsdorf POW magazine *The Clarion* humorously pointed out, onions were "as scarce as an African native skating round the North Pole" in British camps.[180] A Jewish prisoner therefore specialized in supplying the POWs with onions in return for cigarettes.[181] Similarly, the teenage inmate Wolf W. arranged a deal with two Polish laborers, who brought him bread rolls that he resold to British POWs. He shared the additional bread rations he was able to procure with fellow prisoners. Even this kind of small-scale bartering was invariably accompanied by German demands for bribes, however. An SS guard who claimed he was "hungry" took some of the rolls for himself in return for not filing a penal report.[182]

Bartering was occasionally combined with the Allied resistance effort, and Jewish prisoners also played their part in it. The Belgian Jewish inmate Jules Fainzang was recommended as an intermediary by French POWs when the British urgently required an electronic device for a secret wireless radio in their camp. Fainzang utilized his contacts with Polish workers, who agreed to buy the device in the nearest town, to enable the British to receive radio messages. Fainzang's reward, a carton of cigarettes, was unfortunately confiscated by an SS patrol.[183] From late 1943, Czech workers supplying Blechhammer's second economy markets with products from Bohemia that had been rationed in Silesia, like eggs, butter, ham, sausages, and alcohol, strongly relied on Jewish prisoners to barter with British POWs and French laborers. They received some of the food in return.[184]

The Jewish elder Demerer ran large-scale bartering operations, primarily to gain money for the camp's bribing fund. Bartering and bribery were closely intertwined, as trafficking contraband goods was facilitated by bribing guards, and the revenues thereof were required as bribes.[185] As Demerer did not work on the construction site himself, several Kapos were delegated to barter for him. One of them was the Belgian Jewish Kapo Goldberg, whose intimidating demeanor permitted him to control the bread prices on the market. If POWs or civilian workers asked for more than the fixed sum of 6 RM, Goldberg and his fellow Kapos beat them up.[186] The prisoners were also instructed to cut off chunks from conveyor belts, which were exchanged for bread and cigarettes by their Kapos.[187]

Individual trafficking without Demerer's special protection was riskier, prompting such prisoners to fabricate food cans with false bottoms or to add secret pockets to their jackets.[188] During the Schmelt camp phase, work details were regularly flogged for bartering. Threats by camp leader Hoffmann to execute those involved in such undertakings were reportedly not put into practice. However, the clandestine exchange of goods temporarily ceased, and some contacts were lost.[189] Under the SS, over forty penal reports related to bartering were forwarded to Berlin. Typical punishments included floggings, extra hard work for up to ten consecutive Sundays, and transfer to a penal commando unit.[190] Many SS guards were nonetheless susceptible to bribes and refrained from reporting prisoners if they could pocket the contraband goods themselves.[191] The greatest threat was posed by the works policemen, who were given license to kill Jewish prisoners on the spot following the decrees on plundering and sabotage of July 1944.[192] Moreover, dishonest trading partners occasionally took advantage of Jewish prisoners and robbed them of their last possessions: "A single thought was on the mind of the immense number of prisoners: survive and eat, eat to survive.... To guards and laborers with contacts to the outside world, these people, who lacked everything, were a temptation. And they, too, were driven by a single idea: to make money with them."[193]

As an example of this, the young prisoner Israel Rosengarten was deceived by a British POW for whom he and a fellow prisoner had made a beret. The POW never gave them the agreed remuneration of prunes and raisins and simply avoided them. Rosengarten's next deal with a British POW ended even worse. He had procured razor blades from Czech workers for the POW and was paid with prunes. However, as soon the exchange had taken place, a Wehrmacht soldier guarding the POWs came along, rifle-butted Rosengarten, and took away the prunes. This strange coincidence led him to suspect that the POW had bribed the guard to take back his prunes.[194]

In May 1944 the Jewish prisoner Israel Wächter made an exceptional decision: he reported a German foreman to the authorities for cheating on him! The foreman, Felix Ochmann, was a member of the German Air Force and had promised Wächter to supply him with bread, honey, and confitures from his father's bakery for a considerable amount of gold. Wächter and several fellow prisoners were ready to invest their valuables. However, as soon as Wächter had handed over the gold, Ochmann announced that he had no intention of delivering the goods and went off. Wächter's outraged exclamation "Catch the thief!" immediately alarmed the guards, who found the gold on Ochmann and arrested him. Ochmann was put on trial before a military tribunal in Breslau, and Israel Wächter was called up as a witness. Wächter's courage nonetheless entailed negative consequences for himself. The Political Department of Blechhammer sent a report to the WVHA, and he was sentenced to twenty-five lashes and punitive work for the possession of valuables.[195]

Aside from a lack of resources, the considerable dangers outlined above deterred most prisoners from bartering.[196] The teenage inmate Felix G. always went straight to sleep when bartering comrades started to prepare their extra food in the evenings, so he would not give in to the temptation of doing it himself.[197] The Jewish camp physician Dr. Wollenberg had other motives for rejecting clandestine trading. As a former officer of the German Army and a veteran of the First World War, he still identified with a military code of honor and was appalled when he learned that the other doctors lived on contraband food, like the sardines they offered him on his first night in Blechhammer: "My delight at the sardines was spoiled. I had a feeling that these were the first and last ones I would see during my time in the camp. But I did not starve, ... even though neither in Blechhammer, nor in any other camp did I 'make money.'"[198]

Prisoners who had the means but did not want to become involved in second economy deals could turn to the Fogiel family, a father and his three sons from Belgium, who offered to exchange money for food.[199] Similarly, two prisoners from the Netherlands specialized in selling the diamonds many of their compatriots had brought with them.[200]

Kapo Walter Redock, a "green triangle" from Auschwitz who headed the clothing chamber, was prohibited from leaving the camp himself but delegated Jewish prisoners to barter garments from the magazine for him on the construction site. In late 1944 four inmates offered rucksacks procured by Redock to British POWs, who were preparing for the evacuation.[201]

Contraband goods were also sold in one of the barracks that served as a clandestine "shop." The inmates called it the "stock exchange," as the prices varied depending on the quantity of available products. The prices were generally higher than on the construction site. One piece of bread bought four potatoes, for instance.[202] Almost anything was on offer, even live chicken, chocolate, fruit, white bread, English cigarettes, condensed milk, sardines, and alcohol. A bottle of alcohol was worth up to 400 RM.[203] The stock exchange was a place where the camp's social strata became palpable: "The affluent sold English chocolate, and the poorest offered their soup rations."[204] Fat allocations from the camp kitchen embezzled by the cooks were resold there as well. In stark contrast to bartered food, these fats had been deducted from the standard rations.[205] The German camp leadership attempted several times to raid the barracks, but the prisoners always set watches and hid the goods in time.[206]

Many German laborers bartered goods they clandestinely manufactured during their normal work at the OHW, utilizing the company's raw materials and tools. Jewish inmates allocated to them were often forced to assist in these illegal dealings. The OHW management apparently knew of their workforce's illicit enterprises but only seemed to object to the use of Jewish prisoners for this purpose. On December 15, 1943, following a complaint by Speer's Ministry of Armament and War Production, Otto

Stoltzenburg of the building supervisory board issued an official warning to all contractors that their employees faced prosecution if they continued to assign Jewish prisoners to such tasks.[207] The Germans nevertheless proceeded with their second economy businesses, and Jewish prisoners fabricated electric stoves, repaired clocks, or fixed bicycles for them.[208] The survivor Stanley B. was forced to mend jewelry for his German foreman, who owned a jeweler's shop in Hamburg. The foreman did not pay him and carefully avoided giving out his name. Sometimes he passed on food to Stanley in a manner that reminded the latter of how "a bone is given to a dog."[209] German workers also specifically chose prisoners with a good command of English to barter with British POWs for them in return for cigarettes.[210] The inmates' enforced participation in the Germans' bartering put them at risk of being punished or even killed on the spot for alleged "plundering."[211] Several prisoners were thus reported to Berlin and sentenced to floggings. As the Germans involved often denied that the prisoners had acted on their orders, even more severe punishments ensued.[212] Despite the risks, some Jewish prisoners followed the Germans' example and fabricated electric stoves, which they sold to fellow inmates so they could prepare their bartered food.[213] Others made rings from silver spoons or coins, crafted bowls, or manufactured waterproof vests from pilfered plastic foil for British POWs or Germans.[214]

Following the Auschwitz takeover, the SS ordered that the camp be refurbished. Instead of providing the required material and tools, they advised the Jewish elder to steal everything from the OHW plant.[215] This was the birth of the so-called Organization Niewes. Under the auspices of the deputy Jewish elder Jozef Niewes, the prisoners pilfered paint, nails, tools, lamps, and clocks in return for extra food. His large-scale trafficking operations prompted some prisoners to change the acronym "OT" for Organisation Todt inscribed on his barracks to "ON" for "Organization Niewes." In postwar testimony, Niewes delineated his efforts to improve the camp infrastructure: "We had the nicest shoemaker's workshop. . . . We had a well-equipped infirmary with an operating theatre, dental care and so on. Everything was of the best material and all pilfered, for the Germans gave us nothing."[216]

Niewes was a polarizing figure, but his organizational skills mollified many of his critics. Despite considering him "a mixture of a merchant and a thief," the survivor Gabriel Zvi Lifschitz credited Niewes for the significant improvements to the camp. Niewes seized on the pandemonium caused by the air raids on the plant to carry out more and more daring thefts. He even had some prisoners steal a horse-drawn cart loaded with logs. The sudden abundance of paint permitted the inmates to individually decorate their beds or make hand-painted Dutch clogs.[217] However, Niewes rarely handed out the additional food he had promised. If prisoners complained, they were simply beaten, and many began to loathe him for exploiting them.[218] Moreover, the pilfering inmates had to assume the full risk for their actions. Ironically, they were flogged by the SS, who had ordered the thefts in the first place, if they were caught by the works police or German foremen.[219] To evade detection, the booty was even concealed underneath the dead and dying inmates, who were taken back from the construction site on a handcart.[220] Both Niewes and members of the SS came out to the factory to earmark tools or machines for theft. The SS men also had the prisoners pilfer objects for their private use, like clocks and bicycles.[221] It is unknown whether the SS ordered prisoners to steal from entrepreneurs in other Auschwitz subcamps as well, or if these criminal acts were inspired by the general climate of dishonesty prevailing at the OHW. The Jewish survivor Leo Voss summed up the corrupt moral values of the factory staff in his postwar memoir:

> "*Klauen*" [stealing] is a system, "*organisieren*" [pilfering] an everyday term; everybody is involved in it: directors, accountants, clerks, foremen, workers, they all steal ... the prisoners steal for themselves or by order of the guards or the camp leadership. Whole wagon-loads of material, tools and food are being stolen by these noble gentlemen, and nails, hammers, and paint for their garden fence on top. Whoever gets caught is punished without mercy. But not because he stole, but because he allowed himself to be caught. "*Lass Dich nur nicht erwischen!*" ["Don't let yourself be caught!"] is the standard rule given out by the guard, who nearly batters the prisoner to death he himself commanded to steal.[222]

CLANDESTINE ART

Several remarkable artists, some already well known and accomplished, others about to start their careers, were interned in Blechhammer. Their creative talent became a key factor in their survival. Creating clandestine artworks for fellow inmates, prisoners of war, civilian workers, and the SS helped them to obtain lifesaving extra food and clothing.

It is estimated that out of the approximately one hundred thousand works of art made during the Holocaust by the inmates of camps and ghettos or in hiding, only a small percentage may have been preserved. They were lost during confiscations, deportations, and death marches; in bombings; or in unsafe hiding places, or they perished along with the artists. The artworks saved by smuggling them out of camps were often scattered all over the world.[223] They are rare, individual testimonies and reflections of their time, both in their subject matter and in what they reveal about the artist. During the Shoah, artists had to face unprecedented conditions of violence, suffering, death, deprivation, and dehumanization, affecting not only themselves but also their creative intentions, styles, subjects, and access to materials. Janet Blatter distinguishes between the art *of* the Holocaust, representing works created by victims of the Shoah between 1939 and 1945, and the Holocaust *in* art, referring to all general depictions of the Shoah by survivors or others made either after the war or during the war, but from a safe distance.[224]

Of the numerous artworks clandestinely made by Blechhammer prisoners, only a set of cartoons by Bil Spira that he gave to a British POW have been preserved as art of the Holocaust under Blatter's definition.[225] From the other surviving artists, only works made after the war still exist. These postwar works are equally important sources, not only because they depict individual victims and perpetrators, but also because they reflect the artists' struggle to cope with the trauma of the Shoah. They nonetheless tend to use a different iconography resembling the stereotypes of war art. The depiction of violent scenes showing Nazis as perpetrators is a dominant characteristic. The central theme of mass atrocity also reveals the postwar artists' much more informed view. By contrast, the art of the Holocaust typically focused on relatively benign camp routines and images of everyday objects.[226] Moreover, postwar artists utilize a wider range of materials, allowing for a degree of finish seldom achieved in works made in the camps.[227]

Contrary to Auschwitz, where artists' workshops and even a camp "museum" had been established, all artworks had to be clandestinely made in Blechhammer.[228] The Auschwitz commandant's order of July 1943 prohibiting the SS from commissioning artworks for private purposes was largely ignored.[229] Several SS men at Blechhammer were keen on obtaining works of art, usually portraits of their wives or girlfriends, in return for some food. On these occasions, the prisoner artists were given high-quality paper and pencils or paint, which they later reused for art they offered to civilians, POWs, or fellow inmates. If nothing else was available, they also drew on paper bags, cardboard, and scrap paper. In addition to securing the artists' physical survival, clandestine art served to chronicle events in the camp and render images of prisoners. Confronted with their own mortality and the deaths of their friends and families, the inmates found that such portraits helped to preserve a part of themselves, or the memory of those who had perished, for posterity. Depicting traumatizing camp scenes enabled the artists to cope better with their feelings.[230] Art temporarily offered consolation and a respite from the unbearable strains of camp life, not merely for the artist but also for those being portrayed. The child survivor Walter Spitzer stressed the prisoners' need to reconnect with their former selves and to escape from the horrors surrounding them: "They wanted to see their face, it was a way of seeing their face, for there weren't any photographs in the camp, they probably also wanted to have something that seemed like art to them, even if it was just lousy, not really great art by a guy like me, . . . but it made them dream a little."[231]

However, the debatable notion of art as "spiritual resistance" against dehumanization does not sufficiently reflect the complex hierarchies in the camps and the social divisions they created. It is important to remember that, similar to musical entertainment, artworks were very much the privilege of more resourceful prisoners.[232]

Most prisoner artists had been influenced by modernist movements such as expressionism, cubism, dadaism, surrealism, and abstract art. They had typically left their places of origin (and their Jewish background) behind to study in cultural centers like Paris. Curiously, these trends do not figure prominently in the art of the Holocaust, which appears to be self-contained and is difficult to classify into conventional categories by school or style. At the same time, no "Holocaust style" of its own developed. Although the artists stuck to styles familiar to them and their cultural education subliminally influenced their witnessing, their works tend to portray scenes in more realistic detail, largely avoiding abstract forms, albeit refusing to adopt the Nazi-approved sentimental realism. Possibly this was done to secure concise evidence for the outside world. Moreover, the artists had been forcefully dislodged from artistic communities and were disconnected from cultural frameworks, such as universities or museums. In the camps, the artists nevertheless formed distinct groups based on the diverse yet fragmentary remnants of their past cultural identities.[233]

In Blechhammer, an alternative artistic "community" was inadvertently created by the camp leader. Those apt with the brush were usually assigned to painting jobs at the OHW or in housing estates for the German workforce. Already established prisoner artists seized the opportunity to transform their workplace in the basement of the plant's power station into an art studio. Their German foreman Böse, who was a painter himself, encouraged them to create art instead of working. Böse spent most of his time painting landscapes, which he would sell to German civilian workers to support his family. He often prepared meals for the prisoners. Among the Jewish artists was a thirty-five-year-old restorer from Arnhem named Cohen, who was very knowledgeable and lectured the younger members of the group on Dutch artists like Rembrandt. He perished on the death march to Gross-Rosen.[234] Jonas Moscou (Amsterdam, 1900) painted in the "Dutch style," and his works were very popular among British and French POWs, as well as Italian laborers, who supplied him with oil paint. His talent was equally exploited by the SS and higher echelon Wehrmacht guards, who even provided him with a little studio but rarely remunerated him. However, his comparatively privileged position as an artist did not save him when he contracted typhus. While Moscou was in the infirmary, he was selected for Auschwitz, where he was murdered on September 30, 1943.[235] An elderly painter in bad health named Kohn had fled to France from Nazi Germany and was eventually deported. He was greatly admired for his watercolors but peculiarly refused to depict anything but tulips. The flowers symbolized the beauty of life before the camps, which he tried to convey to fellow prisoners.[236]

Wilhelm "Bil" Spira (Vienna, 1913–Puteaux, Paris, 1999) had drawn cartoons for left-wing Viennese newspapers like *Das kleine Blatt* as a student and later studied arts at Vienna's Kunstgewerbeschule. From 1934, he did the layout for the Sunday edition of the socialist paper *Arbeiter-Zeitung*. In 1938 he was arrested by the Gestapo, but he managed to escape to Paris under the assumed identity Willy Freier, which he retained for some time after the war. In Paris, he joined a group of artists-in-exile headed by the famous Jewish writer Joseph Roth. Spira made numerous caricatures of fellow artists during this time.[237] After the German invasion, he fled to the unoccupied south of France and worked as a forger for Varian Fry of the Emergency Rescue Committee, set up by Thomas Mann and others in 1940 to help artists and intellectuals on the Gestapo blacklist emigrate to a safe destination via Spain. In 1941 he was denounced to the Gestapo shortly before it would have been his turn to leave the country, leading to his arrest and internment in the Vernet camp.[238] On September 3, 1942, Spira was deported from Drancy; he came to Blechhammer in early 1944 via the Schmelt camp Laurahütte. He survived two death marches to Buchenwald and Terezín, where he was liberated by the Red Army in 1945. After the liberation, Spira returned to Paris and resumed his work as a cartoonist for various Swiss and French newspapers, such as *Der Nebelspalter* and *Jours de France*.

In Blechhammer, Spira earned himself some extra soup by making portraits of the absent husbands of civilian women working in the kitchens. Despite his assignment to the painters' group, he mostly drew in his spare time. While he was busy making a portrait one Sunday, he was surprised by an SS man. Liking what he saw, the latter requested a portrait of his wife in return for offering Spira a job as a "shoeshine boy." Each night after work, Spira had to clean the SS men's boots that were lined up in the corridor of their quarters, accompanied by some dinner leftovers. Spira shared the extra food with an emaciated teenage prisoner from his barracks. As word of his talent had spread, another SS man approached him. The infamous block leader Tom Mix wanted Spira to create a "cheerful" painting for his room. He left the motif up to the artist. Spira suggested painting a girl having catcalls shouted at her by construction workers, to which he agreed. Tom Mix procured some watercolors and brushes and secretly let Spira paint in a storage room on the building site. However, the almost finished artwork was destroyed when the room was hit by a bomb. Camp leader Klipp soon commissioned him to make a drawing of his wife from a photograph, supplying Spira with high-quality pencils and paper.[239]

Spira bartered cartoons for cigarettes with British POWs. In early 1944 he regularly met the British prisoner of war Charles Hayward during truck rides to the construction site of a housing estate for OHW and IG Farben workers in Heydebreck. Hayward, a nonsmoker, decided to invest his cigarette allocations in artworks offered to him by Spira. He was looking for a "souvenir" from the camp, something that would be "interesting for people at home," as he pointed out in a postwar interview. Altogether, he acquired eleven cartoons depicting foreign and unfree laborers at the OHW. In addition to British POWs, these encompassed inmates of the work education camp, the penitentiary subcamp, and Jewish prisoners. Unlike the portraits, the cartoons were not commissioned but were randomly drawn by Spira in advance. They strongly mirror his background as a political caricaturist. In his portrayal of the Jews, Spira focused on the violence meted out by Jewish functionary prisoners to their own comrades, not on the atrocities committed by German camp personnel. The absence of German perpetrators is typical of the art of the Holocaust,[240] for most artists considered this subject too risky. A recurring theme in Spira's cartoons was the working Jewish children, whose exploitation frequently caused an outcry among the other laborers, particularly the British POWs.[241] Possibly this was an underlying reason Spira added them, letting the outside world know of their internment in the camp.

Unlike his commissioned works, the cartoons directed at British POWs were obviously intended as testimonies to the victims of the Nazi camps. Spira could not be sure he would survive the camps; however, his cartoons had a fair chance of being brought back to the free world in the hands of British POWs. Charles Hayward managed to do just that. He even developed a special strategy for smuggling things into camps by always volunteering to be the first to have his kit searched. Hidden in a chocolate tin, Spira's cartoons thus safely reached Hayward's London home after the war. Spira's identity and fate nevertheless remained unknown to him.[242]

Unaware that some of his cartoons had been preserved, Spira delineated the tragic loss of his artworks from the camps in his postwar autobiography. During the liberation of Terezín, they were burned together with his clothes to combat lice. He had tried in vain to convince the Soviet soldier in charge of the delousing to spare his drawings: "I pointed out that the drawings did not just have an artistic value but were also important testimonies. Drawing was prohibited in German camps, and I had preserved unique evidence. So, did my liberators really intend to spoil my liberation and destroy what I had been able to save from the camp despite being searched?"[243]

In 2009, ten years after Spira's death, the Hayward family donated his cartoons to the Imperial War Museum in London, where they were shown in an exhibition on Holocaust art. They assumed that the cartoonist, known only by his signature "Bill," had perished in the Shoah.[244] As a result of this research project on Blechhammer, it was finally possible to identify the cartoons as Spira's, thus facilitating their integration into his pre- and post-Holocaust artistic cycles. Most recently, the cartoons were exhibited in Spira's hometown, Vienna.[245]

Among the youngest budding artists at Blechhammer was Walter Spitzer (Cieszyn, 1927–Paris, 2021), who had developed an early interest in the fine arts. He was taken to Laurahütte and Blechhammer after the liquidation of the Strzemieszyce ghetto in June 1943, during which his mother was shot. His father had died before the war. Spitzer was liberated in Buchenwald in January 1945 and immediately volunteered to serve with the

US Signal Corps. He later settled in Paris to study at the École des Beaux Arts and became a renowned painter and sculptor. Among his works is the official memorial for the Jews of France, who were rounded up for deportation in the Vél-d'Hiver cycling arena.

In Blechhammer, Spitzer started out as a welder. As they had to work at great heights, many prisoners on that detail fell to their deaths or were sent to Auschwitz due to fractured bones. His friendship with the Jewish elder's daughter Halina Demerer enabled Spitzer to transfer into the painters' detail. Already accomplished artists, like David Brainin, taught him how to earn extra food by making portraits from photographs for civilian female workers. He sacrificed most of his family's valuables, which had been deposited with non-Jewish neighbors in Cieszyn, to procure pencils and watercolors, with the assistance of Czech laborers. Hiding in a pipe, Spitzer used the thirty-minute lunch break at the factory for making portraits. Stricter punishments for contacts between Jews and other workers after the Auschwitz takeover made him temporarily abandon his clandestine production of artworks, until he found a friend ready to negotiate the deals for him. Shortly before the death march, his friend managed to swap some of Spitzer's paintings for a pair of shoes and lambswool socks from British POWs for him, which presumably saved his life. In retrospect, Spitzer identified his comparatively "privileged" life as an artist as a key factor in his survival.[246]

Spitzer lost all the artworks he made in the camps, but he started a series of paintings depicting scenes from Blechhammer and Buchenwald soon after his liberation. His immediate postwar artistic cycle predominantly depicts atrocities, executions, selections for Auschwitz, and individual perpetrators.[247] Spitzer's powerful works exemplify the survivors' attempts to come to terms with the traumatic past through their art.[248]

Jakob Zim (Cymberknopf), born in Sosnowiec in 1920, was conscripted for forced labor in the ghetto. His ability to draw and paint initially secured him a job as a draftsman at the local German police station. By mid-1941 he was forced to leave, but he managed to set up a workshop for applied arts with the help of a German who admired his artistic talent. The workshop offered a temporary refuge to 120 ghetto inhabitants, among them his two brothers. Following the liquidation of the Sosnowiec ghetto in August 1943, Zim was sent to camp Annaberg, where he secretly continued to paint. However, he never created art for bartering but exclusively to have a respite from the atrocious life in the camp. Like many prisoner artists, Zim drew his inspiration from a well-known painting and adapted it to his own situation. He chose an artwork by the Polish Jewish painter Josef Budko entitled *No One Cries Like Me*. When his painting was discovered by guards in January 1944, he was flogged and sent to Blechhammer as a punishment. There, he was reunited with his younger brother Nathan. They were both liberated in Buchenwald. During the death march, Zim drew on his artistic talent as a core inner strength to help him survive. After the war, he resolved to communicate his experiences in the camps through painting. Zim migrated to Israel and studied at the

Bezalel Academy of Art and Design in Jerusalem. He won many prizes as a graphic designer and artist and exhibited his work internationally.[249] A visit to Poland inspired a series of abstract paintings commemorating his childhood and the Shoah.[250]

Michel Sima (Michael Smajewski, Słonim, Poland/Belarus, 1912) left the traditional Jewish orthodox environment of his childhood in 1929 to study sculpture at the Académie de la Grande Chaumière in Paris. After one year at the academy, he felt he could learn more by working directly with artists in their studios. Sima thus got to know many artists and writers and was invited to join the circle formed around Francis Gruber, Moise Kisling, and Pierre Tal-Coat. Ossip Zadkine, one of the leading cubist sculptors of his time, accepted him as a student. In Zadkine's studio, Sima met Jean Cocteau, Paul Eluard, and Francis Picabia. Eluard gave him the pseudonym "Sima," an anagram derived from the French word for "friends," *amis*. It symbolized Sima's sincere friendship with the other artists. Sima had truly arrived in the world of the most influential artists in Paris when he met Picasso and Gertrude Stein.

In 1940 the German invasion of France forced him to leave Paris, and he fled to the nonoccupied zone in the south. Together with his friend Picabia he prepared an exhibition in Cannes, but he was arrested before its launch on August 22, 1942. Sima was deported from Drancy and taken to Blechhammer in the same year. In May 1945 he returned to France, physically and mentally shattered. The Nazis had destroyed all the artworks he had left behind in Paris, and the camps had robbed him of the strength to continue as a sculptor. Picasso suggested that he should take a series of photographs to document his work-in-progress instead. Sima thus successfully used photography as a new means of expression. In the following years, he portrayed the works of artists like Matisse, Jacques Cocteau, and Marc Chagall, resulting in the publication *21 visages d'artistes* in 1959. He made a fresh attempt at creating sculptures in 1967, using olive wood instead of stone this time. He died in the Ardèche region in 1987. Sima is said to have been the least known photographer who made some of the best-known photographs. In Blechhammer, his artistic proficiency helped him to survive. He carved the portraits of the girlfriends and wives of German airmen stationed nearby into sheets of metal in return for food.[251] Sima also used the daily march to work to chisel small stones he held in the hollow of his hands into tiny sculptures, usually erotic couples and nude women, for British POWs.[252] Extremely small sculptures like these had been characteristic of Sima's artistic style of the 1930s. They were "reminiscent of butterfly wings and extraordinary ornaments made for a lilliputian palace," as stated in the preface to the catalog of his last exhibition in France.[253]

Later, Sima was placed in Blechhammer's carpentry workshop, entitling him to certain privileges. All carpenters were accommodated in a wing of the infirmary, with only two men sharing each bedroom. They had proper beds with a spring mattress and were not required to attend the strenuous roll calls. When the SS camp leader discovered

Sima's talent for creating beautiful wood carvings, he commissioned an intricate chandelier and supplied him with the special carving knives he required. As Sima was remunerated with food from the SS kitchen, he tried to prolong the work as much as possible. The evacuation of January 1945 prevented him from finishing it, and the camp leader left without the chandelier. Sima secretly stayed behind in the camp. In the critical period between the evacuation and the arrival of the Red Army, he sacrificed the chandelier to have firewood for his comrades and himself.[254] Despite certain material benefits and the soothing qualities offered by their creativity, an estimated two-thirds of the artists held in camps and ghettos perished in the Holocaust, and most of their artworks disappeared with them. And even if the artists survived, they usually lost what they had created. The Blechhammer artists were no exception in this respect. The rare preservation of Bil Spira's cartoons underscores the important role played by clandestine contacts with non-Jews, who not only supplied prisoner artists with lifesaving food, but whose less vulnerable status permitted them to safeguard such unique art from inside the Nazi camps.[255]

CONCLUSION

In February 1946, former OHW employee Heinz Ebers was interrogated by British intelligence. He recounted the following episode, apparently to vindicate himself. Ebers told of his encounter with three liberated concentration camp prisoners in the vicinity of Bergen-Belsen. The men started a conversation, and when Ebers mentioned that he had worked for the OHW, one of them purportedly exclaimed: "I owe my life to you, then!" The former prisoner, whose family had been murdered in Auschwitz, was allegedly convinced that he had escaped certain death by working at the plant. Ebers claimed that the three men later admitted that they had planned to mug him but had changed their minds after the conversation. He contended that this encounter was proof of the favorable conditions granted to Jews at the OHW and the lifesaving function of their work deployment.[1]

Ebers's story was obviously fabricated, as male Blechhammer prisoners were evacuated to Buchenwald and were unlikely to have wound up in Bergen-Belsen. Contrary to its intended purpose, the narrative clearly corroborates his derogatory view of Jews, whom he portrayed as "marauders" and a security threat. This is nonetheless an early example of the apologetic argumentation that industrialists had saved lives by accepting Jews as a workforce.

Plants like the Oberschlesische Hydrierwerke had been established in Upper Silesia for ideological purposes from the outset. The protracted war changed their function from offering employment opportunities to Germans in a borderland area to assisting in the mass murder of the Jews in the region and detaining other political or ethnic groups rated as "dangerous" by the Nazi regime. Both Schmelt and the Auschwitz administration relied on the OHW's infrastructure and increasingly drew on their staff as auxiliaries. The utilization of Jewish workers was inexorably intertwined with the implementation of the Final Solution, and the OHW played its part in turning the Holocaust into a reality. The company's complicity began with its consent to have a Schmelt camp erected on its premises in spring 1942 that eventually became Auschwitz's second largest satellite and culminated in senior members of the management shooting Jewish prisoners during the evacuation of January 1945.

Blechhammer was set up during the most expansive phase of Schmelt's system, when Speer's calls for higher productivity and the first ghetto liquidations pumped more and more Jewish prisoners into these camps. Their vital status in the war economy secured the OHW ever larger contingents of such workers. After three-quarters of the Schmelt camps had been disbanded, Blechhammer was among the fifteen camps that were important enough to be taken over by Auschwitz in early 1944. At this point, an estimated fifty thousand Jewish women and men from Eastern Upper Silesia, the Netherlands, Belgium, and France had perished in Schmelt's system. The OHW management had lent its private industrial terrain to be used as a collection point for taking unfit, or simply superfluous, Schmelt prisoners as well as children, pregnant women, and the elderly from the ghettos to the gas chambers of Auschwitz in 1943.

Under Schmelt and Auschwitz alike, the prisoners allocated to the OHW quickly succumbed to the lethal conditions. However, it was not simply the combination of hard labor and too little food that killed them. Polish penitentiary prisoners (among them Jews arrested in the Łódź ghetto) were subjected to the same amount of work on similar rations, but their mortality did not exceed 20 percent.[2] Death tolls of up to 95 percent in Blechhammer's camp for Jews point to other underlying causes that did not affect the penitentiary prisoners. A major contributor was the systematic murder of injured, sick, or emaciated prisoners either by using water-related methods in the camp or in the gas chambers of Auschwitz. Contracts between the SS and the industrial clients contained a paragraph stating that permanently unfit prisoners could be sent back to Auschwitz. Analogous to the euphemistic terminology commonly used by the SS to obfuscate their crimes, the document avoided spelling out that these prisoners would be killed. Affidavits by former OHW employees nonetheless corroborate that the gassings of Jewish inmates were an open secret at the plant.[3] Moreover, German and ethnic German foremen not only maltreated Jewish prisoners but intentionally worked or bludgeoned them to death, without being reprimanded. The OHW management likewise tolerated the camp guards' ubiquitous violence against the prisoners. From summer 1944, decrees on plundering permitted the company's works police under the deputy director, Heinrich Schlick, to lynch unfree laborers.

As one of the most important Schmelt camps and Auschwitz subcamps, Blechhammer illustrates the practical implications of two seemingly opposite policies: the intense exploitation of Jewish labor in wartime Upper Silesia and the mass murder of the Jewish people. A constant influx of fresh prisoners allowed the OHW to increase its Jewish workforce while simultaneously contributing to the genocide. The lives of Jewish workers were assigned little value, both economically and as human beings. Their overall treatment by camp leaders, guards, the OHW management, and civilian foremen was not in line with Speer's alleged "economic rationalization" efforts. Franciszek Piper fittingly described Jewish forced labor in industrial camps as the "protracted hell" of the death camps.[4]

Only a small fraction of the OHW's German and ethnic German workforce was ready to aid Jewish prisoners, for varying and at times purely opportunistic reasons. Many British and French POWs, along with other foreign laborers, extended a crucial lifeline to the Jews. Next to the material aspects, these gestures of solidarity strengthened the inmates' will to persevere. The Jewish elder Karl Demerer also did his best to ameliorate the conditions in the camp. However, his strategy of bribing the camp leadership invariably drew him into the Nazis' perfidious system of dividing the prisoners and projecting their crimes onto functionary inmates. Inner resources, like artistic creativity, spirituality, and political convictions, helped individual prisoners keep going. These immense human efforts notwithstanding, the few survivors of Blechhammer and other Nazi camps owed their lives to the fact that they were liberated in time.[5]

Those who narrowly lived through the agony of the Schmelt camps always stressed that they had been even more "hellish" than the concentration camps.[6] These survivors' experiences are still not sufficiently reflected by Holocaust scholarship, which continues to marginalize camps outside the concentration camp system, like the Schmelt camps. Thus, Blechhammer's two-year history as a Schmelt camp is all too often eclipsed by its ten-month status as an Auschwitz satellite in academic literature.

The Holocaust was not a uniform process; there were regional and temporal specificities and a wide array of perpetrators and collaborators. The Schmelt camps were integral, not antithetical, to the Shoah in Eastern Upper Silesia. Young people died there even before their next of kin were deported to Auschwitz from the ghettos. Schmelt's staff, first and foremost his deputy Heinrich Lindner, were chiefly responsible for both, detaining the able-bodied in these camps and organizing the ghetto liquidations. Schmelt's half a dozen coworkers could draw on the support of hundreds of German order policemen and their ethnic German auxiliaries, and they also found civilians like Dr. Erich Hoffmann and Haunschild, who readily participated in camp killings or selected prisoners for Auschwitz. Blechhammer formed part of an extensive network of camps that remains largely unexplored. In the immediate vicinity of Auschwitz, Schmelt's killing infrastructure (which has been understudied) facilitated the murder of the Jews of Eastern Upper Silesia and up to nine thousand Jewish men from western Europe. Beyond the typical concentration camp settings, this also underscores the connivance and collaboration of a wide spectrum of German society in the Holocaust. Schmelt's system also reflects how some ethnically mixed parts of the Upper Silesian population and ethnic Germans were prompted to prove their "Germanness" by participating in the genocide. This microhistory endeavors to unravel the functions and inner workings of one of these camps. However, Blechhammer's history will only become fully comprehensible when more is known about the other Schmelt camps, their interactions, and their changing purposes in the Shoah.

When all ghettos in Eastern Upper Silesia had been liquidated and most of their inhabitants had been murdered in Auschwitz, the Schmelt camps were no longer required. Drawing on the remaining twenty-five thousand Schmelt inmates and, later, on Jews held in Auschwitz, Blechhammer's prisoner population of thirty-two hundred was steadily increased to almost six thousand during the course of 1944. The former Schmelt camp's second life as an Auschwitz satellite was a result of Speer's pressure on Himmler to increase the number of concentration camp prisoners working in the war industry. In parallel to this, the mass murder of the European Jews at Auschwitz reached its devastating peak.

Apart from French resistance fighters interned there from fall 1944, Blechhammer remained an exclusively Jewish camp. The only difference was that the new prisoners now came from Auschwitz, not Sosnowiec. The takeover initially brought increased reliability and slightly improved living conditions but also entailed stricter discipline with more vigilant camp personnel. In summer 1944 the onset of Allied airstrikes added two new threats to the prisoners' lives: exposure to bombs and the laws on sabotage and plundering, which led to lynchings and public hangings. The SS camp leader Otto Brossmann used the first execution to instill absolute horror in the prisoners. SS men like Tom Mix instigated new levels of violence against the inmates that also spread to German and ethnic German foremen on the OHW construction site. The haste to build shelters and fix bomb damage, coupled with lowered food rations, consumed the prisoners' last physical reserves. Those requiring treatment in the camp infirmary, along with the victims of a typhus outbreak, were taken to Auschwitz in two-weekly intervals or killed by phenol injections. On the eve of the evacuation in January 1945, the second camp leader, Kurt Klipp, surprisingly opted to disobey superior orders and to spare the lives of three hundred infirmary patients and over one hundred female prisoners. He was nevertheless responsible for several massacres of prisoners refusing to go on the death march and had those who fell out en route ruthlessly killed. When Klipp's group was already miles away on their trek, he could rely on the collaboration of the OHW works police and Wehrmacht units, who continued to murder in the camp. During Blechhammer's final days, the deadly alliance between the Nazi regime and the industrialists reached its tragic climax.

In the thirty-four months of its existence, the Blechhammer camp saw a swift succession of leaders and authorities and underwent several transformations. While the perpetrators were exchanged (and apparently were highly interchangeable), the camp's dual function remained the same: to supply the German war industry with cheap laborers and decimate the Jewish population through the lethal conditions of their work deployment.

ABBREVIATIONS

ACICR: Archive du Comité International de la Croix Rouge (Archive of the ICRC)
AEL: Arbeitserziehungslager (work education camp)
AFZ: Archiv für Zeitgeschichte, ETH Zürich (Archive for Contemporary History, ETH Zurich)
AN: Archives Nationales, Paris Pierrefitte-sur-Seine (French National Archives, Paris Pierrefitte-sur-Seine)
APK: Archiwum Państwowe w Katowicach (State Archive Katowice)
APMO: Archiwum Państwowe Muzeum Auschwitz-Birkenau w Oświęcimiu (The Archive of the State Museum Auschwitz-Birkenau in Oświęcim)
APO: Archiwum Państwowe w Opolu (State Archive Opole)
APWR: Archiwum Państwowe w Wrocławiu Oddział Kamieniec-Ząbkowicki (State Archive Wrocław-Kamieniec Ząbkowice)
AWFA: Australians at War Film Archive, Canberra
BAL: Bayer AG: Corporate History & Archives Leverkusen
BARCH: Bundesarchiv (German Federal Archives)
DAF: Deutsche Arbeitsfront (German Labor Front)
DEGOB: Deportáltakat Gondozó Országos Bizottság (National Committee for Attending Deportees)
DOEW: Dokumentationsarchiv Österreichischer Widerstand (Documentary Archive of Austrian Resistance Fighters)
FO.: folio (reference to unbound archival documents)
FVA: Fortunoff Video Archive for Holocaust Testimonies at Yale University
GFH: Beit Lohamei HaGhettaot (Ghetto Fighters' House Museum)
HHSTAW: Hessisches Hauptstaatsarchiv Wiesbaden (Central State Archive of Hesse)
HSSPF: Höhere SS- und Polizeiführer (Higher SS and Police Leader)
ICRC: International Committee of the Red Cross
IPN: Instytut Pamięcki Narodowej (Institute of National Remembrance)
ITS: International Tracing Service
IWM: Imperial War Museum London
LAA: Bundesarchiv/Lastenausgleichsarchiv Bayreuth (German Federal Archives' Offsite Storage Depot)

LHA: Landesarchiv Münster (County Archive Münster)
NA: National Archives Kew
NARA: National Archives and Records Administration, College Park, MD
NIOD: Nederlands Instituut voor Oorlogs-, holocaust- en genocide studies (The Netherlands Institute for War, Holocaust and Genocide Studies)
OESTA: Österreichisches Staatsarchiv (Austrian State Archive)
OHW: Oberschlesische Hydrierwerke (Upper Silesian Hydrogenation Works)
PIŻ: Polish Research Institute Archive Lund
POW: prisoner of war
RAB: Reichsautobahngesellschaft (Reich Motorway Company)
RM: Reichsmark (official currency of the German Reich)
RSHA: Reichssicherheits-Hauptamt (Reich Security Main Department)
SA: Sturmabteilung (storm troopers)
SCHA: Schering-Archiv (Schering Archive)
SOKA: Státní okresní archiv Trutnov (District Archive Trutnov)
SS: Schutzstaffel (protection squadron)
STA M: Staatsarchiv München (State Archive Munich)
STA N: Staatsarchiv Nürnberg (State Archive Nuremberg)
STA OL: Staatsarchiv Oldenburg (State Archive Oldenburg)
STA WÜ: Staatsarchiv Würzburg (State Archive Würzburg)
SWA: Wiesenthal Archiv, Vienna
USAF: United States Air Force
USHMM: United States Holocaust Memorial Museum
VHA: Visual History Archive, USC Shoah Foundation
VVA: Voice/Vision Holocaust Survivor Oral History Archive, University of Michigan, Dearborne
WL: The Wiener Library for the Study of the Holocaust & Genocide, London
YVA: Yad Vashem Archives, Jerusalem
ŽMP: Židovski Muzeum v Praze (Jewish Museum Prague)

NOTES

INTRODUCTION

1. Leo B., HVT-1824, FVA.
2. Steinbacher, "East Upper Silesia," 239–66; and Madajczyk, *Okkupationspolitik*, 390–405.
3. Gruner, *Jewish Forced Labor*, 294.
4. Korherr report, YVA TR 19127; and Die Deportationstransporte während der sogenannten Cosel Periode, StA Wü 2012-009, no. 37, fos. 1128–31.
5. Michman, "Jewish Leadership," 326; Bulletin of the Central Office of the Jewish Councils in Eastern Upper Silesia, no. 2, September 30, 1940, APK 12/1600, no. 3, fo. 23; and Fulbrook, *Small Town*, 62.
6. Szternfinkiel, *Zagłada*, 1946, 25; trial of Schmelt Office staff, BArch B 162/20513; and report of the first police precinct of Sosnowiec on a raid in the Jewish ghetto (*Judenaktion*), November 5, 1941, APK 12/807, no. 316, fo. 36.
7. Steinbacher, *Musterstadt Auschwitz*, 138; and Gruner, *Jewish Forced Labor*, 217.
8. Isaac Cohensius, GFH 12032 R M-Hol., no. 416; and Grużlewska, *Annaberg*, 100.
9. Die Deportationstransporte während der sogenannten Cosel Periode, StA Wü 2012-009, no. 37, fos. 1128–31; and Maurits Broeks, NIOD 250d/450.
10. Annual business report of the RAB, printed in Weiss, "Oberste Bauleitung."
11. Miron and Shulhani, *Yad Vashem Encyclopedia*, 745; and Nitzah Ranz, interview 11814, VHA.
12. Gutterman, *Narrow Bridge*, 50.
13. Gruner, *Jewish Forced Labor*, 222; and Konieczny, "Zwangsarbeit der Juden," 104.
14. Protocol of the Wannsee Conference, January 20, 1942, printed in Klein, *"Wannsee-Konferenz,"* 31.
15. Pohl, "Holocaust," 156.
16. The Hebrew biblical term *Shoah* ("destruction") was used by Jews from 1940 to refer to the genocide of European Jewry. The expression *Holocaust*, derived from the ancient Greek word for "burnt offering," was employed in the English-speaking world from 1950 for the Nazi mass murder of Jews in Europe. Lately, other victims of Nazi persecution, like Sinti and Roma and political prisoners, have been included (Bauer, *Rethinking the Holocaust*, 10). In the following, the terms Shoah and Holocaust are alternately used to describe the Nazi genocide of the European Jews.
17. There are only a few monographs; see Grużlewska, *Annaberg*; Maj, *Więzniowie*; Weiss, *Bus-*

chvorwerk; and recently, Holc, *Weavers.* For short articles, see, Weiss, "From *Reichsautobahnlager*"; Weiss, "Reichsautobahnlager Geppersdorf"; and Weiss, "Johannsdorf."

18. Bauer, *Rethinking the Holocaust,* 90.
19. Rudorff, "Arbeit und Vernichtung," 38.
20. Lehnstaedt, "Coercion and Incentive," 400–30.
21. Steinbacher, *Musterstadt Auschwitz,* 279.
22. Friedlander, *Memory.*
23. Langer, *Holocaust Testimonies,* 6–9.
24. BArch R 9348 Oberschlesische Hydrierwerke AG Blechhammer.
25. BArch R 9348, R 4601; and APK 12/807, 12/1600, 12/771, 12/119.
26. APMO D-AU I-2, D-AU I, II, III; and BArch R 9348, R 4601.
27. NIOD 250d, 250k, 244; AN F/9/5565, F/9/5583–88, 736 MI 1-3; WL 055-EA, 053-EA; DEGOB; YVA O.3, O.33, M.1., M.49; GFH 12032 R M-Hol., no. 416, Isaac Cohensius; APMO Oświedzienia, f. 48; ŽMP; and PIZ.
28. FVA; VHA; VVA; and IWM Sound Archive.
29. To name but a few, see Clary, *Holocaust*; Fainzang, *Mémoire*; Kichka, *Adolescence*; Koenig, *Vorhof*; Obréjan, *Homme*; Prochownik, *Mémoires*; Rosengarten, *Overleven*; Spira, *Legende*; Spitzer, *Dessin*; Wajnblum, *My Destiny*; and Wollenberg, *Alptraum.*
30. StA M SpkA K 739 Erich Hoffmann; IfZ F 13-7-8 Aufzeichnungen Rudolf Höss; APMO Hoess Trial, vol. 21; IPN GK 184/262; HHStAW Abt. 461 no. 37638, vol. 151, Frankfurter Auschwitzprozess; and LHA Verfahren gegen Schmelt (205 AR-Z 78/60), nos. 4859–84; see also BArch B 162/20513; StA Wü 2012-009, 33–37 Tötungsdelikte; IfZ Ga 05.02/1-3; and BArch 162/18172–73.
31. OHW quarterly management reports, February–March 1942, BArch R 9348/7; Message on a visit by Speer at the OHW by General Plenipotentiary Carl Krauch to OHW director Josenhans, July 30, 1942, BArch R 9348/60; and Schütz and Gruber, *Mythos,* 90.
32. Hoess Trial, vol. 21, APMO.
33. Ministry of Finance, Handakten Nasse, BArch R 2/17835.
34. OMGUS dossier on Max Josenhans, July 5, 1949, NARA RG-065 105 11219; and discussion on the possible cooperation between Buna and Schlesien–Benzin (OHW) in Ludwigshafen, January 16, 1941, IfZ NI-11784.
35. Dr. Heinrich Karl Schlick (Karlsruhe, 1905–Mannheim, 1977) initially worked for IG Farben. HA PA Dr. Dr. Heinrich Schlick, HO 243827; and OHW organigram, BArch R 9348/95 (2).
36. Drobisch, "Werkschutz," 223; Koenig, *Vorhof,* 115–16; and additional declaration by Kurt Karl Schumann, NA WO 309/978.
37. Overy, *War and Economy,* 18.
38. Drobisch, "Werkschutz"; and Mallmann and Paul, *Herrschaft.*
39. Letter by Schmauser to Himmler, April 20, 1942, BArch B 162/20513; and Matthäus, "Beteiligung," 178.

40. Westermann, *Hitler's Police Battalions*; Matthäus, "Beteiligung"; Mallmann and Musial, *Genesis*; Curilla, *Judenmord*; and Fransecky, *Flucht*.
41. Dobosiewicz, *Gusen*, 270–80.
42. Orth, *System*, 134–37; and Hördler, *Ordnung*, 155.
43. Karl Demerer, StA M SpkA K 739; and Samson Rauchwerger, BArch B 162/8869, fo. 2016.
44. Steinbacher, "East Upper Silesia," 252, 259; Gruner, *Jewish Forced Labor*, 226; and Rudorff, *KZ Auschwitz*, 17.
45. Bernhard Bart, interview 1661, VHA; and Jakob Thaler, YVA M.49 2071.
46. For instance, SS-Ansiedlungsstab and Einwandererzentralstelle. Herta Seidelmann, LHA 4878, fo. 203; and Heinemann, *"Rasse,"* 138–217.
47. Harten, *Himmlers Lehrer*, 14–22.
48. Salomon Lierens, NIOD 250d/673; and interrogation of Margarethe Neugebauer, BArch B 162/20513, fo. 34.
49. Schmauser to Himmler, April 20, 1942, BArch B 162/20513, fo. 21; and Perz, "Wehrmacht," 69–81.
50. Beorn, *Marching into Darkness*, 234–46.
51. Wollenberg, *Alptraum*, 123; Koenig, *Vorhof*, 110; and Harten, *Himmler's Lehrer*, 14–22.
52. Trial of Erich Hoffmann, StA M SpkA K 739.
53. Sofsky, *Order*, 131; and Brown, *Judging "Privileged" Jews*, 2–11.
54. Karl Demerer, YVA O.3 3635; BArch B 162/18175; and Abraham Jonas Walg, NIOD 250d/920.
55. Etienne Rosenfeld, YVA O.33 2070; and Oskar Langer, BArch B 162/8866, fo. 820.
56. Bankier, *Germans*, 123–31; Bergen, "Nazi Concept," 575; and Browning, "Holocaust: Basis and Objective of the *Volksgemeinschaft*?," 225.
57. Circular by Plenipotentiary Carl Krauch to all synthetic fuel plants, July 23, 1941, BArch R 9348/6; internal memorandum by the RAB building supervisory board Breslau, June 12, 1942, BArch R 9348/60; and Salomon Staszewski, NIOD 250d/864.
58. Karl Demerer, YVA O.3 3637.
59. Halpin, *Jewish Doctors*, 115–35.
60. Levi, *Drowned*, 22–33.
61. Siegel, "Coercion-Resistance Spectrum," 1–20.
62. Wollenberg, *Alptraum*, 76.
63. Karl Demerer, BArch B 162/18175; and Abraham Jonas Walg, NIOD 250d/920.
64. Piper, *Auschwitz*, 124.
65. Jakob Thaler, YVA M.49 2071; and Weindling, *Epidemics*, 312.
66. Rachel Brukner Frydrych, YVA O.3 3664; and Gucia Ferst, interview 34207, VHA.
67. Rosa Schwarzberg, interview 9645, VHA; trial of Erich Hoffmann, StA M SpkA 739; Kubica, "Children," 324; Shik, "Sexual Abuse," 223; Katz, "Thoughts," 293–313; Rosa Schwarzberg, interview 9645, VHA; and trial of Erich Hoffmann, StA M SpkA 739.
68. Kubica, "Kinder," 324.

69. Sali Montag, BArch B 162/8864, fos. 429–31; and Jozef Niewes, NIOD 250d/716.
70. Fulbrook, *Small Town*, 290; and Steinbacher, *Musterstadt Auschwitz*, 300.
71. Rudolf Höss, BArch B 162/20513, fo. 119.
72. Szternfinkiel, *Zagłada*, 75.
73. Isaac Arbeid/Arthur Salomons, NIOD 250d/815; Rose Rotmensh, interview 8669, VHA.
74. Gussie Zaks, interview 3093, VHA; and Rudolf Höss, BArch B162/20513, fo. 119.
75. Grużlewska, *Annaberg*, 104.
76. Calfactors were given lighter work, such as camp chores. They often attended to functionary prisoners. Gunter Faerber, interview 41847, VHA; Koenig, *Vorhof*, 119; and Demerer, *Kind*, 50–52.
77. Buser, *Überleben*, 192–96.
78. Grużlewska, *Annaberg*, 88; and Erna Ellert, StA M SpkA K 739.
79. Ernest Nives, interview 588, VHA; and Karl Demerer, YVA O.3 3635.
80. S. Kaufmann, LHA 4861.
81. Abraham Herzberg, NIOD 250d/577.
82. Interrogation of Johannes Hassebroek, LHA 4883. The Korherr report still listed 50,570 Schmelt prisoners in January 1943 (Korherr report, YVA TR. 19 127, fo. 13). Czech, *Kalendarium*, 174–232; Piper, "Nebenlager Blechhammer," 26; and Piper, *Zahl*, 183.
83. Rudorff, "Arbeit und Vernichtung"; and Lehnstaedt, "Coercion."
84. OHW strength reports, BArch R 9348/23.
85. Krakowski, "Satellite Camps," 51–60; and interrogation of Heinrich Schäfer, August 18, 1945, IPN GK 184/262.
86. Karl Demerer, BArch B162/18175; Rosengarten, *Overleven*, 153; Siegfried Hermann, interview 38621, VHA; and Jacques G., HVT-2845, FVA.
87. Lasik, "Organisationsstruktur," 179, 349; and IfZ Ga.05.02/02, fo. 147.
88. SS personnel file Kurt Klipp, BArch B 162/8863; and Lasik, "Organisationsstruktur," 355.
89. Piper, "Nebenlager Blechhammer," 25; and Orth, "Concentration Camp Personnel," 47–49.
90. Harten, *Himmlers Lehrer*, 298; and private papers by Dr. Schlick, BArch R 9348/121.
91. Circular by Oswald Pohl, October 26, 1943, BArch NS 3/386; and Piper, *Arbeitseinsatz*, 291.
92. Bloxham, "Jewish Slave Labor," 178; and Herbert, "Arbeit und Vernichtung," 384–426.
93. Gerlach, *Extermination*, 207–8.
94. Wagner, "Work," 140; and Hördler, *Ordnung*, 12.
95. Bauer, *Holocaust*, 55; and Katz, *Holocaust in Historical Context*, 184, 200. Similarly, see Hilberg, *Destruction*, 587; and Kaienburg, *"Vernichtung."*
96. Sofsky, *Order*, 170.
97. Based on estimates by Franciszek Piper in "Nebenlager Blechhammer," 32.
98. The average mortality of Germans and similar status groups was 0.3 percent. Mantelli, "Wanderarbeit," 53.

99. Wachsmann, *Hitler's Prisons*, 280; interrogation of Johannes Josef Stera, August 19, 1976, BArch B 162/18172, fo. 1513; and Stanisław Rogulski, interview 224, PIZ.
100. Kochavi, *Captivity*, 33.
101. Lasik, "Organisationsstruktur," 282–95; Aufzeichnungen Rudolf Hoess, IfZ F 13-7-8; Abram Szeftel, APMO Oświedcienia, f. 48, fo. 154; and Kurt Klappholz, IWM Sound Archive, interview 9425.
102. Fainzang, *Mémoire*, 26; and Czech, "Rolle," 20; see also Lifton, *Nazi Doctors*, 239.
103. Fainzang, *Mémoire*, 73; Nathan Gipsman, interview 166, VHA; and Flusser, "Rückblick," 68.
104. OHW strength reports, BArch R 9348/23; see also Hilberg, *Destruction*, 587.
105. Lasik, "Organisationsstruktur," 217; Eliazer Content, NIOD 250d/481; and Sam Weinstock, BArch B 162/8864, fo. 457.
106. Weinberg, *Boy 30529*, 96; and Kurt Baum, interview 29790, VHA. See also Laub and Auerhahn, "Knowing," 36.
107. Friedlander, *Memory*, 131.
108. Private Papers: George Didcock, IWM 10/6/1; and Prochownik, *Mémoires*, 115–20.
109. Gendarmerie department Blechhammer to Gendarmerie department Oppeln on Ukrainian auxiliary policemen at the OHW, April 22, 1944, APO Rej. Opolska 1191, I/1172; Radchenko, "'We Emptied Our Magazines into Them,'" 63–98; and Wollenberg, *Alptraum*, 128.
110. Directive on sheltering by OHW director Josenhans, September 4, 1944, BArch R 9348/117; and Maurits Bremer, NIOD 250d/448.
111. Piper, *Arbeitseinsatz*, 289; and Joseph Braasem, NIOD 250d/446.
112. Hayes, "Ambiguities," 15; and Spoerer, "Unternehmen," 68.
113. Guidelines on the Work Deployment of Prisoners of War in the Reich Highway Company, November 11, 1939, and OHW circular to contractors, November 16, 1943, BArch R 9348/57.
114. Contract between the SS WVHA and Ost Maschinenbau GmbH Sosnowiec, April 26, 1944, printed in Piper, *Arbeitseinsatz*, annex 22; and affidavits by Friedrich Pook and Karl Kulicke, NA WO 309/978.
115. Overy, *War and Economy*, 18.
116. Deposition of Kurt Karl Schumann, NA WO 309/978, and interrogation of Karl Czapla, October 7, 1976, BArch B 162/8863, fos. 1529–31; and Etienne Rosenfeld, YVA O.33 2070.
117. Keller, "*Volksgemeinschaft and Violence*," 274–91.
118. Abram Szeftel, APMO Oświedcienia, f. 48, 158; and Piper, "Nebenlager Blechhammer," 38.
119. Czech, *Kalendarium*, 979, 990.
120. Winter, "Die SS," 101; and Blatman, *Death Marches*, 94.
121. Strzelecki, *Endphase*, 277.
122. Bauer, "Death Marches," 497–99; and Kolb, *Bergen-Belsen*, 42.
123. Karl Demerer, BArch B 162/18175.

124. Rachel Brukner Frydrych, YVA O.3 3664.
125. Trunk, *Judenrat*, 244; Karl Demerer, YVA O.3 3635; and Jozef Niewes, NIOD 250d/716.
126. Rosengarten, *Overleven*, 122.
127. Samuel Abrams, NIOD 250d/386; and Paul Hertz, NIOD 250d/576.
128. André B., HVT-2842, FVA; and Leo Young Papers, USHMM 1992.A0016/RG-10.048*01.
129. Josek Melcer, interview 48401, VHA; and Jenny Sandberg, interview1667, VHA.
130. Davidowicz, "Holocaust Landscape," 25.
131. Gilbert, *Music*, 4–7; and Berger, *Surviving the Holocaust*, 3–5.
132. Peter Sturm, YVA O.33 2380; and Maurice Moshe Szmidt, YVA O.3 3474.
133. Leo Weiniger, NIOD 244/1486; and Bravo, Davite, and Jalla, "Myth," 99.
134. Gunter Faerber, interview 41847, VHA; Rosengarten, *Overleven*, 106; and Rosen, *Holocaust's Jewish Calendars*, 90–161.
135. Greenberg, "Ultra-Orthodox Responses," 11–26.
136. Sam Silberberg, USHMM 2006.248; and Henry K., HVT-3000, FVA.
137. Rahe, "Jewish Religious Life," 115.

CHAPTER 1

1. Kaczmarek, *Historia*, 97–105; and Tambor, *Mowa*, 67–228.
2. Muschol, *Herrschaft*, 13–134.
3. Correspondence between the OHW and the Hohenlohe Trust, November 1942, BArch R 9348/90.
4. Sikora, "Gau," 258; and Office of the chief administrator of Oppeln, August 15, 1940, APO Rej. Opolska 1191, I/5465, fo. 293.
5. Rogmann, "Aufgaben," 442–46; and Tooley, *Identity*, 14–15.
6. Hayes, "Carl Bosch," 358–61; Birkenfeld, *Treibstoff*, 133; and Carr, *Arms*, 58–63.
7. Minutes of a meeting between the Hard Coal Syndicate and the Office for Economic Development, March 30, 1939, Ministry of Finance, Handakten Nasse, BArch R 2/17835.
8. On the syndicates' premeditated function in this respect, see Dr. Alfred Pott, "Neuordnung und Aufbau im oberschlesischen Raum," keynote address to students of Economics and Administration, Schlesische Friedrich-Wilhelms-University Breslau, February 7, 1941, SchA B5 345.
9. Ministry of Finance, *Handakten Nasse*, BArch R 2/17835; note to the director of Borsig-Kokswerke Dr. Hans Berckemeyer, July 1944, SchA B2 704. Sikora and Meyer erroneously state that Göring had obtained 100 percent of the OHW shares. Sikora, *Waffenschmiede*, 100; 109; and Meyer, *Hitler's Holding*, 324, 329.
10. Letter by OHW deputy director Dr. Heinrich Schlick to director Duisberg of IG Farben Leverkusen, June 9, 1942, BArch R 9348/111; and cooperation agreement between the OHW and IG Farben Heydebreck, September 12, 1944, BAL 019-387, 303.
11. Ministry of Finance, *Handakten Nasse*, BArch R 2/17835; and Stranges, "History," 11.
12. Correspondence between the OHW and the Navy High Command (OKM), May 1941,

BArch R 9348/11; and OHW quarterly management reports, May–July 1941, BArch R 9348/6.
13. Denazification file, September 30, 1946, StA Lu EL 902/22 Bü 1423 Josenhans; Karl Kulicke on the professional activities of OHW leaders, July 31, 1946, NA WO 309/978; and speeches by Josenhans on September 11 and October 29, 1942, BArch R 9348/95.
14. Walter, "Raum," 177–81; Schanetzky, *Kanonen*, 32; and Heuel, *Stand*, 507.
15. Note on Hans Deichmann by Josenhans, August 5, 1946, StA Lu EL 902/22 Bü 1423 Josenhans.
16. Discussion on the possible collaboration between Buna and Schlesien-Benzin (OHW) in Ludwigshafen, January 16, 1941, IfZ NI-11784.
17. Minute of a meeting between Krauch, Eckell, Ambros, and ter Meer at the Reich Office for Economic Development, July 5, 1940, BAL 1638.
18. Discussion on the possible collaboration between Buna and Schlesien-Benzin (OHW) in Ludwigshafen, January 16, 1941, IfZ NI-11784.
19. Meeting between Krauch and ter Meer, February 6, 1941, IfZ NI-11113.
20. Wagner, *IG Auschwitz*, 43–44.
21. Hayes, *Industry*, 347–48; Hayes, "IG Farben," 134–37; Wagner, *IG Auschwitz*, 53; and Kilian, *Buna-Werk*.
22. Minute of a meeting between Josenhans and Dr. Dürrfeld, September 18, 1943, BArch R 9348/95.
23. Steinbacher, *Auschwitz*, 54.
24. Note on awards to OHW members, July 1942, BArch R 9348/116.
25. Simon Blein, NIOD 250d/433.
26. Letter to Director Pott by Karl Kulicke, December 1945, NA WO 309/978.
27. OMGUS dossier on Josenhans by James A. Duffey, May 7 and July 5, 1949, NARA RG-065 105 11219; denazification file, September 30, 1946, StA Lu EL 902/22 Bü 1423 Josenhans; Jacobson, *Operation Paperclip*, 142–65; and Hunt, *Secret Agenda*, 22–40.
28. Affidavit by Josenhans before the Notary General of County Pike and Missouri, December 23, 1947, NARA RG-065 105 11219.
29. FBI inquiry by Peyton Ford, 1949, NARA RG-065 105 11219.
30. Obituary of Hildegard Gussmann, *The Evening Independent*, St. Petersburg, Florida, April 26, 1966.
31. OHW organigram, BArch R 9348/95 (2).
32. Lindner, *Hoechst*, 198–205; and statement by engineer Jähne to IG Farben, November 7, 1955, HA PA Dr. Dr. Heinrich Schlick, HO 243827.
33. Denazification trial of Dr. Schlick, Spruchkammer Main-Taunus, February 26, 1948, and Schlick to IG Farben, October 28, 1950, HA PA Dr. Dr. Heinrich Schlick, HO 243827.
34. The National Socialist Lawyers' Association (NS-Rechtswahrerbund) to Schlick, spring 1941, BArch R 9348/77; and Heyen, *Parole*, 7–16.
35. Correspondence between Schlick and the Ratibor propaganda office, December 9, 1944,

and exchange of Christmas cards between Schlick and SS Obersturmbannführer R. Kügler, December 29, 1944, BArch R 9348/121.
36. Invitations to comradeship evenings, August 19, and November 25, 1944, BArch R 9348/121; and Georges Czaczkes, interview 3328, VHA.
37. Invitiation by Klipp and reply card by Schlick, December 1944, BArch R 9348/121.
38. Correspondence between Dr. Schlick and Dr. Bertrams, June 9 and July 4, 1944, BArch R 9348/121.
39. OHW organigram, BArch R 9348/95 (2); Gestapo: *Richtlinien für die sicherheitspolizeiliche Tätigkeit der Abwehrbeauftragten*, 1939, BArch R 58/797; Drobisch, "Dokumente," 215; and Mallmann and Paul, *Herrschaft*, 291.
40. Statement by Karl Kulicke, July 31, 1946, and depositions of Karl Kulicke, August 1 and 16, 1946, NA WO 309/978.
41. *Reichsgesetzblatt*, I:1387; and Drobisch, "Werkschutz," 219–22.
42. Depositions of Kurt Karl Schumann, August 16, 1946, and September 25, 1947, NA WO 309/978.
43. OHW circular to contractors, July 15, 1944, BArch R 9348/117; Private Papers: George Didcock, IWM 10/6/1; and Koenig, *Vorhof*, 115–16.
44. British War Crimes Group Minden, November 28, 1947, NA WO 309/978.
45. Keller, *Volksgemeinschaft*, 274–91.
46. Lindner, *Hoechst*, 198–205; and correspondence between Schlick and IG Farben, 1959–61, HA PA Dr. Dr. Heinrich Schlick HO 243827.
47. Herbert, "Einleitung," 7–9.
48. Spitzer, *Dessin*, 74.
49. Borrie, *Captivity*, 90.
50. Ste. Croix, "Slavery," 19–22.
51. OHW circular on special terms of contract for construction works, November 16, 1943, BArch R 9348/57.
52. Durand, *Captivité*, 214; Gelber, "Palestinian POWs," 136; Streit, "Kriegsgefangene," 286; Piper, "Nebenlager Blechhammer," 32; and Die Deportationstransporte während der sogenannten Cosel Periode, StA Wü 2012-009, no. 37, fos. 1128–31.
53. OHW quarterly management reports, November 1–December 31, 1941, BArch R 9348/7.
54. OHW special terms of contract for construction works, November 16, 1943, BArch R 9348/57.
55. Circular by Mineralöl-Bau, August 6, 1940, BArch R 9348/45; OHW circular on reduced output factors, November 16, 1943, BArch R 9348/57; and Piper, *Arbeitseinsatz*, 349. Gruner stresses the RAB's impact on payment schemes but does not differentiate between German standard wages and reduced output factors. Gruner, *Jewish Forced Labor*, 222.
56. OHW strength reports, BArch R 9348/23; OHW quarterly management reports, BArch R 9348/23; and Plenipotentiary Krauch to Mineralöl-Bau, August 24, 1940, BArch R 9348/60.

57. OHW strength reports, BArch R 9348/23.
58. OHW quarterly management reports, April 1–June 30, 1942, BArch R 9348/6; Schütz and Gruber, *Mythos*, 80–84; and Circular by the Ministry of Labor to regional employment agencies, May 24, 1940, APO Rej. Opolska, 1191, I/1465, fo. 142.
59. Strzelecki, "Deportation," 8; Silberklang, *Gates*, 78–80; and Steinbacher, "East Upper Silesia," 237–49.
60. Fulbrook, *Small Town*, 167; and Trunk, *Judenrat*, 100–106.
61. Michman, "*Judenräte*," 296–300.
62. Hans Dreier, born in Königsberg (East Prussia) in 1907, was an order police officer who joined the SS before working for Gestapo Kattowitz. He was killed in action in May 1945. Trial against Schmelt Office staff, LHA 4879.
63. Bulletin of the Central Office of Jewish Councils in Eastern Upper Silesia, no. 1, September 15, 1940, APK 12/1600, no. 3, fo. 1.
64. Friedman, "Messianic Complex," 353–64; and Israel Welner, interview 26908, VHA.
65. Unger, *Reassessment*, 17–19; and Michman, "Jewish Leadership," 326–27.
66. Szternfinkiel, *Zagłada*, 26; Friedlander, *Years*, 41; and *Bulletin of the Central Office of the Jewish Councils in Eastern Upper Silesia*, no. 2, September 30, 1940, APK 12/1600, no. 3. fos. 6–9.
67. Namysło, "Einfluss," 311; and Niewyk and Nicosia, *Columbia Guide*, 185–86. The Jewish councils of Vilna and Białystok followed the same strategy. See Bender, *Jews*, 283.
68. Trunk, *Judenrat*, 75–78.
69. Steinbacher, *Musterstadt Auschwitz*, 138–39; and Gruner, *Jewish Forced Labor*, 217.
70. For instance, SS-Ansiedlungsstab and Einwandererzentralstelle. Interrogation of Herta Seidelmann, LHA 4878, fo. 203; and Heinemann, "*Rasse*," 138–217.
71. The Polish historian Artur Eisenbach coined the alternative term "Organization Schmelt" in 1953, possibly alluding to the influential "Organisation Todt." See Eisenbach, *Polityka*.
72. Trial of Schmelt Office staff, BArch B 162/20513, fo. 116; and interrogation of Herta Seidelmann, LHA 4878, fo. 203.
73. Interrogation of A. Hitschler, LHA 4877, fos. 1255–56; Paul Hertz, NIOD 250d/576; and Hartog Soep, NIOD 250d/851.
74. Helen Israel, interview 21038, VHA.
75. Laib Bratt, BArch B 162/20513, fo. 77; and Samuel Reifer, YVA M. 49 4311. On the massacre, see Krakowski, "Fate," 315–18; and Silberklang, *Gates*, 90–91.
76. S. Kaufmann, LHA 4861, fo. 107; and Max Glücksmann, YVA M.1. 679.
77. Paul Hertz, NIOD 250d/576; and Trial of Schmelt Office staff, BArch B 162/20513, fos. 107–19.
78. Eisenbach, *Polityka*, 212.
79. Interrogation of Walter Tschechne, LHA 4877, fo. 1299.
80. Paul Hertz, NIOD 250d/576; and interrogation of Albert Hitschler, LHA 4877, fos. 1252–53.

81. Isaac Cohensius, GFH 12032 R M-Hol., no. 416; Gruzlewska, *Annaberg*, 100; and Josef Niewes, NIOD 250d/716.
82. Interrogations of Albert Hitschler, July 13, 1954, and February 14, 1964, LHA 4877, fos. 1252–58.
83. Albert Youra, interview 31491, VHA.
84. Israel Wolnerman, interview 21328, VHA.
85. Statement of A. Hitschler, October 20, 1954, LHA 4877, fo. 1306.
86. Biuro Informacyjne W. Schimmelpfeng, APWr 11620.
87. Miron and Shulhani, *Yad Vashem Encyclopedia*, 744; and Samuel Reifer, YVA M.49 4311.
88. Bulletin of the Central Office of Jewish Councils in Eastern Upper Silesia, February 15, 1941, APK 12/1600, no. 18, fos. 5–16; and Trunk, *Judenrat*, 128–29.
89. Szternfinkiel, *Zaglada*, 26; and Yahil, *Holocaust*, 208.
90. The Chief administrator of Kattowitz, September 30, 1941, APK 12/807, fo 21; Steinbacher, *Musterstadt Auschwitz*, 166; and Strzelecki, "Deportation," 11.
91. Sam Seltzer, interview 13798, VHA; and Szternfinkiel, *Zaglada*, 25.
92. Protocol of the "Wannsee Conference," January 20, 1942, printed in Kampe, *Wannsee-Konferenz*, 31–32.
93. Commander of the order police Sosnowiec, December 13, 1941, APK 12/807, no. 316, fos. 103–7; and Hoess Trial, vol. 21, 181–85, APMO.
94. Fulbrook, *Small Town*, 203, 221–22; and Długoborski and Piper, *Auschwitz 1940–1945*, 1:69.
95. Miron and Shulhani, *Yad Vashem Encyclopedia*, 715; and Trunk, *Judenrat*, 420–31.
96. Gruner, *Jewish Forced Labor*, 294; similarly, Griffioen and Zeller, *Jodenvervolging*, 434.
97. Piper, *Zahl*, 183; and Czech, *Kalendarium*, 174–232.
98. Fulbrook, *Small Town*, 237–44; and Nitzah Rantz, interview 11814, VHA.
99. Leon Introligator, interview 19589, VHA; interrogation of Walter Tschechne, LHA 4877, fo. 1301; military district VIII, November 4, 1941, APO Rej. Opolska 1191, I/1465, fo. 77; and travel report Wawra, September 24–27, 1941, BArch R 4602/4131.
100. RAB annual business report 1942, printed in Weiss, "Oberste Bauleitung," 7.
101. The census of the Korherr report counted 50,570 Schmelt camp prisoners in January 1943. Korherr report, YVA TR 19 127, fo. 13.

CHAPTER 2

1. OHW quarterly management reports, November 1–December 31, 1941, BArch R 9348/7. Todt was also the RAB's founder. Seidler, *Fritz Todt*, 24–27; and Schütz and Gruber, *Mythos*, 90.
2. Samson Rauchwerger, BArch B 162/8869, fos. 2114–15; and Oskar Langer, BArch B 162/8866, fos. 819–20.
3. OHW strength reports to General Plenipotentiary Krauch, BArch R 9348/23.
4. Westermann, *Hitler's Police*, 92–121; Matthäus, "Beteiligung," 168–74; and Mallmann, "Mißgeburten," 77–82.
5. Harten, *Himmlers Lehrer*, 14–22.

6. Salomon Lierens, NIOD 250d/673; Hartog Soep, NIOD 250d/851; and Gucia Ferst, interview 34207, VHA.
7. Schmauser became HSSPF of Silesia in May 1941. Birn, *Höheren SS- und Polizeiführer*, 346; letter by Schmauser to Himmler, April 20, 1942, BArch B 162/20513, fo. 121; Steinbacher, *Musterstadt Auschwitz*, 282; Curilla, *Judenmord*, 140; Salomon Lierens, NIOD 250d/673; and Isaac Cohensius, GFH 12032 R M-Hol, no. 416.
8. Oskar Langer, BArch B 162/8866, fo. 820.
9. Browning, *Ordinary Men*, 3–9.
10. Matthäus, "Beteiligung," 178.
11. Pelt and Dwork, *Auschwitz*, 179; and Heinemann, "*Rasse*," 205.
12. Schmidt, "Reichskommissar," 199–223.
13. Black and Gutman, "Racial Theory"; and Schiessl, "Volksdeutsche."
14. Hoffmann claimed Rettinghausen had had a predecessor, whose identity is unclear. Statement of Erich Hoffmann, December 13, 1946, StA M SpkA K 739; and interrogation of Margarethe Neugebauer, June 26, 1962, BArch B 162/20513, fo. 34.
15. Report of the Commission for the Investigation of Nazi Crimes of the Israeli Police, Tel Aviv, August 2, 1964, APMO, fo. 8; and Samson Rauchwerger, BArch B 162/8869, fo. 2016.
16. Oskar Langer, BArch B 162/8866, fo. 820.
17. Karl Demerer, StA M SpkA K 739.
18. Koenig, *Vorhof*, 111; and Karl Demerer, YVA O.3 3635.
19. Despite using swastika armbands on its uniforms, Organisation Todt was no party organization and not only accepted a significant number of foreigners within its ranks but also served as a testing ground for the rehabilitation of *Wehrunwürdige* (soldiers expelled from the Wehrmacht). See Seidler, *Organisation Todt*, 144, 171.
20. Statement of Erich Hoffmann, 1947, StA M SpkA K 739.
21. Interrogation of Margarethe Neugebauer, BArch B 162/20513, fo. 34; and Gucia Ferst, interview 34207, VHA.
22. The order police units deployed in the annexed territories received ideological schooling by the SS from 1940. Harten, *Himmlers Lehrer*, 14–22.
23. Statement of Erich Hoffmann, StA M SpkA K 739.
24. Jozef Niewes, NIOD 250d/716.
25. Statement of Erich Hoffmann, 1947, StA M, SpkA K 739.
26. Maurits Bremer, NIOD 250d/448; and Wollenberg, *Alptraum*, 120–21.
27. See Albert Youra, interview 31491, VHA.
28. David Leo W., HVT-1687, FVA; Walter Ziegler, USHMM 2006.70.191; and Karl Demerer, BArch B 162/18175.
29. Gucia Ferst, interview 34207, VHA; and anonymous testimony, YVA M.49 610.
30. Oskar Langer, BArch 162/8866, fos. 819–20. Jewish POWs from Mandate Palestine serving in the British Army were held in Ehrenforst from December 1941. Pinchas Bleier, interview 45393, VHA.

31. Todt to director Schönleben, July 22, 1941, BArch R 4601/788.
32. Isaac Cohensius, GFH 12032 R M-Hol., no. 416.
33. Maurits Broeks, NIOD 250d/450; and Hans Bonn, NIOD 250d/445.
34. Salomon Lierens, NIOD 250d/673.
35. Rosa Schwarzberg, interview 9645, VHA; and anonymous testimony, YVA M.49 610.
36. Gruner, *Jewish Forced Labor*, 224; and police commando of section I Sosnowiec, May 1, 1942, APK 12/807, 316, fo. 191.
37. Sofsky, *Order*, 131; and Brown, *Judging "Privileged" Jews*, 2–11.
38. Karl Demerer, YVA O.3 3635; Karl Demerer, BArch B 162/18175; and Abraham Jonas Walg, NIOD 250d/920.
39. Gilbert, *Music*, 4, 158–59; and Fackler, *"Des Lagers Stimme,"* 366.
40. Arthur Salomons/Isaac Arbeid, NIOD 250d/815; and Clary, *Holocaust*, 86.
41. Weiss, "Oberste Bauleitung," 4–5; and Isaac Cohensius, GFH 12032 R M-Hol., no. 416.
42. Interrogation report of Otto Stoltzenburg, NA WO 309/978; OHW organigram, BArch R 9348/95; and Walter Ziegler, USHMM 2006.70.191.
43. Anonymous testimony, YVA M.49 610.
44. Oskar Langer, BArch B 162/8866, fos. 819–20; Sol W., HVT-1543, FVA; and anonymous testimony, YVA M.49 610.
45. OHW strength reports, March 1, 1942, BArch R 9348/23.
46. Rosengarten, *Overleven*, 117. Rosengarten's view is supported by Doris Bergen's study. See Bergen, "Nazi Concept," 575.
47. Oskar Langer, BArch B 162/8866, fos. 819–20; and Etienne Rosenfeld, YVA O.33 2070.
48. Wollenberg, *Alptraum*, 76.
49. Karl Demerer, YVA O.3 3635; BArch B 162/18175; Dr. Cohensius, LHA 4866, fo. 1053; Wollenberg, *Alptraum*, 78; Fainzang, *Mémoire*, 26–27; and Isaac Cohensius, GFH 12032 R M-Hol., no. 416.
50. Szternfinkiel, *Zagłada*, 26; Wollenberg, *Alptraum*, 76–77; and Abram Rosmarin, interview 11009, VHA.
51. Bernhard Bart, interview 1661, VHA.
52. Czech, "Rolle," 17; Heberer, "'Aktion T 4,'" 167–69; Grode, *"Sonderbehandlung 14f13,"* 252–53; Klee, "Von der T 4," 147–48; and Friedlander, *Origins*, 284–86.
53. Grode, *"Sonderbehandlung 14f13"*; Friedlander, *Origins*; and Heberer, "'Aktion T 4.'"
54. Klee, "Von der T 4"; Hinz-Wessels, "Jüdische Opfer"; and Czech, "Nazi Medical Crimes."
55. Kłudzinski, "'Aktion 14f13,'" 136–46; Piper, *Auschwitz 1940–1945*, 3:140–41; Klee, *Dokumente*, 260; and Czech, "Rolle," 17–18.
56. Czech, "Rolle," 20; and Garbe, "Konzentrationslager," 328.
57. Piper, *Auschwitz 1940–1945*, 3:124; and Czech, "Rolle," 21–39.
58. Gruner, *Jewish Forced Labor*, 226; Steinbacher, "East Upper Silesia," 252, 259; and Rudorff, "Arbeit und Vernichtung," 28.

59. Rudorff, *KZ Auschwitz*, 17.
60. Heinz Joseph, NIOD 250d/854.
61. Max Glücksmann, YVA M.1 679.
62. Herta Seidelmann, LHA 4878, fo. 203; and Heinemann, "*Rasse*," 138–217.
63. Harten, *Schulung*, 14–22.
64. Interrogation of Margarethe Neugebauer, BArch B 162/20513, fo. 34.
65. Karl Demerer, StA M SpkA K 739; and Samson Rauchwerger, BArch B 162/8869, fo. 2016.
66. Dobosiewicz, *Vernichtungslager*, 270–80.
67. Isaac Cohensius, GFH 12032 R M-Hol., no. 416; Wollenberg, *Alptraum*, 103–6; and Hirsch Bornstein, LHA 4877, fo. 51.
68. Arthur Salomons, NIOD 250d/815.
69. Strzelecka, "Frauen," 213; and Gutterman, *Narrow Bridge*, 161–62.
70. Gucia Ferst, interview 34207, VHA.
71. Chaja Pelzmann, BArch B 162/8866, fo. 889; and Gucia Ferst, interview 34207, VHA.
72. Rachel Brukner Frydrych, YVA O.3 3664.
73. Waxman, *Women*, 113; see also Ofer and Weitzman, *Women*.
74. Helen Israel, interview 21038, VHA; and Gucia Ferst, interview 34207, VHA.
75. Sinnreich, "Rape," 109.
76. Shik, "Sexual Abuse," 223.
77. Katz, "Thoughts," 302–5.
78. Sinnreich, "Rape," 109.
79. Kubica, "Kinder," 324.
80. Year Hammer, interview 18278, VHA.
81. Rosa Schwarzberg, interview 9645, VHA.
82. Voss, *Het fluitje*, 80–81.
83. Statement of Erich Hoffmann, December 13, 1946, StA M SpkA K 739.
84. Gucia Ferst, interview 34207, VHA.
85. Rosa Schwarzberg, interview 9645, VHA. The rape and murder of Sala Fischel was confirmed by several witnesses heard in the Munich trial of Erich Hoffmann in 1947. See statements by Szlama Palluck, Basia Palluck, Lucie Noher, and Karl Demerer, StA M SpkA 739.
86. Gucia Ferst, interview 34207, VHA.
87. Statement of Erich Hoffmann, StA M SpkA K 739; and OHW quarterly management reports, July 1–September 15, 1942, BArch R 9348/6.
88. OHW quarterly management reports, July 1–September 15, 1942, BArch R 9348/6.
89. Anonymous testimony, YVA M.49. 610; Jakob Thaler, YVA M.49. 2071; Gabriel Zvi Lifschitz, NIOD 250d/674; and Wollenberg, *Alptraum*, 76.
90. Gutterman, "Jews," 53–83; and statement of Wolf Leitner, StA M SpkA K 739.
91. Weindling, *Epidemics*, 312.
92. Czech, "Rolle," 20.

93. Sol W., HVT-1543, FVA.
94. Jakob Thaler, YVA M.49.2071.
95. Jeremias Samentini, NIOD 250d/816; and Hoess Trial, APMO, vol. 21, fo. 181.
96. Karl Demerer, BArch B 162/18175; and statement by Erich Hoffmann, StA M SpkA K 739.
97. Rosa Schwarzberg, interview 9645, VHA.
98. OHW strength reports, June 1–September 1, 1942, BArch R 9348/23; Oskar Langer, BArch B 162/8866, fo. 820; and Samson Rauchwerger, BArch B 162/8869, fo. 2016.
99. David Leo W., HVT-1687, FVA; Walter Ziegler, USHMM 2006.70.191; Samson Rauchwerger, BArch B 162/8869, fo. 2016; and Karl Demerer, YVA O.3 3635. At least one transport from Blechhammer passed through Brande in transit in late 1942. See Weiss, "From *Reichsautobahnlager*," 111.

CHAPTER 3

1. StA M SpkA K 739.
2. See directive by Krauch to Riedmüller, January 30, 1942, and minute of the meeting between Dr. Riedmüller, Dr. Urbanek, and Dr. Carstaedt, February 18, 1942, BArch R 9348/60, 50.
3. Minute of the meeting between Dr. Riedmüller, Dr. Urbanek, and Dr. Carstaedt, February 18, 1942, and memorandum by Otto Stoltzenburg to Dr. Urbanek, April 2, 1942, BArch R 9348/50.
4. Hoess Trial, APMO, vol. 21, fo. 181.
5. Eichmann announced his plans to deport 135,000 Jews (later reduced to 90,000) from the Netherlands, Belgium, and France on June 11, 1942. Griffioen and Zeller, "Deportations," 449. In October 1942 Speer's Ministry of Armaments and War Production informed the Silesian industrialists that a transfer of Jewish skilled laborers from the west was currently underway. Hayes, "Ambiguities," 13.
6. The term "Cosel period" was coined by Dutch historians in 1947. Landesberger, de Haas, and Selowsky, *Auschwitz*.
7. A memorial plaque was set up on the platform in September 2016. See http://www.holocaustlimburg.nl/cosel (October 2016). Thanks to Herman van Rens and Edward Haduch for sharing this information. See also Rens and Wilms, *Tussenstation Cosel*.
8. Salomon van Velzen, NIOD 250k/854; Harry Fransman, interview 2548, VHA; Marcus Samuel Frank, NIOD 250d/528; Siegfried Hermann, interview 38261, VHA; and Clary, *Holocaust*, 65–67.
9. Die Deportationstransporte während der sogenannten Cosel-Periode, StA Wü 2012-009, no. 37, fos. 1128–31; and Hermann Kluger, YVA M.68 4031627.
10. Hoess Trial, APMO, vol. 21, fo. 181; cable by Hoess to Eichmann, NA HW 16/21, 7 October 1942, items 1–4; Breitman, *Official Secrets*, 112; and August König, BArch B 162/4103, fos. 698–99.
11. Klarsfeld, *Mémorial*, 331.
12. Griffioen and Zeller, "Anti-Jewish Policy," 452–53; and Pinot, *Convois*, 47–48.

13. Egon Altmann, 20100/00119, DOEW; Peter Sturm, 20100/12040, DOEW; Wollenberg, *Alptraum*, 36–38; Spira, *Legende*, 105–10; and Fry, *Surrender*, 44–45.
14. Griffioen and Zeller, "Anti-Jewish Policy," 452–53; Pinot, *Convois*, 48, 268; and Piper, "Nebenlager Blechhammer," 28.
15. The Cosel selections affected transports numbers 6–9 (departures from Malines on August 29, September 1, 10, and 12, 1942), and 12–13 (both October 10, 1942). Meinen, *Shoah*, 84, 239.
16. The respective transports departed from Westerbork on August 28 and 31, September 4, 7, 11, and 14, October 2, 5, 16, 23, and 30, November 2, 6, 10, 16, 24, 30, and December 8, 1942. Die Deportationstransporte während der sogenannten Cosel-Periode, StA Wü 2012-009, no. 37, fos. 1128–31.
17. Hans Bonn, NIOD 250d/445; Maurits Bremer, NIOD, 250d/448; and Heinrich Demler, BArch B 162/4102, fos. 249–50.
18. Nathan de Vries, NIOD 250d/915; Felix G., HVT-3458, FVA; and Heinrich Falke, BArch B 162/4102, fo. 325.
19. Isaac Cohensius, GFH 12032 R M-Hol, no. 416.
20. Hartog Salomon Ereira, NIOD 250d/519; and Samuel Abrams, NIOD 250d/386.
21. Kurt Baum, RG-50.154*0005, USHMM; and Koenig, *Vorhof*, 95–96.
22. Fainzang, *Mémoire*, 14.
23. The message was intercepted by British intelligence. NA HW 16/21, October 7, 1942, items 1–4; and Breitman, *Official Secrets*, 112.
24. Die Deportationstransporte während der sogenannten Cosel-Periode, StA Wü 2012-009, no. 37, fos. 1128–31.
25. In October 1942, 11,965 Jews were deported. Griffioen and Zeller, "Anti-Jewish Policy," 456; and Moore, *Victims*, 98–99.
26. Hoess Trial, APMO, vol. 21, fo. 181. The escapes alleged by Hoess were not corroborated by testimonies.
27. Steinbacher, *Musterstadt Auschwitz*, 256; and Rudorff, *KZ Auschwitz*, 35–36.
28. S. L. Toneman, NIOD 250d/887; Jacob de Boers, NIOD 250d/441; and Hessel Goldberg, NIOD 250d/553.
29. Rafael Lewin, interview 27687, VHA; and Salomon Ruben Swaab, NIOD 250k/872.
30. Hoess Trial, APMO, vol. 21, fo. 181.
31. Jakob Thaler, YVA M. 49. 2071.
32. Jeremias Samentini, NIOD 250d/816; and Jacques op den Berg, NIOD 250d/726.
33. Czech, *Kalendarium*, 321.
34. Borrie, *Captivity*, 171.
35. Hans Hanenkamp, BArch B 162/4102, fo. 403; Johann Hönle, BArch B 162/4103, fo. 456; Hoess Trial, APMO, vol. 21, fo. 181.
36. Die Deportationstransporte während der sogenannten Cosel-Periode, StA Wü 2012-009, no. 37, fo. 1130.

37. Wolfgang Curilla also shares this view. Curilla, *Ordungspolizei*.
38. The transports ran on August 24–26; August 31–September 2, September 7–9, 14–16, 21–23, and October 19–21; and November 16–18, 1943.
39. Walter Meyer, BArch B 162/4102, fo. 415; Konrad von Salzen, BArch B 162/4103, fo. 697; and Johann Hönle, BArch B 162/4103, fo. 456.
40. Erna Ellert, StA M SpkA 739; Czech, *Kalendarium*, 593; and Wollenberg, *Alptraum*, 118–19.
41. August König, BArch B 162/4103, fos. 698–99; Ernst Heins, BArch B 162/4103, fo. 386; and Eberhard Pohland, BArch B 162/4103, fo. 424.
42. Karl Demerer, YVA O.3 3536; Memoirs of R. Stoppelman, YVA O.33/4272; Die Deportationstransporte während der sogenannten Cosel-Periode, StA Wü 2012-009, no. 37, fo. 1130.
43. Boom, "'Auschwitz Reservation,'" 385–407; and Hermann Leefsma, interview 11033, VHA.
44. Gabriel Zvi Lifschitz, NIOD 250d/674.
45. Salomon Ruben Swaab, NIOD 250k/854.
46. Kurt Baum, USHMM, RG-50.154*0005; Kurt Rosendahl, YVA O.33 7003; and Courtois and Rayski, *Qui savait quoi?*, 122–65.
47. Spira, *Legende*, 126; and Koenig, *Vorhof*, 95–96.
48. The testimony was featured in the movie *Les Héretiers* (*Once in a Lifetime*, France, 2014, directed by Marie-Castille Mention Schaar) based on the true story of French students participating in an essay prize contest on the Holocaust. Léon Zyguel had been invited into their class to speak about his experiences in Nazi camps and played himself in the movie adaptation.
49. Bettelheim, "Trauma," 31–33; Laub, "Event," 76–82; and Greenspan, *Listening to Holocaust Survivors*, 7.
50. Abraham Spiero, NIOD 250d/859; Nathan de Vries, NIOD 250d/915; and Felix G., HVT-3458, FVA. On the Annaberg transit camp, see Grużlewska, *Annaberg*, 90–103.
51. Etienne Rosenfeld, YVA O.33 2070, fo. 109; Mozes Vischjäger, NIOD 250d/908; Hartog Salomon Ereira, NIOD 250d/519; and Felix G., HVT-3458, FVA.
52. Die Deportationstransporte während der sogenannten Cosel-Periode, StA Wü 12012-009, no. 37, fos. 1128–31; Isaac Arbeid/Arthur Salomons, NIOD 250d/815; Maurits Bremer, NIOD 250d/448; Barend van Delft, NIOD 250d/495; Brommet, NIOD 250d/453; and Clary, *Holocaust*, 69–71.
53. Marcus Samuel Frank, NIOD 250d/528; Mendel Meyer, NIOD 250d/695; and Maurits Broeks, NIOD 250d/450.
54. Joseph Braasem, NIOD 250d/446; Marcus Samuel Frank, NIOD 250d/528; Piet Nieuwes, NIOD 250d/715; Jozef Niewes, NIOD 250d/716; Karl Demerer, YVA O.3 3635; and Alexander Kuechel, interview 19, VHA.
55. Hayes, "Ambiguities," 13.
56. Hans Bonn, NIOD 250d/445; Raphael Montezinos, NIOD 250k/854; Paul Hertz, NIOD 250d/576; and Wollenberg, *Alptraum*, 47.

57. Salomon Lierens, NIOD 250d/673.
58. Hartog Soep, NIOD 250d/851; and Gucia Ferst, interview 34207, VHA.
59. Joseph Braasem NIOD 250d/446; and Piet Nieuwes, NIOD 250d/715. On Knoll, see Szternfinkiel, *Zagłada*, 23.
60. Salomon Lierens, NIOD 250d/673.
61. Stephenson, *Women*, 112.
62. Interrogation of Margarethe Neugebauer, June 26, 1962, BArch B 162/20513, fo. 34.
63. The chief of the German order police Daluege to HSSPF Schmauser, September 9, 1942, APO 1191/1486, fos. 70–74.
64. Joseph Braasem, NIOD 250d/446.
65. Abraham Aussen, NIOD 250d/389; and Joseph Braasem, NIOD 250d/446.
66. Penal reports concerning the Blechhammer subcamp, BArch B 162/8867.
67. Paul Hertz, NIOD 250d/576; and Memoirs of R. Stoppelman, YVA O.33 4272.
68. Obréjan, *Homme*, 60.
69. Isaac Cohensius, GFH 12032 R M-Hol, no. 416.
70. Salomon Lierens, NIOD 250d/673.
71. Karl Demerer, StA M SpkA K 739.
72. Piet Nieuwes, NIOD 250d/715.
73. Gutterman, *Narrow Bridge*, 50; and Wollenberg, *Alptraum*, 119.
74. Marcus Samuel Frank, NIOD 250d/528; Samuel Lifschitz, NIOD 250/674; and Spitzer, *Dessin*, 71.
75. Piet Nieuwes, NIOD 250d/715; and Jozef Niewes, NIOD 250d/716.
76. Salomon Lifschitz, NIOD 250d/674.
77. Jozef Niewes, NIOD 250d/716; Piet Nieuwes, NIOD 250d/715; Helen Israel, interview 21038, VHA; and Fainzang, *Mémoire*, 68–69.
78. Leo Weiniger, NIOD 244/1486.
79. Salomon Staszewski, NIOD 250d/864; Efraim Roseboom, NIOD 250d/805; and Maurits Bremer, NIOD 250d/448.
80. Artur Salomons/Isaac Arbeid, NIOD 250d/815.
81. OHW circular, July 14, 1942, and Memoirs of R. Stoppelman, YVA O.33 4272.
82. Samuel Abrams, NIOD 250d/386; Joseph Braasem, NIOD 250d/446; and Piet Nieuwes, NIOD 250d/715.
83. BArch R 4601/42, no. 1173; Schütz and Gruber, *Mythos*, 80–84; and Wollenberg, *Alptraum*, 115.
84. S. Kaufmann, LHA 4861, fo. 1030.
85. Wollenberg, *Alptraum*, 146.
86. Paul Hertz, NIOD 250d/576; Trunk, *Judenrat*, 475–88; and Levi, *Drowned*, 22–33.
87. See Gutterman, "Jews," 53–83.
88. Hartog Salomon Ereira, NIOD 250d/519; and Salomon Staszewski, NIOD 250d/864.
89. Etienne Rosenfeld, YVA O.33 2070.

90. Louis Waterman, NIOD 250d/922.
91. Wolf W., HVT-2989, FVA.
92. Charge of the Central Committee against Icek Rosenzweig, YVA M.21 73.
93. Arthur Salomons/Isaac Arbeid, NIOD 250d/815.
94. Paul Hertz, NIOD 250d/576; Joseph Braasem, NIOD 250d/446; Samuel Abrams, NIOD 250d/386; and Chaim Weitzenfeld, interview 35967, VHA.
95. Simon Blein, NIOD 250d/433.
96. Joseph Braasem, NIOD 250d/446; Rosengarten, *Overleven*, 167–68; Paul Hertz, NIOD 250d/576; Hans Bonn, NIOD 250d/445; Jacques op den Berg, NIOD 250d/726; and Jacob de Wolf, NIOD 250d/946.
97. Wajnblum, *My Destiny*, 126.
98. Joseph Braasem, NIOD 250d/446; and Salomon Staszewski, NIOD 250d/864.
99. Arthur Salomons/Isaac Arbeid, NIOD 250d/815; and Gunter Faerber, interview 41847, VHA.
100. Memoirs of R. Stoppelman, YVA O.33 4274.
101. Wollenberg, *Alptraum*, 64–65, 75, 109–10.
102. Maurice Perlman was born in Botosany, Romania, in 1905. He was arrested in September 1942 with his wife, Marta Hershkowici. AN 736 MI 2, Au 6; and Isidore Emanuel Moppes, NIOD 250d/703.
103. Hans Bonn, NIOD, 250d/445; and Joseph Braasem, NIOD 250d/446.
104. Wollenberg, *Alptraum*, 76.
105. Szlama Palluck, StA M SpK 739; and Samuel Abrams, NIOD 250d/386.
106. Szlama Palluck, StA M SpK 739.
107. Abram Szeftel, APMO Oświedcienia, f. 48, fos. 154–59.
108. Grużlewska, *Annaberg*, 88.
109. Isaac Cohensius, GFH 12032, R M-Hol., no. 416.
110. Wollenberg, *Alptraum*, 76.
111. Grużlewska, *Annaberg*, 88–89; Joseph Braasem, NIOD 250d/446; Hans Bonn, NIOD 250d/445; and Marcus Samuel Frank, NIOD 250d/528.
112. Abram Blachinskzi, StA M SpkA K 739; Arthur Salomons/Isaac Arbeid, NIOD 250d/815; and Salomon Lierens, NIOD 250d/673.
113. Piper, "Nebenlager Blechhammer," 32.
114. OHW quarterly management reports, July 1–September 15, 1942, BArch R 9348/6; Szymon Szafir, WL 055-EA-1026; and Marcus Samuel Frank, NIOD 250d/528.
115. Leo Weiniger, NIOD 244/1486; and Arthur Salomons/Isaac Arbeid, NIOD 250d/815.
116. Marcus Samuel Frank, NIOD 250d/528; Moshe Erlikh, YVA O.3 11891; and Obréjan, *Homme*, 65–66.
117. Hans Bonn, NIOD 250d/445; Etienne Rosenfeld, YVA O.33 2070; and Seidler, *Organisation Todt*, 171.

118. Maurits Bremer, NIOD 250d/448.
119. Etienne Rosenfeld, YVA O.33 2070.
120. Myron B., HVT-1507, FVA; Spitzer, *Dessin*, 84, Gerrit Aardewerk, NIOD 250d/384; and Rosengarten, *Overleven*, 180.
121. Jonas Pampel, NIOD 250d/741.
122. Intermediary report no. 1 by the Israeli police, August 2, 1964, APMO.
123. Ida Frydman, interview 35134, VHA.
124. Gucia Ferst, interview 34207, VHA.
125. Piet Nieuwes, NIOD 250d/715; and Karl Demerer, BArch B 162/18175.
126. Maurits Bremer, NIOD 250d/448.
127. Czech, *Kalendarium*, 352.

CHAPTER 4

1. Westermann, *Police*, 92–121; Matthäus, "Beteiligung," 168–74; and Klemp, *"Nicht ermittelt,"* 29–79.
2. Directive by Himmler, October 31, 1939, APO 1191/1486, fos. 21–27; Himmler to Schmelt, September 18, 1941, APO 1191/1486, fos. 14–15; and Klemp, *"Nicht ermittelt,"* 76.
3. Schmauser to Himmler, April 20, 1942, BArch B 162/20513, fos. 21–22.
4. Daluege to Schmauser, September 9, 1942, APO 1191/1486, fos. 70–74; and Schmauser to Schmelt, September 29, 1942, APO 1191/1486, fos. 82–83.
5. Schmauser to the inspector of the order police Breslau, November 30, 1942, APO 1191/1486, fo. 105.
6. Guidelines for the training of police guard battalions, forwarded by the police director of Oppeln to Schmelt, December 30, 1942, APO 1191/1486, fo. 142.
7. Schmauser to Schmelt, February 1, 1943, APO 1191/1486, fo. 127.
8. Chief of the order police, Berlin, April 8, 1943, APO 1191/1486, fo. 149; and Schmelt to Schmauser, October 6, 1943, APO 1191/1486, fo. 222.
9. Klemp, *"Nicht ermittelt,"* 46, 78–79.
10. Perz, "Wehrmacht," 69–75, 81.
11. Eliazer Content, NIOD 250d/481; and Wollenberg, *Alptraum*, 123.
12. Lasik, "Organisationsstruktur," 194–96.
13. Statement by Erich Hoffmann, December 13, 1946, StA M SpkA K 739; and Wollenberg, *Alptraum*, 121.
14. Koenig, *Vorhof*, 110–11; and Spitzer, *Dessin*, 67.
15. Louis Schuitevorder, NIOD 250d/835.
16. Wollenberg, *Alptraum*, 123; and Mozes Jacob van Dam, NIOD 250d/491.
17. Rosengarten, *Overleven*, 131.
18. Wollenberg, *Alptraum*, 123.
19. Maurits Bremer, NIOD 250d/448; and Bernhard Littwack, interview 26341, VHA.

20. Perz, "Wehrmachtsangehörige," 177–78.
21. Wollenberg, *Alptraum*, 130.
22. Overy, *War and Economy*, 26–31.
23. Interrogation of Otto Stoltzenburg, NA WO 309/978; and deposition of Karl Kulicke, April 19, 1947, NA WO 309/378.
24. Drobisch, "Werkschutz," 221.
25. Stoltzenburg to Dr. Urbanek, April 13, 1943, BArch R 9348/50; and OHW quarterly management report, June 30, 1943, BArch R 9348/7.
26. Karl Demerer, YVA O.3 3635.
27. Wollenberg, *Alptraum*, 119; and Bernhard Littwack, interview 26341, VHA.
28. Korherr report, YVA TR 19 127, fo. 13.
29. OHW strength reports 1943–1944, BArch R 9348/23; Piper, "Nebenlager Blechhammer," 26.
30. Dr. Urbanek, November 16, 1943, BArch R 9348/57.
31. Rosengarten, *Overleven*, 132.
32. Arthur Salomons/Isaac Arbeid, NIOD 250d/815.
33. Karl Demerer, BArch B 162/18175; Leo Weiniger, NIOD 244/1486; and Piper, "Ausbeutung," 156–57.
34. Leo Weiniger, NIOD 244/1486.
35. Gerrit Aardewerk, NIOD 250d/384; and Jerrit A., HVT-208, FVA.
36. Leo Weiniger, NIOD 244/1486.
37. Dr. Urbanek, OHW social department, November 16, 1943, BArch R 9348/57.
38. Circular by Oswald Pohl, October 26, 1943, BArch NS 3/386.
39. Lasik, "Organisationsstruktur," 173; Piper, *Arbeitseinsatz*, 291; and Wachsmann, *KL*, 65–471.
40. David Leo W., HVT-1687, FVA.
41. Joseph Braasem, NIOD 250d/446; Maurits Bremer, NIOD 250d/448; and Arthur Salomons, NIOD 250d/815.
42. Leo Weiniger, NIOD 244/1486; and Louis Waterman, NIOD 250d/922.
43. Kurt Klappholz, IWM Sound Archive, 9425; and Wollenberg, *Alptraum*, 116. On the psychological effects of starvation, see, Guetzkow and Bowman, *Men*, 24.
44. Spitzer, *Dessin*, 94–95.
45. Strzelecki, "Deportation," 40–41.
46. Leo Weiniger, NIOD 244/1486.
47. Rosengarten, *Overleven*, 134.
48. Sofsky, *Order*, 130.
49. Maurits Bremer, NIOD 250d/448; and Louis Waterman, NIOD 250d/922.
50. Abraham Jonas Walg, NIOD 250d/920; and Private Papers by Dr. Schlick, July 7, 1943, BArch R 9348/111.

51. NI-036, ITS Doc. ID 24/0047 (accessed via the USHMM); and *Mitteilungen der österreichischen Lagergemeinschaft*, May 1962, SWA.
52. Joseph Braasem, NIOD 250d/446.
53. Salomon Lierens, NIOD 250d/673.
54. Müller to Josenhans, June 12, 1942, BArch R 9348/60.
55. Hessel Goldberg, NIOD 250d/553.
56. Maurice Moshe Szmidt, YVA O.3 3474.
57. Salomon Staszewski, NIOD 250d/864; and Person, "Jews," 225–46.
58. Heyman Joseph Leefsma, NIOD 250d/657; Helmo Trzesniewsky, BArch B 162/8864, fo. 422; Karl Kaye, BArch B 162/8864, fo. 434; and Spitzer, *Dessin*, 79.
59. Rosengarten, *Overleven*, 115; and Fainzang, *Mémoire*, 72.
60. Adam, *"Arbeiterfrage,"* 349.
61. Maurits Bremer, NIOD 250d/448; and Fainzang, *Mémoire*, 111.
62. Jacques G., HVT-2845, FVA; Louis Schuitevoerder, NIOD 250d/835; and Jacques op den Berg, NIOD 250d/726.
63. Wollenberg, *Alptraum*, 123–24; and Rosengarten, *Overleven*, 131.
64. Hans Bonn, NIOD 250d/445.
65. Jakob Gesang, BArch B 162/8864, fos. 382–84.
66. Maurits Broeks, NIOD 250d/450.
67. Maurits Bremer, *Een Dag in Blechhammer*, NIOD 250d/448; Kurt Klappholz, IWM Sound Archive 9425; and Tooley, *National Identity*, 14.
68. Bil Spira, IWM ART 17120.
69. Rosengarten, *Overleven*, 117. In his autobiography, Rosengarten stated that the master had been in the S.A., but it seems more likely that he was an RAB employee. They also wore the military-style khaki outfits and berets of Organisation Todt from 1939. Jewish inmates often confused OT uniforms with those of the S.A. and wrongly assumed that the swastika armband indicated membership in the Nazi party. Seidler, *Organisation Todt*, 171.
70. Joseph Braasem, NIOD 250d/446.
71. Affidavit of Helga Kulicke, NA WO 309/798.
72. Interrogation of A. Hitschler, LHA 4877, fos. 1255–56.
73. Wollenberg, *Alptraum*, 123–24; and statement by Erich Hoffmann, 13 December 1946, StA M SpkA K 739.
74. Sofsky, *Order*, 170; and Piper, *Arbeitseinsatz*, 291.
75. Halpin, *Jewish Doctors*, 115–35.
76. Levi, *Drowned*, 22–33.
77. Siegel, "Coercion-Resistance Spectrum," 1–20.
78. Isaac Cohensius was born in Oude-Tonge, the Netherlands, on November 14, 1910. Ende, *Vergeet niet dat je arts bent*, 297; Isaac Cohensius, GFH 12032 R M-Hol, no. 416; Dr. Cohensius, April 5, 1948, LHA 4866, fo. 1053; and Abraham Jonas Walg, NIOD 250d/920.

79. Louis Schuitevoerder, NIOD 250d/835; and Wollenberg, *Alptraum*, 76.
80. Isaac Cohensius, GFH, 12032 R M-Hol, no. 416; and statement by Dr. Cohensius, April 5, 1948, LHA 4866, fo. 1053.
81. Dr. Moses Auerhahn was born in Olkusz in 1900. After the war, he remained in Poland and polonized his name to Marian Głuszecki. YVA M.49 3721281 3321; Joseph Braasem, NIOD 250d/446; Abraham Spiero, NIOD 250d/859; Efraim Roseboom, NIOD 250d/805; and Fainzang, *Mémoire*, 58.
82. Fainzang, *Mémoire*, 26–27, 45; Lion Gosler, NIOD 250d/555; Maurice Moshe Szmidt, YVA O.3 3474; and Simon Overste, NIOD 250d/735.
83. Louis Waterman, NIOD 250d/922; and Jonas Pampel, NIOD 250d/741.
84. Leo Weiniger, NIOD 244/1486.
85. Wollenberg, *Alptraum*, 83–84.
86. M. Fajon, AN 736 MI 3.
87. Kurt Klappholz, IWM Sound Archive, 9425.
88. Shik, "Sexual Abuse," 234–35; and Chatwood, "Stories," 162–63.
89. Fainzang, *Mémoire*, 26–27, 57–59.
90. Fanny Pillersdorf, interview 7560, VHA.
91. Samuel Abrams, NIOD 250d/386; Maurits Bremer, NIOD 250d/448; and Brommet NIOD/250d/453.
92. Wollenberg, *Alptraum*, 105–6, 133.
93. Maurits Bremer, NIOD 250d/448.
94. Jozef Niewes, NIOD 250d/716; Brommet, NIOD 250d/453; Marcus Samuel Frank, NIOD 250d/528; Hans Bonn, NIOD 250d/445; and Joseph Braasem, NIOD 250d/446.
95. Trial of Erich Hoffmann, StA M SpkA K 739.
96. Ezriel Rabinowitsch, StA M SpkA K 739.
97. Ezriel Zygmunt Rabinowicz, interview 32755, VHA; and Buser, "Karl Demerer," 476–77.
98. See, Sofsky, *Order*, 131, 136.
99. Wollenberg, *Alptraum*, 70, 105.
100. See Fulbrook, *Reckonings*, 231–65.
101. Appeal by Erich Hoffmann, September 3, 1947, StA M SpkA K 739.
102. Waxman, *Women*, 141; and Trial of Erich Hoffmann, IPN GK 164/4600.
103. Wollenberg, *Alptraum*, 70, 105.
104. Office of the Attorney-General of Mannheim, November 13, 1963, BArch B 162/8863; and Karl Demerer, June 9, 1964, BArch B 162/18175.
105. See, Levi, *Drowned*, 29.
106. Dr. Bernhard Littwack was born in Ortelsburg, East Prussia, in 1902. After the Nazi rise to power, he emigrated to France. He was arrested in 1942 when he tried to cross the Spanish border holding an immigration visa to Mexico and was deported from Drancy. Bernhard Littwack, interview 26341, VHA; and Wollenberg, *Alptraum*, 117.
107. Dr. Wolf Lajtner was born in Dąbrowa, Poland, in 1914. From 1940 he was a camp physi-

cian in Geppersdorf and then accompanied inmates to the Russian front. From 1942 until August 1943 he was in Parschnitz. Wolf Lajtner, LHA 4876, fos. 2415–17.

Dr. Hans-Werner Wollenberg, born in Königsberg, East Prussia, in 1891, served as military physician in the First World War and was awarded the Iron Cross. In Nazi Germany he had to give up his medical practice in Berlin, and he emigrated to France in 1938. He was deported from Drancy in September 1942 and went through camps Johannsdorf and Brande before Blechhammer. Wollenberg, *Alptraum*.

108. Dr. Wolf Lajtner, LHA 4876, fos. 2415–17; Wolf Leitner, StA M SpkA K 739; Abraham Schaufeld, IWM Sound Archive, 17470; and Bernhard Littwack, interview 26341, VHA.
109. Maurits Bremer, NIOD 250d/448.
110. Erna Ellert, StA M SpkA K 739.
111. Erna Ellert, StA M SpkA K 739; and Czech, *Kalendarium*, 593.
112. Statement of Dora Hirsch before the Attorney-General of Kiel, February 10, 1956, ITS (accessed via USHMM), Document ID 48/0069.
113. Lang, *Frauen*, 83–167; and Weindling, *Victims*, 139–52.
114. Erna Ellert, StA M SpkA K 739. Ellert referred to Eduard Wirths, the SS area chief physician of Auschwitz from November 1942 until January 1945. SS physicians routinely supervised the killing process. See Dirks, "Karrieresprung," 143–67.
115. Dr. Wolf Lajtner, LHA 4876, fo. 2417.
116. According to Wollenberg, the transport left Blechhammer on September 13, but the sick were presumably added to a Westerbork convoy on September 14–16, 1943. Wollenberg, *Alptraum*, 118–19.
117. Vaccine mandate for OHW workers by the Public Health Authority, September 16, 1943, BArch R 9348/99.
118. Rudolf Weigl (1883–1957) was recognized as a Righteous Among the Nations by Yad Vashem in 2003. Gutman, *Encyclopedia*, supp. vol. 2, 629. On his activities see also Roland, *Courage*, 148–49; Weindling, *Epidemics*, 345–63; and Weindling, "Delousing."
119. Ernest Wolf, AN 736 MI 3.
120. Wollenberg, *Alptraum*, 122.
121. Bernhard Littwack, interview 26341, VHA; and Wollenberg, *Alptraum*, 133.
122. Sam Green, BArch B 162/8864, fo. 297; Gita Brandsztedter-Sztulbergowa, APMO, Oświedcienia, f. 48, fo. 151; and Jakob Gesang, BArch B 162/8864, fo. 384.
123. Karl Kaye, BArch B 162/8864, fo. 335.
124. Karl Demerer, Trial of Erich Hoffmann, StA M SpkA 739.
125. Aron Schlos, Trial of Erich Hoffmann, StA M SpkA 739.
126. Louis Waterman, NIOD 250d/922.
127. Sofsky, *Order*, 221.
128. Charge of the Central Committee against Icek Rosenzweig, YVA M. 21 73; and Wollenberg, *Alptraum*, 100–12.
129. Leo B., HVT-1824, FVA.

130. Piper, *Auschwitz 1940–1945*, vol. 3, 124; and Dirks, "Karrieresprung," 151–53.
131. Karl Demerer, BArch B 162/18175; and Abraham Jonas Walg, NIOD 250d/920.
132. Maurits Bremer, NIOD 250d/448.
133. Wollenberg, *Alptraum*, 125; and Leo Weiniger, NIOD 244/1486.
134. Gita Brandsztedter-Sztulbergowa, APMO, Oświedcienia, f. 48, fo. 151.
135. Karl Demerer, YVA O.3 3635.
136. Kubica, "Kinder," 324.
137. Sali Montag, BArch B 162/8864, fos. 429–31; and Jozef Niewes, NIOD 250d/716.
138. Fainzang, *Mémoire*, 74.
139. Jonas Pampel, NIOD 250d/741; Herman Boekdrukker, NIOD 250d/1060; and Isaac Cohensius, GFH 12032 R M-Hol, no. 416.
140. M. Frankenhuis, NIOD 250d/532.
141. See Rahe, "Jewish Religious Life," 86; and Bauer, *Holocaust*, 42–45.

CHAPTER 5

1. Fulbrook, *Small Town*, 291; Rudolf Höss, BArch B162/20513, fo. 119; Protocol of the Wannsee Conference, January 20, 1942, printed in Klein, *"Wannsee-Konferenz."*
2. Max Glücksmann, YVA M.1. 679.
3. Pohl, *Judenverfolgung*, 338–41; Yones, *Smoke*, 183–85; and Longerich, *Holocaust*, 380.
4. Hördler, *Ordnung*, 279–84; and Steinbacher, *Musterstadt Auschwitz*, 305.
5. Fulbrook, *Small Town*, 291.
6. Arthur Salomons and Isaac Arbeid, NIOD 250d/815; and Wolf W., HVT-2989, FVA.
7. Gutman, *Encyclopedia of the Holocaust*, 769–70; Henry G., HVT-2384, FVA; Alix H., HVT-210, FVA; and Spitzer, *Dessin*, 66.
8. Gutman, *Encyclopedia of the Holocaust*, 322–23; and Dora Wajs, The Zagórz Concentration Camp, http://www.jewishgen.org/yizkor/Klobuck/klo250.html (August 2017).
9. Ruth Wysocki, interview 42818, VHA; Ann C., HVT-0340, FVA; Gucia Ferst, interview 34207, VHA; and Cadok Plawner, YVA O.3 3679.
10. Langer defined "choiceless choices" as unresolvable choices deliberately imposed by the perpetrators, which did not offer any genuine options. Langer, *Versions*, 72.
11. Rifka Osher, interview 33425, VHA; Year Hammer, interview 18278, VHA; Gucia Ferst, interview 34207; and Lola Lackmann, interview 16283, VHA.
12. Arthur Salomons/Isaac Arbeid, NIOD 250d/815; Jozef Niewes, NIOD 250d/716; Sala Frydrych, interview 4081, VHA; and Cadok Plawner, YVA O.3 3679.
13. Helen Reiber, interview 20189, VHA.
14. Art G., HVT-382, FVA; Ann C., HVT-0340, FVA; and Ann Cyncynatus, interview 19710.
15. Gutman, *Encyclopedia of the Holocaust*, 742–46; reports on deportations from Sosnowiec, Schupo-AK I, August 13, 1942, and First Police Precinct Sosnowiec, August 20, 1942, APK 12/807, no. 316, fos. 208–22, 294.
16. Rose Rotmensh, interview 8669, VHA; and Pincus W., HVT-1419, FVA. The women mur-

dered in winter 1943 were held in the camp for the sick and convalescent set up in September 1943. Gucia Ferst, interview 34207, VHA.
17. Lola Lackmann, interview 16283, VHA; and Gussie Zaks, interview 3093, VHA.
18. S. Kaufmann, LHA 4861.
19. Sara Chrapot, interview 19997, VHA. Anna Hájková identified consensual sexual barter as characteristic of the ghetto economy. See Hájková, "Sexual Barter," 503–33.
20. Karl Demerer, YVA O.3 3635; and Jozef Niewes, NIOD 250d/716.
21. Grużlewska, *Annaberg*, 104.
22. Kubica, "Children," 413–17; Kubica, "Kinder," 268–99, 316–23, 349, 351; and Buser, *Überleben*, 127–60.
23. Karl Demerer, YVA O.3 3635; and Demerer, *Kind*, 50–52.
24. Demerer, *Kind*, 54–56.
25. Jozef Niewes, NIOD 250d/716; Artur Salomons and Isaac Arbeid, NIOD 250d/815; and David F., HVT-0663, FVA.
26. Spitzer, *Dessin*, 63; and Gunter Faerber, interview 41847, VHA.
27. Gunter Faerber, interview 41847, VHA.
28. Kubica, "Kinder," 298–99; and Aufzeichnungen Rudolf Hoess, IfZ F 13-7-8.
29. Jozef Niewes, NIOD 250d/716; Joseph Braasem, NIOD 250d/446; David F., HVT-0663, FVA; and Maurits Bremer, NIOD 250d/448.
30. Gunter Faerber, interview 41847, VHA; and Wollenberg, *Alptraum*, 121.
31. Wollenberg, *Alptraum*, 121.
32. See Keren, "Family Camp."
33. Kubica, "Kinder," 305; and Buser, *Überleben*, 192–96.
34. Maurits Bremer, NIOD 250d/448; Art G., HVT-382, FVA; Gunter Faerber, interview 41847, VHA; and Wollenberg, *Alptraum*, 120–21. Kurt Moses, born in Cologne, Germany, in 1928, had fled to France with his father and was arrested in August 1942. AN 736 MI 2, Au 6.
35. Trial of Erich Hoffmann, StA M SpkA K 739.
36. Wysoki, Ruth, interview 42818, VHA; Sala Frydrych, interview 4081, VHA; Ann Cyncynatus, interview 19710, VHA; Ruth Flaum, interview 6247, VHA; Gussie Zaks, interview 3093; Sara Chrapot, interview 19997; Lola Lackmann, interview 16283, VHA; and Gutterman, *Narrow Bridge*, 161–62.
37. Karl Demerer, YVA O.3 3635; Helen Israel, interview 21038, VHA; Esther Lijek, interview 20470, VHA; Ida Frydman, interview 35134, VHA; Gucia Ferst, interview 34207, VHA
38. Fainzang, *Mémoire*, 75–76.
39. Miron/Shulhani, *Yad Vashem Encyclopedia*, 28.
40. Grużlewska, *Annaberg*, 88; and Wollenberg, *Alptraum*, 76.
41. Grużlewska, *Annaberg*, 13–16, 88–89; Magnichever, Wolf, AN F/9/5586; and Hans Bonn, NIOD 250d/445.
42. SokA Archive of Factory Alois Haase, box 5, nos. 112–15.

43. Wollenberg, *Alptraum*, 83–113; Hirsch Bornstein, LHA 4877, fo. 51; and Weiss, "From *Reichsautobahnlager*," 107. Pompe (Schmiedeberg/Silesia, 1899–Schweinfurt, 1964) was installed as guard duty officer in Brande in late 1942, followed by tenures in Blechhammer and Schmiedeberg. He was a veteran of the First World War with a prosthetic leg. Pompe was never tried for his crimes. Weiss, "From *Reichsautobahnlager*," 113–14.
44. Charge of the Central Committee against Icek Rosenzweig, YVA M. 21 73; and Wollenberg, *Alptraum*, 100–12.
45. Person, "Jews," 225–46; and Levi, *Drowned*, 29.
46. Sofsky, *Order*, 221.
47. Wollenberg, *Alptraum*, 83; and Erna Ellert, StA M SpkA K 739.
48. See Gruźlewska, *Annaberg*, 88; and Wollenberg, *Alptraum*, 76.
49. Maurits Bremer, NIOD 250d/448.
50. Abraham Herzberg, NIOD 250d/577; Karl Demerer, BArch B 162, 18175; Isaac Cohensius, GFH 12032 R M-Hol, no. 416; Ernest Wolf, AN 736 MI 3; Maurice Mosze Szmidt, YVA O.3 3474; Hartog Tertaas, NIOD 250d/883; and Erna Ellert, StA M SpkA K 739.
51. Maurice Mosze Szmidt, YVA O.3 3474.
52. Gucia Ferst, interview 34207, VHA.
53. Weiss, "From *Reichsautobahnlager*," 113; Wollenberg, *Alptraum*, 99; and Jozef Niewes, NIOD 250d/716.
54. Gucia Ferst, interview 34207, VHA.
55. Czech, *Kalendarium*, 321.
56. Ernest Nives, interview 588, VHA.
57. S. Kaufmann, LHA 4861.
58. Rudolf Höss, BArch B162/20513, fo. 119.
59. Karl Demerer, YVA O.3 3635.
60. Charles/Chil Feder, BArch B 162/8864, fo. 449.
61. S. Kaufmann, LHA 4861.
62. Abraham Herzberg, NIOD 250d/577.
63. Johannes Hassebroek, LHA 4883. The Korherr report still listed 50,570 Schmelt prisoners in January 1943. YVA TR. 19 127, fo. 13.
64. Czech, *Kalendarium*, 174–232; Piper, "Nebenlager Blechhammer," 26; and Piper, *Zahl*, 183.
65. Keller, *Volksgemeinschaft*, 226–39.
66. Die Deportationstransporte während der sogenannten Cosel Periode, StA Wü 2012-009, no. 37, fos. 1128–31. Rudorff referred to Schmelt camps as "unintentional safe havens" (*nicht intendierte Überlebensorte*). Rudorff, "Arbeit und Vernichtung," 38.
67. Gruner, *Forced Jewish Labor*, 294.
68. Lehnstaedt, "Coercion," 400–30; Gruner, *Forced Jewish Labor*, 214–29; Gutterman, *Narrow Bridge*, 47. On criticism of this argumentation, see Bauer, *Holocaust*, 90.
69. Steinbacher, *Musterstadt Auschwitz*, 279.

CHAPTER 6

1. Piper, "Nebenlager Blechhammer," 24.
2. Interrogation of Johannes Hassebroek, LHA 4883; Steinbacher, *Musterstadt Auschwitz*, 305; and Sprenger, *Groß-Rosen*, 133.
3. Piper, "Nebenlager Blechhammer," 24.
4. Hans Bonn, NIOD 250d/445; Simon Overste, NIOD 250d/735; Hertog Tertaas, NIOD 250d/883; and S. L. Toneman, NIOD 250d/887.
5. Leo Weiniger, NIOD 244/1486; and Maurits Bremer, NIOD 250d/448.
6. Trial of Schmelt Office Staff, BArch B 162/20513, fo. 116; and Grużlewska, *Annaberg*, 104–20.
7. Denazifiaction trial of Erich Hoffmann; Aron Auerbach, StA M SpkA K 739; and Karl Demerer, BArch B 162/18175.
8. Interrogation of Heinrich Schäfer, Romilly (France), August 18, 1945, IPN GK 184/262.
9. IfZ Ga 05.02/2, fo. 147; and Lasik, "Organisationsstruktur," 349–50.
10. Jozef Niewes, NIOD 250d/716; Fainzang, *Mémoire*, 87; Paul Hertz, NIOD 250d/576; and Jakob Perlmutter, BArch B 162/8866, fo. 903.
11. Database of the International Research and Documentation Centre for War Crimes Trials at the University of Marburg, www.uni-marburg.de/icwc/forschung/2weltkrieg/polen (June 4, 2019); see also Kobierska-Motar, *Ekstradycja*.
12. SS personnel file of Kurt Klipp, BArch B 162/8863; interrogation of Karl Masseli, BArch B 162/8864, fo. 1557; Karl Demerer, BArch B 162/18175; StA Wü 2012-009, 33, fos. 153–68; Lasik, "Organisationsstruktur," 355; and Hördler, *Ordnung*, 50.
13. Lasik, "Organisationsstruktur," 179.
14. Piper, "Nebenlager Blechhammer," 25; and Lasik, "Organisationsstruktur," 337–54.
15. Franz Ludwig, IPN GK 184/262; Orth, "Concentration Camp Personnel," 47–49; Perz, "Wehrmacht," 69–81; Perz, "Wehrmachtsangehörige," 175–77; and Rudolf Höss, IfZ F 13-8-12.
16. Interrogation of Heinrich Schäfer, IPN GK 184/262; and Luzer Markowicz, APMO Oświedcienia, f. 48, fo. 72.
17. Lasik, "Organisationsstruktur," 220–41.
18. Jansen and Weckbecker, *Volksdeutsche Selbstschutz*, 43–193.
19. SS personnel file Olejak, BArch B 162/8863, fos. 143–44; trial investigation of murders of Blechhammer inmates, IfZ Ga 05.02/1, fos. 48–126; and Lasik, "Organisationsstruktur," 254.
20. Interrogation of Karl Masseli, July 18, 1977, BArch B 162/8864, fo. 1557.
21. Josef Bienenstock, BArch B 162/8864.
22. Investigation report on manslaughter in Blechhammer camp, StA Wü 2012-009, 33, fos. 6832–43; trial investigation of the murder of Blechammer inmates, IfZ Ga 05.02/1, fo. 153; and SS personnel file of Czapla, BArch B 162/8863, fo. 1529.
23. Hördler, *Ordnung*, 178–79.

24. Marcus Samuel Frank, NIOD 250k/854; and Isaac Arbeid, NIOD 250k/854.
25. Lasik, "Organisationsstruktur," 227, 247–51; BArch B 162/8863, fos. 152–53; and Salomon Lierens, NIOD 250d/673.
26. Interrogation of Karl Masseli, May 23, 1973, BArch B 162/8864, fos. 1555–59; and July 18, 1977, BArch B 162/8866, fo. 921.
27. Tuchel, "Registrierung," 127–38; Lasik, "Organisationsstruktur," 194–218; and Trial against Bittner, BArch B 162/1817.
28. Investigation report by the Israeli Police, August 2, 1964, APMO, fos. 9–10; and Sam Weinstock, BArch B 162/8864, fo. 457.
29. Michael Schafir, YVA M.21/555.
30. Trial of Bittner, BArch B 162/1817.
31. Lasik, "Organisationsstruktur," 267–69; Anna/Chana May, BArch B 162/8866, fo. 888; Izchak Niewiem, BArch B 162/8866, fo. 887; Isaac Arbeid/Arthur Salomons, NIOD 250d/815; and index of SS members, BArch B 162/8866, fo. 967.
32. Sigbert Weisz, NIOD 250k/854; and Jakob Gesang, BArch B 162/8864, fo. 384.
33. Interrogation of Adolf Schindler, StA Wü 2012-009, 37, fos. 2567–69; and biographical data on Walter Redock, StA Wü 2012-009, 35, fos. 1542–48.
34. Lasik, "Organisationsstruktur," 282–95. Eduard Wirths (Würzburg, 1909) was the area chief physician of Auschwitz from September 1942 until January 1945. He committed suicide in September 1945. Dirks, "Karrieresprung," 143–67.
35. HHStAW, 461/37638, no. 151, no. 54, fos. 9694–97; and Fainzang, *Mémoire*, 88. Scherpe was involved in the murder of 121 Polish and Jewish children from Zamość between January and March 1943. Strzelecka, "Häftlingsspitäler," 397.
36. BArch B 162/8863, fos. 139–40; and Piper, "Nebenlager Blechhammer," 26.
37. Piper, "Nebenlager Blechhammer," 25–26.
38. Piper, *Arbeitseinsatz*, 111; and Lieske, *Opfer*.
39. Biographical note on Walter Redock, StA Wü 2012-009, 35, fos. 1542–48; Lasik, "Organisationsstruktur," 262; and Fainzang, *Mémoire*, 83.
40. Sali Montag, BArch B 162/8864, fo. 429; Isaac Arbeid, NIOD 250d/815; and Fainzang, *Mémoire*, 99–100.
41. Rosengarten, *Overleven*, 150.
42. Grinband, *XIe Commandement*, 143.
43. Karl Demerer, YVA O.3 3635; Czech, *Kalendarium*, 747; Spitzer, *Dessin*, 113; Wajnblum, *My Destiny*, 133–35; Leo Weiniger, NIOD 244/1486; and B. Swaaf, NIOD 250d/881.
44. Gita Brandszteter-Sztulbergowa, APMO Oświedcienia, f. 48, fos. 151–52; and Roza Plawner, interview 24454, VHA.
45. Rosengarten, *Overleven*, 153–54; and Piper, "Nebenlager Blechhammer," 26–27.
46. Karl Demerer, YVA O.3 3635; Helen Pinczewski, interview 6014, VHA; Roza Plawner, interview 24454, VHA; Rachel Brukner Frydrych, YVA O.3 3664; and Fainzang, *Mémoire*, 92.

47. Czech, *Kalendarium*, 747; see prisoner database of the Auschwitz Museum and Memorial, auschwitz.org/muzeum/informacja-o-wiezniach/ (19 January 2016).
48. Fainzang, *Mémoire*, 87.
49. Nathan de Vries, NIOD 250d/915; Maurits Bremer, NIOD 250d/448; Piper, "Nebenlager Blechhammer," 24; and Koenig, *Vorhof*, 140–41.
50. Arthur Salomons, NIOD 250d/815; and Fainzang, *Mémoire*, 82.
51. ITS (via USHMM), Doc. ID 7/001/0373.
52. Fainzang, *Mémoire*, 83; and Jonas Pampel, NIOD 250d/741.
53. Lasik, "Organisationsstruktur," 206–9; and Jonas Pampel, NIOD 250d/741.
54. Obréjan, *Homme*, 122.
55. Josef Bienenstock, BArch B 162/8864, fo. 316; Maurits Bremer, NIOD 250d/448; and Sigbert Weisz, NIOD 250k/854.
56. Kurt Klappholz, IWM Sound Archive 9425.
57. Fainzang, *Mémoire*, 112.
58. Rosengarten, *Overleven*, 176–77; and Sam Silberberg, USHMM 2006.248.
59. Demerer, *Kind*, 70–71.
60. Fainzang, *Mémoire*, 82.
61. Nessou, *Griechenland*, 290–306; Bowman, *Agony*, 80–94; Czech, "Deportation," 5–27; Molho, *Holocaust*, 68–69; and interrogation of Otto Wende, April 23, 1961, HHStAW 461/37638, vol. 49, fos. 8662–63.
62. Bowman, *Agony*, 114–15, 131; and Piper, "Nebenlager Blechhammer," 28.
63. Mazower, *Salonica*, 434–35; and Kounio, *Liter*, 23–28.
64. Fainzang, *Mémoire*, 82.
65. Kárný, "Familienlager," 133–221; Keren, "Family Camp," 428–40; Weinberg, *Boy 30529*, 81–83; Oto Hostovsky, ŽMP; and Arthur Salomons/Isaac Arbeid, NIOD 250d/815.
66. The War-Time Experiences of Otto Deutsch, online collection ŽMP.
67. Oto Hostovsky, ŽMP; The War-Time Experiences of Otto Deutsch, online collection, ŽMP; and Flusser, "Rückblick," 64.
68. Oto Hostovsky, ŽMP.
69. Kárný, "Familienlager," 134.
70. Maquisards groups were formed in rural parts of France. Merged into the Forces Françaises de l'Interieur, they supported the Allied D-Day landings of June 1944. Postwar myths created by Gaullists greatly exaggerated the numbers of men evading the German compulsory labor conscriptions (STO) of 1942 and 1943 in these settings, who represented no more than 10 percent of the Maquisards. See Kedward, *Search*; and Arnaud, *STO*, 15.
71. Report by CICR delegate Dr. Landolt to the International Red Cross Geneva, January 14, 1945, ACICR; Klein, Joseph, AN F/9/5585; and Benaroya, Roland, AN F/9/5583. Altogether, one thousand French political prisoners were transferred from Dachau to Auschwitz in this period. Courtesy of the Archives of the Dachau Concentration Camp Memorial.
72. Lieb, *Krieg*, 387–90.

73. Fainzang, *Mémoire*, 115–16.
74. Benaroya, Roland, AN F/9/5583.
75. Georges Czaczkes, interview 3328, VHA.
76. Obréjan, *Homme*, 165; and Wolf W., HVT-2989, FVA. The Red Cross was allegedly never allowed to enter the Auschwitz concentration camp. See IKRK, *Tätigkeit*, 17.
77. Report by CICR delegate Dr. Landolt to the International Red Cross Geneva, January 14, 1945, ACICR.
78. Oto Hostovsky, ŽMP; and André Lapeyre, AN F/9/5565.

CHAPTER 7

1. Karl Demerer, BArch B 162/18175; Samuel Abrams, NIOD 250d/386; and Jacques G., HVT-2845, FVA.
2. Siegfried Herrmann, interview 38621, VHA.
3. Rosengarten, *Overleven*, 153–54; and Grinband, *XIe Commandement*, 143.
4. Isaac Arbeid/Arthur Salomons, NIOD 250d/815; Paul Hertz, NIOD 250d/576; Luzer Markowicz, APMO Oświedcienia, f. 48, fo. 73; Aron Goldfinger, APMO Oświedcienia, f. 48, fo. 81; Lucjan Radzik, APMO Oświedcienia, f., 48, fo. 42; and Oto Hostovsky, ŽMP.
5. Circular by Oswald Pohl to concentration camp commandants, October 26, 1943, BArch NS 3/386.
6. Memoirs of R. Stoppelman, YVA O.33 4272; and Siegfried Herrmann, interview 38261, VHA.
7. Flusser, "Rückblick," 64; Emanuel Luftglas, APMO Oświedcienia, f. 48, fo. 143; and Koenig, *Vorhof*, 117.
8. Sofsky, *Order*, 170.
9. Hans Bonn, NIOD 250d/445; and Samuel Abrams, NIOD 250d/386.
10. See Guetzkow and Bowman, *Men*, 30; Myron B., HVT-1507, FVA; and Jacob de Boers, NIOD 250d/441.
11. Leo Weiniger, NIOD 244/1486.
12. Paul Hertz, NIOD 250d/576; and Leo Weiniger, NIOD 244/1486.
13. Maurits Bremer, NIOD 250d/448.
14. Koenig, *Vorhof*, 112; and Fainzang, *Mémoire*, 52.
15. Abram Szeftel, APMO Oświedcienia, f. 48, fo. 156; Etienne Rosenfeld, YVA O.33 2070; and The War-Time Experiences of Otto Deutsch, online collection ŽMP.
16. Etienne Rosenfeld, YVA O.33 2070.
17. Invoice by the architect Erich Draub, October 1, 1944, BArch R 9348/87; Maurits Bremer, NIOD 250d/448; Simon Winnik, NIOD 250d/940; and Karl Demerer, YVA O.3 3536.
18. Fainzang, *Mémoire*, 97, 108.
19. Stahl, *Sehnsucht*, 294–302; and Blanc, *Fake Silk*, 145–47.
20. Weindling, *Victims*, 76.

21. The War-Time Experiences of Otto Deutsch, online collection ŽMP.
22. Sigbert Weisz, NIOD 250k/854; Jakob Gesang, BArch B 162/8864, fo. 384; and Josef Bienenstock, StA Wü 2012-009, 33, fo. 313.
23. Johann Sindelar, StA Wü 2012-009, 37, fo. 2182.
24. Simon Winnik, NIOD 250d/940.
25. Fainzang, *Mémoire*, 115; and Leo Weiniger, NIOD 244/1486.
26. Circular by Oswald Pohl to concentration camp commandants, October 26, 1943, BArch NS 3/386.
27. Janek M., HVT-2333, FVA; and Fainzang, *Mémoire*, 71.
28. Leo Weiniger, NIOD 244/1486.
29. Philip Venetianer, NIOD 250d/903.
30. Koenig, *Vorhof*, 112; and Oto Hostovsky, ŽMP.
31. Jozef Niewes, NIOD 250d/716; Paul Hertz, NIOD 250d/576; and Spitzer, *Dessin*, 124.
32. Lustiger, *Schmerz*, 37.
33. The War-Time Experiences of Otto Deutsch, online collection ŽMP.
34. Maurits Bremer, *Een Dag in Blechhammer*, NIOD 250d/448; Luzer Markowicz, APMO Oświedcienia, f. 48, fos. 73–74; and Joseph Kahn/Kokotek, interview 17526, VHA.
35. Aron Goldfinger, APMO Oświedcienia, f. 48, fo. 81; and Henry K., HVT-3000, FVA.
36. Jacob de Boers, NIOD 250d/441; Maurits Bremer, *Een Dag in Blechhammer*, NIOD 250d/448; Arthur Salomons and Isaac Arbeid, NIOD 250d/815; and Memoirs of R. Stoppelman, YVA O.33 4272.
37. Emanuel Luftglas, APMO Oświedcienia, f. 48, fo. 143; Hans Bonn, NIOD 250d/445; Simon Winnik, NIOD 250d/940; Hartog Tertaas, NIOD 250d/883; Maurits Bremer, *Een Dag in Blechhammer*, NIOD 250d/448; and Arthur Salomons and Isaac Arbeid, NIOD 250d/815.
38. Sigmund W., HVT-55, FVA.
39. Joseph Kahn/Kokotek, interview 17526, VHA.
40. Maurits Bremer, *Een Dag in Blechhammer*, NIOD 250d/448.
41. Simon Blein, NIOD 250d/433.
42. Heyman Bronner, interview 24272, VHA; Leo Weiniger, NIOD 244/1486; and Luzer Markowicz, APMO Oświedcienia, f. 48, fos. 73–74.
43. Note on Brossmann's visit to the OHW, April 20, 1944, BArch R 9348/117.
44. Rosengarten, *Overleven*, 151.
45. Investigation report on manslaughter in Blechhammer, StA Wü 2012-009, 35, fo. 1550, 37, fo. 2555.
46. Koenig, *Vorhof*, 131.
47. Sam Weinstock, BArch B 162/8864, fo. 456.
48. Joseph Braasem, NIOD 250d/446.
49. Fainzang, *Mémoire*, 89.

50. Investigation report on manslaughter in Blechhammer, StA Wü 2012-009, 35, fo. 1550, 37, fo. 2555; Joseph Braasem, NIOD 250d/446; and interrogation of Karl Masseli, BArch B 162/8864, fo. 1559.
51. Nathan de Vries, NIOD 250k/854; Arthur Salomons, NIOD 250k/854; Raphael Montezinos, NIOD 250k/854; Joseph Hijman Klos, NIOD 250k/854; Max Nunes Nabarro, NIOD 250k/854; Marcus Samuel Frank, NIOD 250k/854; and Joseph Braasem, NIOD 250d/446.
52. Maurice Moshe Szmidt, YVA O.3 3474.
53. Wallis, *British POWs*, 99.
54. Nathan de Vries, NIOD 250k/854.
55. Heinz Joseph, NIOD 250k/854.
56. Peter Sturm, YVA O.33 2380; and Isaac Arbeid, NIOD 250k/854.
57. Interrogation of Karl Masseli, BArch B 162/8864, fo. 1557; and investigation report on manslaughter in Blechhammer camp, StA Wü 2012-009, 35, fo. 1550, 37, fo. 2555.
58. Michał Kula, APMO Pr. H., vol. 2, fo. 97; and Piper, *Auschwitz 1940–1945*, 3:140–41.
59. Karl Czapla, StA Wü 2012-009, 35, fos. 6832–43.
60. Koenig, *Vorhof*, 130.
61. Salomon Lierens, NIOD 250d/673; and Maurits Bremer, *Een Dag in Blechhammer*, NIOD 250d/448.
62. Maurits Broeks, NIOD 250d/450; and BArch B 162/8866, fo. 839.
63. Beorn, *Darkness*, 234–46.
64. Hördler, *Ordnung*, 228–29; Strebel, *Ravensbrück*; Wagner, *Produktion*; and Buggeln, *Arbeit*.
65. Garrison order (*Standortbefehl*) 17/44, June 9, 1944, printed in Frei et al., *Standort- und Kommandanturbefehle*, 453.
66. Weinberg, *Boy 30529*, 83.
67. Simon Winnik, NIOD 250d/940.
68. Interrogation of Heinrich Schäfer, Romilly, August 18, 1945, IPN GK 184/262; and letter from Erwin Lagus to Simon Wiesenthal, February 17, 1965, SWA.
69. Salomon Kaufmann, NIOD 250d/622; and Siegfried Herrmann, interview 38261, VHA.
70. Perz, "Wehrmachtsangehörige," 177–78.
71. Rosengarten, *Overleven*, 151.
72. Franz Ludwig, IPN GK 184/262; Heinrich Tille, IPN GK 184/262; and Piet Nieuwes, NIOD 250d/715.
73. Janek M., HVT-2333, FVA.
74. Jacques op den Berg, NIOD 250d/726.
75. Paul Hertz, NIOD 250d/576.
76. Oto Hostovsky, ŽMP; Sigmund W., HVT-55, FVA; Monty G., HVT-2427, FVA; and Alix H., HVT-210, FVA.

77. KL-AU III, work deployment, vol. 11, APMO.
78. Maurits Bremer, *Een Dag in Blechhammer*, NIOD 250d/448.
79. Louis Waterman, NIOD 250d/922.
80. Restitution claims of Blechhammer survivors against IG Farben were dismissed, as they no longer worked on their housing projects under Auschwitz and had never worked on the plant's construction site itself. IG Farben's legal representatives cynically argued that only Auschwitz prisoners were eligible for payments, as Auschwitz alone was "symbolic" of atrocities. Notes on Restitution Claims against IG Farben, June 6, 1962, NIOD 250k/894; *Mitteilungen der österreichischen Lagergemeinschaft*, May 1962, SWA; and Joseph Braasem, NIOD 250d/446.
81. Koenig, *Vorhof*, 121–23; Rosengarten, *Overleven*, 144–61; and Joseph Braasem, NIOD 250d/446.
82. Piper, *Arbeitseinsatz*, 345; and circular by Oswald Pohl to concentration camp commandants, October 26, 1943, BArch NS 3/386.
83. Leo Weiniger, NIOD 244/1486.
84. Piper, *Arbeitseinsatz*, 349; Dr. Urbanek on reduced output factors, November 16, 1943, BArch R 9348/57; and legal dispute on unpaid wages, BArch R 9348/33.
85. Louis Schuitevoerder, NIOD 250d/835; Heinz Issen, NIOD 250d/595; Maurits Bremer, NIOD 250d/448; and Leo Weiniger, NIOD 244/1486.
86. Rosengarten, *Overleven*, 136–37.
87. Translation of Karl Kulicke's deposition of August 1, 1946, NA WO 309/378.
88. Penal reports, BArch B 162/8867; Aufzeichnungen Rudolf Hoess, IfZ F 13-8-12; and Lucjan Radzik, APMO Oświedcienia, f. 48, fo. 42.
89. Penal reports, BArch B 162/8867, fos. 1112, 1123, 1128; and Maurits Broeks, NIOD 250d/450.
90. Penal reports, BArch B 162/8867, fos. 1227–28; and Lasik, "Organisationsstruktur," 242–43.
91. Abraham Walg, interview 5476, VHA.
92. Emanuel Luftglas, APMO Oświedcienia, f. 48, fo. 142; and Nathan Gipsman, interview 166, VHA.
93. Strzelecka, "Strafen," 459–64.
94. Rosengarten, *Overleven*, 117.
95. Rosengarten, *Overleven*, 143–44.
96. Strzelecka and Setkiewicz, "Bau," 143; Barend van Delft, NIOD 250d/495; Eliazer Content, NIOD 250d/481; and Jacob de Wolf, NIOD 250d/946.
97. Eliazer Content, NIOD 250d/481.
98. Strzelecka, "Strafen," 459.
99. H. Joseph, NIOD 250k/854; and Abraham Walg, interview 5476, VHA.
100. Harry Fransman, interview 2548, VHA; and H. Joseph, NIOD 250k/854.
101. Aufzeichnungen Rudolf Höss, IfZ, F 13-8-56.

102. Dr. Alfred Hyrsz was born in Horice in 1882. BArch B 162/8868; Fainzang, *Mémoire*, 83; and Kurt Klappholz, IWM Sound Archive, 9425.
103. Abram Szeftel, APMO Oświedcienia, f. 48, fos. 154–59.
104. Kurt Klappholz, IWM Sound Archive, 9425.
105. Maurice Moshe Szmidt, YVA O.3 3474.
106. Efraim Roseboom, NIOD 250d/805.
107. Kurt Baum, interview 29790, VHA.
108. Flusser, "Rückblick," 48–68.
109. Josef Bienenstock, BArch B 162/8864, fos. 315–17; Karl Demerer, YVA O.3 3635, fo. 10; and Lasik, "Organisationsstruktur," 210.
110. Abram Szeftel, APMO Oświedcienia, f. 48, fo. 155.
111. Kurt Klappholz, IWM Sound Archive, 9425.
112. Karl Demerer, YVA O.3 3635; and Jozef Niewes, NIOD 250d/716.
113. Josef Bienenstock, BArch B162/8864, fo. 315.
114. Hartog Tertaas, NIOD 250d/883; and Maurits Bremer, NIOD 250d/448.
115. Fainzang, *Mémoire*, 73; Flusser, "Rückblick," 68; and Abram Szeftel, APMO Oświedcienia, f. 48, fo. 157.
116. Efraim Roseboom, NIOD 250d/805.
117. Fainzang, *Mémoire*, 80–81.
118. Simon Winnik, NIOD 250d/940; and Romney, "Ethical Problems," 324.
119. Abram Szeftel, APMO Oświedcienia, f. 48, fo. 157.
120. Nathan Gipsman, interview 166, VHA.
121. Spira, *Legende*, 136.
122. Abraham Schaufeld, IWM Sound Archive, 17470.
123. Flusser, "Rückblick," 68; and Kolb, *Bergen-Belsen*, 42.
124. Menachem Miedzygorski, BArch B 162/8864, fo. 313.
125. Charles/Chil Feder, BArch B162/8864, fo. 452.
126. Fainzang, *Mémoire*, 116–17; and Salomon Ruben Swaab, NIOD 250k.
127. Fainzang, *Mémoire*, 45–46. On the collaboration of non-Jewish prisoner physicians, see Lifton, *Nazi Doctors*, 239.
128. See Siegel, "Coercion-Resistance Spectrum," 1–20.
129. Kremer was shot on the death march in 1945. Testimony on Aron Kremer, YVA O.89 59. On prisoner physicians' noncompliance, see Romney, "Problems," 328–31.
130. Wolf W., HVT-2989, FVA.
131. Flusser, "Rückblick," 68.
132. Wolf W., HVT-2989, FVA.
133. Siegfried Hermann, interview 38261, VHA.
134. Spira, *Legende*, 136–37; and Fainzang, *Mémoire*, 105–6.
135. Abram Szeftel, APMO Oświedcienia, f. 48, fo. 158.

136. Kubica, "Kinder," 324.
137. Karl Demerer, YVA O.3 3635.
138. Gita Brandszteter-Sztulbergowa, APMO Oświedcienia, f. 48, fos. 151–52.
139. Year Hammer, interview 18278, VHA; and Fainzang, *Mémoire*, 92.
140. Gita Brandszteter-Sztulbergowa, APMO Oświedcienia, f. 48, fos. 151–52; and Fainzang, *Mémoire*, 77.
141. Esther Drexler, interview 11703, VHA.
142. Aufzeichnungen Rudolf Hoess, IfZ F 13-7-8.
143. Gita Brandszteter-Sztulbergowa, APMO Oświedcienia, f. 48, fos. 151–52; and Helen Wakshlag, interview 4093, VHA.
144. Rozka Kam, interview 17201, VHA.
145. Sali Montag, BArch B 162/8864, fos. 429–30.
146. Ida Russ, interview 35966, VHA; and Gita Brandszteter-Sztulbergowa, APMO Oświedcienia, f. 48, fos. 151–52.
147. Yera Hammer, interview 18278, VHA.
148. Year Hammer, interview 18278, VHA; and Gita Brandszteter-Sztulbergowa, APMO Oświedcienia, f. 48, fos. 151–52. See also, Chatwood, "Stories," 162–63.
149. Weinberg, *Boy 30529*, 81; and Demerer, *Kind*, 58. Altogether, ninety out of five hundred boys from the "family camp" were selected for labor. The others were killed. Kárný, "Familienlager," 201.
150. Koenig, *Vorhof*, 119–20.
151. Koenig, *Vorhof*, 119–20.
152. Demerer, *Kind*, 58, 60.
153. Ludwig Hamburger, YVA O.3610.
154. Art G., HVT-382, FVA.
155. See Bravo, Davite, and Jalla, "Myth," 99.
156. König, *Vorhof*, 120.
157. Most survivors stated that the youngest prisoners were eleven years old. See Jozef Niewes, NIOD 250d/716.
158. Demerer, *Kind*, 60, 68.
159. Spira, *Legende*; and Bil Spira, IWM ART 17120–29.
160. Arthur Salomons, NIOD 250d/815; Joseph Braasem, NIOD 250d/446; Maurits Bremer, NIOD 250d/448; Memoirs of R. Stoppelman, YVA O.33 4272; and Bil Spira cartoon, IWM ART 17123. Unlike in Auschwitz, the adult prisoners of Blechhammer reportedly did not supply the children with extra food or toys. See Buser, *Überleben*, 189.
161. Karl Demerer, YVA O.3 3635.
162. Hans Mertens (Wesermünde/Bremerhaven, 1903) joined the Highway Company's building supervisory board at Breslau in 1934. He received the war service medal (first class) in 1945. Karl Demerer called him up as a witness in the trial against Erich Hoffmann, but Mer-

tens refused to appear. Denazification trial of Hans Mertens, StA Ol, Rep. 980, Best. 351, no. 25571; and letter by Mertens to the denazification court, July 10, 1947, StA M SpkA K 709.
163. Demerer, *Kind*, 69.
164. Art G., HVT-382, FVA.

CHAPTER 8

1. Bomb Group Mission Reports USAF, NARA RG-18, box 2624.
2. Nathan de Vries, NIOD 250d/915; and Rosengarten, *Overleven*, 162–67.
3. Szyje Bartnowski, YVA M.11 338.
4. *Personendezentralisierung bei Tagalarm*, July 11, 1944, BArch R 9348/41; and directive by OHW director Josenhans, September 4, 1944, BArch R 9348/117.
5. OHW circular, June 26, 1944, BArch R 9348/117.
6. Koenig, *Im Vorhof der Vernichtung*, 126–27; and Oto Hostovsky, ŽMP.
7. Diary entry for July 9, 1944, Private Papers: George Didcock, IWM, 10/6/1.
8. Gunter Faerber, interview 41847, VHA.
9. Oto Hostovsky, ŽMP; Fainzang, *Mémoire de Deportation*, 103; Henry K., HVT-3000, FVA; and Lustiger, *Sing mit Schmerz und Zorn*, 36.
10. Arthur Salomons/Isaac Arbeid, NIOD 250d/815.
11. Rosengarten, *Overleven*, 166.
12. Maurits Bremer, NIOD 250d/448.
13. Nathan de Vries, NIOD 250d/915; Clary, *Holocaust to Hogan's Heroes*, 88; Gerrit Aardewerk, NIOD 250d/384; Jacob de Boers, NIOD 250d/441; Spira, *Legende vom Zeichner*, 135–36; and Oto Hostovsky, ŽMP.
14. Abraham Schaufeld, IWM Sound Archive, 17470.
15. Spira, *Legende vom Zeichner*, 158.
16. Kurt Baum, USHMM RG-50.154*005; Oto Hostovsky, ŽMP; Leo Weiniger, NIOD 244/1486; and Clary, *Holocaust to Hogan's Heroes*, 88.
17. Arthur Salomons and Isaac Arbeid, NIOD 250d/815; and Maurits Bremer, NIOD 250d/448.
18. Bomb Group Mission Reports USAF, NARA RG-18, box 2624; Maurits Bremer, NIOD 250d/448; The War-Time Experiences of Otto Deutsch, online collection, ŽMP; and Arthur Salomons and Isaac Arbeid, NIOD 250d/815.
19. Jacob de Boers, NIOD 250d/441; The War-Time Experiences of Otto Deutsch, online collection, ŽMP; Luzer Markowicz, APMO Oświedcienia, f. 48, fo. 72; and Rosengarten, *Overleven*, 162–67.
20. Flusser, "Rückblick," 69.
21. Oto Hostovsky, ŽMP.
22. Private Papers: George Didcock, IWM, 10/6/1.
23. Arthur Salomons/Isaac Arbeid, NIOD 250d/815; and Maurits Bremer, NIOD 250d/448.
24. Aron Goldfinger, APMO Oświedcienia, f. 48, fos. 82–83.

25. Oto Hostovsky, ŽMP.
26. Arthur Salomons/Isaac Arbeid, NIOD 250d/815.
27. Private Papers: George Didcock, IWM, 10/6/1; and Oto Hostovsky, ŽMP.
28. Kurt Klappholz, IWM Sound Archive, 9425.
29. Circular of the OHW retinue department, August 22, 1944, BArch R 9348/117.
30. Ernest Nives, interview 588, VHA; Gerson F., HVT-2975, FVA; Leo B., HVT-1824, FVA; Jacob de Boers, NIOD 250d/441; and Rosengarten, *Overleven*, 162-167.
31. Piętka, "Fire Brigade Kommando," 179–83.
32. Simon Blein, NIOD 250d/433.
33. Maurits Bremer, NIOD 250d/448.
34. Joseph Braasem, NIOD 250d/446; and Nathan de Vries, NIOD 250d/915.
35. Piper, *Arbeitseinsatz der Häftlinge*, 289; and Strzelecka and Setkiewicz, "Bau, Ausbau und Entwicklung," 142–43.
36. Paul Hertz, NIOD 250d/576; Maurits Bremer, NIOD 250d/448; The War-Time Experiences of Otto Deutsch, online collection, ŽMP; and Joseph Braasem, NIOD 250d/446.
37. Rosengarten, *Overleven*, 175–76.
38. Jonas Pampel, NIOD 250d/741; Maurits Bremer, NIOD 250d/448; and Josef Bienenstock, BArch B 162/8864.
39. Siegfried Herrmann, interview 38261, VHA.
40. Jonas Pampel, NIOD 250d/741; and Michał Kasprzak, APMO Oświedcienia, f. 48, fo. 60.
41. Simon Blein, NIOD 250d/433; Maurits Bremer, NIOD 250d/448; and Koenig, *Im Vorhof der Vernichtung*, 126.
42. Author's interview with Charles Hayward, June 22, 2010; and Private Papers: George Didcock, IWM, 10/6/1.
43. Simon Blein, NIOD 250d/433.
44. Karl Demerer, YVA O.3 3635; Max Morichay Knobler, BArch B 162/1817; and Private Papers: George Didcock, IWM, 10/6/1. See also Hoffmann, *Fliegerlynchjustiz*, 170–74.
45. *Zehn Gebote für SS-Blockführer*, USHMM RG 15.154, 209 279 (ŹIH zespol 209). See also Abraham Schaufeld, IWM Sound Archive, 17470.
46. Sigbert Weisz, NIOD 250k/854; Salomon Ruben Swaab, NIOD 250k/854; Jakob Perlmutter, BArch B 162/8866, fo. 904; and The War-Time Experiences of Otto Deutsch, online collection, ŽMP.
47. Karl Demerer, BArch 162/18175; Jakob Gesang, BArch 162/8864, fos. 382–84; and Nathan Gipsman, interview 166, VHA.
48. Penal reports, BArch B 162/8867.
49. Gendarmerie Heydebreck to commander of Gendarmerie Oppeln, July 10, 1944, APO, Rej. Opolska, I/1172, fo. 42; Radchenko, "'We Emptied Our Magazines,'" 90–91; and Rossoliński-Liebe, *Stepan Bandera*, 256.
50. Circular by Dr. Schlick, February 12, 1944, BArch R 9348/117; and Golczewski, "Organe der deutschen Besatzungsmacht," 190.

51. Wollenberg, *Alptraum wurde zum Alltag*, 128; interrogation of Johannes Josef Stera, BArch B 162/18172, fo. 920; and Maurits Bremer, *Een Dag in Blechhammer*, NIOD 250d/448. Prisoners' gold teeth were regarded as the property of the Auschwitz administration and were extracted after their deaths. Piper, "Ausbeutung der Häftlinge," 153.
52. Kurt Baum, interview 29790, VHA.
53. Commander of Gendarmerie Oppeln to Gendarmerie Warthenau, October 3, 1944, APO Rej. Opolska 1191, I/1171, fo. 15.
54. Private Papers: George Didcock, IWM, 10/6/9; and OHW circular, July 15, 1944, BArch R 9348/117.
55. Ludwig Hamburger, YVA O.36 10.
56. Willner, Eddie, interview 30082, VHA; and Private Papers: George Didcock, IWM, 10/6/1.
57. Louis Waterman, NIOD 250d/922.
58. Maurice Moshe Szmidt, YVA O.3 3474.
59. Prochownik, *Mémoires Barbelées*, 115–20.
60. Koenig, *Im Vorhof der Vernichtung*, 115–16.
61. OHW circular, July 14, 1944, BArch R 9348/41; and Rosengarten, *Overleven*, 166.
62. Jakob Gesang, BArch B 162/8864, fos. 382–84.
63. Samuel David Beller, YVA O.3 10840.
64. Affidavit of Friedrich Pook, NA WO 309/978; statement by Karl Kulicke, January 19, 1946, NA WO 309/978; and deposition of Ludwig Hecker, NA WO 309/978.
65. Aron Goldfinger, APMO, Oświedcienia, f. 48, fo. 83.
66. Lion Gosler, NIOD 250d/555.
67. Israel Feldman, BArch B 162/8866, fos. 1556–58.
68. Leo Weiniger, NIOD 244/1486.
69. Private Papers: George Didcock, IWM, 10/6/1.
70. Interrogation of Karl Masseli, BArch B 162/8866, fos. 803–4.
71. Aufzeichnungen Rudolf Höss, IfZ, F 13-7-8.
72. Overy, *Bombing War*, 141–42.

CHAPTER 9

1. Laub, "Event," 76–82.
2. Langer, *Testimonies*; and Greenspan, *Listening to Holocaust Survivors*, 6–7.
3. Portelli, "Peculiarities," 100; Bravo, Davite, and Jalla, "Myth," 105–8; and Halbwachs, *Memory*.
4. Blank, Walther, and Isemann, "Past," 55–57.
5. Friedlander, *Memory*, 131–32; and Portelli, "Peculiarities," 104.
6. Greenspan, *Listening to Holocaust Survivors*, 7.
7. Levi, *Drowned*, 12.
8. Soraci, et al., "Impairment," 286–87.
9. Westermann, *Genocide*, 24–45.

10. Leo Weiniger, NIOD 244/1486.
11. Gilbert, *Music*, 187.
12. Levi, *Drowned*, 13–18.
13. Loftus and Davis, "Sources," 222–23.
14. Levi, *Drowned*, 12.
15. IfZ Ga 05.02/1; and BArch B 162/8863.
16. Interrogation of Karl Czapla, October 27, 1960, StA Wü 2012-009, no. 34.
17. Interrogation of Karl Czapla, October 7, 1976, BArch B 162/8864, fo. 1530.
18. Interrogation of Karl Masseli, July 18, 1977, BArch B 162/8864, fo. 1588.
19. Letter by Heinrich Schäfer to Erwin Lagus, January 29, 1965, SWA.
20. Interrogation of Adolf Schindler, June 22, 1977, BArch B 162/8864, fos. 1553–1554; and Josef Bienenstock, BArch B 162/8864, fo. 317.
21. Laub, "Bearing Witness," 59–63.
22. Oulton and Takarangi, "(Mis)Remembering," 15–17.
23. Fulbrook, *Reckonings*, 231–65.
24. See Borrie, *Captivity*, 137–38, 171; and J. Driscoll, IWM Sound Archive, 17435.
25. Laub, "Event," 81.
26. Private Papers: George Didcock, IWM 10/6/1.
27. Wallis, *British POWs*, 97–98.
28. Maurits Bremer, NIOD 250d/448; Ernest Nives, interview 588; VHA; and Fainzang, *Mémoire*, 114.
29. Karl Demerer, YVA O.3 3635; Fainzang, *Mémoire*, 113–14; Rachel Brukner Frydrych, YVA O.3 3664; Obréjan, *Homme*, 137–38; Erwin Lagus, letter to Simon Wiesenthal, December 2, 1965, SWA; and Ernest Nives, interview 588, VHA.
30. Stanley B., HVT-401, FVA; Josef Bienenstock, BArch B 162/8864, fo. 316–17; Israel Feldman, BArch B 162/8866, fo. 806; and Izchak Niewim, BArch B 162/8866, fo. 888.
31. Bergen, *History*, 137.
32. Stanley B., HVT-401, FVA; Karl Demerer, YVA O.3 3635; Fainzang, *Mémoire*, 113–14; Erwin Lagus, letter to Simon Wiesenthal, December 2, 1965, SWA; and Rachel Brukner Frydrych, YVA O.3 3664.
33. Horst Schade, YVA O.33 1097.
34. Sofsky, *Order*, 220–21.
35. Barend van Leuwen, NIOD 250k/854; Salomon van Velzen, NIOD 250k/854; Abraham Aussen, NIOD 250d/399; Heyman Joseph Leefsma, NIOD 250d/657; Jacques op den Berg, NIOD 250d/726; and Jeremias Samentini, NIOD 250d/816.
36. NIOD 250k.
37. André B., HVT-2842, FVA; Maurits Bremer, NIOD 250d/448; Ernest Inow, BArch B 162/8869, fo. 1508; Ernest Nives, interview 588, VHA; Fainzang, *Mémoire*, 113–14; and Isaac Arbeid, NIOD 250k/854.
38. Fainzang, *Mémoire*, 113–14.

39. Greenspan, "Listening to Holocaust Survivors," 85–87, 161–62.
40. Grinband, *XIe Commandement*, 151; Abram Fiszel, BArch B 162/8866, fo. 866; and Erwin Lagus, letter to Simon Wiesenthal, SWA.
41. Felix G., HVT-3458, FVA; and Grinband, *XIe Commandement*, 148–51.
42. Ernest Nives, interview 588, VHA.
43. Oulton and Takarangi, "Experiences," 15–17.
44. Abram Stone, BArch B 162/8864, fo. 371.
45. Bernard Simmeren, NIOD 250d/841.
46. Loftus and Davis, "Sources," 196–97.
47. Private Papers: George Didcock, IWM 10/6/1; and interrogation of Karl Masseli, July 18, 1977, BArch B 162/8864, fo. 1588.
48. Leo Weiniger, NIOD 244/1486; Salomon van Velzen, NIOD 250k/854; Maurits Bremer, NIOD 250d/448; Heyman Joseph Leefsma, NIOD 250d/657; Jean Georges Czaczkes, interview 3328, VHA; and Koenig, *Vorhof*, 127–28.
49. Louis Waterman, NIOD 250d/922.
50. Steiner, "Reflections," 60–61; Felix G., HVT-3458, FVA; and Karl Demerer, YVA O.3 3635.
51. Frankl, *Seelsorge*, 78–79.
52. Penal reports, BArch B 162/8867; and Private Papers: George Didcock, IWM 10/6/1.
53. Felix G., HVT-3458, FVA; Heyman Joseph Leefsma, NIOD 250d/657; and Fainzang, *Mémoire*, 113–14.
54. Ernest Koenig, interview, VHA.
55. Nathan de Vries, NIOD 250k/854; Max Nunes Nabarro, NIOD 250k/854; Louis Waterman, NIOD 250d/922; Abram Stone, BArch B 162/8864, fo. 371; Natan Gipsman, BArch B 162/8864, fos. 403–4; Fainzang, *Mémoire*, 113–14; and Aba Sztulberg, APMO Oświedcienia, f. 48, fo. 113.
56. Izchak Niewim, BArch B 162/8866, fo. 888; and Joseph Braasem, NIOD 250d/446.
57. H. Joseph, NIOD 250k/854.
58. Pickel, "Perpetrators," 340; and Oulton and Takarangi, "Experiences," 12.
59. Joseph Braasem, NIOD 250k/854.
60. Sofsky, *Order*, 221.
61. Josef Habermann, BArch B 162/8864, fo. 1546; and Josef Bienenstock, BArch B 162/8864, fos. 316–17.
62. Maurits Bremer, NIOD 250d/448.
63. Leo Weiniger, NIOD 244/1486; and Stanley B., HVT-401, FVA.
64. Stanley B., HVT-401, FVA.
65. Langer, *Holocaust*, 175–78.
66. Grinband, *XI3 Commandement*, 148–51.
67. Ernest Nives, interview 588, VHA.
68. Erwin Lagus, letter to Simon Wiesenthal, SWA.

69. Obréjan, *Homme*, 137–38.
70. Memoirs of R. Stoppelman, YVA O.33 4272.
71. What he believed to be the first execution was more likely the third or fourth hanging of a prisoner named Katz. Demerer, *Kind*, 65–66.
72. Spira, *Legende*, 143.
73. Leo Weiniger, NIOD 244/1486.
74. Weinberg, *Boy 30529*, 96.
75. Fainer and Leach, *Sixty Years*, 37–38.
76. Greenspan, *Listening to Holocaust Survivors*, 32.
77. Reich, "Narratives," 463–67.
78. Langer, *Holocaust*, 163–65.
79. Felix G., HVT-3458, FVA.
80. Ernest Nives, interview 588, VHA.
81. Portelli, "Peculiarities," 100; and Bravo, Davite, and Jalla, "Myth," 105–8.
82. Loftus and Davis, "Sources," 211–12.
83. Nathan de Vries, NIOD 250k/854.
84. Isaac Arbeid, NIOD 250k/854.
85. Jacques op den Berg, NIOD 250d/726.
86. Hersh Fogel, interview 8021, VHA.
87. Jeffrey Shandler, "Speaking of the Past: Yiddish in Video Interviews," Guest Lecture, Department of Jewish Studies at the University of Vienna, June 14, 2016.
88. Greenspan, *Listening to Holocaust Survivors*, 13.
89. Aron Goldfinger, APMO Oświedcienia, f. 48, fo. 82.
90. Henry K., HVT-3000, FVA.
91. Barend van Leeuwen, NIOD 250k/854; Salomon van Velzen, NIOD 250k/854; Marcus Samuel Frank, NIOD 250k/854; Max Nunes Nabarro, NIOD 250k/854; Jonas Pampel, NIOD 250d/741; Abram Stone, BArch B 162/8864, fo. 371; Spitzer, *Dessin*, 121; and Fainzang, *Mémoire*, 113–14.
92. Oto Hostovsky, ŽMP.
93. See Bravo, Davite, and Jalla, "Myth," 105.
94. Maurits Bremer, NIOD 250d/448.
95. Koenig, *Vorhof*, 127–28.
96. Stawski, *My Life*, 40.
97. Steiner, "Reflections," 58.
98. Laub and Auerhahn, "Knowing," 36; Laub, "Witness," 70–71.
99. Kurt Baum, interview 29790, VHA; Obréjan, *Homme*, 137–38; Arthur Salomons, NIOD 250k/854; Felix G., HVT-3458, FVA; Karl Demerer, YVA O.3 3635; Hyman Joseph Leefsma, NIOD 250d/657; Louis Waterman, NIOD 250d/922; Natan Gipsman, BArch B 162/8864, fos. 403–4; Abram Fiszel, BArch B 162/8866, fo. 866; Joseph Ebner, *Number 176520*, 58;

Joseph Braasem, NIOD 250k/854; Aba Sztulberg, APMO Oświedcienia, f. 48. fo.113; and Rachel Brukner Frydrych, YVA O.3 3664.

100. Erwin Lagus, SWA.
101. Josef Bienenstock, BArch B 162/8864, fos. 316–17; Izchak Niewim, BArch B 162/8866, fo. 888; and Israel Feldman, BArch B 162/8866, fo. 806.
102. Grinband, *XIe Commandement*, 148–51; and Leo Weiniger, NIOD 244/1486.
103. Leo Weiniger, NIOD 244/1486; and Weinberg, *Boy 30529*, 96.
104. Rosen, *Holocaust's Jewish Calendars*, 90–161.
105. Koenig, *Vorhof*, 127–28.
106. Langer, *Holocaust*, 175–78.
107. Alfred Meier, *Jom Kippur 1944 im KZ (Blechhammer-Auschwitz)*, WL 055-EA-1032.
108. Isaac Arbeid, NIOD 250k/854; Marcus Samuel Frank, NIOD 250k/854; Karl Demerer, YVA O.3 3635; and Israel Feldman, BArch B 162/8866, fo. 806. On the importance of Jewish calendars during the Holocaust, see Rosen, *Holocaust*.
109. Portelli, "Peculiarities," 102.
110. Marcus Samuel Frank, NIOD 250k/854; Grinband, *XIe Commandement*, 151–52; Karl Demerer, YVA O.3 3635; Morichay/Max Knobler, BArch B 162/1817; Mordechay Rudoler, BArch B 162/8864, fos. 319–20; Isaac Arbeid, NIOD 250k/854; Maurits Bremer, NIOD 250d/448; Louis Waterman, NIOD 250d/922; and Abram Stone, BArch B 162/8864, fos. 371–72.
111. Private Papers: George Didcock, IWM 10/6/1.
112. Morichay/Max Knobler, BArch B 162/1817; and Josef Bienenstock, BArch B 162/8864, fo. 317.
113. Mordechay Rudoler, BArch B 162/8864, fos. 319–20.
114. Weinberg, *Boy 30529* 95–96.
115. Kalman Landau, *3 Heftlinge ferurteilt zum Galgen*, drawing, 1945, AfZ, S Biographien und Sachthemen/78.
116. Jehuda Mesiri, BArch B 162/1817; Henry S., HVT-0578, FVA; Menachem Miedzygorski, BArch B 162/8864, fo. 313; Karl Kaye, BArch B 162/8864, fo. 434; and Luzer Markowicz, APMO Oświedcienia, f. 48, fo. 75.
117. Paul Leibel, AN F/9/5586; Obréjan, *Homme*, 139–43; Grinband, *XIe Commandement*, 151–52; Samuel Abrams, NIOD 250d/386; Simon Winnik, NIOD 250d/940; Israel Feldman, BArch B 162/8866, fo. 888; Etienne Rosenfeld, YVA O.33 2070; Fainzang, *Mémoire*, 115; and Rosengarten, *Overleven*, 174–75.
118. Nathan P., HVT-2848, FVA.
119. Greenspan, "Listening to Holocaust Survivors," 84–87, 161–62.
120. Prochownik, *Mémoires*, 125–26.
121. Nathan P., HVT-2848, FVA.
122. Grinband, *XIe Commandement*, 151–52; Nathan P., HVT-2848; and Etienne Rosenfeld, YVA O.33 2070.

123. Prochownik, *Mémoires*, 220.
124. The button cover was gifted to the United States Holocaust Memorial Museum. USHMM ID irn 517247, no. 2005.257.1.
125. Wieviorka, "Heroes," 112–16.
126. Portelli, "Peculiarities," 100.
127. Private Papers: George Didcock, IWM 10/6/8.
128. Hans Bonn, NIOD 250d/445; André B., HVT-2842, FVA; Abraham Aussen, NIOD 250d/399; Steiner, "Reflections," 61; Léon Brotfeld, AN F/9/5583; Albert Aelion, AN F/9/5583; Jacques Bonaziz, AN F/9/5583; Max Nunes Nabarro, NIOD 250k/854; and Sigbert Weisz, NIOD 250d/854.
129. Emanuel Luftglas, APMO Oświedcienia, f. 48, fo. 142.
130. Laub, "Witness," 61–63.
131. Henry K., HVT-3000, FVA; and Kichka, *Adolescence*, 127–28.
132. Spitzer, *Dessin*, 122, 105.
133. Etienne Rosenfeld, YVA O.33 2070.
134. Emanuel Luftglas, APMO Oświedcienia, f. 48, fo. 142.
135. Wolf W., HVT-2989, FVA; and interrogation of Karl Czapla, October 27, 1960, StA Wü 2012-009, no. 34.
136. Private Papers: George Didcock, IWM 10/6/1.
137. Jakob Perlmutter, BArch B 162/8866, fo. 904; Aron Goldfinger, APMO Oświedcienia, f. 48, fo. 82; Stawski, *My Life*, 40; and Max Good, interview 6120, VHA.
138. Aron Goldfinger, APMO Oświedcienia, f. 48, fo. 82.
139. Demerer, *Kind*, 65–66.
140. Kurt Klappholz, IWM Sound Archive 9425.
141. Obréjan, *Homme*, 165, 170–71.
142. Wolf W., HVT-2989, FVA.
143. Laub, "Event," 76–80; Laub and Auerhahn, "Knowing," 32–36; Oulton and Takarangi, "Experiences," 11–12; and Pezdek and Taylor, "Memory," 165.
144. Loftus and Davis, "Sources," 210–11; Blank, Walter, and Isemann, "Past," 55–57; and Soraci et al., "Impairment," 281.
145. Laub, "Witness," 58.
146. Robert Clary, interview 95, VHA.
147. Clary, *Holocaust*, 88–89.
148. Clary, *Holocaust*, 90–91.
149. Stanley B., HVT-401, FVA.
150. See Portelli, "Peculiarities," 100.
151. Kurt Baum, National Council of Jewish Women Sarasota-Manatee Section Holocaust Oral History Project, 1988, USHMM RG-50.154*0005.
152. Kurt Baum, interview 29790, VHA.
153. Spitzer, *Dessin*, 121.

154. Rudolf Neumann, BArch B 162/8864, fo. 1539.
155. Werner Simon Albert Rudersdorf, BArch B 162/8864, fo. 1542.
156. Lawrence Langer defined the "impromptu self" as a self-preserving survival mode. Langer, *Holocaust*, 175–78.
157. Fainer, *Sixty Years*, 37–38.
158. Raphael Montezinos, NIOD 250k/854.
159. Weinberg, *Boy 30529*, 96.
160. Siegfried Parsser, NIOD 250d/744.
161. Maurits Bremer, NIOD 250d/448.
162. The War-Time Experiences of Otto Deutsch, online collection, ŽMP.
163. André B., HVT-2842, FVA; Helmo Trzesniewsky, BArch B 162/8864, fo. 422; Josef Habermann, BArch B 162/8864, fo. 1544; and Stawski, *My Life*, 41.
164. Sigbert Weisz, NIOD 250k/854; and Salomon van Velzen, NIOD 250k/854.
165. Menachem Miedzygorski, StA Wü 2012-009, no. 33, fo. 312; and Etienne Rosenfeld, YVA O.33 2070.
166. Louis Waterman, NIOD 250d/922; Wolf W., HVT-2989, FVA; and Henry K., HVT-3000, FVA.
167. Karl Kaye, BArch B 162/8864, fo. 434.
168. H. Joseph, NIOD 250k/854.
169. Koenig, *Vorhof*, 114–15, 127–28.
170. Koenig, *Vorhof*, 127–28.
171. Rosa Plawner, interview 24454, VHA; and Yera Hammer, interview 18278, VHA.
172. Ida Rus, interview 35966, VHA; Rosa Plawner, interview 24454, VHA; and Helen Wakshlag, interview 4093, VHA.
173. Esther Drexler, interview 11703, VHA.
174. Helen Pinczewski, interview 6014, VHA.
175. Anna/Chana May, BArch B 162/8866, fos. 867–68.
176. Rozka Kam, interview 17201, VHA.
177. Gita Brandsztedter-Sztulbergowa, APMO Oświedcienia, f. 48, fo. 152.
178. Waxman, *Women*, 123–24.
179. Rachel Brukner Frydrych, YVA O.3 3664; her husband testified at the same time she did; see Arie Frydrych, YVA O.3 3665.

CHAPTER 10

1. Fainzang, *Mémoire*, 117; Rosengarten, *Overleven*, 178; and Leo Weiniger, NIOD 244/1486.
2. Patterson, "Final Chapter," 159.
3. Lasik, "Organisationsstruktur," 297–99; and Harten, *Himmlers Lehrer*, 298.
4. Garrison order no. 22/44, August 18, 1944, HHStAW 461/37638, 118.

5. Hartog Soep (Harry Pos), NIOD 250d/851; and interrogation of Karl Czapla, StA Wü 2012-009, no. 33, fos. 6832–43.
6. Fackler, *"Des Lagers Stimme,"* 346.
7. Rosengarten, *Overleven*, 178–79.
8. Gilbert, *Music*, 187.
9. Leo Weiniger, NIOD 244/1486.
10. Wajnblum, *My Destiny*, 143.
11. Frankl, *Man's Search*, 67–68.
12. Isaac Arbeid, NIOD 250d/815; Spira, *Legende*, 144; Clary, *Holocaust*, 91; and Spitzer, *Dessin*, 93.
13. Maurits Bremer, NIOD 250d/448.
14. Hartog Salomon Ereira, NIOD 250d/519; and Spira, *Legende*, 144.
15. Clary, *Holocaust*, 91.
16. Hartog Soup (Harry Pos), NIOD 250d/851; and Fackler, *"Des Lagers Stimme,"* 359.
17. Maurits Bremer, NIOD 250d/448.
18. Isaac Arbeid, NIOD 250d/815; Ida Russ, interview 35966, VHA; and Karl Demerer, YVA O.3 3536.
19. Hartog Soup (Harry Pos), NIOD 250d/851.
20. Clary, *Holocaust*, 86.
21. Novitch, Davidowicz, ands Freudenheim, *Resistance*, 52.
22. Spitzer, *Dessin*, 94.
23. Jura Soyfer (Kharkiv, 1912) settled in Vienna in 1920 and became a renowned playwright. He was taken to Dachau and Buchenwald for being a Communist in 1938 and died of typhus a year later. His name has become synonymous with Austrian anti-fascist satire. Jarka, *Jura Soyfer*, 195–249.
24. Spira, *Legende*, 47, 144; and Spira, "Lebensbericht," 36–43.
25. Weniger, *Bühne*, 331.
26. Spira, *Legende*, 148.
27. Clary, *Holocaust*, 92.
28. Clary, *Holocaust*, 2–25, 91–141.
29. Spitzer, *Dessin*, 93.
30. Hartog Salomon Ereira, NIOD 250d/519; and Spira, *Legende*, 144.
31. Maurits Bremer, NIOD 250d/448. *Ein Lied geht um die Welt* was performed by the famous Jewish tenor Joseph Schmidt in a German movie of the same title released in 1933. Schmidt left Germany one year later. An English version entitled *My Song Goes Round the World* came out in 1934.
32. Isaac Arbeid, NIOD 250d/815.
33. Karl Demerer, YVA O.3 3635.

34. Karl Czapla, BArch 162/8863, fo. 1528.
35. Steiner, "Reflections," 61–62.
36. Clary, *Holocaust*, 91.
37. Leo Weiniger, NIOD 244/1486.
38. Kuna, *Musik*, 351.
39. Fackler, "Music," 7; and John, "Music," 280.
40. Fainzang, *Mémoire*, 117; and Karl Czapla, BArch B 162/8869, fo. 1528.
41. Fackler, *"Des Lagers Stimme,"* 344.
42. Karl Czapla, BArch 162/8863, fo. 1528.
43. Kuna, *Musik*, 42; and Fackler, *"Des Lagers Stimme,"* 345–46.
44. Georges Czaczkes, interview 3328, VHA.
45. Isaac Arbeid, NIOD 250d/815; and Fackler, "Music," 5.
46. Isaac Arbeid, NIOD 250d/815; Spitzer, *Dessin*, 93; and Rosengarten, *Overleven*, 178.
47. Georges Czaczkes, interview 3328, VHA.
48. Siegfried Herrmann, interview 38261, VHA; and Henry G., HVT-2384, FVA.
49. Wieczorek, "Like the Wind Drives Dead Leaves," 193–94; and John, "Music," 282.
50. Leo Weiniger, NIOD 244/1486.
51. Koenig, *Vorhof*, 114.
52. Oto Hostovsky, ŽMP.
53. Knapp, *Frauenlager*, 114; and Gilbert, *Music*, 184–85.
54. Georges Czaczkes, interview 3328, VHA; and Fackler, *"Des Lagers Stimme,"* 355.
55. Herbert Heinzelmann, "Wie das Kino einst den 'Alten Fritz' zeigte," *Nürnberger Zeitung*, December 26, 2011.
56. Sam Silberberg, USHMM 2006.248; and Karl Czapla, BArch B 162/8869, fo. 1528.
57. Kuna, *Musik*, 34.
58. Jakob Gesang, BArch B 162/8864, fo. 384; and Obréjan, *Homme*, 42.
59. Louis Waterman, NIOD 250d/922.
60. Hartog Soep (Harry Pos), NIOD 250d/851.
61. Invitations to comradeship evenings on August 19, November 25, and December 31, 1944, BArch R 9348/121.
62. Georges Czaczkes, interview 3328, VHA.
63. Fainzang, *Mémoire*, 59.
64. Isaac Arbeid, NIOD 250d/815.
65. Fackler, "Music," 16; and Gilbert, *Music*, 4.
66. Fainzang, *Mémoire*, 98. The song was composed by Oskar Schima in 1938.
67. Maurits Bremer, NIOD 250d/448. "I Can't Give You Anything but Love, Baby" was written by Jimmy McHugh and Dorothy Fields in 1928.
68. Dr. Schlick to head of NSDAP propaganda department, December 9, 1944, BArch R 9348/121.
69. Kichka, *Adolescence*, 144–45.

CHAPTER 11

1. Strzelecki, *Endphase*, 31–37, 92–100; and Madajczyk, *Okkupationspolitik*, 572.
2. Appendix to Bracht's directive of December 21, 1944, printed in Strzelecki, *Endphase*, 320–21; and Blatman, *Death Marches*, 79–81.
3. Affidavit by Franz Xaver Kraus, printed in Czech, *Kalendarium*, 990.
4. Strzelecki, *Endphase*, 142, 161.
5. Maurits Bremer, NIOD 250d/448; Paul Hertz, NIOD 250d/576; Oto Hostovsky, ŽMP; Peter Sturm, YVA O.33 2380; Maurice Moshe Szmidt, YVA O.3 3474; Strzelecki, *Endphase*, 162; and Ulrich Arnhem, ŽMP.
6. A. Schweid, WL 053-EA-0906.
7. Thirty-two hundred prisoners were originally evacuated from Jaworzno. Piper, "Nebenlager Neu-Dachs," 104. A survivor estimated that about one thousand of his comrades had been shot on the march from Jaworzno to Blechhammer. Jacob Bromet, NIOD 250d/451.
8. SS personnel file of Hans Stefan Olejak, BArch B 162/8863, fo. 143; and trial investigations regarding the murders of Blechhammer inmates, IfZ Ga 05.02/1, fols. 48–126.
9. Maurits Bremer, NIOD 250d/448.
10. Maurits Bremer, NIOD, 250d/448.
11. Anonymous testimony 3146, DEGOB; and Stone, *Liberation*, 30.
12. Strzelecki, *Endphase*, 142–43.
13. A. Schweid, WL 053-EA-0906.
14. Berthold Gersons, NIOD 250k/854; and Hartog Kalkoeve, NIOD 250d/612.
15. Ernest Nives, interview 588, VHA.
16. Ulrich Arnheim, ŽMP; and Mozes Jacob van Dam, NIOD 250d/491.
17. Jacob Bromet, NIOD 250d/451.
18. Wechter, Musia, YVA M. 49/2257; and anonymous testimony, DEGOB 1055.
19. Joseph K., HVT-866, FVA.
20. Simon S., HVT-1356, FVA.
21. Koenig, *Vorhof*, 134–35.
22. Interrogation of Karl Czapla, October 7, 1976, BArch B 162/8863, fos. 1529–31.
23. Isaac Arbeid, NIOD 250k/854.
24. Leo Weiniger, NIOD 244/1486.
25. Sam Green, BArch B 162/8864, fo. 296.
26. Etienne Rosenfeld, YVA O.33/2070; and Ernest Nives, interview 588, VHA.
27. See Blatman, *Death Marches*, 427–28.
28. Paul Hertz, NIOD 250d/576.
29. Gita Brandsztedter-Sztulbergowa, APMO Oświedcienia, f. 48, fols. 150–53.
30. Rachel Brukner Frydrych, YVA O.3/3664.
31. Etienne Rosenfeld, YVA O.33 2070.
32. Abram Szeftel, APMO Oświedcienia, f. 48, fo. 158.
33. International Red Cross report, January 14, 1945, ACICR.

34. Jacob Bromet, NIOD 250d/451.
35. Oto Hostovsky, ŽMP; anonymous testimony, DEGOB 1685; and Martin Shlanger, VVA.
36. Anonymous testimony, DEGOB 1055; and Voss, *Fluitje*, 252–53.
37. Deposition of Kurt Karl Schumann, NA WO 309/978; and Private Papers: Dr. Schlick, BArch R 9348/121.
38. Abram Caransa, NIOD 250d/461.
39. Deposition of Heinrich Schlick, NA WO 309/978.
40. Keller, *Volksgemeinschaft*, 274–91; also Blatman, *Death Marches*, 407–37.
41. Report of the British War Crimes Group, July 18, 1947, NA WO 309/978.
42. Langer, *Holocaust*, 175–78.
43. Hans Rehfisch, interview 26241, VHA; similarly, Martin Shlanger, VVA; and Abram Caransa, NIOD 250d/461.
44. Abram Szeftel, APMO Oświedcienia, f. 48, fo. 158; Israel Feldman, BArch B 162/8866, fos. 807–8; Voss, *Fluitje*, 21, 251; and The War-Time Experiences of Otto Deutsch, ŽMP.
45. Sofsky, *Order*, 130.
46. Koenig, *Vorhof*, 137.
47. Jakob Gesang, BArch B 162/8864, fo. 382.
48. Czech, *Kalendarium*, 972, 976, 979, 990; Levi, *If This Is the Man*, 187–88; Strzelecki, "Arbeitslager Gleiwitz IV," 168; Strzelecka, "Arbeitslager Gleiwitz I," 105–6; and Blatman, *Death Marches*, 90.
49. Lasik, "Organisationsstruktur," 179; and Wachsmann, *KL*, 465–71.
50. Karl Demerer, BArch B 162/18175.
51. Winter, "SS," 101.
52. Krakowski, "Death Marches," 486; and Blatman, *Death Marches*, 264–67.
53. Arthur Salomons, NIOD 250k/872.
54. Oto Hostovsky, ŽMP.
55. Arthur Salomons, NIOD 250k/872; Emanuel Svinkelstein, BArch B 162/8866, fo. 895; and Peter Sturm, YVA O.3/2380.
56. Isidore Emanuel Moppes, NIOD 250d/703; and Jacques op den Berg, NIOD 250d/726.
57. Oto Hostovsky, ŽMP.
58. Abraham Spiero, NIOD 250d/859; Efraim Roseboom, NIOD 250d/805; Anna (Chana) May, BArch B 162/8866, fo. 868; Ernest Wolf, AN 736 MI 3; and The War-Time Experiences of Otto Deutsch, ŽMP.
59. Ernest Nives, interview 588, VHA.
60. The War-Time Experiences of Otto Deutsch, ŽMP; and Ernest Wolf, AN 736 MI 3.
61. Voss, *Fluitje*, 250–51.
62. Jacques op den Berg, NIOD 250d/726; and Voss, *Fluitje*, 253.
63. Ernest Wolf, AN 736 MI 3.
64. Interrogation of Karl Czapla, October 7, 1976, BArch B 162/8863, fos. 1529–31.

65. Rosengarten, *Overleven*, 190.
66. Etienne Rosenfeld, YVA O.33/2017.
67. Philip Venetianer, NIOD 250d/903.
68. Interrogations of Franz Ludwig, and Heinrich Tille, IPN GK 184/262.
69. Etienne Rosenfeld, YVA O.33/2070.
70. Interrogation of Karl Masseli, July 18, 1977, BArch B 162/8864, fos. 1558–62.
71. Philip Venetianer, NIOD 250d/903.
72. Gita Brandsztedter-Sztulbergowa, APMO Oświedcienia, f. 48, fos. 150–53; and Interrogation of Adolf Schindler, StA Wü 2012-009, 33, fo. 2567.
73. Luzer Markowicz, APMO Oświedcienia, f. 48, fos. 76–77.
74. Nathan de Vries, NIOD 250d/915.
75. Bernard Appelbaum, AN 736 MI 3.
76. Anna May, BArch B 162/8866, 868.
77. Etienne Rosenfeld, YVA O.33/2070.
78. Cadok Plawner, YVA O.3/3679; see also Strzelecki, *Endphase*, 163. Strzelecki erroneously stated that the massacre had taken place on January 23 but confirmed the approximate number of casualties.
79. Jacob Bromet, NIOD 250d/451; and Oskar Langer, BArch B 162/8866, fos. 824–25.
80. Jacob Shweizman, BArch B 162/8866, fol. 828; and Cadok Plawner, YVA O.3/3679.
81. The Polish convicts had temporarily been held in the work education camp (AEL) of Blechhammer, which functioned as a transit camp for penitentiaries. Their planned transfer to Auschwitz under the Ministry of Justice's "annihilation through labor" act was averted by the evacuation. Some of them dodged the AEL's march west, during which their comrades were shot on January 22, 1945. Gestapo orders to kill them had obviously been delegated to the OHW works police. Interrogation of Paul Heurich, HHStAW, Abt. 461, no. 37638, vol. 49, fo. 8623. See also Lotfi, *KZ der Gestapo*, 294.
82. Jacques op den Berg, NIOD 250d/726; and Voss, *Fluitje*, 254–60.
83. Mozes Vischjager, NIOD 250d/908; and Ernest Wolf, AN 736 MI 3.
84. The War-Time Experiences of Otto Deutsch, ŽMP.
85. Bergh, *Kronprinz*, 107–8.
86. Anonymous testimony, DEGOB 1055.
87. Johannes Martini, Das I. Volkssturmbataillon Cosel, LAA Ost-Dok. 10/790; and Tessin, *Verbände*, 41.
88. Hijman Cozijn, NIOD 250d/485.
89. Voss, *Fluitje*, 264.
90. Berthold Gersons, NIOD 250k/854; Voss, *Fluitje*, 264; and Vilem Hostovsky, YVA O.33/3432.
91. Anonymous testimony, DEGOB 1055; and Bert Wilner, YVA M.1/2307.
92. Zev H., HVT-0622, FVA. Altogether, 11,500 prisoners were taken to Leitmeritz and Helm-

brechts in seventeen transports from Gross-Rosen then. Konieczny, *KL Gross-Rosen*, 323.
93. Koenig, *Vorhof*, 141–42.
94. Abram Szeftel, APMO Oświedcienia, f. 48, fol. 158.
95. Oto Hostovsky, ŽMP; and The War-Time Experiences of Otto Deutsch, ŽMP.
96. Israel Feldman, BArch B 162/8866, fo. 807; Mendel Meyer, NIOD 250d/695; and Ernest Wolf, AN 736 MI 3.
97. Blatman, *Death Marches*, 93; and Czech, *Kalendarium*, 983. Piper does not support Blatman's version of an alleged massacre either. Piper, "Nebenlager Blechhammer," 38.
98. Based on Joachim Neander's concept of "local liquidation orders" to shoot unfit prisoners on death marches, Blatman defines "local liquidation units" as marauding, lower echelon SS men, or soldiers with "limitless power." Blatman, *Death Marches*, 94.
99. Jacob de Boers, NIOD 250d/441.
100. Beorn, *Darkness*, 234–46.
101. Winter, "SS," 101.
102. Vilem Hostovsky, YVA O.33/3432; and Koenig, *Vorhof*, 141.
103. Levi, *If This Is the Man*, 186.
104. Vilem Hostovsky, YVA O.33/3432. 3432; similarly, Abram Szeftel, APMO Oświedcienia, f. 48, fo. 158.
105. Guetzkow and Bowman, *Men*, 45; and Kronenberg, NIOD 250d/643.
106. Koenig, *Vorhof*, 140.
107. Abram Caransa, NIOD 250d/461.
108. Ernest Wolf, AN 736 MI 3.
109. Oto Hostovsky, ŽMP; and Levi, *If This Is the Man*, 189–192; see also Bacon, *Lives*, 151–155.
110. Oto Hostovsky, ŽMP.
111. A Schweid, WL 053-EA-0906; and Greenberg, "Responses," 11–26.
112. Hartog Kalkoeve, NIOD 250d/612; and A. Schweid, WL 053-EA-0906.
113. Wechter, Musia, YVA M.49/2257; and Chaim Orszanski, YVA M.11/396.
114. Mozes Jacob van Dam, NIOD 250d/491; and Abram Szeftel, APMO Oświedcienia, f. 48, fo. 158.
115. Abram Caransa, NIOD 250d/461.
116. Walter Fantl Brumlik, interview 29561, VHA.
117. Stone, *Liberation*, 30; and Levi, *If This Is the Man*, 219.
118. Zacharias Hammelburg, NIOD 250d/570.
119. Mendel Meyer, NIOD 250d/695.
120. Oto Hostovsky, ŽMP.
121. Abram Szeftel, APMO Oświedcienia, f. 48, fo. 158; and Philip Venetianer, NIOD 250d/903.
122. Voss, *Fluitje*, 263. Some of the bodies were exhumed and buried in a mass grave at the Polwies Communal Cemetery in Opole in 1958. Exhumation Protocols by the Polish Red Cross, courtesy of Edward Haduch.

123. Mozes Jacob van Dam, NIOD 250d/491.
124. Mendel Meyer, NIOD 250d/695.
125. Karl Demerer, BArch B 162/18175; and interrogation report of Franz Ludwig, IPN GK 184/262.

CHAPTER 12

1. Strzelecki, *Endphase*, 142, 161.
2. Directive by Bracht, December 21, 1944, 5–6, printed in Strzelecki, *Endphase*, 324–25.
3. Paul Hertz, NIOD 250d/576; Leo Weiniger, NIOD 244/1486; Henry F., HVT-1332, FVA; and Samuel David Beller, YVA O.3 10840.
4. Maurits Bremer, NIOD 250d/448; and A. Schweid, WL 053-EA-0906.
5. Fainzang, *Mémoire*, 132.
6. Jakob Perlmutter, BArch B 162/8866, fo. 907.
7. Strzelecki, *Endphase*, 153; Blatman, *Death Marches*, 95; and Bauer, "Death Marches," 499. In a verdict against the SS man Reischenbeck in 1958, the county court of Munich assumed that the Auschwitz commandant Richard Baer had issued a general killing order to camp leaders. Orth, *System*, 276–77.
8. Interrogation of Simon Rodis, IPN GK 164/2282, fos. 51, 55; and interrogation of Wilhelm Menzel, NA WO 311/268.
9. Further members of the rear guard were Franz Ludwig; Scharführer Klingberg, Engemann, and Heger; Rottenführer Pichen, Kurt Müller, and Unterscharführer Pach, Pillach, Patzer, Pilz, Zwar, Zöllner, Bretschneider, Leipner, and Wallach. Interrogations of Heinrich Tille and Franz Ludwig, IPN GK 184/262.
10. Henry G., HVT-2384, FVA; Mozes Vischjager, NIOD 250d/908; and B. Swaaf, NIOD 250d/881.
11. Interrogation of Franz Ludwig, IPN GK 184/262; interrogation of Karl Masseli, BArch B 162/8864, fos. 1559–61; and Natan Gipsman, BArch B 162/8864, fo. 406.
12. Helmo Trzesniewsky, BArch B 162/8864, fos. 422–23; and Ernst Inow, BArch B 162/8869, fo. 1510.
13. Peter Sturm, YVA O.33 2380; Sigbert Weisz, NIOD 250k/854; and Isaac Arbeid, NIOD 250k/854.
14. Strzelecki, *Endphase*, 138; interrogation of Karl Czapla, October 7, 1976, BArch B 162/8863, fos. 1530–33; and Isaac Arbeid, NIOD 250k/854.
15. Meijer van Dijk, NIOD 250d/498; and Maurice Moshe Szmidt, YVA O.3 3474.
16. Paul Hertz, NIOD 250d/576; and Jacob de Boers, NIOD 250d/441.
17. Maurice Moshe Szmidt, YVA O.3 3474; Fainzang, *Mémoire*, 127; and Yera Hammer, interview 18278, VHA.
18. Jacob de Boers, NIOD 250d/441; Ludwig Hamburger, YVA O.3610; and Simon Winnik, NIOD 250d/940.

19. Leo Weiniger, NIOD 244/1486; and Ludwig Hamburger, YVA O.3610.
20. Paul Hertz, NIOD 250d/576; Strzelecka and Setkiewicz, "Bau," 144; and Krakowski, "Death Marches," 481.
21. The trek's itinerary was Neustadt—Ziegenhals—Neisse—Ottmachau—Frankenstein—Gräditz—Schweidnitz—Gross-Rosen. Piper, "Nebenlager Blechhammer," 36; Jacob de Boers, NIOD 250d/441; and Arthur Salomons, NIOD 250d/872.
22. Maurice Moshe Szmidt, YVA O.3 3474; and Helmo Trzesniewsky, BArch B 162/8864, fos. 422–23.
23. Leo Weiniger, NIOD 244/1486.
24. Ludwig Hamburger, YVA O.36 10.
25. Leo Weiniger, NIOD 244/1486.
26. Rafael Lewin, interview 27867, VHA.
27. Nathan Ben-Brith, YVA 108-3313 F; and Spira, *Legende*, 147–48.
28. Fainzang, *Mémoire*, 127.
29. Maurice Moshe Szmidt, YVA O.3 3474.
30. Ida Russ, interview 35966, VHA; and Maurice Moshe Szmidt, YVA O.3 3474.
31. Isaac Arbeid, NIOD 250k/854; Henry F., HVT-1332, FVA; and Jerrit A., HVT-208, FVA.
32. Steiner, "Reflections," 66; Leo Weiniger, NIOD 244/1486; and Samuel David Beller, YVA O.3 10840.
33. Spitzer, *Dessin*, 132–34; Clary, *Holocaust*, 94; Weinberg, *Boy 30529*, 101; and Jonas Pampel, NIOD 250d/741.
34. Paul Hertz, NIOD 250d/576; and Peter Sturm, YVA O.3 2380.
35. Paul Hertz, NIOD 250d/576; interrogation of Karl Masseli, BArch B 162/8864, fos. 1559–61; and Peter Sturm, YVA O.3 2380.
36. Simon Winnik, NIOD 250d/940; Sigbert Weisz, NIOD 250k/854; Menachem Miedzygorski, BArch B 162/8864, fo. 314; and Regina Borenstein, interview 29809, VHA.
37. Leo Weiniger, NIOD 244/1486.
38. Piper, "Nebenlager Blechhammer," 38.
39. Arthur Salomons, NIOD 250k/872; Moszek Gerszonowicz, NIOD 250d/550; Ernst Inow, BArch B 162/8869, fo. 1510; and Emanuel Svinkelstein, BArch B 162/8866, fo. 895.
40. Jakob Perlmutter, BArch B 162/8866, fo. 907; Peter Sturm, YVA O.3 2380; Arthur Salomons, NIOD 250k/872; and Maurice Moshe Szmidt, YVA O.3 3474.
41. Abraham Schaufeld, IWM Sound Archive, 17470.
42. Hartog Tertaas, NIOD 250d/883.
43. Karl Demerer, YVA O.3 3635.
44. Esther Drexler, interview 11703, VHA; Konieczny, *KL Gross-Rosen*, 322; Sprenger, *Gross-Rosen*, 288–91; Blatman, *Death Marches*, 97–98; and Strzelecki, *Endphase*, 99.
45. Ida Russ, interview 35966, VHA; Esther Drexler, interview 11703, VHA; Spira, *Legende*, 150–51; Jacques G., HVT-2845, FVA; Salomon Lierens, NIOD 250d/673; Jonas Pampel,

NIOD 250d/741; Gerrit Aardewerk, NIOD 250d/384; Karl Demerer, YVA O.3 3635; Josef Bienenstock, BArch B 162/8864, fo. 318; Kurt Bachmann, *Elendszug von Auschwitz in das KZ Buchenwald*, BArch B162/8864, fo. 1563; and Weinberg, *Boy 30529*, 103.
46. Sprenger, *Gross-Rosen*, 290–91.
47. Karl Demerer, BArch B 162/18175; Franz Ludwig, IPN GK 184/262; Arthur Salomons, NIOD 250k/872; and Krakowski, "Death Marches," 481.
48. Hermann Boekdrukker, NIOD 250d/1060.
49. Salomon Lierens, NIOD 250d/673; Simon Blein, NIOD 250d/433; Arthur Salomons, NIOD 250k/872; Hartog Soep, NIOD 250d/851; Mozes Engelsman, NIOD 250d/514; Spira, *Legende*, 152–55; Clary, *Holocaust*, 96–97; and Hackett, *Buchenwald*, 316–17.
50. Karl Demerer, YVA O.3 3635; Barend van Delft, NIOD 250d/495; Joseph Braasem, NIOD 250d/446; Maurits Broeks, NIOD 250d/450; and Salomon Lierens, NIOD 250d/673.
51. Spira, *Legende*, 154–55; Kurt Bachmann, *Elendszug von Auschwitz in das KZ Buchenwald*, BArch B162/8864, fo. 1563; and Greiser, *Todesmärsche*, 55.
52. Arthur Salomons, 250k/872; Ida Russ, interview 35966, VHA; Peter Sturm, YVA O.3 2380; and Karl Czapla, BArch B 162/8863, fos. 1530–33.
53. Rachel Brukner Frydrych, YVA O.3 3664; Regina Borenstein, interview 29809, VHA; Fainzang, *Mémoire*, 124; and Ernst Inow, BArch B 162/8869, fo. 1510.
54. Arthur Salomons, NIOD 250k/872.
55. Helen Wakshlag, interview 4093, VHA; Ida Russ, interview 35966, VHA; Yera Hammer, interview 18278, VHA; and Esther Drexler, interview 11703, VHA.
56. Kolb, *Bergen-Belsen*, 43–46; Hördler, *Ordnung*, 360; and Lattek, "Bergen-Belsen," 43–56. See also Celinscak, *Distance*.
57. Ida Russ, interview 35966, VHA.
58. Rachel Brukner Frydrych, YVA O.3 3664.
59. Lattek, "Bergen-Belsen," 56; and Kolb, *Bergen-Belsen*, 42.
60. Strzelecki, *Endphase*, 169–70; and Krakowski, "Death Marches," 489.
61. Leo Weiniger, NIOD 244/1486; Kichka, *Adolescence*, 153; and John R., HVT-1295, FVA.
62. Greiser, *Todesmärsche*; and Winter, "Camps."
63. Felix G., HVT-3458, FVA.
64. Rosengarten, *Overleven*, 197; Aba Sztulberg, APMO Oświedcienia, f. 48, fo. 114; Leo Weiniger, NIOD 244/1486; and André B., HVT-2842, FVA.
65. Karl Kaye, BArch B 162/8864, fo. 436.
66. Siegfried Hermann, interview 38261, VHA.
67. Marcus Samuel Frank, NIOD 250d/528.
68. Heyman Joseph Leefsma, NIOD 250d/657.
69. Stanley B., HVT-401, FVA.
70. Sam Silberberg, USHMM 2006.248.
71. Henry S., HVT-0578, FVA.

72. See Winter, "SS," 101.
73. Blatman, *Death Marches*, 93–94.
74. Krakowski, "Death Marches," 486–87; Strzelecki, *Endphase*, 153; Blatman, *Death Marches*, 95; and Neander, *Konzentrationslager*, 100.
75. Interrogation of Wilhelm Menzel, NA WO 311/268. The attorney general of Kattowitz, Haffner, issued a shooting directive to penitentiary subcamps. Statement by Simon Rodis, IPN GK 164/2282.
76. Krakowski, "Death Marches," 486–87.
77. Strzelecki, *Endphase*, 277–78.
78. Bauer, "Death Marches," 497–99; and Kolb, *Bergen-Belsen*, 42.

EPILOGUE

1. Laub, "Event," 76–82; Sofsky, *Order*, 17–24; and Des Pres, *Survivor*, 108.
2. See Davidowicz, "Holocaust Landscape," 25.
3. Gilbert, *Music*, 4–7; and Berger, *Surviving*, 3–5.
4. See, Bajohr, *Parvenüs*, 134–35; and Friedlander, *Years*, 42.
5. Trunk, *Judenrat*, 244.
6. Lifschitz, NIOD 250d/674.
7. Arthur Salomons, NIOD 250d/ 815.
8. Piet Nieuwes, NIOD 250d/715.
9. Jozef Niewes, NIOD 250d/716.
10. Paul Hertz, NIOD 250d/ 576; SS payrolls, BArch B162/8863; and Jozef Niewes, NIOD 250d/716.
11. Arthur Salomons, NIOD 250d/815.
12. Samuel Abrams, NIOD 250d/386; and Lucas Wurms, NIOD 250d/952.
13. Maurits Broeks, NIOD 250d/450.
14. Gabriel Zvi Lifschitz, NIOD 250d/674.
15. Wolf W., HVT-2989, FVA.
16. Paul Hertz, NIOD 250d/576; Jozef Niewes, NIOD 250d/716; and Karl Demerer, YVA O.3 3635.
17. Samuel Abrams, NIOD 250d/386; Marcus Samuel Frank, NIOD 250d/528; Maurice Moshe Szmidt, YVA O.3 3474; and Abraham Herzberg, NIOD 250d/577.
18. Gross, *Society*, 145.
19. Rosengarten, *Overleven*, 146–47.
20. Simon Overste, NIOD 250d/735; Louis Waterman, NIOD 250/922; Hartog Tertaas, NIOD 250d/883; and Isidore Emanuel van Moppes, NIOD 250d/703. See also Friedländer, *Years*, 42.
21. Jozef Niewes, NIOD 250d/716; Paul Hertz, NIOD 250d/576; Abraham Spiero, NIOD

250d/859; Hartog Salomon Ereira, NIOD 250d/519; Salomon Staszewski, NIOD 250d/864; and SS penal reports, BArch B 162/8867.
22. Bajohr, *Parvenüs*, 134–35.
23. Arthur Salomons, NIOD 250d/815; Jozef Niewes, NIOD 250d/716; Lucas Wurms, NIOD 250d/952; and Ann C., HVT-0340, FVA.
24. Karl Demerer, YVA O.3 3635.
25. Rachel Brukner Frydrych, YVA O.3 3664; Wolf W., HVT-2989, FVA; and Piet Nieuwes, NIOD 250d/715.
26. Lifschitz, NIOD 250d/674.
27. Joseph Braasem, NIOD 250d/446.
28. Abraham Spiero, NIOD 250d/859; and Joseph Braasem, NIOD 250d/446.
29. Rosengarten, *Overleven*, 180.
30. Appeal by Hoffmann, September 3, 1947, and statements by Wilhelm Pfeiffer, Karl Demerer, StA M SpkA K 739.
31. See, Rosengarten, *Overleven*, 119.
32. OHW quarterly management reports, May–July 1940, BArch R 9348/6.
33. Rosengarten, *Overleven*, 142; and André B., HVT-2842, FVA.
34. See for instance, The Diary of Lance-Bombardier Edward Charles Stirling, IWM 824699/22/1; Private Papers: George Didcock, IWM 10/6/1; and J. Driscoll IWM Sound Archive, 17435.
35. Wallis, *British POWs*, 104–5.
36. Kochavi, *Captivity*, 22–28, 34; and Levine, *Captivity*, 84.
37. White, "'Even in Auschwitz,'" 285.
38. Kurt Klappholz, IWM Sound Archive, 9425.
39. Rachel Brukner Frydrych, YVA O.3 3664.
40. Koenig, *Vorhof*, 120; Fainzang, *Mémoire*, 63; and Wollenberg, *Alptraum*, 121.
41. Wallis, *British POWs*, 116.
42. Hessel Goldberg, NIOD 250d/553.
43. Gelber, "Palestinian POWs," 111.
44. Pinchas Bleier, interview 45393, VHA; Moshe Erlikh, interview 18332, VHA; and Borrie, *Captivity*, 95.
45. Rosengarten, *Overleven*, 126.
46. Salomon Staszewski, NIOD 250d/864.
47. Oskar Langer, BArch B 162/8866, fos. 819–20. By contrast, a British POW deployed in Monowitz was rifle-butted by an SS man for supporting a collapsing Jewish prisoner, who was subsequently shot. White, "'Even in Auschwitz,'" 276.
48. Salomon Staszewski, NIOD 250d/864; and SS penal report on Wolf Lesorgen for having accepted ten cigarettes from a British POW, BArch B162/8867.

49. Wallis, *British POWs*, 104–5.
50. Frankl, *Seelsorge*, 78–79; and Berger, *Surviving*, 3–5.
51. Memoirs of R. Stoppelman, YVA O.33 4272.
52. Nathan Ben-Brith, YVA 108-3313F; Maurice Mosze Szmidt, YVA O.3 3474; and Steiner, "Reflections," 59–60.
53. Prochownik, *Mémoires*, 106.
54. Lester Berke, interview 2187, VHA.
55. Kushner, *Persistence*, 107–33; and Wallis, *British POWs*, 124.
56. See Bravo, Davite, and Jalla, "Myth," 104.
57. André Lapeyre, AN F/9/5565; and M. Fajon, AN 736 MI 3.
58. Spitzer, *Dessin*, 85.
59. Fainzang, *Mémoire*, 61.
60. Leo Weiniger, NIOD 244/1486.
61. BArch RH 49/14; and Samuel Jas, NIOD 250d/600.
62. Aron Goldfinger, APMO Oświedcienia, f. 48, fo. 82.
63. Rosengarten, *Overleven*, 119.
64. Moszek Gerszonowicz, NIOD 250d/550.
65. Salomon Szaszewski, NIOD 250d/864.
66. Koenig, *Vorhof*, 117–29.
67. Max Bachner, interview 4343, VHA.
68. Rosengarten, *Overleven*, 119–21; and Salomon Lierens, NIOD 250d/673.
69. Hessel Goldberg, NIOD 250d/553.
70. Brommet, NIOD 250d/453; and André B., HVT-2842, FVA.
71. Obréjan, *Homme*, 75–84.
72. Maurits Bremer, *Een Dag in Blechhammer*, NIOD 250d/448.
73. Grinband, *XIe Commandement*, 145.
74. Gerson F., HVT-2975, FVA.
75. Kurt Klappholz, IWM Sound Archive 9425.
76. Henry G., HVT-2384, FVA.
77. Joseph Ebner, *Number 176520*, 47–53.
78. Grinband, *XIe Commandement*, 145–46.
79. Koenig, *Vorhof*, 132.
80. Penal report on Cudek Plawner, BArch B 162/8867.
81. Doris L. Bergen, "Collaboration with Whom? German Presence and Absence in the East" (keynote address presented to the conference Collaboration in Eastern Europe during World War II and the Holocaust, Vienna Wiesenthal Institute for Holocaust Studies, December 5–7, 2013).
82. Rosa Schwarzberg, interview 9645, VHA; and Trunk, *Judenrat*, 128–29.
83. Joseph Braasem, NIOD 250d/446.

84. Wollenberg, *Alptraum*, 129; Mozes Jacob van Dam, NIOD 250d/491; Hessel Goldberg, NIOD 250d/553; Sigmund W., HVT-55, FVA; and Rosengarten, *Overleven*, 120.
85. Maurits Broeks, NIOD 250d/450; Heinz Michaelis, NIOD 250d/697.
86. NIOD 247/280; and Max (Maurits) Stodel, interview 1413, VHA.
87. Felix G., HVT-3458, FVA.
88. Leo Young Papers, USHMM 1992.A0016/RG-10.048*01.
89. Joseph Braasem, NIOD 250d/446; and Isaac Arbeid, NIOD 250d/815.
90. Samuel Abrams, NIOD 250d/386.
91. Etienne Rosenfeld, YVA O.33 2070.
92. SS penal report on Paul Weil, BArch B 162/8867.
93. Obréjan, *Homme*, 170–71.
94. Chaja Pelzmann, BArch B 162/8866, fo. 889.
95. Wollenberg, *Alptraum*, 119.
96. Louis Waterman, NIOD 250d/922.
97. Koenig, *Vorhof*, 130; Clary, *Holocaust*, 84–85; John R., HVT-1295, FVA; Myron B., HVT-1507, FVA; and Harry Fransman, interview 2548, VHA.
98. Rosengarten, *Overleven*, 156–57; and Maurice Moshe Szmidt, YVA O.3 3474.
99. Gutman, *Encyclopedia of the Righteous*: Poland, 260.
100. Josek Melcer, interview 48401, VHA.
101. Wolf W., HVT-2989, FVA.
102. SS penal report on Josef Lajtner, BArch B 162/8867.
103. OHW circular, August 22, 1944, BArch R 9348/117.
104. Luzer Markowicz, APMO Oświedcienia, f. 48, fos. 75–76.
105. Emanuel Luftglas, APMO Oświedcienia, f. 48, fo. 142; and interrogation of Karl Czapla, October 27, 1960, StA Wü 2012-009, no. 34.
106. Kichka, *Adolescence*, 127–28; Maurice Moshe Szmidt, YVA O.3 3474; and Wolf W., HVT-2989, FVA.
107. Salomon Staszewski, NIOD 250d/864.
108. Jenny Sandberg, interview 1667, VHA.
109. Dr. Heinrich Schlick, *Beobachtungen im Ausländereinsatz*, February 10, 1943, BArch R 9348/111.
110. Hessel Goldberg, NIOD 250d/553.
111. Sam Silberberg, USHMM, 2006.248; Koenig, *Vorhof*, 124, 133; Lucjan Radzik, APMO Oświedcienia, f. 48, fo. 4; Wolf W., HVT-2989, FVA; and Maurits Bremer, NIOD 250d/448.
112. Leo Weiniger, NIOD 244/1486.
113. Rosengarten, *Overleven*, 164.
114. Fainzang, *Mémoire*, 108.
115. Henry F., HVT-1332, FVA; Maurits Bremer, NIOD 250d/448; Siegfried Hermann, inter-

view 38261, VHA; Abram Szeftel, APMO Oświedcienia, f. 48, fo. 5; and Paul Hertz, NIOD 250d/576.
116. Sigmund W., HVT-55; FVA.
117. Oto Hostovsky, ŽMP; and Spira, *Legende*, 143.
118. Leo Weiniger, NIOD 244/1486
119. Bravo, Davite, and Jalla, "Myth," 99; and Frankl, *Seelsorge*, 78–79.
120. Leo Weiniger, NIOD 244/1486.
121. SS penal report on Max Voss, BArch B 162/8867.
122. Dr. Heinrich Schlick in a letter to R. Kügler, January 12, 1945, BArch R 9348/121.
123. Koenig, *Vorhof*, 133.
124. Louis Waterman, NIOD 250d/922.
125. Siegfried Hermann, interview 38261, VHA.
126. Bauer, *Holocaust*, 42–45; and Tal, "Roots," 182–83.
127. Rahe, "Jewish Religious Life," 86–87; and Koenig, *Vorhof*, 124.
128. Gunter Faerber, interview 41847, VHA.
129. Rosengarten, *Overleven*, 106–7.
130. Demerer, *Kind*, 57; and Monty G., HVT-2427, FVA.
131. Gucia Ferst, interview 34207, VHA. See also Rosen, *Holocaust's Jewish Calendars*, 90–161.
132. Maurits Bremer, NIOD 250d/448; Gucia Ferst, interview 34207, VHA; Rosengarten, *Overleven*, 174–75; and Ernest Nives, interview 588, VHA.
133. Gucia Ferst, interview 34207, VHA.
134. Prochownik, *Mémoires*, 128–29.
135. Jerrit A., HVT-208, FVA; Kurt Klappholz, IWM Sound Archive, 9425; and Esther Drexler, interview 11703, VHA.
136. Kichka, *Adolescence*, 118; Fainzang, *Mémoire*, 108; and Etienne Rosenfeld, YVA O.33 2070.
137. Rahe, "Jewish Religious Life," 115–16.
138. Katz, *Holocaust in Historical Context*, 362–75.
139. Greenberg, "Responses," 12–20.
140. Sam Silberberg, USHMM 2006.248.
141. Greenberg, "Responses," 15.
142. Koenig, *Vorhof*, 128.
143. Prochownik, *Mémoires*, 128.
144. Spira, *Legende*, 143; and Jonas Pampel, NIOD 250d/741.
145. Henry K., HVT-3000, FVA.
146. Koenig, *Vorhof*, 131.
147. Fainzang, *Mémoire*, 45, 77–104; and Rahe, "Jewish Religious Life," 114.
148. Jacques G., HVT-2845, FVA.
149. Maurice Moshe Szmidt, YVA O.3 3474.
150. Kurt Baum, interview 29790, VHA.
151. Flusser, "Rückblick," 48.

152. See http://www.dkp-koeln.de/index.php/geschichte-dkpkoeln/60–kurt-bachmann (May 3, 2014).
153. Weniger, *Bühne*, 331.
154. Kurt Baum, USHMM RG-50.154*0005.
155. Kurt Baum, interview 29790, VHA.
156. Spira, *Legende*, 148.
157. Peter Sturm, YVA O.33 2380.
158. Hartog Salomon Ereira, NIOD 250d/519; and Hessel Goldberg, NIOD 250d/553.
159. Peukert, "Arbeiterwiderstand," 159–69.
160. Irmer, "*Allemand cochon*," 260.
161. SS penal report on Josef Wolmark, BArch B 162/8867.
162. Richard Overy, "*No Stab in the Back!* Race, Labor and the National Socialist Regime Under the Bombs, 1940–1945" (keynote address presented to the conference Race and Labor in Modern German History, Birkbeck College, London, March 27, 2014).
163. Statement by Karl Demerer to the Israeli police, February 15, 1973, YVA O.3 3635.
164. Deposition of Karl Demerer, June 9, 1964, BArch B 162/18175.
165. Gabriel Zvi Lifschitz, NIOD 250d/674; Hans Bonn, NIOD 250d/445; and Paul Hertz, NIOD 250d/576.
166. Rosengarten, *Overleven*, 122, 144; and Koenig, *Vorhof*, 119.
167. Wolf W., HVT-2989, FVA.
168. The state of Israel enacted several laws against alleged Jewish collaborators in 1949 and 1950. Former functionary prisoners were likewise brought before Jewish "Honor Courts" by fellow survivors in displaced persons camps. Waxman, *Women*, 141.
169. See, Bravo, Davite, and Jalla, "Myth," 104–5.
170. Bartuschka, *Zurückstellung*, 477.
171. I am very grateful to Prof. Dalia Ofer (The Hebrew University of Jerusalem) for suggesting the use of "second economy" rather than "black market," for the abovementioned reasons.
172. Sigmund W., HVT-55, FVA; Spitzer, *Dessin*, 89; Jacob de Wolf, NIOD 250d/946; and Abraham Jonas Walg, NIOD 250d/920.
173. Moszek Gerszonowicz, NIOD 250d/550; and Maurice Moshe Szmidt, YV O.3 3474.
174. Rosengarten, *Overleven*, 122.
175. SS penal report on Samuel Lille, BArch B 162/8867.
176. SS penal report on Leo Luria, BArch B 162/8867.
177. Efraim Roseboom, NIOD 250d/805; Nathan P., HVT-2848, FVA; Salomon Lierens, NIOD 250d/673; Paul Hertz, NIOD 250d/576; and SS penal report on Willem Vos, BArch B 162/8867.
178. Private Papers: George Didcock, IWM 10/6/1. The British Red Cross was also aware of the excessive barter in POW camps. *Clarion*, May 5, 1943, 8.
179. Prochownik, *Mémoires*, 109.
180. "Cookery Nook by Cheffie," *Clarion*, May 5, 1943, 11.

181. Efraim Roseboom, NIOD 250d/805.
182. Wolf W., HVT-2989, FVA.
183. Fainzang, *Mémoire*, 99.
184. Koenig, *Vorhof*, 122; and Rosengarten, *Overleven*, 141.
185. Simon Blein, NIOD 250d/433; and Louis Waterman, NIOD 250d/922.
186. Louis Schuitevoerder, NIOD 250d/835; Gabriel Zvi Lifschitz, NIOD 250d/674; Clary, *Holocaust*, 89; and Paul Hertz, NIOD 250d/576.
187. Salomon Lierens, NIOD 250d/673; and Koenig, *Vorhof*, 117.
188. Rosengarten, *Overleven*, 125; and Prochownik, *Mémoires*, 110.
189. Fainzang, *Mémoire*, 68, 89.
190. SS penal reports, BArch B 162/8867; and Jacob de Wolf, NIOD 250d/946.
191. Prochownik, *Mémoires*, 112; B. Swaaf, NIOD 250d/88; Hans Bonn, NIOD 250d/445; Jacob de Boers, NIOD 250d/441; Fainzang, *Mémoire*, 99; and Rosengarten, *Overleven*, 181.
192. OHW circular, July 15, 1944, BArch R 9348/117; and Prochownik, *Mémoires*, 115–20.
193. Prochownik, *Mémoires*, 108.
194. Rosengarten, *Overleven*, 157–61.
195. SS penal report on Israel Wächter, BArch B 162/8867; and Prochownik, *Mémoires*, 113–14.
196. Koenig, *Vorhof*, 122.
197. Felix G., HVT-3458, FVA.
198. Wollenberg, *Alptraum*, 116.
199. Clary, *Holocaust*, 85; Abraham Jonas Walg, NIOD 250d/920; and Wollenberg, *Alptraum*, 116.
200. Maurits Bremer, NIOD 250d/448; and Louis Waterman, NIOD 250d/922.
201. Rosengarten, *Overleven*, 181.
202. Koenig, *Vorhof*, 119; Maurice Moshe Szmidt, YVA O.3. 3474; Rosengarten, *Overleven*, 122; and Jacob de Boers, NIOD 250d/441.
203. Simon Blein, NIOD 250d/433; Joseph Braasem, NIOD 250d/446; Hans Bonn, NIOD 250d/445; and Paul Hertz, NIOD 250d/576.
204. Maurits Bremer, NIOD 250d/448.
205. Louis Waterman, NIOD 250d/922; and Arthur Salomons, NIOD 250d/815.
206. Simon Blein, NIOD 250d/433.
207. BArch R 9348/117.
208. Jacob de Boers, NIOD 250d/441; and SS penal reports on Efroim Zonszajn and Hersz Posmantir, BArch B 162/8867.
209. Stanley B., HVT-401, FVA.
210. Wolf W., HVT-2989, FVA.
211. Koenig, *Vorhof*, 115–16.
212. Henry F., HVT-1332, FVA; and SS penal reports on Efroim Zonszajn and Hersz Posmantir, BArch B 162/8867.

213. Wolf W., HVT-2989, FVA; Maurits Bremer, NIOD 250d/448; and SS penal report on Mathias Jarzombek, BArch B 162/8867.
214. Alix H., HVT-210, FVA; Lifschitz, NIOD 250d/674; Spitzer, *Dessin*, 81; and Abraham Schaufeld, IWM Sound Archive, 17470.
215. Leo Weiniger, NIOD 244/1486.
216. Jozef Niewes, NIOD 250d/716.
217. Gabriel Zvi Lifschitz, NIOD 250d/674.
218. Efraim Roseboom, NIOD 250d/805; Simon Blein, NIOD 250d/433; and Mendel Meyer, NIOD 250d/695.
219. SS penal report on Kasimierski, BArch B162/8867.
220. Leo Weiniger, NIOD 244/1486; and Efraim Roseboom, NIOD 250d/805.
221. Efraim Roseboom, NIOD 250d/805; Clary, *Holocaust*, 91; Spira, *Legende*, 144; Hartog Salomon Ereira, NIOD 250d/519; Salomon Lierens, NIOD 250d/673; and Maurice Moshe Szmidt, YVA O.3 3474.
222. Voss, *Fluitje*, 54.
223. Milton, "Legacy," 34–43.
224. Blatter, "Art," 20–35.
225. Wilhelm Spira, IWM ART 17120–17129.
226. Blatter, "Art," 35.
227. Sujo, *Legacies*, 79.
228. Szymanska, "Kunst," 73–97, 85.
229. Wendland, *Lager*, 35; and garrison order 24/43, printed in Frei et al., *Standort- und Kommandanturbefehle*, 303.
230. Wendland, *Lager*, 50–52; and Spira, *Legende*, 158–59.
231. Walter Spitzer, 1986, http://www.buchenwald.de/index.php?pageid=21&articleid=7, (September 6, 2010).
232. Gilbert, *Music*, 4–7; and Ida Frydman, interview 35134, VHA. See also Davidowicz, "Holocaust," 25.
233. Freudenheim, "Art," 35; and Amishai-Maisels, "Complexities," 25.
234. Spitzer, *Dessin*, 90, 133.
235. Salomon Lierens, NIOD 250d/673; and Hartog Salomon Ereira, NIOD 250d/519.
236. Spitzer, *Dessin*, 87.
237. Winkler-Bessone, *Bil Spira*, 10–14.
238. Fry, *Surrender*, 44–45; and Spira, *Legende*, 105–10.
239. Spira, *Legende*, 138–43.
240. See Blatter, "Art," 35.
241. See Koenig, *Vorhof*, 119.
242. Interview with Charles Hayward, June 22, 2010.
243. Spira, *Legende*, 158.

244. IWM ART 17120–17130. *Unspeakable: The Artist as Witness to the Holocaust* (exhibition, IWM London, 2009). The cartoons can be viewed online on the museum's website (https://www.iwm.org.uk).
245. The Jewish Museum of Vienna showed the cartoons in the exhibition *Die Drei mit dem Stift. Lily Renée, Bil Spira und Peter Paul Porges* in 2019.
246. Spitzer, *Dessin*, 76–133.
247. Most of Spitzer's postwar works are held by the Ghetto Fighters' House Museum (GFH).
248. Davidowicz, "Holocaust," 27.
249. http://www1.yadvashem.org/yv/en/remembrance/2010/zim.asp (September 21, 2010); and Amishai-Maisels, "Complexities," 25.
250. Fischer, *Jakob Zim*, 193.
251. Billeter and Fischer, *Michel Sima*, 16–22, 199–203.
252. Spitzer, *Dessin*, 87.
253. Printed in Billeter and Fischer, *Michel Sima*, 18.
254. The War-Time Experiences of Otto Deutsch, ŽMP online collection.
255. Davidowicz, "Holocaust," 27.

CONCLUSION

1. Heinz Ebers, February 19, 1946, NA WO 309/978.
2. Stanisław Rogulski, interview 224, PIZ.
3. Contract between the SS WVHA and Ost Maschinenbau GmbH Sosnowiec, April 26, 1944, printed in Piper, *Arbeitseinsatz*, annex 22; and affidavits by Friedrich Pook, Karl Kulicke, NA WO 309/978.
4. Piper, *Arbeitseinsatz*, 291.
5. Silberklang, *Gates*, 434; and Pohl, "Holocaust," 163.
6. Jacques G., HVT-2845, FVA.

UNPUBLISHED SOURCES

Archives

Archiv für Zeitgeschichte, ETH Zurich (AfZ)
 Kalman Landau, *3 Heftlinge ferurteilt zum Galgen*, drawing, 1945, S Biographien und Sachthemen/78
Archives du Comitée International de la Croix Rouge Geneva (ACICR)
 Report of an ICRC (International Committee of the Red Cross) inspection of E 3 Blechhammer, December 13, 1941, ACICR, CSC Allemagne, Wk. VIII, DT
Archives Nationales, Paris Pierrefitte-sur-Seine (AN)
 F/9/5565 Blechhammer: témoignages, documentation
 F/9/5583–5588 témoignages de déportés au retour des camps
 736 MI 1-3 dossier AU-16/2 Blechhammer Kommandos: rapports, témoignages, listes du déportés
Archiwum Państwowe Muzeum Auschwitz-Birkenau w Oświęcimu (APMO)
 D-AU I-2/1-I-2/5423 Häftlingspersonalbögen
 D-AU I, II, III Strafmeldungen
 KL-AU III, vol. 11: Arbeitseinsatz Blechhammer
 Oświedcienia, f. 48
 Hoess Trial, vol. 21
 Michał Kula, Pr. H., vol. 2, fo. 97
Archiwum Państwowe w Katowicach (APK)
 12/119 Regierung Kattowitz
 12/807 Polizeipräsident Sosnowitz
 12/1600 Ältestenrat Dabrowa
 12/771 Landrat Bendsburg
Archiwum Państwowe w Opolu (APO)
 1191 Rejencja Opolska (1816–1945)
 I-64 Landratsamt Cosel (1803–1944)
 586 II-120 Oberschlesische Hydrierwerke AG Blechhammer (1935–1944)
Archiwum Państwowe w Wrocławiu Oddział Kamieniec-Ząbkowicki (APWr)
 11620 Biuro Informacyjne W. Schimmelpfeng: Broemel & Sohn

Bayer AG: Corporate History & Archives Leverkusen (BAL)
   019-387 Verträge Ludwigshafen
   330-0905 Vorbereitung I.G.-Prozess
   1638

Beit Lohamei HaGhettaot/Ghetto Fighters' House Museum (GFH)
   12032 R M-Hol, no. 416 Isaac Cohensius

Bundesarchiv (BArch)
   R 9348 Oberschlesische Hydrierwerke AG Blechhammer
   R 9361/III-98175 Personalfragebogen Kurt Klipp
   R 9361/III-144120 Personalfragebogen Hans Stefan Olejak
   R 2/15464 Oberschlesische Hydrierwerke AG Blechhammer
   R2/15464a Oberschlesische Hydrierwerke AG Blechhammer (Vorstandsberichte)
   R2/17835 Oberschlesische Hydrierwerke AG Blechhammer (Handakten Nasse)
   R 3901/20244 Reichsarbeitsministerium
   R 50-I Organisation Todt
   R 58/797 Reichssicherheitshauptamt
   R 4601/4602 Reichsautobahnbehörde
   RD 19/3 Allgemeine Erlass-Sammlung des Chefs der Sicherheitspolizei und des SD
   DN 5/3071 OHW Abwicklung Weißenfels
   RH 53-8/18 Wehrkreiskommando VIII Breslau
   RW 20-8 Rüstungsinspektion VIII Breslau
   NS 3/386
   B 162/
      18172 Mordverbrechen in Blechhammer
      18173 Mord auf Evakuierungsmarsch
      18175 Karl Demerer
      20513 Verfahren gegen Heinrich Lindner
      8863–8869 Zeugenaussagen Blechhammer
      4100–4103 Verfahren gegen das Reserve-Polizeibataillon 105

Bundesarchiv/Lastenausgleichsarchiv Bayreuth (LAA)
   Ost-Dok. 1 Gemeindeschicksalsberichte: Kriegsende in Blechhammer und Heydebreck

Deportáltakat Gondozó Országos Bizottság (DEGOB)
   Online Database of Testimonies

Dokumentationsarchiv des Bundes jüdischer Verfolgter des Naziregimes/Simon Wiesenthal Archiv (SWA)
   Korrespondenz mit Erwin Lagus, 1965
   Otto Brossmann

Auschwitz I: Mitteilungsblatt der Österreichischen Lagergemeinschaft, Mai 1962

Dokumentationsarchiv Österreichischer Widerstand (DOEW)

20100 Karteikarten des KZ-Verbands (Organisationskomitee der wegen ihrer Abstammung Verfolgten)

Hessisches Hauptstaatsarchiv Wiesbaden (HHStAW)

Abt. 461 No. 37638: 1. Frankfurter Auschwitzprozess

Bd. 49 Vernehmungsniederschrift Paul Heurich

Bd. 151 Vollstreckungsheft Herbert Scherpe

Hoechst-Archiv Frankfurt/Main (HA)

PA Dr. Dr. Heinrich Schlick (HO 243827)

Imperial War Museum London (IWM)

ART 17120–17129 Wilhelm "Bil" Spira

Sound Archive: 9425/16614/17470/17435/18360

Private Papers: George Didcock, 10/6/1; Edward Charles Stirling, 824699/22/1

Institut für Zeitgeschichte München (IfZ)

NI-11784   NI-11117
NI-11120   NI-11112
NI-11125   NI-11113

ZS 1750 Zeugenaussage Lager Blechhammer

Ga 05.02/1–3 Anklageschrift über die Tötung von Häftlingen

F 13-7-8 Aufzeichnungen Rudolf Höss

Instytut Pamięcki Narodowej (IPN)

GK 164/2282

GK 164/2127

GK 184/262

GK 294/48

Kr-11-1-261-1-1 Otto Brossmann

International Tracing Service (ITS) (accessed via WL and USHMM)

1837000 Doc. IDs 52017901, 52018001, 52018101, International Red Cross Geneva, Auschwitz Records, Maquisards in Blechhammer

Landesarchiv Baden-Württemberg/Staatsarchiv Ludwigsburg (StA Lu)

EL 902/22 Bü 1423 Max Josenhans

Landesarchiv Münster (LHA)

Verfahren gegen Schmelt (205 AR-Z 78/60) nos. 4861, 4866, 4877–4883

National Archives and Records Administration, College Park, MD (NARA)

RG-065 105 11219 Max Josenhans

RG-18 Box 2624 Bomb Group Mission Reports

National Archives Kew (NA)

WO 309/978/1843 War Crimes Group

WO 311/187/268/1014/1138 Military Deputy, Judge Advocate General's War Crimes Files
TS 26/356/642 War Crimes at Blechhammer
AIR 40/1938 Synthetic Oil Plant Blechhammer
AIR 51/221/222 Mediterranean Allied Air Forces

Nederlands Instituut voor Oorlogs-, holocaust- en genocide studies (NIOD)
244 Europese dagboeken en egodocumenten
250d Kampen en gevangenissen
250k Concentratiekampen buiten Nederland

Österreichisches Staatsarchiv (OeSta)
Materie 2611-2625/8 Karton 180 Reichsautobahnen

Polish Research Institute Archive Lund (PIŹ)
Survivor Testimonies Collection

Schering-Archiv Berlin (SchA)
B5 345 Dr. Alfred Pott: "Neuordnung und Aufbau im oberschlesischen Raum"
B2 704

Staatsarchiv München (StA M)
SpkA K 739 Erich Hoffmann

Staatsarchiv Nürnberg (StA N)
NI-9108
NI-14189
NI-14190

Staatsarchiv Oldenburg (StA Ol)
Rep. 980, Best. 351, no. 25571 Denazification trial of Hans Mertens

Staatsarchiv Würzburg (StA Wü)
2012-009 Ermittlungsakten, 33-37: Tötungsdelikte im Zwangsarbeitslager Blechhammer

Státní okresní archiv Trutnov (SOkA)
"Krankenrevier," Archive of Factory Alois Haase, box 5, nos. 112–15

United States Holocaust Memorial Museum, Washington, DC (USHMM)
Testimonies
RG-50.120
2005.384
2006.248
1992.A0016/RG-10.48*01 Leo Young Papers

The Wiener Library for the Study of the Holocaust & Genocide, London (WL)
Eyewitness Accounts
055-EA-1032, 1026
053-EA-0906, 0919

Yad Vashem Archives, Jerusalam (YVA)
    O.3 and O.33 Testimonies Collection
    M. Trial Document Collection
    TR Document Collection

Židowski Muzeum v Praze (ŽMP)
    Oto Hostovsky, Vzpomniky na K.L.: Terezín, Osvětim, Blechhammer, inv.č. 80, puvodní stroj.něm., 53 fol.
    The War-Time Experiences of Otto Deutsch, online collection

Digital Oral History Archives

Australians at War Film Archive, Canberra (AWFA)
Fortunoff Video Archive for Holocaust Testimonies at Yale University (FVA)
Visual History Archive, USC Shoah Foundation, 2011, VHA online, accessed 2016–2018 via the University of Vienna (VHA)
Voice/Vision Holocaust Survivor Oral History Archive, University of Michigan/Dearborn (VVA)

Author's Interview

Interview with Charles Hayward, London, June 22, 2010

BIBLIOGRAPHY

Adam, Alfons. *"Die Arbeiterfrage soll mit Hilfe von Häftlingen gelöst werden": Zwangsarbeit in KZ-Außenlagern auf dem Gebiet der heutigen Tschechischen Republik.* Berlin: Metropol, 2013.

Adler, H. G. *Theresienstadt: Das Antlitz einer Zwangsgemeinschaft.* Göttingen: Wallstein, 2005. First published 1960.

Amishai-Maisels, Ziva. "The Complexities of Witnessing." In *After Auschwitz—Responses to the Holocaust in Contemporary Art*, edited by Monica Bohm-Duchen, 25–49. Sunderland: Lund Humphries, Northern Centre for Contemporary Art, 1995.

Arnaud, Patrice. *Les STO: Histoire des Français requis en Allemagne nazie, 1942–1945.* Paris: CNRS Édition, 2010.

Bacon, Ewa K. *Saving Lives in Auschwitz: The Prisoners' Hospital in Buna-Monowitz.* West Lafayette, IN: Purdue University Press, 2017.

Bajohr, Frank. *Parvenüs und Profiteure: Korruption in der NS-Zeit.* Frankfurt/Main: S. Fischer, 2001.

Bankier, David. *The Germans and the Final Solution: Public Opinion under Nazism.* Oxford: Blackwell Publishers, 1992.

Bartuschka, Marc. *"Unter Zurückstellung aller möglichen Bedenken . . .": Die NS-Betriebsgruppe "Reichsmarschall Hermann Göring" (REIMAHG) und der Zwangsarbeitereinsatz 1944/1945.* Göttingen: Wallstein, 2011.

Bauer, Yehuda. "The Death Marches, January–May 1945." In *The Nazi Holocaust*, edited by Michael R. Marrus, 9:491–514. Westport, CT: Meckler, 1989.

Bauer, Yehuda. *Rethinking the Holocaust.* New Haven, CT: Yale University Press, 2001.

Bender, Sara. *The Jews of Białystok during World War II and the Holocaust.* Waltham, MA: Brandeis University Press, 2008.

Beorn, Waitman Wade. *Marching into Darkness: The Wehrmacht and the Holocaust in Belarus.* Cambridge, MA: Harvard University Press, 2014.

Bergen, Doris L. "The Nazi Concept of *Volksdeutsche* and the Exacerbation of Anti-Semitism in Eastern Europe, 1939–1945." In *Journal of Contemporary History* 29, no. 4 (October 1994): 569–82.

Bergen, Evans. *The National History of Nonsense.* New York: Vintage Books, 1958.

Berger, Ronald J. *Surviving the Holocaust: A Life Course Perspective.* New York: Routledge, 2011.

Bergh, van den, Siegfried. *Der Kronprinz von Mandelstein.* Frankfurt/Main: Fischer Taschenbuch, 1996.

Bettelheim, Bruno. "Trauma and Reintegration." In *Surviving and Other Essays*, edited by Bruno

Bettelheim, 19–37. New York: A. Knopf, 1979.

Billeter, Erika, and Kuno Fischer, eds. *Michel Sima: Künstler im Atelier*. Berne: Benteli-Verlag, 2008.

Birkenfeld, Wolfgang. *Der synthetische Treibstoff 1933–1945*. Göttingen: Musterschmidt, 1964.

Birn, Ruth Bettina. *Die Höheren SS und Polizeiführer: Himmlers Vertreter im Reich und in den besetzten Gebieten*. Düsseldorf: Droste, 1986.

Black, Peter, and Martin Gutman. "Racial Theory and Realities of Conquest in the Occupied East: The Nazi Leadership and Non-German Nationals in the SS and Police." In *The Waffen-SS: A European History*, edited by Jochen Böhler and Robert Gerwarth, 16–41. London: Oxford University Press, 2017.

Blanc, Paul David. *Fake Silk. The Lethal History of Viscose Rayon*. New Haven, CT and London: Yale University Press, 2016.

Blank, Hartmut, Eva Walther, and Simon D. Isemann. "The Past Is a Social Construction." In *False and Distorted Memories*, edited by Robert E. Nash and James Ost, 55–72. London: Routledge, 2017.

Blatman, Daniel. *The Death Marches: The Final Phase of Nazi Genocide*. Cambridge, MA: The Belknap Press of Harvard University Press, 2011.

Blatman, Daniel. *Die Todesmärsche 1944/45: Das letzte Kapitel des nationalsozialistischen Massenmords*. Hamburg: Rowohlt Verlag, 2011.

Blatter, Janet. "Art from the Whirlwind." In *Art of the Holocaust*, edited by Janet Blatter and Sybil Milton, 20–35. London: Pan Books, 1982.

Bloxham, Donald. "Jewish Slave Labor and Its Relationship to the 'Final Solution.'" In *"Remembering for the Future": The Holocaust in an Age of Genocide*, edited by John K. Roth and Elisabeth Maxwell, 163–86. New York: Palgrave, 2001.

Boom, van der, Bart. "'The Auschwitz Reservation': Dutch Victims and Bystanders and Their Knowledge of the Holocaust." In *Holocaust & Genocide Studies* 31, no. 3 (Winter 2017): 385–407.

Borrie, John. *Despite Captivity. A Doctor's Life as Prisoner of War*. London: William Kimber, 1975.

Bowman, Steven B. *The Agony of Greek Jews, 1940–1945*. Stanford, CA: Stanford University Press, 2009.

Bravo, Anna, Lilia Davite, and Daniele Jalla. "Myth, Impotence and Survival in the Concentration Camps." In *The Myths We Live By*, edited by Raphael Samuel and Paul Thompson, 95–110. London: Routledge, 1990.

Breitman, Richard. *Official Secrets: What the Nazis Planned, What the British and Americans Knew*. New York: Hill and Wang, 1998.

Brown, Adam. *Judging "Privileged" Jews: Holocaust Ethics, Representation and the "Grey Zone"*. New York: Berghahn Books, 2013.

Browning, Christopher. "The Holocaust: Basis and Objective of the *Volksgemeinschaft*?" In *Visions of Community in Nazi Germany: Social Engineering and Private Lives*, edited by Martina Stebel and Berhard Gotto, 217–25. Oxford: Oxford University Press, 2014.

Browning, Christopher. *Ordinary Men. Reserve Police Battalion 101 and the Final Solution in Poland*. New York: HarperCollins, 1992.
Browning, Christopher. *Remembering Survival: Inside a Nazi Slave-Labor Camp*. London: W. W. Norton, 2010.
Buggeln, Marc. *Arbeit und Gewalt: Das Außenlagersystem des Konzentrationslagers Neuengamme*. Göttingen: Wallstein, 2009.
Buggeln, Marc. *Slave Labor in Nazi Concentration Camps*. Oxford: Oxford University Press, 2014.
Buggeln, Marc. "Unfreie Arbeit im Nationalsozialismus: Begrifflichkeiten und Vergleichsaspekte zu den Arbeitsbedingungen im Deutschen Reich und in den besetzten Gebieten." In *Arbeit im Nationalsozialismus*, edited by Marc Buggeln and Michael Wildt, 231–52. Munich: De Gruyter Oldenbourg, 2014.
Buser, Verena. "Karl Demerer—przywólca elity obozowej w Blechhammer." In *Elity i przedstawiciele społeczności Żydowskiej podczas II wojny światowej*, edited by Martyn Grądzki-Rejak and Aleksandra Namysło, 465–78. Cracow: IPN, 2017.
Buser, Verena. *Überleben von Kindern und Jugendlichen in den Konzentrationslagern Sachsenhausen, Auschwitz und Bergen-Belsen*. Berlin: Metropol, 2001.
Carr, William. *Arms, Autarky and Aggression: A Study in German Foreign Policy, 1933–1939*. London: Edward Arnold, 1983. Reprinted with corrections.
Castle, John. *The Password Is Courage*. London: W. W. Norton, 1954.
Celincsak, Marc. *Distance from the Belsen Heap: Allied Forces and the Liberation of a Nazi Concentration Camp*. Toronto: University of Toronto Press, 2015.
Chatwood, Kirsty. "(Re-) Interpreting Stories of Sexual Violence: The Multiple Testimonies of Lucille Eichengreen." In *Life, Death, and Sacrifice: Women and Family in the Holocaust*, edited by Esther Hertzog, 161–80. Jerusalem: Gefen, 2008.
The Clarion. Lamsdorf POW magazine. January 1943–45.
Clary, Robert. *From the Holocaust to Hogan's Heroes*. Lanham, MD: Madison Books, 2001.
Courtois, Stephane, and Adam Rayski. *Qui savait quoi? L'extermination des Juifs, 1941–1945*. Paris: La Découverte, 1987.
Curilla, Wolfgang. *Der Judenmord in Polen und die deutsche Ordnungspolizei, 1939–1945*. Paderborn: Schöningh, 2011.
Curilla, Wolfgang. *Die deutsche Ordnungspolizei im westlichen Europa, 1940–1945*. Paderborn: Schöningh, 2020.
Czech, Danuta. "Deportation und Vernichtung der griechischen Juden." In *Hefte von Auschwitz* 11 (1970): 5–37.
Czech, Danuta. "Die Rolle des Häftlingskrankenbaulagers im KL Auschwitz II." *Hefte von Auschwitz* 15 (1975): 5–112.
Czech, Danuta. *Kalendarium der Ereignisse im Konzentrationslager Auschwitz-Birkenau 1939–1945*. Reinbeck: Rohwolt Verlag, 1989.
Czech, Herwig. "Nazi Medical Crimes, Eugenics, and the Limits of the Racial State Paradigm."

In *Beyond the Racial State: Rethinking Nazi Germany*, edited by Devin O. Pendas, Mark Roseman, and Richard F. Wetzell, 213–38. Cambridge: Cambridge University Press, 2017.

Daniel, Curt. "'The Freest Theatre in the Reich': In the German Concentration Camps." In *Theatrical Performance during the Holocaust*, edited by Rebecca Rovit and Alvin Goldfarb, 150–56. Baltimore, MD: Johns Hopkins University Press, 1999.

Davidowicz, Lucy S. "The Holocaust Landscape." In *Spiritual Resistance: Art from Concentration Camps, 1940–1945*, edited by Miriam Novitch, Lucy S. Davidowicz, and Tom L. Freudenheim, 23–32. Philadelphia: Jewish Publication Society of America, 1981.

Dean, Martin. *Collaboration in the Holocaust: Crimes of the Local Police in Belorussia and the Ukraine, 1941–1944*. New York: St. Martin's Press, 2000.

Demerer, Heinrich. *Als Kind in NS-Konzentrationslagern: Aufzeichnungen*. Edited by Verena Walter. Berlin: Metropol, 2009.

Des Pres, Terrence. *The Survivor: An Anatomy of Life in the Death Camps*. Oxford: Oxford University Press, 1976.

Dirks, Christian. "Karrieresprung Vernichtungslager: Dr. Horst Fischer in Auschwitz." In *NS-Täter aus interdisziplinärer Perspektive*, edited by Helgard Kramer, 143–70. Munich: Martin Meidenbauer, 2006.

Długoborski, Wacław, and Franciszek Piper. *Auschwitz 1940–1945: Studien zur Geschichte des Konzentrations- und Vernichtungslagers Auschwitz*. Vol. 1. Oświęcim: State Museum Auschwitz-Birkenau Press, 1999.

Dobosiewicz, Stanisław. *Vernichtungslager Gusen*. Vienna: BMI, 2007.

Drobisch, Klaus. "Der Werkschutz—betriebliches Terrororgan im faschistischen Deutschland." *Jahrbuch für Wirtschaftsgeschichte* 4 (1965): 217–47.

Drobisch, Klaus. "Dokumente zur direkten Zusammenarbeit zwischen Flick-Konzern und Gestapo bei der Unterdrückung der Arbeiter." In *Jahrbuch für Wirtschaftsgeschichte* 3 (1963): 212–25.

Durand, Yves. *La Captivité. Histoire des prisonniers de guerre français, 1939–1945*. Forges-les-Eaux: A.G.M., 1980.

Eisenbach, Artur. *Hitlerowska Polityka Zagłady Żydów*. Warsaw: Książka i Wiedza, 1961.

Ende, van den, Hannah. *Vergeet niet dat je arts bent: Joodse artsen in Nederland, 1940–1945*. Amsterdam: Boom, 2015.

Fackler, Guido. *"Des Lagers Stimme"—Musik im KZ: Alltag und Häftlingskultur in den Konzentrationslagern 1933–1936, Darstellung der weiteren Entwicklung bis 1945*. Bremen: Edition Temmen, 2000.

Fackler, Guido. "Music in Concentration Camps 1933–1945." *Music & Politics* 1, no. 1 (Winter 2007): 1–25.

Fainer, Ben, and Mark W. Leach. *Silent for Sixty Years: Ben Fainer—Holocaust Survivor*. Charleston, SC: B. Fainer, 2013.

Fainzang, Jules. *Mémoire de Déportation*. Paris: L'Harmattan, 2002.

Ferencz, Benjamin. *Less Than Slaves: Jewish Forced Labor and the Quest for Compensation.* Cambridge, MA: Harvard University Press, 1997.

Fischer, Yona, ed. *Jakob Zim.* Tel Aviv: Yedioth Ahronoth, 2003.

Flusser, Jindřich. "Ein Rückblick." *Terezín Studies and Documents (Theresienstädter Studien und Dokumente)* 6 (1999): 43–75.

Frankl, Viktor E. *Ärztliche Seelsorge.* 5th ed. Vienna: Deuticke, 1948.

Frankl, Viktor E. *Man's Search for Meaning: An Introduction to Logotherapy.* 2nd ed. New York: Washington Square Press, 1963.

Fransecky, Tanja von. *Flucht von Juden aus Deportationszügen in Frankreich, Belgien und den Niederlanden.* Berlin: Metropol, 2014.

Frei, Norbert, Thomas Grotum, Jan Parcer, Sybille Steinbacher, and Bernd C. Wagner, eds. *Standort- und Kommandanturbefehle des Konzentrationslagers Auschwitz 1940–1945.* Munich: K.G. Saur, 2000.

Freudenheim, Tom L. "Art from Concentration Camps." In *Spiritual Resistance: Art from Concentration Camps, 1940–1945,* edited by Miriam Novitch, Lucy S. Davidowicz, and Tom L. Freudenheim, 33–38. Philadelphia: Jewish Publication Society of America, 1981.

Friedlander, Henry. *The Origins of the Nazi Genocide: From Euthanasia to the Final Solution.* Chapel Hill: University of North Carolina Press, 1995.

Friedlander, Saul. *Memory, History and the Extermination of the Jews of Europe.* Bloomington: Indiana University Press, 1993.

Friedlander, Saul. *The Years of Extermination: Nazi Germany and the Jews.* New York: HarperCollins, 2007.

Friedman, Philip. "The Messianic Complex of a Nazi Collaborator in a Ghetto: Moses Merin of Sosnowiec." In *Roads to Extinction, Essays on the Holocaust,* edited by Ada June Friedman, 353–64. New York: The Jewish Publication Society, 1980.

Fry, Varian. *Surrender on Demand.* New York: Random House, 1945.

Fulbrook, Mary. *Reckonings: Legacies of Nazi Persecution and the Quest for Justice.* New York: Oxford University Press, 2018.

Fulbrook, Mary. *A Small Town Near Auschwitz: Ordinary Nazis and the Holocaust.* Oxford: Oxford University Press, 2012.

Garbe, Detlev. "Die Konzentrationslager als Stätten des Massenmordes: Zur Geschichte der anderen Tötungsverfahren und der notwendigen Einordnung des Gasmordes." In *Neue Studien zu nationalsozialistischen Massentötungen durch Giftgas: Historische Bedeutung, technische Entwicklung, revisionistische Leugnung,* edited by Günther Morsch and Bertrand Perz, 316–34. Berlin: Metropol, 2011.

Gelber, Yoav. "Palestinian POWs in German Captivity." *Yad Vashem Studies* 14 (1981): 89–137.

Gerlach, Christian. *The Extermination of the European Jews.* Cambridge: Cambridge University Press, 2016.

Gilbert, Shirli. *Music in the Holocaust: Confronting Life in the Nazi Ghettos and Camps.* Oxford:

Clarendon Press, 2005.

Golczewski, Frank. "Organe der deutschen Besatzungsmacht: Die ukrainischen Schutzmannschaften." In *Die Bürokratie der Okkupation: Strukturen der Herrschaft und Verwaltung im besetzten Europa*, edited by Wolfgang Benz, Johannes Houwink ten Cate, and Gerhard Otto, 173–96. Berlin: Metropol, 1998.

Goldfarb, Alvin. "Theatrical Activities in Nazi Concentration Camps." *Performing Arts Journal* 1, no. 2 (Fall 1976): 3–11.

Grabowski, Jan. "Jewish Criminality and Jewish Criminals in the Warsaw Ghetto." In *Lebenswelt Ghetto: Alltag und soziales Umfeld während der nationalsozialistischen Verfolgung*, edited by Imke Jansen, Katrin Steffen, and Joachim Tauber, 117–30. Wiesbaden: Harrassowitz, 2013.

Greenberg, Gershon. "Ultra-Orthodox Responses During and Following the War." In *Wrestling with God: Jewish Theological Responses During and After the Holocaust*, edited by Steven T. Katz, Shlomo Biderman, and Gershon Greenberg, 11–26. Oxford: Oxford University Press, 2007.

Greenspan, Henry. "Listening to Holocaust Survivors: Interpreting a Repeated Story." *Shofar: An Interdisciplinary Journal of Jewish Studies* 17, no. 4 (Summer 1999): 83–88.

Greenspan, Henry. *On Listening to Holocaust Survivors: Recounting and Life History*. Westport, CT: Praeger, 1998.

Greiser, Katrin. *Die Todesmärsche von Buchenwald: Räumung, Befreiung und Spuren der Erinnerung*. Göttingen: Wallstein, 2008.

Griffioen, Pim, and Ron Zeller. "Anti-Jewish Policy and Organization of the Deportations in France and the Netherlands, 1940–1944: A Comparative Study." *Holocaust and Genocide Studies* 20, no. 3 (December 2006): 437–73.

Griffioen, Pim, and Ron Zeller. *Jodenvervolging in Nederland, Frankrijk en België, 1940–1945: Overeenkomsten, verschillen, oorzaken*. Amsterdam: Boom, 2011.

Grinband, Simon. *XIe Commandement: "Tu n'oublieras point."* Paris: La Pensée Universelle, 1986.

Grode, Walter. *Die "Sonderbehandlung 14f13" in den Konzentrationslagern des Dritten Reichs: Ein Beitrag zur Dynamik faschistischer Vernichtungspolitik*. Frankfurt/Main: Peter Lang, 1987.

Gross, Jan T. *Polish Society under German Occupation: The General Government 1939–1944*. Princeton, NJ: Princeton University Press, 1979.

Gruner, Wolf. *Jewish Forced Labor under the Nazis: Economic Needs and Racial Aims 1938–1944*. New York: Cambridge University Press, 2006.

Grużlewska, Anna. *Annaberg: Obóz Pracy Na Górze Świętej Anny*. Opole: Muzeum Śląska Opolskiego, 2017.

Guetzkow, Harold Steere, and Paul Hoover Bowman. *Men and Hunger: A Psychological Manual for Relief Workers*. Elgin, IL: Brethren Publishing House, 1946.

Gutman, Israel, ed. *Encyclopedia of the Holocaust*. Vol. I. New York: Macmillan, 1990.

Gutman, Israel, ed. *Encyclopedia of the Righteous among the Nations: Rescuers of Jews during the Holocaust, Poland*. Jerusalem: Yad Vashem, 2004.

Gutman, Israel, ed. *Encyclopedia of the Righteous among the Nations: Rescuers of Jews during the Holocaust*. Vol. 1, *2000–2005*. Jerusalem: Yad Vashem, 2010.

Gutman, Israel, ed. *Encyclopedia of the Righteous among the Nations: Rescuers of Jews during the Holocaust*. Supplementary vol. 2. Jerusalem: Yad Vashem, 2010.

Gutterman, Bella. "Jews in the Service of Organisation Todt in the Campaign to Occupy the Soviet Union (October 1941–March 1942)." *Yad Vashem Studies* 29 (2001): 53–83.

Gutterman, Bella. *A Narrow Bridge to Life: Jewish Forced Labor and Survival in the Gross-Rosen Camp System, 1940–1945*. New York: Berghahn Books, 2008.

Hackett, David A. *The Buchenwald Report*. Boulder, CO: Westview Press, 1995.

Hájková, Anna. "Sexual Barter in Times of Genocide: Negotiating the Sexual Economy of the Theresienstadt Ghetto." *Signs: Journal of Women in Culture and Society* 38, no. 3 (Spring 2013): 503–33.

Halbwachs, Maurice. *On Collective Memory*. Chicago: University of Chicago Press, 1992.

Halpin, Ross W. *Jewish Doctors and the Holocaust: The Anatomy of Survival in Auschwitz*. Berlin: Hebrew University Magnes Press Jerusalem, De Gruyter Oldenbourg, 2019.

Harten, Hans-Christian. *Die weltanschauliche Schulung der Polizei im Nationalsozialismus*. Paderborn: Schöningh, 2018.

Harten, Hans-Christian. *Himmlers Lehrer: Die Weltanschauliche Schulung in der SS, 1933–1945*. Paderborn: Ferdinand Schöningh, 2014.

Hayes, Peter. "The Ambiguities of Evil and Justice: Degussa, Robert Pross and the Jewish Slave Labourers at Gleiwitz." In *Gray Zones: Ambiguity and Compromise in the Holocaust and its Aftermath*, edited by Jonathan Petropoulos and John Roth, 7–25. New York: Berghahn Books, 2005.

Hayes, Peter. "Carl Bosch and Carl Krauch: Chemistry and the Political Economy of Germany, 1925–1945." *Journal of Economic History* 47, no. 2 (June 1987): 353–63.

Hayes, Peter. "Die IG Farben und die Zwangsarbeit von KZ-Häftlingen im Werk Auschwitz." In *Konzentrationslager und deutsche Wirtschaft, 1939–1945*, edited by Hermann Kaienburg, 129–48. Opladen: Leske und Budrich, 1996.

Hayes, Peter. *Industry and Ideology: IG Farben in the Nazi Era*. 2nd ed. Cambridge: Cambridge University Press, 2001.

Heberer, Patricia. "Von der 'Aktion T4' zum Massenmord an den europäischen Juden." In *Neue Studien zu nationalsozialistischen Massentötungen durch Giftgas: Historische Bedeutung, technische Entwicklung, revisionistische Leugnung*, edited by Günter Morsch and Bertrand Perz, 165–75. Berlin: Metropol, 2011.

Heinemann, Isabel. *"Rasse, Siedlung, deutsches Blut": Das Rasse- & Siedlungshauptamt der SS und die rassenpolitische Neuordnung Europas*. Göttingen: Wallstein, 2003.

Herbert, Ulrich. "Arbeit und Vernichtung: Ökonomisches Interesse und Primat der 'Weltanschauung' im Nationalsozialismus." In *Europa und der "Reichseinsatz": Ausländische Zivilarbeiter, Kriegsgefangene und KZ-Häftlinge in Deutschland 1938–1945*, edited by Ulrich Herbert,

384–426. Essen: Klartext Verlag, 1991.

Herbert, Ulrich. "Einleitung." In *Europa und der "Reichseinsatz": Ausländische Zivilarbeiter, Kriegsgefangene und KZ-Häftlinge in Deutschland 1938–1945*, edited by Ulrich Herbert, 7–25. Essen: Klartext Verlag, 1991.

Herbert, Ulrich. *Fremdarbeiter: Politik und Praxis des "Ausländer-Einsatzes" in der Kriegswirtschaft des Dritten Reiches*. Berlin: J. H. W. Dietz Nachf., 1985.

Heuel, Eberhard. *Der umworbene Stand: Die ideologische Integration der Arbeiter im Nationalsozialismus, 1933–1935*. Frankfurt/Main: Campus Verlag, 1989.

Heyen, Franz-Josef, ed. *Parole der Woche: Eine Wandzeitung im Dritten Reich, 1936–1943*. Munich: dtv, 1983.

Hilberg, Raul. *The Destruction of the European Jews*. New York: Harper Colophon Books, 1961.

Hinz-Wessels, Annette. "Jüdische Opfer der 'Aktion T4' im Spiegel der überlieferten 'Euthanasie'-Krankenakten im Bundesarchiv." In *Die nationalsozialistische Euthanasie "Aktion T4" und ihre Opfer. Geschichte und ethische Konsequenzen für die Gegenwart*, edited by Maike Rotzoll, Gernot Holendorf, Petra Fuchs, Paul Richter, Christoph Mundt, and Wolfgang U. Eckhart, 143–46. Paderborn: Schöningh, 2010.

Hoffmann, Georg. *Fliegerlynchjustiz: Gewalt gegen abgeschossene alliierte Flugzeugbesatzungen, 1943–1945*. Paderborn: Ferdinand Schöningh, 2015.

Holc, Janine P. *The Weavers of Trautenau: Jewish Female Forced Labor in the Holocaust*. Waltham, MA: Brandeis University Press, 2023.

Holroyd, R., ed., on behalf of Ministry of F. and P. and T.I.I.C. *Report on Investigations by Fuels and Lubricants Teams at the I.G. Farben Works at Leuna*. CIOS Target No. 30/402. Washington, DC: US Department of the Interior/Bureau of Mines, 1945.

Hördler, Stefan. *Ordnung und Inferno: Das KZ-System im letzten Kriegsjahr*. Göttingen: Wallstein, 2015.

Hunt, Linda. *Secret Agenda: The United States Government, Nazi Scientists and Project Paperclip, 1945–1990*. New York: St. Martin's Press, 1991.

Internationales Komitee vom Roten Kreuz (IKRK). *Die Tätigkeit des IKRK zugunsten der in den deutschen KZ-Lagern inhaftierten Zivilpersonen, 1939–1945*. Geneva: International Committee of the Red Cross, 1947.

Irmer, Thomas. "*Allemand cochon*—Widerständiges Verhalten von ausländischen Zwangsarbeiterinnen und Zwangsarbeitern am Beispiel AEG/Telefunken in Berlin." In *Der vergessene Widerstand der Arbeiter, Gewerkschaftler, Kommunisten, Sozialisten, Trotzkisten, Anarchisten und Zwangsarbeitern*, edited by Hans Coppi and Stefan Heinz, 248–63. Berlin: Karl-Dietz Verlag, 2012.

Jacobson, Annie. *Operation Paperclip: The Secret Intelligence Program That Brought Nazi Scientists to America*. New York: Little, Brown, 2014.

Jansen, Christian, and Arno Weckbecker. *Der volksdeutsche Selbstschutz in Polen, 1939–1940*. Munich: R. Oldenbourg, 1992.

Jarka, Horst. *Jura Soyfer: Leben, Werk, Zeit.* Vienna: Löcker-Verlag, 1987.

Jewish Historical Institute Warsaw, ed. *Faschismus-Getto-Massenmord: Dokumentation über Ausrottung und Widerstand der Juden in Polen während des Zweiten Weltkrieges.* East Berlin: Ruetten & Loening, 1962.

John, Eckhard. "Music and Concentration Camps: An Approximation." *Journal of Musicological Research* 20, no. 4 (2009): 269–323.

Joseph Ebner, Deanne. *Number 176520: The Story of Paul Argiewicz, a Teenage Holocaust Survivor.* Salem, WI: Blue Thread, 2008.

Kaczmarek, Ryszard. *Historia Polski, 1914–1989.* Warsaw: Wydawnictwo Naukowa, 2010.

Kaienburg, Hermann. *"Vernichtung durch Arbeit": Der Fall Neuengamme; Die Wirtschaftsbestebungen der SS und ihre Auswirkungen auf die Existenzbedingungen der KZ-Gefangenen.* Bonn: Verlag J. H. W. Dietz, 1990.

Kampe, Norbert, and Peter Klein. *Die Wannsee-Konferenz am 20. Januar 1942: Dokumente, Forschungsstand, Kontroversen.* Cologne: Böhlau, 2013.

Kárný, Miroslav. "Das Theresienstädter Familienlager in Birkenau." *Hefte von Auschwitz* 20 (1997): 133–237.

Katz, Steven T. *The Holocaust and New World Slavery: A Comparative History.* Vol. 1. New York: Cambridge University Press, 2019.

Katz, Steven T. *The Holocaust in Historical Context.* Vol. 1. New York: Oxford University Press, 1994.

Katz, Steven T. "Thoughts on the Intersection of Rape and Rassenschande during the Holocaust." *Modern Judaism* 32, no. 3 (October 2012): 293–313.

Kedward, H. R. *In Search of the Maquis: Rural Resistance in Southern France, 1942–1944.* Oxford: Clarendon Press, 2003.

Keller, Rolf. *Sowjetische Kriegsgefangene im Deutschen Reich, 1941–1942: Behandlung und Arbeitseinsatz zwischen Vernichtungspolitik und kriegswirtschaftlichen Zwängen.* Göttingen: Wallstein, 2011.

Keller, Sven. *Volksgemeinschaft am Ende: Gesellschaft und Gewalt 1944–45.* Munich: Oldenbourg, 2013.

Keller, Sven. "*Volksgemeinschaft* and Violence: Some Reflections on Interdependencies." In *Visions of Community in Nazi Germany: Social Engineering & Private Lives,* edited by Martina Steber and Bernhard Gotto, 226–39. Oxford: Oxford University Press, 2014.

Keren, Nili. "The Family Camp." In *Anatomy of the Auschwitz Death Camp,* edited by Yisrael Gutman and Michael Berenbaum, 428–40. Bloomington: Indiana University Press, 1994.

Kichka, Henri. *Une Adolescence Perdue dans la Nuit des Camps.* Waterloo: Renaissance du Livre, 2014.

Kilian, Andreas. *Buna-Werk Auschwitz: Die maßgeblichen Entscheidungsgründe der IG Farben für die Standortwahl Dwory-Monowitz.* Hamburg: Disserta Verlag, 2015.

Klarsfeld, Serge. *Mémorial de la Déportation des Juifs de France.* Paris: Klarsfeld, 1978.

Klarsfeld, Serge. *Vichy-Auschwitz: Die Zusammenarbeit der deutschen Behörden bei der "Endlösung der Judenfrage" in Frankreich*. Nördlingen: Greno, 1989.

Klarsfeld, Serge, and Steinberg, Maxime. *Mémorial de la Déportation des Juifs de Belgique*. Brussels: Union des déporté juifs en Belgique et filles et fils de la déportation, Beate Klarsfeld Foundation, 1982.

Klee, Ernst. *Auschwitz, die NS-Medizin und ihre Opfer*. Frankfurt/Main: S. Fischer, 1997.

Klee, Ernst, ed. *Dokumente zur "Euthansie"*. Frankfurt/Main: Fischer Taschenbuch, 1986.

Klee, Ernst. "Von der 'T4' zur Judenvernichtung: Die 'Aktion Reinhardt' in den Vernichtungslagern Belzec, Sobibor und Treblinka." In *Die "Euthanasie-Zentrale" in der Tiergartenstraße 4*, edited by Götz Aly, 136–46. Berlin: Edition Hentrich, 1989.

Klein, Peter. *Die "Wannsee-Konferenz" am 20. Januar 1942: Eine Einführung*. Berlin: Metropol, 2017.

Klemp, Stefan. *"Nicht ermittelt"—Polizeibataillone und die Nachkriegsjustiz*. 2nd, rev. ed. Essen: Klartext-Verlag, 2011.

Kłudzinski, Stanisław. "'Die 'Aktion 14f13': Der Transport von 575 Häftlingen von Auschwitz in das 'Sanatorium Dresden.'" In *Die "Euthanasie-Zentrale" in der Tiergartenstraße 4*, edited by Götz Aly, 147–52. Berlin: Edition Hentrich, 1989.

Knapp, Gabriele. *Das Frauenlager in Auschwitz: Musikalische Zwangsarbeit und ihre Bewältigung*. Hamburg: von Bockel Verlag, 1996.

Kobierska-Motar, Elżbieta. *Ekstradycja przestępców wojennych do Polski z czterech stref okupacyjnych Niemiec, 1946–1950*. Warsaw: Główna Komisja Badania Zbrodni Przeciwko Narodowi Polskiemu, 1992.

Kochavi, Arieh J. *Confronting Captivity: Britain, the United States and their POWs in Nazi Germany*. Chapel Hill: University of North Carolina Press, 2005.

Koenig, Ernest. *Im Vorhof der Vernichtung: Als Zwangsarbeiter in den Außenlagern von Auschwitz*. Frankfurt/Main: S. Fischer, 2000.

Kolb, Eduard. *Bergen-Belsen, 1943–1945*. Göttingen: Vandenhoek & Ruprecht, 1996.

Konieczny, Alfred. "Die Zwangsarbeit der Juden in Schlesien im Rahmen der 'Organisation Schmelt.'" In *Sozialpolitik und Judenvernichtung: Gibt es eine Ökonomie der Endlösung? Beiträge zur nationalsozialistischen Gesundheitspolitik*, edited by Götz Aly, 5:91–110. Berlin: Rotbuch, 1987.

Konieczny, Alfred. *KL Gross-Rosen: Das Nazi-Konzentrationslager in Niederschlesien 1940–1945*. Wałbrzych: Muzeum Gross-Rosen, 2011.

Konieczny, Alfred, and Herbert Szurgacz, eds. *Documenta Occupationis X: Praca Przymusowa Polaków Pod Panowaniem Hitlerowskim 1939–1945*. Poznań: Instytut Zachodni, 1976.

Kounio, Heinz Salvator. *Ein Liter Suppe und 60 Gramm Brot: Das Tagebuch des Gefangenen 109565*. Berlin: Hentrich & Hentrich, 2016.

Krakowski, Shmuel. "The Death Marches in the Period of the Evacuation of Camps." In *The Nazi Holocaust*, edited by Michael R. Marrus, 9:476–90. Westport, CT: Meckler, 1989.

Krakowski, Shmuel. "The Fate of Jewish Prisoners of War in the September 1939 Campaign." *Yad Vashem Studies* 12 (1977): 297–333.

Krakowski, Shmuel. "The Satellite Camps." In *Anatomy of the Auschwitz Death Camp*, edited by Yisrael Gutman and Michael Berenbaum, 50–60. Bloomington: Indiana University Press, 1994.

Kubica, Helena. "Children." In *Anatomy of the Auschwitz Death Camp*, edited by Yisrael Gutman and Michael Berenbaum, 412–27. Bloomington: Indiana University Press, 1994.

Kubica, Helena. "Kinder und Jugendliche im KL Auschwitz." In *Auschwitz 1940–1945: Studien zur Geschichte des Konzentrations- und Vernichtungslagers Auschwitz*, edited by Tadeusz Iwasko, Helena Kubica, Franciszek Piper, Irena Strzelecka, and Andrzej Strzelecki, 2:251–351. Oświęcim: State Museum Auschwitz-Birkenau Press, 1999.

Kuna, Milan. *Musik an der Grenze des Lebens, Musikerinnen und Musiker aus böhmischen Ländern in nationalsozialistischen Konzentrationslagern und Gefängnissen*. 2nd ed. Frankfurt/Main: Zweitausendeins, 1998.

Kushner, Tony. *The Persistence of Prejudice: Antisemitism in British Society during the Second World War*. Manchester: Manchester University Press, 1989.

L'Agence Centrale des Prisonniers de Guerre. *Rapport du Comité International de la Croix-Rouge sur son activité pendant la seconde guerre mondiale (1er septembre 1939–30 juin 1947)*. 3 vols. Geneva: International Committee of the Red Cross, 1948.

Landesberger, L., A. de Haas, and K. Selowsky. *Auschwitz*. The Hague: Nederlandsche Roode Kruis, 1947–53.

Lang, Hans-Joachim. *Die Frauen von Block 10: Medizinische Versuche in Auschwitz*. Hamburg: Hoffmann und Kampe, 2011.

Langer, Lawrence. *Holocaust Testimonies: The Ruins of Memory*. New Haven, CT: Yale University Press, 1991.

Langer, Lawrence. "Redefining Heroic Behavior: The Impromptu Self and the Holocaust Experience." In *The Holocaust: Origins, Implementations, Aftermath*, edited by Omer Bartov, 235–51. London and New York: Routledge, 2000.

Langer, Lawrence. *Versions of Survival: The Holocaust and the Human Spirit*. Albany: State University of New York Press, 1982.

Lasik, Alexander. "Die Organisationsstruktur des KL Auschwitz." In *Auschwitz 1940–1945: Studien zur Geschichte des Konzentrations- und Vernichtungslagers Auschwitz*, edited by Wacław Długoborski, Alexander Lasik, and Franciszek Piper, 1:165–317. Oświęcim: State Museum Auschwitz-Birkenau Press, 1999.

Lattek, Christine. "Bergen-Belsen: From 'Privileged' Camp to Death Camp." In *Bergen-Belsen in History and Memory*, edited by Jo Reilly, Tony Kushner, David Cesarani, and Colin Richmond, 37–72. London: Frank Cass, 1997.

Laub, Dori. "Bearing Witness or the Vicissitudes of Listening." In *Testimony: Crises of Witnessing in Literature, Psychoanalysis and History*, edited by Shoshana Felman and Dori Laub, 57–74.

New York: Routledge, 1992.

Laub, Dori. "An Event without a Witness: Truth, Testimony and Survival." In *Testimony. Crises of Witnessing in Literature, Psychoanalysis and History*, edited by Shoshana Felman and Dori Laub, 75–92. New York: Routledge, 1992.

Laub, Dori, and Nanette Auerhahn. "Knowing and Not Knowing: Forms of Traumatic Memory." In *Psychoanalysis and Holocaust Testimony*, edited by Dori Laub and Andreas Hamburger, 32–43. London: Routledge, 2017.

Lehnstaedt, Stephan. "Coercion and Incentive: Jewish Ghetto Labor in East Upper Silesia." *Holocaust & Genocide Studies* 24, no. 3 (December 2010): 400–30.

Lehnstaedt, Stephan. "Jüdische Arbeit im Generalgouvernement, Warthegau und Ostoberschlesien." In *Lebenswelt Ghetto. Alltag und soziales Umfeld während der nationalsozialistischen Verfolgung*, edited by Imke Hansen, Katrin Steffen, and Joachim Tauber, 210–26. Wiesbaden: Harrassowitz, 2013.

Levi, Primo. *The Drowned and the Saved*. London: Abacus, 1989.

Levi, Primo. *If This Is a Man/The Truce*. London: Everyman's Library, 1999.

Levine, Alan J. *Captivity, Flight and Survival in World War Two*. Westport, CT: Greenwood, 2000.

Ley, Astrid. "Die 'Aktion 14f13' in den Konzentrationslagern." In *Neue Studien zu nationalsozialistischen Massentötungen durch Giftgas: Historische Bedeutung, technische Entwicklung, revisionistische Leugnung*, edited by Günter Morsch and Bertrand Perz, 231–43. Berlin: Metropol, 2011.

Lieb, Peter. *Konventioneller Krieg oder NS-Weltanschauungskrieg? Kriegführung und Partisanenbekämpfung in Frankreich, 1943–1944*. Munich: Oldenbourg, 2002.

Lieske, Dagmar. *Unbequeme Opfer? "Berufsverbrecher" als Häftlinge im Konzentrationslager Sachsenhausen*. Berlin: Metropol, 2016.

Lifton, Robert. *The Nazi Doctors: Medical Killing and the Psychology of Genocide*. London: Macmillan, 1986.

Lindner, Stephan H. *Hoechst: Ein I.G. Farben Werk im Dritten Reich*. Munich: C. H. Beck, 2005.

Lotfi, Gabriele. *KZ der Gestapo: Arbeitserziehungslager im Dritten Reich*. Stuttgart: Deutsche Verlagsanstalt, 2000.

Loftus, Elizabeth, and Deborah Davis. "Internal and External Sources of Misinformation in Adult Witness Memory." In *The Handbook of Eyewitness Psychology*, edited by Michael P. Toglia, Jon D. Read, David F. Ross, and R. C. L. Lindsay, 1:195–238. Mahwah, NJ: Lawrence Erlbaum Associates, 2006.

Longerich, Peter. *Holocaust: The Nazi Persecution and Murder of the Jews*. Oxford: Oxford University Press, 2010.

Loose, Ingo. *Kredite für NS-Verbrechen: Die deutschen Kreditinstitute in Polen und die Ausraubung der polnischen und jüdischen Bevölkerung, 1939–1945*. Munich: Oldenbourg, 2007.

Ludewig-Kedmi, Revital. *Opfer und Täter zugleich? Moraldilemmata jüdischer Funktionshäftlinge in der Shoah*. Giessen: Psychosozial-Verlag, 2001.

Lustiger, Arno. *Sing mit Schmerz und Zorn. Ein Leben für den Widerstand.* Berlin: Aufbau-Verlag, 2004.

Madajczyk, Czesław. *Die Okkupationspolitik Nazideutschlands in Polen 1939–1945.* Cologne: Pahl-Rugenstein, 1988.

Madajczyk, Czesław, ed. *Vom Generalplan Ost zum Generalsiedlungsplan: Dokumente.* Munich: K G Saur, 1994.

Maier, Dieter. *Arbeitseinsatz und Deportation: Die Mitwirkung der Arbeitsverwaltung bei der nationalsozialistischen Judenverfolgung in den Jahren 1938–1945.* Berlin: Edition Hentrich, 1994.

Maj, Henryka. *Więźniowie obozu pracy przymusowej w Klein-Mangersdorf w prowincji górnośląskiej w latach 1941–1942.* Niemodlin: Niemodlińskie Towazystwo Regionalne, 2011.

Mallmann, Klaus-Michael. "'Mißgeburten, die nicht auf diese Welt gehören': Die deutsche Ordungspolizei in Polen, 1939–1941." In *Genesis des Genozids: Polen 1939–1945*, edited by Klaus-Michael Mallmann and Bogdan Musial, 71–89. Darmstadt: WBG, 2004.

Mallmann, Klaus-Michael, and Bogdan Musial. *Genesis des Genozids: Polen 1939–1945.* Darmstadt: WBG, 2004.

Mallmann, Klaus-Michael, and Gerhard Paul. *Herrschaft und Alltag: Ein Industrierevier im Dritten Reich.* Bonn: J. H. W. Dietz Nachf., 1991.

Mantelli, Brunello. "Von der Wanderarbeit zur Deportation: Die italienischen Arbeiter in Deutschland 1938–1945." In *Europa und der "Reichseinsatz": Ausländische Zivilarbeiter, Kriegsgefangene und KZ-Häftlinge in Deutschland 1938–1945*, edited by Ulrich Herbert, 51–90. Essen: Klartext Verlag, 1991.

Matthäus, Jürgen. "Die Beteiligung der Ordnungspolizei am Holocaust." In *Täter im Vernichtungskrieg: Der Überfall auf die Sowjetunion und der Völkermord an den Juden*, edited by Wolf Kaiser, 166–85. Munich: Ullstein, 2002.

Mazower, Mark. *Salonica, City of Ghosts: Christians, Muslims and Jews.* London: HarperCollins, 2004.

Megargee, Geoffrey P., ed. *Encyclopedia of Camps and Ghettos, 1933–45.* Vol. 1. Bloomington: Indiana University Press, 2009.

Meinen, Insa. *Die Shoah in Belgien.* Darmstadt: WBG, 2009.

Meyer, August. *Hitlers Holding: Die Reichswerke Hermann Göring.* Hamburg: Europa Verlag, 1999.

Michman, Dan. "Jewish Leadership in Extremis." In *Historiography of the Holocaust*, edited by Dan Stone, 319–40. Basingstoke: Palgrave Macmillan, 2004.

Michman, Dan. "*Judenräte* und *Judenvereinigungen* unter nationalsozialistischer Herrschaft: Aufbau und Anwendung eines verwaltungsmäßigen Konzepts." *Zeitschrift für Geschichtswissenschaft* 46 (1998): 293–304.

Milton, Sybil. "The Legacy of Holocaust Art." In *Art of the Holocaust*, edited by Janet Blatter and Sybil Milton, 34–43. London: Pan Books, 1982.

Miron, Guy, and Shlomit Shulhani, eds. *The Yad Vashem Encyclopedia of Camps and Ghettos during the Holocaust*. Vol. 2. Jerusalem: Yad Vashem, 2009.

Molho, Rena. *Der Holocaust der griechischen Juden: Studien zur Geschichte und Erinnerung*. Bonn: J. H. W. Dietz, 2016.

Moore, Bob. *Victims and Survivors: The Nazi Persecution of the Jews in the Netherlands, 1940–1945*. London: Arnold, 1997.

Muschol, Bernhard. *Die Herrschaft Slawentzitz/Ehrenforst in Oberschlesien: Piastisches Kammergut im Spätmittelalter, sächsischer Adelsbesitz und Hohenlohesche Residenz in der Neuzeit*. Sigmaringen: Jan Torbecke, 1993.

Namysło, Aleksandra. "Der Einfluss der Zentrale der Jüdischen Ältestenräte in Ostoberschlesien auf das Verhalten der Juden." In *Der Judenmord in den eingegliederten polnischen Ostgebieten, 1939–45*, edited by Jacek Andrzej Młynarczyk and Jochen Böhler, 311–28. Osnabrück: fibre, 2010.

Namysło, Aleksandra. "Ostoberschlesien: Organisation und Formen von Beschäftigung der jüdischen Bevölkerung (1939–1945)." In *Arbeit in den nationalsozialistischen Ghettos*, edited by Jürgen Hensel and Stephan Lehnstaedt, 139–59. Osnabrück: fibre, 2013.

Neander, Joachim. *Das Konzentrationslager "Mittelbau" in der Endphase der nationalsozialistischen Diktatur: Zur Geschichte des letzten im "Dritten Reich" gegründeten selbständigen Konzentrationslagers unter besonderer Berücksichtigung seiner Auflösungsphase*. Clausthal-Zellerfeld: Papierflieger, 1997.

Nessou, Anestis. *Griechenland 1941–1944: Deutsche Besatzungspolitik und Verbrechen gegen die Zivilbevölkerung—eine Beurteilung nach dem Völkerrecht*. Göttingen: V&R Unipress, 2009.

Niewyk, Donald L., and Francis Nicosia. *The Columbia Guide to the Holocaust*. New York: Columbia University Press, 2000.

Novitch, Miriam, Lucy Dawidowicz, and Tom L. Freudenheim, eds. *Spiritual Resistance: Art from Concentration Camps 1940–1945*. Philadelphia: Jewish Publishing Society of America, 1981.

Obréjan, Maurice. *Un Homme trois fois français*. Brissac: Editions du Petit Pavé, 2005.

Ofer, Dalia, and Leonor Weitzman, eds. *Women in the Holocaust*. New Haven, CT: Yale University Press, 1998.

Orth, Karin. "The Concentration Camp Personnel." In *Concentration Camps in Nazi Germany: The New Histories*, edited by Nikolaus Wachsmann and Jane Caplan, 44–57. London: Routledge, 2010.

Orth, Karin. *Das System der nationalsozialistischen Konzentrationslager: Eine politische Organisationsgeschichte*. Hamburg: Hamburger Edition, 1999.

Oulton, Jacinta M., and Melanie K. T. Takarangi. "(Mis)Remembering Negative Emotional Experiences." In *False and Distorted Memories*, edited by Robert E. Nash and James Ost, 9–22. London: Routledge, 2017.

Overmans, Rüdiger. "German Treatment of Jewish Prisoners of War in the Second World War." In *Wartime Captivity in the Twentieth Century. Archives, Stories, Memories*, edited by

Anne-Marie Pathé and Fabien Théofilakis, 45–53. New York: Berghahn, 2016.

Overmans, Rüdiger. *Rotarmisten in deutscher Hand*. Paderborn: Ferdinand Schöningh, 2012.

Overy, Richard J. *The Bombing War: Europe 1939–1945*. London: Penguin, 2013.

Overy, Richard J. *War and Economy in the Third Reich*. Oxford: Clarendon Press, 1994.

Patterson, Michael. "The Final Chapter: Theatre in the Concentration Camps of Nazi Germany." In *Theatre in the Third Reich, the Prewar Years: Essays on Theatre in Nazi Germany*, edited by Glen W. Gadberry, 157–65. Westport, CT: Greenwood, 1995.

Pelt, Robert-Jan van, and Dwork, Debórah. *Auschwitz: 1270 to the Present*. New York: W. W. Norton, 1996.

Person, Katarzyna. "Jews Accusing Jews: Denunciations of Alleged Collaborators in Jewish Honor Courts." In *Jewish Honor Courts: Revenge, Retribution and Reconciliation in Europe and Israel after the Holocaust*, edited by Laura Jokusch and Gabriel N. Finder, 225–46. Detroit: Wayne State University Press, 2015.

Perz, Bertrand. "Wehrmacht und KZ-Bewachung." *Mittelweg* 36, no. 5 (1995): 69–81.

Perz, Bertrand. "Wehrmachtsangehörige als KZ-Bewacher." In *Die Wehrmacht im Rassenkrieg: Der Vernichtungskrieg hinter der Front*, edited by Walter Manoschek, 168–81. Vienna: Picus, 1996.

Peukert, Detlev. "Der deutsche Arbeiterwiderstand, 1933–1945." In *Der deutsche Widerstand, 1933–1945*, 2nd ed., edited by Klaus-Jürgen Müller, 157–78. Paderborn: Ferdinand Schöningh, 1986.

Pezdek, Kathy, and Jennifer Taylor. "Memory of Traumatic Events in Children and Adults." In *Memory and Suggestibility in the Forensic Interview*, edited by Mitchell L. Eisen, Jodi A. Quas, and Gail S. Goodman, 165–84. London: Lawrence Erlbaum Associates, 2002.

Pickel, Kerri L. "Remembering and Identifying Menacing Perpetrators: Exposure to Violence and the Weapon Focus Effect." In *The Handbook of Eyewitness Psychology*, edited by Michael P. Toglia, Jon D. Read, and David F. Ross, 339–60, vol. 2. Mahwah, NJ: Lawrence Erlbaum Associates, 2007.

Piętka, Bohdan. "The Fire Brigade Kommando (Feuerwehrkommando) at KL Auschwitz." *Auschwitz Studies* 26 (2012): 179–98.

Pinot, Jean-Luc. *Convois: La déportation des Juifs de France*. Paris: Éditions du Détour, 2019.

Piper, Franciszek. *Arbeitseinsatz der Häftlinge aus dem KL Auschwitz*. Oświęcim-Brzezinka: State Museum Oświęcim-Brzezinka Press, 1995.

Piper, Franciszek. *Auschwitz 1940–1945: Studien zur Geschichte des Konzentrations- und Vernichtungslagers*. Vol. 3. Oświęcim: State Museum Auschwitz-Birkenau Press, 1999.

Piper, Franciszek. "Das Nebenlager Blechhammer." *Hefte von Auschwitz* 10 (1967): 19–39.

Piper, Franciszek. "Das Nebenlager Neu-Dachs." *Hefte von Auschwitz* 12 (1970): 55–111.

Piper, Franciszek. "Die Ausbeutung der Häftlinge." In *Auschwitz 1940–1945: Studien zur Geschichte des Konzentrations- und Vernichtungslagers Auschwitz*, edited by Tadeusz Iwasko, Helena Kubica, Franciszek Piper, Irena Strzelecka, and Andrzej Strzelecki, 2:83–167. Oświęcim:

State Museum Auschwitz-Birkenau Press, 1999.

Piper, Franciszek. *Die Zahl der Opfer von Auschwitz*. Oświęcim-Brzezinka: State Museum Oświęcim-Brzezinka Press, 1993.

Pohl, Dieter. "The Holocaust and the Concentration Camps." In *Concentration Camps in Nazi Germany: The New Histories*, edited by Jane Caplan and Nikolaus Wachsmann, 149–66. London: Routledge, 2010.

Pohl, Dieter. *Nationalsozialistische Judenverfolgung in Ostgalizien*. Munich: Oldenbourg, 1996.

Portelli, Alessandro. "The Peculiarities of Oral History." *History Workshop Journal* 12, no. 1 (Autumn 1981): 96–107.

Prochownik, Nathan. *Mémoires Barbelées: Et Après . . .* Paris: L'Harmattan, 1995.

Radchenko, Yuri. "'We Emptied Our Magazines into Them': The Ukrainian Auxiliary Police and the Holocaust in the Generalbezirk Charkow, 1941–1943." *Yad Vashem Studies* 41, no. 1 (2013): 63–98.

Rahe, Thomas. "Jewish Religious Life in Bergen-Belsen." In *Bergen-Belsen in History and Memory*, edited by Jo Reilly, Tony Kushner, David Cesarani, and Colin Richmond, 85–121. London: Frank Cass, 1997.

Reich, Walter. "Unwelcome Narratives: Listening to Suppressed Themes in American Holocaust Testimonies." *Poetics Today* 27, no. 2 (2006): 463–72.

Reichsgesetzblatt. Edited by Reichsministerium des Inneren. Berlin: Reichsdruckerei, 1943.

Rens, Herman van, and Annelies Wilms. *Tussenstation Cosel: Joodse Mannen uit West-Europa naar Dwangsarbeiderskampen in Silezië, 1942–1945*. Hilversum: Maaslandse Monografieen, 2020.

Rogmann, Heinz. "Bevölkerungspolitische Aufgaben in Schlesien." *Zeitschrift für Raumforschung und Raumordnung* 8/9 (August/September 1939): 442–46.

Roland, Charles G. *Courage under Siege: Starvation, Disease and Death in the Warsaw Ghetto*. New York: Oxford University Press, 1992.

Romney, Claude Jacquelien. "Ethical Problems Encountered by Auschwitz Prisoner Doctors." In *Remembering for the Future: The Holocaust in an Age of Genocides*, edited by John K. Roth and Elisabeth Maxwell, 319–34. New York: Palgrave Macmillan, 2001.

Rosen, Alan. *The Holocaust's Jewish Calendars: Keeping Time Sacred, Making Time Holy*. Bloomington: Indiana University Press, 2019.

Rosengarten, Israel. *Overleven: Relaas van een zestienjaarige joodse Antwerpenaar*. Rotterdam: De Vries-Brouwers, 1996.

Rossoliński-Liebe, Grzegorz. *Stepan Bandera: The Life and Afterlife of a Ukrainian Nationalist. Fascism, Genocide, and Cult*. Stuttgart: ibidem, 2014.

Rudorff, Andrea. "Arbeit und Vernichtung Reconsidered: Die Lager der Organisation Schmelt für polnische Jüdinnen und Juden aus dem annektierten Teil Oberschlesiens." *SozialGeschichte Online* 7 (2012): 10–39.

Rudorff, Andrea. "Blechhammer (Blachownia)." In *Der Ort des Terrors: Geschichte der nationalsozialistischen Konzentrationslager*, edited by Barbara Distel and Wolfgang Benz, 5:186–90. Munich: C. H. Beck, 2007.

Rudorff, Andrea. *Das KZ Auschwitz 1942–1945 und die Zeit der Todesmärsche 1944/45: Die Verfolgung und Ermordung der europäischen Juden durch das nationalsozialistische Deutschland, 1933–1945*. Vol. 16, Berlin: De Gruyter Oldenbourg, 2018.

Rudorff, Andrea. "Das Lagersystem der 'Organisation Schmelt' in Schlesien." In *Der Ort des Terrors: Geschichte der nationalsozialistischen Konzentrationslager*, edited by Barbara Distel and Wolfgang Benz, 9:155–60. Munich: C. H. Beck, 2009.

Rutowska, Maria. "Die Aussiedlung von Polen und Juden aus den in das deutsche Reich eingegliederten Gebieten ins General Gouvernement in den Jahren 1939–1941." In *Umgesiedelt—Vertrieben. Deutschbalten und Polen 1939–1945 im Warthegau*, edited by Eckhart Neander and Andrzej Sakson, 43–51. Marburg: Herder Institut, 2010.

Schanetzky, Tim. *Kanonen statt Butter: Wirtschaft und Konsum im Dritten Reich*. Munich: C. H. Beck, 2015.

Schiessl, Christoph. "The Volksdeutsche of Eastern Europe as Nazi Collaborators during World War II." In *German-Occupied Europe in the Second World War*, edited by Raffael Scheck, Fabien Théofilakis, and Julia Torrie, 195–212. New York: Routledge, 2019.

Schmidt, Ute. "Der 'Reichskommissar für die Festigung deutschen Volkstums': Fallbeispiel: Transfer der Bessarabiendeutschen." In *Das organisierte Chaos: "Ämterdarwinismus" und "Gesinnungsethik"; Determinanten nationalsozialistischer Besatzungsherrschaft*, edited by Johannes Houwink ten Cate and Gerhard Otto, 199–230. Berlin: Metropol, 1999.

Schulte, Jan Erik. *Zwangsarbeit und Vernichtung: Das Wirtschaftsimperium der SS; Oswald Pohl und das SS-Wirtschaftsverwaltungs-Hauptamt, 1933–1945*. Paderborn: Ferdinand Schöningh, 2001.

Schütz, Erhard, and Eckhard Gruber. *Mythos Reichsautobahn: Bau und Inszenierung der 'Straßen des Führers', 1933–1941*. Berlin: Links, 1996.

Seidler, Franz W. *Die Organisation Todt: Bauen für Wehrmacht und Staat, 1938–1945*. Koblenz: Bernard und Gräfe, 1987.

Seidler, Franz W. *Fritz Todt: Baumeister des Dritten Reiches*. Dortmund: Bublies, 2000. First published 1986.

Shik, Na'ama. "Sexual Abuse of Jewish Women in Auschwitz-Birkenau." In *Brutality and Desire. War and Sexuality in Europe's Twentieth Century*, edited by Dagmar Herzog, 221–46. London: Palgrave Macmillan, 2009.

Siegel, Sari. "The Coercion-Resistance Spectrum: Analyzing Prisoner-Functionary Behavior in Nazi Camps." *Journal of Genocide Research* 23, no. 1 (2021): 17–36.

Sikora, Mirosław. "Der Gau Oberschlesien in der Raumplanung der NS-Verwaltung, 1939–1944." In *Industrialisierung und Nationalisierung: Fallstudien zur Geschichte des oberschlesischen Industrialreviers im 19. und 20. Jahrhundert*, edited by Lutz Budraß, Barbara Kalinowska-Wójcik, and Andrzej Michalczyk, 249–84. Essen: Klartext, 2013.

Sikora, Mirosław. *Die Waffenschmiede des "Dritten Reiches": Die deutsche Rüstungsindustrie in Oberschlesien während des Zweiten Weltkrieges.* Essen: Klartext, 2014.

Silberklang, David. *Gates of Tears: The Holocaust in the Lublin District.* Jerusalem: The International Institute for Holocaust Research, Yad Vashem, 2013.

Sinnreich, Helene J. "The Rape of Jewish Women During the Holocaust." In *Sexual Violence Against Jewish Women during the Holocaust*, edited by Sonja Hedgepeth and Rochelle G. Saidel, 108–23. Waltham, MA: Brandeis University Press, 2010.

Sofsky, Wolfgang. *The Order of Terror: The Concentration Camp.* Princeton, NJ: Princeton University Press, 2013.

Soraci, Sal A., Michael T. Carlin, J. Don Read, Terri Krangel Pogoda, Yvonne Wakeford, Sarah Cavanagh, and Lisa Skin. "Psychological Impairment, Eyewitness Testimony and False Memories: Individual Differences." In *The Handbook of Eyewitness Psychology*, edited by Michael P. Toglia, Jon D. Read, David F. Ross, and R. C. L. Lindsay, 1:261–97. Mahwah, NJ: Lawrence Erlbaum Associates, 2007.

Spira, Bil. *Die Legende vom Zeichner.* Vienna: Döcker-Verlag, 1997.

Spira, Willi Bil. "Ein kleiner Lebensbericht." In *Zwischenwelt2: Die Welt des Jura Soyfer*, edited by Herbert Arlt, Konstantin Kaiser, and Gerhard Scheit, 36–43. Vienna: Theodor Kramer, 1991.

Spitzer, Walter. *Sauvé par le Dessin.* Lausanne, Paris: L'Harmattan, 2004.

Spoerer, Mark. "Profitierten Unternehmen von KZ-Arbeit? Eine kritische Analyse der Literatur." *Historische Zeitschrift* 303/I, 268, no. 1 (January 1999): 61–95.

Sprenger, Isabell. *Groß-Rosen: Ein Konzentrationslager in Schlesien.* Cologne: Böhlau, 1996.

Stahl, Christine. *Sehnsucht Brot: Essen und Hungern im KZ-Lagersystem Mauthausen.* Vienna: Edition-Mauthausen, 2010.

Stawski, Moniek. *My Life.* N.p.: n.p., n.d.

Ste. Croix, G. E. M. de. "Slavery and Other Forms of Unfree Labour." In *Slavery and Other Forms of Unfree Labour*, edited by Léonie Archer, 19–32. London: Routledge, 1988.

Steinbacher, Sybille. *Auschwitz: Geschichte und Nachgeschichte.* Munich: C. H. Beck, 2004.

Steinbacher, Sybille. "East Upper Silesia." In *The Greater German Reich and the Jews: Nazi Persecution in the Annexed Territories, 1935–1945*, edited by Wolf Gruner and Jürgen Osterloh, 239–66. New York: Berghahn Books, 2015.

Steinbacher, Sybille. *Musterstadt Auschwitz: Germanisierungspolitik und Judenmord in Ostoberschlesien.* Munich: K. G. Saur, 2000.

Steiner, John M. "Reflections on Experiences in Nazi Death Camps: Slave Laborer at the Blechhammer Synfuel Plant." In *Jahrbuch Dokumentationsarchiv des Österreichischen Widerstandes*, 57–78. Vienna: De Gruyter Oldenbourg, 1996.

Stephenson, Jill. *Women in Nazi Germany.* Harlow: Pearson Education, 2001.

Stone, Dan. *The Liberation of the Camps: The End of the Holocaust and its Aftermath.* New Haven, CT: Yale University Press, 2015.

Stranges, Anthony N. "A History of the Fischer-Tropsch Synthesis in Germany, 1926–1945."

Studies in Surface Science Catalysis 163 (December 2007): 1–27.

Strebel, Bernhard. *Das KZ Ravensbrück: Geschichte eines Lagerkomplexes*. Paderborn: Ferdinand Schöningh, 2003.

Streit, Christian. "Sowjetische Kriegsgefangene in deutscher Hand: Ein Forschungsüberblick." In *Die Tragödie der Gefangenschaft in Deutschland und in der Sowjetunion, 1941–1956*, edited by Klaus-Dieter Müller, Konstantin Nikischkin, and Günther Wagenlehner, 281–90. Cologne: Böhlau, 1998.

Strzelecka, Irena. "Arbeitslager Gleiwitz I." *Hefte von Auschwitz* 14 (1973): 75–106.

Strzelecka, Irena. "Die Häftlingsspitäler im KL Auschwitz (HKB)." In *Auschwitz 1940–1945: Studien zur Geschichte des Konzentrations- und Vernichtungslagers Auschwitz*, edited by Tadeusz Iwasko, Helena Kubica, Franciszek Piper, Irena Strzelecka, and Andrzej Strzelecki, 2:353–422. Oświęcim: State Museum Auschwitz-Birkenau Press, 1999.

Strzelecka, Irena. "Frauen im KL Auschwitz." In *Auschwitz 1940–1945: Studien zur Geschichte des Konzentrations- und Vernichtungslagers Auschwitz*, edited by Tadeusz Iwasko, Helena Kubica, Franciszek Piper, Irena Strzelecka, and Andrzej Strzelecki, 2:213–50. Oświęcim: State Museum Auschwitz-Birkenau Press, 1999.

Strzelecka, Irena. "Strafen und Folter." In *Auschwitz 1940–1945: Studien zur Geschichte des Konzentrations- und Vernichtungslagers Auschwitz*, edited by Tadeusz Iwasko, Helena Kubica, Franciszek Piper, Irena Strzelecka, and Andrzej Strzelecki, 2:451–70. Oświęcim: State Museum Auschwitz-Birkenau Press, 1999.

Strzelecka, Irena, and Piotr Setkiewicz. "Bau, Ausbau und Entwicklung des KL Auschwitz und seiner Nebenlager." In *Auschwitz 1940–1945: Studien zur Geschichte des Konzentrations- und Vernichtungslagers Auschwitz*, edited by Wacław Długoborski, Franciszek Piper, Irena Strzelecka, Piotr Setkiewicz, and Alexander Lasik, 1:73–154. Oświęcim: State Museum Auschwitz-Birkenau Press, 1999.

Strzelecki, Andrzej. "Arbeitslager Gleiwitz III." *Hefte von Auschwitz* 14 (1973): 129–50.

Strzelecki, Andrzej. "Arbeitslager Gleiwitz IV." *Hefte von Auschwitz* 14 (1973): 151–69.

Strzelecki, Andrzej. *Die Endphase des KL Auschwitz: Evakuierung, Liquidierung und Befreiung des Lagers*. Oświęcim-Brzezinka: State Museum in Oświęcim-Brzezinka Press, 1995.

Strzelecki, Andrzej. "The Initial Deportation of Zagłębie Jews to KL Auschwitz as Recorded in Nazi Documents." *Auschwitz Studies* 26 (2012): 7–48.

Sujo, Glenn. *Legacies of Silence: The Visual Arts and Holocaust Memory*. London: Wilson, 2001.

Szternfinkiel, Natan Eliasz. *Zagłada Żydów Sosnowca*. Katowice: Centralna Żydówska Komisja Historicznej, 1946.

Szymanska, Irena. "Kunst im Konzentrationslager Auschwitz." *Terror und Kunst: Zeugnis, Überlebenshilfe, Rekonstruktion und Denkmal, Dachauer Hefte* 18 (November 2002): 73–97.

Tal, Uriel. "Religious and Anti-Religious Roots of Modern Anti-Semitism." In *Religion, Politics and Ideology in the Third Reich: Selected Essays in Memoriam by Saul Friedländer*, 171–90. London: Routledge, 2004.

Tambor, Jolanta. *Mowa Górnoślązaków oraz ich świadomość językowa I etniczna*. Katowice: Wydawnictwo Uniwersytetu Śląskiego, 2008.
Terry, Nicholas. "Conflicting Signals: British Intelligence on the 'Final Solution' through Radio Intercepts and Other Sources, 1941–1942." *Yad Vashem Studies* 32 (2004): 351–96.
Tessin, Georg. *Verbände und Truppen der deutschen Wehrmacht und der Waffen-SS im Zweiten Weltkrieg 1939–1945*. Osnabrück: Biblio-Verlag, 1998.
Tooley, T. Hunt. *National Identity and Weimar Germany: Upper Silesia and the Eastern Border, 1918–1922*. Lincoln: University of Nebraska Press, 1997.
Treue, Wilhelm. "Hitlers Denkschrift zum Vierjahresplan." *VfZ* 3 (1955): 204–10.
Trunk, Isaiah. *Judenrat: The Jewish Councils in Eastern Europe under Nazi Occupation*. New York: Stein & Day, 1977.
Tuchel, Johannes. "Registrierung, Mißhandlung und Exekution: Die Politische Abteilung in den Konzentrationslagern." In *Die Gestapo im Zweiten Weltkrieg, "Heimatfront" und besetztes Europa*, edited by Gerhard Paul and Klaus-Michael Mallmann, 127–40. Darmstadt: Wissenschaftliche Buchgesellschaft, 2000.
Unger, Michal. *Reassessment of the Image of Mordechai Chaim Rumkowski*. Jerusalem: The International Institute for Holocaust Research, Yad Vashem, 2004.
Voss, Leo. *Het fluitje*. Rijswijk: Kramers, 1946.
Vourkoutiotis, Vasilis. "What the Angels Saw: Red Cross and Protecting Power Visits to Anglo-American POWs, 1939–1945." *Journal of Contemporary History* 40, no. 4 (2005): 689–706.
Wachsmann, Nikolaus. *Gefangen unter Hitler: Justizterror und Strafvollzug im NS-Staat*. Rev. trans. Munich: Siedler, 2004.
Wachsmann, Nikolaus. *Hitler's Prisons: Legal Terror in Nazi Germany*. New Haven, CT: Yale University Press, 2004.
Wachsmann, Nikolaus. *KL: A History of the Nazi Concentration Camps*. London: Little, Brown, 2015.
Wagner, Bernd C. *IG Auschwitz: Zwangsarbeit und Vernichtung von Häftlingen des Lagers Monowitz 1941–1945*. Munich: K G Saur, 2000.
Wagner, Jens-Christian. *Produktion des Todes: Das KZ Mittelbau-Dora*. Göttingen: Wallstein, 2001.
Wagner, Jens-Christian. "Work and Extermination in the Concentration Camps." In *Concentration Camps in Nazi Germany: The New Histories*, edited by Jane Caplan and Nikolaus Wachsmann, 127–48. London: Routledge, 2010.
Wajnblum, Emanuel. *My Destiny*. South Melbourne: Corporated Printers, 1998.
Wallis, Russell. *British POWs and the Holocaust: Witnessing the Nazi Atrocities*. London: I. B. Tauris, 2017.
Walter, Oliver. "Raum und Gemeinschaft. Die Mobilisierung der deutschen Wirtschaftseliten im 'Totalen Krieg.'" In *Der Ort der "Volksgemeinschaft" in der deutschen Gesellschaftsgeschichte*,

edited by Detlev Schmiechen-Ackermann, Marlies Buchholz, Bianca Roitsch, and Christian Schröder, 168–81. Paderborn: Ferdinand Schöningh, 2018.

Waxman, Zoë Vania. *Women in the Holocaust: A Feminist History*. Oxford: Oxford University Press, 2017.

Weigelt, Andreas, Klaus-Dieter Müller, Thomas Schaarschmidt, and Mike Schweitzer. *Todesurteile sowjetischer Militärtribunale gegen Deutsche (1944–47): Eine historisch-biographische Studie*. Göttingen: Vandenhoek & Ruprecht, 2015.

Weinberg, Felix. *Boy 30529: A Memoir*. London: Verso, 2013.

Weindling, Paul. "Delousing and Resistance." In *Jewish Medical Resistance in the Holocaust*, edited by Michael A. Grodin, 49–58. Oxford: Berghahn Books, 2014.

Weindling, Paul. *Epidemics and Genocide in Eastern Europe, 1890–1945*. Oxford: Oxford University Press, 2000.

Weindling, Paul. *Victims and Survivors of Nazi Human Experiments: Science and Suffering in the Holocaust*. London: Bloomsbury, 2015.

Weiss, Aharon. "Jewish Leadership in Occupied Poland—Postures and Attitudes." *Yad Vashem Studies* 12 (1977): 335–65.

Weiss, Aharon. "The Relations between the Judenrat and the Jewish Police." In *Patterns of Jewish Leadership in Nazi Europe, 1933–1945*, edited by Yisrael Gutman, 201–17. Jerusalem: Yad Vashem, 1979.

Weiss, Hermann F. *Buschvorwerk im Riesengebirge: Eine Gemeinde in Niederschlesien von den Kriegsjahren bis zur Vertreibung*. Herbholzheim: Centaurus-Verlag, 2006.

Weiss, Hermann F. "Die Oberste Bauleitung Reichsautobahnen in Breslau und der Holocaust." 2012. http://www.breslau-wroclaw.de.

Weiss, Hermann F. "From *Reichsautobahnlager* to Schmelt Camp: Brande, a Forgotten Holocaust Site in Western Upper Silesia, 1940–1943." *Yad Vashem Studies* 39, no. 2 (2011): 81–119.

Weiss, Hermann F. "Johannsdorf: A Forgotten Forced Labor Camp for Jews in Western Upper Silesia, 1940–1943." *Śląsnik Kwartalnik Historyczny Sobótka* 75, no. 1 (2020): 93–121.

Weiss, Hermann F. "Reichsautobahnlager Geppersdorf (Upper Silesia), 1940–1942." *Śląsnik Kwartalnik Historyczny Sobótka* 67, no. 1 (2012): 55–71.

Wendland, Jörn. *Das Lager von Bild zu Bild: Narrative Bildserien von Häftlingen aus NS-Zwangslagern*. Cologne: Böhlau, 2017.

Weniger, Kay. *Zwischen Bühne und Baracke: Lexikon der verfolgten Theater-, Film- und Musikkünstler*. Berlin: Metropol, 2008.

Westermann, Edward B. *Drunk on Genocide: Alcohol and Mass Murder in Nazi Germany*. Ithaca, NY: Cornell University Press, 2021.

Westermann, Edward B. *Hitler's Police Battalions: Enforcing Racial War in the East*. Lawrence: University Press of Kansas, 2005.

Weyrauch, Walter Otto. *Gestapo V-Leute: Tatsachen und Theorien des Geheimdienstes; Untersuchungen zur Geheimen Staatspolizei während der NS-Herrschaft*. Frankfurt/Main: Fischer

Taschenbuch, 1992.

White, Joseph Robert. "'Even in Auschwitz... Humanity Could Prevail': British POWs and Jewish Concentration Camp Inmates at IG Auschwitz, 1943–1945." *Holocaust and Genocide Studies* 15, no. 2 (Fall 2002): 266–95.

Wieczorek, Slawomir. "'Like the Wind Drives Dead Leaves': Music in Concentration Camps." In *Böse Macht Musik: Zur Ästhetik des Bösen in der Musik*, edited by Katharina Wisotzki and Sara R. Falke, 191–99. Bielefeld: Transcript, 2012.

Wieviorka, Annette. "On Testimony." In *Holocaust Remembrance. The Shapes of Memory*, edited by Geoffrey Hartman, 23–32. Oxford: Blackwell Publishers, 1994.

Wieviorka, Olivier. *The French Resistance*. Cambridge, MA: The Belknap Press of Harvard University Press, 2016.

Wieviorka, Olivier. "To Exalt Heroes or to Commemorate Victims? The Evolution of the French Memory from the Liberation until Nowadays." In *Das soziale Gedächtnis und die Gemeinschaft der Überlebenden: Bergen-Belsen in vergleichender Perspektive*, edited by Janine Doerry, Thomas Kubetzky, and Katja Seybold, 112–23. Göttingen: Wallstein, 2014.

Winkler-Bessone, Claude. *Bil Spira: Pariser Impressionen (1935–1939); Zeichnungen und Karikaturen*. Munich: Edition Kappa, 1998.

Winter, Martin Clemens. "Die SS als Negativfolie in Narrativen der Todesmärsche." In *Die SS nach 1945: Entschuldungsnarrative, populäre Mythen, europäische Erinnerungsdiskurse*, edited by Jan Erik Schulte and Michael Wildt, 99–115. Göttingen: V+R Unipress, 2018.

Winter, Martin Clemens. "Evacuating the Camps: The Last Collective Crime of Nazi Society." *Dapim: Studies on the Holocaust* 29, no. 3 (2015): 138–53.

Wolf, Gerhard. "*Volk* Trumps Race: The *Deutsche Volksliste* in Annexed Poland." In *Beyond the Racial State: Rethinking Nazi Germany*, edited by Devin O. Pendas, Mark Roseman, and Richard F. Wetzell, 431–54. Cambridge: Cambridge University Press, 2017.

Wollenberg, Hans-Werner. *... und der Alptraum wurde zum Alltag: Autobiographischer Bericht eines jüdischen Arztes über NS-Zwangsarbeitslager in Schlesien (1942–1945)*. Edited by Manfred Brusten. Pfaffenweiler: Centaurus-Verlag, 1992.

Yahil, Leni. *The Holocaust: The Fate of European Jewry, 1932–1945*. New York: Oxford University Press, 1987.

Yones, Eliyahu. *Smoke in the Sand: The Jews of Lvov in the War Years, 1939–1944*. Jerusalem: Gefen Publishing House, 2004.

Zakic, Mirna. "The Price of Belonging to the *Volk*: *Volksdeutsche*, Land Redistribution and Aryanization in the Serbian Banat, 1941–1944." In *Journal of Contemporary History* 49, no. 2 (2014): 320–40.

INDEX

AEG (Allgemeine Elektricitäts-Gesellschaft), 62, 139
Annaberg,
    transit camp, 11, 12, 54, 57, 89, 178
    sick camp, 61, 85, 93
    seat of Schmelt Office, 98
"annihilation through labor," 4, 14, 19, 52
Auerhahn, Dr. Moses, Jewish physician,
    head surgeon in Blechhammer, 76, 128
    protest against women's tough working conditions, 132
    comforting traumatized girl before her murder by SS, 132
Auschwitz concentration camp,
    criminal Kapos, 110, 132, 178, 183, 186, 195
    medical experiments on women from Blechhammer, 80
    medical supervision of Blechhammer under Schmelt, 10, 11, 40, 45, 79, 82, 83
    prisoner transfer from Birkenau's "family camp" BIIb, 114, 129, 134, 169, 186
    prisoner transfer of Greek Jews, 114
    prisoners' feelings towards takeover, 110, 111, 116
    transports of Blechhammer prisoners to gas chambers, 10, 12, 41, 43, 56, 93, 131, 210

Bergen-Belsen concentration camp,
    fate of women from Blechhammer, 202, 203
Bismarckhütte, punishment camp,
    transfer of Blechhammer prisoners, 127
Braasem, Joseph "Jopie," 59, 60, 74, 122, 211
Brainin, David, artist, 175–77, 241
Brande Schmelt camp, 12, 79
    atrocities, 94, 95
Broemel & Sohn camp administration, 31, 32, 37, 109
Brossmann, Otto, SS camp leader,
    biography, 13, 14, 99
    prisoner work deployment, 121
    plan to kill female prisoners, 111, 211
    responsibility for executions, 146
burials of prisoners, 61, 62, 84, 225

children in Blechhammer,
    rescued during ghetto liquidations, 12, 87, 88, 210, 211
    selected during Cosel period, 12, 91
    as calfactors and "apprentices," 90, 91
    deaths by overworking, 135
    alleged "misbehavior," 91
    sexual abuse, 12, 92
    the children's work detail, 134, 135
    British POWs' protests against working children, 213, 240
    bombing victims, 137
    aid-giving by adults, 213, 217
Clary, Robert, artist, 165, 175, 176
Cohensius, Dr. Isaac, Jewish physician,
    biography, 75
    maltreatment of patients, 76
    transfer to Gräditz, 82
Cosel men, 52, 54–57, 60–63, 75, 97, 218, 228
Cosel period, 45, 48–54, 64, 80, 91
Czaczkes, Georges (Johnny Georgeslo), artist, 115, 178
Czapla, Karl, SS deputy camp leader,
    biography, 105
    camp theater, 174, 177, 180
    responsibility for hangings, 146, 163, 164
    death march, 181, 183, 186, 195, 198

death bath procedure, *see* water-induced murders
dysentery outbreaks, 10, 44–47, 51, 60, 129, 184, 228
Demerer, Halina, 90, 241
Demerer, Heinrich, 12, 135, 154, 164, 225
Demerer, Karl, Jewish elder,
 biography, 9, 39
 bribery as survival strategy, 18, 88, 111, 122, 208–12, 246
 rejection of violence, 59, 72, 117, 132, 175
 saving prisoners, 44, 70, 149, 150, 172
 child rescue, 12, 88, 90, 135
 privileges, 71, 90
 barter, 230–36
 organization of cultural events, 175–77, 180
 Dr. Ritter, murder allegations, 78, 79
 enforced participation in camp killings, 82
 transfer of wife and daughter to Peterswaldau, 93
 during death march, 190, 194, 200, 201
 witness in Hoffmann's trial, 99
Dreier, Hans, Gestapo Sosnowiec, 2, 3, 29, 259

Ellert, Erna, nurse,
 transfer to Blechhammer, 80
 attempted murder of, 80, 81
Ems, deputy Jewish elder, 57
ethnic Germans,
 status and mortality, 15, 27
 identification with Nazism, 9
 in order police or SS, 35, 105
 violence against Jews, 40
female prisoners,
 work deployment in Schmelt camps, 42, 43
 gender-specific selections for Auschwitz, 43, 83, 84
 sexual abuse, 43, 44, 133, 134
 murder of pregnant women, 43, 44, 84
 maltreatment, 60, 133
 edema from kitchen work, 63, 132
 strangling of unfit women, 80
 water-induced mass killings, 95
 medical experiments on women from Blechhammer in Auschwitz, 80
 transfers to future Gross-Rosen sub-camps, 84, 92, 93
 planned murders due to tattoo errors, 111, 112
 under Auschwitz, 132, 133
 witnessing executions, 170–72
 during death march, 197, 202
 in Bergen-Belsen, 202, 203
Flusser, Jindřich, Jewish medical orderly, 129
food allocations,
 in first half of 1942, 37, 38
 in second half of 1942, 58
 alleged improvements in 1943, 70
 in 1944, 115, 116
 embezzlement, 38, 58, 70
food experiments, 117, 119

German workforce
 anti-Semitic assaults, 63, 74, 141–43
 aid to Jews, 72, 229, 235, 216–18
Gestapo Kattowitz, 2, 29, 86
 Oppeln, 26
Gleiwitz camps, 89, 179
 Degussa use of Jewish labor, 54
 treks to Blechhammer, 181–93, 195
Gross-Rosen concentration camp,
 takeover of Schmelt camps, 11, 84, 85, 92, 93, 96 98
 during death marches, 17, 115, 189, 193–195, 200–02

Haunschild,
 unclear identity and nicknames, 31
 participation in selections, 3, 42, 43, 61, 85, 87, 96, 246
 Cosel selections, 50, 54, 91
 camp killings, 78, 246
Hitschler, Albert, RAB social ombudsman, 31, 74

Hoffmann, Dr. Erich Walter Fritz,
Schmelt camp leader,
  biography, 8–12, 36, 37
  food mismanagement, 38, 58, 70
  prisoner work deployment, 40, 68, 74, 75
  dysentery outbreak, 44, 46
  false claims about new camp, 47
  sexual abuse of female prisoners, 44, 46
  collaboration in selections, 50–52, 54, 62, 63, 82, 83, 95
  maltreatment of prisoners, 56, 60, 68, 69, 74, 75, 78, 80, 82, 83, 95, 220
  Dr. Ritter, murder allegations, 78, 79
  attempted murder of Dr. Lajtner and nurse Erna Ellert, 80, 81
  water-induced murders, 57, 59, 61, 82
  order to strangle inmates, 80, 94, 95
  destruction of religious artifacts, 225
  acceptance of bribes, 88, 209, 212, 213
  postwar trial, 78, 79, 99, 212
Hohenlohe, Prince,
  ancestry, 20, 21
  sale of land to OHW, 21
  lease of land for Jewish camp, 47, 48, 69
  Jewish "graveyard," 61
Hohenlohe trust, 47
Hoess, Rudolf, Auschwitz commandant,
  complaint about Cosel stops, 50, 51
  on disbanding of Schmelt camps system, 85
  on standard punishments in Auschwitz, 126, 127
  on "nonmedical" activities of medical staff, 127
  on alleged causes of German workers' assaults against Jews, 143
"horse dealer," *see* Haunschild
hyperphagia, 70, 191
Hyrsz, Dr. Alfred/Arnost, Jewish head physician
  arrival in Blechhammer, 128
  construction of operating table, 130
  adverse attitude to lethal injections, 131

IG Farben,
  ties to Nazi regime, 21, 26
  personnel at OHW, 22, 24–26
  Mineralöl-Bau building supervision, 73
  Heydebreck plant, 22, 25, 71, 72, 140, 239
  decision not to use Jewish laborers at Heydebreck, 125
  Auschwitz-Monowitz plant, 30
  joint expansion plans to Auschwitz, 23, 24
  staff visits to Auschwitz, 25
Iwanter, Dr. Jerzy, Jewish physician,
  arrival in Blechhammer, 76
  harsh treatment of patients, 76, 129
  spoliation, 76, 129
  sexual abuse of teenage prisoner, 77
  identity conflicts as Jewish convert to Catholicism, 131, 228
  collaboration in giving lethal injections, 131

Jaworzno subcamp, 14, 99, 105
  trek to Blechhammer, 17, 182–93, 195
Jewish councils (*Judenräte*),
  forced formation, 2, 9, 29
  The Central Office of the Jewish Councils in Eastern Upper Silesia, 29, 218
  "salvation through labor," 2, 29–33
  Zionist resistance, 30, 32, 88
Jewish policemen,
  in Schmelt camps, 58, 59
  forced collaboration in killings, 78, 131
  postwar trials before Jewish Honor Courts, 94
Johannsdorf transit camp, 54
Josenhans, Max, OHW director,
  biography, 6, 23–24
  conformity with Nazi regime, 24, 121
  discovery of Auschwitz-Monowitz site, 22, 23
  cooperation with IG Farben Auschwitz-Monowitz, 23, 24

Kapo Manni/Mouni, criminal Kapo,
  biography, 110
  musical performances, 180
Kapo Walter, see Redock, Walter
Klettendorf, Schmelt camp,
  training of prisoners, 33
  prisoner transfer, 42
Klipp, Kurt, SS camp leader,
  biography, 14, 99–104
  relations to industrialists, 25
  responsibility for hangings, 146
  establishment of camp theater, 173, 177
  spoliation, 209
  protection of infirmary patients, 17, 185, 190, 205, 247
  death march, 181, 183, 186, 195, 200
Knauer, police guard, 55
Krauch, Carl, 21, 47
Kuczinsky, Friedrich Karl, Schmelt Office, 31–33

Lajtner, Dr. Wolf, Jewish physician,
  biography and transfer to Blechhammer, 80
  attempted murder of, 80, 81
Landau, Kalman, artist, 161
Langenbielau, Schmelt camp,
  female prisoner transfer, 92
Leinkenjost, Hermann, see "Tom Mix"
lethal injections, 15, 41, 109–111, 128, 131, 202
Levi, Primo,
  the "gray zone," 10, 75, 131
  on repressed memory, 145
  on survival in evacuated Monowitz subcamp, 190, 191
Lindner, Heinrich, Schmelt's deputy,
  biography, 3, 30
  SD school instructor, 35, 55, 56
  police guard supervision, 35
  selections, 7, 11, 43, 49, 63, 85, 87, 89
  ghetto deportations, 32, 33
  Cosel period, 49, 50
  appointment of Jewish functionaries, 57
  camp killings, 43, 94
  arrest and suicide, 98
"Lion of Buna," see Veittes, Paul
Littwack, Dr. Bernhard, Jewish physician,
  head physician in Blechhammer, 80
  transfer to Gräditz, 82
Ludwig, Alfred, Schmelt Office worker
  biography, 31
  female prisoners' work deployment, 31
  ban on relatives visiting inmates, 38, 39
  protection of Jewish elder's family, 90, 93

Maquisards (French resistance fighters), 115, 184, 194
Mareck, police guard duty officer,
  restrained behavior, 67
  participation in selections, 82, 83
  delegation of camp killings, 82
  spoliation, 209
  forcing religious Jews to eat on Yom Kippur, 226
Masseli, Karl, SS block leader
  biography, 105
  prisoner work deployment, 142, 143
  identities of fellow SS men, 123
  participation in hangings, 147, 151
  involvement in shootings during evacuation, 187
  responsibility for casualties on death march, 199
Merin, Moshe Moniek, head of Central Office of Jewish Councils in Eastern Upper Silesia,
  biography, 2, 29
  "salvation through labor," 2, 29, 33
  ghetto deportations, 32, 33, 86, 88
  resistance against, 32
Mertens, Hans, RAB employee, 135
Mineralöl-Bau, 22, 28, 31, 73
"Mikvenik," see Rettinghausen, Walter

Neu-Dachs subcamp, see Jaworzno
Neusalz, Schmelt camp,
  female prisoner transfer, 89, 92

INDEX 345

Niewes, Jozef, deputy Jewish elder,
  biography, 57, 58
  polarizing personality traits, 57, 71
  burial detail, 84
  child rescue, 88
  bribery as survival strategy, 209
  "Organization Niewes" trafficking operation, 235, 236
Niederkirch, Schmelt camp,
  prisoner transfer from, 54
  transit camp, 76

Oberschlesische Hydrierwerke,
  synthetic fuel program, 21, 22 47, 136
  management, 22–26
  planned expansion to Auschwitz-Monowitz, 6, 23, 25
Olejak, Hans Stefan, SS deputy camp leader,
  biography, 100, 105, 105-09
  maltreatment of prisoners, 132
  responsibility for hangings, 146, 161
  alleged return during death march, 182
order police (*Ordungspolizei*),
  prehistory, 34, 35
  ideological training, 7, 8, 42, 55
  guard duties in Schmelt camps, 3, 7, 35
  participation in selections, 7, 35
  camp killings, 35
  maltreatment of prisoners, 35
  during Cosel period, 49, 50
  Ukrainian auxiliaries, 16, 140, 141
  transfer to rapid response units, 57, 65–67
Organisation Todt,
  use of Jewish Schmelt prisoners in Russia, 45, 49, 80
  provision of Jewish laborers to OHW, 34
  pseudo-military uniforms, 62
Ottmuth, Schmelt camp,
  transit camp, 39, 54, 176
  sick camp, 93

Perlman, Dr. Maurice, Jewish dentist, 60, 129
Peterswaldau, Schmelt camp
  female prisoner transfer, 84, 93, 132

Pfeiffer, Wilhelm, deputy Schmelt camp leader, 12, 37, 212
  child molestation, 92
Pohl, Oswald, WVHA,
  alleged improvements in concentration camps, 70
  bonus payment to Kurt Klipp, 100
  order to evacuate Auschwitz camps, 181
Pompe, Kurt Bruno, guard duty officer of Brande,
  water-induced murders in Brande, 94
  transfer to Blechhammer, 94
  murder of pregnant women, 95
Pott, Dr. Alfred, OHW chairman, 21, 22
pregnancies and childbirth, 11, 43, 44, 79, 80, 84, 88, 89, 95, 97, 132, 133, 222, 245
Preussag, OHW investor, 6, 22
prisoners of war,
  British, 17, 27, 28, 62, 90, 121, 123, 126, 136, 139, 140, 148, 176, 188, 210, 212–15, 217, 223–24, 231–35, 238–42, 246
  "Palestinian," 15, 38, 214
  French, 27, 69, 115, 188, 215, 223, 231, 232–35, 238-42, 246
  Soviet, 27, 32, 33, 41, 44, 117, 119, 212, 215

Quirin, Peter, SS medical orderly,
  biography, 110
  ill-treatment of Jewish doctor, 130
  lethal injections, 131
  murder of a girl, 132

"rationalization," 15, 19, 65, 68, 72, 85, 246
Redock, Walter, criminal Kapo,
  biography, 110
  supervision of clothes depot, 119
  supervision of tailor's shop, 133
  crematorium supervision, 113
  spoliation, 209,
  abusive behavior towards female prisoners, 133
  collaboration in atrocities during evacuation, 187
reduced output factors, 16, 17, 28, 126

Reich Highway Company (*Reichsautobahngesellschaft*),
  building supervisory board Breslau, 3, 10, 31, 40, 48, 68, 72, 135, 235
  use of Jewish labor in Silesia, 28–33
  thoroughfare (*Durchgangsstrasse*) IV, 3, 28
  transit camps for Jews, 11, 49, 51–54, 75, 178
Reichswerke-Hermann-Göring, OHW investor, 22
Rettinghausen, Walter, police guard duty officer,
  unclear identity, 35
  maltreatment of prisoners, 38, 60
  participation in selections, 63
  water-induced murders, 42, 57, 82
  transfer from Blechhammer, 67
Ritter, Dr., Jewish physician,
  transfer to Blechhammer, 45
  maltreatment of patients, 60
  murder of, 78, 79, 212
Romani Kapo, *see* Kapo Manni/Mouni
Rumkowski, Chaim, elder of ghetto Łódź, 2, 29

Sakrau, Schmelt camp,
  transit camp, 53, 54
  sick camp, 93
Schatzlar, Schmelt camp,
  female prisoner transfer, 92
Schindler, Adolf, SS head of crematorium/clothes depot,
  biography, 109
  maltreatment of prisoners, 119, 133
  the crematorium, 113
  fabrication of operating table, 130
  participation in hangings, 147, 161
  shootings on death march, 187
Schlesien-Benzin, *see* Oberschlesische Hydrierwerke
Schlick, Dr. Heinrich, OHW deputy director,
  biography, 6, 25, 26
  counter-intelligence officer, 25, 224
  conformity with Nazi ideology, 14, 25, 143, 180
  commander of works police, 26, 141, 245
  prisoner work deployment, 40, 67, 121
  collaboration in massacre of Jewish prisoners, 184
Schmauser, Heinrich, HSSPF Silesia,
  commander of police guards in Schmelt camps, 7, 35, 66
  intervention in Cosel stops, 51
  Auschwitz takeover preparations, 98
  order to evacuate Auschwitz camps, 181
  order to murder infirmary patients, 17, 181, 185, 189, 205
Schmelt, Albrecht, head of Schmelt Office,
  biography, 30
  establishment of camp system, 2, 3
  labor conscriptions, 32, 42
  annihilatory policies, 4, 11, 45, 60, 84
  Cosel period and rivalry with Auschwitz, 48, 50
  withdrawal of police guards, 66
  embezzlement accusations and suicide, 98
Schmelt Office,
  establishment and staff, 3, 31, 55
  controversy on annihilatory functions, 4, 97, 246
  collaboration with Reich Highway Company, 3, 31, 55
  Jewish labor conscription, 32
  conditions in camps, 38, 40, 57, 59, 61, 71, 94
  selections, 42, 97
  Cosel period, 48, 50–52
  introduction of Wehrmacht guards, 67, 68
  camp killings, 45, 78, 82, 84, 97
  protection of Jewish elder's family, 90
  relocation to Annaberg, 89, 98
Schmidt, Otto Ewald Albin, head of SS Political Department,
  biography, 109
  torture of prisoners, 127, 128, 142, 151
  assault against Jewish girl, 133

participation in hangings, 151, 161
shootings on death march, 195, 197
Schumann, Kurt Karl, works police leader, 26, 184
SD school Blechhammer, 8, 35, 37, 42, 55, 56
Seibersdorf Schmelt camp,
  camp song, 40
  Blechhammer guard as camp leader, 56, 57
  "zero-sick-policy," 76
  prisoner transfer to Blechhammer, 75, 84
selections,
  for Auschwitz, 7, 10, 13, 31, 33, 37, 41, 43, 75, 77, 82, 83, 97, 110, 115, 130, 131, 136, 166, 210, 229
  for work in Schmelt camps, 50–53
  of ghetto inhabitants in Blechhammer, 86–90
  gender-specific, 43, 63, 84
sexual assaults,
  against boys, 77, 92
  against women, 11, 43, 84, 89, 133, 134
Sima, Michel, artist, 242, 243
"slave trader," see Haunschild
Sosnowiec ghetto uprising, 87, 88
Sosnowiec transit camp, 32, 54
Speer, Albert, Minister, RAB director,
  exploitation of Jewish labor, 4, 6, 12
  initiator of Cosel period, 4, 48, 49
  "rationalization" and alleged improvements in camps, 13–15, 65, 68, 70, 85, 97, 125, 234, 246, 247
  use of Wehrmacht soldiers as guards, 8, 66, 67, 100
  role of RAB transit and sick camps in Holocaust, 89, 93, 94
Spira, Wilhelm "Bil," artist, 53, 74, 135, 137, 154, 175, 198, 238–40
spirituality, 18, 84, 159, 160, 191, 192, 207, 224–28
Spitzer, Walter, artist, 164, 167, 175, 199, 240, 241
Stoltzenburg, Otto, RAB employee, biography, 68, 69

new camp for Jews, 48
Jewish work deployment, 68, 69, 235
maltreatment of prisoners, 74
Szeftel, Dr. Abram, Jewish physician,
  biography, 128
  maltreatment by SS, 130, 132
  rescue of prisoner from selection, 130
  protecting infirmary patients after evacuation, 184, 189

Todt, Fritz, Minister, RAB director, 3, 6, 35, 38
"Tom Mix," unidentified SS block leader,
  nickname and possible identity, 122, 123
  maltreatment of prisoners, 122, 177, 247
  participation in hangings, 152, 153, 156, 165, 166
  spoliation, 211, 239
  shootings on death march, 195
transit camp in Blechhammer, 86–89
typhus outbreaks, 78, 81, 82, 115, 131, 178, 220, 238

United States Air Force pilots, lynching, 140
Upper Silesia,
  industrialization and "Germanization" policy, 21, 27
  Nazi anti-Jewish policy, 28–33
Upper Silesians,
  ethnic minority and political instrumentalization of, 20, 21
  as overseers of Jews, 73, 75, 217
Upper Silesian Hard Coal Syndicate, OHW investor, 6, 21, 22

Veittes, Paul, SS block leader,
  biography, 121
  controversy around removal, 211

Wallner, Simon, Jewish dentist, 40, 60
warlike building (*kriegsmäßiges Bauen*), 9, 72
water-induced murders, 7–9, 13, 42, 56–59, 82, 94

Wehrmacht guards,
    collaboration in the Holocaust, 8, 97, 123, 124, 227
    as Schmelt camp guards, 8, 65, 67, 173
    ambivalent behavior towards prisoners, 67, 68, 69, 91, 123, 124
    maltreatment of prisoners, 73
    participation in selections, 83, 220
    spoliation, 238
    incorporation in SS guard battalion, 14, 100
    on death march, 195
Wehrmacht massacres, 17, 188-190, 205, 247
WVHA (*Wirtschafts-Verwaltungshauptamt*),
    alleged improvements in concentration camps, 14, 70, 93, 116, 119
    decrees on selections, 10, 40, 83
    decrees on prisoners' work deployments, 69, 125
    takeover negotiations, 98, 130
    subcamp administration, 110
    punishment of prisoners, 126–28, 140, 151, 233
Wollenberg, Dr. Hans-Werner, Jewish physician,
    arrival in Blechhammer, 80
    attitude to children in camp, 91, 92
    rejection of bartered food, 234
    transfer to Gräditz, 82
works police (*Werkschutz*),
    prehistory, 6, 26
    leadership in Blechhammer, 26
    monitoring Jewish prisoners at work, 15
    lynchings and shootings, 26, 141–43, 170, 233, 236
    voluntary works police, 68
    massacre of Jewish inmates, 17, 184, 188, 193, 205, 247

"Yeke Potz," *see* Ems

Zim, Jakob, artist, 241

ABOUT THE AUTHOR

SUSANNE BARTH RECEIVED A PHD IN HISTORY FROM CARL-VON-OSSIETZKY UNIversity in Oldenburg (Germany), from where she also obtained a master's degree in history and political science. She is a postdoctoral researcher at the Institute for History and Contemporary Studies at Södertörn University in Sweden. Her thesis, "The Oberschlesische Hydrierwerke and the Auschwitz Subcamp Blechhammer, 1939–1945," was awarded the Belgian Prix Fondation Auschwitz-Jacques Rozenberg, 2021–2022. Her research was funded by a Claims Conference Saul Kagan Fellowship in Advanced Shoah Studies, a European Union Holocaust Research Infrastructure (EHRI) Fellowship at the Netherlands' Institute for War, Holocaust, and Genocide Studies (NIOD) in Amsterdam, a stand-alone project grant from the German Research Association (Deutsche Forschungsgemeinschaft, DFG), a two-week research fellowship for PhD candidates at the International Center for Holocaust Research at Yad Vashem, a junior fellowship at the Vienna Wiesenthal Center for Holocaust Studies (VWI), and a doctoral fellowship from the Fondation pour la Mémoire de la Shoah. Her articles have been published in *Shofar: An Interdisciplinary Journal of Jewish Studies* (Summer 2021), *S:I.M.O.N. Shoah: Interventions, Methods, Documentation* (2017, vol. 2), and *European History Quarterly* (forthcoming).

She closely collaborates with the research initiative and museum Blechhammer-1944 Association (Stowarzyszenie Blechhammer-1944) in Kędzierzyn-Koźle, Poland. The museum reconstructs the history of the Blechhammer camp complex. From 2012 to 2013, she was the second vice chairwoman of a memorial for the victims of the Nazi "euthanasia" killings in Wehnen near Oldenburg (Gedenkstätte Alte Pathologie).

Her main research area is the intertwining of industrial labor and genocide in the Nazi period, with a particular focus on the Schmelt camp system and the subcamps of Auschwitz. A key aspect in this context is to investigate the collaboration of civilians and policemen. She is also interested in the inmates' survival strategies and the dynamics of their relationships with other prisoner groups.

www.ingramcontent.com/pod-product-compliance
Lightning Source LLC
Chambersburg PA
CBHW061423300426
44114CB00014B/1521